# The College Writer

## A Guide to Thinking, Writing, and Researching

Australia • Brazil • Canada • Mexico • Singapore • United Kingdom • United States

**Seventh Edition**

John Van Rys
Redeemer University

Verne Meyer
Dordt University

Randall VanderMey
Westmont College

Pat Sebranek

**The College Writer: A Guide to Thinking, Writing, and Researching, Seventh Edition with 2021 MLA and 2020 APA Updates**

**John Van Rys, Verne Meyer, Randall VanderMey, and Pat Sebranek**

Product Director: Catherine van der Laan

Product Manager: Matt Filimonov

Learning Designer: Leslie Taggart

Subject Matter Expert: Anne Alexander

Product Assistant: Celia Smithmier

Marketing Manager: Kina Lara

Senior Content Developer: Kathy Sands-Boehmer

Development Editor: Mark Connelly

IP Analyst: Ashley Maynard

IP Project Manager: Carly Belcher, Kelli Besse

Art Director: Lizz Anderson

Production Service: Thoughtful Learning

Compositor: Tim Kemper, Thoughtful Learning

Text and Cover Designer: Mark Lalumondier, Thoughtful Learning

Cover Image: archideaphoto/Shutterstock.com

© 2022, 2018, 2015 Cengage Learning, Inc. ALL RIGHTS RESERVED.

No part of this work covered by the copyright herein may be reproduced or distributed in any form or by any means, except as permitted by U.S. copyright law, without the prior written permission of the copyright owner.

---

For product information and technology assistance, contact us at **Cengage Customer & Sales Support, 1-800-354-9706 or support.cengage.com.**

For permission to use material from this text or product, submit all requests online at **www.copyright.com.**

---

Library of Congress Control Number: 2020943783

Student edition:
ISBN: 978-0-357-50584-7

Loose-leaf edition:
ISBN: 978-0-357-50587-8

**Cengage**
200 Pier 4 Boulevard
Boston, MA 02210
USA

Cengage is a leading provider of customized learning solutions with employees residing in nearly 40 different countries and sales in more than 125 countries around the world. Find your local representative at: **www.cengage.com.**

To learn more about Cengage platforms and services, register or access your online learning solution, or purchase materials for your course, visit **www.cengage.com.**

The content in this textbook for which Cengage holds the copyright has been updated to better fit MLA and APA guidelines for language that is inclusive and bias free. This updating could not be applied to content for which Cengage does not own the copyright, including excerpts from articles as well as student papers.

Printed at CLDPC, USA, 08-22

# Brief Contents

Preface **xxii**

## I. The Writing Process  1

| 1 | Getting Started **3** |
| 2 | Reading Critically **19** |
| 3 | Viewing Critically **35** |
| 4 | Planning Your Piece **47** |
| 5 | Drafting: From Paragraphs to Essays **59** |
| 6 | Revising Your Draft **73** |
| 7 | Polishing Your Prose **89** |
| 8 | One Writer's Process **109** |

## II. Modes of Writing  125

| 9 | Forms of College Writing **127** |
| 10 | Personal Writing **137** |
| 11 | Analytical Writing: Definition **163** |
| 12 | Analytical Writing: Classification **185** |
| 13 | Analytical Writing: Process **205** |
| 14 | Analytical Writing: Compare and Contrast **227** |
| 15 | Analytical Writing: Cause and Effect **247** |
| 16 | Reading Literature: A Case Study in Analysis **271** |
| 17 | Persuasive Writing: Strategies for Argumentation **295** |
| 18 | Persuasive Writing: Positions, Actions, and Solutions **321** |

### Bonus Online Chapters

| A | Taking Essay Tests |
| B | Writing for the Workplace |
| C | Preparing Oral Presentations |
| D | Multimodal Projects |

## III. Research and Writing  357

| 19 | Planning Your Research **359** |
| 20 | Doing Research **375** |
| 21 | Practicing Research Ethics **411** |
| 22 | Drafting Research Papers **429** |
| 23 | MLA Style **453** |
| 24 | APA Style **491** |

## IV. Handbook  521

| 25 | Understanding Grammar **523** |
| 26 | Constructing Sentences **545** |
| 27 | Avoiding Sentence Errors **555** |
| 28 | Marking Punctuation **571** |
| 29 | Checking Mechanics **595** |
| 30 | Using the Right Word **617** |
| 31 | Multilingual and ESL Guidelines **633** |

Index **665**

# Contents

Thematic Contents for Readings **xvi**
Preface **xxii**

## I. The Writing Process

### 1 Getting Started 3

The Writing Process:
    From Start to Finish **4**
  *Consider the Writing Process* **4**
  *Adapt the Process to Your Project* **5**
Aiming for Writing Excellence **6**
  *Common Traits of College Writing* **6**
  *Common Traits in Action* **7**
  Sample: *"Hair Today, Gone Tomorrow"* **7**
Understanding Your Project **8**
  *Analyze the Rhetorical Situation* **8**
  *Study the Assignment* **9**
Developing a Topic **10**
  *Limit the Subject Area* **10**
  *Conduct Your Search* **10**
  *Explore Possible Topics* **11**
  *Freewrite to Discover and Develop a Topic* **12**
Researching Your Topic **14**
  *Find Out What You Already Know* **14**
  *Ask Questions* **15**
  *Identify Possible Sources* **16**
  *Track Sources* **17**
Getting Started: Applications **18**
  *Learning-Objectives Checklist* **18**

### 2 Reading Critically 19

Cultivating Critical-Thinking Habits **20**
  *Adopt a Critical-Thinking Mindset* **20**
  *Ask Probing Questions* **21**
  *Activate a Thinking Pattern* **21**
Using the SQ3R Reading Strategy **22**
  *Survey* **22**
  *Question* **22**
  *Read* **23**
  *Recite* **23**
  *Review* **23**
Critical Thinking Through Reading **24**
  *Maintain Focus and Attention* **24**
  Sample: *"Why Change Is So Hard: Self-Control Is Exhaustible,"* Dan Heath **24**
  *Map the Text* **26**
  *Outline the Text* **26**
  *Evaluate the Text* **27**
Taking Notes Actively **28**
  *Annotate the Text* **28**
  *Create a Double-Entry Notebook* **29**
Responding to a Text **30**
  *Guidelines for Response Writing* **30**
Summarizing a Text **31**
  *Guidelines for Summary Writing* **31**
Engaging with Social Media **32**
  *Revisit the Rhetorical Situation* **32**
  *Beware of Bias* **33**
  *Avoid Confirmation Bias* **33**
Reading Critically: Applications **34**
  *Learning-Objectives Checklist* **34**

### 3 Viewing Critically 35

Viewing an Image Actively **36**
  *Follow Active-Viewing Steps* **36**
  *View a Sample Image* **37**
Interpreting an Image **38**
  *Interpret a Sample Image* **39**
Evaluating an Image **40**
  *Consider the Purpose* **40**
  *Evaluate the Quality* **40**
  *Determine the Value* **40**
  *Evaluate a Sample Image* **41**
Critiquing a Video **42**
  *Before Viewing* **42**
  *During Viewing* **42**
  *After Viewing* **43**
Detecting Misinformation **44**
  *Deepfakes* **44**
  *Deceptive Edits* **44**
  *Out-of-Context Images* **44**
  *Doctored Images* **45**
  *Visual Misinformation:*

Contents

       *A Case Study*  45
   Viewing Critically: Applications  46
       *Learning-Objectives Checklist*  46

### 4 Planning Your Piece  47

   Forming Your Thesis Statement  48
       *Find a Focus*  48
       *State Your Thesis*  48
       *Refine Your Thesis*  49
   Developing a Plan or an Outline  50
       *Discover Organization in Your Thesis*  50
       *Refer Back to Your Prewriting*  50
       *Structure Your Writing for the Development of Ideas*  50
       *Consider Inductive and Deductive Patterns*  51
   Experimenting with Mapping Methods  52
       *Quick Lists*  52
       *Topic Outline*  53
       *Sentence Outline*  54
       *Writing Organizers*  55
   Planning the Design of Your Project  55
       *Consider the Rhetorical Situation*  55
       *Choose Design Elements*  56
       *Consider Multimodal Elements*  57
   Planning Your Piece: Applications  58
       *Learning-Objectives Checklist*  58

### 5 Drafting: From Paragraphs to Essays  59

   Basic Essay Structure: Major Moves  60
   Tips for Drafting  61
   Drafting Paragraphs  61
       *Types of Paragraphs*  61
       *Use a Basic Pattern for Body Paragraphs*  62
       *Vary Your Paragraph Style*  63
   Opening Your Draft  64
       *Engage Your Reader*  64
       *Establish Your Direction*  64
       *Get to the Point*  65
   Developing the Middle  66

       *Advance Your Thesis*  66
       *Test Your Ideas*  66
       *Make Writing Moves*  67
   Ending Your Draft  70
       *Reassert the Main Point*  70
       *Urge the Reader*  70
       *Complete and Unify Your Message*  71
   The Last Step in Drafting: Your Working Title  71
   Drafting: Applications  72
       *Learning-Objectives Checklist*  72

### 6 Revising Your Draft  73

   Tips for Revising Your Work  74
       *Use Practical Strategies*  74
       *Consider Your Overall Approach*  74
   Revising Your Ideas  75
       *Test Your Ideas*  75
       *Test Your Evidence*  76
   Revising Your Organization  77
       *Check Your Overall Plan*  77
       *Revisit Your Opening*  77
       *Test the Flow of Ideas*  78
       *Revisit Your Closing*  78
   Revising Your Voice  79
       *Check the Level of Commitment*  79
       *Check the Intensity*  79
   Strengthening Your Body Paragraphs  80
       *Remember the Basics*  80
       *Keep the Purpose in Mind*  80
       *Check for Unity*  81
       *Check for Coherence*  83
       *Check for Completeness*  85
   Revising Collaboratively  86
       *Know Your Role*  86
       *Provide Appropriate Feedback*  86
       *Respond According to a Plan*  87
   Revising Your Draft: Applications  88
       *Learning-Objectives Checklist*  88

### 7 Polishing Your Prose  89

   Tips for Polishing Your Prose  90

Contents

   *Use Tools and Methods That Work*   90
   *Proofread Plus*   90
Strengthening Sentence Style   91
   *Recognize Sentence Style Problems*   91
Edit Sentences to Give Them an Academic Style   92
   *Fix Primer Style*   94
   *Fix Repetitive Patterns with Varied Structures*   96
   *Fix Overuse of the Passive Voice*   98
   *Fix Unparallel Structure*   99
   *Fix Weak Constructions*   100
   *Eliminate Wordiness*   101
Fixing Weak Wording   102
   *Substitute Specific Words*   102
   *Replace Jargon and Clichés*   103
   *Replace Questionable Wording with Plain English*   104
   *Replace Biased Words with Fair and Inclusive Language*   105
Polishing Your Prose: Applications   108
   *Learning-Objectives Checklist*   108

**8 One Writer's Process   109**
Ariana's Assignment and Response   110
   *Ariana Examined the Assignment*   110
   *Ariana Explored and Narrowed Her Assignment*   111
Ariana's Planning   112
   *Ariana Focused Her Topic*   112
   *Ariana Researched the Topic*   112
   *Ariana Decided How to Organize Her Writing*   113
Ariana's First Draft   114
Ariana's Revision   116
Ariana's Edited Draft   118
Angela's Proofread Draft   119
Angela's Finished Essay   120
One Writer's Process: Applications   123
   *Learning-Objectives Checklist*   123
Traits of College Writing: A Checklist   124

## II. Modes of Writing

**9 Forms of College Writing   127**
Three Curricular Divisions   128
Writing in the Humanities   129
   *The Purpose of Inquiry*   129
   *Forms of Humanities Writing*   129
   *Humanities Research Methods*   129
Writing in the Social Sciences   130
   *The Purpose of Inquiry*   130
   *Forms of Social-Science Writing*   130
   *Social-Science Research Methods*   130
Writing in the Natural and Applied Sciences   131
   *The Purpose of Inquiry*   131
   *Forms of Natural-Science Writing*   131
   *Natural-Science Research Methods*   131
The Rhetorical Modes   132
   *The Modes as Thinking Frameworks*   132
   *The Modes at Work*   133
Multimodal Projects   134
   *Modes: Methods of Communication*   134
   *Forms of Multimodal Projects*   134
Forms of College Writing: Applications   136
   *Learning-Objectives Checklist*   136

**10 Personal Writing   137**
Meeting the Mode   138
   Sample: *"Spare Change," Teresa Zsuffa*   138
   *Converse with the Mode*   141
Strategies for Writing Personal Essays   142
   *The Rhetorical Situation*   142
   *Principles of Narration*   142
   *Principles of Description*   144
   *Principles of Reflection*   145
   *Patterns for Personal Essays: Thesis Thinking*   146
   *Patterns for Personal Essays: Writing Moves*   147

Personal Essays: Learning Writers' Moves  149
   Exploring Our Relationship with Death  149
   Sample: "Speaking Ill of the Dead," Rachel Ten Hove  149
   Exploring an Immigrant Identity  152
   Sample: "It Took Me 18 Years to Embrace My Name," Fiza Pirani  152
   Examining a Failed Institution  156
   Sample: "What I Learned in Prison," James Kilgore  156
DIY: Craft Your Own Personal Essay  160
   Planning  160
   Drafting  161
   Revising  161
   Polishing  161
   Publishing  161
The Personal Essay: Applications  162
   Learning-Objectives Checklist  162

## 11 Analytical Writing: Definition  163

Meeting the Mode  164
   Sample: "The Gullible Family," Mary Bruins  164
   Converse with the Mode  165
Strategies for Writing Definition Essays  166
   The Rhetorical Situation  166
   Principles of Definition Writing  166
   Patterns for Definition Essays: Thesis Thinking  168
   Patterns for Definition Essays: Writing Moves  169
Definition Essays: Learning Writers' Moves  170
   Explaining a Misunderstood Term  170
   Sample: "How 'Namaste' Flew Away from Us," Kumari Devarajan  170
   Examining the Changing Meaning of a Social Phrase  173
   Sample: "The History of 'Coming Out': From Secret Gay Code to Popular Political Protest," Abigail Saguy  173
   Defining Ethnic and Racial Attitudes  177
   Sample: "Dead Indians," Thomas King  177
DIY: Craft Your Own Definition Essay  182
   Planning  182
   Drafting  183
   Revising  183
   Polishing  183
   Publishing  183
Definition Essays: Applications  184
   Learning-Objectives Checklist  184

## 12 Analytical Writing: Classification  185

Meeting the Mode  186
   Sample: "Why We Lift," Hillary Gammons  186
   Converse with the Mode  187
Strategies for Writing Classification Essays  188
   The Rhetorical Situation  188
   Principles of Classification Writing  188
   Patterns for Classification Essays: Thesis Thinking  189
   Patterns for Classification Essays: Writing Moves  190
Classification Essays: Learning Writers' Moves:  191
   Analyzing Forms of Music  191
   Sample: "Latin American Music: A Diverse and Unifying Force," Kathleen Marsh  191
   Analyzing Artificial Intelligence  195
   Sample: "Understanding the Four Types of AI: From Reactive Robots to Self-Aware Beings," Arend Hintze  195
   Approaches to Literary Criticism  199
   Sample: "Four Ways to Talk About Literature," John Van Rys  199
DIY: Craft Your Own Classification Essay  202
   Planning  202
   Drafting  203
   Revising  203
   Polishing  203

*Publishing* **203**
Classification Essays: Applications **204**
*Learning-Objectives Checklist* **204**

## 13 Analytical Writing: Process **205**

Meeting the Mode **206**
- Sample: *"American Lumpia: Filipino Egg Roll,"* Andrea Santiago **206**
- *Converse with the Mode* **208**

Strategies for Writing Process Essays **209**
- *The Rhetorical Situation* **209**
- *Principles of Process Writing* **209**
- *Patterns for Process Essays: Thesis Thinking* **210**
- *Patterns for Process Essays: Writing Moves* **211**

Process Essays: Learning Writers' Moves **212**
- *Analyzing a Cultural Practice* **212**
- Sample: *"Chasing the Stoke,"* Tim Zekveld **212**
- *Analyzing a Natural Process* **216**
- Sample: *"Yogurt: Milk & Mayhem,"* Nina Mukerjee Furstenau **216**
- *Analyzing a Policy* **220**
- Sample: *"The Emancipation of Abe Lincoln,"* Eric Foner **220**

DIY: Craft Your Own Process Essay **224**
- *Planning* **224**
- *Drafting* **224**
- *Revising* **225**
- *Polishing* **225**
- *Publishing* **225**

Process Essays: Applications **226**
- *Learning-Objectives Checklist* **226**

## 14 Analytical Writing: Compare and Contrast **227**

Meeting the Mode **228**
- Sample: *"Modern Arranged Marriages,"* Ariana King **228**
- *Converse with the Mode* **229**

Strategies for Writing Compare-Contrast Essays **230**
- *The Rhetorical Situation* **230**
- *Principles of Compare-Contrast Writing* **230**
- *Patterns for Compare-Contrast Essays: Thesis Thinking* **232**
- *Patterns for Compare-Contrast Essays: Writing Moves* **233**

Compare-Contrast Essays: Learning Writers' Moves **234**
- *Analyzing Two Cultures* **234**
- Sample: *"Beyond the Polite Smile,"* Janice Pang **234**
- *Analyzing Human Compassion* **236**
- Sample: *"Why We Care About Whales,"* Marina Keegan **236**
- *Analyzing Internet Bullying* **240**
- Sample: *"How the Internet Has Changed Bullying,"* Maria Konnikova **240**

DIY: Craft Your Own Compare-Contrast Essay **244**
- *Planning* **244**
- *Drafting* **244**
- *Revising* **245**
- *Polishing* **245**
- *Publishing* **245**

Compare-Contrast Essays: Applications **246**
- *Learning-Objectives Checklist* **246**

## 15 Analytical Writing: Cause and Effect **247**

Meeting the Mode **248**
- Sample: *"Adrenaline Junkies,"* Sarah Hanley **248**
- *Converse with the Mode* **249**

Strategies for Writing Cause-Effect Essays **250**
- *The Rhetorical Situation* **250**
- *Principles of Cause-Effect Writing* **250**
- *Patterns for Cause-Effect Essays: Thesis Thinking* **252**
- *Patterns for Cause-Effect Essays: Writing Moves* **253**

Cause-Effect Essays: Learning Writers' Moves **254**

*Analyzing Password Protection* **254**
Sample: *"1$_Your_P@$$wOrd_Cl3v3r?,"* Scott Reichelt **254**
*Analyzing the African American Experience of Baseball* **259**
Sample: *"On the 100th Anniversary of the Negro Leagues: A Look Back at What Was Lost,"* Rob Ruck **259**
*Analyzing a Trend* **263**
Sample: *"The Rise of the New Groupthink,"* Susan Cain **263**
DIY: Craft Your Own Cause-Effect Essay **268**
*Planning* **268**
*Drafting* **269**
*Revising* **269**
*Polishing* **269**
*Publishing* **269**
Cause-Effect Essays: Applications **270**
*Learning-Objectives Checklist* **270**

**16** Reading Literature: A Case Study in Analysis **271**
Strategies for Analyzing Literature and the Arts **272**
*The Rhetorical Situation* **272**
*Principles of Literary-Analysis Writing* **272**
*Patterns for Literary-Analysis Essays: Thesis Thinking* **275**
*Patterns for Literary-Analysis Essays: Writing Moves* **276**
Analyzing Literature: Learning Writers' Moves **277**
*Analyzing a Poem* **277**
Sample: *"Let Evening Come,"* Jane Kenyon **277**
Sample: *"'Let Evening Come': An Invitation to the Inevitable,"* Sherry Mantel **278**
Sample: *"The World Is Too Much With Us,"* William Wordsworth **280**
*Analyzing a Short Story* **281**
Sample: *"'A Clean, Well-Lighted Place': Emotional Darkness,"* by Julia Jansen **281**
*Analyzing a Film* **284**

Sample: *"The Revenant: A Brutal Masterpiece,"* by James C. Schaap **284**
Literary Terms **288**
Poetry Terms **291**
DIY: Craft Your Own Literary Analysis **292**
*Planning* **292**
*Drafting* **292**
*Revising* **293**
*Polishing* **293**
*Publishing* **293**
Analyzing Literature: Applications **294**
*Learning-Objectives Checklist* **294**

**17** Persuasive Writing: Strategies for Argumentation **295**
Meeting the Mode **296**
Sample: *"America Needs a Ministry of (Actual) Truth,"* Josh Wilbur **296**
*Converse with the Mode* **300**
Structuring Arguments **301**
*Understand Toulmin Argumentation* **301**
*Toulmin Patterns* **302**
*Understand Rogerian Argumentation* **302**
*Rogerian Patterns* **303**
*Choose an Approach* **304**
Engaging the Opposition **305**
*Make Concessions* **305**
*Develop Rebuttals* **305**
*Consolidate Your Claim* **305**
Arguing Through Appeals **306**
*Appeal to Ethos* **306**
*Appeal to Pathos* **306**
*Appeal to Logos* **307**
Making and Qualifying Claims **308**
*Distinguish Claims from Facts and Opinions* **308**
*Distinguish Three Types of Claims* **308**
*Develop a Supportable Claim* **309**
Supporting Your Claims **310**
*Gather Evidence* **310**

Use Evidence  311
Identifying Logical Fallacies  313
  Distorting the Issue  313
  Sabotaging the Argument  314
  Drawing Faulty Conclusions from the Evidence  315
  Misusing Evidence  315
  Misusing Language  316
  Identifying Fallacies in Others' Arguments  317
  Sample: "Executive Deception: Four Fallacies About Divestment, and One Big Mistake," Kathleen Dean Moore  317
Strategies for Argumentation: Applications  320
  Learning-Objectives Checklist  320

**18** Persuasive Writing: Positions, Actions, and Solutions  321
Meeting the Mode  322
  Sample: "Evening the Odds," Dave DeHaan  322
  Converse with the Mode  323
Strategies for Persuasive Writing  324
  The Rhetorical Situation  324
  Principles: Taking a Stand  324
  Principles: Calling for Action  325
  Principles: Proposing a Solution  326
  Patterns for Persuasive Essays: Thesis Thinking  328
  Patterns for Persuasive Essays: Writing Moves  329
Persuasive Essays: Learning Writers' Moves  330
  Solving the Problem of E-Waste  330
  Sample: "Remedying an E-Waste Economy," Rachel DeBruyn  330
  Addressing a Racial Problem  334
  Sample: "Reaction GIFs of Black People Are More Problematic Than You Think," Naomi Day  334
  Debating *Latinx*  338
  Sample: "Why 'Latinx' Is Succeeding While Other Gender-Neutral Terms Fail to Catch On," Katy Steinmetz  338

  Sample: "Can We Please Stop Using 'Latinx'? Thanx," Kurly Tlapoyawa  341
  Calling for Action on Cannabis  345
  Sample: "Is Marijuana as Safe as We Think?," Malcolm Gladwell  345
DIY: Craft Your Own Persuasive Essay  353
  Planning  353
  Drafting  354
  Revising  355
  Polishing  355
  Publishing  355
Persuasive Essays: Applications  356
  Learning-Objectives Checklist  356

## Online Bonus Chapters

**A** Taking Essay Tests  A-1
Reviewing for Tests  A-2
  Perform Daily Reviews  A-2
  Perform Longer Weekly Reviews  A-2
Forming a Study Group  A-3
Considering the Testing Situation  A-4
Taking the Essay Test  A-5
  Look for Key Words  A-5
  Plan and Write the Essay-Test Answer  A-7
Writing Under Pressure: The Essay Test  A-10
Taking an Objective Test  A-11
Tips for Coping with Test Anxiety  A-12

**B** Writing for the Workplace  B-1
Writing Emails and Messages  B-2
  Choosing the Right Medium  B-2
  Messaging Effectively  B-2
  Emailing Effectively  B-3
Writing Business Letters  B-4
  Parts of the Business Letter  B-4
Writing Memos  B-6
Applying for a Job  B-7
  Sample Letter of Application  B-7
  Sample Recommendation-Request Letter  B-8
  The Application Essay  B-9

Preparing a Résumé **B-11**
   *Sample Résumé* **B-12**
   *Sample Electronic Résumé* **B-13**

### C Preparing Oral Presentations **C-1**

Organizing Your Presentation **C-2**
   *Prepare an Introduction* **C-2**
   *Develop the Body* **C-3**
   *Come to a Conclusion* **C-4**
   *Hold a Q & A Session* **C-4**
Writing Your Presentation **C-5**
   *Sample Speech* **C-6**
   **Sample:** *"Save Now or Pay Later," Burnette Sawyer* **C-6**
   *Use Visual Aids* **C-8**
Developing Digital Presentations **C-9**
Overcoming Stage Fright Checklist **C-10**

### D Multimodal Projects **D-1**

Meeting Multimodal Texts **D-2**
   *Converse with the Mode* **D-3**
Strategies for Crafting Multimodal Texts **D-4**
   *The Rhetorical Situation* **D-4**
   *Principles of Multimodality* **D-4**
   *Patterns for Multimodal Texts: Thesis Thinking* **D-6**
   *Patterns for Multimodal Texts: Composing Moves* **D-7**
Multimodal Texts: Learning Composers' Moves **D-8**
   *Poking Fun at Technology Dependency* **D-8**
   **Sample:** *"Slowpoke," Jen Sorensen* **D-9**
   *Blogging About a Historical Figure* **D-10**
   **Sample:** *"'Hamilton,'—About Alexander and Eliza's Last Goodbye," Neely Tucker* **D-10**
Craft Your Own Multimodal Text **D-13**
Multimodal Projects: Applications **D-15**
   *Learning-Objectives Checklist* **D-15**

## III. Research and Writing

### 19 Planning Your Research **359**

Your Project: Writing a Research Proposal **360**
   *Understand the Parts of a Research Proposal* **360**
   **Sample:** *"Film Studies 201 Proposal: Jane Austen's* Pride and Prejudice *as Fiction and Film," Gwendolyn Mackenzie* **360**
Research: An Overview **362**
   *The Research Process* **362**
   *The Research Frame of Mind* **363**
Getting Focused **364**
   *Establish a Narrow, Manageable Topic* **364**
   *Brainstorm Research Questions* **364**
   *Develop a Working Thesis* **365**
Understanding Primary, Secondary, and Tertiary Sources **366**
   *Primary Sources* **366**
   *Secondary Sources* **366**
   *Tertiary Sources* **367**
Exploring Information Resources and Sites **368**
   *Consider Different Information Resources* **368**
   *Consider Different Information Sites* **369**
Planning Keyword Searches **370**
   *Choose Keywords Carefully* **370**
   *Learn Keyword Strategies* **371**
Building a Working Bibliography **372**
   *Select an Efficient Approach for Your Project* **372**
Developing a Research Plan **373**
   *Choose Research Methods* **373**
   *Get Organized to Do Research* **373**
Planning Your Research: Applications **374**
   *Learning-Objectives Checklist* **374**

### 20 Doing Research **375**

Your Project: Creating an Annotated

Bibliography **376**
   *The Elements of an Annotated Bibliography* **376**
   *Sample Annotated Bibliography* **376**
   Sample: *"Project on Alice Munro's* Runaway: *An Annotated Bibliography"* **376**
Working with Your Sources **378**
   *Engage Your Sources* **378**
   *Choose a Note-Taking System* **379**
   *Summarizing, Paraphrasing, and Quoting Source Material* **382**
   *Rate Source Reliability and Depth* **385**
   *Evaluate Each Source* **386**
   *Test Free-Web Sources* **387**
   *Sample Evaluations* **388**
Doing Primary Research **390**
   *Methods of Primary Research* **390**
   *Principles for Doing Primary Research* **391**
   *Conduct Surveys* **392**
   *Analyze Texts, Documents, Records, and Artifacts* **394**
   *Conduct Interviews* **396**
   *Make Observations* **398**
Doing Library Research **399**
   *Search the Catalog* **400**
   *Locate Resources by Call Numbers* **401**
   *Work with the Books You Find* **402**
   *Consult Reference Resources* **403**
   *Find Articles Via Databases* **404**
Doing Free-Web Research **405**
   *Using Search and Metasearch* **405**
   *Use Search Engines Effectively* **406**
   *Understanding the Uses and Limits of Wikipedia* **408**
Doing Research: Applications **410**
   *Learning-Objectives Checklist* **410**

## 21 Practicing Research Ethics **411**

Your Project: Writing a Literature Review **412**
   *Guidelines for Writing a Literature Review* **412**
   Sample: *"Assertiveness Use and Abuse Experience of Haitian Women: A Literature Review,"* Kadee Rowe **413**
Research Ethics: A Primer **418**
   *Participation in Information Culture* **418**
   *Your Research-Writing Responsibilities* **419**
Developing Credibility Through Source Use **420**
   *Writing with Poor Use of Sources* **420**
   *Writing with Strong Use of Sources* **421**
Recognizing Plagiarism **422**
   *What Is Plagiarism?* **422**
   *What Does Plagiarism Look Like?* **422**
Understanding Why Plagiarism Is Serious **424**
   *Academic Dishonesty* **424**
   *Theft from the Academic Community* **424**
   *Present and Future Harm* **424**
Avoiding Plagiarism **425**
Avoiding Other Source Abuses **426**
   *Sample Source Abuses* **426**
   *Related Academic Offenses* **427**
Practicing Research Ethics: Applications **428**
   *Learning-Objectives Checklist* **428**

## 22 Drafting Research Papers **429**

Papers with Documented Research: Quick Guide **430**
Reviewing Your Findings **431**
   *Deepen Your Thinking on the Topic* **431**
   *Sharpen Your Working Thesis* **431**
Considering Methods of Organization **432**
   *Organizational Practices That Consider Sources* **432**

Traditional Organizational Patterns   433
Considering Drafting Strategies   434
   Choose a Drafting Method   434
   Respect Your Sources While Drafting   434
   Reason with the Evidence   435
Using Source Material in Your Writing   436
   Integrate Source Material Carefully   436
   Effectively Document Your Sources   438
   Mark Changes to Quotations   439
   Sample Research Paper: A Humanities Essay   440
   **Sample:** "Chipping Away at Our Privacy?," Lucas Koomans   440
Sample Research Paper: Science IMRAD Report   445
   **Sample:** "The Effects of the Eastern Red Cedar on Seedlings and Implications for Allelopathy," Dana Kleckner, Brittany Korver, Nicolette Storm, and Adam Verhoef   445
Drafting a Research Paper: Applications   452
   Learning-Objectives Checklist   452

## 23  MLA Style   453

MLA Documentation: Quick Guide   454
   In-Text Citation: The Basics   454
   Works Cited: Nine Core Elements   455
Guidelines for In-Text Citations   456
   Citations for Regular Sources   456
   Citations for Sources Without Traditional Authorship and/or Pagination   457
Sample In-Text Citations   458
Guidelines for Works-Cited Entries   464
   Works-Cited Template   464
   Works-Cited Components   464

Supplemental Elements   467
Sample Works-Cited Entries   468
   Books   468
   Periodical Articles   470
   Interviews and Personal Correspondence   471
   Multimedia Works   472
   Government Publications, Reference Works, and Other Documents   473
   Two or More Works by the Same Author   474
MLA Format Guidelines   475
   MLA Format at a Glance   475
   Whole-Paper Format and Printing Issues   476
   Typographical Issues   477
   Page-Layout Issues   478
   Formatting Non-Print Media   479
Sample MLA Paper   479
   Sample Paper: Format, In-Text Citation, and Works-Cited List   480
   **Sample:** "Consequences of Childhood Staples: Do Barbies and Disney Princesses Do More Harm Than Good to Girls' Self-Esteem?," Annie Sears   480
MLA Style: Applications   490
   Learning-Objectives Checklist   490

## 24  APA Style   491

APA Documentation: Quick Guide   492
   In-Text Citation: The Basics   492
   References: The Basics   493
Guidelines for In-Text Citations   494
   The Form of an Entry   494
   Points to Remember   494
   Sample In-Text Citations   494
Guidelines for APA References   498
Sample Reference Entries   499
   Books and Other Documents   499
   Print Periodical Articles   502
   Online Sources   504

*Other Sources (Primary, Personal, and Multimedia)* **507**
APA Format Guidelines **509**
Sample APA Paper **510**
Sample: "The Silent Sibling: How Current Autism Intervention Neglects Typically-Developing Siblings," Julia Sweigert **510**
*Sample Title Page* **510**
*Sample Abstract* **511**
APA Style: Applications **520**
*Learning-Objectives Checklist* **520**

# IV. Handbook

## 25 Understanding Grammar **523**

Noun **523**
  *Classes of Nouns* **523**
  *Forms of Nouns* **524**
  **Exercises** **526**
Pronoun **527**
  *Classes of Pronouns* **528**
  *Forms of Personal Pronouns* **529**
  **Exercises** **531**
Verb **532**
  *Classes of Verbs* **532**
  *Forms of Verbs* **533**
  *Verbals* **536**
  *Irregular Verbs* **537**
  **Exercises** **538**
Adjective **539**
Adverb **540**
Preposition **541**
Conjunction **542**
Interjection **542**
  **Exercises** **543**

## 26 Constructing Sentences **545**

Using Subjects and Predicates **545**
  *The Subject* **545**
  *The Predicate (Verb)* **547**
  **Exercises** **548**
Using Phrases **549**
  *Types of Phrases* **549**

Using Clauses **551**
  *Types of Clauses* **551**
Using Sentence Variety **552**
  *Kinds of Sentences* **552**
  *Structure of Sentences* **553**
  **Exercises** **554**

## 27 Avoiding Sentence Errors **555**

Subject–Verb Agreement **555**
Pronoun–Antecedent Agreement **559**
  **Exercises** **560**
Shifts in Sentence Construction **561**
Fragments, Comma Splices, and Run-Ons **562**
  **Exercises** **564**
Misplaced and Dangling Modifiers **565**
Ambiguous Wording **566**
  **Exercises** **567**
Nonstandard Language **568**
  **Exercises** **569**
Avoiding Sentence Problems Review **570**

## 28 Marking Punctuation **571**

Period **571**
Ellipsis **572**
Question Mark **573**
  **Exercises** **574**
Comma **575**
  **Exercises** **580**
Semicolon **581**
Colon **582**
Hyphen **583**
Dash **585**
  **Exercises** **586**
Quotation Marks **587**
Italics (Underlining) **589**
Parentheses **590**
Diagonal **590**
Brackets **591**
Exclamation Point **591**
Apostrophe **592**
  **Exercises** **594**

**29 Checking Mechanics 595**

Capitalization   595
  Exercises   599
Plurals   600
Numbers   602
  Exercises   604
Abbreviations   605
Acronyms and Initialisms   607
  Exercises   608
Basic Spelling Rules   609
Commonly Misspelled Words   610
Steps to Becoming a Better Speller   615
  Exercises   616

**30 Using the Right Word 617**

  Exercises   620
  Exercises   624
  Exercises   628
  Exercises   632

**31 Multilingual and ESL Guidelines 633**

Five Parts of Speech   633
Noun   633
  *Articles and Other Noun Markers*   634
  Exercises   636
Verb   637
  *Objects and Complements of Verbs*   638
  Exercises   643
Adjective   644
Adverb   645
Preposition   646
  Exercises   647
Understanding Sentence Basics   648
Sentence Problems   649
  Exercises   651
Numbers, Word Parts, and Idioms   652
  *Numbers*   652
  *Prefixes, Suffixes, and Roots*   653
  Exercises   654
  *Idioms*   655
  Exercises   658
  Mixed Review Exercises   659

Index   665

# Thematic Contents for Readings

## Character and Conscience
"Beyond the Polite Smile" by Janice Pang   234
"Chipping Away at Our Privacy?" by Lucas Koomans   440
"'A Clean Well-Lighted Place': Emotional Darkness" by Julia Jansen   281
"Consequences of Childhood Staples: Do Barbies . . . ?" by Annie Sears   480
"Dead Indians" by Thomas King   177
"The Emancipation of Abe Lincoln" by Eric Foner   220
"Executive Deception: Four Fallacies About Divestment . . ." by Kathleen Dean Moore   317
"Homelessness Doesn't Equate to Inhumanity" by Ariana King   120
"How the Internet Has Changed Bullying" by Maria Konnikova   240
"It Took Me 18 Years to Embrace My Name" by Fiza Pirani   152
"Reaction GIFs of Black People Are More Problematic Than You Think" by Naomi Day   334
"Remedying an E-Waste Economy" by Rachel DeBruyn   330
"*The Revenant*: A Brutal Masterpiece" by James C. Schaap   284
"The Silent Sibling: How Current Autism Intervention Neglects . . . " by Julia Sweigert   510
"Spare Change" by Teresa Zsuffa   138
"What I Learned in Prison" by James Kilgore   156
"Why Change Is So Hard" by Dan Heath   24
"Why We Care About Whales" by Marina Keegan   236

## Community and Culture
"American Lumpia: Filipino Egg Roll" by Andrea Santiago   206
"America Needs a Ministry of (Actual) Truth" by Josh Wilbur   296
"Assertiveness Use and Abuse Experience of Haitian Women" by Kadee Rowe   413
"Beyond the Polite Smile" by Janice Pang   234
"Can We Please Stop Using 'Latinx'? Thanx" by Kurly Tlapoyawa   341
"Chasing the Stoke" by Tim Zekveld   212
"Chipping Away at Our Privacy?" by Lucas Koomans   440
"Consequences of Childhood Staples: Do Barbies . . . ?" by Annie Sears   480
"Dead Indians" by Thomas King   177
"The Emancipation of Abe Lincoln" by Eric Foner   220
"The History of 'Coming Out'" by Abigail Saguy   173
"Homelessness Doesn't Equate to Inhumanity" by Ariana King   120
"How the Internet Has Changed Bullying" by Maria Konnikova   240
"How 'Namaste' Flew Away From Us" by Kumari Devarajan   170
"It Took Me 18 Years to Embrace My Name" by Fiza Pirani   152
"Latin American Music: A Diverse and Unifying Force" by Kathleen Marsh   191
"Modern Arranged Marriages" by Ariana King   228
"On the 100th Anniversary of the Negro Leagues" by Rob Ruck   259
"Reaction GIFs of Black People Are More Problematic Than You Think" by Naomi Day   334
"Remedying an E-Waste Economy" by Rachel DeBruyn   330
"The Rise of the New Groupthink" by Susan Cain   263
"Spare Change" by Teresa Zsuffa   138
"What I Learned in Prison" by James Kilgore   156

"Why 'Latinx' Is Succeeding . . ." by Katy Steinmetz   338
"Why We Care About Whales" by Marina Keegan   236
"Why We Lift" by Hillary Gammons   186
"Yogurt: Milk & Mayhem" by Nina Mukerjee Furstenau   216

## Disease, Death, and Coping
"'A Clean Well-Lighted Place': Emotional Darkness" by Julia Jansen   281
"Dead Indians" by Thomas King   177
"Is Marijuana as Safe as We Think?" by Malcolm Gladwell   345
"Let Evening Come" by Jane Kenyon   277
"The Silent Sibling: How Current Autism Intervention Neglects . . ." by Julia Sweigert   510
"Speaking Ill of the Dead" by Rachel Ten Hove   149
"Why We Care About Whales" by Marina Keegan   236

## Diversity and Equity
"Beyond the Polite Smile" by Janice Pang   234
"Can We Please Stop Using 'Latinx'? Thanx" by Kurly Tlapoyawa   341
"Dead Indians" by Thomas King   177
"The Emancipation of Abe Lincoln" by Eric Foner   220
"The History of 'Coming Out'" by Abigail Saguy   173
"How the Internet Has Changed Bullying" by Maria Konnikova   240
"It Took Me 18 Years to Embrace My Name" by Fiza Pirani   152
"On the 100th Anniversary of the Negro Leagues" by Rob Ruck   259
"Reaction GIFs of Black People Are More Problematic Than You Think" by Naomi Day   334
"The Rise of the New Groupthink" by Susan Cain   263
"The Silent Sibling: How Current Autism Intervention Neglects . . ." by Julia Sweigert   510
"Spare Change" by Teresa Zsuffa   138
"What I Learned in Prison" by James Kilgore   156
"Why 'Latinx' Is Succeeding . . ." by Katy Steinmetz   338

## Education and Learning
"America Needs a Ministry of (Actual) Truth" by Josh Wilbur   296
"Consequences of Childhood Staples: Do Barbies . . . ?" by Annie Sears   480
"The Effects of the Eastern Red Cedar . . ." by Dana Kleckner, et al.   445
"The Emancipation of Abe Lincoln" by Eric Foner   220
"Executive Deception: Four Fallacies About Divestment . . ." by Kathleen Dean Moore   317
"Film Studies 201 Proposal . . ." by Gwendolyn Mackenzie   360
"Four Ways to Talk About Literature" by John Van Rys   199
"How the Internet Has Changed Bullying" by Maria Konnikova   240
"'Let Evening Come': An Invitation to the Inevitable" by Sherry Mantel   278
"The Rise of the New Groupthink" by Susan Cain   263
"The Silent Sibling: How Current Autism Intervention Neglects . . ." by Julia Sweigert   510
"Understanding the Four Types of AI" by Arend Hintze   195
"Why Change Is So Hard" by Dan Heath   24

## Environment and Nature

"The Effects of the Eastern Red Cedar . . . " by Dana Kleckner, et al.   **445**
"Evening the Odds" by Dave DeHaan   **322**
"Remedying an E-Waste Economy" by Rachel DeBruyn   **342**
"Why We Care About Whales" by Marina Keegan   **236**
"The World Is Too Much With Us" by William Wordsworth   **280**

## Ethics and Ideology

"America Needs a Ministry of (Actual) Truth" by Josh Wilbur   **296**
"Can We Please Stop Using 'Latinx'? Thanx" by Kurly Tlapoyawa   **341**
"Chipping Away at Our Privacy?" by Lucas Koomans   **440**
"Consequences of Childhood Staples: Do Barbies . . . ?" by Annie Sears   **480**
"Dead Indians" by Thomas King   **177**
"The Emancipation of Abe Lincoln" by Eric Foner   **220**
"Evening the Odds" by Dave DeHaan   **322**
"Executive Deception: Four Fallacies About Divestment . . ." by Kathleen Dean Moore   **317**
"Homelessness Doesn't Equate to Inhumanity" by Ariana King   **120**
"How the Internet Has Changed Bullying" by Maria Konnikova   **240**
"Is Marijuana as Safe as We Think?" by Malcolm Gladwell   **345**
"Reaction GIFs of Black People Are More Problematic Than You Think" by Naomi Day   **334**
"Remedying an E-Waste Economy" by Rachel DeBruyn   **330**
"*The Revenant*: A Brutal Masterpiece" by James C. Schaap   **284**
"Spare Change" by Teresa Zsuffa   **138**
"What I Learned in Prison" by James Kilgore   **156**
"Why We Care About Whales" by Marina Keegan   **236**

## Ethnicity and Identity

"American Lumpia: Filipino Egg Roll" by Andrea Santiago   **206**
"Assertiveness Use and Abuse Experience of Haitian Women" by Kadee Rowe   **413**
"Beyond the Polite Smile" by Janice Pang   **234**
"Can We Please Stop Using 'Latinx'? Thanx" by Kurly Tlapoyawa   **341**
"Chasing the Stoke" by Tim Zekveld   **212**
"Dead Indians" by Thomas King   **177**
"The Emancipation of Abe Lincoln" by Eric Foner   **220**
"The History of 'Coming Out'" by Abigail Saguy   **173**
"How 'Namaste' Flew Away From Us" by Kumari Devarajan   **170**
"It Took Me 18 Years to Embrace My Name" by Fiza Pirani   **152**
"Latin American Music: A Diverse and Unifying Force" by Kathleen Marsh   **191**
"On the 100th Anniversary of the Negro Leagues" by Rob Ruck   **259**
"Reaction GIFs of Black People Are More Problematic Than You Think" by Naomi Day   **334**
"*The Revenant*: A Brutal Masterpiece" by James C. Schaap   **284**
"The Rise of the New Groupthink" by Susan Cain   **263**
"Speaking Ill of the Dead" by Rachel Ten Hove   **149**
"What I Learned in Prison" by James Kilgore   **156**
"Why 'Latinx' Is Succeeding . . . " by Katy Steinmetz   **338**
"Yogurt: Milk & Mayhem" by Nina Mukerjee Furstenau   **216**

## Family and Friends

"American Lumpia: Filipino Egg Roll" by Andrea Santiago    **206**
"Beyond the Polite Smile" by Janice Pang    **234**
"Consequences of Childhood Staples: Do Barbies . . . ?" by Annie Sears    **480**
"It Took Me 18 Years to Embrace My Name" by Fiza Pirani    **152**
"Modern Arranged Marriages" by Ariana King    **228**
"The Silent Sibling: How Current Autism Intervention Neglects . . ." by Julia Sweigert    **510**
"Speaking Ill of the Dead" by Rachel Ten Hove    **149**

## Fashion and Lifestyle

"Adrenaline Junkies" by Sarah Hanley    **248**
"Chasing the Stoke" by Tim Zekveld    **212**
"Chipping Away at Our Privacy?" by Lucas Koomans    **440**
"Consequences of Childhood Staples: Do Barbies . . . ?" by Annie Sears    **480**
"Evening the Odds" by Dave DeHaan    **322**
"How 'Namaste' Flew Away From Us" by Kumari Devarajan    **170**
"Latin American Music: A Diverse and Unifying Force" by Kathleen Marsh    **191**
"Remedying an E-Waste Economy" by Rachel DeBruyn    **330**
"The Rise of the New Groupthink" by Susan Cain    **263**
"Spare Change" by Teresa Zsuffa    **138**
"Why Change Is So Hard" by Dan Heath    **24**
"Why We Lift" by Hillary Gammons    **186**

## Gender and Integrity

"Assertiveness Use and Abuse Experience of Haitian Women" by Kadee Rowe    **413**
"Can We Please Stop Using 'Latinx'? Thanx" by Kurly Tlapoyawa    **341**
"Consequences of Childhood Staples: Do Barbies . . . ?" by Annie Sears    **480**
"Reaction GIFs of Black People Are More Problematic Than You Think" by Naomi Day    **334**
"Spare Change" by Teresa Zsuffa    **138**
"Why 'Latinx' Is Succeeding . . ." by Katy Steinmetz    **338**
"Why We Lift" by Hillary Gammons    **186**

## Humor and Humanity

"America Needs a Ministry of (Actual) Truth" by Josh Wilbur    **296**
"The Gullible Family" by Mary Bruins    **164**
"1$_Your_P@$$wOrd_Cl3v3r?" by Scott Reichelt    **254**

## Language and Literature

"Can We Please Stop Using 'Latinx'? Thanx" by Kurly Tlapoyawa    **341**
"'A Clean Well-Lighted Place': Emotional Darkness" by Julia Jansen    **281**
"Dead Indians" by Thomas King    **177**
"Film Studies 201 Proposal . . ." by Gwendolyn Mackenzie    **360**
"Four Ways to Talk About Literature" by John Van Rys    **199**
"The History of 'Coming Out'" by Abigail Saguy    **173**
"How 'Namaste' Flew Away From Us" by Kumari Devarajan    **170**
"The Gullible Family" by Mary Bruins    **164**

"'Let Evening Come': An Invitation to the Inevitable" by Sherry Mantel   278
"Let Evening Come" by Jane Kenyon   277
"*The Revenant*: A Brutal Masterpiece" by James C. Schaap   284
"Why 'Latinx' Is Succeeding . . ." by Katy Steinmetz   338
"The World Is Too Much With Us" by William Wordsworth   280

## Memory and Tradition
"American Lumpia: Filipino Egg Roll" by Andrea Santiago   206
"America Needs a Ministry of (Actual) Truth" by Josh Wilbur   296
"Beyond the Polite Smile" by Janice Pang   234
"Can We Please Stop Using 'Latinx'? Thanx" by Kurly Tlapoyawa   341
"Chasing the Stoke" by Tim Zekveld   212
"Consequences of Childhood Staples: Do Barbies . . . ?" by Annie Sears   492
"Dead Indians" by Thomas King   177
"How 'Namaste' Flew Away From Us" by Kumari Devarajan   170
"It Took Me 18 Years to Embrace My Name" by Fiza Pirani   152
"On the 100th Anniversary of the Negro Leagues" by Rob Ruck   259
"Speaking Ill of the Dead" by Rachel Ten Hove   149
"Why 'Latinx' Is Succeeding . . ." by Katy Steinmetz   338
"Yogurt: Milk & Mayhem" by Nina Mukerjee Furstenau   216

## Science and Health
"Adrenaline Junkies" by Sarah Hanley   248
"America Needs a Ministry of (Actual) Truth" by Josh Wilbur   296
"Consequences of Childhood Staples: Do Barbies . . . ?" by Annie Sears   480
"The Effects of the Eastern Red Cedar . . ." by Dana Kleckner, et al.   445
"Is Marijuana as Safe as We Think?" by Malcolm Gladwell   345
"Let Evening Come" by Jane Kenyon   277
"Remedying an E-Waste Economy" by Rachel DeBruyn   330
"The Silent Sibling: How Current Autism Intervention Neglects . . ." by Julia Sweigert   510
"Understanding the Four Types of AI" by Arend Hintze   195
"Why Change Is So Hard" by Dan Heath   24
"Why We Care About Whales" by Marina Keegan   236
"Why We Lift" by Hillary Gammons   186
"Yogurt: Milk & Mayhem" by Nina Mukerjee Furstenau   216

## Technology and Our Time
"America Needs a Ministry of (Actual) Truth" by Josh Wilbur   296
"Chipping Away at Our Privacy?" by Lucas Koomans   440
"Homelessness Doesn't Equate to Inhumanity" by Ariana King   120
"How the Internet Has Changed Bullying" by Maria Konnikova   240
"1$_Your_P@$$wOrd_Cl3v3r?" by Scott Reichelt   254
"*The Revenant*: A Brutal Masterpiece" by James C. Schaap   284
"Reaction GIFs of Black People Are More Problematic Than You Think" by Naomi Day   334
"Understanding the Four Types of AI" by Arend Hintze   195
"What I Learned in Prison" by James Kilgore   156

## Work and Play

"Adrenaline Junkies" by Sarah Hanley   **248**
"Chasing the Stoke" by Tim Zekveld   **212**
"Consequences of Childhood Staples: Do Barbies . . . ?" by Annie Sears   **480**
"Evening the Odds" by Dave DeHaan   **322**
"How 'Namaste' Flew Away From Us" by Kumari Devarajan   **170**
"Is Marijuana as Safe as We Think?" by Malcolm Gladwell   **345**
"1$_Your_P@$$wOrd_Cl3v3r?" by Scott Reichelt   **254**
"Latin American Music: A Diverse and Unifying Force" by Kathleen Marsh   **191**
"On the 100th Anniversary of the Negro Leagues" by Rob Ruck   **259**
"The Rise of the New Groupthink" by Susan Cain   **263**
"Understanding the Four Types of AI" by Arend Hintze   **195**
"Why We Lift" by Hillary Gammons   **186**

# Acknowledgements

The authors express their gratitude to the following reviewers of *The College Writer*, 7th Edition.

Gary Beagle, *Southcentral Kentucky Community and Technical College*
Robert Galin, *University of New Mexico*
Rebecca Hoffman, *Northeast Wisconsin Technical College*
Jonathan Joy, *Ashland Community and Technical College*
Debra Justice, *Ashland Community and Technical College*
Gail McGrady, *Southcentral Kentucky Community and Technical College*
Kelly Paul, *West Kentucky Community and Technical College*
Rachel Pierce, *Miles College*
Amber Ridgeway, *Southwestern Oregon Community College*

# Preface

Wherever students are in their writing process or however confident they feel about writing, *The College Writer* is a resource they can turn to for guidance and support. Valuable for student writers of any skill level, this book is a fully updated four-in-one text with major sections on the writing process, modes of writing, research and writing, and grammar, punctuation, and usage. Throughout the text, numerous student and professional writing samples highlight important features of academic writing—from organization to documentation—and model strategies students can use in their own papers.

The seventh edition features increased attention to the role of critical reading and paragraph writing in the composing process, updated sample essays focused on timely and inclusive topics, a stronger emphasis on evaluating and composing multimodal texts, and friendly organization that directly leads students through the process of composing critical academic and research-based essays. The text is available as a multimedia online learning experience, featuring an e-book, audio, video, exercises, models, web links, and bonus chapters on multimodal projects, taking tests, writing for the workplace, and preparing oral presentations.

## New Features

- **Twenty-one NEW sample essays,** 8 from students and 13 from professionals, offer fresh perspectives on relevant, current topics—from embracing identity to culturally significant food to problematizing racialized Internet GIFs. Perfect for discussion, these essays will also inspire students' writing. New professional writers include Fiza Pirani, Thomas King, Abigail C. Saguy, Kumari Devarajan, Arend Hintze, Nina Mukerjee Furstenau, Rob Ruck, William Wordsworth, Josh Wilbur, Naomi Day, Katy Steinmetz, and Kurly Tlapoyawa. New student writers tackle topics such as homelessness, online security, food and identity, and arranged marriages.

- **REORGANIZED chapters in Part 1, "The Writing Process,"** help students fully integrate critical thinking, reading, and viewing into their writing process. The **NEW chapter 2, "Reading Critically,"** introduces students to active-reading strategies for analyzing, evaluating, and responding to texts. This chapter also gives special attention to engaging with social media and detecting bias. The **NEW chapter 3, "Viewing Critically,"** shows students how to actively view, understand, and critique images and video. New pages feature strategies for detecting visual misinformation.

- **An ENHANCED chapter 5, "Drafting: From Paragraphs to Essays,"** features increased attention to crafting opening, body, and closing paragraphs, highlighting how paragraphs serve as a line of reasoning and showing how to link them together into a full essay. Additions to the chapter help students examine paragraphs at the sentence level, showing how different types of sentences—topic, reasoning, evidence, and concluding—can interact to create strong academic paragraphs.

- **Chapters in Part II, "Modes of Writing," feature REWORKED pedagogy and increased writing instruction** to help students to more effectively produce thoughtful, energetic college-level prose. The chapters now begin with a brief teaching model that introduces students to the mode. Following the teaching model, the chapters include increased instruction on thesis development and mode-specific writing moves and strategies. Students then see those moves in action as they read and respond to exemplary sample essays from student and professional writers. New reading topics address current issues of interest and concern to a diverse student body. As culminating support, students receive process-based writing instructions for creating their own essay within the mode.

- **Each chapter in Part III, "Research and Writing," now includes a specific form of research writing** that students can complete while they receive instruction on how to find and engage with sources ethically. **NEW research forms include a literature review and annotated bibliography.** The progression of chapters in Part III highlights the interplay of writing and research, not just in the final large research-paper project but throughout the research process.

- **ENHANCEMENTS to chapters in Part III also include additional material on research ethics,** including examining online sources critically, identifying misinformation, recognizing filter bubbles and confirmation bias, and questioning the "fake news" and "alternative facts" concepts.

- **UPDATED instruction in Chapter 23, "MLA Style," updates coverage to the *MLA Handbook*, 9th edition; Chapter 24, "APA Style," aligns with changes in the *APA Style Guide*, 7th Edition.** Also included in Chapter 7 are the new guidelines on inclusive language for both systems.

## Key Features

- *The College Writer* **provides students with a concise yet complete overview of the writing process.** The text's unique "at-a-glance" visual format presents each major concept in a one- or two-page spread, with examples illustrating explanations, and then the opportunity for hands-on practice, with writing assignments or practice exercises.

- **Consistent attention to the rhetorical situation**—writer, reader, message, medium, and context—gives students a tool to analyze the works of others and create their own works.

- **"Learning Objectives" at the beginning of each chapter help students focus on key learning points;** main headings throughout the chapter reinforce those points; and "Learning-Objective Checklists" enable students to track their performance.

- **"Common Traits of College Writing," introduced in chapter 1 and then underlying much of the instruction in the text, help students understand and achieve college-level writing.** These traits are also in sync with the "WPA Outcomes Statement for First-Year Composition."

- **An ENHANCED person-to-person style engages students directly with instruction that connects to the writing that they are doing.** Particularly in chapter openings, direct address aims to thoughtfully and sometimes humorously create a framework for understanding the chapter's topic and its importance.
- **Increased emphasis on thesis creation encourages students to organize their thinking as they write.**
- **Activities and projects help students fully engage with readings, complete their own writing, and extend their learning through critical thinking.** After each sample essay, "Reading for Better Writing" questions ask students to connect the reading to their own life and experiences, show comprehension of the content, study writing moves and strategies within the piece, and brainstorm related topics and approaches for their own project. End-of-chapter activities extend students' learning through applications such as Photo Op, Wise Words, Living Today, Public Texts, Writing Reset, and Major Work.
- **High-interest academic writings from students and professionals help writers understand and create a scholarly tone.** Throughout the text, the authors offer examples of writing for different disciplines as well as in different work contexts.
- **An ENHANCED Chapter 17, "Persuasive Writing: Strategies for Argumentation," strengthens instruction in argumentative writing.** The chapter includes attention to the contrast between Toulmin and Rogerian approaches to argument, along with a sample argument and a fallacy-focused essay.
- **An ENHANCED Chapter 18, "Persuasive Writing: Positions, Actions, Solutions," also strengthens instruction in argumentative writing.** The chapter offers more instruction on the principles involved in forms of persuasive writing, along with new sample essays that cluster around the environment, cultural identity, online culture, and drug legalization.
- **The Research section gives students all the tools they need to do twenty-first century research,** including working with digital databases; understanding the differences between primary, secondary, and tertiary sources; working effectively with sources, while avoiding plagiarism; learning to evaluate diverse sources; and documenting their research in MLA (9th edition) or APA (7th edition) format.
- **The Handbook covers key points of grammar, sentence structure, sentence errors, punctuation, mechanics, and usage, as well as multilingual and ESL guidelines.** These topics are reinforced by exercises available both in the text and online.
- **Charts, graphs, and photos help visual learners grasp concepts and cultivate visual literacy in all students.** These elements range from the high-interest chapter-opening photos to mode-specific graphic organizers.
- **The entire text is available as a multimedia eBook, featuring audio, video, exercises, models, and web links.**

# New to This Edition

**New Sample Essays:** Twenty-one new sample essays include works by professionals such as Fiza Pirani, Thomas King, Abigail C. Saguy, Arend Hintze, Nina Mukerjee Furstenau, Rob Ruck, Josh Wilbur, Naomi Day, Katy Steinmetz, and Kurly Tlapoyawa.

**Increased Instruction on Crafting Strong Paragraphs:** The seventh edition features support for creating well-developed opening, body, and closing paragraphs, highlighting how paragraphs serve as a line of reasoning and showing how to link them together into a full essay. Additions help students examine paragraphs at the sentence level, showing how different types of sentences can interact to create strong academic paragraphs.

---

62 The Writing Process

### Use a Basic Pattern for Body Paragraphs

In much of your academic writing, you want to write full-bodied paragraphs—rich like a quality cup of coffee. These paragraphs are typically longer than two or three sentences. And the sentences tend to be substantial—full of careful thinking and discussions of information. Such body paragraphs normally combine these kinds of sentences:

1. **A topic sentence:** Each paragraph typically has one, often the first sentence. It states the focus and main idea of the paragraph while often offering a transition from the previous paragraph.
2. **Reasoning sentences:** These typically elaborate your thinking about the topic sentence—explaining what you mean, what you've learned about it. Essentially, reasoning is what's happening in your head as you reflect on the main idea.
3. **Evidence sentences:** These statements present information in support of your reasoning: facts, statistics, examples, illustrations, quotations, case studies, and more. Evidence is what you've gathered through reading, viewing, researching, and experiencing. In that sense, it's what exists outside your head. You weave evidence sentences into your reasoning. Note: sometimes sentences blend reasoning and evidence. Don't get hung-up on the distinction: learning to weave reasoning and evidence together is the main lesson.
4. **Concluding sentence:** The final sentence often wraps up the discussion of the paragraph's topic, summarizing the point that you've developed in the reasoning and evidence sentences.

**Example:** Read the paragraph below from "Chasing the Stoke" in chapter 13. Notice how Tim Zekveld builds his thinking out of these four types of sentences. Note, too, how the paragraph has forward momentum, moving from A (the topic sentence) to A+ (the concluding sentence), all through the dance of reasoning and evidence.

> **Topic sentence** — In Hawaii, surfing began as a joyous thanksgiving to the ocean for its providence and sustenance. Dating as far back as 800 AD, surfing was commonplace in Hawaiian society. **Reasoning sentences** — Men, women, and children of every social status—from the commoner to the king—would surf regularly as a means of leisure and a form of ritual. When the ocean had provided food for their clan or had affected the people in a catastrophic way, Hawaiians would, while surfing the face of a wave, turn around and bow, wetting their head in the curl (Peralta). This ritual was a physical act meant to pay homage to the ocean, showing immense humility and reverence to their life force. **Evidence sentences** — Surfing on carved wooden boards measuring sixteen feet or longer and weighing well over a hundred pounds, the ancient Hawaiians would paddle into waves varying from three to thirty feet (Young 11). Captain James Cook, on viewing a Hawaiian surf in 1777, wrote, "I could not help concluding that this man felt the most supreme pleasure while he was being driven on so fast and so smoothly by the sea" (qtd. in Peralta). **Concluding sentence** — The joy that Captain Cook had witnessed, paired with the unfathomable respect that Hawaiians had for the ocean, fused into one term: aloha.

**Enhanced Instruction on Reading and Viewing Critically:** Chapter 2, "Reading Critically," introduces active-reading strategies for analyzing, evaluating, and responding to texts. Special attention is given to engaging with social media and detecting bias. Chapter 3, "Viewing Critically," shows students how to actively view, understand, and critique images and video. New pages feature strategies for detecting visual misinformation.

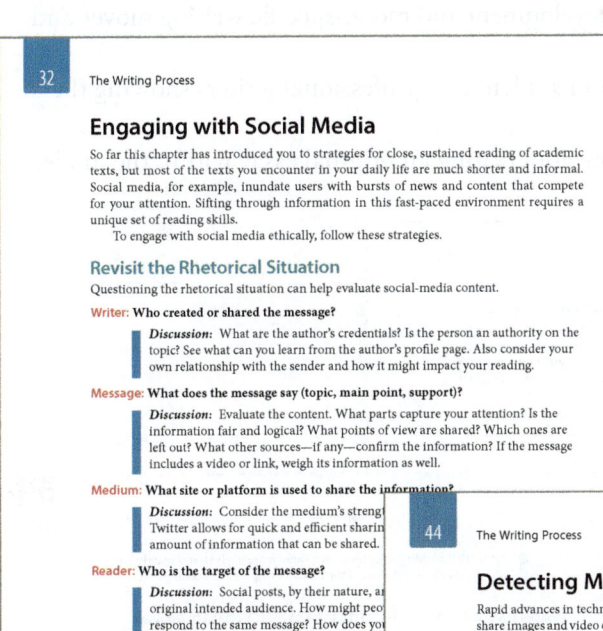

**Increased Instruction in the Modes of Academic Writing:** Chapters in Part II, "Modes of Writing," feature reworked pedagogy and enhanced writing instruction to help students more effectively produce thoughtful, energetic college-level prose. Each chapter in Part II includes . . .

- A brief teaching model to introduce students to the mode.
- Increased instruction on thesis development and mode-specific writing moves and strategies.
- New exemplary sample essays from student and professional writers showing the mode in action.
- Process-based writing instructions for creating an original essay within the mode.

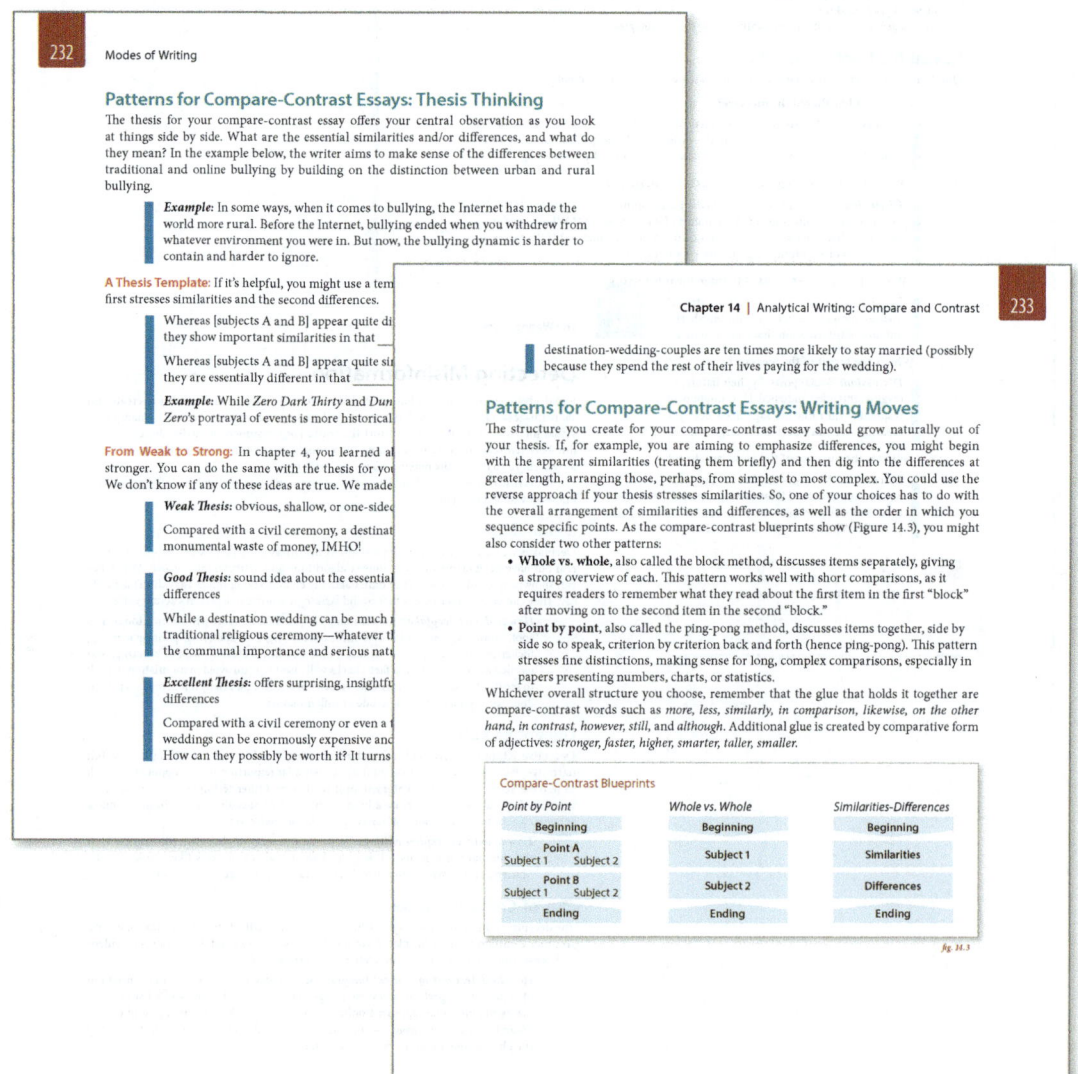

**Updated Instructions on MLA Documentation and Style (9th edition) and APA Documentation and Style (7th edition):** Clear instructions and illustrations help students understand and use the current MLA and APA systems for documenting research writing. The new systems are introduced through easy-reference quick guides, presented through clear examples, and modeled in new student essays.

---

492   Research and Writing

## APA Documentation: Quick Guide

The APA system involves two parts: (1) an in-text citation within your paper when you use a source and (2) a matching bibliographic entry at the end of your paper. Note these features of the APA author-date system:

- **It uses signal phrases and parenthetical references** to set off source material from your own thinking and discussion. A signal phrase names the author and places the material in context (e.g., "As Jung described it, the collective unconscious…").
- **It's date-sensitive.** Because the publication dates of resources are especially important in social-science research, the publication year is included in the parenthetical reference and after the authors' names in the reference entry.
- **It's smooth, unobtrusive, and orderly.** APA in-text citations identify borrowed material while keeping the paper readable. Moreover, alphabetized reference entries at the end of the paper make locating source details easy.

You can see these features at work in the example below. The parenthetical material "Pascopella, 2011, p. 32" tells the reader these things:

- The borrowed material came from a source authored by Pascopella.
- The source was published in 2011.
- The specific material can be found on page 32 of the source.
- Full source details are in the reference list under the surname Pascopella.

**1. In-Text Citation in Body of Paper**

> In newcomer programs, "separate, relatively self-contained educational interventions" (Pascopella, 2011, p. 32) are implemented to meet the academic and transitional needs of recent immigrants before they enter mainstream English Language Development.

**2. Matching Reference Entry at End of Paper**

> Pascopella, A. (2011). Successful strategies for English language learners. *District Administration, 47*(2), 29-44.

### In-Text Citation: The Basics

Follow these basic rules for in-text citation.

1. Refer to the author(s) and date of publication by using one of these methods:

   **Last name(s), publication date in parentheses:**

   > ELLs normally spend just three years in 30-minute "pull-out" English language development programs (Calderón et al., 2011).

   **Last name(s) cited in text with publication date in parentheses:**

   > In "Key Issues for Teaching English Learners in Academic Classrooms," Carrier (2005) explained that it takes an average of one to three years to reach conversational proficiency in a second language, but five to seven years to reach academic proficiency.

**New Forms of Research Writing and Increased Attention to Research Ethics:** Each chapter in Part III, "Research and Writing," now includes a specific form of research writing that students can complete while they receive instruction on how to find and engage with sources ethically. The progression of chapters in Part III highlights the interplay of writing and research, not just in the final large research-paper project but throughout the research process.

| Part III Research Focus | Writing Form |
|---|---|
| 19. Planning Your Research | *Research Proposal* |
| 20. Doing Research | *Annotated Bibliography* |
| 21. Practicing Research Ethics | *Literature Review* |
| 22. Drafting Research Papers | *Humanities Essay* and *Science IMRAD Report* |
| 23. MLA Style | *MLA Paper* |
| 24. APA Style | *APA Paper* |

---

418    Research and Writing

### Research Ethics: A Primer

When it comes to the wise and fair treatment of information, we live in complicated times. Consider both your participation in the larger information culture and your specific responsibilities in your research writing.

#### Participation in Information Culture

We are all citizens of a larger information culture—a world of stories, news, studies, social media posts, blogs, documentaries, advertising campaigns, politics, and more. What should citizenship look like and how it applies to this world? We might start with the Golden Rule and how it applies to this world: Do unto others as you would have them do unto you. It begins with respect, tolerance, and neighborliness in the spaces where information gets shared, discussed, and debated.

Consider a difficult and controversial topic such as the COVID-19 pandemic. What would a healthy information culture look like? Here are some principles:

**Seek out, rely on, and share ethically-sourced information:** Learn where information comes from. It's easy to passively rely on social media as a source, as it often feeds us what we want to hear—a lot of it junk-food information. Instead, become a more active information consumer—seeking out trustworthy, respected, ethically-produced sources. These typically come from organizations that have the well-being of individuals and society, as well as advancing knowledge, as part of their mission: government agencies, universities, nonprofits, media entities with high standards and moderate leanings. They're not perfect, but they do what's humanly possible to share information people can count on.

> *Example:* To get reliable information on COVID-19, you would go to a source such as the CDC—the Centers for Disease Control and Prevention, a government agency whose mission is "Saving Lives, Protecting People." Be suspicious of resources such as the video, "Plandemic: The Hidden Agenda Behind COVID-19"—produced by a well-known conspiracy theorist, featuring a discredited scientist from the National Cancer Institute, and spread on social media.

**Avoid misinformation:** Put simply, don't believe it, create it, or share it. Of course, you need to recognize misinformation when you see it. Develop your nose for falsehood, a healthy suspicion, so that you can practice the smell test: Does something seem too good to be true? Too crazy? Too connected to the source's self-interest? Bottom line: Never call a lie the truth, the truth a lie. When you hear phrases such as "That's just your opinion" or "It's all relative" or "These are just alternative facts," don't accept them: While it's sometimes difficult to get at, truth exists. If you need help knowing whether something is misinformation, turn to fact-checking organizations (e.g., FactCheck.org and PolitiFact), as well as reliable sources that might confirm or counter the information in question.

> *Example:* To test the truth-content of the video "Plandemic," a quick Google search will take you to reputable news articles and a Wikipedia entry that explain the falsehoods and errors in the film.

# MindTap© English for *The College Writer*, 7th Edition

The MindTap for *The College Writer*, Seventh Edition, engages students with additional activities, videos, worksheets, modules, and readings to help them succeed.

## Activities for Understanding and Applying Chapter Content

- "Check Your Understanding" exercises after each chapter help students and instructors assess learning by asking students to apply what they have learned to very short scenarios of writing. Students get three sets of activities, so they have ample practice. Problems are auto-graded and report to the gradebook.
- "Collaborate" activities can be used in the online and face-to-face classroom. In the face-to-face classroom, collaborative activities are designed to take up to 30 minutes to complete. Online, the focus is on completing an activity, asynchronously, within one week. Worksheets give students a way to record their ideas, and optional individual reflection questions ask students to summarize what they have learned about the subject, the process of collaboration itself, or themselves.

## Videos That Offer Writing and Research Help

- "Watch a Video" activities in most Part II chapters show students how authentically the need to use rhetorical strategies arises. Animated stories are used to provoke thought and summarize key elements of each mode.
- In Part III on research and documentation, "Watch a Video" activities consist of very short videos with 10-item, auto-graded quizzes afterward. Videos are narrated by instructors from across the curriculum.

## Worksheets to Help Students Stay Focused and Organized

- "Writing Organizers" in Part II chapters are worksheets with open-ended questions that help students stay organized and focused on the most important elements of what they need to do. These Word docs can be downloaded, printed or filled out onscreen, and then uploaded to the instructor if desired. "Thesis Templates" help students draft well-formed thesis statements for each mode.
- "Research Organizers" in Part III chapters perform the same function as the Writing Organizers. Topics include developing a search strategy, evaluating sources using the CRAAP test, and editing and proofreading MLA and APA citations.

## Modules for Both Foundational and Advanced Topics

- The Just in Time Plus series includes 43 units on foundational topics that range from writing an essay to using commas correctly to paraphrasing, summarizing, and quoting. Each unit includes an introductory Video Tutorial (4-5 minutes), a Quick Review of instructional text (2-5 pages), and an Assignment (10-15 minutes) to check understanding of the topic. Assignments are auto-graded. A diagnostic pre-test and post-test help the instructor determine which students should study which units. Students get a report of their results, and instructors see reports for individual students and for the entire class.

- Focused Support for Key Topics includes 9 topics in argument, evaluating sources, and critical thinking. Each unit includes a Reading of instructional text; a Video Example of a student working with the topic; an auto-graded Review Activity; an annotated student essay; and two professional readings with discussion questions.

### 50 More Readings to Customize Your Course

- Ten themes, each with five readings, are supported by two kinds of apparatus for maximum flexibility: an extensive set of open-ended questions for before, during, and after reading, including annotation guides; and a separate, short (5-item) reading comprehension quiz that is auto-graded.
- The themes are Fake News on Social Media, Media Bias, The Value of College, Social Justice, Cultural Appropriation, Place and Identity, Nature and the Environment, Gender Identity, Writing About Writing, and Public Discourse.
- Readings range from 1100 to 1300L, or approximately 9th grade reading level to 13.5.

## Resources for Teaching

The MindTap for *The College Writer*, Seventh Edition, includes a full suite of instructor resources to help you plan and implement your course:

### For Setting Up the Course

- "MindTap Table of Contents with Learning Objectives" can help you quickly locate the resources you want to include to meet your course objectives.
- "Sample Syllabi" for courses that integrate MindTap resources are available for 4-week, 8-week, and 16-week courses. Syllabi for the co-req section are also provided.
- "Instructor's Manual" provides syllabi for the course using only the print text, along with teaching tips applicable to a variety of teaching contexts.
- "Customizing Your MindTap Course" is a video narrated by an English instructor on how to add, move, and hide content to arrive at the exact course configuration that will help your students the most.

### For Teaching the Course

- "Reading Instruction in the Writing Classroom" helps instructors quickly get up to speed on how to teach reading and writing together.
- "Co-Req Activities You Can Do on the Spot" are five- to twenty-minute activities organized by topic that can be done in the co-req section with no instructor preparation.
- "Success with Collaborative Activities" is a brief guide to setting up groups and running them, and it includes talking points and answer keys for the Collaborate activities.
- "Discussion Board Prompts" are prompts that require critical thinking at the application, analysis, evaluation, and synthesis levels of Bloom's Taxonomy. These can be used in class or in an LMS discussion board.
- "50 Readings Answer Key" provides answers and talking points to the open-ended questions in the 50 Readings module.

# I. The Writing Process

## The Writing Process

### 1 Getting Started
- The Writing Process: From Start to Finish — 4
- Aiming for Writing Excellence — 6
- Understanding Your Project — 8
- Developing a Topic — 10
- Researching Your Topic — 14
- Getting Started: Applications — 18

### 2 Reading Critically
- Cultivating Critical-Thinking Habits — 20
- Using the SQ3R Reading Strategy — 22
- Critical Thinking Through Reading — 24
- Taking Notes Actively — 28
- Responding to a Text — 30
- Summarizing a Text — 31
- Engaging with Social Media — 32
- Reading Critically: Applications — 34

### 3 Viewing Critically
- Viewing an Image Actively — 36
- Interpreting an Image — 38
- Evaluating an Image — 40
- Critiquing a Video — 42
- Detecting Misinformation — 44
- Viewing Critically: Applications — 46

### 4 Planning Your Piece
- Forming Your Thesis Statement — 48
- Developing a Plan or an Outline — 50
- Experimenting with Mapping Methods — 52
- Planning the Design of Your Project — 55
- Planning Your Piece: Applications — 58

### 5 Drafting: From Paragraphs to Essays
- Basic Essay Structure: Major Moves — 60
- Tips for Drafting — 61
- Drafting Paragraphs — 61
- Opening Your Draft — 64
- Developing the Middle — 66
- Ending Your Draft — 70
- The Last Step in Drafting: Your Working Title — 71
- Drafting: Applications — 72

### 6 Revising Your Draft
- Tips for Revising Your Work — 74
- Revising Your Ideas — 75
- Revising Your Organization — 77
- Revising Your Voice — 79
- Strengthening Your Body Paragraphs — 80
- Revising Collaboratively — 86
- Revising Your Draft: Applications — 88

### 7 Polishing Your Prose
- Tips for Polishing Your Prose — 90
- Strengthening Sentence Style — 91
- Edit Sentences to Give Them an Academic Style — 92
- Fixing Weak Wording — 102
- Polishing Your Prose: Applications — 108

### 8 One Writer's Process
- Ariana's Assignment and Response — 110
- Ariana's Planning — 112
- Ariana's First Draft — 114
- Ariana's Revision — 116
- Ariana's Edited Draft — 118
- Ariana's Proofread Draft — 119
- One Writer's Process: Applications — 123
- Traits of College Writing: A Checklist — 124

# Chapter 1

## Getting Started

At the start of her wonderful book, *The Writing Life*, Annie Dillard says, "When you write, you lay out a line of words." Writing is that simple, isn't it? And that complicated.

As a student, you know how difficult it can be to arrive at a line of words that sound right and make sense. Getting there requires a whole process. Done well, it's a process of discovery. Your line of words becomes what Dillard calls "a miner's pick, a woodcarver's gouge, a surgeon's probe." That's the aim of the writing process—discovery, both for you and your reader. Discovery happens when you give ample time to each step in the process.

This chapter introduces the writing process and then focuses on helping you start any writing project through prewriting strategies. As with many things in life, completing the first step right sets you up for the whole journey.

**Visually Speaking** Painting is the process of converting infinite possibilities into a single image. How is writing similar? How is it different? What is the starting point for painting? For writing? Consider these questions as you examine Figure 1.1.

### Learning Objectives

By working through this chapter, you will be able to

- outline the writing process.
- determine how to follow the process for different projects.
- summarize seven traits of strong, college-level writing.
- analyze the rhetorical situation behind writing tasks.
- interpret the nature and requirements of specific writing assignments.
- generate topics for writing projects.
- conduct research for writing projects.

*Chamille White / Shutterstock.com*

*fig. 1.1*

# The Writing Process: From Start to Finish

It's easy to feel overwhelmed by a writing project—especially if the form of writing is new to you, the topic is complex, or the paper must be long. However, using the writing process will relieve some of that pressure by breaking down the task into manageable steps.

## Consider the Writing Process

Figure 1.2 maps out the basic steps in the writing process. As you work on your writing project, periodically review this diagram to keep yourself on task.

**Steps in the Writing Process**

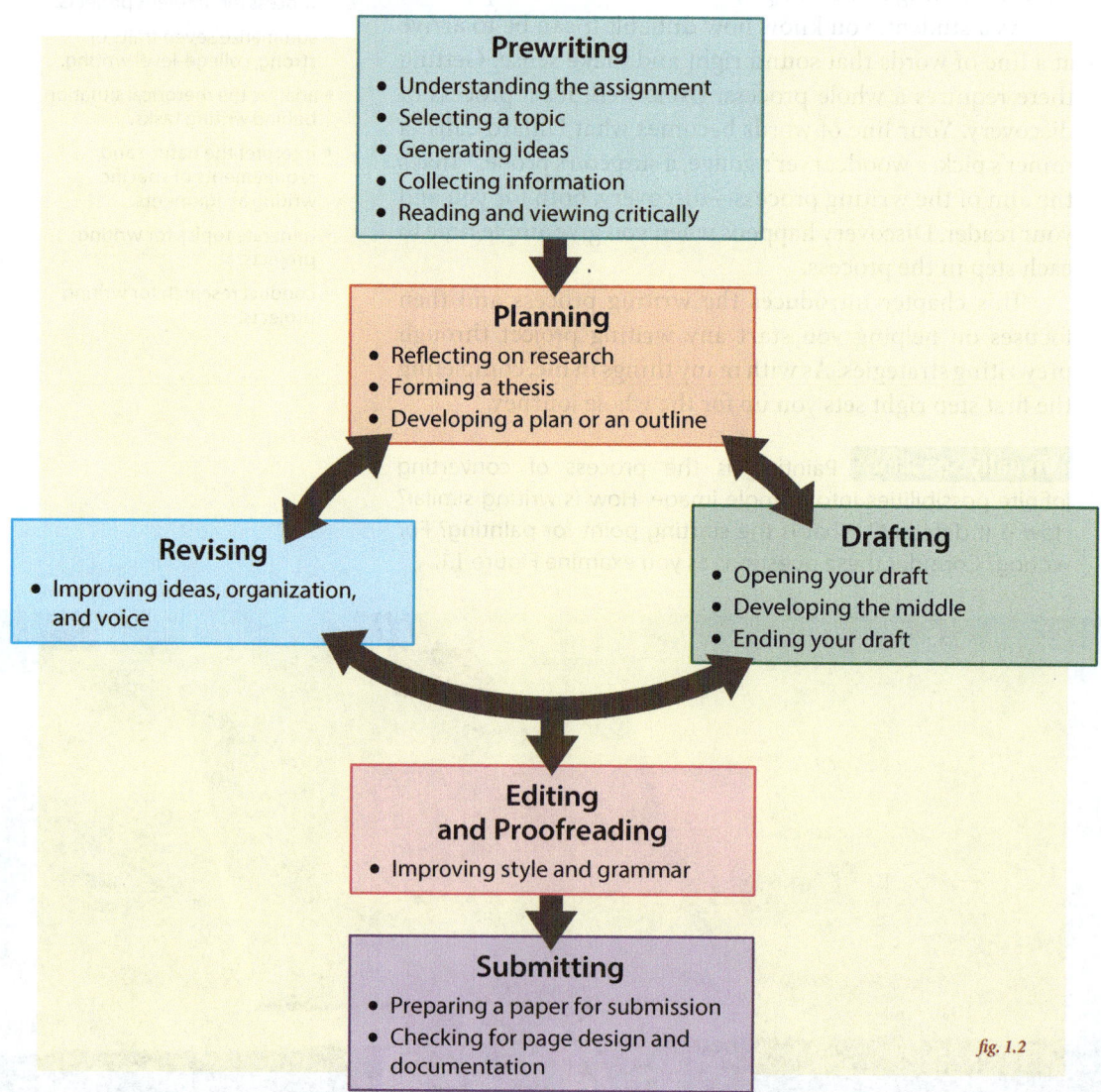

*fig. 1.2*

## Adapt the Process to Your Project

The writing process shown on the previous page is flexible, not rigid. As a writer, you need to adapt the process to your situation and assignment. To do so, consider these essential principles.

- **Writing tends not to follow a straight path.** While writing begins with an assignment or a need and ends with a reader, the journey in between is often indirect. The steps in the Figure 1.2 flowchart show that when you write, you sometimes move back and forth between steps, meaning that the process is recursive. For example, during the revision phase, you may discover that you need to draft a new paragraph or do more research.
- **Each assignment presents distinct challenges.** A personal essay may develop best through clustering or freewriting; a literary analysis through close reading of a story; a lab report through the experimental method; and a position paper through reading of books and journal articles, as well as through careful and balanced reasoning. Moreover, an assignment may or may not involve extensive research and working with sources.
- **Writing can involve collaboration.** From using your roommate as a sounding board for your topic choice to working with a group to produce a major report, college writing is not solitary writing. In fact, many colleges have a writing center to support you.
- **Each writer works differently.** Some writers do extensive prewriting before drafting, while others do not. You might develop a detailed outline, whereas someone else might draft a brief list of topics. Experiment with the strategies introduced in chapters 1–7, adopting those that help you.
- **Good writing can't be rushed.** Although some students regard pulling an all-nighter as a badge of honor, good writing takes time. A steady, disciplined approach will generally produce the best results. For example, by brainstorming or reading early in a project, you stimulate your subconscious mind to mull over issues, identify problems, and project solutions—even while your conscious mind is working on other things. Similarly, completing a first draft early enough gives you time to revise objectively.
- **Different steps call for attention to different writing issues.** As you use the writing process, at each stage keep your focus where it belongs:
  1. While getting started, planning, and drafting, focus on global issues: ideas, structure, voice, format, and design.
  2. During revising, fix big content problems by cutting, adding, and thoroughly reworking material. (Our experience is that students benefit the most from revising—but spend the least time doing it!)
  3. While editing and proofreading, pay attention to specific details—word choice, sentence smoothness, and grammatical correctness. Worrying about these issues too early in the writing process interrupts the flow of drafting and wastes time on material that may later be deleted.

# Aiming for Writing Excellence

What makes your writing strong enough to engage and enlighten readers? You can measure writing excellence by the depth of what you learn through writing, as well as by what your reader gains through reading. However, while the world of writing is so diverse that no formula or prescription can state definitively what makes for strong writing, we can point to common traits that describe such writing. Consider the relevance of these traits at the beginning of any writing project.

## Common Traits of College Writing

Quality writing shows strengths in the traits below, which range from global issues to local, sentence-level issues.

- **Strong ideas** are what you discover and develop through your writing. They are what make your content substantial and meaningful. These elements include a clear, sharp thesis or theme; strong and balanced reasoning; and accurate, supportive information that is properly credited.

- **Logical organization** creates the structure and flow of your writing. Through organization, reasoning is delivered through a clear chain of ideas, a unified whole. Typically, an engaging opening focuses discussion, the middle effectively develops the main idea, and a closing offers conclusions and points forward—all in paragraphs that are well developed (unified, coherent, and complete).

- **Engaging voice** refers to how your writing "sounds" to readers—the attitude, pacing, and personality that come through. An engaging voice sounds authentic and natural, engaged with the topic. Moreover, the tone—whether serious, playful, or sarcastic—is confident but also sincere and measured, fitting the writing occasion.

- **Clear word choice** carries your meaning. In your writing, the vocabulary should fit the topic, purpose, and audience. Phrasing should be clear throughout—language that readers will understand, using precise terminology and plain English whenever possible.

- **Smooth sentences** express complete thoughts in a good blend of sentence lengths (short and punchy, long and thoughtful) and patterns (loose, balanced, and periodic). Such sentences use phrases and clauses in logical and expressive ways—energetically, economically, gracefully.

- **Correct writing** follows the conventions of language (grammar, punctuation, mechanics, usage, and spelling), as well as standards of citation and documentation (e.g., MLA, APA).

- **Professional document design** refers to the appearance of your writing on the page, the screen, and so on. Such design includes the document's format (e.g., essay, lab report, presentation, website), its page layout (e.g., margins, headings, bullets, white space), its typography (typefaces, type sizes, and type styles), and its use of tables and visuals.

## Common Traits in Action

What do these common traits look like in a typical piece of academic writing? Study the process essay below to discover how it represents strong freshman-level college writing.

**Ideas**
Clear focus, engaging thesis, and precise content (including visual)

**Organization**
Lively opening, well-structured middle, and thoughtful closing

**Voice**
Informed and engaging tone

**Words**
Precise, lively, and clear phrasing, including in the title

**Sentences**
Smooth, varied, and graceful constructions

**Correctness**
Error-free prose

**Design**
Attractive format, page layout, and diagram

### Hair Today, Gone Tomorrow

Imagine a field of grass covered with two layers of soil: first a layer of clay, and on top of that a layer of rich, black dirt. Then imagine that 100,000 little holes have been poked through the black dirt and into the clay, and at the bottom of each hole lies one grass seed.

Slowly each seed produces a stem that grows up through the clay, out of the dirt, and up toward the sky. Now and then every stem stops for a while, rests, and then starts growing again. At any time about 90 percent of the stems are growing and the others are resting. Because the field gets shaggy, sometimes a gardener comes along and cuts the grass.

Your skull is like that field of grass, and your scalp (common skin) is like the two layers of soil. The top layer of the scalp is the epidermis, and the bottom layer is the dermis. About 100,000 tiny holes (called follicles) extend through the epidermis into the dermis.

At the base of each follicle lies a seed-like thing called a papilla. At the bottom of the papilla, a small blood vessel drops like a root into the dermis. This vessel carries food through the dermis into the papilla, which works like a little factory using the food to build hair cells. As the papilla makes cells, a hair strand grows up through the dermis past an oil gland. The oil gland greases the strand with a coating that keeps the hair soft and moist.

Most of the hairs on your scalp grow about one-half inch each month. If a strand stays healthy, doesn't break off, and no barber snips it, the hair will grow about 25 inches in four years. At that point hair strands turn brittle and fall out. Every day between 25 and 250 hairs fall out of your follicles, but nearly every follicle grows a new one.

Around the clock, day after day, this process goes on . . . unless your papillae decide to retire. In that case you reach the stage in your life—let's call it "maturity"—that others call "baldness."

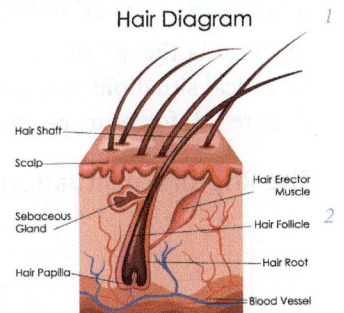

Hair Diagram

# Understanding Your Project

To start strong, you need to spend some time getting your writing project in focus. What exactly is the nature of your writing task? Answering this question will set you on the right path for your writing. Two steps will help you get off on the right foot: analyzing the rhetorical situation and studying the assignment.

## Analyze the Rhetorical Situation

Rhetoric is the art of using language effectively. Your writing is effective when it fits the rhetorical situation: your role, goal, audience, and context. Discover the rhetorical situation (Figure 1.3) for your specific project by answering the questions that follow.

**The Rhetorical Situation**

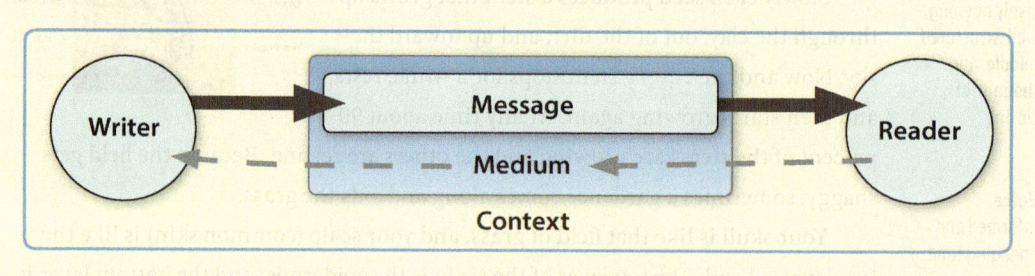

*fig. 1.3*

- **What's your role as the writer in this project?** Are you writing as a concerned citizen, a student, a friend relating a story, a reporter providing news, or a blogger giving an opinion? Your role affects the level of language you should use, the voice you adopt, the kinds of information you'll include, and so on.
- **What's your goal?** What do you want to happen because of your writing? Is your goal to inform, entertain, or persuade? Some combination of these? What actions and outcomes do you want to result from this project? Your goals determine your approach.
- **Who are your readers?** Consider whether it's your instructor, your classmates, or some other group. Then reflect on questions like these, which will help you make choices about what to include in your writing and how to organize it, as well as your voice and style:
  - What do my readers know about my topic, and what do they need or want to know?
  - What are their attitudes toward the topic and toward me?
  - How well do they read English, at what level, especially in relation to the special language of this topic?
  - How will they use my writing—for enjoyment, instruction, debate, something else?
- **What's the medium for your message?** What form of writing is your project? A traditional essay? A research paper, case study, or lab report? Or is it a multimodal project—some combination of written report, audio or video segments, web page, presentation, and so on? In what context will you develop and share your project?

## Study the Assignment

College instructors generally personalize their writing assignments, but most will spell out these essentials: (1) the objective, (2) the task, (3) the requirements, and (4) suggested approaches and topics. An important step in your prewriting, then, is to study the assignment carefully so you can meet or exceed the expectations. Use these questions to guide you:

- **What are the key words?** Certain words—especially verbs—explain what main action you must perform in your writing. Pay attention to these signals:

| | |
|---:|:---|
| **Analyze:** | Break down a topic into subparts, showing how those parts relate. |
| **Argue:** | Defend a claim with logical arguments. |
| **Classify:** | Sort a large group into well-defined subgroups. |
| **Compare/contrast:** | Point out similarities and/or differences. |
| **Define:** | Give a clear, thoughtful explanation or meaning of something. |
| **Describe**: | Show in detail what something is like. |
| **Evaluate:** | Weigh the truth, quality, or usefulness of something. |
| **Explain:** | Give reasons, list steps, or discuss the causes of something. |
| **Interpret:** | Tell in your own words what something means. |
| **Reflect:** | Share your well-considered thoughts about a subject. |
| **Summarize**: | Restate someone else's ideas very briefly in your own words. |
| **Synthesize:** | Connect facts or ideas to create something new. |

- **What are the choices, restrictions, and deadlines?** The assignment may offer a list of options and approaches related to topics, while also restricting those options in some way. Your assignment will undoubtedly specify a due date, but it may also set interim deadlines for topic selection, research, a first draft, etc. Include these in your planning.
- **What types of writing does the assignment specify?** Perhaps it's a traditional essay, but it could also be any number of forms: a personal reflection, a research report, a creative alternative or experimental piece. What are the specific qualities and features of the form? And what are the expectations about how you will submit and/or present your project?
- **How does the assignment fit in the course?** Consider the value of the project as a percentage of the final grade. Explore its connection to course learning outcomes, as well as to earlier and later assignments.
- **How will the assignment be evaluated?** Look for assessment criteria in the assignment. Have these expectations clearly in mind as you move forward with the project.

 Your project will likely be more successful—as well as more meaningful and enjoyable—if you can discover or cultivate a personal interest in the assignment. Consider ways to connect the project to your curiosity, your chosen field of study, or your life outside of school.

# Developing a Topic

For some assignments, finding a suitable topic may require little thinking on your part. If an instructor asks you to summarize an article in a scholarly journal, you know what you will write about—the article in question. But suppose the instructor asks you to analyze a feature of popular culture in terms of its impact on society. You won't be sure of a specific writing topic until you explore the possibilities. Keep the following points in mind when you conduct a topic search. Your topic must . . .

- meet the requirements of the assignment.
- be limited in scope.
- seem reasonable (that is, be within your means to research).
- genuinely interest you.

## Limit the Subject Area

Many of your writing assignments may relate to general subject areas you are currently studying. Your task, then, is to select a specific topic related to the general area of study—a topic limited enough that you can treat it with sufficient depth in the number of pages and preparation time allowed for the assignment. The following examples show the difference between general subjects and limited topics:

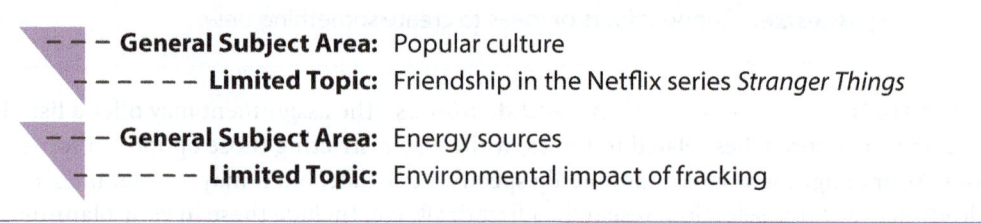

**General Subject Area:** Popular culture
**Limited Topic:** Friendship in the Netflix series *Stranger Things*

**General Subject Area:** Energy sources
**Limited Topic:** Environmental impact of fracking

## Conduct Your Search

Finding a writing idea that meets the requirements of the assignment should not be difficult, if you know how and where to look. Follow these steps:

1. **Check your class notes and handouts** for ideas related to the assignment.
2. **Consult indexes, guides, and other library references.** Subscription databases such as EBSCOhost, for example, list current articles published on specific topics and where to find them. Databases include sources suitable for college papers and exclude social media and advertising found in general online searches.
3. **Search the Internet.** Type in a keyword or phrase (the general subject stated in the assignment) and see what you can find.
4. **Discuss the assignment** with your instructor or an information specialist.
5. **Use one or more of the prewriting strategies** described on the following pages to generate possible writing ideas.

## Explore Possible Topics

You can generate topic possibilities by using the following strategies. These same strategies can be used when you've chosen a topic and want to develop it further.

### Journal Writing

Write in a journal on a regular basis. Reflect on your personal feelings, develop your thoughts, and record the happenings of each day. Periodically go back and underline ideas that you would like to explore in writing assignments. In the following journal-writing sample, the writer came up with an idea for a writing assignment about the societal impacts of popular culture.

> I saw a really disturbing story on Twitter this morning. I've been thinking about it all day. In California a little girl was killed when she was struck by a car driven by a man distracted by a billboard ad for lingerie featuring a scantily clothed woman. Not only is it a horrifying thing to happen, but it also seems to me all too symbolic of the way that sexually charged images in the media are putting children, and especially girls, in danger. That reminds me of another story I read this week about preteen girls wanting to wear the kinds of revealing outfits that they see influencers wearing on Instagram and celebrities wearing on the covers of magazines aimed at teenagers. Too many of today's media images give young people the impression that sexuality should begin at an early age. This is definitely a dangerous message.

### Listing

Freely list ideas as they come to mind, beginning with a key concept related to the assignment. (Brainstorming—listing ideas in conjunction with members of a group—is often an effective way to extend your lists.) The following is an example of a student's list of ideas for possible topics on the subject of news reporting:

> **Aspect of popular culture: News reporting**
>
> Fake news, misinformation, clickbait
> Sensationalism
> Sound bites rather than in-depth analysis
> Focus on the negative
> Shouting matches pretending to be debates
> Problems with social media as a primary news source
> Lack of observation of people's privacy
> Bias and polarization
> Contradictory health news confusing to readers
> Little focus on "unappealing" issues like poverty
> Celebration of "celebrity"

## Clustering

When you create a cluster, you visualize connections between concepts, things, and events. To begin the clustering process, write a key word or phrase related to the assignment in the center of your paper. Circle it, and then cluster ideas around it. Circle each idea as you record it, and draw a line connecting it to the closest related idea. Keep going until you run out of ideas and connections. Figure 1.4 shows a student's cluster on the subject of sports:

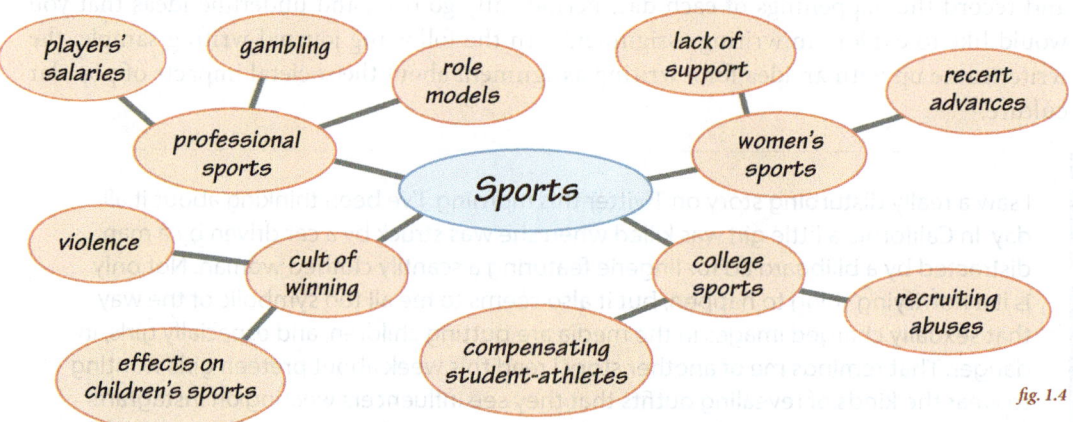

fig. 1.4

 After four or five minutes of listing or clustering, scan your work for an idea to explore in freewriting. A writing idea should begin to emerge during this freewriting session.

# Freewrite to Discover and Develop a Topic

Freewriting is the writing you do without having a specific outcome in mind. You simply write down whatever pops into your head as you explore your topic. Freewriting can serve as a starting point for your writing, or it can be combined with any of the other prewriting strategies to help you select, explore, focus, or organize your writing. If you get stuck at any point during the composing process, you can return to freewriting as a way of generating new ideas.

### Reminders

- **Freewriting helps you get your thoughts down on paper.**
  (Thoughts are constantly passing through your mind.)
- **Freewriting helps you develop and organize these thoughts.**
- **Freewriting helps you make sense out of things that you may be studying or researching.**
- **Freewriting may seem awkward at times, but just stick with it.**

## The Process

- **Write nonstop and record whatever comes into your mind.** Follow your thoughts instead of trying to direct them.
- **If you have a particular topic or assignment to complete, use it as a starting point.** Otherwise, begin with anything that comes to mind.
- **Don't stop to judge, edit, or correct your writing;** that will come later.
- **Keep writing even when you think you have exhausted all of your ideas.** Switch to another angle or voice, but keep writing.
- **Watch for a promising idea to emerge.** Learn to recognize the beginnings of a good idea, and then expand that idea by recording as many related thoughts and specific details as possible.

## The Result

- **Review your writing and underline the ideas you like.** These ideas will often serve as the basis for future writings.
- **Determine exactly what you need to write about.** Once you've figured out what you are required to do, you may then decide to do a second freewriting exercise.
- **Listen to and read the freewriting of others.** Learn from your peers.

## Freewriting

Write nonstop for ten minutes or longer to discover possible writing ideas. Use a key concept related to the assignment as a starting point. You'll soon discover potential writing ideas that might otherwise have never entered your mind. Note in the following example that the writer doesn't stop writing even when he can't think of anything to say. Note also that he doesn't stop to correct typos and other mistakes.

> Popular culture. What does that include? Movies, music, video games, podcasts, television. I like all of those. Nothing's better than spending a night binge-watching Netflix. Hmm . . . Maybe there's something to that topic. Have binge-watching habits changed the way TV series are written and produced? What features make a show more binge-worthy than others? Those questions might be fun to write about. What else? What if I examined how my experience of a show changed by watching just one episode a week rather than binging two or three or SIX in a row? That topic could be interesting, but gathering data would take too long. So . . . what else comes to mind? Well, binge-watching isn't always a good thing. Maybe I could write about how the easy access of streaming TV is creating a generation of nonreaders. Or maybe I could focus on whether people aren't getting much physical exercise because they are too hooked on too many shows. Also, all that screen time . . . that can't be good. What are the effects? I feel like I've gathered some good ideas here.

# Researching Your Topic

Writer and instructor Donald Murray said that "writers write with information. If there is no information, there will be no effective writing." How true! Before you can develop a thoughtful piece of writing, you must gain a thorough understanding of your topic; to do so, you must carry out the necessary reading, reflecting, and researching. Writing becomes a satisfying experience once you can speak with authority about your topic. While the "Research and Writing" section in Part 3 of *The College Writer* offers in-depth instruction on this topic, the following pages introduce these strategies:

- Determining what you already know about the topic
- Listing questions you would like to answer during your research
- Identifying and exploring possible sources of information
- Tracking and effectively working with your sources

## Find Out What You Already Know

Use one or more of the following strategies to determine what you already know about a writing topic.

1. **Focused freewriting:** At this point, you can focus your freewriting by (1) exploring your limited topic from different angles or (2) approaching your freewriting as if it were a quick draft of the actual paper. A quick version will tell you how much you know about your topic and what you need to find out.
2. **Clustering:** Try clustering with your topic serving as the nucleus word. Your clustering should focus on what you already know. (See Figure 1.4.)
3. **Five W's of writing:** Answer the five W's—Who? What? When? Where? and Why?—to identify basic information on your subject. Add How? to the list for better coverage.
4. **Directed writing:** Write whatever comes to mind about your topic, using one of the modes listed below. (Repeat the process as often as you need to, selecting a different mode each time.)

> **Describe it:** What do you see, hear, feel, smell, and taste?
> **Compare it:** What is it similar to? What is it different from?
> **Associate it:** What connections between this topic and others come to mind?
> **Analyze it:** What parts does it have? How do they work together?
> **Argue it:** What do you like about the topic? What do you not like about it? What are its strengths and weaknesses?
> **Apply it:** What can you do with it? How can you use it?

## Ask Questions

To guide your collecting and researching, you may find it helpful to list questions about your topic that you would like to answer. Alternatively, you can use the questions that follow to guide your research.

|  | Description | Function | History | Value |
|---|---|---|---|---|
| **Problems** | • What is the problem?<br>• What type of problem is it?<br>• What are its parts?<br>• What are the signs of the problem? | • Who or what is affected by it?<br>• What new problems might it cause in the future? | • What is the current status of the problem?<br>• What or who caused it?<br>• What or who contributed to it? | • What is its significance? Why?<br>• Why is it more (or less) important than other problems?<br>• What does it symbolize or illustrate? |
| **Policies** | • What is the policy?<br>• How broad is it?<br>• What are its parts?<br>• What are its most important features? | • What is the policy designed to do?<br>• What is needed to make it work?<br>• What are or will be its effects? | • What brought about this policy?<br>• What are the alternatives? | • Is the policy workable?<br>• What are its advantages and disadvantages?<br>• Is it practical?<br>• Is it a good policy? Why or why not? |
| **Concepts** | • What is the concept?<br>• What are its parts?<br>• What is its main feature?<br>• Whom or what is it related to? | • Who has been influenced by this concept?<br>• Why is it important?<br>• How does it work? | • When did it originate?<br>• How has it changed over the years?<br>• How might it change in the future? | • What practical value does it have?<br>• Why is it superior (or inferior) to similar concepts?<br>• What is its social worth? |

*ajt / Shutterstock.com*

## Identify Possible Sources

Finding meaningful sources is one of the most important steps you will take as you prepare to write. Listed below are tips that will help you identify good sources:

1. **Give yourself enough time.** Finding good sources of information may be time-consuming. For example, you may need to get important books and articles through interlibrary loan if they aren't available digitally or in the library.
2. **Be aware of the limits of your resources.** Print material may be out-of-date. Online information may be more current, but it may not always be reliable.
3. **Use your existing resources to find additional sources of information.** Pay attention to books, articles, and individuals mentioned in reliable sources of information you find as you research.
4. **Ask for help.** The specialists in your school library can help you find information that is reliable and relevant. These people are trained to find information; don't hesitate to ask for their help.
5. **Bookmark useful websites.** Include reference works and academic resources related to your major.
6. **Use ethically sourced information.** You've heard of ethically sourced coffee, chocolate, and clothing. Take the same attitude to your information. Make sure it comes from reputable information suppliers: scholarly studies and academic journals from databases, reliable media sources, expert websites, and so on.

### Explore Different Sources of Information

Of course, books and websites are not the only possible sources of information. Primary sources such as interviews, observations, and surveys may lead you to a more thorough and meaningful understanding of a topic.

| Primary Sources | Secondary Sources |
|---|---|
| Interviews | Articles |
| Observations | Reference resources |
| Participation | Books |
| Surveys | Websites |
| Original documents and artifacts | Documentaries |

### Carry Out Your Research

As you conduct your research, seek a variety of reliable sources. It's also a good idea to choose an efficient note-taking method before you start. You will want to take good notes on the information you find and record all the publishing details necessary for citing your sources. Of course, you'll need to work with your sources by reading and viewing them critically.

Reserve a special part of a notebook or file on your computer to question, evaluate, and reflect on your research as it develops. Reflection helps you make sense of new ideas, refocus your thinking, and evaluate your progress.

## Track Sources

Follow these strategies for tracking sources and taking notes.

- **Track resources in a working bibliography.** Once you find a useful book, journal article, news story, or web page, record identifying information for the source.

- **Use a note-taking system that respects sources.** Essentially, your note-taking system should help you keep an accurate record of useful information and ideas from sources while also allowing you to engage those sources with your own thinking.

- **Distinguish summaries, paraphrases, and quotations.** As you read sources, you will find material that answers your questions and helps you achieve your writing purpose. At that point, decide whether to summarize, paraphrase, or quote the material:
  - **A summary** pulls just the main points out of a passage and puts them in your own words: Summarize source material when it contains relevant ideas and information that you can boil down.
  - **A paraphrase** rewrites a passage point by point in your own words: Paraphrase source material when all the information is important but the actual phrasing isn't especially important or memorable.
  - **A quotation** records a passage from the source word for word: Quote when the source states something crucial and says it well. Note: In your notes, always identify quoted material by putting quotation marks around it.

Summarizing, paraphrasing, and quoting are treated more fully in chapter 20. Here is a brief example, with the original passage coming from Coral Ann Howells' *Alice Munro*, published in 1998 by Manchester University Press as part of its Contemporary World Writers series.

> **Original:** "To read Munro's stories is to discover the delights of seeing two worlds at once: an ordinary everyday world and the shadowy map of another imaginary or secret world laid over the real one, so that in reading we slip from one world into the other in an unassuming domestic sort of way."
>
> **Summary:** Munro's fiction moves readers from recognizable reality into a hidden world.
>
> **Paraphrase:** Reading Munro's fiction gives readers the enjoyment of experiencing a double world: day-to-day reality and on top of that a more mysterious, fantastic world, with the result that readers move smoothly between the worlds in a seamless, ordinary way.
>
> **Quotation:** Munro's fiction takes us into "the shadowy map of another imaginary or secret world laid over the real one."

# Getting Started: Applications

Once you have used the instruction in this chapter to get started on a writing project, there might be more to think about. Through the activities below, apply what you have learned.

1. **Wise Words:** Writer Ralph Fletcher shares, "When I write, I am always struck at how magical and unexpected the process turns out to be." Would you describe the writing process you follow as "magical" and "unexpected"? Explain.
2. **Writing Reset:** Reread one of your recent essays. Does the writing show that you thoroughly understood your subject, met the needs of your readers, and achieved your purpose? How does it measure against the traits of strong writing? What traits in your writing are strong? Which need work?
3. **Living Today:** Getting started techniques help you engage with topics thoughtfully. Many areas of contemporary life—whether in health, the environment, the arts, or work—could benefit from our thoughtful engagement. Select one of these broad subject areas and engage it by doing the following: Brainstorm possible topics and select one. Then explore what you know about that topic and what you need to learn.
4. **Photo Op:** This chapter opens with a photograph (Figure 1.1) and a diagram of the writing process (Figure 1.2). With these images in mind, find or make a photo, diagram, or other graphic that captures your sense of the writing process as a whole or of getting started in particular.

## Learning-Objectives Checklist ✓

Have you achieved this chapter's learning objectives? Check your progress with the items below, revisiting topics in the chapter as needed. I have . . .

\_\_\_\_ outlined the writing process, from getting started to submitting.

\_\_\_\_ adapted the writing process to a specific writing project, taking into account the assignment challenges and my own writing habits.

\_\_\_\_ differentiated seven traits of strong, college-level writing and assessed my relative strengths and weaknesses with respect to these traits.

\_\_\_\_ analyzed the rhetorical situation for a specific writing project so as to make good decisions about my approach, tone, and content.

\_\_\_\_ identified an assignment's key words, options, and restrictions, and related the assignment to course goals, other assignments, and my own interests.

\_\_\_\_ developed and chosen a strong topic for a writing project by limiting the subject, conducting an exploratory search, and using prewriting techniques.

\_\_\_\_ identified what I already know about the topic, generated questions to research, formulated a list of possible resources, and worked with those sources, while carefully tracking my use of these sources.

# Chapter 2

# Reading Critically

Nobody likes to be criticized. While we might agree that some politicians, celebrities, and billionaires deserve it, it's likely that even they feel thin-skinned about criticism.

It doesn't help that in our digital age criticism is loud, proud, and emotional. Digital trolls make the trolls in *The Hobbit* look like little lost lambs. Social media pours misinformation on debates like gasoline on a wildfire, twisting facts, hurling insults, and taking quotes out of context. People are called out, shamed, and canceled.

None of that noise is intelligent criticism. True critical thinking involves attentive listening, careful analyzing, and measured evaluating. Such thinking is at the heart of thoughtful reading and viewing, which are central to the process of developing thoughtful, truthful writing.

Where do you start? In this chapter, with learning the art of careful, critical reading.

**Visually Speaking** Review Figure 2.1. What reading habits are on display? How do you know? What reading habits do you typically follow? Are any present in the picture?

## Learning Objectives

By working through this chapter, you will be able to

- implement strategies to think critically about topics.
- practice SQ3R to read texts critically.
- take notes through annotation and a double-entry notebook.
- actively read different written texts.
- produce personal responses to texts.
- objectively summarize texts.
- thoughtfully engage with social media.

Rawpixel.com / Shutterstock.com

fig. 2.1

# Cultivating Critical-Thinking Habits

Anti-vaccination campaigns. Conspiracy theories about virus outbreaks. Panic buying of toilet paper. Is this what critical thinking looks like? More like indiscretion based on emotion and misinformation. Such thinking ignores real science, expert voices, and common sense.

True critical thinking, on the other hand, is fair and balanced. It poses questions effectively and explores all the relevant data and ideas to arrive at a sensible conclusion. Critical thinkers are aware of their own perspectives, testing them while being open to other points of view. It's the kind of thinking enormously helpful to your writing projects.

## Adopt a Critical-Thinking Mindset

Train your mind to think critically, and the substance of your writing will improve.

1. **Be curious.** Ask "Why?" Cultivate your ability to wonder; question what you see, hear, and read—both inside and outside the classroom.

2. **Be creative.** Don't settle for obvious answers. Look at things in a fresh way, asking "what-if" questions, such as "What if Ophelia didn't die in *Hamlet*?"

3. **Be open to new ideas.** Approach thinking as you would approach a road trip—looking for the unexpected and musing over mysteries.

4. **Value others' points of view.** Look at an issue from another person's perspective and weigh it against your own. Examine how the core of the person's perspective compares to the core of yours, and how each basis for thought might lead to different conclusions.

5. **Get involved.** Read quality books, journals, and news articles. Watch documentaries. Join book clubs, film clubs, or political and social-action activities.

6. **Focus.** Sharpen your concentration, looking for details that distinguish a topic and reveal key questions related to its nature, function, and impact.

7. **Be rational.** Choose a logical thinking pattern like the one on the next page, and then work through the steps to deepen your understanding of a topic.

8. **Make connections.** Use writing to explore how and why topics or issues are related. Use comparisons to identify and name these relationships.

9. **Tolerate ambiguity.** Respectfully analyze issues not readily resolved—and acknowledge when your position requires further research or thought.

10. **Test the evidence.** Be properly skeptical about all claims. Look for corroboration (or verification) in other sources. Consider how your textbooks and instructors select, examine, and present evidence.

11. **Develop research-based conclusions.** Focus on understanding issues, assessing their history, development, function, and impact. During the process, gather details that lead to and support a reasonable conclusion.

12. **Assess results.** Consider each paper you do as a benchmark that reflects your progress in developing your thinking and writing skills. Test new papers against earlier ones.

## Ask Probing Questions

Whatever the topic, good questions trigger critical thinking about it. They open up the issue and guide you toward in-depth answers. To learn this art, practice these strategies:

**Push beyond closed questions to open ones.** Closed questions seek a limited response—a simple fact, a "yes" or a "no." Such questions are important, but critical thinking asks open questions that invite brainstorming and discussion, triggering a flow of ideas.
- *Closed:* Would someone feel an earthquake measuring 3.0 on the Richter scale?
- *Open:* How might a major earthquake impact San Francisco?

**Ask "educated" questions.** Educated questions are informed, precise, and clear. They invite debate and interpretation.
- *Broad question:* What's wrong with social media?
- *Educated question:* Does the 16 percent rise in instances of online bullying during the past five years correlate to a rise in teenage suicides?

**Keep a question journal.** Divide a notebook page or split a digital document. On one side, write questions about a topic. On the other side, freewrite your thoughts about the questions.

**Write Q&A drafts.** Turn your topic into a main question, then draft an answer. As you draft, feel free to break it down into secondary questions behind the main question, and answer those in turn. Once you're done, assess what answers need more thought and information.

## Activate a Thinking Pattern

Thinking critically includes several components. Learn how to activate them.

**Determine your thinking purpose.** What's the central issue you wish to settle, the problem to explore, the idea to understand, and so on? What outcome do you want? Study any assignment directions to guide your thinking pattern.

**Explore relevant and reliable information.** What data in what forms are available? Is this information accurate, precise, and connected to your question? Are you exploring with an open mind or just looking for evidence to support what you already believe?

**Draw sensible, logical conclusions from the evidence.** What's the best way to interpret the available information? To what logical conclusions does it lead, through what reasoning?

**Consider your perspective—your point of view.** From what point of view are you looking at the issue? Are there other perspectives you need to consider? Are your ego, interests, and desires getting in the way of helpful empathy for those with another point of view? Are assumptions coloring your conclusions?

**Explore the consequences of your conclusions.** To what outcomes do your conclusions naturally lead? What do they imply about the issue and its relation to life?

**Evaluate your conclusions.** Are they clear and clearly based on quality, ethically-sourced information? Are your conclusions both deep and broad, logical and fair?

# Using the SQ3R Reading Strategy

Your coursework and writing projects involve reading a lot of material—textbooks, novels, scholarly books, news articles, and even social media posts. For important reading assignments, it pays to approach them systematically. **SQ3R—Survey, Question, Read, Recite,** and **Review**—is one system that activates your critical thinking as you read. Here's how it works.

## Survey

The first step is to preview the material. Check the rhetorical situation (Figure 2.2) for clues:

**Rhetorical Situation**

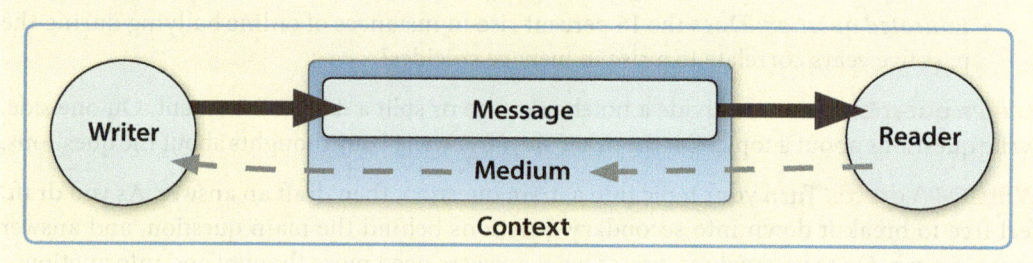

fig. 2.2

Read about the author. Then read the title and the opening and closing paragraphs to get a sense of the main points. Glance at all other pages, noting headings, topic sentences in paragraphs, boldface type, illustrations, charts, maps, and other cues to the content and organization.

**Benefits:** Surveying helps you (1) focus on the writer's message, (2) identify the text's organization, and (3) anticipate how the text will develop.

## Question

As you survey, ask questions that you hope to answer as you read.

- **Read any questions that accompany the reading.** Look at the end of the reading or in a study guide.
- **Turn headings into questions.** If a subhead says, "The Study," ask, "How was the study conducted?"
- **Imagine test questions for major points.** If the reading discusses self-control, ask, "What conclusions does the author draw about self-control?"
- **Ask journalistic questions:** *Ask who, what, where, when, why,* and *how?* Whose attitudes are changing? What are their attitudes? Where is the change strongest? When is it occurring? Why is it happening? How?

## Read

As you encounter facts and ideas, ask these questions: What does this mean? How do the ideas relate to each other and to what I know? What's coming next?

Keep track of your answers by taking notes, annotating the text, mapping, or outlining. Read difficult parts slowly; reread them if necessary. Look up unfamiliar words or ideas, and use your senses to imagine the events, people, places, or things you are reading about. Imagine talking with the writer.

Separate fact from opinion. Where does the author state objective evidence you can verify? Where does the author express personal points of view? Express agreement, lodge complaints, ask for proof—and imagine the writer's response or look for it in the text.

***Benefits:*** Engaging actively with the text in this way will draw you deeper into the world of the writing. You'll trigger memories and make surprising connections.

## Recite

After finishing a page, section, or chapter, recite the key points aloud. Answering *who, what, where, when, why,* and *how* questions is a quick way of testing yourself on how well you understood what you read. You can also recite by listing key points or writing a summary.

***Benefits:*** Reciting tests your comprehension, drives the material deeper into your long-term memory, and helps you connect the content with what you already know.

## Review

As soon as you finish reading the material, double-check the questions you posed in the "question" stage of SQ3R. Can you answer them? Glance over any notes you made as well. But don't stop there if the reading is especially important. You will remember the material much better by spacing out your reviews; spend a few minutes reviewing each text over the next few days. Consider the following helpful memory techniques:

- **Visualize the concepts in concrete ways.** *Example:* If a text discusses a study about self-control, imagine a television panel discussing the topic.
- **Draw diagrams or develop clusters.** *Example:* Make a chart.
- **Explain the material in your own words.** *Example:* Write a summary.
- **Teach it to someone:** *Example:* Review the main points with a friend.
- **Use acronyms or rhymes.** *Example:* "*i* before *e* except after *c*."

***Benefits:*** Research shows that reviewing within 24 hours helps considerably to move information from your short-term memory to your long-term memory. You will also improve your memory if you create a network of associations with the information you want to remember, if you link the memory to two or more senses, or if you reorganize the material while still retaining the substance with accuracy.

# Critical Thinking Through Reading

While the SQ3R method gives you a specific system for reading important works, you can generally improve your reading skills by simply reading more actively. Below and on the pages that follow you'll find several strategies for active reading.

## Maintain Focus and Attention

Active reading relies on conditions and practices that keep your attention engaged and your focus sharp. Follow these tips:

- **Remove distractions.** Engaged reading requires that you disengage from all distractions such as your cell phone, social media, or TV.
- **Take your time.** Read in stretches of about 45 minutes, followed by short breaks. And when you break, think about what you've read, what might come next, and why.
- **Put your reading in context.** Where and when was this text written and published? Who is the author, and why did this person write the piece? What are the writer's qualifications to address this topic? Why are you reading it?
- **Preview, read, review.** In a compressed version of SQ3R, preview the text: scan the title, opening and closing paragraphs, headings, topic sentences, and graphics. Next, read the text carefully, asking questions such as "What does this mean?" and "Why is this important?" Finally, review what you have learned and what questions remain unanswered.
- **Read aloud.** Do so for especially difficult parts of the text.
- **Write while reading.** Take notes, especially when working on research projects. Annotate the text by highlighting main points, writing a "?" beside puzzling parts, or jotting key insights in the margin.

### Sample Text

The following article by Dan Heath appeared in the June 2, 2010 edition of *Fast Company*. Read the essay, using the active reading tips above and answering the questions that follow.

#### Why Change Is So Hard: Self-Control Is Exhaustible

1   You hear something a lot about change: People won't change because they're too lazy. Well, I'm here to stick up for the lazy people. In fact, I want to argue that what looks like laziness is actually exhaustion. The proof comes from a psychology study that is absolutely fascinating.

##### The Study

2   So picture this: Students come into a lab. It smells amazing—someone has just baked chocolate-chip cookies. On a table in front of them, there are two bowls. One has the fresh-baked cookies. The other has a bunch of radishes. Some of the students are asked to eat some cookies but no radishes. Others are told to eat radishes but no cookies, and while

they sit there, nibbling on rabbit food, the researchers leave the room—which is intended to tempt them and is frankly kind of sadistic. But in the study none of the radish-eaters slipped—they showed admirable self-control. And meanwhile, it probably goes without saying that the people gorging on cookies didn't experience much temptation.

Then, the two groups are asked to do a second, seemingly unrelated task—basically a kind of logic puzzle where they have to trace out a complicated geometric pattern without raising their pencils. Unbeknownst to the group, the puzzle can't be solved. The scientists are curious how long individuals will persist at a difficult task. So the cookie-eaters try again and again, for an average of 19 minutes, before they give up. But the radish-eaters—they only last an average of 8 minutes. What gives?

**The Results**

The answer may surprise you: The radish-eaters ran out of self-control. Psychologists have discovered that self-control is an exhaustible resource. And I don't mean self-control only in the sense of turning down cookies or alcohol; I mean a broader sense of self-supervision—any time you're paying close attention to your actions, like when you're having a tough conversation or trying to stay focused on a paper you're writing. This helps to explain why, after a long hard day at the office, we're more likely to snap at our spouses or have one drink too many—we've depleted our self-control.

And here's why this matters for change: In almost all change situations, you're substituting new, unfamiliar behaviors for old, comfortable ones, and that burns self-control. Let's say I present a new morning routine to you that specifies how you'll shower and brush your teeth. You'll understand it and you might even agree with my process. But to pull it off, you'll have to supervise yourself very carefully. Every fiber of your being will want to go back to the old way of doing things. Inevitably, you'll slip. And if I were uncharitable, I'd see you going back to the old way and I'd say, "You're so lazy. Why can't you just change?"

This brings us back to the point I promised I'd make: That what looks like laziness is often exhaustion. Change wears people out—even well-intentioned people will simply run out of fuel.

---

### Reading for Better Writing

1. *Connections:* Think about your own life. Which activities require you to exert a great deal of self-control? How might this article help you with those struggles?
2. *Comprehension:* What is the thesis of this essay? Can you restate it in a single sentence? How does that thesis grow out of the findings of the psychology study that the essay discusses? Summarize those findings.
3. *Reading Strategies:* Which active-reading practices did you follow when reading this essay? Which ones helped you understand and engage the essay fully? Compare your notes and annotations with a classmate's.

**Your Project:** Dan Heath's essay explains the results of a research study. For your own writing, consider finding a research report on a topic that interests you. Then use the active reading strategies in this chapter to write an essay like Heath's.

## Map the Text

If you are visually oriented, you may understand a text best by mapping out its important parts. One way to do so is by "clustering." Start by naming the main topic in an oval at the center of the page. Then branch out using lines and "balloons," where each balloon contains a word or phrase for one major subtopic. Branch out in further layers of balloons to show even more subpoints, as in Figure 2.3. If you wish, add graphics, arrows, drawings—anything that helps you visualize the relationships among ideas.

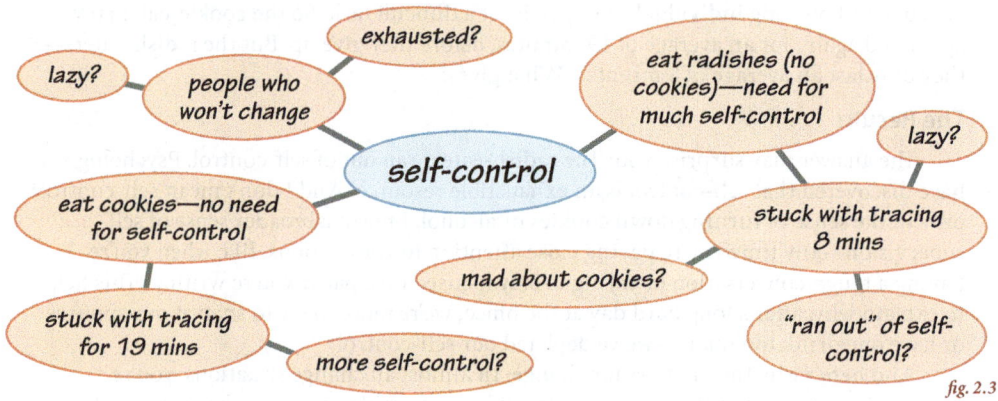

fig. 2.3

## Outline the Text

Outlining is the traditional way of showing all the major parts, points, and subpoints in a text. An outline uses parallel structure to show main points and subordinate points.

### Sample Outline for "Why Change Is So Hard: Self-Control Is Exhaustible"

1. Introduction: Change is hard not because of laziness but because of exhaustion.
2. A study tests self-control.
   a. Some students must eat only cookies—using little self-control.
   b. Some students must eat only radishes—using much self-control.
   c. Both sets of students have to trace a pattern without lifting the pencil—an unsolvable puzzle.
      - Cookie-only students last an average of 19 minutes before quitting.
      - Radish-only students last an average of 8 minutes before quitting.
3. Results show that self-control is exhaustible.
   a. Avoiding temptation and working in a hard, focused way require self-control.
   b. Change requires self-control.
   c. Failure to change often results from exhaustion of self-control.

## Evaluate the Text

Critical reading does not mean disproving a text or disapproving of it. It means thoughtfully inspecting, weighing, and evaluating the writer's ideas. To strengthen your reading skills, learn to evaluate texts using the following criteria.

1. **Judge the reading's credibility.** What form of writing is this text? Did you access it through a reliable or a questionable source? Where was the piece published? How reliable is the author? How current is the information? How accurate and complete does it seem to be? In addition, consider the author's tone of voice, attitude, and apparent biases.

   > *Discussion:* Dan Heath, the author of "Why Change Is So Hard" is a *New York Times* best-selling author, a consultant to the Aspen Institute, and a monthly columnist for *Fast Company*. How do these credentials affect your reading of the article? How does the article itself build or break credibility?

2. **Put the reading in a larger context.** Do other sources support the text's ideas? Which details of background, history, and social context help you understand the text's perspective? Have things changed or remained the same since the text's publication? What allusions (references to people, events, and so on) does the writer use? Why?

   > *Discussion:* "Why Change Is So Hard" centers around a single psychological study and draws from it specific conclusions about self-control. What other studies have attempted to track self-control? Is this a new subdiscipline in psychological research, or a well-established one?

3. **Evaluate the reasoning and support.** Is the reasoning clear and logical? Are the examples and other supporting details appropriate and enlightening? Are inferences (what the text implies) consistent with the tone and message? (Look especially for ulterior motives or sarcasm that undercut what is said explicitly.)

   > *Discussion:* In "Why Change Is So Hard," Heath identifies exhaustion of self-control as the reason for the difference between the performance of the two test groups. What other explanations could there be for the difference in performance between the two groups of subjects? Is Heath's reasoning sound and convincing?

4. **Reflect on how the reading challenges you.** Which of your beliefs and values does the reading call into question? What discomfort does it create? Does your own perspective skew your evaluation?

   > *Discussion:* What self-control issues have you faced? What might this article have to say about those who work two jobs, run single-parent households, serve extended terms in war zones, or otherwise must exert superhuman levels of self-control? What social changes could help keep people from "snapping"?

**fyi** For additional help evaluating texts, see chapter 20, "Doing Research."

# Taking Notes Actively

Critical reading can happen when you engage the text through note-taking. While there are many different methods, two popular ones are annotating the text and using a double-entry notebook. Both help you slow down, absorb what you're reading, and reflect on it.

## Annotate the Text

Whether you're working with a print-out of a text or working digitally with a pdf, annotating means commenting in the margin, underlining or highlighting portions of the text, and tracking key points. Here are some other common annotation strategies:

- **Ask questions.** Sometimes a simple "?" in the margin will do. Other times it's best to write out the question in full. What doubts, concerns, and confusions do you encounter as you read?
- **Make connections.** Draw arrows to link ideas, or make notes like "see page 36" to link related passages.
- **Add personal asides.** Record what you think and feel while reading.
- **Define terms.** When you encounter a word you don't know, you may be able to sense the meaning from the context; however, you'll want to clarify such terms and define them in the margin if they're especially important.
- **Create a marginal index.** Write key words in the margin to identify themes, parts of the piece, and so on.

### Sample Annotations

> ### Why Change Is So Hard: Self-Control Is (Exhaustible)
>
> *[Hmm? What does exhaustible mean?]*
>
> You hear something a lot about change: People won't change because they're too lazy. Well, I'm here to stick up for the lazy people. In fact, I want to argue that what looks like laziness is actually (exhaustion). The proof comes from a psychology study that is absolutely fascinating.
>
> *[I like this writer's voice.]*
> *[Oh, so our self-control eventually gets tired?]*
>
> ### The Study
>
> So picture this: Students come into a lab. It smells amazing—someone has just baked chocolate-chip cookies. On a table in front of them, there are two bowls. One has the fresh-baked cookies. The other has a bunch of radishes. Some of the students are asked to eat some cookies but no radishes. Others are told to eat radishes but no cookies, and while they sit there, nibbling on rabbit food, the researchers leave the room—which is intended to tempt them and is frankly kind of sadistic. But in the study none of the radish-eaters slipped—they showed admirable self-control. And meanwhile, it probably goes without saying that the people gorging on cookies didn't experience much temptation.
>
> *[Maybe they just don't like radishes?]*

# Create a Double-Entry Notebook

A double-entry notebook involves parallel note-taking—notes from the text you're reading beside your own brainstorming, reaction, and reflection. You can do this note-taking in a physical notebook, or you set up parallel columns on your computer. Follow these steps:

1. **Divide your notebook pages in half with a vertical line.**
2. **Record notes on your reading in the left column.** Put bibliographic information identifying the text at the top. Underneath, take notes—summarizing, paraphrasing, and quoting material from the text. Identify each note with a page number or other locating detail from the text.
3. **Explore your responses to the reading in the right column.** You can generate these responses as you take notes on the text. Or you can complete your note-taking on the text and then go back to work on your reflection. Think about what the text is saying, why the point is important, whether you agree with it, and how the material relates to other ideas and other readings you've done. Consider questions like these:
   - How does this text relate to the writing project I'm working on?
   - What specific information is particularly striking? What about ideas and explanations in the piece?
   - How does the text connect with my experiences, values, and beliefs?
   - How might this material be useful to my writing project?

## Sample Double-Entry Notebook Page

| | |
|---|---|
| Dan Heath, "Why Change Is So Hard: Self-Control Is Exhaustible." <u>Fast Company</u>. June 2, 2010.<br>• It's not laziness but exhaustion that makes it difficult for people to change<br>• The experiment shows this: part 1, students faced with two bowls, one of cookies and the other or radishes --> one group told to eat cookies but no radishes, the second group radishes but no cookies. Part 2: all students asked to complete a puzzle without a solution--> a test of endurance<br>• Results: cookie students last 19 minutes average; radish students only 8 minutes<br>• Reason for difference: radish students ran out of self-control | This article hit home when it comes to junk food. I try to resist chips and chocolate, eat healthier snacks (fruit and veggies), but I fall off the wagon again and again. Is it self-control fatigue, or is something else going on with me? Maybe it's connected to feeling blue? The irony is I feel even more blue after giving in.<br><br>Heath says it's about running out of self-control. I'm in school, so what tests my self-control here? The temptation to skip class when I'm behind on readings and homework? The stress of getting assignments done and studying for tests? Guilt over wasting time on my phone? |

# Responding to a Text

In a sense, when you read a text, you enter into a dialogue with it. Your response expresses your turn in the dialogue. Such a response can take varied forms, from a journal entry to a blog to a posting in an online-comments forum.

## Guidelines for Response Writing

On the surface, responding to a text seems perfectly natural—just let it happen. But it can be a bit more complicated. A written response typically is not the same as a private diary entry but is instead shared with other readers, who may be in your class or elsewhere, including online. To develop a fitting response, keep in mind common expectations for this kind of writing, as well as your instructor's requirements, if the response is for a course:

1. **Be honest.** Although you want to remain sensitive to the context in which you will share your response, be bold enough to be honest about your reaction to the text—what it makes you think, feel, and question. To that end, a response usually allows you to express yourself directly using the pronoun "I."

2. **Be fluid.** Let the flow of your thoughts guide you in what you write. Don't stop to worry about grammar, punctuation, mechanics, and spelling. These can be quickly cleaned up before you share or submit your response.

3. **Be reflective.** Generally, the goal of a response is to offer thoughtful reflection as opposed to knee-jerk reaction. Show, then, that you are engaging the text's ideas, relating them to your own experience, looking both inward and outward. Avoid a shallow reaction that comes from skimming the text or misreading it.

4. **Be selective.** By nature, a response must limit its focus; it cannot exhaust all your reactions to the text. So zero in on one or two elements of your response, and run with those to see where they take you in your dialogue with the text.

**Sample Response**

Here is part of a student's response to Dan Heath's "Why Change Is So Hard." Note the informality and explanatory tone.

> Heath's report of the psychological experiment is very vivid, referring to the smell of chocolate-chip cookies and hungry students "gorging" on them. He uses the term "sadistic" to refer to making the radish-eaters sit and watch this go on. I wonder if this mild torment plays into the student's readiness to give up on the later test. If I'd been rewarded with cookies, I'd feel indebted to the testers and would stick with it longer. If I'd been punished with radishes, I might give up sooner just to spite the testers.
> 
> Now that I think of it, the digestion of all that sugar and fat in the cookies, as opposed to the digestion of roughage from the radishes, might also affect concentration and performance. Maybe the sugar "high" gives students the focus to keep going?

# Summarizing a Text

Writing a summary disciplines you by making you pull only essentials from a reading—the main points, the thread of the argument. By doing so, you create a brief record of the text's contents and exercise your ability to comprehend, analyze, and synthesize.

## Guidelines for Summary Writing

Writing a summary requires sifting out the least important points, sorting the essential ones to show their relationships, and stating those points in your own words. Follow these guidelines:

1. **Skim first; then read closely.** First, get a sense of the whole, including the main idea and strategies for support. Then read carefully, taking notes as you do.

2. **Capture the text's argument.** Review your notes and annotations, looking for main points and clear connections. State these briefly and clearly, in your own words. Include only what is essential, excluding most examples and details. Don't say simply that the text talks about its subject; tell what it says about that subject.

3. **Test your summary.** Aim to objectively provide the heart of the text; avoid interjecting your own opinions and presence as a writer. Don't confuse an objective summary of a text with a response to it. Check your summary against the original text for accuracy and consistency.

**Sample Summary**

Below is a student's summary of Dan Heath's "Why Change Is So Hard." Note how the summary writer includes only main points and phrases them in her own words. She departs from the precise order of details, but records them accurately.

> In the article "Why Change Is So Hard," Dan Heath argues that people who have trouble changing are not lazy, but have simply exhausted their self-control. Heath refers to a study in which one group of students was asked to eat cookies and not radishes, while another group in the same room was asked to eat radishes and not cookies. Afterward, both groups of students were asked to trace an endless geometric design without lifting their pencils. The cookie-only group traced on average 19 minutes before giving up, but the radish-only group traced on average only 8 minutes. They had already used up their self-control. Heath says that any behavioral change requires self-control, an exhaustible resource. Reverting to old behavior is what happens due not to laziness but to exhaustion.

**INSIGHT** Writing formal summaries—whether as part of literature reviews or as abstracts—is an important skill, especially in the social and natural sciences. See chapter 21 for a sample literature review and chapter 22 for a sample abstract.

## Engaging with Social Media

So far this chapter has introduced you to strategies for close, sustained reading of academic texts, but most of the texts you encounter in your daily life are much shorter and informal. Social media, for example, inundate users with bursts of news and content that compete for your attention. Sifting through information in this fast-paced environment requires a unique set of reading skills.

To engage with social media ethically, follow these strategies.

### Revisit the Rhetorical Situation

Questioning the rhetorical situation can help evaluate social-media content.

**Writer:** Who created or shared the message?

> *Discussion:* What are the author's credentials? Is the person an authority on the topic? See what can you learn from the author's profile page. Also consider your own relationship with the sender and how it might impact your reading.

**Message:** What does the message say (topic, main point, support)?

> *Discussion:* Evaluate the content. What parts capture your attention? Is the information fair and logical? What points of view are shared? Which ones are left out? What other sources—if any—confirm the information? If the message includes a video or link, weigh its information as well.

**Medium:** What site or platform is used to share the information?

> *Discussion:* Consider the medium's strengths and weaknesses. For instance, Twitter allows for quick and efficient sharing, but a character limit restricts the amount of information that can be shared.

**Reader:** Who is the target of the message?

> *Discussion:* Social posts, by their nature, are designed to spread beyond their original intended audience. How might people outside of the target group respond to the same message? How does your own subject position impact your reading? Are you a part of the target audience?

**Context:** What is the purpose of the message—to entertain, to inform, to persuade?

> *Discussion:* Messages that are meant to educate or inform are typically more neutral and unbiased than messages meant to entertain or persuade. However, even "neutral" messages share one point of view and exclude others. Ask yourself: Who benefits from sending this message?

**fyi** You don't need to closely read every post that comes across a social feed—no one has that kind of time. Save your careful analysis for information you are considering adopting or sharing with others.

## Beware of Bias

As a responsible social media user, you must stay alert for bias and misinformation. Otherwise, you risk believing something based on faulty or incomplete information. The following questions can help you detect partial or one-sided information. The more times you can answer "yes," the more likely it is that you've discovered biased content.

- Is the language extreme, characterized by all-or-nothing statements?
- Does the message appeal to emotion rather than reason or logic?
- Does the message simplify or generalize information?
- Does the message offer a one-sided or limited view?
- Does the logic of the message seem fuzzy or distorted?
- Does the message make claims without proof?

## Avoid Confirmation Bias

While you should inspect the messages you read for bias, you should also consider the biases you bring to the reading situation, which can lead to confirmation bias. Confirmation bias refers to the tendency to seek and interpret information in ways that affirm something you already believe in. The more invested you are in hoping a story is true or false, the harder it becomes to judge the information fairly or objectively.

To test for confirmation bias, consider these questions:

1. **What news does the message share?** Is the topic something you care about?
2. **What is your initial reaction to the message?**
3. **How does the news make you feel?** Be cautious of information that makes you feel overly emotional—for or against the subject.
4. **What do you already know about the topic?** Is this something you have a lot of background knowledge of or experiences with?
5. **How strongly do you hope the news is true?**

Strongly hope it's false — Strongly hope it's true

6. **How strongly does the claim confirm something you already believe?**

Completely disconfirms — Completely confirms

7. **Overall, how believable is the claim?**

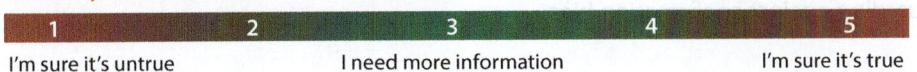
I'm sure it's untrue — I need more information — I'm sure it's true

### Confirmation Bias Scale

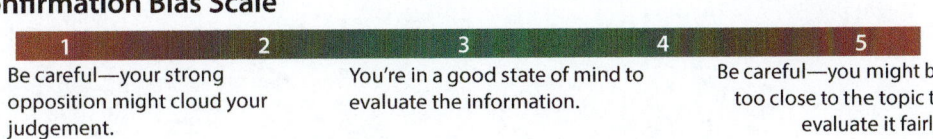
Be careful—your strong opposition might cloud your judgement. — You're in a good state of mind to evaluate the information. — Be careful—you might be too close to the topic to evaluate it fairly.

# Reading Critically: Applications

Apply what you have learned about reading critically by completing these activities.

1. **Wise Words:** Northrop Frye has argued that "[n]obody is capable of free speech unless he knows how to use language, and such knowledge is not a gift: It has to be learned and worked at." How does Frye's claim relate to the discussions of critical thinking and reading in this chapter?
2. **Public Texts:** Active reading is required to make sense of many texts. Find a story, article, or report related to an issue that you find important. Then use the active reading strategies to understand, analyze, and evaluate the text.
3. **Photo Op:** This chapter offers tips on how to create conditions for productive critical reading. What would your ideal reading environment look like? Draw a sketch of this space, or find or take a photo of such a place. Make a list of features that would make this an effective reading location; identify rituals and reading practices you would follow here.
4. **Living Today:** With what recreational activities, games, and hobbies are you thoroughly familiar? Choose one, and find an article or story about it. First write a personal response to the piece. Then write a summary of it.
5. **Major Work:** Consider your major and your future career. What is the focus of this field of study and this profession? What critical reading skills are required and valued in this area? Research these questions, as needed.

## Learning-Objectives Checklist ✓

Have you achieved this chapter's learning objectives? Check your progress with the following items, revisiting topics in the chapter as needed. I have . . .

____ adopted a critical-thinking mindset, learned to ask probing questions, and practiced a critical-thinking pattern.

____ used SQ3R for important reading assignments in my courses and research projects.

____ read texts actively through focused attention, mapping, outlining, and evaluating.

____ annotated texts and taken effective notes through a double-entry notebook.

____ responded to written texts in an honest, fluid, reflective, and selective way.

____ objectively summarized texts in my own words, distinguishing main arguments and key supporting points from secondary content.

____ evaluated social media by questioning the rhetorical situation, detecting bias, and guarding against confirmation bias.

# Chapter 3

# Viewing Critically

It would be hard to exaggerate how much visual media have come to dominate our lives. On top of movies and television, we have social media dedicated to photos and videos, and devices that give us instant access to visual media. Many of us also contribute to this visual ecosystem—posting selfies, recording TikToks, and videoing milestones using smartphones and other devices. In fact, it seems our phone is the filter through which many of us experience life—or perhaps a barrier between us and reality.

Because visual media are pervasive and powerful, it's never been more important than now to cultivate strong critical-viewing skills: learning how to view images and videos fully, analyze them carefully, and evaluate them fairly. Like never before, your thinking and writing skills depend on your critical-viewing skills.

By working through this chapter, you will be able to
- actively view images.
- analyze the meaning of visual images.
- effectively critique visual images.
- effectively critique videos.
- detect visual misinformation.

**Visually Speaking** Figure 3.1 shows people engaged with smartphones. What message does the image convey? Why do you think the creator added emojis and other icons? Imagine you had to write an essay about this image. What title would you use?

Rawpixel.com / Shutterstock.com

fig. 3.1

# Viewing an Image Actively

Images are created to communicate, just as words are. Most images in everyday life are made to communicate very quickly—ads, signs, Instagram posts, GIFs, and so forth. Other images require contemplation, such as the *Mona Lisa*. When you view an image, view actively and critically. Follow the steps below, and see the same steps in action on the next page.

## Follow Active-Viewing Steps

**Survey the image.** See the image as a whole so that you can absorb its overall idea. Look for the image's focal point—what your eye is drawn to. Also consider the relationship between the image's foreground and background, its left content and right content, and its various colors.

**Inspect the image.** Let your sight touch every part of the image, as if you were reading Braille. Hints of its meaning may lurk in the tiny details as well as in the relationship between the image's parts.

**Question the image.** Think in terms of each part of the rhetorical situation.
- **Designer:** Who created the image? Why did the person create it?
- **Message:** What is the subject of the image? What is the purpose?
- **Medium:** How was the image originally shown? How is it currently shown?
- **Viewer:** Who is the intended viewer? Why are you viewing the image?
- **Context:** When and where did the image first appear? When and where does it appear now? How does the image relate to its context?

**Understand the purpose.** Different images have different purposes. Ask yourself, "What is this image meant to do?" and then decide on an appropriate response.
- **Arouse curiosity?** Open your imagination, but stay on guard.
- **Entertain?** Look for the pleasure or the joke, but be wary of excess or of ethically questionable material in the image.
- **Inform or educate?** Search for key instructions, noting what's left out.
- **Illustrate?** Relate the image to the words or concept being illustrated: Does the image clarify or distort the meaning?
- **Persuade?** Examine how the image appeals to the viewer's needs, from safety and satisfaction to self-worth. Are the appeals manipulative, clichéd, or fallacious? Do they play on emotions to bypass reason?
- **Summarize?** Look for the essential message in the image: Does that main idea correspond with the written text?

**Evaluate the caption.** Many photographs are accompanied with captions. Some simply identify a time and place. Others provide a brief narrative to influence how viewers should interpret the image. Examine the words used in captions for truth and bias.

catwalker / Shutterstock.com

# View a Sample Image

Chris Krenzke / Thoughtful Learning

**The use of *minors* as *miners* is no *minor* problem.**

*fig. 3.2*

## Discussion ▼

Figure 3.2 by Chris Krenzke and the caption by Verne Meyer effectively combine humor with instruction. Originally published in a high school writing handbook, the image's aim is to teach students about a specific word-usage problem while also entertaining them. The image is line art in the "comic" genre, using a humorous scene to convey a serious message. Here are some thoughts on how you might actively view this image:

1. **Survey.** The image tells a story of heavily burdened children working under the demanding supervision of an authoritarian male. That story moves from left to right, from breaking rocks to loading rocks to carrying rocks toward a likely distant destination, the destination pointed to by the man. The black-and-white medium accentuates the starkness.

2. **Inspect.** In terms of the illustration's details, each figure is striking. The individual children share a thinness in their bodies and a strain in their faces. The four children in the line are pictured as beasts of burden bent over by bags that dwarf them. The repetition of figures emphasizes the trudging repetition of their work, and each child in line is pressed farther toward the ground. As for the man, his back is straight and his posture tall. His enormous chin, large nose, overly long but skinny arm, and sharply pointed finger suggest a negative authority. His stubbly face and his caveman clothing add to this figure's prehistoric character.

3. **Question.** Who is the artist Chris Krenzke? When did he first create this image? In what book was it published? When? Why did Krenzke use this caveman style? Who or what do "minors," "miners," and "minor" refer to in the illustration?

4. **Relate.** The connection between the sentence and the image becomes clear when the viewer realizes that "minors" are children not of a legal age to work, "miners" refers to an occupation, and "minor" means insignificant. But the image prompts other connections: the history of horrific child-labor practices during the Industrial Revolution as well as continuing child-labor issues in today's global economy. With these allusions, Krenzke succeeds in deepening the instruction offered by his art.

# Interpreting an Image

Interpreting an image follows naturally from viewing or "reading" the image. Interpreting means figuring out what the image or design is meant to do, say, or show. Interpreting requires you to think more deeply about each element of the rhetorical situation shown in Figure 3.3, and about possible complications with each element.

*fig. 3.3*

- **Designer:** Who created the image—a photographer, a painter, a designer, a smartphone user? Why did the person create it? What other people might have been involved—editors, patrons?

    *Complications:* The designer might be unknown or a group.

- **Message:** What is the subject of the image? How is the subject portrayed? What is the main purpose of the image—to entertain, inform, persuade, entice, or shock? What are the image's various meanings? Does a caption accompany the image? If so, does the text offer an objective identification or a subjective narrative?

    *Complications:* The message might be mixed, implied, ironic, unwelcome, or distorted. The subject might be vague, unfamiliar, complex, or disturbing. The caption may subconsciously influence your interpretation of the image.

- **Medium:** What is the image—a painting, a cartoon panel, a photo? How might the image have been modified over time? What visual language has the sender used?

    *Complications:* The medium might be unusual or unfamiliar, or more than one medium may be involved.

- **Viewer:** Whom was the image made for? Are you part of the intended audience? What is your relationship with the designer? Do you agree with the message? How comfortable are you with the medium? What is your overall response to the image?

    *Complications:* You might be uninterested in, unfamiliar with, or biased toward the message.

- **Context:** What was the context in which the image was first presented? What context surrounds the image now? Does the image fit its context or fight it?

    *Complications:* The context may be disconnected, ironic, changing, or multilayered.

## Interpret a Sample Image

*fig. 3.4*

### Discussion

Figure 3.4 shows a woman walking her dog in an empty market in Tel Aviv, Israel, during the COVID-19 outbreak of 2020. She approaches a sign that reads "Don't Panic." The image's power is marked by the contrasts between the sign, the woman's protective mask, and the empty stalls aligning the market. Both the sign and the masked woman suggest something out of the ordinary is occurring. The sign encourages patrons not to panic, but the need for this message implies some people believe there is reason to panic. Many of the photo's details show evidence of alarm. The stalls on both sides of the walkway are boxed up. No vendors are present. No smoke billows from grills. Few people occupy the space. One of these people, of course, is the woman walking her dog. Her mask implies health precautions are necessary. Then again, she also abides by the sign's message. Her posture is relaxed. She is doing a perfectly ordinary activity—going on a stroll with her dog. Her yellow bag suggests she recently visited a store. Behind her, a man rides a bike. Two other people walk. These other people don't wear masks. Life goes on, even during a pandemic.

**Designer:** Photographed by Oded Balilty; supplied to the Associated Press
**Message:** A woman in a mask walks a dog in an open-air market during the COVID-19 crisis. A large "Don't Panic" sign hangs near the entrance.
**Medium:** Digital color photograph
**Viewer:** The original intended viewers were reading news about the virus.
**Context:** This photo was taken in Tel Aviv, Israel on Monday, March 23, 2020. The Associated Press shared it with news organizations that were documenting the COVID-19 crisis.

# Evaluating an Image

As a critical thinker, you must do more than understand and interpret an image you encounter: You must assess its quality, truthfulness, and value. In other words, you must evaluate it. When you have done that well, you can fairly say you have thought it through. The following questions will guide your assessment.

## Consider the Purpose

What purpose does the visual image best seem to serve?

- **Ornamentation:** Makes the page or screen more pleasing to the eye
- **Illustration:** Supports points made in the accompanying text
- **Revelation:** Gives an inside look at something or presents new data
- **Explanation:** Uses imagery or graphics to clarify a complex subject
- **Instruction:** Guides the viewer through a complex process
- **Persuasion:** Influences feelings or beliefs
- **Entertainment:** Amuses the viewer

## Evaluate the Quality

Essentially, how good is the image?

- **Is the image done with skill?** A map, for example, should be accurately and attractively drawn, should use color effectively, and should be complete enough to serve its purpose.
- **Does the image measure up to standards of quality?** For example, there's a big difference between an average person's selfie and a shot by a professional photographer.
- **Is it backed by authority?** Does the designer have a good reputation? Does the publication or institution have good credentials?
- **How does the image compare to other images like it?** Are clearer or more accurate images available?
- **What are its shortcomings?** Are there gaps in its coverage? Does it twist the evidence? Does it convey clichéd or fallacious information? Does it present stereotypes or appeal to common prejudices?
- **Could you think of a better way to approach the image's subject?** If you were to produce the visual, what might you improve?

## Determine the Value

What is the image's tangible and intangible worth? Its benefits and drawbacks?

- **Is the visual worth viewing?** Does it enrich the document by clarifying or otherwise enhancing its message?
- **Does the visual appeal to you?** Listen to authorities and peers, but also consider your own perspective.

## Evaluate a Sample Image

### Discussion

Evaluating an image such as the WWII poster in Figure 3.5 aimed at U.S. servicemen reveals its strong stereotypes of both men and women, stereotypes related to the historical period. As with all images, evaluation begins with understanding and interpreting the poster.

In the poster's center is a woman in evening dress, her hair done up, wearing jewels and a corsage. She is seated, at ease, looking at us. Perhaps she represents beauty, both sensual attractiveness and sophistication. The colors used to present her are pale and muted, except for her blue eyes and red lips.

Surrounding the woman are three men, individually dressed in the uniforms of Army, Air Force, and Navy. Drinking and smoking, the men seem to be competing for her attention.

The poster implies that all service personnel were male, which was not true even in WWII, when WACs and WAVEs served in the armed forces. It cautions that these male members of the armed forces should be wary in seemingly innocent social situations, since even a beautiful woman, whom popular stereotypes of the day characterized as "dumb," might not be what she appears. Such a woman might, in fact, be a spy—an idea perhaps inspired by the famous case of WWI spy Mata Hari. The statement that "careless talk costs lives" is a version of another common phrase from the period: "Loose lips sink ships."

Evaluating this poster involves considering its original context while assessing it from our current perspective. In the heat of WWII, this poster could be considered a fair piece of military persuasion. Today, however, what is striking are the gender stereotypes at work in both image and words. Not only are service personnel today both male and female, in every branch of the armed forces, but they fulfill the same roles, including combat positions. With respect to the men, the image implies that in social situations (which are assumed to include smoking and drinking), they are untrustworthy and apt to boast or compete in the presence of an attractive woman. With respect to women, the image both denounces and warns, implying that women, especially attractive women, are cunning and dangerous. In addition, the absence of racial diversity is striking, as numerous African Americans and other people of color served in the armed forces during the war. Today, such stereotypes press us to question the quality, truthfulness, and value of the image.

*National Archives, London, Great Britain*

fig. 3.5

# Critiquing a Video

Our hunger for video is insatiable. Just take a second to consider these statistics: Every minute, 500 hours of new video content are uploaded to YouTube (Figure 3.6). The average young person watches 68 videos every day (Figure 3.7). Overall, we spend one-third of our time online watching videos.

*fig. 3.6*

Marketers, advertisers, political candidates, and special interest groups are keenly aware of these statistics and increasingly use video to pitch products and ideas. Since videos are both ever-present and persuasive, it is crucial that you know how to view them critically.

Yet, developing a critical eye for videos presents an even bigger challenge than photographs and other images. Instead of having to interpret a static image, you must take stock of movements, sound, and a host of other special effects. The viewing process that follows can help.

## Before Viewing

Establish a viewing mindset.

- **Consider how you discovered the video.** Did you actively search for it, or did it appear by chance? Social media sites, search engines, streaming services, and advertisers use algorithms to display videos that cater to your age, location, interests, and previous viewing habits.
- **Analyze the title, title screen, and other contextual information.** If you're watching an online video, how many views and comments accompany it? When was it posted? What are commenters saying about it? What is the ratio of likes to dislikes?
- **Activate your prior knowledge.** What do you already know about the topic, medium (YouTube, network television, etc.), or genre (news, comedy, horror, etc.)? What do you want to know?
- **Identify your viewing purpose.** Why are you watching this video? For entertainment? For education? Both?

## During Viewing

Practice active viewing strategies.

- **Limit distractions.** Give the video your full attention.
- **Scan the full frame.** Particularly in movies, everything that appears in a frame is constructed to create a specific effect on the viewer.
- **Gauge your emotions.** How do different parts of the video make you feel? Note the parts that raise your emotions. Consider the action, dialogue, music, color, and camera focus.
- **Take notes.** Jot down key moments and insights as they appear.

## After Viewing

Analyze and evaluate what you just watched.

- **Rewatch key parts or the whole thing.** Your first viewing will help you understand the video. Your second viewing will help you critique the video. Consider rewatching parts with the sound off and pausing at key points. What new things do you notice?
- **Revisit the rhetorical situation.** Ask questions about each of the main parts.

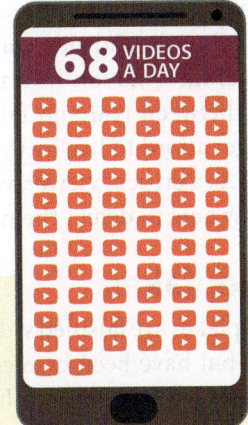

*fig. 3.7*

> - **Creator:** Who created the video—a director, a corporation, a lobbyist, a smartphone user? What other people might have been involved?
>
>   *Tips:* Note the opening and closing credits. Check the online username.
>
> - **Message:** What story does the video share? How does it tell it? What people and ideas are included and excluded? Is the information trustworthy?
>
>   *Tips:* Consider the techniques the video uses to create interest and stir emotions. For instance, did it include a lot of patriotic imagery? Were the colors and music ominous? If you watched this video for educational purposes, seek other sources to see if they support the information presented in the video. Evaluate the language used in headlines, captions, and voice overs for bias.
>
> - **Medium:** Is it a short viral video on Instagram? A news clip on PBS? A full-length documentary?
>
>   *Tips:* Consider the strengths, weaknesses, and authority of the medium.
>
> - **Viewer:** Who is meant to see the video? Are you part of the intended audience? How comfortable are you with the medium?
>
>   *Tips:* Consider why the creator might want or not want you to see the video.
>
> - **Context:** Did the video match your expectations? Do your opinions of the video align with others who watched the video?
>
>   *Tips:* Recheck the comments and rankings for online videos. Read reviews from professional critics.

- **Decide what to do with the video.** Consider the video's worth. Will you recommend and share it with others? Rate or comment on it? Use the information in a writing project? Dismiss the video as fake news?

# Detecting Misinformation

Rapid advances in technology have provided millions of people with the ability to create and share images and video online. Unfortunately, these same advances allow users to manipulate visual information in ways that distort the truth. For consumers of media, discerning the line between real and fake is becoming increasingly difficult, so much so that you can no longer afford to live by the maxim of *seeing is believing*.

As a critical viewer, you should be aware of common types of visual misinformation and know how to detect them.

## Deepfakes

Deepfakes are falsified videos of people—often celebrities or other public figures—that appear real but have been created using complex algorithms and artificial intelligence. Deepfakes can show people doing things they didn't actually do and saying things they didn't actually say. They can create voice clones that sound strikingly similar to a person's actual voice.

> ***How to detect deepfakes:*** As technology improves, deepfakes will become tougher to spot. However, you can look for these obvious signs of doctoring: poor lip syncing, flickering around the edges of faces, muddled fine features, a lack of blinking, and garbled audio. Performing fact-checks will also help you avoid manipulation. Check to see if other sources confirm the veracity of a video, especially if it involves a person doing or saying something crude or inflammatory.

## Deceptive Edits

Deceptive editing involves cutting and rearranging a video and presenting it as a full narrative. For instance, a political ad may cut out a large portion of an opponent's speech to make it seem more inflammatory than it really was. Other techniques involve splicing together disparate videos to create a brand new story, or speeding up the frame to make someone's actions appear more aggressive than they actually were.

> ***How to detect deceptive editing:*** The best way to combat deceptive editing is to view the original video in its full length. Also, go to fact-checkers like Snopes, Media Matters, or *The Washington Post* Fact Checker to get more information.

## Out-of-Context Images

The deceptive editing techniques described above intentionally distort the context of events. Another common form of misplaced context involves recycling old photographs or videos and presenting them as evidence in relation to a current event.

> ***How to detect out-of-context images:*** The best way to discover an image used out of context is to perform a reverse image search. This will show you a list of other places the photo has appeared online. Simply right click on the image, and choose "Search Google for image." Also, read captions and source information to identify the photographer and the original publisher.

## Doctored Images

Doctored or photoshopped images twist the truth by altering existing photos. These changes range from the harmless, like adjusting the color of a shirt, to full-scale distortion, like replacing a torn piece of paper with the U.S. Constitution (see Figure 3.8).

***How to detect doctored images:*** While many doctored photos include obvious distortions, some require closer viewing. Experts recommend looking for shadows, reflections, and edges. These are difficult to reproduce and are often missing, misplaced, or distorted in fake photos. Another strategy is to perform a reverse image search. Since most doctored images use a real image as a source, you can compare the doctored photo to similar images.

## Visual Misinformation: A Case Study

fig. 3.8

*Tyler Mitchell, Teen Vogue (c) Conde Nast*

In 2018, *Teen Vogue* posted a GIF on its Instagram account of Parkland school shooting survivor Emma Gonzalez ripping apart a shooting target as part of a gun control campaign. Soon afterward, an image of the GIF was doctored to make it appear as if the 18-year-old Gonzalez was tearing up the U.S. Constitution. The image was posted anonymously on an influential forum and was quickly spread on social platforms of gun-rights activists.

Notice that the doctored image on the left in Figure 3.8 not only distorts what Gonzalez rips apart but also distorts her facial features, including the coloring under her eyes and face. Another clear sign that this photo is doctored is the fuzziness at the edges of the paper.

By detecting and calling out misinformation for others, you can help stop its spread.

# Viewing Critically: Applications

Apply what you have learned about viewing critically by completing these activities.

1. **Wise Words:** Marshall McLuhan famously said that the medium is the message. Choose one of the visual media you normally "consume" and apply McLuhan's idea to that medium. What kind of message are you consuming with that visual medium?
2. **Front-Page Check:** Browse the front-page images at newseum.org. Choose one striking image to analyze. Then use the strategies from this chapter to carefully view, interpret, and evaluate the image.
3. **Gone Viral:** Pick a favorite viral image or video and follow the viewing strategies from this chapter to perform a rhetorical analysis of it. Who originally created it and for what reason? Does it include any deceptive techniques, such as deepfakes, deceptive editing, doctoring, or missing context? Having performed your analysis, evaluate the ethics of the viral visual.
4. **Living Today:** The introduction to this chapter proposes that "our phone is the filter through which many of us experience life—or perhaps a barrier between us and reality." What are your feelings about this statement? Do you agree? Do you find it hard to live in the moment and tackle responsibilities when your phone is nearby? Do you ever feel like you're capturing too much visual information rather than experiencing it?
5. **Multimodal Storytelling:** Imagine that you could turn an essay assignment into a multimodal story. How might you enhance the essay with images, graphics, videos, and other visual elements? Which visuals would you include? How would you ensure you were using them ethically? What medium would work best for delivering the story (a Google Site, a blog, a poster board)? Propose your multimodal story to your instructor.

## Learning-Objectives Checklist ✓

Have you achieved this chapter's learning objectives? Check your progress with the following items, revisiting topics in the chapter as needed. I have . . .

\_\_\_\_ viewed images actively by surveying and inspecting them.
\_\_\_\_ carefully interpreted images by deeply analyzing the rhetorical situation and its complications—designer, message, medium, viewer, and context.
\_\_\_\_ critiqued visual images by assessing their purpose, value, and quality.
\_\_\_\_ critiqued videos by following a close-viewing process.
\_\_\_\_ detected misinformation, such as deepfakes, doctored images, deceptive editing, and out-of-context images.

# Chapter 4

# Planning Your Piece

When we go on a trip, some of us are meticulous, even obsessive, planners—every detail mapped out, every minute accounted for. Then again, some of us fly by the seat of our pants, to use a phrase from the early days of aviation when pilots had no fancy instruments—not even a radio—to guide them.

In writing, author and instructor Ken Macrorie calls for a blend of these two approaches for your writing journey: "Good writing," says Macrorie, "is formed partly through plan and partly through accident." In other words, too much planning can get in the way of the discovery aspect of writing, while not enough planning can harm the focus and coherence of your piece. As a writing pilot, you end up in Antarctica when you needed to be Albuquerque.

**Visually Speaking** Carefully study Figure 4.1. What does the photograph suggest about the role that planning plays in military life? What might be some of its benefits and drawbacks? Does such planning parallel planning to write? How might planning your writing be different from what you see in the image?

## Learning Objectives

By working through this chapter, you will be able to

- generate a thoughtful thesis to guide the direction of your writing.
- refine your thesis so that it has greater substance and nuance.
- develop a plan or outline grounded in your thesis, research, and other prewriting.
- choose between inductive and deductive patterns for your writing.
- choose a mapping method, from a quick list to a writing organizer.
- map out possible design and media elements for your writing.

U.S. Air Force photo/Master Sgt. Jack Braden

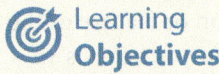

fig. 4.1

# Forming Your Thesis Statement

After you have completed enough research and collecting, you may begin to develop a more focused interest in your topic. If all goes well, this narrowed focus will give rise to a thesis for your writing. A thesis statement identifies your central idea. It usually highlights a special condition or feature of the topic, expresses a specific claim about it, or takes a stand.

State your thesis in a sentence that effectively expresses what you want to explore or explain in your essay. Sometimes a thesis statement develops early and easily; at other times, the true focus of your writing emerges only after you've written your first draft. If responding to an assignment prompt, make sure your topic and the thesis statement you develop meet the prompt's requirements and expectations.

## Find a Focus

A general subject area is typically built into your writing assignments. Your task, then, is to find a limited writing topic and examine it from a particular angle or perspective. (You will use this focus to form your thesis statement.) Figure 4.2 shows this process.

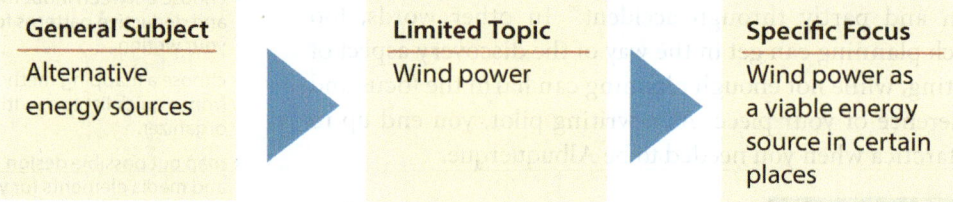

fig. 4.2

## State Your Thesis

You can use the formula in Figure 4.3 to write a thesis statement for your essay. A thesis statement sets the tone and direction for your writing. Keep in mind that at this point you're writing a *working thesis statement*—a statement in progress, so to speak. You may change it as your thinking on the topic evolves.

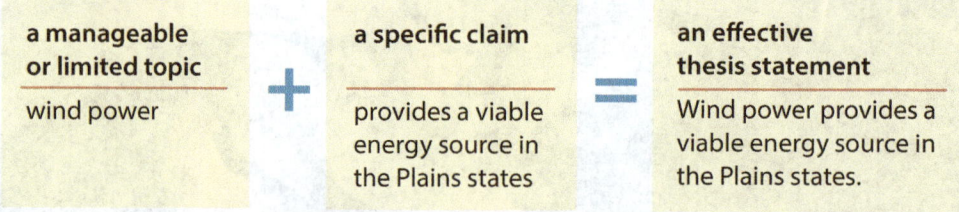

fig. 4.3

**Working with Sources** Sometimes your writing can take direction specifically from your sources. You may consider making your thesis a response to a specific source. For example, if one source is especially strong or especially contrary to your own thinking, you could shape your thesis as an affirmation of the strong source's authority or as a rebuttal to the contrary source's claims.

## Refine Your Thesis

Once you have drafted your working thesis, you can move on to thinking about organizing your essay. However, it may be helpful to pause, consider why the thesis is so important, and find ways to strengthen your working thesis before moving forward. Consider the following:

**Why is the thesis so important for your writing?** The thesis is the controlling idea of your essay—the main point or assertion about the topic. As such, the thesis is central to your essay. It sets a direction for your writing and represents your contribution to the larger "conversation" on the topic. Without a solid thesis, an essay lacks direction, purpose, and pressure; it too easily falls into traps of diffusion and disorganization. With a good thesis, an essay takes on purpose, becomes naturally organized, and takes the reader on a journey.

**How can you discover, develop, and refine your thesis?** You can improve your chances of developing a strong thesis by doing the following:

- **Reflect on your findings.** Prewriting strategies and research (including critical reading and viewing) should generate ideas and information for your writing. Both during and after these activities, reflect on all this material. What patterns and connections come to the surface? These connections might hold the key idea that you are looking for.
- **Ask the right questions.** The thesis can be thought of as an answer to a question. But not all questions are the same, nor are all questions equal. What are the most meaningful questions about your topic?
- **Apply concepts from the field.** Some writing calls for a practical, concrete thesis (e.g., the steps that should be followed to create an attractive and informative web page). However, most essay writing centers on concepts and principles (e.g., the key principles of web design). What are the central concepts at the heart of your topic? What principles are common in the field of knowledge to which the topic belongs? Can you apply concepts from other fields of knowledge to your topic?

**What is the difference between a weak and a strong thesis?** A strong thesis is narrowly focused rather than broad, making it manageable for the assignment. It is challenging rather than simplistic—rarely a simple summary, a straightforward statement of fact, or a pure opinion (a taste or preference that cannot really be argued). Here are three examples:

**Weak thesis:** lacks depth, functions as a cliché, offers a broad or vague generalization

> Writing is an important skill.

**Good thesis:** demonstrates some higher level thinking, such as analysis and argument

> Reading and writing function symbiotically: strengthening one skill improves the other.

**Strong thesis:** shows complexity, tension, or even risk (surprise, challenge, paradox)

> In a college or university, writing needs to become much more than an academic exercise: it must function as part of an authentic internal and communal dialogue on consequential issues.

# Developing a Plan or an Outline

Your approach to planning may differ from one type of writing to another. For a short personal essay, a few brief points may be all you need to get started; by contrast, for a major research project, you may want to develop a full, formal outline. Whatever choices you make, planning gives you a map to get started—a helpful tool for preventing writer's block and keeping you on course. To do effective planning, consider the following strategies.

## Discover Organization in Your Thesis

A working thesis sets a direction for your writing. With this in mind, your goal is to shape the essay as a unified whole around the thesis. To find that unity, ask questions like these:

- **What support is implied in the phrasing of my working thesis?** Examine the key terms and phrases for hints of where your writing needs to go. Try turning those elements into questions, and then order those questions logically.
- **Does my thesis naturally suggest a specific method of development?** For example, in terms of your assignment, you may have drafted a working thesis that calls for support in a problem-solution, cause-effect, or compare-contrast pattern. This concept is explored more fully in Part II of this text, "Modes of Writing."
- **Where should I place my thesis in relation to the overall structure of my writing?** Frequently, the thesis is placed at the end of the introduction, paving the way for elaboration and support. Some writers prefer to provide details and evidence before stating their thesis. For example, stating a controversial point without support may alienate readers, causing them to dismiss your ideas without reading on. Presenting evidence first invites your reader on the journey, showing how you arrived at your point of view.

## Refer Back to Your Prewriting

What organizational hints are in your notes? Explore how your notes suggest a way of proceeding. See how points collect under key ideas.

## Structure Your Writing for the Development of Ideas

A strong essay is much more than a static list of points in support of a thesis, each point standing alone and equal in weight. You may recognize this approach as the five-paragraph hamburger: introduction (top bun), three supporting points (meat), and conclusion (bottom bun). If this is the type of essay that you are used to cooking up, it's time to take your cooking skills to the next level. A more mature essay is about idea development, with each idea building upon or deepening the previous one. Start by asking these questions:

- **How can I help my reader understand my line of thinking?** To deepen your reader's understanding of your topic, structure your writing for your reader, not for yourself. You might, for example, begin by explaining historical context, by defining key terms, or by reviewing commonly held positions. Only then can you proceed.

- **How can I build sections that move from the known to the new?** Consider how you might "scaffold" your essay by building each new point on top of the previous one, now understood by the reader. This strategy is the "known-new" pattern.

## Consider Inductive and Deductive Patterns

From whole essays to individual paragraphs, you can organize your writing in two common but opposite thinking patterns: induction and deduction. Induction begins with specific information, reasons with it, and builds toward a specific conclusion: your main point comes at the end of your paragraph. This pattern works well if you wish to begin with questions and build toward answers, as shown in the diagram in Figure 4.4.

Deduction, the opposite, is the traditional pattern for academic paragraphs and essays. The writing begins with an idea—a specific point, principle, or concept—and then applies it to specific information through reasoning. In your paragraph, you begin with a topic sentence and develop your thinking from that; in your essay, you offer your thesis in the introduction, then explore, develop, and support that idea moving forward. Deduction is thus strong on logical clarity and direction, induction on inquiry. Compare the two in Figure 4.4.

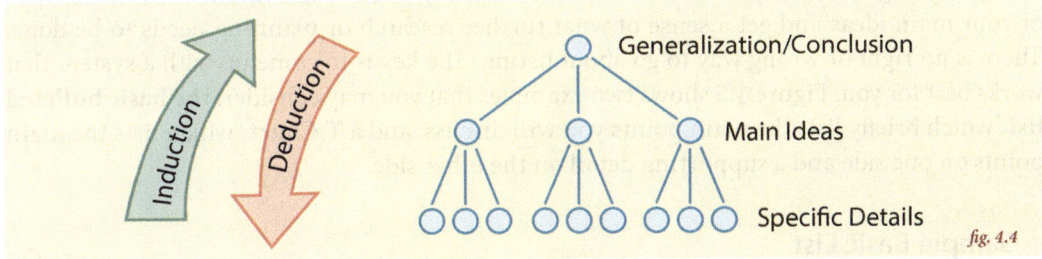

*fig. 4.4*

**Induction:** specific details to conclusion

1   Dr. Smith stood beside a fellow neurobiologist on the campus of Washington University in St. Louis. While engrossed in conversation, Smith noticed from the corner of his eye an undergraduate walking in their direction. At first he thought nothing of it, but as she approached, it dawned on him that she was looking directly at him. "Strange," he thought. He tried to ignore her and continue his conversation, but when she was about 20 feet away he heard her laugh. Upon hearing the sound, the unfamiliar undergraduate who had been staring so intently at him morphed into his daughter. Smith had been unable to recognize her.

**Deduction:** general concept explained through specifics

2   Dr. Smith suffers from a unique condition known as *prosopagnosia*, or face blindness. Historically, most documented cases have been due to brain damage suffered after maturity from head trauma, stroke, or degenerative diseases. Recently, however, studies have demonstrated that many more people suffer from prosopagnosia without experiencing neurological damage (Avidan et al., 2005). Smith suffers from this form of face blindness, known as congenital prosopagnosia. Although he spent the vast majority of his life unaware of his condition, Dr. Smith, now 54 years old, acknowledges that it all makes sense in retrospect.

# Experimenting with Mapping Methods

You may be comfortable with using one strategy to organize all your essays—traditional outlining, for example. However, trying other methods may unlock creative possibilities that you had not imagined. Below is a list of four mapping strategies, each of which is elaborated on the pages that follow.

- **Quick List:** A brief listing of main points (See Figure 4.5.)
- **Topic Outline:** A more formal plan, including main points and essential details (See Figure 4.6.)
- **Sentence Outline:** A formal plan, including main points and essential details, written as complete sentences (See Figure 4.7.)
- **Writing Organizers:** An arrangement of main points and essential details in an appropriate chart or diagram (See Figure 4.8.)

## Quick Lists

Though listing is the simplest of all the methods of organization, it can help you take stock of your main ideas and get a sense of what further research or planning needs to be done. There is no right or wrong way to go about listing. The key is to come up with a system that works best for you. Figure 4.5 shows two examples that you may consider: **the basic bulleted list,** which briefly lists the main points you will discuss, and a **T Chart,** which lists the main points on one side and a supporting detail on the other side.

**Sample Basic List**

**Topic:** Different ways to discuss literature ———— Topic

- Focus on the text itself
- Focus on the text and the reader
- Focus on the author of the text ———— Main Points
- Focus on ideas outside of literature

**Sample T Chart**

**Topic:** Different ways to discuss literature ———— Topic

| Approach | Emphasis |
|---|---|
| Text-centered approach | Structure and rules |
| Audience-centered approach | Relationship between reader and text |
| Author-centered approach | The writer's life |
| Idea-centered approach | Interpretation via specific ideology or field of knowledge |

*fig. 4.5*

## Topic Outline

If you have a good deal of information to sort and arrange, you may want to use a **topic outline** for your planning. In a topic outline, you state each main point and essential detail as a word or phrase. Before you start constructing your outline, write your working thesis statement at the top of your paper to help keep you focused on the subject. (Do not attempt to outline your opening and closing paragraphs unless you are specifically asked to do so.)

An effective topic outline is parallel in structure, meaning the main points (I, II, III) and essential details (A, B, C) are stated in the same way. Notice how the sample outline in Figure 4.6 uses a parallel structure, making it easy to follow.

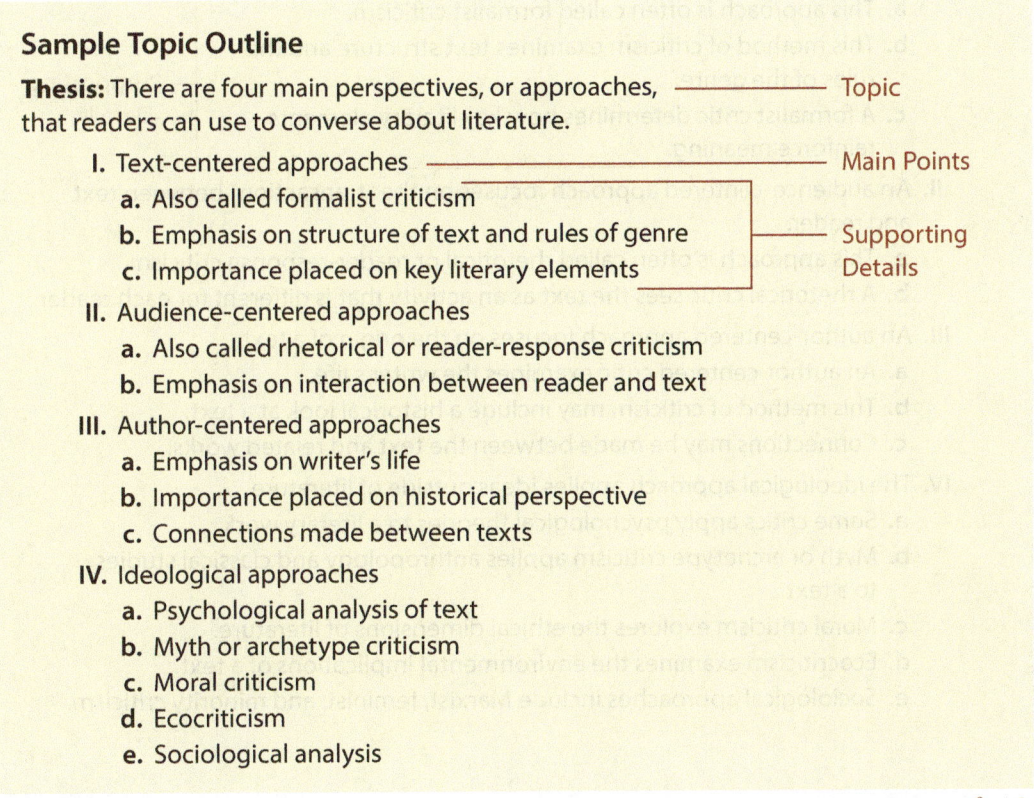

fig. 4.6

**INSIGHT** Planning is adaptable. Some writers prefer to generate an outline before they begin writing, while others prefer to make a more detailed outline after having written a draft. In the latter strategy, an outline can serve as a tool for evaluating the logic and completeness of the paper's organization.

Another adaptation to your planning might be to begin with a brief outline—a basic list of topics, say—and then as you begin drafting for a specific topic, sketch an outline of what to explore for that section of your piece. When you're finished drafting that section, then move on to the next topic, create an outline for it, and start drafting again.

# Sentence Outline

A **sentence outline**, such as the one in Figure 4.7, uses complete sentences to explain the main points and essential details in the order that they will be covered in the main part of your essay. Such an outline can help you develop your ideas when writing the paper.

**Sample Sentence Outline**

**Thesis:** There are four main perspectives, or approaches, that readers can use to converse about literature. ——— *Thesis*

    I. A text-centered approach focuses on the literary piece itself. ——— *Main Points*
        a. This approach is often called formalist criticism.
        b. This method of criticism examines text structure and the rules of the genre. ——— *Supporting Details*
        c. A formalist critic determines how key literary elements reinforce meaning.
    II. An audience-centered approach focuses on the "transaction" between text and reader.
        a. This approach is often called rhetorical or reader-response criticism.
        b. A rhetorical critic sees the text as an activity that is different for each reader.
    III. An author-centered approach focuses on the origin of a text.
        a. An author-centered critic examines the writer's life.
        b. This method of criticism may include a historical look at a text.
        c. Connections may be made between the text and related works.
    IV. The ideological approach applies ideas outside of literature.
        a. Some critics apply psychological theories to a literary work.
        b. Myth or archetype criticism applies anthropology and classical studies to a text.
        c. Moral criticism explores the ethical dimensions of literature.
        d. Ecocriticism examines the environmental implications of a text.
        e. Sociological approaches include Marxist, feminist, and minority criticism.

*fig. 4.7*

**Working with Sources** — When your writing project involves sources, the planning phase will include a great deal of sorting through material. Outlining can help you organize your primary and secondary sources to best support your thesis. As you organize your research in your outline, ask these questions:

- Where and how should I work with primary sources—interviews, surveys, analyses, observations, experiments, and other data I have collected?
- Where and how should I bring in secondary sources—scholarly books, journal articles, and the like?

## Writing Organizers

Writing organizers can help you map out ideas and illustrate relationships among them, as well as help you arrange your information, as in Figure 4.8. You'll find a number of these organizers in Part 2 of *The College Writer*, "Modes of Writing."

▼ Note how this line diagram breaks out the topic, main ideas, and supporting details for use in building an essay of classification.

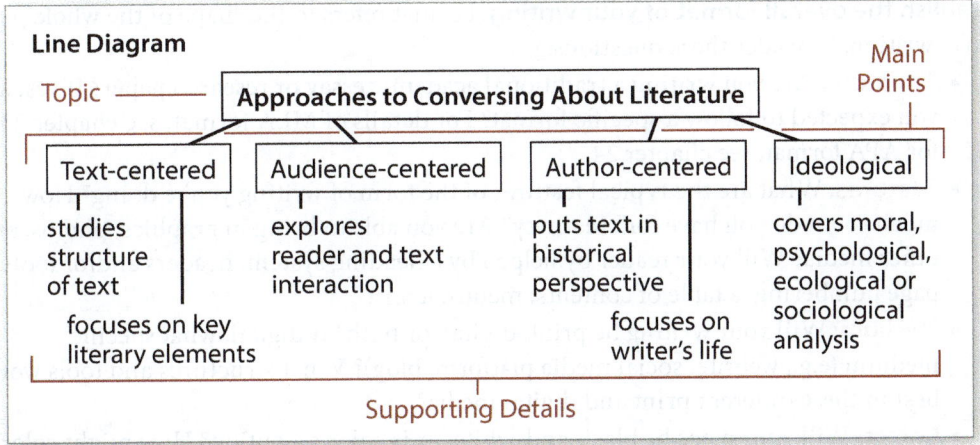

*fig. 4.8*

# Planning the Design of Your Project

Before you start drafting, it is also helpful to think through the overall design of your project. That design might be specified by your assignment, or you may have some freedom to develop one. The next pages introduce the main elements of design.

## Consider the Rhetorical Situation

You want your design to be reader-friendly and fit the parameters of the assignment. It should invite readers in, help them navigate your piece, map out the structure of your thinking, and promote understanding of that thinking. For these reasons, your design choices should be rhetorically driven:

1. **What are your goals?** What do you want this piece of writing to accomplish? To inform, analyze, persuade—or all of these? Is your writing clarifying complex information? Are you aiming for a particular tone (e.g., scholarly, entertaining)?
2. **Who are your readers?** What are their needs, values, and experiences? What will they be looking for, and how will they use it? How will they access your writing? Where, and on what device? Will they be reading deeply, or searching, skimming, following links? Will readers be focused or distracted, motivated or reluctant?
3. **What is the context?** What kind of document are you creating? What are its traditional parts and features? Will your writing be print, digital, or both? How will it be produced and shared? Where will it be shared, posted, or published?

## Choose Design Elements

Sometimes, designing your piece is simple: you just follow a template supplied to you. Generally, though, good design involves careful decisions about three elements: format, layout, and typography. Poor design fails on all three—perhaps offering readers a big block of dense text without divisions, without techniques to organize, divide, and highlight different parts of the writing. To achieve reader-friendly design, start making plans now.

**Establish the overall format of your writing.** Format refers to the shape of the whole piece you're writing. Consider these questions:

- **Structure:** Are you writing a traditional academic essay or research paper? If yes, are you expected to follow a specific format? For details of MLA format, see chapter 23; for APA format, see chapter 24.
- **Features:** What are the typical features of the form of writing you're doing? How much room do you have for creativity? Are you able to bring in graphics, photos, and other media? Will your reader by helped by a heading system, headers and/or footers, page numbering, a table of contents, menus, icons?
- **Medium:** Will your writing be print, digital, or both? If digital, what specific medium (e.g., website, social media platform, blog)? What structures and tools work best in these different print and digital media?
- **Colors:** Will your piece be black-and-white, or is color an option? How might color be useful?

**Develop an attractive and accessible layout.** Layout—how you arrange material on a page or screen—determines whether your writing is attractive, readable, and accessible. Consider these choices:

- **Orientation:** Portrait orientation (vertical) is traditional for print documents (including academic essays and reports), while landscape (horizontal) is common for computer screens. But either orientation can be used for print or digital pieces.
- **Columns:** While essays and reports are typically a single column, other projects may benefit from being presented in multiple columns. Consider these common column options: two even (useful for comparisons), two uneven (main text plus secondary information), or three even (e.g., brochure panels).
- **Spacing:** A healthy use of white space helps the reader engage your writing. It might be the double-spacing typically used with academic papers, along with the healthy margins around the text. In other writing, white space is accomplished with shorter paragraphs in a block style and space between paragraphs, by use of headings to separate sections, and by presenting material in bulleted or numbered lists.
- **Visuals:** These range from tables to graphs (line, bar, and pie) to images such as maps, diagrams, and photos. You can use them to make information accessible, clarify complex ideas, and dramatize important points. As you plan your writing, consider the visual story you might tell, as well as how you will position and discuss such visuals within your writing. As with spacing, align visuals so they appear in the appropriate size to be seen clearly without overwhelming the page.

**Consider your typographical options.** Typography refers to the actual print on the page or screen. Your aim with typographical planning is to create a positive impression, make reading easy, and clarify your content.

- Typeface refers to the look of the letters (e.g., Arial, Courier, Times Roman). Some are serif, like this, with finishes on the letters; others, like this, are sans serif, without finishes. Choose an attractive typeface that is above all readable. Times New Roman is traditional for academic writing; a sans serif, such as Arial, is often best for writing that will be read on a screen.
- Type size for normal reading conditions is 10 or 12 points. For subheadings, headings, and titles, gradually increase the size. For difficult reading conditions and presentations, go big—18 to 36 points, or even larger.
- Type styles refer to special effects you can use to highlight material in some way. IT MIGHT BE UPPER CASE, EMPHATIC IN SOME SITUATIONS, CONSIDERED SHOUTING IN OTHERS. **It might be boldface used to make words, phrases, and heading stand out.** *Or it might be italics for book titles and key statements.* Or underlining for headings and emphasis. Maybe color for warnings or for headings.

## Consider Multimodal Elements

At some point, you may be assigned a multimodal writing project. Such a project goes beyond written words to include components in other media, whether aural (sound), visual (photos, illustrations, or videos), or even spatial and gestural (models, performances). These components might be physical or digital. (For more on multimodal projects, see online chapter D.)

If you think about it, all writing is already multimodal. As the discussion above about format, layout, and typography suggests, written words on the page or screen have a visual dimension and potentially an aural dimension if used in presentations. If your instructor assigns a more complex multimodal project, they will undoubtedly offer instruction on your media choices: their nature, as well as the techniques, technologies, and software needed to create them. Consider these key questions to help you plan your multimodal project:

1. **Media Choices:** Given your research and prewriting, which media will help you tell the story of your topic or create a full experience of your thesis in words, sounds, and images?
2. **Media Relationships:** How might different media work together to create a coherent project? What media components would complement each other? Which would create useful and interesting contrasts? Will components be equal in contribution, or will one dominate and others supplement? How might you link components to each other?
3. **Project Genre:** What type of overall project will you produce from your components? Is it a fairly simple type? Examples: a graphic narrative, a brochure, a poster, a presentation, a podcast, social media. Or might it be a more complex genre? Examples: a website, a film, an animation, a music video.

# Planning Your Piece: Applications

Once you have used the instruction in this chapter to plan your piece, there may be more that you can think about. Through the following activities, apply what you have learned.

1. **Wise Words:** At the beginning of this chapter, Ken Macrorie claims that "good writing is formed partly through plan and partly through accident." Do you agree? Why or why not? Relate Macrorie's idea to your own writing experiences. How might you improve the way you plan your writing?
2. **Photo Op:** Recall the photograph on the chapter's opening page. Find another photograph or a short video that similarly portrays in an interesting and insightful way something about the practice of planning.
3. **Living Today:** A lot of the writing we do regularly now happens in digital environments, whether in the form of texts, Tweets, memes, blogs, or emails. To what degree is such writing spontaneous? What role does or should planning play?
4. **Public Texts:** This chapter explains how the thesis sets the direction for your writing. Is this principle true for more than essays? Find and study a magazine article, a blog, a web page, a workplace document, or a government report. Determine the document's main idea, outline the document's structure, and explore whether that structure follows effectively from the main idea.
5. **Major Work:** In many disciplines, it is a common practice early in a paper to "survey the literature" on the topic: i.e., the major studies done by scholars and researchers. For example, in a literary analysis, you might survey common interpretations of a key issue in the literary work before you offer your own interpretation. In the social and natural sciences, you might write a report called a literature review—a report that surveys, summarizes, and synthesizes the studies on a topic. In your major, is a literature survey or review common? Research this question, aiming to find out the typical features and qualities of such writing.

## Learning-Objectives Checklist ✓

Have you achieved this chapter's learning objectives? Check your progress with the following items, revisiting topics in the chapter as needed. I have . . .

____ generated a thoughtful thesis to guide the direction of my writing.
____ refined that thesis so that it has greater substance and nuance.
____ developed a plan or outline grounded in my thesis, research, and other prewriting.
____ considered when and how to use inductive and deductive patterns in my writing.
____ implemented a specific mapping method for my piece, whether a basic list, T-chart, topic outline, sentence outline, or writing organizer.
____ mapped the design of my piece, including the format, layout, and typography.
____ planned any components and media to use, to the extent that my project is multimodal.

# Chapter 5

# Drafting: From Paragraphs to Essays

French novelist Anatole France once said that one of his first drafts could have been written by a schoolboy, his next draft by a bright college student, his third draft by a superior graduate, and his final draft "only by Anatole France." Think in those terms as you write your first draft. Your main objective is to get ideas down; you'll have a chance later to improve your writing, to make it uniquely yours.

This chapter provides instruction for drafting strong paragraphs and whole essays. You'll find specific advice for creating the three main parts of essays and arranging information—the writing moves that enable you to develop your thinking and impact readers.

So get started. It's time to lay down that line of words. You're ready.

**Visually Speaking** How is drafting like sketching? Note the hand with the pencil in Figure 5.1. What does it suggest about the process of drafting? Then again, are there important differences between sketching and drafting?

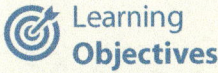

## Learning Objectives

By working through this chapter, you will be able to

- explain the parts or "major moves" of essays.
- draft four types of paragraphs: introduction, body, transition, and conclusion.
- craft substantial body paragraphs comprised of four types of sentences: topic, reasoning, evidence, and concluding.
- vary your paragraphs' length and style to fit the type and medium of your writing.
- compose an effective opening.
- generate a substantial middle.
- produce an effective closing.
- brainstorm a working title.

*Sergey Sarychev / Shutterstock.com*

*fig. 5.1*

# Basic Essay Structure: Major Moves

Figure 5.2 lists the main writing moves that occur during the development of a piece of writing. Use it as a general guide that you adapt as needed for all of your drafting. Note that especially the middle moves listed offer strategies to use, not a set pattern to follow.

### Opening

**Engage your reader.**
Stimulate and direct the reader's attention.

**Establish your direction.**
Identify the topic and put it in perspective.

**Get to the point.**
Narrow your focus and state your thesis or main idea (your formal thesis may appear later). Suggest how your support will unfold.

### Middle

**Advance your thesis.**
Provide background information, if needed. Cover your main points, creating a line of thinking.

**Test your ideas.**
Raise questions and consider alternatives.

**Support your main points.**
Add substance and build interest.

**Build a coherent structure.**
Start new paragraphs and arrange the support.

**Use different levels of detail.**
Clarify and complete each main point.

### Ending

**Reassert the main point and unify your message.**
Remind the reader of the purpose, rephrase the thesis, and relate the parts of your discussion.

**Urge the reader.**
Gain the reader's acceptance and look ahead.

*fig. 5.2*

# Tips for Drafting

Remember that drafting works best when it focuses on discovery—achieved partly through plan, partly by accident. Note, too, that it's perfectly okay to write a "shitty first draft," as Anne Lamott puts it. Most writers do. Relax. Take a breath, and hit your keyboard or paper with these strategies:

- **Review the assignment** to see if you missed anything during your planning.
- **Use your outline, writing plan, or diagram** as a general guide, but don't feel bound by it. Develop main points, but allow new ideas to emerge gradually.
- **Write freely.** Don't stress about correctness. Concentrate on developing your ideas, not on producing a clean copy. You can highlight or underline mistakes to fix later.
- **Start with a part that feels comfortable.** There's no rule that says you have to start at the beginning. To loosen up, draft a section you feel confident about. Then move on to harder parts. You might even leave the introduction for last.
- **Include as much detail as possible**, continuing until you reach a logical end point.
- **Complete your first draft** in one or two sittings. Reward yourself with short breaks.
- **Use the most natural voice you can** so the writing will flow smoothly. If your voice is too formal during drafting, you might stall or be tempted to stop and edit.
- **Quote sources accurately** by copy-and-pasting or by transcribing carefully.

# Drafting Paragraphs

The basic unit of drafting is the paragraph—that grouping of sentences created by laying down a line of words. The paragraph breaks your drafting into manageable chunks, each a mile marker along the journey. To meet these mile markers, know what kinds of paragraphs to draft, activate a basic pattern for body paragraphs, and learn to vary your paragraph style.

## Types of Paragraphs

Your drafting will lead you to write four types of paragraphs:

- **Introductory paragraphs** open your essay or a section of a longer project. The introduction gives your work a focus and welcomes readers into your discussion.
- **Body paragraphs** do the heavy lifting of your writing—developing the thesis of your essay with a rich blend of reasoning and information. See the basic pattern that follows, plus "Developing the Middle" (pages 66–69). Note, too, that revising your body paragraphs for unity, coherence, and completeness is addressed in chapter 6.
- **Transition paragraphs** are useful in longer projects when you have distinct sections or clusters of paragraphs. In two or three sentences, you might summarize one section and turn to the next section's focus—like the bridge in a song.
- **Concluding paragraphs** bring your essay or a portion of a longer work to a close. In closing, the conclusion drives home the main point of your writing and explores its larger significance, directing the reader outward and onward.

## Use a Basic Pattern for Body Paragraphs

In much of your academic writing, you want to write full-bodied paragraphs—rich like a quality cup of coffee. These paragraphs are typically longer than two or three sentences. And the sentences tend to be substantial—full of careful thinking and discussions of information. Such body paragraphs normally combine these kinds of sentences:

1. **A topic sentence:** Each paragraph typically has one, often the first sentence. It states the focus and main idea of the paragraph while often offering a transition from the previous paragraph.
2. **Reasoning sentences:** These typically elaborate your thinking about the topic sentence—explaining what you mean, what you've learned about it. Essentially, reasoning is what's happening in your head as you reflect on the main idea.
3. **Evidence sentences:** These statements present information in support of your reasoning: facts, statistics, examples, illustrations, quotations, case studies, and more. Evidence is what you've gathered through reading, viewing, researching, and experiencing. In that sense, it's what exists outside your head. You weave evidence sentences into your reasoning. Note: sometimes sentences blend reasoning and evidence. Don't get hung-up on the distinction: learning to weave reasoning and evidence together is the main lesson.
4. **Concluding sentence:** The final sentence often wraps up the discussion of the paragraph's topic, summarizing the point that you've developed in the reasoning and evidence sentences.

**Example:** Read the paragraph below from "Chasing the Stoke" in chapter 13. Notice how Tim Zekveld builds his thinking out of these four types of sentences. Note, too, how the paragraph has forward momentum, moving from A (the topic sentence) to A+ (the concluding sentence), all through the dance of reasoning and evidence.

---

**Topic sentence**

In Hawaii, surfing began as a joyous thanksgiving to the ocean for its providence and sustenance. Dating as far back as 800 AD, surfing was commonplace in Hawaiian society.

**Reasoning sentences**

Men, women, and children of every social status—from the commoner to the king—would surf regularly as a means of leisure and a form of ritual. When the ocean had provided food for their clan or had affected the people in a catastrophic way, Hawaiians would, while surfing the face of a wave, turn around and bow, wetting their head in the curl (Peralta). This ritual was a physical act meant to pay homage to the ocean, showing immense humility and reverence to their life force.

**Evidence sentences**

Surfing on carved wooden boards measuring sixteen feet or longer and weighing well over a hundred pounds, the ancient Hawaiians would paddle into waves varying from three to thirty feet (Young 11). Captain James Cook, on viewing a Hawaiian surf in 1777, wrote, "I could not help concluding that this man felt the most supreme pleasure while he was being driven on so fast and so smoothly by the sea" (qtd. in Peralta).

**Concluding sentence**

The joy that Captain Cook had witnessed, paired with the unfathomable respect that Hawaiians had for the ocean, fused into one term: aloha.

## Vary Your Paragraph Style

The body-paragraph pattern is just that—a pattern, not a formula that must be imitated in every paragraph. In fact, you'll want to match your paragraph length and style to the type of writing, the nature of the audience, and the medium in which you share the work.

**For most academic essays, and research papers, use traditional paragraphing.** Your paragraphs may vary in length, but they should be substantial presentations of ideas supported by thoughtful reasoning and compelling evidence. Most often, the first lines of these paragraphs are indented five spaces and the lines double-spaced. Paragraphs are linked with formal transitions, such as "however" and "furthermore."

**For less formal essays, use shorter paragraphs with lighter links.** Articles from newspapers, magazines, and websites often use short paragraphs with simple transitions. Because people often "skim" rather than "read," two or three sentence paragraphs can be more effective. Online paragraphs are presented in a block style to set them off visually, with links embedded in them for exploring connections and supporting evidence. The example below is from "The History of Coming Out," published online in *The Conversation*.

> By presenting coming out as a way to end internalized self-hatred and achieve a better life, the LGBTQ movement helped to encourage people to come out, despite associated risks. It also showed how coming out could be used to build solidarity and recruit other queer people.
>
> For instance, in 1978, in his campaign to defeat a California initiative that would have banned gay teachers from working in state public schools, openly gay elected government official Harvey Milk urged people to "Come Out, Come Out, Wherever You Are."

**For personal essays, be fluid in your paragraphing.** Personal essays unfold seamlessly. Vary paragraph lengths, though generally shorter is better, using the start of a new paragraph as a turn in the story or discussion. Note how the short, varied paragraphs in "Spare Change" by Teresa Zsuffa propel the narrative forward and signal speaker changes.

> I check my watch—quarter past eight. I just missed an express shuttle, and the next bus to Niagara Falls, where my father lives, won't be leaving for another forty-five minutes. Something pulls me back to the woman, and against all sworn Torontonian rules, I ask if she needs help.
>
> Her dull brown eyes light up. "I need to find the Old City Hall."
>
> "Okay," I nod. "I'll take you." I lead her through the glass doors into the city's busiest mall. It's the fastest way from Dundas to Queen Street, and from there she will need to walk only a few blocks west. As we're walking, I'm aware of the stares I'm getting from people I'll never see again.
>
> "So where are you from?" I ask.
>
> "Sudbury." And I'm instantly speechless. What is this woman doing so far from home?

# Opening Your Draft

The opening paragraph is one of the most important elements in any composition. It should accomplish at least three essential things: (1) engage the reader; (2) establish your direction, tone, and level of language; and (3) introduce your line of thought.

**Advice:**
- The conventional way of approaching the first paragraph is to view it as a kind of "funnel" that draws a reader in and narrows to a main point. In some situations, the final sentence explicitly states your thesis.

**Cautions:**
- Don't feel bound by the conventional pattern, which may sound stale if not handled well.
- Don't let the importance of the paragraph paralyze you. Relax and write.
- Avoid "false titles": introductions that just announce the topic—"This paper is about drugs. Opioid deaths are increasing."

The information that follows will help you develop your opening. For additional opening strategies, you can refer to the sample essays in Part II of this text, "Modes of Writing."

## Engage Your Reader

Your readers will be preoccupied with other thoughts until you seize, stimulate, and direct their attention. Here are some effective ways to "hook" readers:

- **Mention little-known facts about the topic.**
  > Beads may have been what separated human ancestors from their Neanderthal cousins. Yes, beads.

- **Pose a challenging question.**
  > Why would our human ancestors spend days carving something as frivolous as beads while Neanderthals spent days hunting mammoths?

- **Offer a thought-provoking quotation.**
  > "The key thing in human evolution is when people start devoting just ridiculous amounts of time to making these [beads]," says archeologist John Shea of Stony Brook University.

- **Tell a brief, illuminating story.**
  > When I walked into the room, I had only to show my hand to be accepted by the group of strangers there. The Phi Delta Kappa ring on my finger—and on all of our fingers—bound us across space and time as a group. Our ancestors discovered the power of such ornamentation forty thousand years ago.

## Establish Your Direction

The direction of your line of thought should become clear in the opening part of your writing. Here are some moves you might make to set the right course:

- **Identify the topic (issue).** Show a problem, a need, or an opportunity.
- **Deepen the issue.** Connect the topic, showing its importance.
- **Acknowledge other views.** Tell what others say or think about the topic.

## Get to the Point

You may choose to state your main point up front, or you may wait until later to introduce your thesis. For example, you could work inductively by establishing an issue, a problem, or a question in your opening and then build toward the answer—your thesis—in your conclusion. In any case, the opening should at least hint at the central issue or thesis of your paper. Here are three ways to get to the point:

1. **Narrow your focus.** Point to what interests you about the topic.
2. **Raise a question.** Answer the question in the rest of the essay.
3. **State your thesis.** If appropriate, craft a sentence that boils down your thinking to a central claim. You can use the thesis sentence as a "map" for the organization of the rest of the essay. (Even if your thesis sentence appears later in the essay, your opening should clearly set up your main point.)

**Weak Opening**

This sample opening comes from a student's essay about Trevor Noah's memoir, *Born a Crime*. The assignment asks the writer to analyze the tools Noah developed in response to the constraints of his environment. While this opening introduces the topic, the writing isn't engaging and doesn't establish a clear focus or thesis about Noah's tools.

> I would like to tell you about Trevor Noah. He grew up in South Africa, where he had a tough life. He has written a memoir about that life called *Born a Crime*. Now he's made it big in America. You could say he's living the American dream as a comedian with his own show, *The Daily Show*.

**Strong Opening**

In the following opening, the writer uses the first paragraph to engage the reader in Noah's life. The paragraph highlights in concrete terms the hardships Noah experienced, references the title of Noah's memoir effectively, references three tools Noah developed to face difficulties, and ends with a sharply stated thesis that sets up a theme for the rest of the essay.

> Trevor Noah is an award-winning author, comedian, podcaster, and host of *The Daily Show*. Looking at Noah's successful career you would never know the social hardships he faced as a child. He was born near the end of Apartheid in South Africa, a period when systematic racism and segregation were ways of life and having a mixed child was illegal. Because his mother was Black and his father was White, Noah was literally "born a crime." His racial classification separated him from most groups he interacted with as a young person. However, through his understanding of multiple languages, humor, and entrepreneurial mindset, Noah learned how to adapt to the various racial and social restrictions around him. Noah became a chameleon who could overcome a social system set up for him to fail.

# Developing the Middle

The middle of an essay is the place where you do the "heavy lifting." In this part you develop the main points that support your thesis statement or main point.

**Advice:**
- As you write, you will likely make choices that were unforeseen when you began. Use "scratch outlines" (temporary jottings) along the way to show where your new ideas may take you.

**Cautions:**
- Writing that lacks effective detail gives only a vague image of the writer's intent.
- Writing that wanders loses its hold on the essay's purpose.

For both of these reasons, always keep your thesis in mind when you develop the main part of your writing. Your goal is to build a coherent structure—a sequence of paragraphs that develop your thesis clearly and logically .

## Advance Your Thesis

If you stated a thesis in the opening, you can advance it in the middle paragraphs by covering your main points and supporting them in these ways.

**Explain:** Provide important facts, details, and examples.
**Narrate:** Share a brief story or re-create an experience to illustrate an idea.
**Describe:** Tell in detail how someone appears or how something works.
**Define:** Identify or clarify the meaning of a specific term or idea.
**Analyze:** Examine the parts of something to better understand the whole.
**Compare:** Provide examples to show how two things are alike or different.
**Argue:** Use logic and evidence to prove that something is true or untrue.
**Reflect:** Express your thoughts or feelings about something.
**Cite authorities:** Add expert analysis or personal commentary.

## Test Your Ideas

When you write a first draft, you're testing your initial thinking about your topic. You're determining whether your thesis is valid and whether you have enough compelling information to support it. Here are ways to test your line of thinking as you write:

- **Raise questions.** Try to anticipate your readers' questions.
- **Consider alternatives.** Look at your ideas from different angles; weigh various options; reevaluate your thesis.
- **Answer objections.** Directly or indirectly deal with possible problems that a skeptical reader might point out.

## Make Writing Moves

Drafting the body of your essay can involve using a range of writing moves. Many of these are addressed in "Modes of Writing," beginning in chapter 10; however, to start, here are some common ones.

### Developing an Analogy or Comparison

An analogy is a comparison that a writer uses to explain a complex or unfamiliar phenomenon. For example, in this paragraph, Rob King compares our immune system to mall security.

> The human body is like a mall, and the immune system is like mall security. Because the mall has hundreds of employees and thousands of customers, security guards must rely on photo IDs, name tags, and uniforms to decide who should be allowed to open registers and who should have access to the vault. In the same way, white blood cells and antibodies need to use DNA cues to recognize which cells belong in a body and which do not. Occasionally security makes mistakes, wrestling Kookie the Klown to the ground while new clothes "walk" out of the mall, but these problems amount only to allergic reactions or little infections. If security guards become hypervigilant, detaining every customer and employee, the situation is akin to leukemia, in which white blood cells attack healthy cells. If guards become corrupt, letting thieves run amok, the situation is akin to AIDS. Both systems—mall security and human immunity—work by correctly differentiating friend from foe.

### Developing an Example or Illustration

An example allows you to flesh out an idea by exploring an instance of it that clarifies its various facets. In the following passage from "The Rise of the New Groupthink," Susan Cain illustrates how charisma can blind people to actual sources of creativity.

> Culturally, we're often so dazzled by charisma that we overlook the quiet part of the creative process. Consider Apple. In the wake of Steve Jobs's death, we've seen a profusion of myths about the company's success. Most focus on Mr. Jobs's supernatural magnetism and tend to ignore the other crucial figure in Apple's creation: a kindly, introverted engineering wizard, Steve Wozniak, who toiled alone on a beloved invention, the personal computer.
>
> Rewind to March 1975: Mr. Wozniak believes the world would be a better place if everyone had a user-friendly computer. This seems a distant dream—most computers are still the size of minivans, and many times as pricey. But Mr. Wozniak meets a simpatico band of engineers that call themselves the Homebrew Computer Club. The Homebrewers are excited about a primitive new machine called the Altair 8800. Mr. Wozniak is inspired, and immediately begins work on his own magical version of a computer. Three months later, he unveils his amazing creation for his friend, Steve Jobs. Mr. Wozniak wants to give his invention away free, but Mr. Jobs persuades him to co-found Apple Computer.

## Presenting and Interpreting Evidence

You may be familiar with the phrase "marshalling evidence," which suggests that this writing move is something of a military campaign. When you pull together, present, and analyze a range of evidence (e.g., statistics, historical records, and expert testimony), you advance your ideas by building a foundation on which your reasoning can stand. In the following paragraph from "The Emancipation of Abe Lincoln," Eric Foner offers evidence of Lincoln's complex efforts to end slavery.

> Lincoln's plan sought to win the cooperation of slave holders in ending slavery. As early as November 1861, he proposed it to political leaders in Delaware, one of the four border states (along with Kentucky, Maryland and Missouri) that remained in the Union. Delaware had only 1,800 slaves; the institution was peripheral to the state's economy. But Lincoln found that even there, slave holders did not wish to surrender their human property. Nonetheless, for most of 1862, he avidly promoted his plan to the border states and any Confederates who might be interested.
>
> Lincoln also took his proposal to black Americans. In August 1862, he met with a group of black leaders from Washington. He seemed to blame the presence of blacks in America for the conflict: "but for your race among us there could not be war." He issued a powerful indictment of slavery—"the greatest wrong inflicted on any people"—but added that, because of racism, blacks would never achieve equality in America. "It is better for us both, therefore, to be separated," he said. But most blacks refused to contemplate emigration from the land of their birth.

## Applying a Concept

A lot of academic writing involves explaining and applying concepts—the key ideas that make sense of subjects. For example, an environmental science student might analyze corn production using the concept of sustainability, or an English student might explain a character's fate through the concept of hubris. In the following passage from "How the Internet Has Changed Bullying," Maria Konnikova applies the concept of rural bullying, which she has just explained as distinct from urban bullying, to the relatively new phenomenon of cyberbullying.

> In some ways, when it comes to bullying, the Internet has made the world more rural. Before the Internet, bullying ended when you withdrew from whatever environment you were in. But now, the bullying dynamic is harder to contain and harder to ignore. If you're harassed on your Facebook page, all of your social circles know about it; as long as you have access to the network, a ceaseless stream of notifications leaves you vulnerable to victimhood. Bullying may not have become more prevalent—in fact, a recent review of international data suggests that its incidence has declined by as much as ten percent around the world. But getting away from it has become more difficult.

## Stretching an Idea

When you stretch an idea, you are making a writing move that explores the boundaries and portability of the idea. Can it be stretched to include elements and dimensions not normally associated with it? Might it be transported from one field of knowledge to another? Should you shift the direction of discussion by turning the idea upside down? In the following paragraph from an essay titled "Fatherless America," David Blankenhorn explores the possible ramifications of fatherlessness for American society, not just specific families.

> If this trend continues, fatherlessness is likely to change the shape of our society. Consider this prediction. After the year 2000, as people born after 1970 emerge as a large proportion of our working-age adult population, the United States will be a nation divided into two groups, separate and unequal. The two groups will work in the same economy, speak a common language, and remember the same national history. But they will live fundamentally divergent lives. One group will receive basic benefits—psychological, social, economic, educational, and moral—that are denied to the other group.
>
> The primary fault line dividing the two groups will not be race, religion, class, education, or gender. It will be patrimony. One group will consist of those adults who grew up with the daily presence and provision of fathers. The other group will consist of those who did not. By the early years of the next [twenty-first] century, these two groups will be roughly the same size.

## Exploring a Tension

This writing move attends to the gaps, disagreements, dualisms, and elements of confusion within your topic. Such tensions are often big and obvious, but they may also be small and subtle. Both kinds are worthy of your attention. Such a move may call out the tension, explore its meaning, and possibly seek to resolve it. In the following paragraph from "Death from Below," an article about shark attacks, Brian Phillips introduces opposing, contradictory themes in how the media cover them.

> Like almost all shark-related media coverage, the summer-of-shark-attacks dossier is depressing and contradictory. It has to be, because it's designed to serve two opposing agendas. It needs to scare us a little, because the fascination that makes sharks prime box-office draws hinges on sharks being real-life sea monsters and thus categorically terrifying. But it also needs to live up to the statistical and ecological responsibility not to vilify sharks. The result is the distinctive, smug tone of self-correcting sensationalism that we associate with shark-attack pseudo-journalism: DID YOU KNOW that these BEINGS OF PURE EVIL AND MALEVOLENCE who WILL NEVER EVER BOTHER YOU also totally YEARN TO EAT YOUR CHILDREN and are VITAL TO THE HEALTH OF OUR PLANET??

# Ending Your Draft

Closing paragraphs can be important for tying up loose ends, clarifying key points, or signing off with the reader. In a sense, the entire essay is a preparation for an effective ending; the ending helps the reader look back over the essay with new understanding and appreciation. Many endings leave the reader with fresh food for thought.

**Advice:**
- Because the ending can be so important, draft a variety of possible endings. Choose the one that flows best from a sense of the whole.

**Cautions:**
- If your thesis is weak or unclear, you will have a difficult time writing a satisfactory ending. To strengthen the ending, strengthen the thesis.
- You may have heard this formula for writing an essay: "Say what you're going to say, say it, then say what you've just said." Remember, though, if you need to "say what you've just said," say it in new words.
- You may be tempted to begin your conclusion with "In conclusion." As a general rule, don't. This phrase is clichéd. Aim to be more subtle and inventive in beginning your ending.

The information that follows will help you develop your ending. For more ideas, you can refer to the sample essays in Part II of this book.

## Reassert the Main Point

If the topic is complicated, your reader may need you to reassert your main point at the end. Show that you are fully addressing the issues that you forecasted earlier in the essay.

- **Remind the reader.** Recall what you first set out to do; check off the key points you've covered; or answer any questions left unanswered.
- **State or rephrase the thesis.** If you have stated your thesis previously, deepen and expand your main point.
- **Revisit your opening.** Your opening may include an interesting fact, question, quotation, or story. In your ending, you could refer to that element again, offering a final thought about it to bring your writing full circle.

## Urge the Reader

Your reader may still be reluctant to accept your ideas or argument. The ending is your last chance to gain the reader's acceptance. Here are some possible strategies:

- **Show the implications.** Follow further possibilities raised by your train of thought; be reasonable and convincing.
- **Look ahead.** Suggest other possible connections.
- **List the benefits.** Point readers to the benefits of accepting or applying your ideas.
- **Call for action.** Urge your reader to put your ideas to work or change their behavior.

**INSIGHT** When your writing comes to an effective stopping point, conclude the essay. Don't tack on another idea.

## Complete and Unify Your Message

Your final paragraphs are your last chance to refocus, unify, and reinforce your message. Draft the closing carefully, not merely to finish the essay but to further advance your purpose.

### Weak Ending

The following ending does not focus on and show commitment to the essay's main idea. Rather than reinforcing this idea, the writing leads off in a new direction.

> I realize I've got to catch my bus. I've spent too much time talking to this woman whose life is a wreck. I give her some spare change and then head off. She doesn't follow me. Toronto is a great city, but sometimes you have weird experiences there. Once a street vendor gave me a free falafel. What a weird city!

### Strong Ending

What follows are final paragraphs from "Spare Change." (See chapter 10 for the full essay.) Listen to their tone, watch how they reconsider the essay's ideas, and note how they offer further food for thought. These are a revision of the weak paragraph above.

> I tell her I need to get going. She should go, too, or she'll be late for the hearing. Before getting up, I reach into my wallet and give her two TTC passes and some spare change. I walk her to the street and point her toward Old City Hall. She never thanks me, only looks at me one last time with immense vulnerability and helplessness. Then she walks away.
>
> I wonder as I hurry towards the station if she'll be okay, if her boyfriend really will get out of jail, and if her grandmother will ever take her back. Either way, I think as I cross Bay Street, what more can I do? I have a bus to catch.

# The Last Step in Drafting: Your Working Title

When you began drafting, you may have put at the top "History Essay" or "Psyche Paper." Once you finish your draft, it's time to consider a working title as it contains the first words your reader meets. Your title should engage your reader, signal your focused topic, and point toward your thesis.

**For a personal or informal essay,** make the title short and suggestive, possibly clever (but not too clever). Is there a key word or phrase from your draft that suggests a title? Examples: "Spare Change," "Hair Today, Gone Tomorrow."

**For more academic essays,** make the title engaging, but above all, make it precise—containing the key words signaling your topic and focus. Often, such titles are made of a title and subtitle, separated by a colon in this pattern: main topic or theme + colon + subtopic, focus, or question. Examples: "The Emancipation of Abe Lincoln," "American Lumpia."

# Drafting: Applications

Once you have used the instruction in this chapter to draft your writing, there may be more that you can think about. Through the following activities, apply what you have learned.

1. **Wise Words:** Patricia T. O'Connor says, "All writing begins life as a first draft, and first drafts are never any good. They're not supposed to be." Is this claim true? Why or why not? What do you hope to accomplish with a first draft? How can you make drafting more effective?
2. **Photo Op:** Recall the photograph on the chapter's opening page. Find another photograph or a short video that portrays something about your practices when drafting, or the challenges you face when you sit down to do so.
3. **Making Moves:** Review the chart in Figure 5.2 and the "writing moves" from this chapter. Based on your own reading and writing, can you identify, name, and describe an additional writing move? Can you supply an example of that move?
4. **Writing Reset:** Choose one of the sample essays in Part II of this text. After analyzing the opening, middle, and closing strategies that the writer uses, imagine alternatives to what you find there. Sketch out these alternatives and explain how they would change the writing.
5. **Major Work:** Find one or two examples of the kinds of writing done in or related to your field of study—scholarly articles, online reports, websites, and so on. What writing moves seem to be valued in your field? Why?

## Learning-Objectives Checklist ✓

Have you achieved this chapter's learning objectives? Check your progress with the following items, revisiting topics in the chapter as needed. I have . . .

\_\_\_\_ identified the parts or "major moves" of an essay.

\_\_\_\_ recognized four types of paragraphs: introduction, body, transition, and conclusion.

\_\_\_\_ crafted substantial body paragraphs comprised of four types of sentences: topic, reasoning, evidence, and concluding.

\_\_\_\_ varied my paragraphs' length and style to fit the type and medium of my writing.

\_\_\_\_ composed an opening that engages my readers, sets a direction, and introduces my line of thought through a theme or thesis.

\_\_\_\_ generated a substantial middle that advances my theme or thesis through a series of writing moves.

\_\_\_\_ produced a closing that reasserts my main point in a fresh way, conveys the point's relevance to readers, and unifies my writing.

\_\_\_\_ brainstormed a working title that engages my reader, indicates my topic, and points toward my theme or thesis.

# Chapter 6

# Revising Your Draft

So, you've finished a draft of your paper. What's next? A quick spellcheck before you click print, post, or send? Sorry, it's not that simple. You should consider revising that draft.

Revision means *seeing again*. And experts suggest that it takes 48 to 72 hours before you can see your writing with fresh eyes. That's why it's so important to give ample time to all steps of the writing process, including revision—which, in our experience, many students don't understand and simply skip.

Because revision is re-seeing your draft, it involves examining critically the global issues in your writing—the strength of the content, organization, and voice. It's also about the shape, depth, and direction of each paragraph. In other words, revising takes true grit, the kind of grit this chapter will help you develop.

**Visually** Speaking   Revision requires that you develop a clear vision of your draft. As suggested by Figure 6.1, how is that vision like putting on a pair of glasses?

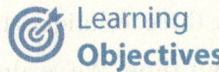
**Learning Objectives**

By working through this chapter, you will be able to

- practice tips for effectively revising your writing.
- improve the content of your writing—the ideas and information.
- reshape the organization so that your writing flows better from beginning to end.
- strengthen the commitment and intensity of your voice.
- improve the unity, coherence, and completeness of your body paragraphs.
- exchange useful feedback with a peer on your first drafts.

cla78 / Shutterstock.com

*fig. 6.1*

# Tips for Revising Your Work

How do you get started on revising effectively? Begin with the strategies below.

## Use Practical Strategies

Here are three techniques to implement as part of your revision practices.

**Take your time.** We've already advised you to wait two to three days after your draft. In addition, do your revising in manageable chunks of time—a half hour, say. Set a timer and work steadily. This approach makes revising doable and takes away the pressure of getting every problem fixed in one sitting. In addition, time away from revising allows your unconscious, the "back of your mind," to work on solving problems you've identified.

**Revisit your rhetorical situation.** Consider whether something in your draft doesn't fit the situation. Is there something problematic in your draft's approach? Consider these questions:

- **Purpose:** Does the entire draft contribute to your writing goals? Is there material that is extraneous? Does the draft veer off on a tangent?
- **Subject:** In terms of your treatment of the topic, what's good, what's bad, and what's ugly? When you look hard, what do you see?
- **Readers:** What would your audience hear in this draft? Would it engage them throughout, give them what they need?
- **Assignment:** Does the draft meet all the requirements of the assignment? Does it show the necessary features of the form you're writing? Does it fully address the instructor's directions?

**Examine your draft from different points of view.** You can get a fresh perspective by looking at your writing through different lenses:

- **On screen:** Digital tools offer you the power and flexibility to make changes and rework passages.
- **On paper:** At some point, it's best to double- or triple-space your draft and print it. Words on paper encourage a thoughtful interaction with them.
- **Out loud:** Read your writing aloud; record it. Hearing your writing will help you identify the problem areas, the stumbling blocks. It is easier to "hear" than "see" missing and misspelled words, grammar errors, and awkward phrases.
- **Others' eyes:** Ask a peer for feedback, or visit your school's Writing Center.

## Consider Your Overall Approach

Sometimes it's better to start fresh if your writing contains stretches of uninspired ideas. Consider a fresh start if your first draft shows one of these problems:

- **The topic is worn-out.** An essay titled "Lead Poisoning" may not sound very interesting. Unless you can approach it with a new twist ("Get the Lead Out!"), consider cutting your losses and finding a fresh topic.

- **The approach is stale.** If you've been writing primarily to get a good grade, finish the assignment, or sound cool, start again. Try writing to learn something, prompt real thinking in readers, or touch a chord.
- **Your voice is predictable or fake.** Avoid the bland "A good time was had by all" or the phony academic "When one studies this significant problem in considerable depth . . ." Be real. Be honest. Trust your true voice.
- **The draft sounds boring.** Maybe it's boring because you pay an equal amount of attention to everything and hence stress nothing. Try condensing less important material and expanding what's important.
- **The essay is formulaic.** In other words, it follows the "five-paragraph" format. This handy organizing frame may prevent you from doing justice to your topic and thinking. If your draft is dragged down by rigid adherence to a formula, try a more original approach.

**INSIGHT** Even a weak first draft will have something to salvage. Look for a key word, phrase, sentence, or paragraph that contains the seed of a new draft, and run with it.

## Revising Your Ideas

As you review your draft for content, make sure the ideas are fully developed. From your main claim or thesis to your reasoning and your evidence, strengthen your thinking.

### Test Your Ideas

Review the ideas in your writing, making sure that each point is logical, complete, and clear.

#### Complete Thinking

Have you answered readers' basic questions? Have you supported the thesis? The original passage that follows is too general; the revision is clearly more complete.

> **Original Passage** (Too general)
> As soon as you receive a minor cut, the body's healing process begins to work. Blood from tiny vessels fills the wound and begins to clot. In less than 24 hours, a scab forms.
>
> **Revised Version** (More specific)
> As soon as you receive a minor cut, the body's healing process begins to work. In a simple wound, the first and second layers of skin are severed along with tiny blood vessels called capillaries. As these vessels bleed into the wound, minute structures called platelets help stop the bleeding by sticking to the edges of the cut and to one another, forming a plug. The platelets then release chemicals that react with certain proteins in the blood to form a clot. The blood clot, with its fiber network, begins to join the edges of the wound together. As the clot dries out, a scab forms, usually in less than 24 hours.

## Strong Thesis

Make sure that your writing centers on one main issue or thesis, and the thesis is strong. To refine your thesis, refer to "Forming Your Thesis Statement" in chapter 4. Although the following original passage lacks a thesis, the revision has a clear, thoughtful one.

> **Original Passage** (Lacks a thesis)
> Teen magazines are popular with young girls. These magazines contain a lot of how-to articles about self-image, fashion, and boy-girl relationships. Girls read them to get advice on how to act and how to look. Girls who don't really know what they want are the most eager readers.
>
> **Revised Version** (Identifies a specific thesis statement)
> Adolescent girls often see teen magazines as handbooks on how to be teenagers. These magazines influence the ways they act and the ways they look. For girls who are unsure of themselves, these publications can exert an enormous amount of influence. Unfortunately, the advice about self-image, fashion, and boys found within their pages may do more harm than good.

## Test Your Evidence

The quality and extent of the evidence you've woven into your draft is critical. Test the information you've used against these criteria. The evidence should be . . .

- _____ **Accurate:** Each detail is correct and precise, preferably verifiable in more than one source. The information is solid.
- _____ **Authoritative:** The evidence clearly comes from a credible, reliable source in terms of author, institutional affiliation, print or online publisher, and so on.
- _____ **Close to the original source:** At best, the evidence is based on a direct report of it; the further the evidence used is distant from the original source (a report of a report of evidence), the greater the risk of distortion, of the evidence becoming hearsay.
- _____ **Current:** The evidence is reliably up-to-date, a measurement determined by the nature of the topic.
- _____ **Relevant:** The evidence is clearly related to the point you are making; the information isn't "beside the point."
- _____ **Representative:** The information is typical of the whole body of evidence, not an anomaly put forward as the norm, an exception treated as the rule.
- _____ **Sufficient:** The evidence is complete enough to make the point clearly and convincingly; the amount of information is neither too skimpy nor too extensive (overkill). The weight of evidence is compelling.
- _____ **Appropriate:** The evidence is suited to fulfill the needs of the assignment and meet the instructor's expectations.

If evidence fails these tests, you may need to look deeper, rethink your reasoning, and go back to your research—testing your sources and perhaps even doing more research.

# Revising Your Organization

Good writing has structure. It leads readers effectively from one point to the next. When revising for organization, consider four areas: the overall plan, the opening, the flow of ideas, and the closing.

## Check Your Overall Plan

Look closely at the sequence of ideas or events that you share. Does that sequence advance your thesis? Do the points build effectively? Have you arranged them to build your reader's understanding of the topic? Are there gaps in the support or points that stray from your original purpose? If you find such problems, consider the following actions:

- **Refine the focus or emphasis** by rearranging material within the text.
- **Fill in the gaps with new material.** Revisit your planning notes and the assignment requirements.
- **Delete material that wanders** away from your purpose.
- **Use an additional (or different) method of organization.** For example, if you are comparing two subjects, add depth to your analysis by contrasting them as well. If you are describing a complex subject, show the subject more clearly and fully by distinguishing and classifying its parts.

**INSIGHT** What is the best method of organization for your essay? Your reader's needs and the type of writing you are doing will usually determine the choice. For example, a personal narrative is often organized by time. Typically, however, you combine and customize methods to develop a writing idea. For instance, within a comparison essay you may do some describing or classifying.

## Revisit Your Opening

Reread your opening paragraph(s). Is the opening organized effectively? Does it engage readers, establish a direction for your writing, and express your thesis or focus? The original opening that follows doesn't build to a compelling thesis statement, but the revised version engages the reader and leads to the thesis.

> **Original Opening** (Lacks interest and direction)
> The lack of student motivation is a common subject in the news. Educators want to know how to get students to learn. Today's higher standards mean that students will be expected to learn even more. Another problem in urban areas is that large numbers of students are dropping out. How to interest students is a challenge.
>
> **Revised Version** (Effectively leads readers into the essay)
> How can we motivate students to learn? How can we get them to meet today's rising standards of excellence? How can we, in fact, keep students in school long enough to learn? The answer to these problems is quite simple. Give them money. Pay students to study and learn and stay in school.

## Test the Flow of Ideas

Look closely at the start and finish of each paragraph. Have you connected your thoughts clearly? (A list of transition words appears later in this chapter.) Typically in academic writing, the first sentence in a paragraph sets a new direction for your writing, but that sentence also links back to the previous paragraph, often its last sentence. The original opening words of the paragraph sequence below, from an essay of description, offer no links for readers. The revised versions use strong transitions indicating spatial organization (order by location).

> **Original First Words in the Four Middle Paragraphs**
> There was a huge, steep hill . . .
> Buffalo Creek ran . . .
> A dense "jungle" covering . . .
> Within walking distance from my house . . .
>
> **Revised Versions** (Words and phrases connect ideas)
> Behind the house, there was a huge, steep hill . . .
> Across the road from the house, Buffalo Creek ran . . .
> On the far side of the creek bank was a dense "jungle" covering . . .
> Up the road, within walking distance from my house . . .

## Revisit Your Closing

Reread your closing paragraph(s). Look at your ending side by side with your opening. Do you offer an effective summary, reassert your main point in a fresh way, and provide readers with food for thought as they leave your writing? Or is your ending a bland mirror image or restatement of your opening? Is your closing abrupt, repetitive, or directionless? The original ending that follows is uninspiring; it adds little to the main part of the writing. The revision summarizes the main points in the essay and then urges the reader to think again about the overall point of the writing.

> **Original Ending** (Sketchy and flat)
> *Native Son* deals with a young man's struggle against racism. It shows the effects of prejudice. Everyone should read this book.
>
> **Revised Version** (Effectively ends the writing)
> *Native Son* deals with a young man's struggle in a racist society, but also with so much more. It shows how prejudice affects people, how it closes in on them, and what some people will do to find a way out. Anyone who wants to better understand racism in the United States should read this book.

**INSIGHT** To generate fresh ideas for your closing, freewrite answers to questions like these: Why is the topic important to me? What should my readers have learned? Why should this issue matter to readers? What evidence or appeal will help readers remember my message and act on it? How does the topic relate to broader issues in society, history, or life?

# Revising Your Voice

Generally, readers more fully trust writing that speaks in a committed but measured voice. To develop such a voice, keep the focus on your topic, offering the reader rich information and sound thinking.

## Check the Level of Commitment

Consider how and to what degree your writing shows that you care about the topic and reader. The original passage that follows lacks a personal voice, revealing nothing about the writer's connection to—or interest in—the topic. The revision shows the opposite.

> **Original Passage** (Lacks voice)
> Cemeteries can teach us a lot about history. They make history seem more real. There is an old grave of a Revolutionary War veteran in the Union Grove Cemetery. . . .
>
> **Revised Version** (Personal, sincere voice)
> I've always had a special feeling for cemeteries. It's hard to explain any further than that, except to say history never seems as real as it does when I walk among many old gravestones. One day I discovered the grave of a Revolutionary War veteran. . . .

## Check the Intensity

All writing—including academic writing—is enriched by an appropriate level of intensity, or even passion. In the original passage that follows, the writer's concern for the topic is unclear because the piece sounds neutral. In contrast, the revised version exudes energy.

> **Original Passage** (Lacks feeling and energy)
> The Dream Act could make a difference for people. It just takes a long time to get any bill through Congress. This bill probably will never get approved. Instead of passing the Dream Act, the country will probably just deport high school students from other countries.
>
> **Revised Version** (Expresses real feelings)
> Given such debates, it might be a long time before the bill becomes law, thereby dashing the dreams of nearly 65,000 high school students like Maria who can't wait another year because they may already be in deportation proceedings. We need to step up and educate our representatives about the importance of passing the Dream Act on its own instead of including the bill along with other resolutions. We need to urge them to debate and approve the Dream Act now, thereby making Maria's dreams—and the dreams of thousands of students like her—a reality.

**INSIGHT** Each academic discipline has standards, codes, and expected language used in academic and professional writing. Reviewing the language in textbooks, handouts, and professional articles can guide you in developing the appropriate voice for your project.

# Strengthening Your Body Paragraphs

While drafting, you may have constructed paragraphs that are loosely held together, poorly developed, or unclear. As well as revisiting your opening and closing paragraphs, you should take a close look at your body paragraphs for focus, unity, and coherence.

## Remember the Basics

A paragraph should be a concise unit of thought. Revise a paragraph until it . . .

- is organized around a controlling idea—often stated in a topic sentence that also links back to the previous paragraph in some way.
- consists of supporting sentences that (a) develop the controlling idea through reasoning or (b) offer evidence related to that reasoning.
- concludes with a sentence that summarizes the main point and prepares readers for the next paragraph or main point.
- serves a specific function in a piece of writing—opening, supporting, developing, illustrating, countering, describing, or closing.

### Sample Paragraph

Tumor cells can hurt the body in a number of ways. First, a tumor can grow so big that it takes up space needed by other organs. Second, some cells may detach from the original tumor and spread throughout the body, creating new tumors elsewhere. This happens with lymphatic cancer—a cancer that's hard to control because it spreads so quickly. A third way that tumor cells can hurt the body is by doing work not called for in their DNA. For example, a gland cell's DNA code may tell the cell to produce a necessary hormone in the endocrine system. However, if cancer damages or distorts that code, sick cells may produce more of the hormone than the body can use—or even tolerate (Braun 4). Cancer cells seem to have minds of their own, and this is why cancer is such a serious disease.

## Keep the Purpose in Mind

Use these questions to evaluate the purpose and function of each paragraph:

- What function does the paragraph fulfill? How does it add to your line of reasoning or the development of your thesis?
- Would the paragraph work better if it were divided in two—or combined with another paragraph?
- Does the paragraph flow smoothly from the previous paragraph, and does it lead effectively into the next one?

## Check for Unity

A unified paragraph is one in which all the details help to develop a single main topic or achieve a single main effect. Test for unity by following these guidelines.

### Topic Sentence

Very often the topic of a paragraph is stated in a single sentence called a "topic sentence." Check whether your paragraph needs a topic sentence. If the paragraph has a topic sentence, determine whether it is clear, specific, and well focused. Figure 6.2 presents a formula for writing good topic sentences:

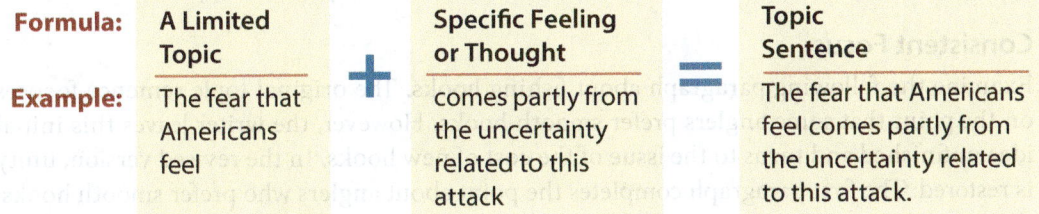

*fig. 6.2*

### Placement of the Topic Sentence

Normally the topic sentence is the first sentence in the paragraph. However, it can appear elsewhere in a paragraph.

> **Middle Placement:** Place a topic sentence in the middle when you want to build up to and then lead away from the key idea.
>
> During the making of *Apocalypse Now*, Eleanor Coppola created a documentary about the filming called *Hearts of Darkness: A Filmmaker's Apocalypse*. In the first film, the insane Colonel Kurtz has disappeared into the Cambodian jungle. As Captain Willard searches for Kurtz, the screen fills with horror. **However, as *Hearts of Darkness* relates, the horror portrayed in the fictional movie was being lived out by the production company.** For example, in the documentary, actor Larry Fishburne shockingly says, "War is fun. . . . Vietnam must have been so much fun." Then toward the end of the filming, actor Martin Sheen suffered a heart attack. When an assistant informed investors, the director exploded, "He's not dead unless I say he's dead."
>
> **End Placement:** Place a topic sentence at the end when you want to build to a climax, as in a passage of narration or persuasion.
>
> When anglers stop to reflect on why they find fishing enjoyable, most realize that what they love is the feel of a fish on the end of the line, not necessarily the weight of the fillets in their coolers. Fishing has undergone a slow evolution over the last century. While fishing used to be a way of putting food on the table, most of today's anglers do so only for the relaxation that it provides. The barbed hook was invented to increase the quantity of fish people could land to better feed their families. **This need no longer exists, so barbed hooks are no longer necessary.**

## Supporting Sentences

All the sentences in the body of a paragraph should support the topic sentence by reasoning about that idea or supplying evidence (facts, statistics, examples, etc.) related to that reasoning. The closing sentence, for instance, will often summarize the paragraph's main point or emphasize a key detail. If any sentences shift the focus away from the topic, revise the paragraph in one of the following ways:

- **Delete the material** from the paragraph.
- **Rewrite the material** so that it clearly supports the topic sentence.
- **Create a separate paragraph** using the material that doesn't fit.
- **Revise the topic sentence** so that it relates more closely to the support.

## Consistent Focus

Examine the following paragraph about fishing hooks. The original topic sentence focuses on the point that some anglers prefer smooth hooks. However, the writer leaves this initial idea unfinished and turns to the issue of the cost of new hooks. In the revised version, unity is restored: The first paragraph completes the point about anglers who prefer smooth hooks; the second paragraph addresses the issue of replacement costs.

**Original Paragraph** (Lacks unity)

According to some anglers who do use smooth hooks, their lures perform better than barbed lures as long as they maintain a constant tension on the line. Smooth hooks can bite deeper than barbed hooks, actually providing a stronger hold on the fish. Some people have argued that replacing all of the barbed hooks in their tackle would be a costly operation.

**Revised Version** (Unified)

According to some anglers who do use smooth hooks, their lures perform better than barbed lures as long as the anglers maintain a constant tension on the line. Smooth hooks can bite deeper than barbed hooks, actually providing a stronger hold on the fish. These anglers testify that switching from barbed hooks has not noticeably reduced the number of fish that they are able to land. In their experience, and in my own, enjoyment of the sport is actually heightened by adding another challenge to playing the fish (maintaining line tension).

Some people have argued that replacing all of the barbed hooks in their tackle would be a costly operation. While this is certainly a concern, barbed hooks do not necessarily require replacement. With a simple set of pliers, the barbs on most conventional hooks can be bent down, providing a cost-free method of modifying your existing tackle. . . .

**INSIGHT** Paragraphs that contain unrelated ideas lack unity and are hard to follow. As you review each paragraph for unity, ask yourself these questions: Is the topic of the paragraph clear? Does each sentence relate to the topic? Are the sentences organized in the best possible order?

# Check for Coherence

When a paragraph is coherent, the parts stay together. A coherent paragraph flows smoothly because each sentence is connected to others by patterns in the language such as repetition and transitions. To strengthen the coherence in your paragraphs, check for the following issues.

## Effective Repetition

To achieve coherence in your paragraphs, consider using repetition—repeating words or synonyms where necessary to remind readers of what you have already said. You can also use parallelism—repeating phrase or sentence structures to show the relationships among ideas. At the same time, you will add a unifying rhythm to your writing.

> **Ineffective:** The floor was littered with discarded soda cans, newspapers that were crumpled, and wrinkled clothes.
> **Effective:** The floor was littered with discarded soda cans, crumpled newspapers, and wrinkled clothes. (Three parallel phrases are used.)
> **Ineffective:** Reading the book was enjoyable; to write the critique was difficult.
> **Effective:** Reading the book was enjoyable; writing the critique was difficult. (Two similar structures are repeated.)

## Clear Transitions

Linking words and phrases like "next," "on the other hand," and "in addition" connect ideas by showing the relationship among them. There are transitions that show location and time, compare and contrast things, emphasize a point, conclude or summarize, and add or clarify information. Note the use of transitions in the following examples:

> **The transition is used to emphasize a point.**
> The paradox of Scotland is that violence had long been the norm in this now-peaceful land. In fact, the country was born, bred, and came of age in war.
>
> **The transition is used to show time or order.**
> The production of cement is a complicated process. First, the mixture of lime, silica, alumina, and gypsum is ground into very fine particles.

**INSIGHT** Another way to achieve coherence in your paragraphs is to use pronouns effectively. A pronoun forms a link to the noun it replaces and ties that noun (idea) to the ideas that follow. However, don't overuse pronouns or rely too heavily on them in establishing coherence in your paragraphs.

## Transitions and Linking Words

The words and phrases in Figure 6.3 can help you tie together words, phrases, sentences, and paragraphs.

**Words used to show location:**

| | | | |
|---|---|---|---|
| above | behind | down | on top of |
| across | below | in back of | onto |
| against | beneath | in front of | outside |
| along | beside | inside | over |
| among | between | into | throughout |
| around | beyond | near | to the right |
| away from | by | off | under |

**Words used to show time:**

| | | | |
|---|---|---|---|
| about | during | next | today |
| after | finally | next week | tomorrow |
| afterward | first | second | until |
| as soon as | immediately | soon | when |
| at | later | then | yesterday |
| before | meanwhile | third | simultaneously |

**Words used to compare things (show similarities):**

| | | |
|---|---|---|
| also | in the same way | likewise |
| as | like | similarly |

**Words used to contrast things (show differences):**

| | | | |
|---|---|---|---|
| although | even though | on the other hand | still |
| but | however | otherwise | |

**Words used to emphasize a point:**

| | | | |
|---|---|---|---|
| again | for this reason | particularly | to repeat |
| even | in fact | to emphasize | truly |

**Words used to conclude or summarize:**

| | | | |
|---|---|---|---|
| all in all | finally | in summary | therefore |
| as a result | in conclusion | last | to sum up |

**Words used to add information:**

| | | | |
|---|---|---|---|
| additionally | and | equally important | in addition |
| again | another | finally | likewise |
| along with | as well | for example | next |
| also | besides | for instance | second |

**Words used to clarify:**

| | | | |
|---|---|---|---|
| for instance | in other words | put another way | that is |

*fig. 6.3*

*Note:* Use transitions to link, expand, or intensify an idea, but don't add elements carelessly, creating run-on or rambling sentences.

## Check for Completeness

A paragraph's sentences should support and expand on the main point. If a paragraph does not seem complete, add information to deepen the reasoning and add more evidence.

### Supporting Details

If some of your paragraphs are incomplete, they may lack details. There are numerous kinds of details, including the following:

| | | | |
|---|---|---|---|
| facts | paraphrases | explanations | definitions |
| anecdotes | statistics | comparisons | summaries |
| analyses | quotations | examples | analogies |

Add details based on the type of writing you are engaged in.

> **Describing:** Add details that help readers see, smell, taste, touch, or hear it.
> **Narrating:** Add details that help readers understand the events and actions.
> **Explaining:** Add details that help readers understand what it means, how it works, or what it does.
> **Persuading:** Add details that strengthen the logic of your argument.

### Specific Details

The original paragraph that follows fails to answer fully the question posed by the topic sentence. In the revised paragraph, the writer uses an anecdote to answer the question.

> **Original Paragraph** (Lacks completeness)
> So what is stress? Actually, the physiological characteristics of stress are some of the body's potentially good self-defense mechanisms. People experience stress when they are in danger. In fact, stress can be healthy.
>
> **Revised Version** (Full development)
> So what is stress? Actually, the physiological characteristics of stress are some of the body's potentially good self-defense mechanisms. Take, for example, a man who is crossing a busy intersection when he spots an oncoming car. Immediately his brain releases a flood of adrenaline into his bloodstream. As a result, his muscles contract, his eyes dilate, his heart pounds faster, his breathing quickens, and his blood clots more readily. Each one of these responses helps the man leap out of the car's path. His muscles contract to give him exceptional strength. His eyes dilate so that he can see more clearly. His heart pumps more blood and his lungs exchange more air—both to increase his metabolism. If the man were injured, his blood would clot faster, ensuring a smaller amount of blood loss. In this situation and many more like it, stress symptoms are good (Curtis 25–26).

**INSIGHT** If a paragraph is getting long, divide it at a natural stopping point. The topic sentence can then function as the thesis for that part of your essay or paper.

# Revising Collaboratively

Every writer can benefit from feedback from an interested audience, especially one that offers constructive and honest advice during a writing project. Members of an existing writing group already know how valuable it is for writers to share their work. Others might want to start a writing group to experience the benefits. Your group might collaborate online or in person. In either case, the information on the next two pages will help you get started.

## Know Your Role

Writers and reviewers should know their roles and fulfill their responsibilities during revising sessions. Essentially, the writer should briefly introduce the draft and solicit honest responses. Reviewers should make constructive comments in response to the writing.

## Provide Appropriate Feedback

Feedback can take many forms, including the three approaches described here.

- **Basic Description:** In this simple response, reviewers listen or read attentively and then simply describe what they hear or see happening in the piece. Reviewers offer no criticism of the writing.

    **Ineffective:** "That was interesting. The piece was informative."
    **Effective:** "First, the essay introduced the challenge of your birth defect and how you have had to cope with it. Then in the next part you . . ."

- **Summary Evaluation:** Here reviewers read or listen to the piece and then provide a specific evaluation of the draft.

    **Ineffective:** "Gee, I really liked it!" or "It was boring."
    **Effective:** "Your story at the beginning really pulled me in, and the middle explained the issue strongly, but the ending felt a bit flat."

- **Thorough Critique:** Reviewers assess the ideas, organization, and voice in the writing. Feedback should be detailed and constructive. Such a critique may also be completed with the aid of a review sheet or checklist. As a reviewer, be prepared to share specific responses, suggestions, and questions. But also be sure to focus your comments on the writing, rather than the writer.

    **Ineffective:** "You really need to fix that opening! What were you thinking?"
    **Effective:** "Let's look closely at the opening. Could you rewrite the first sentence so it grabs the reader's attention? Also, I'm somewhat confused about the thesis statement. Could you rephrase it so it states your position more clearly?"

## Respond According to a Plan

Using a specific plan or scheme like the following will help you give clear, helpful, and complete feedback.

- **OAQS Method:** Use this simple four-step scheme—**O**bserve, **A**ppreciate, **Q**uestion, and **S**uggest—to respond to your peers' writing.

  1. **O**bserve means to notice what another person's essay is designed to do, and to say something about its design or purpose. For example, you might say, "Even though you are writing about your boyfriend, it appears that you are trying to get a message across to your parents."

  2. **A**ppreciate means to praise something in the writing that impresses or pleases you. You can find something to appreciate in any piece of writing. For example, you might say, "In this paragraph, you make a very convincing point about our reliance on fossil fuels" or "With your description here, I can actually see his broken tooth and understand how dramatic it is."

  3. **Q**uestion means to ask whatever you want to know after you've read the essay. You might ask for background information, a definition, an interpretation, or an explanation. For example, you might say, "Can you tell us what happened when you got to the emergency room?"

  4. **S**uggest means to give helpful advice about possible changes. For example, you might say, "With a little more physical detail—especially more sounds and smells—your third paragraph could be the highlight of the whole essay."

### Asking the Writer Questions

Reviewers should ask the following types of questions while reviewing a piece of writing:

- **To help writers reflect on their purpose and audience . . .**
  Why are you writing this?
  Who will read this, and what do they need to know?

- **To help writers focus their thoughts . . .**
  What message are you trying to get across?
  Do you have more than one main point?
  What are the most important examples?

- **To help writers think about their information . . .**
  What do you know about the subject?
  Does this part say enough?
  Does your writing cover all of the basics? (*Who? What? Where? When? Why?* and *How?*)

- **To help writers with their openings and closings . . .**
  What are you trying to say in the opening?
  How else could you start your writing?
  How do you want your readers to feel at the end?

# Revising Your Draft: Applications

Once you have used the instruction in this chapter to revise your writing, there may be more that you can think about. Through the following activities, apply what you have learned.

1. **Wise Words:** Doris Lessing has stated that when it comes to writing, "The more a thing cooks, the better." In what sense is revision a crucial stage in that cooking process? Using Lessing's cooking metaphor as a starting point, explore how revision should function in your own writing. How should you let your writing cook?
2. **Photo Op:** As noted at the start of the chapter, revision is about seeing again. What does it mean to "re-see" something after some time? Look through your photos from a year or more ago. What do you see in them now? How has your vision changed? In what ways is such changed understanding similar to the perspective needed to revise your writing effectively?
3. **Living Today:** This chapter discusses the concept of voice. How is voice a reflection of the speaker or writer? Consider a public figure whose speeches or writings you admire. Study one of their oral or written statements. What qualities of voice do you discern, and what creates those qualities?
4. **Public Texts:** This chapter explains that strong paragraphs, especially body paragraphs, are unified, coherent, and complete. But do these requirements apply to more than academic essays? Find a print or digital document from a business, government agency, educational institution, or other organization. What paragraphing principles seem to be at work?

## Learning-Objectives Checklist ✓

Have you achieved this chapter's learning objectives? Check your progress with the following items, revisiting topics in the chapter as needed. I have . . .

___ practiced strategies for effectively revising my writing.
___ examined my ideas for a clear thesis and complete development.
___ evaluated the overall organization of my draft, including whether the opening engages readers and sets a direction, the middle clearly traces a line of reasoning, and the closing effectively ends the draft.
___ improved the voice in my draft, addressing issues of commitment and intensity.
___ examined each paragraph to ensure that it is an effective unit of thought, unified in its topic or effect, coherent through transitions, and complete in its details.
___ exchanged helpful feedback on a draft by collaborating with classmates through techniques such as the OAQS method.

# Chapter 7

# Polishing Your Prose

You've worked hard to draft your paper. You've even taken the time to revise it—making tough choices about the content, organization, and voice. "Now, can I run a spellchecker?" you ask. Not quite. Unless you want the dreaded CS (comma splice) and the critical "choppy" peppering the margins of your writing. (Professors can be so picky.)

You need to also polish your writing and fine-tune your prose by editing and proofreading so that all the notes you've sounded are strong and clear. But polishing isn't really about preventing professors from finding mistakes in your paper. It's about doing your best to avoid confusion for your readers, to offer them the clarity and force of your meaning—as well as to make the good impression that error-free writing offers.

That said, it's surely true that profs can be picky, oh so cruel—especially the ones who love red ink. This chapter will help you keep the red ink away from your work.

**Visually Speaking** Piano tuning requires special skills and tools (Figure 7.1). What skills and tools do you need to edit and proofread your writing? How are tuning a piano and polishing writing similar and different?

## Learning Objectives

By working through this chapter, you will be able to

- practice polishing tips.
- strengthen sentence style.
- repair primer style by combining and/or expanding sentences.
- fix repetitive sentence patterns through variety.
- use both active and passive voice of verbs effectively.
- fix missing parallelism.
- repair nominalizations, expletives, and negatives.
- cut wordiness in your prose.
- replace weak nouns and verbs with stronger choices.
- replace jargon and clichés with fresh, clear wording.
- use plain English.
- replace biased wording with fair language.
- proofread for errors.

PhotoHouse / Shutterstock.com

fig. 7.1

# Tips for Polishing Your Prose

After you have revised your writing, you need to edit it so that the style is clear, concise, energetic, and varied; and proofread it so that it's error-free.

## Use Tools and Methods That Work

Here are three tips that will help you edit and proofread effectively:

1. **Do it at the right time, and give yourself the time.** Leave time between revising and editing (at least 24 hours) to give yourself a fresh view of your writing. Also, don't rush through editing. Doing it well takes patience and concentration.
2. **Review your draft from multiple points of view.** On-screen editing offers you tremendous power and flexibility. Then again, at some point you need to see your words in print on a page. Consider increasing print size and line spacing to create white space that helps you see your writing and make changes. Finally, read or have a classmate read your paper aloud: hearing your words will help you sense where your sentences fall flat or your grammar breaks down.
3. **Use software editing tools.** Without relying on them exclusively, use wisely such tools as spell-check, grammar-check, find-and-replace functions, and track-changes. For example, spell-check will not catch usage errors such as *it's* versus *its*.

## Proofread Plus

Effective proofreading relies on your studied, absorbed, or intuitive sense of grammar and syntax (how sentences are put together). Here, you'll find just a brief checklist of errors to look for in your writing. For in-depth help, see the Handbook section of *The College Writer*.

### Proofreading Checklist

- \_\_\_\_ correct end punctuation with sentences (periods, question marks).
- \_\_\_\_ proper use of commas in compound sentences, after introductory phrases and clauses, between items in a series, and so on.
- \_\_\_\_ correct use of semicolons and colons for more complex sentence arrangements.
- \_\_\_\_ proper use of quotation marks and italics for quoted material, titles, and dialogue.
- \_\_\_\_ correct use of apostrophes in contractions, plurals, and possessive nouns.
- \_\_\_\_ proper capitalization, plural forms, presentation of numbers, and spelling.
- \_\_\_\_ no typographical errors.
- \_\_\_\_ correct use of commonly misused words: *it's/its*; *there/they're/their*; and so on.
- \_\_\_\_ agreement of subjects and verbs in person and number.
- \_\_\_\_ consistent verb tenses (past, present, future, and so on).
- \_\_\_\_ agreement of pronouns with their antecedents in number, person, and gender.
- \_\_\_\_ complete and distinct sentences: no fragments, comma splices, or run-ons.
- \_\_\_\_ clear rather than confusing phrasing: no misplaced or dangling modifiers (adjectives, adverbs), no vague pronouns, no incomplete comparisons.

# Strengthening Sentence Style

E. B. White advised writers, "The approach to style is by way of plainness, simplicity, orderliness, sincerity." To achieve this style in your sentences, you need to learn how to identify the opposite in them—weaknesses.

## Recognize Sentence Style Problems

Here are seven weaknesses to identify in your writing. The fixes are on the following pages.

- **A Style That Doesn't Fit the Context:** If you're writing is falsely academic or overly informal, you've missed the Goldilocks middle you need to aim for in most writing.

  > **An Example:** These politicians, they've made a helluva mess of this virus stuff.
  > **The Fix:** a natural academic style

- **Primer Style:** If a section of your prose is made up of short, simplistic sentences, the thinking and rhythm are choppy.

  > **An Example:** People must practice social distancing. It means staying apart. The distance should be six feet. That is about two meters.
  > **The Fix:** combining sentences and/or expanding sentences

- **Bland, Repetitive Patterns:** If your sentences seem to start the same way and repeat the same structure, your prose will lack energy and interest.

  > **An Example:** COVID-19 started in WuHan, China. The virus soon found its way onto cruise ships. The virus then travelled around the globe.
  > **The Fix:** varied sentence openings, lengths, kinds, and arrangements

- **Overuse of the Passive Voice of Verbs:** If your sentence subject is being acted upon by the verb rather than doing the action, the result is sluggish writing.

  > **An Example:** Healthcare workers are especially threatened by COVID-19.
  > **The Fix:** active voice except in special circumstances

- **Lack of Parallelism in Syntax:** When parts of your sentence should be parallel (in the same form) but aren't, the result is a structure that is out of whack.

  > **An Example:** Social distancing involves avoiding crowded spaces, limiting trips outside of the home, and to keep six feet apart from other people.
  > **The Fix:** parallel structure

- **Weak Patterns:** When your sentences are dominated by nominalizations (nouns that should be verbs), expletives (sentences beginning *It is* and *There is*), or negative constructions (too much *no*, *not*, *neither/nor*), the result is sluggish writing.

  > **An Example:** It is imperative that the government enforce strict quarantine laws. There is no possibility of defeating the virus without coordinated action. There is a national catastrophe on the horizon.
  >
  > **The Fix:** energized constructions

- **Wordy Sentences:** If your sentences aren't concise, your writing lacks energy and taxes the reader's attention.

  > **An Example:** The world finds itself in an unprecedented and never-before-seen extremely difficult situation from a public health point of view.
  >
  > **The Fix:** cutting deadwood, redundancy, unnecessary modifiers; replacing wordy phrases and clauses with shorter phrases or single words

## Edit Sentences to Give Them an Academic Style

Most college writing requires an academic style. Such a style isn't stuffy; you're not trying to impress readers with ten-dollar words. In addition, this style isn't colloquial or slang. Rather, it facilitates a thoughtful, engaged discussion of the topic. Consider these issues:

### Personal Pronouns

Academic writing generally avoids using personal pronouns like *I*, *you*, and *we*. Instead, writers focus on the topic and reveal their attitudes indirectly. Personal pronouns are acceptable in reading responses, personal essays, and opinion-editorials written for a broad audience.

> **No:** I really think that the problem of the homeless in Chicago is serious, given the number of people who are dying, as I know from my experience where I grew up.
>
> **Yes:** Homelessness in Chicago often leads to death. This fact demands the attention of more than lawmakers and social workers; all citizens must address the problems of their suffering neighbors.

### Technical Terms and Jargon

Technical terms and jargon—"insider" words—can be the specialized vocabulary of a subject, a discipline, a profession, or a social group. As such, jargon can be difficult to read for "outsiders."

- **The rule:** Use technical terms with readers inside your profession or discipline; avoid specialized jargon with all others.

> **Technical:** The power washer delivers 2200 psi p.r., runs off standard a.c. lines, comes with 100 ft. h.d. synthetic-rubber tubing, and three adjustable s.s. tips.
>
> **Simple:** The power washer has a pressure rating of 2200 psi (pounds per square inch), runs off a common 200-volt electrical circuit, comes with 100 feet of hose, and includes three nozzles.

### Level of Formality

Most academic writing (especially research papers, literary analyses, lab reports, and argumentative essays) should meet the standards of formal English. Formal English is characterized by a serious tone; careful attention to word choice; longer and more complex sentences reflecting complex thinking; strict adherence to traditional conventions of grammar, mechanics, and punctuation; and avoidance of contractions.

You may write other papers (personal essays, commentaries, journals, and reviews) in which informal English is appropriate. Informal English is characterized by a personal tone, the occasional use of popular expressions, shorter sentences, contractions, and personal references (*I, we, you*), but it still adheres to basic conventions.

> **Formal**
> Formal English, modeled in this sentence, is worded correctly and carefully so that it can withstand repeated readings without seeming tiresome, sloppy, or cute.
>
> **Informal**
> Informal English sounds like one person talking to another person (in a somewhat relaxed setting). It's the type of language that you're reading now. It sounds comfortable and real, not affected or breezy.

*Tip:* In academic writing, generally avoid slang—words considered outside standard English because they are faddish, familiar to few people, and sometimes insulting.

### Unnecessary Qualifiers

Using qualifiers (such as *mostly, often, likely,* or *tends to*) is an appropriate strategy for developing defendable claims in argumentative writing. However, when you "overqualify" your ideas or add intensifiers (*really, truly*), the result is insecurity—the impression that you lack confidence in your ideas. The cure? Say what you mean, and mean what you say.

> **Insecure:** I totally and completely agree with the new security measures at sporting events, but that's only my opinion.
>
> **Secure:** I agree with the new security measures at sporting events.

**fyi** Each academic discipline has its own vocabulary and its own vocabulary resources. Such resources include dictionaries, glossaries, or handbooks. Check your library for the vocabulary resources in your discipline.

# Fix Primer Style

A series of short, simplistic sentences creates a choppy effect called primer style (named after the kind of book used to teach young children to read). When you come across primer style in your own writing, try two fixes: combining sentences and/or expanding one or more of your simplistic sentences.

## Combine Simple Sentences:

Effective sentences often contain several basic ideas that work together to show relationships and make connections. Here are five basic ideas followed by seven examples of how the ideas can be combined into effective sentences.

1. The longest and largest construction project in history is the Great Wall of China.
2. The project took 1,700 years to complete.
3. The Great Wall of China is 1,400 miles long.
4. It is between 18 and 30 feet high.
5. It is up to 32 feet wide.

- Use a **series** to combine three or more similar ideas.

    > The Great Wall of China is **1,400 miles long,** between **18 and 30 feet high,** and up to **32 feet wide.**

- Use a **relative pronoun** *(who, whose, that, which)* to introduce subordinate (less important) ideas.

    > The Great Wall of China, **which is 1,400 miles long and between 18 and 30 feet high,** took 1,700 years to complete.

- Use an **introductory phrase** or **clause**.

    > **Having taken 1,700 years to complete,** the Great Wall of China is the longest construction project in history.

- Use a **semicolon** (and a conjunctive adverb if appropriate).

    > The Great Wall took 1,700 years to complete**;** it is 1,400 miles long and up to 30 feet high and 32 feet wide.

- Repeat a **key word** or phrase to emphasize an idea.

    > The Great Wall of China is the longest construction **project** in history, a **project** that took 1,700 years to complete.

- Use **correlative conjunctions** *(either, or; not only, but also)* to compare or contrast two ideas in a sentence.

    > The Great Wall of China is **not only** up to 30 feet high and 32 feet wide **but also** 1,400 miles long.

- Use an **appositive** (a word or phrase that renames) to emphasize an idea.

    > The Great Wall of China—**the largest construction project in history**—is 1,400 miles long, 32 feet wide, and up to 30 feet high.

## Expand Simple Sentences

A second method for fixing primer style involves taking one or more of the simplistic sentences and making them richer in content. You can expand sentences to connect related ideas and make room for new information. Remember that length has no value in and of itself. The best sentence is still the shortest one to say what you want to say. An expanded sentence, however, is capable of saying more—and saying it more expressively.

Modern writers often use an expressive sentence form called the cumulative sentence. A cumulative sentence is made of a general "base clause" that is expanded by adding modifying words, phrases, or clauses. In such a sentence, details are added before and after the main clause, creating an image-rich thought. Here's an example of a cumulative sentence, with the base clause or main idea in boldface:

> In preparation for her Spanish exam, **Julie was studying at the kitchen table,** completely focused, memorizing a list of vocabulary words.

*Discussion:* Notice how each new modifier adds to the richness of the final sentence. Also notice that each of these modifying phrases is set off by a comma. Here's another sample sentence:

> With his hands on his face, **Tony was laughing halfheartedly,** looking puzzled and embarrassed.

*Discussion:* Such a cumulative sentence provides a way to write description that is rich in detail, without rambling. Notice how each modifier changes the flow or rhythm of the sentence.

Here are seven basic ways to expand a main idea:
1. with **adjectives and adverbs:** *halfheartedly, once again*
2. with **prepositional phrases:** *with his hands on his face*
3. with **absolute phrases:** *his head tilted to one side*
4. with **participial (-ing or -ed) phrases:** *looking puzzled*
5. with **infinitive phrases:** *to hide his embarrassment*
6. with **subordinate clauses:** *while his friend talks*
7. with **relative clauses:** *who isn't laughing at all*

**INSIGHT** To edit sentences for more expressive style, it is best to (1) know your grammar and punctuation (especially commas); (2) practice tightening, combining, and expanding sentences using the guidelines in this chapter; and (3) read good writing carefully, looking for models of well-constructed sentences.

## Fix Repetitive Patterns with Varied Structures

To energize your sentences when they follow the same pattern, vary their structures using one or more of the methods shown on this page and the next.

1. **Vary sentence openings.** If a series of sentences begin the same way, move modifying words, phrases, or clauses to the front of some sentences.

   > **Unvaried:** The problem is not just about wasteful irrigation, though. The problem is also about resistance to change. The problem is that many people have fought against restrictions.
   >
   > **Varied:** However, the problem is not just about wasteful irrigation. It's about resistance to change. When governments have tried to pass regulations, many people have fought against restrictions.

2. **Vary sentence lengths.** Short sentences (ten words or fewer) are ideal for making points crisply. Medium sentences (ten to twenty words) should carry the bulk of your thinking. When well crafted, occasional long sentences (more than twenty words) can develop and expand your ideas.

   > **Short:** Museum exhibitions have become increasingly commercial.
   >
   > **Medium:** To the extent that "access" adequately measures museum performance, art as entertainment "has proven a resounding triumph."
   >
   > **Long:** Shows featuring motorcycles, automobiles, the treasures of King Tutankhamen, the works of Van Gogh, and other blockbuster favorites not only have proven immensely popular but have also offered the promise of corporate underwriting and ample commercial tie-ins.

3. **Vary sentence kinds.** The most common sentence is declarative—it states a point. For variety, try exclamatory, imperative, interrogative, and conditional statements.

   > **Declarative:** Historical records indicate that the lost colonists of Roanoke may have been harboring a dangerous virus: influenza.
   >
   > **Conditional:** If the influenza virus was not present in the New World, then the lost colonists of Roanoke likely served as vectors for the disease.
   >
   > **Interrogative:** That being said, we must now turn to a different question: What happened to those lost colonists?
   >
   > **Imperative:** Let us take steps to ensure that the Lumbee People do not share the fate of the colonists who disappeared from Roanoke.
   >
   > **Exclamatory:** Just as John White discovered over 400 years ago, something is terribly wrong! (Note: generally avoid exclamatory sentences in academic writing.)

4. **Vary sentence arrangements.** Where do you want to place the main point of your sentence? You make that choice by arranging sentence parts into loose, periodic, balanced, or cumulative patterns. Each pattern creates a specific effect.

### Loose Sentence

> **Men are frequently mystified by women,** with their unfamiliar rituals, their emotional vitality, and their biological clocks—issues often addressed in romantic comedies.

*Analysis:* This pattern is direct. It states the main point immediately (bold), and then tacks on extra information.

### Periodic Sentence

> While Western culture celebrates romantic love, seen powerfully in its films and romance novels, **in the end, such attraction between a man and a woman fails to sustain a relationship for a lifetime.**

*Analysis:* This pattern postpones the main point (bold) until the end. The sentence builds to the point, creating an indirect, dramatic effect.

### Balanced Sentence

> **The modern romantic comedy often portrays male characters as resistant to or clueless about love**; however, **in Jane Austen's narratives, men's behavior is further complicated by traditional codes of honor.**

*Analysis:* This pattern gives equal weight to complementary or contrasting points (bold); the balance is often signaled by a comma and a conjunction *(and, but)* or by a semicolon. Sometimes, a conjunctive adverb *(however, nevertheless)* or a transitional phrase *(in addition, even so)* follows the semicolon to further clarify the relationship.

### Cumulative Sentence

> In spite of his initially limiting pride, **Mr. Darcy**, now properly proud, **emerges** finally **as the consummate romantic hero**, the anonymous savior of Elizabeth's family, a true gentleman.

*Analysis:* This pattern puts the main idea (bold) in the middle of the sentence, surrounding it with modifying words, phrases, and clauses.

5. **Use positive repetition.** Although you should avoid needless repetition, you might use emphatic repetition to stress a key word that helps you emphasize a point.

### Needlessly Repetitive Sentence

> Each year, more than a million young people who read poorly leave high school unable to read well, functionally illiterate.

### Emphatic Sentence

> Each year, more than a million young people leave high school functionally illiterate, so **illiterate** that they can't read newspapers, job ads, or safety instructions.

# Fix Overuse of the Passive Voice

Most verbs can be in either the active or the passive voice. When a verb is active, the sentence's subject performs the action. When the verb is passive, the subject is acted upon.

> **Active:** Given the global economy, when U.S. consumers stopped buying cars, Japanese carmakers shared in the rapid economic downturn.
>
> **Passive:** Given the global economy, when cars were no longer being bought by U.S. consumers, the rapid economic downturn was shared by Japanese carmakers.

## Weaknesses of Passive Voice

The passive voice tends to be wordy and sluggish because the verb's action is directed backward, not ahead. In addition, passive constructions tend to be impersonal, making people disappear.

> **Passive:** As a sign of economic recovery, 350,000 job gains were experienced in March 2021.
>
> **Active:** As a sign of economic recovery, 350,000 workers gained a job in March 2021.

## Strengths of Passive Voice

Using the passive voice isn't wrong. In fact, the passive voice has some important uses: (1) when you need to be tactful (say, in a bad-news letter), (2) if you wish to stress the object or person acted upon, and (3) if the actual actor is understood, unknown, or unimportant.

> **Active:** The U.S. government bailed out both GM and Chrysler, two struggling automakers.
>
> **Passive:** Both GM and Chrysler, two struggling automakers, were bailed out by the U.S. government.
>
> **Active:** As part of the study, participants drove hybrids for six months.
>
> **Passive:** As part of the study, hybrids were driven for six months.

*Tip:* Avoid using the passive voice unethically to hide responsibility. For example, an instructor who says, "Your assignments could not be graded because of scheduling difficulties," might be trying to evade the truth: "I did not finish grading your assignments because I was binge-watching *The Office*."

## Fix Unparallel Structure

Coordinated sentence elements should be parallel—that is, they should be written in the same grammatical forms. Parallel structures save words, clarify relationships, and present the information in the correct sequence. Follow these guidelines.

1. **For words, phrases, or clauses in a series,** keep elements consistent.

   > **Not parallel:** I have tutored students in Biology 101, also Chemistry 102, not to mention my familiarity with Physics 200.
   > **Parallel:** I have tutored students in *Biology 101, Chemistry 102,* and *Physics 200.*
   > **Not parallel:** I have volunteered as a hospital receptionist, have been a hospice volunteer, and as an emergency medical technician.
   > **Parallel:** I have done volunteer work as *a hospital receptionist, a hospice counselor,* and *an emergency medical technician.*

2. **Use both parts of correlative conjunctions** *(either, or; neither, nor; not only, but also; as, so; whether, so; both, and)* so that both segments of the sentence are balanced.

   > **Not parallel:** *Not only* did Blake College turn 20 this year. Its enrollment grew by 16 percent.
   > **Parallel:** *Not only* did Blake College turn 20 this year, *but* its enrollment *also* grew by 16 percent.

3. **Place a modifier correctly** so that it clearly indicates the word or words to which it refers.

   > **Confusing:** MADD promotes *severely* punishing and eliminating drunk driving because this offense leads to a *great number* of deaths and sorrow.
   > **Parallel:** MADD promotes eliminating and *severely* punishing drunk driving because this offense leads to *many* deaths and *untold* sorrow.

4. **Place contrasting details in parallel structures** (words, phrases, or clauses) to stress a contrast.

   > **Weak contrast:** The average child spends 24 hours in front of a screen each week and reads for 36 minutes.
   > **Strong contrast:** Each week, the average child *spends more than 24 hours in front of a screen but spends much less than an hour in a book.*

## Fix Weak Constructions

Avoid constructions that weaken your writing, including the ones that follow.

### Nominal Constructions

The nominal construction is both sluggish and wordy. Avoid it by changing the noun form of a verb *(description* or *instructions)* to a verb *(describe* or *instruct)*. At the same time, delete the weak verb that preceded the noun.

| Nominal Constructions (noun form underlined) | Strong Verbs (italicized) |
|---|---|
| Engineer Tim Schuster *gave a* description ... | Schuster *described* ... |
| Lydia Balm *provides an* explanation ... | Balm *explains* ... |

> **Sluggish:** In her study of Austen film adaptations, Lydia Balm *provides an* explanation for the narrative power of dance scenes. Dances *offer a* symbolization and visualization of characters in situations of mutual attraction but nonverbalization.
>
> **Energetic:** In her study of Austen film adaptations, Lydia Balm *explains* the narrative power of dance scenes. Dances *symbolize visually* the attraction characters feel for each other but cannot *verbalize*.

### Expletives

Expletives such as "it is" and "there is" are fillers that serve no purpose in most sentences—except to make them wordy and unnatural.

> **Sluggish:** *It is* believed by some people that childhood vaccinations can cause autism. *There are* several websites that promote this point of view quite forcefully. In fact, *it is* also the case that some celebrities advocate this cause.
>
> **Energetic:** Some people believe that childhood vaccinations can cause autism. Some celebrities and several websites forcefully promote this point of view.

### Negative Constructions

Sentences constructed upon the negatives *no, not,* and *neither/nor* can be wordy and difficult to understand. It's simpler to state what *is* the case.

> **Negative:** Hybrid vehicles *are not* completely different from traditional cars, as hybrids *cannot* run without gas and *cannot* rely only on battery power that has *not been created* by the gasoline engine.
>
> **Positive:** Hybrid vehicles are similar to traditional cars, as hybrids do require gas in order to power an internal-combustion engine that in turn powers batteries.

## Eliminate Wordiness

Wordy sentences tax your reader's attention. To tighten your writing so that every word counts, cut the following types of wordiness.

### Deadwood

Deadwood is filler material—verbal "lumber" that you can remove without harming the sentence. Look for irrelevant information and obvious statements.

> **Deadwood:** GM *must undergo a thorough retooling process if it is to be competitive in the fast-paced, rapidly changing world of today's* global marketplace.
> **Concise:** GM must change to meet global challenges.

### Redundancy

Redundancy refers to unnecessary repetition. Check your sentences for words and phrases that say the same thing, doubling up the meaning. Examples: *combine together, new beginner, connect up, green in color, round in shape, plan ahead, descend down.*

> **Redundant:** Avoid the construction site, and *be sure to pick a different route* if you want to avoid riding over nails and *risking a flat tire.*
> **Concise:** If you want to avoid a flat tire, don't drive through the construction site.

### Unnecessary Modifiers

Adjectives and adverbs typically clarify nouns and verbs; however, excessive modifiers make prose dense. Use precise nouns and verbs to avoid the need for modifiers, and avoid intensifying adverbs (*very, extremely, intensely, awfully, especially*).

> **Wordy:** To ensure *very healthy, properly growing* trees, whether *deciduous* or *coniferous*, hire a *licensed, professional* tree surgeon.
> **Concise:** To ensure healthy trees, hire a professional tree surgeon.

### Long Phrases and Clauses

Often, a long phrase or clause can be replaced by a shorter phrase or even a single word. Locate prepositional phrases (*at the beginning of the project*) and relative clauses (*who, which, that* clauses) and replace them when possible with simpler words.

> **Wordy:** Among a variety of different devices that could possibly perform the task of preventing the wastage of water, an interesting one is LEPA, also known by many as low-energy precision application, hence the acronym.
> **Concise:** A second device that prevents water waste is LEPA, or low-energy precision application.

# Fixing Weak Wording

As you edit your writing, check your choice of words carefully. The information on the next five pages will help you edit for word choice.

## Substitute Specific Words

Replace vague nouns and verbs with words that generate clarity and energy.

### Specific Nouns

Make it a habit to use specific nouns for subjects. General nouns *(woman, school)* give the reader a vague, uninteresting picture. More specific nouns *(actor, university)* give the reader a better picture. Finally, very specific nouns *(Meryl Streep, Notre Dame)* are the type that can make your writing clear and colorful.

**General to Specific Nouns**

| Person | Place | Thing | Idea |
|---|---|---|---|
| woman | school | book | theory |
| actor | university | novel | scientific theory |
| Meryl Streep | Notre Dame | *Pride and Prejudice* | relativity |

### Vivid Verbs

Like nouns, verbs can be too general to create a vivid word picture. For example, the verb *looked* does not say the same thing as *stared, glared, glanced,* or *peeked*.

- Whenever possible, use a verb that is strong enough to stand alone without the help of an adverb.

  **Verb and adverb:** John fell down in the student lounge.
  **Vivid verb:** John collapsed in the student lounge.

- Avoid overusing the "be" verbs (*is, are, was, were*) and helping verbs. Often a main verb can be made from another word in the same sentence.

  **A "be" verb:** Cole is someone who follows international news.
  **A stronger verb:** Cole follows international news.

- Use active rather than passive verbs. (Use passive verbs only if you want to downplay who is performing the action in a sentence.)

  **Passive verb:** Another provocative essay was submitted by Kim.
  **Active verb:** Kim submitted another provocative essay.

- Use verbs that show rather than tell.

  **A verb that tells:** Dr. Lewis is very thorough.
  **A verb that shows:** Dr. Lewis prepares detailed, interactive lectures.

## Replace Jargon and Clichés

Replace language that is overly technical or difficult to understand. Also replace overused, worn-out words.

### Use Understandable Language

Jargon is language used in a certain profession or by a particular group of people. It may be acceptable to use if your audience is that group of people, but to most ears jargon will sound technical and unnatural.

> **Jargon:** I'm having conceptual difficulty with these academic queries.
> **Clear:** I don't understand these review questions.

### Use Fresh and Original Writing

Clichés are overused words or phrases. They give the reader no fresh view and no concrete picture. Because clichés spring quickly to mind (for both the writer and the reader), they are easy to write and often fail to convey a precise meaning.

> an axe to grind
> between a rock and a hard place
> easy as pie
>
> piece of cake
> stick your neck out
> throwing your weight around

While clichés fill your writing with tired expressions, using flowery phrases leads to language that is overblown. Such wording is unnecessarily fancy and often sentimental. This type of writing draws attention to itself, interfering with direct communication.

> **Flowery:** The gorgeous beauty of the Great Barrier Reef is fantastically on display in coral of all the colors of the rainbow and in its wondrous variety of delightful tropical fish that soar like eagles through the azure liquid.
> **Fresh:** The beauty of the Great Barrier Reef is displayed in rainbow-colored coral formations and in a rich variety of tropical fish.

### Use Unpretentious Language

Pretentious language aims to sound intelligent but comes off sounding phony. Such language calls attention to itself rather than its meaning; in fact, pretentious words can be so high-blown that meaning is obscured altogether.

> **Pretentious:** Liquid precipitation in the Iberian Peninsula's nation-state of most prominent size experiences altitudinal descent as a matter of course primarily in the region characterized by minimal topographical variation.
> **Plain:** The rain in Spain falls mainly on the plain.

## Replace Questionable Wording with Plain English

In many ways, plain English is the product of the principles discussed on the previous pages: avoiding jargon, technical language, clichés, flowery phrasing, and pretentious wording. However, plain English also counters these ethically questionable uses of language:

### Obfuscation

When writing includes fuzzy terms such as *throughput* and *downlink* that muddy the issue, the result is obfuscation. These words may make simple ideas sound more profound than they really are, or they may make false ideas sound true.

> Through the fully functional developmental process of a streamlined target-refractory system, the military will successfully reprioritize its data throughputs.

(*Objection*: What does this mean?)

### Ambiguity

Especially when it's deliberate, ambiguity makes a statement open to two or more interpretations. While desirable in some forms of writing (like poetry and fiction), ambiguity is usually disruptive in academic writing because it obscures the meaning of the words.

> When the forklift operator placed the pallet on the scale, it broke.

(*Objection*: Does *it* refer to *the scale* or *the pallet*? The meaning is unclear.)

### Euphemisms

A euphemism is an indirect expression that avoids stating an uncomfortable truth. In your academic writing, choose neutral, tactful phrasing, but avoid euphemisms.

> This economically challenged neighborhood faces some issues concerning mind-enhancing substances and scuffles between youths.

(*Translation*: This impoverished neighborhood is being destroyed by drug trafficking and gangs.)

### Doublespeak

When phrasing deliberately seeks either to hide the truth from readers or at least to understate the situation, the result is often doublespeak. Such slippery language is especially a temptation when the writer wields authority, power, or privilege in a negative situation (e.g., a hospital administrator writing a report, as shown in the sentence below). Avoid such verbal misdirection; be clearly honest by choosing precise, transparent phrasing.

> The doctor executed a nonfacile manipulation of newborn.

(*Translation*: The doctor dropped the baby during delivery.)

## Replace Biased Words with Fair and Inclusive Language

Fair language treats all differences with respect and stresses the equality of all people. Start with these general guidelines: (1) focus on characteristics of people relevant for your discussion, not ones "beside the point"; (2) be specific about characteristics, not vague; (3) be sensitive to labels, adopting instead terms people use to describe themselves; and (4) be careful not to set up or imply false hierarchies (normal-abnormal, superior-inferior). Note: The guidelines on these pages follow recommendations from the MLA (Chapter 23) and the APA (Chapter 24).

### Words Referring to Race or Ethnicity

| Acceptable General Terms | Acceptable Specific Terms |
|---|---|
| Indigenous People, Native Americans | Cherokee People, Inuit People, etc. |
| Asian Americans (not Orientals) | Chinese Americans, Japanese Americans, and so on |
| Latinos, Latinas, Latinxs, Hispanics | Mexican Americans, Cuban Americans, and so on |
| African Americans, Black people<br>"African American" is widely accepted, though "Black" is preferred by some. | |
| Anglo Americans (English ancestry), European Americans<br>Use these terms to avoid the notion that "American," used alone, means "White." | |

| Not Recommended | Preferred |
|---|---|
| Eurasian, mulatto | person of mixed ancestry |
| nonwhite | person of color |
| Caucasian | White |
| American (to mean U.S. citizen), when writing to international readers | U.S. citizen |

### Words Referring to Age

| Age Group | Acceptable Terms |
|---|---|
| 12 years and younger | infant, child, girl, boy, transgender girl, etc. |
| between 13 and 17 | adolescent, young person, young man, young woman |
| 18 years and older | adult, woman, man, transgender man, trans woman, etc. |
| Older adults | older adults, older people / persons, persons 65 and older |

## Words Referring to Disabilities or Impairments

Disabilities can be physical, psychological, intellectual, and emotional in nature. As varied as they are, they can be visible or invisible. When referring to people with disabilities, avoid such degrading labels as *crippled, invalid,* and *maimed*. Follow instead these two principles: (1) use language that emphasizes or guards the dignity and worth of all people, and (2) adopt terms that a specific group within the disability community uses to refer to themselves.

| Not Recommended | Preferred |
| --- | --- |
| handicapped | disabled |
| mentally retarded | intellectual disability |
| birth defect | congenital disability |
| stutter, stammer, lisp | speech impairment |
| an AIDS victim | person with AIDS |
| suffering from cancer | person who has cancer |

## Words Referring to Conditions

People with various disabilities and conditions have sometimes been referred to as though they were their condition (*quadriplegics, depressives, epileptics*) instead of people who happen to have a particular disability. As much as possible, refer to the person first, the disability second. There are exceptions, though. In the deaf, blind, and deaf-blind communities, these terms are acceptable and even preferred by some: *Deaf person, hard-of-hearing person, Deaf-Blind person, blind person, visually impaired person, vision-impaired person.*

| Not Recommended | Preferred |
| --- | --- |
| the disabled | people with disabilities |
| cripples | people who have difficulty walking |
| the retarded | people with a developmental disability |
| dyslexics | students with dyslexia |
| neurotics | patients with neuroses |
| subjects, cases | participants, patients |
| quadriplegics | people who are quadriplegic |

## Additional Terms

Make sure you understand the following terms that address specific impairments:

| | | |
| --- | --- | --- |
| **hearing impairment** | = | partial hearing loss, hard of hearing (not deaf, which is total loss of hearing) |
| **visual impairment** | = | partially sighted (not blind, which is total loss of vision) |
| **communicative disorder** | = | speech, hearing, and learning disabilities affecting communication |

### Words Referring to Gender

The approach to gender in language is an evolving one, just as it is in society. Start by understanding that gender refers to a social identity, while sex refers to a biological quality. Use the terms correctly. The basic principles around gender are essentially the same as with other differences: treat all genders—male, female, and nonbinary—with equality and respect in the terms and pronouns you use. First person pronouns (*I* and *we*) and second person (*you*) are straightforward, as they are gender-neutral. Third-person pronouns (*she, he, they*) require a more nuanced approach. Follow these guidelines around gender:

- Use parallel language when referring to gender:

  > The **men** and the **women** rebuilt the school together.
  >
  > **Mr. Robert Gumble, Mrs. Joy Gumble**

  *Note:* The courtesy titles Mr., Ms., Mrs., and Miss should be used according to the person's preference.

- Use non-sexist alternatives to words with sexist connotations. Examples: **humanity** (not *mankind*), **synthetic** (not *man-made*), **artisan** (not *craftsman*). This principle applies to occupations as well: **mail carrier** (not *mailman*), **firefighter** (not *fireman*), **flight attendant** (not *steward* or *stewardess*), etc.

- Do not use masculine-only or feminine-only third-person pronouns (*he, she,* etc.) to refer to a human being in general.

  **Avoid:** A politician can kiss privacy good-bye when **he** runs for office.

  **Solutions:** With greater understanding of gender differences, it is becoming less acceptable to replace "he" with "he or she" as a solution. Instead, fix the problem by changing the sentence to plural or rewriting it to eliminate the pronoun altogether.

  > Politicians can kiss privacy good-bye when **they** run for office.
  >
  > A politician can kiss privacy good-bye when running for office.

**A Note on Singular *They*:** While it is an evolving convention, we recommend that you use the singular *they* in these circumstances: (1) the person about whom you are writing uses *they/them* as their pronouns; (2) you are referring to people whose identified pronouns are not known; or (3) the gender of the person is irrelevant to the context of your writing. The latter two circumstances help you avoid assumptions about an individual's gender. Examples of singular *they*:

> **Person self-identified as nonbinary:** Selena Ramirez can kiss **their** privacy good-bye when **they** run for political office.
>
> **Gender identity not know or irrelevant:** A politician can kiss privacy good-bye when **they** run for office.

# Polishing Your Prose: Applications

After you have used the instruction in this chapter to edit and proofread your essay, apply what you learned to the activities that follow.

1. **Wise Words:** The nineteenth-century British writer Matthew Arnold offers this advice to writers about refining their writing: "Have something to say and say it as clearly as you can. That is the only secret of style." Does your own writing demonstrate such a style? What might you do to strengthen clarity in your writing?

2. **Writing Reset:** Choose a writing assignment that you submitted without doing enough polishing. Edit the sentences for style using the "Strengthening Sentence Style" section as a guide. Then use the "Fixing Weak Words" section to edit the wording. Finally, use the "Proofreading Checklist" on page 90 to correct the essay. What difference does it make to have carefully edited and proofread your work?

3. **Word Play:** Combine some of the following ideas into longer, more mature sentences. Write at least four sentences, using strategies from this chapter.

   > Dogs can be difficult to train. The necessary supplies include a leash and treats. Patience is also a necessity. Dogs like to please their owners. Training is not a chore for dogs. A well-trained dog is a pleasure to its owner.

4. **Photo Op:** To suggest the nature of editing and proofreading, the chapter's opening page (Figure 7.1) contains a photograph of piano tuning. Find another image, graphic, meme, or cartoon that represents this part of the writing process for you.

## Learning-Objectives Checklist ✓

Have you achieved this chapter's learning objectives? Check your progress with the following items, revisiting topics in the chapter as needed. I have . . .

____ practiced tips for effectively polishing my prose.
____ fixed my style when it was inappropriate for the piece and writing context.
____ repaired primer style wherever I could find it by combining and/or expanding sentences.
____ fixed repetitive sentence patterns by varying openings, lengths, kinds, and arrangements.
____ used both active and passive voice of verbs effectively, relying primarily on active.
____ fixed sentences lacking parallel structure.
____ repaired weak constructions such as nominalizations, expletives, and negatives.
____ cut any wordiness I could find in my sentences.
____ replaced weak nouns and verbs with stronger choices.
____ replaced jargon and clichés with fresh, clear wording.
____ replaced questionable wording with plain English.
____ replaced biased wording with fair language.
____ proofread for errors in grammar, punctuation, mechanics, usage, and spelling.

# Chapter 8

# One Writer's Process

In chapter 1, we shared some wisdom from Annie Dillard: "When you write, you lay out a line of words." She later adds that this line of words looks deep inside you. And it probes high above you. When you follow the whole writing process, your writing becomes a tool for such discoveries, and a means of communicating them to the world.

That process can get messy. It doesn't always follow a straight line from assignment to polished essay; it can be recursive, taking you back and forth. You may have to break some eggs, in other words, to come up with a delicious omelet. Broken shells might get on the counter, and milk might spill on the floor. But the main task of the process is to get your ideas cooking. You can clean up after.

Student writer Ariana King got her ideas cooking by using the process outlined in chapters 1–7. This chapter takes us into her kitchen to show her at work from start to finish.

## Learning Objectives

By working through this chapter, you will be able to

- analyze how one writer worked through the writing process to complete an assignment.
- compare this student's process with your own.
- assess how the writing process might help you complete college assignments.

**Visually Speaking** A roundabout or rotary (Figure 8.1) controls the flow of traffic. How might the writing process control the flow of ideas? In what ways is the process similar to a roundabout?

*Malota / Shutterstock.com*

fig. 8.1

# Ariana's Assignment and Response

In this chapter, you will follow student Ariana King as she writes an assigned essay for European Culture and Politics during her semester in France. Start by carefully reading the assignment and discussion below, noting how she thinks through the rhetorical situation.

## Ariana Examined the Assignment

Ariana carefully read her assignment and responded with the notes below.

> "In a two- to three-page essay, explain in English how a modern trend in France impacts culture and politics and reflects the wider European community. Format your paper and document sources in MLA style. You may seek revising help from a classmate or from the online writing center."

**Role**
- I'm writing as a study-abroad student in France for my European Culture and Politics class.

**Subject**
- The subject is a modern trend in France.

**Purpose**
- My purpose is to explain how the trend impacts culture and politics in France and the wider European community. I need to find a trend that I care about and that my instructor and classmates will care about.

**Form**
- I need to write a two- to three-page essay in English.
- I'll need to include a thesis statement as well as references to my sources using MLA style.

**Audience**
- My audience will be my instructor and other study-abroad students in my program.
- I'll need to keep in mind what they already know and what they need to know.

**Context**
- I want to choose a trend that we encounter every day.
- I'll get feedback from Jules and use the online writing center to improve my work.

 For each step in the writing process, choose strategies that fit your writing situation. For example, a personal essay in an English class might require significant time getting started, whereas a lab report in a chemistry class might require little or none.

# Ariana Explored and Narrowed Her Assignment

Ariana explored her assignment and narrowed its focus by clustering and freewriting.

## Ariana's Cluster

When she considered modern trends in France, Ariana first thought of challenges to the established order. She wrote "Challenges" in the middle of a piece of paper and circled it (Figure 8.2). Around it she clustered issues that she might choose as her topic. After reviewing her cluster, she decided to focus on a challenge she encountered daily—homelessness.

fig. 8.2

## Ariana's Freewriting

Next, Ariana used freewriting to connect to the topic of homelessness. She sat in the center of the city where she was studying and let her surroundings inspire her thoughts.

> It's December in Aix-en-Provence. I'm in the Christmas market in Cours Mirabeau. Lights sparkle all around me, carnival rides and hand-crafted ornaments. But, in the darkness, there are people lying in blankets, women holding paper cups in their hands looking down at the ground and dogs looking alert next to their sleeping owners. Most days, I walk straight past them, but tonight I wonder what their story is. No one really talks about them. We're trained not to see them. What must it be like to become invisible in the middle of a crowd?

## Ariana's Narrowed Assignment

Based on her freewriting, Ariana rephrased her assignment to narrow its focus.

> Explain in two or three pages how homelessness in France impacts culture and politics and reflects the wider European community.

## Ariana's Planning

Ariana reviewed her narrowed assignment and reassessed her topic.

> **Narrowed Writing Assignment**
>
> Explain in two or three pages how homelessness in France impacts culture and politics and reflects the wider European community.

### Ariana Focused Her Topic

To focus her topic, Ariana answered the journalistic questions (five Ws and H).

> **Topic:** Homelessness and the French response
> **Who?** - Les sans dominiciles fixes, Parisians, politicians, the UN
> **What?** - Sleeping on the streets
> - 21 percent increase last year in Paris
> - Excluded from services because of drugs/alcohol, mental illness
> **Where?** - Paris and throughout France
> **When?** - Right now
> **Why?** - Recession, refugee crisis, draconian evictions, rising rents
> **How?** - Policies help only "cleanest" of homeless.

### Ariana Researched the Topic

Ariana then did some research to check her information and collect more details for her paper. She recorded all the essential data on each source following MLA format and then listed the specific details related to her topic. Here's one source:

> "France Must Do More for Its Homeless Says UN Housing Expert." *Euronews*, 15 Apr. 2019, www.euronews.com/2019/04/13/france-must-do-more-for-its-homeless-says-un-housing-expert.
>
> Lelani Farha, housing expert for the UN:
> - "Evictions that are happening throughout the country, in a variety of different contexts, are not happening in compliance with international human rights law."
> - "In Calais, I met a population of migrants who are certainly in a kind of trauma" (roughed up by police when sleeping by road or in forest)
> - "People are not even accessing the most basic emergency services. [France must provide] unconditional accommodation to the homeless, rather than moving them through different levels of shelters depending on their work, health, and administrative status."
>
> In 2018, homeless deaths in France reached 566, with more than 100 in Paris.
> Global financial crisis a major cause.
> Refugees from Middle East and Africa increase homeless populations.

## Ariana Decided How to Organize Her Writing

With a focus selected, Ariana used the three guidelines below to choose the best organizational pattern for her writing.

### Guidelines

1. **Review your assignment** and record your response.

   **Assignment:**
   Explain in two or three pages how homelessness in France impacts culture and politics and reflects the wider European community.

   **Response:**
   My assignment clearly states that I need to explain my topic, so I have a general idea of how my paper will be organized.

2. **Decide on a working thesis statement** and think about your essay's possible content and organization.

   **Thesis Statement:**
   The homeless have become invisible, but Parisians and all people must learn to see them instead of just walking by.

   **Reflection:**
   After reading my thesis statement, it's obvious that I'm going beyond just explaining. I also want to advocate for change.

3. **Choose an organizational pattern** and reflect on its potential effectiveness.

   **Reflection:**
   At first, I thought I'd use a cause/effect organizational pattern, focusing on the financial crisis and refugee crisis and the misery caused by homelessness. But it's not just about explaining the problem. It's about finding a solution.

   With a problem/solution organizational pattern, I need to first present the problem clearly so that readers can fully understand it and see why it's important. Then I need to explore solutions to the problem—what the French government has done and what it really needs to do to address the problem. I also want to focus on the humanity of the situation, seeing homeless people as people.

Many essays you write will be organized according to one basic method or approach. However, within that basic structure you may want to include other methods. For example, while developing a comparison essay, you may do some describing or classifying. In other words, you should choose methods of development that (1) help you understand the topic, and (2) help your reader understand your message.

# Ariana's First Draft

After composing her opening, middle, and closing paragraphs, Ariana put together her first draft. She then added a working title and a bibliography—the start of her works-cited page.

## Homeless People Are People

*The writer introduces the topic with startling statistics.*

Homelessness in Paris increased by 21 percent February 2018 to February 2019. The city houses approximately 3,640 homeless sleepers ("In Numbers" 2019). **They are Les sans dominiciles fixes, and Parisians and all people must learn to see them.**

*She provides her thesis statement (boldfaced).*

While people believe that homelessness is due to personal irresponsibility, other factors have contributed. The 2008 financial crisis, increase in refugees and migrants in the city and stagnant wages are major factors (Havana 2018). Skyrocketing housing costs have taken away purchasing power from even those with stable jobs making it ever more difficult to find a place to live.

*The writer describes the cause of the problem.*

While all homeless people in France have a right to housing within six months, immediate needs are not often met because there is no unconditional accommodation available for homeless people much of the time. This means that homeless people often have to wait through bureaucratic processes to obtain the accommodations "fit for their needs."

*She explains the seriousness of the problem.*

The severity of the issue has reached a tipping point. The United Nations Housing Expert Lelani Fahra declared that French policies have failed the homeless. To justify her bold declaration, Farha called out harsh eviction policies that violate human rights as well as the fact that most homeless people do not have access to basic emergency services.

*Throughout, she cites sources of information.*

However, this lack of efficiency concerning homelessness is out of step with French people's views overall. Most citizens feel some sense of solidarity with homeless individuals and believe they could one day be in their shoes (Havana 2018).

Additionally, nearly two-thirds of French people think that the state is responsible for homelessness. As Professor Julien Damon from Sciences Po explains, homelessness is a structural issue for French people. Unlike the English, the French recognize external factors that contribute to the inability to afford permanent housing and do not blame or scorn the homeless (Williamson 2018).

It is such solidarity that inspired several Parisians to create short obituaries for the homeless in 2018 (Williamson 2018). The act called attention to the de facto nature of their invisibility and reminded people that those who died while sleeping on the streets had stories and individual character. After all, homelessness does not take away humanity. The only humanity that is in jeopardy is that of the people who treat homeless people as if they weren't people at all but just inconveniences.

In their battle against homelessness, the French state has provided housing, but what about trying to address the root causes of homelessness? Since President Emmanuel Macron took office, the government has offered more aid to the homeless—but only to the cream of the crop.

Due to the strict qualifications for aid that still plague France's solutions to homelessness, the most vulnerable people are not receiving the help they need. The French administration is ignoring homeless people's humanity. To receive aid, they cannot make mistakes or struggle with anything but homelessness.

True solutions to homelessness must therefore be intersectional, addressing the underlying causes of the issue. Once this happens, homeless people will finally be seen as they truly are—fellow human beings.

*She focuses on the humanity of homeless people.*

*She shows how current solutions have fallen short.*

*The concluding paragraph focuses on the solution.*

## Working Bibliography

"France Must Do More for Its Homeless Says UN Housing Expert." *Euronews.*

Havana, Omar. "This Is Europe: An Image of Homelessness in Paris." *Al Jazeera.*

"In Numbers: How the Homeless Population of Paris Is Growing." *The Local.*

Williamson, Lucy. "Homeless in Paris." *BBC News.*

## Ariana's Revision

After finishing the first draft, Ariana set it aside. When she was ready to revise it, she looked carefully at global issues—ideas, organization, and voice. She wrote notes to herself to help keep her thoughts together. She also noted responses from her classmate Jules and rechecked the assignment to ensure her draft fit the instructor's criteria.

**Ariana's comments**

*Write a smoother opening.*

*Combine these choppy sentences.*

*Move this paragraph after the next one.*

*Add some statistics to quantify this claim.*

### Homeless People Are People

**The invisibility of the homeless is a fairly universal phenomenon, yet the issue is becoming harder to ignore. This is particularly true in Paris.**

Homelessness ~~in Paris~~ increased by 21 percent February 2018 to February 2019. The city houses approximately 3,640 homeless sleepers ("In Numbers" 2019). They are Les sans dominiciles fixes, and Parisians and all people must learn to see them.

While people believe that homelessness is due to personal irresponsibility, other factors have contributed. The 2008 financial crisis, increase in refugees and migrants in the city and stagnant wages ~~are major factors~~ (Havana 2018). Skyrocketing housing costs have taken away purchasing power from even those with stable jobs making it ever more difficult to find a place to live.

While all homeless people in France have a right to housing within six months, immediate needs are not often met because there is no unconditional accommodation available for homeless people much of the time. This means that homeless people often have to wait through bureaucratic processes to obtain the accommodations "fit for their needs."

The severity of the issue has reached a tipping point. The United Nations Housing Expert Lelani Fahra declared that French policies have failed the homeless. To justify her bold declaration, Farha called out harsh eviction policies that violate human rights as well as the fact that most homeless people do not have access to basic emergency services.

However, this lack of efficiency concerning homelessness is out of step with French people's views overall. ~~Most citizens feel~~ **75 percent of French people felt** some sense of solidarity with homeless individuals and ~~believe~~ **56 percent believed** they could one day be in their shoes (Havana 2018).

Additionally, nearly two-thirds of French people think that the state is responsible for homelessness. As Professor Julien Damon from Sciences Po explains, —who see homelessness as a symbol of personal failure—. homelessness is a structural issue for French people. Unlike the English, the French recognize external factors that contribute to the inability to afford permanent housing and do not blame or scorn the homeless (Williamson 2018).

> [Explain what the English think.]

It is such solidarity that inspired several Parisians to create short obituaries for the homeless in 2018 (Williamson 2018). The act called attention to the de facto nature of their invisibility and reminded people that those who died while sleeping on the streets had stories and individual character. After all, homelessness does not take away humanity. ~~The only humanity that is in jeopardy is that of the people who treat homeless people as if they weren't people at all but just inconveniences.~~

> [Cut this sentence.]

As for the continued battle against homelessness, the French state needs to address the root causes of homelessness and not solely provide housing. ~~In their battle against homelessness, the French state has provided housing, but what about trying to address the root causes of homelessness?~~ Since President Emmanuel Macron took office, the government has offered more aid to the homeless—but only to the cream of the crop.

> [Rewrite this sentence.]

Due to the strict qualifications for aid that still plague France's solutions to homelessness, the most vulnerable people are not receiving the help they need. By offering aid only to the "cleanest" of the homeless, The French administration is ignoring homeless people's humanity. To receive aid, they cannot make mistakes or struggle with anything but homelessness.

> [Add a paragraph explaining "cream of the crop."]

True solutions to homelessness must therefore be intersectional, addressing the underlying causes of the issue. Once this happens, homeless people will finally be seen as they truly are—fellow human beings.

> For instance, emergency shelters have been ordered to provide detailed information of their residents, making it easier for the police to deport homeless migrants and refugees. Despite a surge in new shelters, they don't allow couples, dogs, alcohol, and often people with mental illnesses (Williamson 2018).

# Ariana's Edited Draft

When Ariana began editing, she read each of her sentences aloud to check for clarity and smoothness. **The first page of Ariana's edited copy is shown below.**

*Ariana revises her title.*

Homelessness Doesn't Equate to Inhumanity
<s>Homeless People Are People</s>

The invisibility of the homeless is a fairly universal phenomenon, yet the issue is becoming harder to ignore. This is particularly true in Paris. Homelessness increased by 21 percent from February 2018 to February 2019. The city houses approximately 3,640 homeless sleepers ("In Numbers" 2019). They are Les sans dominiciles fixes, and Parisians and all people must learn to see them.

*She qualifies her statement, replacing "people" with "some may."*

While some may <s>people</s> believe that homelessness is due to personal irresponsibility, other factors have contributed: the 2008 financial crisis, increase in refugees and migrants in the city and stagnant wages (Havana 2018). Skyrocketing housing costs have stolen <s>taken away</s> purchasing power from even those with stable jobs making it ever more difficult to find a place to live.

*She improves word choice and combines a choppy sentence.*

The severity of the issue has reached <s>a tipping</s> the point where The United Nations Housing Expert Lelani Fahra declared that French policies have failed the homeless. To justify her bold declaration, Farha called out harsh eviction policies that violate human rights as well as the fact that most homeless people do not have access to basic emergency services ("France" 2019).

While all homeless people in France have a right to housing within six months, immediate needs are not often met because there is no unconditional accommodation <s>available</s> for homeless people <s>much of the time</s>. This means that homeless people often have to wait through bureaucratic processes to obtain the accommodations "fit for their needs."

*Ariana deletes unnecessary words.*

However, this lack of efficiency concerning homelessness is out of step with French people's views overall. In a 2009 survey, 75 percent of French people felt some sense of

*She improves sentence flow.*

# Ariana's Proofread Draft

Ariana reviewed her edited copy for punctuation, agreement issues, and spelling. **The first page of Ariana's proofread essay is shown below.**

## Homelessness Doesn't Equate to Inhumanity

The invisibility of the homeless is a fairly universal phenomenon, yet the issue is becoming harder to ignore. This is particularly true in Paris. Homelessness increased by 21 percent ~~form~~ *from* February 2018 to February 2019. The city houses approximately 3,640 homeless sleepers ("In Numbers" 2019). They are *Les sans dominiciles fixes*, and Parisians and all people must learn to see them.

While some may believe that homelessness is due to personal irresponsibility, other factors have contributed: the 2008 financial crisis, *the* increase in refugees and migrants in the city, and stagnant wages (Havana 2018). Skyrocketing housing costs have stolen purchasing power from even those with stable jobs, making it ever more difficult to find a place to live.

The severity of the issue has reached the point where the United Nations Housing Expert Lelani ~~Fahra~~ *Farha* declared that French policies have failed the homeless. To justify her bold declaration, Farha called out harsh eviction policies that violate human rights, as well as the fact that most homeless people do not have access to basic emergency services ("France" 2019).

While all homeless people in France have a right to housing within six months, immediate needs are often not met because there is no unconditional accommodation for homeless people. This means that homeless people often have to wait through bureaucratic processes to obtain the accommodations "fit for their needs" ("France" 2019).

However, this lack of efficiency concerning homelessness is out of step with French people's views overall. In a 2009 survey, 75 percent of French people felt some

---

*The writer corrects errors that the spell-checker did not pick up.*

*She adds commas in series and before a nonessential phrase.*

*She checks the spelling of names.*

*She adds a missing in-text citation.*

# Ariana's Finished Essay

After proofreading and formatting her essay, Ariana added a heading and page numbers. She also added more documentation and a works-cited list at the end.

King 1

Ariana King

Professor Adrienne Caron

European Culture and Politics

18 December 2020

Homelessness Doesn't Equate to Inhumanity

The invisibility of the homeless is a fairly universal phenomenon, yet the issue is becoming harder to ignore. This is particularly true in Paris. Homelessness increased by 21 percent from February 2018 to February 2019. The city houses approximately 3,640 homeless sleepers ("In Numbers" 2019). They are *les sans dominiciles fixes*, and Parisians and all people must learn to see them.

While some may believe that homelessness is due to personal irresponsibility, other factors have contributed: the 2008 financial crisis, the increase in refugees and migrants in the city, and stagnant wages (Havana 2018). Skyrocketing housing costs have stolen purchasing power from even those with stable jobs, making it ever more difficult to find a place to live.

The severity of the issue has reached the point where the United Nations housing expert Lelani Farha declared that French policies have failed the homeless. To justify her bold declaration, Farha called out harsh eviction policies that violate human rights, as well as the fact that most homeless people do not have access to basic emergency services ("France" 2019).

While all homeless people in France have a right to housing within six months, immediate needs are often not met because there is no unconditional

*Annotations:*
- The header lists the writer, instructor, class, and date.
- The writer states her thesis.
- An appropriate font and type size are used.
- Each claim or supporting point is backed up with reasoning and evidence.

accommodation for homeless people. This means that homeless people often have to wait through bureaucratic processes to obtain the accommodations "fit for their needs" ("France" 2019).

However, this lack of efficiency concerning homelessness is out of step with French people's views overall. In a 2009 survey, 75 percent of French people felt some sense of solidarity with homeless individuals, and 56 percent believed they could one day be in their shoes (Havana 2018).

Additionally, nearly two-thirds of French people think that the state is responsible for homelessness. As Professor Julien Damon from Sciences Po explains, homelessness is a structural issue for French people. Unlike the English—who see homelessness as a symbol of personal failure—the French recognize external factors that contribute to the inability to afford permanent housing and do not blame or scorn the homeless (Williamson 2018).

It is such solidarity that inspired several Parisians to create short obituaries for the homeless in 2018 (Williamson 2018). The act called attention to the de facto nature of their invisibility and reminded people that those who died while sleeping on the streets had stories and individual character. After all, homelessness does not take away humanity.

As for the continued battle against homelessness, the French state needs to address the root causes of homelessness and not solely provide housing. Since President Emmanuel Macron took office, the government has offered more aid to the homeless—but only to the cream of the crop.

King 3

> Throughout, the voice is objective and engaged.

For instance, emergency shelters have been ordered to provide detailed information of their residents, making it easier for the police to deport homeless migrants and refugees. Despite a surge in new shelters, they don't allow couples, dogs, alcohol, and often people with mental illnesses (Williamson 2018).

Due to the strict qualifications for aid that still plague France's solutions to homelessness, the most vulnerable people are not receiving the help they need. By offering aid only to the "cleanest" of the homeless, the French administration is ignoring homeless people's humanity. To receive aid, they cannot make mistakes or struggle with anything but homelessness.

> The writer restates her thesis in the last sentence.

True solutions to homelessness must therefore be intersectional, addressing the underlying causes of the issue. Once this happens, homeless people will finally be seen as they truly are—fellow human beings.

King 4

## Works Cited

> Sources appear, in alphabetical order.

"France Must Do More for Its Homeless Says UN Housing Expert." *Euronews*, 15 Apr. 2019, www.euronews.com/2019/04/13/france-must-do-more-for-its-homeless-says-un-housing-expert.

Havana, Omar. "This Is Europe: An Image of Homelessness in Paris." *Al Jazeera*, 23 Dec. 2018, www.aljazeera.com/indepth/inpictures/europe-image-homelessness-paris-181210131627074.html.

> Each entry follows MLA rules for content, format, and punctuation.

"In Numbers: How the Homeless Population of Paris Is Growing." *The Local*, 19 Mar. 2019, www.thelocal.fr/20190319/in-numbers-how-the-homeless-population-of-paris-is-growing.

Williamson, Lucy. "Homeless in Paris." *BBC News*, 26 Jan. 2018, www.bbc.co.uk/news/resources/idt-sh/Paris_homeless.

# One Writer's Process: Applications

After you have reviewed Ariana's writing process, there may be more to think about. Through the activities below, apply what you have learned.

1. **Wise Words:** Scott Russell Sanders suggests that "essays are experiments in making sense of things." Does Sanders' statement ring true? What makes such experiments flop or succeed? What kinds of "sense" do essays create?
2. **Photo Op:** The chapter's opening page contains an aerial photograph of a roundabout—a bird's-eye view of traffic. What other bird's-eye view image might resemble the writing process for you? What would that image show?
3. **Living Today:** Because she was writing an essay for a college course, Ariana took her writing carefully through all the steps of the full writing process. For your formal writing assignments, you will want to do the same. But what about the many forms of writing that we do today outside the college classroom? In what situations should you use the full writing process? How might you use an abbreviated or condensed process in other situations?
4. **Writing Reset:** How does Ariana's writing process differ from the process you typically follow? Review the work that you did to complete a recent writing assignment. What elements of the process did you complete productively? Where were the weaknesses and gaps? What would you do differently now?
5. **Major Work:** Based on the assignment instructions, Ariana documented and formatted her paper following the MLA system. In your field of study, what system are you expected to follow? What are the key features of that system?

## Learning-Objectives Checklist ✓

Have you achieved this chapter's learning objectives? Check your progress with the following items, revisiting topics in the chapter as needed. I have . . .

\_\_\_\_ analyzed how Ariana worked through the writing process:
- examining the assignment
- narrowing the topic
- researching her topic and organizing her thoughts
- completing her first draft
- revising the draft by herself and then through peer review
- and editing and proofreading her essay.

\_\_\_\_ compared Ariana's process with the process that I normally follow, considering strengths and weaknesses of my own approach.

\_\_\_\_ assessed how I might tailor the writing process shown by Ariana and outlined in chapters 1–7 to my own writing habits and my college writing assignments.

# Traits of College Writing: A Checklist

In chapter 1, you learned about the common traits of excellent college writing. The following checklist is a reminder of those traits. You can use it to evaluate your college writing.

**Stimulating Ideas**     *The writing . . .*
- \_\_\_\_\_ presents interesting and important information.
- \_\_\_\_\_ maintains a clear focus or purpose—centered on a thesis, theme, concern, or question.
- \_\_\_\_\_ develops the focus through a line of thought or reasoning elaborated with sufficient details or evidence.
- \_\_\_\_\_ holds readers' attention (and answers their questions).
- \_\_\_\_\_ addresses the assignment and instructor's requirements.

**Logical Organization**
- \_\_\_\_\_ includes a clear beginning, middle, and ending.
- \_\_\_\_\_ contains specific details, arranged in an order that builds understanding with readers.
- \_\_\_\_\_ uses transitions to link sentences and paragraphs.

**Engaging Voice**
- \_\_\_\_\_ speaks in a sincere, natural way that fits the writing situation.
- \_\_\_\_\_ shows that the writer really cares about the subject.

**Appropriate Word Choice**
- \_\_\_\_\_ contains specific, clear words.
- \_\_\_\_\_ uses a level of language appropriate for the type of writing and the audience.

**Overall Sentence Fluency**
- \_\_\_\_\_ flows smoothly from sentence to sentence.
- \_\_\_\_\_ displays varied sentence beginnings and lengths.
- \_\_\_\_\_ follows a style that fits the situation (e.g., familiar versus academic).

**Correct, Accurate Copy**
- \_\_\_\_\_ adheres to the rules of grammar, spelling, and punctuation.
- \_\_\_\_\_ follows established documentation guidelines.

**Reader-Friendly Design**
- \_\_\_\_\_ exhibits a polished, professional design in terms of overall format, page layout, and typographical choices.
- \_\_\_\_\_ makes the document attractive and easy to read.
- \_\_\_\_\_ is formatted correctly in MLA or APA style.

# II. Modes of Writing

*Sergey Peterman / Shutterstock.com*

## Modes of Writing

**9 Forms of College Writing**
- Three Curricular Divisions — 128
- Writing in the Humanities — 129
- Writing in the Social Sciences — 130
- Writing in the Natural and Applied Sciences — 131
- The Rhetorical Modes — 132
- Multimodal Projects — 134
- Forms of College Writing: Applications — 136

**10 Personal Writing**
- Meeting the Mode — 138
- Strategies for Writing Personal Essays — 142
- Personal Essays: Learning Writers' Moves — 149
- DIY: Craft Your Own Personal Essay — 160
- The Personal Essay: Applications — 162

**11 Analytical Writing: Definition**
- Meeting the Mode — 164
- Strategies for Writing Definition Essays — 166
- Definition Essays: Learning Writers' Moves — 170
- DIY: Craft Your Own Definition Essay — 182
- Definition Essays: Applications — 184

**12 Analytical Writing: Classification**
- Meeting the Mode — 186
- Strategies for Writing Classification Essays — 188
- Classification Essays: Learning Writers' Moves — 191
- DIY: Craft Your Own Classification Essay — 202
- Classification Essays: Applications — 204

**13 Analytical Writing: Process**
- Meeting the Mode — 206
- Strategies for Writing Process Essays — 209
- Process Essays: Learning Writers' Moves — 212
- DIY: Craft Your Own Process Essay — 224
- Process Essays: Applications — 226

**14 Analytical Writing: Compare and Contrast**
- Meeting the Mode — 228
- Strategies for Writing Compare-Contrast Essays — 230
- Compare-Contrast Essays: Learning Writers' Moves — 234
- DIY: Craft Your Own Compare-Contrast Essay — 244
- Compare-Contrast Essays: Applications — 246

**15 Analytical Writing: Cause and Effect**
- Meeting the Mode — 248
- Strategies for Writing Cause-Effect Essays — 250
- Cause-Effect Essays: Learning Writers' Moves — 254
- DIY: Craft Your Own Cause-Effect Essay — 268
- Cause-Effect Essays: Applications — 270

**16 Reading Literature: A Case Study in Analysis**
- Strategies for Analyzing Literature and the Arts — 272
- Analyzing Literature: Learning Writers' Moves — 277
- Literary Terms — 288
- Poetry Terms — 291
- DIY: Craft Your Own Literary Analysis — 292
- Analyzing Literature: Applications — 294

**17 Persuasive Writing: Strategies for Argumentation**
- Meeting the Mode — 296
- Structuring Arguments — 301
- Engaging the Opposition — 305
- Arguing Through Appeals — 306
- Making and Qualifying Claims — 308
- Supporting Your Claims — 310
- Identifying Logical Fallacies — 313
- Strategies for Argumentation: Applications — 320

**18 Persuasive Writing: Positions, Actions, and Solutions**
- Meeting the Mode — 322
- Strategies for Persuasive Writing — 324
- Persuasive Essays: Learning Writers' Moves — 330
- DIY: Craft Your Own Persuasive Essay — 353
- Persuasive Essays: Applications — 356

# Chapter 9

# Forms of College Writing

College professors in nearly all fields assign writing. But why? Because they know that writing helps you learn course material, show your learning, and share your learning. They also know you'll use that knowledge and those skills—both in thinking and writing—in later courses and in the workplace, in your studies and your career.

This chapter introduces the world of college writing. Beginning with an overview of academic divisions and departments, it describes the forms of writing valued in different disciplines. It then lists the modes of writing out of which these forms are built—the modes on which this section of *The College Writer* offers you instruction. Lastly, the chapter introduces projects that require writing, but also other media—multimodal projects.

**Visually Speaking** Study Figure 9.1 and consider the possible comparison between modes of transportation and forms of writing. What might the analogy suggest regarding the distinctions between different forms of writing?

## Learning Objectives

By working through this chapter, you will be able to

- classify fields of study in the college curriculum.
- explain writing in the humanities, the social sciences, and the natural and applied sciences.
- analyze the nature of writing in your own field of study or a major that interests you.
- identify personal, analytical, and argumentative modes of writing.
- transition from one mode to another.
- explain the nature of a multimodal project.

Artens / Shutterstock.com

fig. 9.1

# Three Curricular Divisions

Based on each department's field of study, the college curriculum is generally divided into three groups: humanities, social sciences, and natural and applied sciences. These groups are then subdivided into specific departments, such as biology, chemistry, and physics. Below you will find an explanation of each division, along with its common departments. Think about how your own studies are situated within this world of knowledge.

## Humanities

Scholars and students within this division study human culture, both past and present. They examine topics such as the history of civilization, cultural institutions and trends, religious beliefs and practices, languages and their use, and artwork and performance skills. This division includes the following departments:

| | | | |
|---|---|---|---|
| Archeology | Ethnic Studies | Modern Languages | Theater Arts |
| Asian Studies | Film Studies | Music | Theology |
| Dance | Graphic Design | Philosophy | Visual Arts |
| English | History | Religion | Women's Studies |

## Social Sciences

Scholars and students in this division study human behavior and societies using research strategies adapted from the natural sciences, including experiments. Students study economic systems, correctional programs, and personality disorders. Departments in this division include the following:

| | | | |
|---|---|---|---|
| Anthropology | Economics | Geophysics | Psychology |
| Business | Education | Government | Social Work |
| Communication | Genetics | Health & Phys. Ed. | Sociology |
| Criminology | Geography | Political Science | Urban Planning |

## Natural and Applied Sciences

The natural sciences (such as biology, zoology, and chemistry) focus on specific aspects of nature, such as animal life, plant life, and molecular structures. In contrast, the applied sciences (such as mathematics, computer science, and engineering) consider how to use science-based information to understand concepts and develop artifacts. Here are some of the departments in this division:

| | | | |
|---|---|---|---|
| Agriculture | Biology | Environment | Physics |
| Agronomy | Botany | Forestry | Physiology |
| Anatomy | Chemistry | Mathematics | Public Health |
| Architecture | Computer Science | Nutrition | Space Science |
| Astronomy | Engineering | Oceanography | Zoology |

# Writing in the Humanities

In a humanities class (e.g., English, history, and theater arts), your study and writing likely focus on various types of texts, broadly understood: primary texts, such as poems, novels, historical records, and philosophical essays, as well as secondary sources (books and periodical articles). Such study is largely concerned with the world of ideas, whether creative, historical, or theoretical. Your writing will likely have the character described below.

## The Purpose of Inquiry

Humanities study aims to understand more deeply some aspect of human experience and humanity's place in the world, whether that aspect of experience relates to the artistic and imaginative, the historical, the spiritual, the linguistic, or the world of ethics. As a result, writing in the humanities tends to be thesis-driven, focused on a central idea that is explored through coherent analysis and argument.

## Forms of Humanities Writing

In humanities courses, you will likely write different types of essays and research papers: interpretive analyses and arguments on a specific topic, theoretical studies of key concepts in the discipline, and book reviews or broader bibliographic surveys. Here are typical forms:

- **Analysis of a Text or Art Work:** Such a study closely examines a specific work in order to understand more fully what it means, how it communicates, and so on.
- **A Review of the Literature on a Topic:** This form of research writing identifies and synthesizes the studies that have been published on a specific issue or question.
- **A Book, Film, Music, or Performance Review:** Applying general criteria for excellence, reviews evaluate the quality, impact, strengths, and weaknesses of a specific text or art work.

*Examples:* "Latin American Music: A Diverse and Unifying Force" (chapter 12), "*The Revenant*: A Brutal Masterpiece" (chapter 16), "'Let Evening Come': An Invitation to the Inevitable" (chapter 16), "The Emancipation of Abe Lincoln" (chapter 13), "Dead Indians" (chapter 11)

## Humanities Research Methods

As the forms of writing above suggest, the humanities involve the careful "reading" of primary texts, artifacts, and events. In addition, humanities projects involve a careful investigation of past scholarship on a topic so that writers can add their voice to the ongoing discussion or dialogue. With their focus on "reading," the humanities value skills of interpretation—sensitivity to the primary text, thoughtful use of evidence from the text, attention to the textual context, awareness of theoretical frameworks for understanding texts, insightful theses about texts, and the rhetorical skills involved in analysis and argument. In such research, the following resource may be especially helpful:

- MLA Documentation (chapter 23 and www.mla.org)

# Writing in the Social Sciences

In a social sciences class (e.g., psychology, sociology, business, education), your writing will likely explore some dimension of the way that people behave, individually or within groups, whether the group is just two people or an entire society. While you'll want to learn and follow the professional standards of your particular field of study within the social sciences, your writing will likely have the following character.

## The Purpose of Inquiry

Broadly, the social sciences aim to understand, through using an adapted version of the natural-science experimental method, the rules and conventions that govern human behavior and societies. As such, social-sciences thinking tends to be hypothesis-driven, seeking not only to describe behavior but also to predict it. To that end, the social sciences involve observing, measuring, and testing various forms of behavior.

## Forms of Social-Science Writing

With their focus on behavior and social laws, social scientists typically write reports, often as teams of researchers. Here are specific types of writing that you might do:

- **A Literature Review:** This form of research writing identifies and synthesizes the studies that have been published on a specific behavioral or social issue.
- **An Experiment Report:** Such a report describes a specific experiment designed to test a hypothesis about behavior, and then share and analyze the results.
- **A Field Report:** Whether based on observations, interviews, or surveys, such a report shares insights gathered through such contact with human subjects.
- **A Case Study:** Such a study describes and examines actual individuals and situations so as to understand them more deeply.

***Examples:*** "Why Change Is So Hard: Self-Control Is Exhaustible" (chapter 2), "The Rise of the New Groupthink" (chapter 15), "How the Internet Has Changed Bullying" (chapter 14) "The Silent Sibling" (chapter 24)

## Social-Science Research Methods

Like scholars in the natural sciences, social scientists tend to use the experimental method to test out observation-based hypotheses. Some social-science research, however, is more subjective, involving a speculative approach to the mysteries of human consciousness, emotions, and the like. Because much social-science research is observation-based, much of the thinking is rooted in mathematics, particularly statistical analysis. Focused on testing hypotheses, such research pays careful attention to variables, controls, experiment replication, and case studies. Objective analysis of all the data is valued. The following resources may be especially helpful:

- "Conducting Surveys," "Conducting Interviews," "Making Observations" (chapter 20), and APA Documentation (chapter 24)

# Writing in the Natural and Applied Sciences

In a natural- or applied-science class (e.g., botany, chemistry, engineering, and oceanography), your writing will explore some aspect of the physical, natural world. Such writing seeks to explore and explain the nature of the world that we inhabit and are part of, as well as the natural laws that govern that world. While you'll want to learn and follow the established writing methods and formats of your particular field within the natural or applied sciences, your writing will likely have the following character.

## The Purpose of Inquiry

Broadly, natural science aims to explain observations in the light of current theories, observations that are typically not now explicable. The goal of the scientist—or more likely team of scientists—is to arrive at an explanation, stimulate discussion, and prompt further research. As such, scientific thinking tends to be hypothesis driven: it begins with a possible explanation rooted in current knowledge, makes an experiment-related prediction, observes and measures results, and then accepts, rejects, or modifies the possible explanation.

## Forms of Natural-Science Writing

With their focus on natural phenomena, natural scientists typically write research reports. Here are types of writing that you might do:

- **Lab or Field Reports:** Sometimes called IMRAD reports (introduction, method, results, and discussion), such reports share the results of experiments and measured observations.
- **Literature Reviews:** These reports summarize and synthesize all the current research on a specific topic, perhaps also examining the theories that underlie the topic.
- **Technical Reports:** Applied research might involve writing technical reports aimed at proposing practical solutions to a specific problem or challenge.
- **Popular Articles:** Scientists may explain their knowledge for a general audience in magazines, at news sites, or on organizational websites (government, etc.).

*Examples:* "Hair Today, Gone Tomorrow" (chapter 1), "Understanding the Four Types of AI" (chapter 12), "Yogurt: Milk and Mayhem" (chapter 13), "The Effects of the Eastern Red Cedar on Seedlings and Implications for Allelopathy" (chapter 22)

## Natural-Science Research Methods

Natural scientists practice two predominant research methods: laboratory experiments and field work. Both rooted in objective attention to phenomena, laboratory research follows the strict procedures of the experimental method while field work relies on careful, often quantifiable observation. Both forms of research value insightful hypothesizing, carefully collecting and analyzing data, and thoughtfully relating the results to past research and current theories. These resources may help you with your natural-science writing:

- "Making Observations" (chapter 20) and the Council of Science Editors website (councilscienceeditors.org)

# The Rhetorical Modes

The chapters in this part of *The College Writer* are largely organized by the type of writing: personal essay, analytical essay, and argumentative essay. However, this division also features the rhetorical modes—thinking patterns that characterize writing in part or in whole. These thinking patterns are at work in your academic writing, so learning them and practicing them create a foundation for all of your writing assignments in all your courses.

## The Modes as Thinking Frameworks

Each rhetorical mode involves a thinking move that allows you to deepen your understanding of a topic, to explore it and make claims about it.

### Personal-Writing Modes

Personal-writing modes focus on experience, especially the writer's experience—whether of places, people, or events—with the goal of vividly sharing that experience with readers. (See chapter 10.)

- **Narration** tells a story, whether in the form of a brief anecdote, a personal essay, a short story, or a book-length novel.
- **Description** evokes material reality (e.g., birds outside a window) through appealing to the senses (sight, hearing, touch, taste, and smell).
- **Reflection** involves rumination—a kind of speculation that extends narration and description toward personal and universal meaning.

### Analytical Modes

Analytical modes involve mentally "breaking down" a topic in an effort to reveal structures and logical relationships that hold it together.

- **Definition** seeks to clarify the meaning of a term or concept (e.g., human trafficking, mathematics, excellence). (See chapter 11.)
- **Classification** organizes into categories large or complex sets of things: weight lifters and their motivations, musical genres popular in Latin America, or positions on climate change. (See chapter 12.)
- **Process** analysis explains how a specific phenomenon unfolds in time—stage by stage, step by step. The phenomenon might be natural (the development of cancer), historical (emancipation), or cultural (end-of-life care). (See chapter 13.)
- **Compare-contrast** analysis examines the similarities and/or differences between two or more topics in order to illuminate their distinctiveness and/or their commonalities, whether the topics are cultural characteristics, human and animal suffering, or traditional and cyber bullying. (See chapter 14.)
- **Cause-effect** analysis examines the forces that bring about specific results—focusing on the forces at work (causes), the results (effects), or both. As such, cause-effect reasoning explores why and how questions about a wide range of topics, for example, why creativity requires solitude. (See chapter 15.)

### Argumentative Modes

Argumentative modes are persuasive in nature, aiming to convince readers to accept claims about topics that are typically controversial or at least problematic. (See chapters 17 and 18.)

- **Position papers** take a stand on a topic (e.g., incarceration, a controversial statue on campus), either arguing for a specific claim or arguing against a claim with which the writer disagrees.
- **Call-to-action essays** move beyond taking a position on a controversial topic to pressing readers to take a step in response to that position—a concrete action or a general change in behavior.
- **Problem-solution** analysis proposes specific changes to address a specific challenge. This mode thus presses readers to care about a problem, embrace the recommended solution, and (sometimes) even implement the solution.

## The Modes at Work

In academic writing, a specific rhetorical mode might dominate a piece of writing, giving the essay structure and direction from start to finish, such as in an essay classifying types of student weight lifters. However, the rhetorical modes are more often seamlessly combined in your writing, all serving the specific mental work you are doing with your topic. For example, your main purpose might be to explain how a knuckleball works (cause-effect), but in doing so you also walk through a typical pitch delivery (process) and describe the distinctly different ball movement of other pitches such as fast balls and curve balls (contrast). Indeed, it is fair to say that the rhetorical modes build and rely on each other: analytical writing can contain narrative, descriptive, and reflective elements; argumentative writing, in turn, depends upon effective analytical moves to bolster its claims.

*Example:* To explain the nature of prosopagnosia, student writer Audrey Torrest uses *narration* and *description* to describe its *effects*, and she uses *definition* to identify its *cause*.

> Dr. Smith stood beside a fellow neurobiologist on the campus of Washington University in St. Louis. While engrossed in conversation, Smith noticed from the corner of his eye an undergraduate walking in their direction. At first he thought nothing of it, but as she approached, it dawned on him that she was looking directly at him. "Strange," he thought. He tried to ignore her and continue his conversation, but when she was about 20 feet away he heard her laugh. Upon hearing the sound, the unfamiliar undergraduate who had been staring so intently at him morphed into his daughter. Smith had been unable to recognize her.
>
> Dr. Smith suffers from a unique condition known as prosopagnosia or face blindness. Historically, most documented cases have been due to brain damage experienced after maturity from head trauma, stroke, or degenerative diseases. . . .

# Multimodal Projects

The previous pages introduce the rhetorical modes as thinking patterns you use in your writing, either singly or in combination. But there's another way the word "mode" is important to your writing. You may be assigned a multimodal project in one or more of your courses, and you may develop such projects in the work you do after college. The term "multimodal" uses "mode" to refer to methods of communication. In other words, a multimodal project combines two or more ways of connecting with an audience.

## Modes: Methods of Communication

What are the methods of communication available for your multimodal projects? These modes fall into five categories:

- **The Linguistic Mode:** This refers to any element that is language-based, such as written or spoken words.
- **The Audio Mode:** If the element makes a sound of some sort, it's audio. It can range from a speaker's voice to a sound effect to music, even silence.
- **The Visual Mode:** These elements refer to any material that can be seen—from type on a page to shapes and colors, images and videos.
- **The Gestural Mode:** Broadly conceived, this refers to body language—the messages sent by people's movements, facial expressions, hand motions, and so on.
- **The Spatial Mode:** This mode refers to the arrangement of elements in space, whether on a page or a screen or in a presentation space (e.g., gallery, museum, stage).

As you can see, you have a wide range of choices in what modes to combine and how to combine them. Various elements can be physical or digital; they can be live or recorded. In a sense, you can think of a multimodal project as a meal you are creating for your audience: the various modes are ingredients you combine and cook to create the dishes that together make a coherent dining experience. As such, multimodal projects typically require some training in modes beyond the linguistic—a kind of cooking school in which you learn about visual and auditory literacy, as well as different tools and software that help you create the elements.

## Forms of Multimodal Projects

If you think about it, virtually every writing project is multimodal. Beyond the lingual, any writing you do automatically includes visual elements when words are presented on the page or the screen, even with a traditional essay. (See the discussion of format, page layout, and typography in chapter 4.) Beyond the essay, though, there are many types of multimodal projects that you might produce. Here is a quick overview of basic and complex forms:

- **Basic Multimodal Projects:** posters, instructions, storyboards, infographics, oral presentations, picture books, brochures, slide shows, memes, blogs, podcasts, graphic narratives, ads, newsletters, dances, live storytelling, performances
- **Complex Multimodal Projects:** websites, digital stories, interactive stories, animations, films, documentaries, music videos

## A Sample Multimodal Document

To get you thinking about possibilities for multimodal projects, consider a common multimodal document—instructions. They come with things we buy, explaining how to put them together, use them, clean them, and so on. In fact, we rely on instructions in all walks of life, whether they are on a wall poster or in the form of an online video.

Consider the simple handwashing instructions in Figure 9.2. In terms of the rhetorical modes, you can see how the instructions are a form of process analysis (chapter 13): they break the task of properly washing your hands into a sequence of steps. As for the multimodal elements, note how the poster presents the task in separate numbered steps, combines these with clear and simple drawings reinforcing the words' meaning, and places all this linguistic and visual information against a background of white and light blue. The quality and accuracy of such a multimodal set of instructions can mean the difference between health and illness, even life and death, for ourselves and those around us.

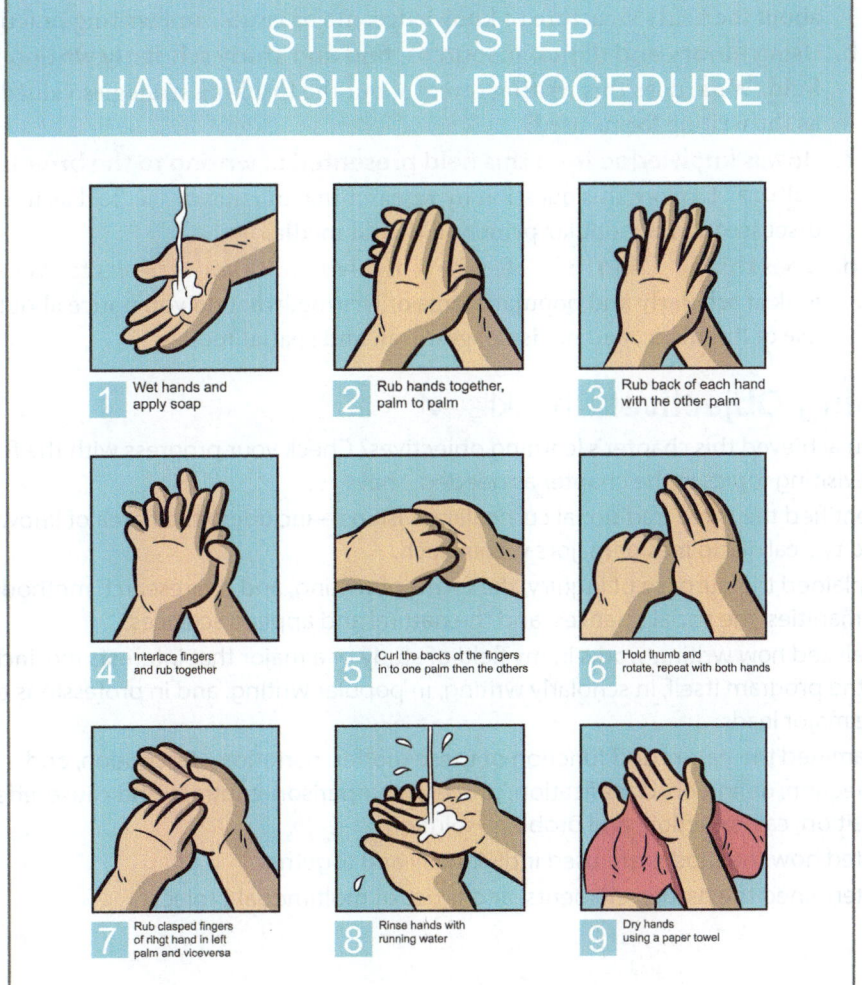

*fig. 9.2*

Modes of Writing

# Forms of College Writing: Applications

After you've read the chapter, apply what you've learned in the situations that follow.

1. **Curricular Survey:** Using its online or print catalog, review your college's curriculum—its organization into divisions, disciplines, and courses. What does that big picture reveal about knowledge, inquiry, and learning in your school? How might you apply that knowledge and learning in your career?
2. **Writing Analysis:** Browse through chapters 10–24, identifying essays, research papers, and other forms of writing that relate to the different divisions and disciplines. Read closely two or three samples that interest you, analyzing the thinking and writing strategies that the authors use.
3. **Major Analysis:** Consider the major that you have chosen, or select a program that interests you. Then research the thinking and writing skills practiced in this field:
    a. **Study the programs and courses in the department.** What do these reveal about the field's structure of knowledge, major issues, and writing practices?
    b. **Using library and digital resources, find and study scholarly writing in this field.** What does this writing reveal about the thinking strategies valued, as well as the writing forms used?
    c. **How is knowledge from this field presented in writing to the broader culture?** Explore this question by researching an issue in the field as it is discussed in the popular print and digital media.
    d. **Does this field and its professions involve multimodal projects?** When you look at scholarly and popular forms of writing, what do you notice about their use of linguistic, audio, visual, gestural, and spatial modes?

## Learning-Objectives Checklist ✓

Have you achieved this chapter's learning objectives? Check your progress with the following items, revisiting topics in the chapter as needed. I have . . .

\_\_\_\_ identified the three traditional curricular divisions—including their area of knowledge and typical disciplines or majors within each.

\_\_\_\_ explained the purpose of inquiry, the forms of writing, and the research methods in the humanities, the social sciences, and the natural and applied sciences.

\_\_\_\_ analyzed how writing works in my field of study or a major that interests me, including in the program itself, in scholarly writing, in popular writing, and in professions to which the major leads.

\_\_\_\_ examined the nature and function of these modes: narration, description, and reflection; definition, classification, process, comparison-contrast, and cause-effect; position, call-to-action, and problem-solution.

\_\_\_\_ noted how the modes are used individually and together.

\_\_\_\_ determined the nature, elements, and types of multimodal projects.

# Chapter 10

# Personal Writing

"It's time to get personal, up close and personal." That's what personal essays say to readers. In them, writers share particular stories from their lives. Paradoxically, the more particular and vivid the story, the more readers can connect with it; the more they can sense the larger truth behind it.

Such personal writing is often called *creative nonfiction*: writing that tells the truth of a real experience using the tools of creative writing—narration, description, and reflection. In different combinations, these modes allow you to tell stories from your life, describe places you've been and people you've known, and reflect on what it all means.

So, as you get ready to write your own personal essay, prepare to relive your past experiences—what you sensed and felt and thought. Be ready to learn something new about those events, about others, and even about yourself. That's the power of personal writing.

**Learning Objectives**

By working through this chapter, you will be able to

- define a personal essay.
- explain techniques of narration, description, and reflection.
- develop a strong theme or thesis for a personal essay.
- identify writing moves and strategies for shaping personal writing.
- craft an engaging personal essay by drawing upon a range of writing moves.

**Visually Speaking** Carefully study the photograph in Figure 10.1. What story does it suggest? What elements of narration, description, and reflection might the story include?

igor.stevanovic / Shutterstock.com

*fig. 10.1*

## Meeting the Mode

A key way to begin understanding what personal writing is and how to write it yourself is by reading and working with a personal essay. The example that follows, "Spare Change," is the first part of student writer Teresa Zsuffa's "A Diary of Chance Encounters." To engage the essay, activate the reading strategies you learned in chapter 2. And as you read, consider these initial questions:

1. What's *personal* about this writing? In what sense is it an essay?
2. How would you describe the experience of reading the essay? What seem to be its goals with readers? What does it offer them?

### Spare Change

This grime is infectious. The smell of old cigarettes and expired perfume is constricting my throat and turning my stomach. But here I am again on the underground subway platform, changing trains at Bloor-Yonge in Toronto, the weight of my backpack thrusting me forward with the Friday morning rush hour crowd. When the subway doors open I hurry inside and look around frantically, as usual. There is an empty seat to my left, but everyone is keeping a safe four-foot distance, as if the seat will suck them in and destroy them if they sit down. Or at least destroy the facade put on with a Ralph Lauren suit, a Coach handbag, or a pair of authentic Gucci sunglasses. Not like the fake five-dollar ones I picked up from a Chinatown vendor just yesterday. The others keep their starry distance; when I sit down, I see why.

She must be about twenty-nine. Her orange track-pants are worn and faded, her T-shirt is far too big, and her powder blue sweatshirt is tied around her waist. Her face and teeth are stained, hair greasy and unkempt. A part of me feels sorry for her. Another part follows the crowd and is careful not to make eye contact.

"Excuse me," she says, perching on the edge of her seat, leaning forward and clasping the metal pole with two hands. No one turns. "Excuse me, which stop do I take to the Old City Hall?" One man shrugs and shakes his head while pretending to check his phone. I feel guilt, but it's easily subdued. After all, she wasn't asking me.

I am deeply engrossed in my Nicholas Sparks novel by the time the driver announces "Dundas Station." As I stuff the book back into my purse and make my way towards the doorway, I'm irritated to see that she also stands up—one stop early for Old City Hall. Doesn't she know she should stay on until Queen? Oh well, she'll figure it out, I reason. The Toronto Transit Commission officers can help her.

I let her off the subway before me. Finally I'm free.

But then she stops on the platform and turns her head, like a puppy making sure her owner is following close behind. No eye contact, I remind myself, and try to walk past but she falls into step with me.

"Can I help you carry your bag?"

I may look like a tourist, but I'm smarter. "No, thanks," I reply.

"Well it just looks pretty heavy." We reach the escalator and the staircase and I take the left side, where I can climb the steps and go up twice as fast as those just standing there on the right and enjoying the ride. But it doesn't work; the woman is still at my heels.

"Are you going somewhere?" she asks.

"Yeah, I have to get to the Greyhound station, I'm going out of town."

"Oh." Now we are standing in front of the underground entrance to the Eaton Center. The Atrium on Bay is to my right, on the other side of which is the bus station and my ticket out of this alien city that is now my home. The woman stands frozen and looks around trying to get her bearings. I start to walk away but hesitate. Looking back, I see her blinking and flinching as people shove past her. She reminds me of a small child lost at a summer carnival.

I check my watch—quarter past eight. I just missed an express shuttle, and the next bus to Niagara Falls, where my father lives, won't be leaving for another forty-five minutes. Something pulls me back to the woman, and against all sworn Torontonian rules, I ask if she needs help.

Her dull brown eyes light up. "I need to find the Old City Hall."

"Okay," I nod. "I'll take you." I lead her through the glass doors into the city's busiest mall. It's the fastest way from Dundas to Queen Street, and from there she will need to walk only a few blocks west. As we're walking, I'm aware of the stares I'm getting from people I'll never see again.

"So where are you from?" I ask.

"Sudbury." And I'm instantly speechless. What is this woman doing so far from home? How did she get here? I ask why she's in the city.

"My boyfriend. He's in jail, and they're letting him go today. I came to take him back home with me after his hearing."

While we walk past Mexx, Aritzia, and Abercrombie, I learn that she had taken a bus from Sudbury the day before and spent the night on a park bench. Her boyfriend is forty-two years old and has been in jail for the past ten months. I don't ask why. She proudly tells me she was a crack addict and that she's been clean for three months.

"I just got out of rehab," she says. "Now maybe my grandma will take me back in."

"Back in?"

"Yeah, she kicked me out. She told me I wasn't allowed to be a hooker anymore, but I got caught bringing someone home once."

I have no idea how to talk to a sex worker, never mind one who is so open about everything she's done, but this woman seems to like me and trust me. The next thing I know, I'm offering to buy her breakfast before she meets up with her boyfriend.

There's a McDonald's at the southernmost side of the Eaton Centre, overlooking the Queen Street entrance. I tell her she can have anything she wants. An Egg McMuffin? Fruit and yogurt? But all she wants is Coke and a hash-brown. I order her two.

We sit down at a freshly wiped table by the window. Beside us, two men in grey suits sip coffee over an array of files and spreadsheets. They pause in their conversation to stare at us—the student traveler and the bedraggled sex worker. I tell the woman a little about my life, and ask more about hers and her grandmother. She says that they used to go to church together, when she was little, but she hasn't been since. She takes another bite of her hash-brown and tells me she's now twenty-one. Only twenty-one, and her boyfriend is forty-two. She talks about the drugs and the providence of God.

"I know that he helped me stop," she says. "I've been clean for three months, can you believe that? That's a miracle! It has to be a miracle."

At this point all I can do is smile.

"I wish I could get my boyfriend to quit," she says, staring off. Then she suddenly leans forward and asks, "Do you know how hard it is? Have you ever done crack?"

"No."

"Pot, at least?"

"No. Sorry." I'm not sure why I'm apologizing for never having tried drugs, but the way her face drops and she shifts her eyes makes me feel guilty. As though I can never fully understand her because I've never experienced the things she has.

"Well you should try it," she urges. "It's really good."

"Maybe one day." I glance at my watch. It's now quarter-to, and I still need to stand in line to buy my ticket and get to the right platform. I wonder why I'm not panicking yet.

> I tell her I need to get going. She should go, too, or she'll be late for the hearing. Before getting up, I reach into my wallet and give her two TTC passes and some spare change. I walk her to the street and point her toward Old City Hall. She never thanks me, only looks at me one last time with immense vulnerability and helplessness. Then she walks away.
>
> I wonder as I hurry towards the station if she'll be okay, if her boyfriend really will get out of jail, and if her grandmother will ever take her back. Either way, I think as I cross Bay Street, what more can I do? I have a bus to catch.

34

35

"Spare Change" by Teresa Zsuffa. Used with permission.

## Converse with the Mode

So, what did you discover about the personal essay? First, you may have noticed that it's *personal* in the sense that it's about *people* and their experiences—possibly about the writer, the "I," but likely about other people, as well. Second, though it's not academic in the traditional sense, it is an *essay*—an attempt to understand something through words—in this case what an experience means. Reading a personal essay feels like you're entering someone's life for awhile, walking around in it, trying to understand it. Now dig a little further in your conversation with "Spare Change."

### Conversation Starters

1. Personal essays come in many forms. How would you describe "Spare Change" as a type of personal essay? What name would you give it?
2. The chapter introduction suggests that personal writing blends narration, description, and reflection. Where and how does Teresa use these modes in her essay?
   - **Narration**—writing that recounts events
   - **Description**—writing that appeals to the senses
   - **Reflection**—writing that shares observations and insights
3. Chapter 5 introduced you to writing moves for essays (openings, middles, and closings). What moves does Teresa make in "Spare Change," and how do they work?
4. "Spare Change" recounts Teresa's particular experience. Though it's specific to her life, how does the essay imply there's something bigger going on, something that you as a reader might relate to?

**Moving On:** In a number of places in this chapter, you'll have the chance to brainstorm possible topics for your own personal essay. For now, start your list by thinking about the topic of "Spare Change" and similar experiences you've had: meaningful encounters with people.

# Strategies for Writing Personal Essays

Personal essays typically present and explore a subjective account of the writer's experience by blending **narration, description,** and **reflection.** This blending often implies a theme or thesis and follows a **fluid organization.** To learn the possibilities for your own personal essay, first think about the **rhetorical situation** and then consider the strategies that follow.

## The Rhetorical Situation

To put your personal essay in context, consider the rhetorical situation that gives rise to it:

**Purpose:** The goal of such writing is to explore topics or issues with which you have a personal connection. Your aim is to deepen your own insight while sharing it with readers.

**Readers:** Most personal essays are written for a general audience, though they may be directed to a specific segment of society. You hope that your personal experience will speak universally—that readers will empathize and connect with it.

**Topic:** You address a meaningful topic that is worth exploring through the lens of personal experience and reflection—often real-life events, people, and places.

> *Example:* In "What I Learned in Prison," James Kilgore focuses on a **topic** important to his own life, the prison system and what it means to be incarcerated. His **purpose** is to reflect on his incarceration experience—what it meant to him personally and professionally—as well as to give his **readers**—the general public—an inside view that may help them understand the truth of that experience and advocate for change to a system that he sees as broken.

## Principles of Narration

Personal essays often center on engaging narratives—stories that focus on meaningful events and people. That's the case, for example, with "Spare Change," the story on the previous pages. Teresa Zsuffa tells a story that stands on its own. The following elements are central to a well-crafted narrative:

**Action:** This refers to the unfolding sequence of events shaped into a meaningful whole, a force that drives narrative forward. Consider these strategies:

- **Handling chronology:** Narrative is time-sensitive, so a good narrative handles time effectively through clear temporal markers, verb tenses, and time transitions (*before, after, then*). Narratives may be written in past ("I drove") or present ("I drive") tense. Moreover, the narrative manages temporal pacing by focusing in on key events and compressing or summarizing less significant action. Finally, the narrative may "escape" strict chronology by beginning in the middle of the action before going back to the beginning, as well as by using flashbacks and foreshadowing.
- **Clarifying action:** Narratives move forward energetically when you use precise, engaging, and suggestive verbs. Example: "Outside the restaurant, Goodman

**leapfrogged** across rocks into the middle of the broad, taupe-colored Panjshir River to **pose**, **mugging** and **clowning**, for pictures. **Driving** back to the base, she **hooted** with delight whenever we **passed** a scatter of scruffy red hens **pecking** listlessly along the roadside or **huddled** in a dirt yard."

- **Shaping a plot:** A narrative's overall pattern may take many forms, but the traditional structure builds tension and complication toward a climactic moment of decision or discovery, followed by aftermath and resolution.

**Character:** While events (what happened and why) are often the focus of a narrative, frequently the narrative's focus is character—what the events reveal about people. Characters need to be well-developed and engaging in order to reveal things about life and human nature. Narrative shows people feeling, thinking, acting, and interacting.

**Dialogue:** Conversations are used in narrative to reveal character, advance the action, and embody the conflict. Typically chosen for significant moments in the action, such dialogue should be natural in word choice, voice, and sentence rhythms (reflecting dialects if needed).

> I once asked Mr. Ebeye if he thought so too. He scratched his patchy beard and grunted. "Do you like your family?" he asked. "I do." He shook his head. "Lucky you."

**Narrative Perspective:** In a personal narrative, you as the writer are typically the narrator—the voice telling the story. However, your voice might be in the foreground (participating in the action) or the background (observing the action).

**Setting:** Action happens and people live within specific places and times—the narrative's setting. Settings put events and characters in physical, historical, and cultural context.

## Sample Narrative Paragraphs

Narratives are useful in all kinds of essay writing—including objective forms like research papers, biographies, and news accounts. For example, a brief narrative, or **anecdote**, can illustrate a concept. In her comparison-contrast essay, Ariana King introduces her essay topic—modern arranged marriages—through a narrative anecdote.

> It's late Thursday night and I'm scrolling through Youtube videos when a new recommendation catches my eye. The show is called *Married at First Sight*, another one of Lifetime's reality television shows where a group of relationship experts matchup a few hopefuls to be married—you guessed it—at first sight.
> 
> While I hate to admit that the show has me hooked, I didn't just watch it for the drama. In the back of my mind, I kept asking myself what this show teaches people about arranged marriages and how that representation is reflected in American culture. Mostly, I wondered why a show about arranged marriage would be such a spectacle now since arranged marriages have been around for ages.

## Principles of Description

Effective descriptive passages (of places, people, and objects) offer precise, evocative details that help readers thoughtfully experience the essay's topic. Such description may aim for fidelity—objectivity through accurate and complete details, including measurements and so on. Or the description may aim to create a dominant impression, a sense of the person, place, or object that is rooted in carefully selected details that work through imagination, association, and symbolism. For example, "Speaking Ill of the Dead" is filled with vivid descriptions of a place (cemetery) and a person (Mr. Ebeye). Such strong description draws attention to different strategies: naming, detailing, ordering, and comparing.

**Naming:** Description identifies things, and to identify things requires naming—among available terms, choosing words that precisely or suggestively clarify what is being described.

**Detailing:** Description appeals to the senses through concrete details, details that may be precise but also rich in connotations and associations. Details that appeal to sight create a mental picture for readers; sounds and smells tend to evoke feelings and memories; taste and touch generate a sense of intimacy.

**Ordering:** While they may involve a single detail, descriptions are often much fuller. In that case, you may need to (1) establish a vantage point from which readers will see the object, (2) orient the object in space, and (3) lead readers systematically through the description (e.g., left to right, top to bottom, back to front).

**Comparing:** You can clarify and deepen descriptions through comparisons. Here are three common options:

- **Simile** is a comparison of two things in which *like* or *as* is used. Example: "My friends have given me an exercise item that looks like a glob of blue putty."
- **Metaphor** is a comparison in which one thing is said to be another, establishing an identity. (Neither *like* nor *as* is used.) Example: "I can't deny the place [health club] was a lekking ground."
- **Personification** is a device in which the author speaks of or describes an animal, object, or idea as if it were a person. Example: "The moon is lonesome without you, but I look at it each night as it rises and see you staring back at me."

### Sample Descriptive Paragraph

While description is vital to personal essays, it's useful in many modes of writing. In this passage from "American Lumpia: Filipino Egg Roll," note how Andrea Taylor appeals to multiple senses as she remembers her family's cooking.

> When I think of lumpia being made at my house, I hold these memories close: the sound of the food processor intertwined with the squish and squash of meat enfolding the remainder of the ingredients; the sight of my mother measuring each ingredient with her experienced eyes; my Lola leaning over a large tub of ground

> pork and beef, using the force of her entire body and the strength of her hands to push the ingredients into the crevices of the meat; the melodic sounds of Mommy and Lola chattering back and forth in their dialect, discussing the welfare of my cousins, aunties, and uncles across the seas back home in the Philippine Islands.

## Principles of Reflection

Strong reflective passages—from single sentences to entire paragraphs—relay your observations and insights regarding the nature, impact, and value of the experience. In some personal essays, reflection is minimal (e.g., essays that are primarily narrative in nature, such as "Spare Change"). However, some essays are rich in reflection, particularly when the writer's purpose is to explore psychological and cultural complexity, as in "It Took Me 18 Years to Embrace My Name" and "What I Learned in Prison." Consider these strategies:

**Natural Observation:** Reflection within a personal essay should have an organic feel—arising naturally out of the material presented, out of the narration and description. That reflection can be thematically implied or openly stated, depending on your purpose.

**Honest Insight:** Your reflection should be meaningful and thought-provoking, as well as generous in its attitude—even empathetic. Such thinking will help your readers connect with and universalize the experience. But be careful: avoid preaching at your reader, offering a simplistic "moral of the story" conclusion, or exaggerating the meaning of the experience.

**Both Deep and High Perspectives:** Thoughtful reflection comes from looking up-close at your experience—at the details, at what went on deep inside. Beware, though, of getting too wrapped up in yourself, as if you're writing in a private diary; after all, your essay is a public account of your experience. It helps if you also zoom outward and upward to see the big picture: the larger context of the events, their social and cultural meaning, even their connection with the past and a possible future—both yours and your reader's.

### Sample Reflective Paragraphs

In the passage below from "It Took Me Eighteen Years to Embrace My Name," Fiza Pirani looks back on her struggle with her name, reflecting on the forces at work within her.

> I was too young or oblivious to know then that internalized racism was at work.
> I convinced myself that embracing the mispronunciation kept me at a healthy distance from my roots—that it was the smart and safe thing to do if we wanted this new country to keep us around.
> Instead, I simply carried the two names—FEE-za and FIZZ-ah—around like one heavy burden, picking and choosing the inflections that best appeased the crowd around me. At school, in the White suburbs of Georgia, I embraced FEE-za and everything the mispronunciation seemed to erase—my color, my language, my religion, and its very meaning: a cool breeze.

## Patterns for Personal Essays: Thesis Thinking

The key idea of a personal essay typically grows out of your questions about the meaning of an experience, and that idea may become clear only as you draft the essay. In fact, you may never fully state your thesis but simply imply it—for example, letting the narrative do the talking. Whatever approach you take, you want to do justice to the fullness and complexity of the experience.

### Sample Thesis

In this thesis, James Kilgore relates that his experience of prison, painful as it was, allows him to share four insights about prison life and the prison system.

> At first I talked about the most painful things: that your children grow up without you, that you never get to hold your lover, kiss your mother, or walk down a quiet street in the rain. But I decided that I didn't like sharing that pain with strangers. I put together four talking points about how prison changes a middle-class, educated white man.

**A Thesis Template:** To get you started on thinking about a theme or thesis for your personal essay, you can use a template such as the one below.

> My experience with _____ *[combination of person, place, event]* impacted me by _____ *[changes in circumstances, understanding, life direction, relationships, etc.]*
>
> *Example:* My experience of working at the Daily Bread Foodbank in Seattle impacted me by showing me how so many people with so many different stories struggle to get by, here in what might be the richest country on Earth.

**From Weak to Strong:** In chapter 4, you learned about refining your thesis to make it stronger. You can do the same with the theme or thesis of your personal essay. *Note:* the examples below are not based in science or research and are simply offered as illustrations. Don't take our word for it!

> *Weak Thesis:* offers a cliché, a trite conclusion, or an obvious statement
>
> Some people make a poor choice when they select a marriage partner.
>
> *Good Thesis:* captures something more insightful about the experience.
>
> Many marriages demonstrate the notion that opposites attract—with painful consequences for everyone involved.

> ***Excellent Thesis:*** goes deeper into the complexities and tensions, offering something surprising.
>
> Because many people seem to marry their opposites, these couples face an uphill battle, especially early in their marriage, to reconcile differences. Strangely, though, such marriages, if they survive the adversity, end up stronger, deeper, and more satisfying than a partnership of like-minded people.

## Patterns for Personal Essays: Writing Moves

If a personal essay centers on a narrative, the organization will largely be determined by chronology, arranged according to the logic of the plot. (See, for example, "Spare Change.") Generally, the structure of a personal essay tends to be fluid—flowing more freely than a traditional academic essay. Consider these writing moves:

**Opening:** The opening seeks to get readers' attention, usher them into the world of the essay, and orient them to the topic through techniques like these: a memory, an image, an idea, a conflict, a puzzle, a moment from the middle or near the end of the story. Remember that personal essays don't always need to open at the beginning of the story; they can start from the middle or end of the action.

**Middle:** The body of the essay may weave together elements of narration, description, and reflection to deepen interest, and possibly to build toward a climax—a moment of discovery or decision. This process may involve

- bringing together "strands" of the past and the present
- introducing tensions, complications, and conflicts
- focusing on key moments, episodes, and encounters (including dialogue)
- foreshadowing what is to come or creating a puzzle to be solved
- comparing events, settings, or characters
- moving from a broad view to a narrow focus or vice versa
- mapping out a journey (possibly there and back again).

**Closing:** Traditional narratives follow the climax with the fallout and resolution (revealing the results of conflict, the outcome). Other narratives, however, aim to be more open-ended. The ending might also focus on authentic reflection (without trite moralism) that leaves readers with food for thought. Finally, it might supply a surprise, a dramatic turn of events, or it might return to the opening in some way.

**Two Tools for Structuring Personal Writing:** In addition to drawing on the writing moves for openings, middles, and closings, you could use a writing organizer such as one of these:

*The ABDCE formula:* If you're not sure how to shape your experience into a story, try this pattern made famous by writer Alice Adams. It might be visualized, as well, as two hills with a small peak and a large peak (Figure 10.2).

1. **Action**—start with an event from the experience that will pull readers in.
2. **Background**—supply the information readers need in order to know who the people are, what's brought them together, and what happened before the event.
3. **Development**—move these people forward through events, shaping these as a plot containing tensions, hurdles, and difficulties.
4. **Climax**—build the conflicts toward a key moment of crisis, discovery, or decision.
5. **Ending**—show how things have changed for the people, what they're left with, what they're facing.

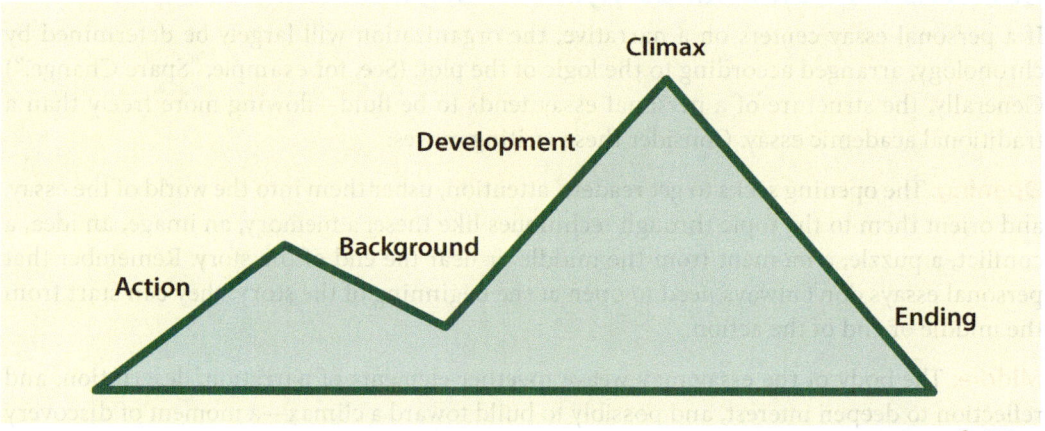

fig. 10.2

*Storyboarding:* A storyboard, like the one in Figure 10.3, is a series of illustrations that map out the sequence of events in a narrative. Used extensively in film, a storyboard of even a few illustrations can help you identify the major scenes in your essay, anchoring them in place and time so that you can write those moments vividly. And you don't need to be a great artist—stick figures will do!

Mila Basenko / Shutterstock.com

fig. 10.3

# Personal Essays: Learning Writers' Moves

One way to get ideas for your own personal essay is to read other writers' personal essays with a writer's eye. By studying their writing moves, you pick up tools for your writing toolbox. In the essays that follow, you'll see how one writer explores a childhood experience of death, another struggles with the cultural complexities of growing up in an immigrant family, and a third gives an insider view on a painful experience—incarceration.

## Exploring Our Relationship with Death

In the essay below, student writer Rachel Ten Hove recounts her childhood experience of death. She presents it through a specific character from her past, Mr. Ebeye, and a specific place where she would go with him—a cemetery.

### Speaking Ill of the Dead

1  Not very many people liked Mr. Ebeye. His teeth always popped out of his mouth when he talked, and his skin was leathery like an elephant's. But I think Mr. Ebeye had a certain fondness for me; I was the only one he ever took to the cemetery.

2  We'd go in the late evenings together, just before it was getting dark, and the lot took on a bluish tinge. The cemetery was a flat, treeless area. The wind would sweep right through and rattle the metal gate on its way out. Because of this, I would have to zip my coat right up to my chin to keep my teeth from chattering. I don't think Mr. Ebeye ever noticed how cold it was; he was always too busy testing the ground of new graves. He'd spend five minutes at each, shuffling around the mound of dirt, and prodding at the chunks of soil with his toe. Then he'd crouch down, as much as his crooked legs would let him, and read the inscription on the tombstone. Sometimes, he'd stay completely quiet while the wind ruffled the few tufts of grey hair left on his head. Other times, he would get back up, wrap my little hand in his calloused one, and walk further into the lot.

3  Peter Kabler was the first person I met in the cemetery. His grave was a modest one: a small piece of limestone shoved into the eroded dirt. The grave marker was supposed to be white but had since faded into a grey that one might mistake as a stepping stone had they not known they were in the cemetery. He was lying in the oldest part of the lot, nestled in the corner where the metal gate was rusted, and the dirt path faded into patches of grass. Sure, he didn't have the nicest plot, but he was by far the liveliest man there. "A world champion cyclist," Mr. Ebeye told me. "Nipped before his time while riding his brand spanking new bike. A complete idiot too. Wasted his money on something that got him killed". I could imagine Peter whipping down the hills of the countryside, then flying when the truck nicked his back tire. Mr. Ebeye said he screamed when he flew into the ditch. I bet he flew faster through the air than he ever could while on his bike. I bet he broke a world record while he was

at it, too. I thought I would like to break a world record someday. "Was he wearing a helmet?" I once asked. Mr. Ebeye had laughed at that, then said, "no helmet could save that fool's soul."

Whenever we reached Peter's grave, we would circle back to the center of the cemetery. The closer we got to the middle, the bigger the tombstones were. More empty plots would appear, and the fake plastic flowers resting on the headstones would become real ones with silky petals and juicy stalks. Sometimes the flowers would be wilted, and Mr. Ebeye would grab them and chuck them in the ditch just outside the metal gates. They sat there in a pile all winter, decomposing. I always hoped they would bloom again in the spring, but they never did.

At the center of the lot, there was a small white church with black swinging doors. The doors were secured shut with a heavy-duty lock and chain. Mr. Ebeye said he could show me inside one day if I wanted to see. It seemed like a good idea; after all, I hadn't formally met Edna Muller yet, and that's where she was currently residing. The church had stained glass windows: reds, blues, and yellows all pieced together to make no particular image. "Edna would have liked that," Mr. Ebeye commented, "being a hippie and all." She was an interesting lady, to say the least. Apparently, she used drugs to "color" her imagination. I wasn't quite sure what Mr. Ebeye meant by that, but she sounded like a fun person to be around. "The old witch didn't wake up one day. Served her right," grumbled Mr. Ebeye. I guess her lifestyle just wasn't for him. It sounded just about right for me, though: a little adventure with a dash of crazy to spice it up.

At the other end of the cemetery, by the gate, was a columbarium. The dirt path circled the concrete pad where eight white pillars were planted in an octagon. Resting inside the structure were small metal boxes with inscribed plates. There were too many names to read on the plates, so Mr. Ebeye and I usually passed by instead. Occasionally, he'd tell me that a family of five were inside the columbarium, but he never introduced me to them. I thought it would be nice to be buried with my family. I once asked Mr. Ebeye if he thought so too. He scratched his patchy beard and grunted. "Do you like your family?" he asked. "I do." He shook his head. "Lucky you."

When we reached the edge of the cemetery, Mr. Ebeye would push open the squeaky metal gate and look back over the hundreds of plots. By this time, it was usually dark. The tombstones were unreadable, and the church's photocell light had turned on. We'd stand there for a few minutes while Mr. Ebeye would comment on how the grass needed cutting or complain about how people were always stealing flowers from the church's flowerbeds. I didn't pay much mind to him at this point. Instead, I wondered if the family of five would go on a midnight walk together or if Peter would visit Edna for a few hours. Sometimes I thought they might all play a game of soccer and use the tombstones as goalposts. I told Mr. Ebeye this once. He scowled at me, saying there were no such things as ghosts. He was probably right, but I liked the idea of it.

As I got older, I stopped going to the cemetery with Mr. Ebeye. I'm not sure if he went by himself, or if he found someone new to bring along with him. Who knows, maybe his legs became too crooked for him to walk there anymore, or maybe he lucked out and got one of those electric wheelchairs to zip around the lot. I never checked the fresh graves for tire marks. What I do know is he eventually claimed his own plot at the cemetery: one of the nice ones near the church, all by himself. His headstone was a reddish granite. The fresh flowers that were placed on his grave quickly wilted and joined the pile in the ditch outside.

It was only then that I finally returned to the cemetery. I walked around, taking our usual route, with a slight detour to stop by his grave. I stood there for a while, staring at the fresh mound of dirt and prodding it with my foot. It felt wrong to do. I tried to conjure up an extravagant story about how he died; maybe he had been thrown from his wheelchair while racing down the road. But I don't think that was the case. As far as I know, he died in his sleep, doing nothing particularly exciting. It bothered me, not being able to think up anything dramatic on his behalf. It was too bad he did nothing thrilling like Edna or Peter. But then, maybe that's the way he wanted it.

I finally moved on, making my way to the edge of the lot. I circled the columbarium twice, searching for the names of the family of five, but finding only two. Then I pushed open the squeaky gate and looked back. Maybe Peter went cycling that night, or maybe the family invited Edna over for a game. Maybe Mr. Ebeye would join them sometime.

Or maybe he'd just stay in his grave.

## Reading for Better Writing

1. *Connections:* In the essay, Ten Hove takes us to a place most people aren't keen to visit—a cemetery. What has been your experience of them, if any? More broadly, have you had to deal with a death of a family member, a friend, or an acquaintance?
2. *Comprehension:* Ten Hove takes us on a walk around the cemetery with Mr. Ebeye in this piece. In your own words, describe Mr. Ebeye, the cemetery, and its "residents."
3. *Writing Moves:*
    a. In the first paragraphs, Ten Hove creates a sense of Mr. Ebeye, the cemetery, and her connection to both. How does she use vivid images and details to do so?
    b. The essay introduces specific dead people and cemetery landmarks. Examine one of each. How does Ten Hove "bring them to life," so to speak?
    c. The narrative structure is that of a journey: if you map it out, what is its shape?
    d. The last three paragraphs signal a number of shifts or changes. What are they, and how do they work to bring the essay to a thoughtful, reflective close?

**Your Project:** Think about your own experiences with death. How have they impacted and shaped you? Or consider places that you visited frequently as a child, places that you returned to as an adult. How are those places important to your life and changes in it?

## Exploring an Immigrant Identity

Fiza Pirani is a freelance journalist and editor for *The Atlanta Journal-Constitution*. Much of her work focuses on mental-health issues. In the following essay published by ZORA, Pirani explores the doubleness of her own immigrant experience as found in her name.

### It Took Me 18 Years to Embrace My Name

1  I don't remember how or when FEE-za was born, but I can imagine my reluctance to correct the teachers who, during roll call, would announce this mispronunciation of my Muslim name with a confidence I didn't know a name could hold. There was no "Did I say that right?" No room for even a reluctant plea for rectification, let alone a chance for me to boldly assert myself as the FIZZ-ah my Pakistani mother birthed in my hometown of Indore, India.

2  The butchering was done with such conviction that I forgot it was a mispronunciation at all. My teachers probably knew better, I thought.

3  But it didn't take long to internalize the inaccuracy and make it mine.

4  "It's actually FEE-za," I valiantly told my parents and younger brother, proud of the mispronunciation I'd adopted sometime during my first childhood years in America—somewhere between New York, Texas, or Georgia—at one of the dozen suburban schools I'd end up attending before high school graduation.

5  My folks didn't seem to care much. "If changing your name makes life easier at your American school, then go for it," their apathy implied.

6  Ease was the goal, after all. After decades of instability, of bouncing from country to country, state to state, and city to city to ensure a future safe and fruitful enough for their children, quiet assimilation to White America was a signifier of success in my parents' eyes.

7  Nikita Redkar, a 26-year-old filmmaker from Austin, Texas, can empathize.

8  Like me, Redkar, who goes by Ni-KEY-da, moved around a lot as a kid and grew up in predominantly White American neighborhoods.

9  "Teachers would look at my name on attendance lists and pause with doubt," she says. Afraid to draw attention to herself, a shy Nikita adopted whichever pronunciation caused the least fuss.

10  Her parents understood, just as my parents did.

11  "Their mentality was to survive, survive, survive," she says. "That was just life in the '90s."

12  Generations of immigrants before us have aspired to do the same. After all, research has consistently shown that immigrants who try their best to "pass" as natives by shedding their accents or changing their names have, historically, fared better within the labor market.

13  And if the recent public charge policy tells us anything at all, it's that our worth as immigrants is directly tied to how much we have in our pockets.

Regret began overwhelming Redkar only in recent years, after she joined a Facebook group for South Asian–identifying women called the Little Brown Diary, a community that has amassed more than 22,000 members from all over the world.

"Seeing women like me embrace their identity to the fullest made me feel like, 'Ah, I fucked up,'" she says.

But Redkar can't help introducing herself as Ni-KEY-da to non-Indians. The original pronunciation of her Sanskrit name, Nee-KEY-tha, sounds unnatural on her own tongue, she says.

And when she does reluctantly introduce herself as Nee-KEY-tha around fellow South Asians, it's certainly not out of pride.

"It's mostly out of fear," she admits. "The fear of them othering me."

It's a strange fear to have, being othered by the people who look most like you. But I know it well.

"You know, that's not your name," my mosque mates and religious education teachers reminded me again and again as I reached adolescence. "Your name is Fiza. FIZZ-ah. Like the movie."

Ah, yes. The movie. A 2000 Bollywood film titled *Fiza*, starring superstars Karisma Kapoor, Jaya Bachchan, and Hrithik Roshan. A movie about a Muslim family in which the protagonist, Fiza (Kapoor), sets out to find her missing brother only to learn that he's joined a terrorist group. That's just the attribution I needed in a post-2001 America, an America emboldened by Islamophobic rhetoric and military action to ensure people like me knew just how far down the ladder we'd fallen, how unlikely we were to catch up with the naturalized citizens we dreamed of becoming.

I was too young or oblivious to know then that internalized racism was at work.

Instead, I simply carried the two names—FEE-za and FIZZ-ah—around like one heavy burden, picking and choosing the inflections that best appeased the crowd around me. At school, in the White suburbs of Georgia, I embraced FEE-za and everything the mispronunciation seemed to erase—my color, my language, my religion, and its very meaning: a cool breeze.

At mosque with my brown-skinned friends and in relationships with brown-skinned men, I reluctantly gave in to FIZZ-ah and still remember enjoying the way my birth name sounded and tasted on their lips. For a brief moment, I'd ache for my name to feel as alluring on my own tongue.

I convinced myself, however, that embracing the mispronunciation kept me at a healthy distance from my roots—that it was the smart and safe thing to do if we wanted this new country to keep us around.

Then I witnessed the sweeping, historical election of America's first Black president.

I remember, quite vividly, remarks from classmates about the new president's Muslim middle name and the implied danger it carried. I remember nods of agreement around the room and quickly assured myself that maybe my peers just didn't know I was born Muslim, that they didn't really mean it like *that*.

My ignorance and naivete revealed that I was, unfortunately, really acing this assimilation thing.

That was the first year I began consciously making room for the growing wedge between the FEE-za I'd absentmindedly molded into and the FIZZ-ah who reminded me there was no escaping my otherness.

I began losing patience for the mispronunciations and grew angry with myself for being so aloof. How would I right what I felt was my wrong?

For Shweta Karikehalli, who spent more than 20 years with her own mispronunciation, the chance to shed SHWAY-da for SHWAY-tha began with a move to a city and a state where no one knew her.

Georgia was just as homogenous as Karikehalli's old Syracuse neighborhood, but for the first time in her life, she started introducing herself to strangers with a name that felt like home.

When you move to a new place or start a new job and have to constantly introduce and reintroduce yourself, you get used to hearing the way your name sounds in your own voice.

"That's where the confidence came from—when I started saying my name correctly out loud," Karikehalli says. "It finally felt natural."

Upon graduating high school, I also began introducing myself to strangers as FIZZ-ah. College orientation gave me plenty of practice to assert myself—even after a new professor's second or third mispronunciation.

But how would I convince the people who'd spent the past 18 years calling me by a butchered version of my name to unlearn it just because I've had some life-altering reckoning?

"It's certainly a lot for someone to grasp," Karikehalli says. Though most of her loved ones have been incredibly understanding, one friend's reluctance to adopt her new pronunciation was enough to momentarily set her back.

"I remember just laughing it off, because it was just uncomfortable," Karikehalli says, wondering if she should have stuck up for herself. In the end, she reasoned that her friend, who is White and has a common American name, might just never understand.

Radhika Gore, on the other hand, vowed to take no prisoners.

"I'm turning 21 soon, and I'm going to stop being afraid of correcting people over and over again," she wrote in a Facebook post, a friendly public service announcement for all to hear. "If I can learn to pronounce and sing words in Spanish, French, German, English, etc., others can and now will have to try harder to say my name correctly."

Gore even included a handy breakdown:

> *Ra — as in rah rah ah ah ah from Lady Gaga's "Bad Romance."*
> *Dhi — I am modifying to my country tis of THEE. Same sound, not difficult.*
> *Ka — rhymes with ra.*

While I don't see a social PSA in my future, Gore's bluntness did inspire me to give my younger brother a nudge. More than a decade after I decided to personally reclaim FIZZ-ah, he's finally beginning to address me as such.

For some, a name might just be a name at the end of the day. My birth name, however, is a family gift I let rust in the back of my closet, unused and neglected for more than half of my life. It represents my roots, my culture, my complicated relationship with religion—all of the Brownness I once wanted to color away, even erase.

As an immigrant old enough to witness the challenges of the migrant experience but too young to remember my birth country, I've accepted that my identity, like my memory, is destined to feel fractured. One place or culture will never feel like the perfect setting for my story. But by claiming this singular name, and wearing it boldly, at least I know this is my story to tell.

## Reading for Better Writing

1. *Connections:* What's in a name? Consider your own. What has been your relationship with it—your struggles, your joys?
2. *Comprehension:* In this essay, Pirani tells the story of her immigrant experience from childhood to adulthood. Describe the different phases and elements of her life journey. How are those phases tied to her name?
3. *Writing Moves:*
   a. The opening paragraphs take us into Pirani's childhood: how do they establish her central struggle?
   b. As Pirani recounts her struggle, she zeroes in on key moments. What are they, and how does each contribute to her gradual change?
   c. Pirani includes in her essay the stories of Nikita Redkar, Shweta Karikehalli, and Radhika Gore. How are the stories presented and what do they add?
   d. In the closing paragraph, Pirani says, "I've accepted that my identity, like my memory, is destined to feel fractured." How is this the theme or thesis for her essay?

**Your Project:** This essay focuses on the fractured identity of an immigrant. Are you yourself an immigrant? Have you experienced such fracturing? Or are you someone who has experienced some other form of fracturing? Add these to your list of possible topics.

"It Took Me 18 Years to Embrace My Name" by Fiza Pirani. Originally appeared at zora.medium.com. Used with permission.

## Examining a Failed Institution

James Kilgore is a lecturer, novelist, and research scholar at the University of Illinois at Urbana-Champaign, as well as a convicted felon who spent six and a half years in prison. In this essay, published in 2015, he describes prison life and his effort to deal with the stigma of having been incarcerated. As you read the essay, note how he reflects on his experiences and uses them to support his critique of current incarceration policies. In addition to this essay, Kilgore has written a number of books, including *Understanding Mass Incarceration: A People's Guide to the Key Civil Rights Struggle of Our Time*.

### What I Learned in Prison

1. I was paroled to Champaign, Illinois in 2009, after serving six and a half years in federal and state prisons in California. When I arrived in Illinois, I ducked questions about my years behind bars. People would ask me where I had been before. "California," I'd say. "What were you doing there?" I'd look away and mumble something about being a writer (I did write a lot in prison) or just say "a lot of things."

2. Since I'm an older white guy, with no tattoos or bulging biceps and all my teeth, no one assumes I'm a thug or a meth cook. Class and race stereotypes help steer people away from specifics.

3. Then one day I met a man at a birthday party who started in on the "where were you before you came to Champaign?" routine. I didn't feel like playing the game anymore. "I was in prison," I told him. He went bug-eyed. All he could do was repeat the word "prison."

4. I, on the other hand, felt great. I realized the power of truth, even if it does come with stigma and judgment. Since we have nearly 20 million people in the United States with felony convictions and an estimated 65 million with some kind of criminal record, people need to get used to dealing with "background" as part of people's biographies. Of course, those millions are not spread evenly. Many black folks either have a family member with a felony or have one themselves. Ditto if you are Native American or transgender. It's not much different in Latino communities, especially if we acknowledge that immigration detention is the same as imprisonment.

5. After that fateful birthday party, people began asking me: "What was prison like?" At first I talked about the most painful things: that your children grow up without you,

that you never get to hold your lover, kiss your mother, or walk down a quiet street in the rain. But I decided that I didn't like sharing that pain with strangers. I put together four talking points about how prison changes a middle-class, educated white man.

First, the abnormal becomes normal. This occurs in ways that you might expect: You get called "inmate" or referred to by your prison number, not your name. You get handcuffed and put in waist chains and leg shackles when you have to leave the prison to see a doctor (and at other times when the guards see fit).

But the most abnormal thing that becomes normal is the endless stream of black, brown, and poor white bodies flowing through those gates. And those bodies will spend 10, 20, 30 years in prison. Some will do life or double life or life without parole. I had one friend who was doing 555 years. Most of those prisoners have not committed crimes that any rational society would punish so severely.

When I was in the federal prison at Lompoc, I was a GED teacher. One of my best students was Weldon Angelos, whose case exposes the madness of mass incarceration. He is serving 55 years for selling marijuana while possessing a gun—with no prior record, a family, and a job. Even his judge says he should never have gotten such a long sentence. I met too many Weldons behind those walls.

Second, there isn't much violence in prison. That always shocks people because they think that men in prison spend their days stabbing and raping each other. But instead, people find ways to live together: to share tight spaces and meager resources in a way that puts getting along at the center of their lives. I have a lot of respect for that.

The minute you arrive at a new prison yard, someone will approach you, find out where you are from, connect you to one of your "homies," and make sure you have the basics needed to survive: soap, deodorant, a couple of Top Ramens, a pair of shower shoes. The assumption is that we all have to live together in this hellhole, so let's find a way to do that; let's make sure no one starves, no one stinks, no one has to walk around in bare feet.

Every prison has a well-developed service economy, all run by prisoners. I have paid for the following from my comrades-in-arms: a massage, getting my shirts ironed, a haircut, a delicious burrito, oatmeal cookies stolen from the kitchen, color portraits of my entire family, a picture frame made from old potato-chip wrappers, and, of course, white lightning and the prison wine known as pruno. People find ways to make money, to barter, to improve their lives through systems of production and cooperation.

You can cram 150 "convicts" into a converted gym and make them sleep on triple bunks, and they will develop a way to get along without violence. They will make rules, carve out territory, and respect boundaries. Anyone who breaks the rules may be forced to do a few burpees or even get "checked" (punched), but the rules are clear. If you put 150 CEOs or MacArthur geniuses in the same space, they wouldn't do half as well.

My next point contradicts Point No. 2: Prisons are steeped in hate and violence. Guards generally loathe prisoners. Since so many prisons are located in rural areas with mostly white populations, whereas those locked up are overwhelmingly poor people of color from big cities, prison hatred has a powerful racial tinge. Most guards have learned how to avoid using the N-word, but institutional racism lurks just below the surface.

Then there is white supremacy. In prison I acquired the social skill of making polite conversation with someone with a swastika tattoo on his forehead or a nicely inked "thank God I'm white" across the back of his neck. Prisons are hotbeds of white supremacy, a special form of hatred that keeps prison populations divided and makes it difficult to mount resistance to the myriad ways in which the institutions violate the rights of their charges. Unfortunately, the ideology spills out into the streets.

While I hate white supremacy, I don't hate all white supremacists. Most are victims of circumstances—but still dangerous.

Finally, in prison you always know someone is benefiting from locking you up. People make money designing those crepe-paper suits they put on you when you move to another prison. Companies like Bob Barker ("America's Leading Detention Supplier") profit from a range of disgusting products, like one-inch razors and canvas shoes with black and white stripes on the side. Other companies make millions designing and building prisons and supplying them with everything from food to toilet paper.

Guards are the most obvious profiteers. They're constantly cooking up overtime schemes. Thousands of guards in California make more than $100,000, and last year more than 100 had paychecks surpassing $180,000. That's a criminal misuse of taxpayers' money.

Prison changed me. I'm a little less fun now, less prone to look for the lighter side of things. I do try. But most days, prison is all I can talk about. I've become an obsessed campaigner against incarceration, against the madness of solving social problems with concrete and steel cages. My obsession may not make me an ideal party guest, but I can't think of a better way to spend my time.

### Reading for Better Writing

1. *Connections:* In his essay, James Kilgore asserts that the incarceration system in the U.S. is exploitative, abusive, and de-humanizing. What have you learned through reading about or experiencing the system? Does your knowledge and/or experience support or contradict Kilgore's claims? Explain.
2. *Comprehension:*
   a. Prisons and penitentiaries are sometimes called "correctional institutions," implying that they strengthen society by "correcting" deviant behavior. Would Kilgore agree with this claim? Why? Cite details in his essay to support your answer.
   b. In paragraph 9, Kilgore says, "Second, there isn't much violence in prison." But in paragraph 13, he says, "My next point contradicts Point No. 2: Prisons are steeped in hate and violence." What does he suggest by these (apparently) contradictory statements?
3. *Writing Moves:* Kilgore develops his personal essay through researched data, personal anecdotes, and reflection. Find an example of each and explain how he uses it to advance his thesis.

**Your Project:** Kilgore's essay critiques what he believes to be an institution that fails to accomplish what it is intended to do. What other institutions are important to you? Consider researching and writing about an institution that you believe either succeeds or fails to achieve its mission.

"What I Learned in Prison" from The Chronicle of Higher Education. *Used by permission of James Kilgore.*

#  DIY: Craft Your Own Personal Essay

## Planning

1. **Select a topic.** Promising topics are experiences that gave you insights into yourself, and possibly into others. To identify such topics, reflect on the essays in this chapter and consider the categories below. Then list whatever experiences come to mind:
   - Times when you felt *secure, hopeful, distraught, appreciated, confident, frightened, exploited,* or *misunderstood.*
   - Times when you made a decision about *lifestyles, careers, education,* or *religion.*
   - Events that tested your *will, patience, self-concept,* or *goals.*
   - Events that changed or confirmed your assessment of *a person, a group,* or *an institution.*

   *Tip:* List topics in response to the following statement: *Reflect on times when you first discovered that the world was strange, wonderful, complex, frightening, small, full, or empty.* How did these experiences affect you?

2. **Get the big picture.** Once you have chosen a topic, gather your thoughts by brainstorming or freewriting in response to questions like these:
   - Where did the experience take place and what specific sights, sounds, and smells distinguish the place?
   - Who else was involved, and what did they look like, act like, do, and say?
   - What were the key or pivotal points in your experiences and why?
   - What led to these key moments and what resulted from them?
   - How did your or others' comments or actions affect what happened?
   - What did others learn from this experience—and what did you learn?
   - Did the experience end as you had hoped? Why or why not?
   - What themes, conflicts, and insights arose from the experience?
   - How do your feelings now differ from your feelings then? Why?

   *Tip:* To find out more details about the event or people involved, sort through photos and videos to trigger memories; talk to someone who shared your experiences; consult your journal, old letters, and saved digital communications, such as texts or social-media posts.

3. **Probe the topic and reveal what you find.** Ask "so-why" questions: *So why does this picture still make me smile?* or *Why does his comment still hurt?* or *Why did I do that when I knew better*—or *Did I know better?* Your readers need to experience what you experienced, so don't hide what's embarrassing, painful, or still unclear.

4. **Get organized.** Review your brainstorming or freewriting, and highlight key details, quotations, or episodes. Then list the main events in chronological order, or create an ABDCE chart or storyboard (see Figures 10.2 and 10.3).

## Drafting

5. **Write the first draft.** Rough out the first draft using writing moves you've learned earlier in the chapter. Consider opening, middle, and closing strategies.

## Revising

6. **Review the draft.** After taking a break, read your essay for truthfulness and completeness. Does it include needed details and questions? Test your narration and description by asking whether the quotations, details, and events are accurate and clear. Test your reflection by asking whether it explains how the experience affected you.
7. **Get feedback.** Ask a classmate to read your paper and respond to it.
8. **Improve the ideas, organization, and voice.** Address these issues:
   - **Ideas:** The essay offers readers an engaging, informative look into your life, personality, and perspective.
   - **Organization:** The essay includes (1) an inviting opening that pictures the setting, introduces the characters, and forecasts the themes; (2) a rich middle that develops a clear series of events, nuanced characters, and descriptions; and (3) a satisfying closing that completes the experience and unifies the essay's ideas. Paragraphs organize details and signal clear temporal transitions.
   - **Voice:** The tone is fair and fits the experience. The voice is genuine and engaging.

## Polishing

9. **Edit and proofread your essay.** Polish your writing by addressing these items:
   - **Words:** The words in descriptive and narrative passages *show* instead of *tell about*; they are precise and rich, helping readers imagine the setting, envision the characters, and vicariously experience the action. The words in reflective passages are insightful and measured.
   - **Sentences:** The sentences in descriptive and reflective passages are clear, varied in structure, and smooth. The sentences in dialogue accurately reflect the characters' personalities, regional diction, and current idioms.
   - **Correctness:** The copy includes no errors in spelling, mechanics, punctuation, or grammar. The essay avoids improper or confusing shifts in tense.
   - **Page Design:** The design is attractive and follows assigned guidelines.

## Publishing

10. **Publish your writing** by sharing it with peers, posting it on a blog, or submitting it to an online journal.

# The Personal Essay: Applications

Once you have finished your narrative essay, there may be more to think about. Consider how to apply what you have learned in the situations below.

1. **Living Today:** *TMI*—too much information. Perhaps you've heard the phrase. In the digital world we inhabit, many of us share personal information regularly, maybe even obsessively, through social media. Is it ever too much information? What you post is part of what's called your digital persona—your presence and personality on the Internet. Do a Google search of your name. Check out the history of your posts. What story do they tell about who you are? How does your digital persona compare to the one you created in your personal essay?

2. **Public Texts:** Public and private organizations use narratives to tell their "stories" or enhance their reputations. For example, a hospital may advertise its obstetrics ward by broadcasting on TV mothers and fathers, who are holding their newly born babies, telling how the birthing process and care of the babies was enhanced by the hospital's exemplary doctors, nurses, and facilities. Critique one or more of these mini-dramas by assessing whether the settings seem "staged," the dialogue sounds authentic, and the characters are believable.

3. **Major Work:** Consider your major and your future career. What is the focus of this field of study and this profession? Where and how do people in this profession use anecdotes or longer narratives? Why will doing it well matter? Research these questions to get the answers you need.

## Learning-Objectives Checklist ✓

Have you achieved this chapter's learning objectives? Check your progress with the items below, revisiting topics in the chapter as needed. I have . . .

\_\_\_\_ defined a personal essay.

\_\_\_\_ practiced techniques of narration, description, and reflection.

\_\_\_\_ developed a strong theme or thesis for my personal essay.

\_\_\_\_ identified writing moves and strategies for shaping my personal writing.

\_\_\_\_ crafted an engaging personal essay that draws upon a range of those writing moves.

# Chapter 11

# Analytical Writing: Definition

What's in a word? Given the war of words we hear most days, given that words can lead to real wars—a heck of a lot.

There are words upon which our lives depend—*Stop*, *Yield*. There are words new to us that we have to grapple to understand—*coronavirus*. There are words that are culturally problematic—*Washington Redskins*. And there are words that are just plain fun—*palooza*.

Definitions clarify and deepen understanding of words for both writers and readers. Defining words clears up verbal fog and misunderstanding. It brings precision and insight to discussions of virtually any topic. It says, "Here's what we're really talking about." A definition might do so in a single sentence or a paragraph; sometimes such definition requires an entire essay—called an extended definition. This chapter will teach you how to write definitions of any length—and help you avoid those verbal wars that are so damaging.

## Learning Objectives

By working through this chapter, you will be able to

- explain what a definition essay is.
- practice techniques of definition.
- develop a strong thesis for a definition essay.
- identify writing moves and strategies for shaping definition writing.
- craft a strong definition essay by drawing upon a range of writing moves.

**Visually Speaking**  Figure 11.1 shows a woman studying a tableau of figures. Can you read the message that the figures convey? Try to define one or more figures.

kravka / Shutterstock.com

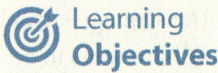

fig. 11.1

## Meeting the Mode

What is a definition essay? That's a question that requires a definition of *definition*, as crazy as that sounds. A good way to begin building that understanding is to read and reflect on a definition essay, such as "The Gullible Family" by Mary Bruins. As you read her essay, activate the strategies you learned in chapter 2 and consider these initial questions:

1. What seems to be Mary's purpose in defining "gullible"?
2. In the end, what does the essay offer you as a reader? How would you describe the experience of reading the essay?

---

### The Gullible Family

The other day, my friend Loris fell for the oldest trick in the book: "Hey, somebody wrote *gullible* on the ceiling!" Shortly after mocking "Gullible Loris" for looking up, I swallowed the news that Walmart sells popcorn that pops into the shapes of cartoon characters. And so, as "Gullible Mary," I decided to explore what our name means, and who else belongs to our Gullible family. What I learned is that the family includes both people and birds, related to each other by our willingness to "swallow."

A gullible person will swallow an idea or argument without questioning its truth. Similarly, the gull (a long-winged, web-footed bird) will swallow just about anything thrown to it. In fact, the word *gullible* comes from *gull*, and this word can be traced back to the Germanic word *gwel* (to swallow). Both *gull* and *gwel* are linked to the modern word *gulp*, which means "to swallow greedily or rapidly in large amounts." It's not surprising, then, that Loris and I, sisters in the Gullible family, both eagerly gulped (like gulls) the false statements thrown to us.

Swallowing things this quickly isn't too bright, and gull (when referring to a bird or person) implies that the swallower is immature and foolish. For example, gull refers to an "unfledged" fowl, which the *Grolier Encyclopedia* describes as either "an immature bird still lacking flight feathers," or something that is "inexperienced, immature, or untried." These words describe someone who is fooled easily, and that's why gull, when referring to a human, means "dupe" or "simpleton." In fact, since 1550, *gullet*, which means "throat," has also meant "fooled."

To illustrate this usage, the *Oxford English Dictionary* quotes two authors who use *gull* as a verb meaning to fool. "Nothing is so easy as to gull the public, if you only set up a prodigy," writes Washington Irving. William Dean Howells uses the word similarly when he writes, "You are perfectly safe to go on and gull imbeciles to the end of time, for all I care."

> Both of these authors are pretty critical of gullible people, but does *gullible* have 5
> only negative connotations? Is there no hope for Gullibles like Loris and me? C. O.
> Sylvester Marson's comments about *gullible* may give us some comfort. He links
> *gullible* to "credulous, confiding, and easily deceived." At first, these adjectives also
> sound negative, but *credulous* does mean "to follow implicitly." And the word credit
> comes from the Latin word *credo* (meaning "I believe"). So what's bad about that? In
> other words, isn't wanting to believe other people a good thing? Why shouldn't Loris
> and I be proud of at least that aspect of our gull blood? We want to be positive—and
> we don't want to be cynics!

"The Gullible Family" by Mary Bruins. Used by permission of the author.

## Converse with the Mode

So, what definition of *definition* did you develop as a result of reading this essay? Is it that defining aims to bring precision to the reader's understanding of a word, while perhaps also exploring its meaning and value in culture through time, maybe even to entertain the reader? That's a good start. The root meaning of *definition* is actually "to set bounds to" (from the Latin *definire*). So what a definition does is explain what distinguishes one word from other words, as well as the possibilities for meaning within the boundary created by the word. To dig a bit deeper, explore these questions about "The Gullible Family."

### Conversation Starters

1. Mary opens her essay with an anecdote and returns to it at the end. In other words, she draws upon modes of personal writing. What does doing so contribute to the essay?
2. Writers of definition essays can use many resources to create their extended definitions. What resources does Mary use? Are there others you imagine she could have turned to?
3. In addition to her opening and closing anecdote, what writing moves does Mary make?

**Moving On:** "Gullible" is a word Mary applies to herself. What words would you apply to your own character? What recent events in your life point toward the qualities of your personality? Begin your list of possible topics for your own definition essay by brainstorming answers to these questions.

**INSIGHT** Be sure to distinguish *definition* from *description*. To *describe* means to show in detail what something is like. To *define* means to explore the nature, scope, and meaning of something. However, description can help you clarify a definition. (See chapter 10 for more.)

# Strategies for Writing Definition Essays

Definition clarifies meaning through an equation: **term *x* = explanation *y***. Your job as a writer is to show that explanation *y* on the right amounts to the same thing as the term (or referent) *x* on the left. Depending on your situation (purpose, readers, and topic), you might develop a succinct one-sentence formal definition or a six-page extended definition.

## The Rhetorical Situation

Put your definition writing in context by reviewing your assignment and your instructor's directions. In particular, analyze the three parts of the rhetorical situation:

- **Purpose:** You may compose a definition for many reasons—to define a misunderstood term, to plumb the meaning of a complex concept, to entertain, or even persuade. For example, defining *addiction* as a disease rather than a crime could potentially change readers' opinions or attitudes on the topic. Overall, your writing purpose and readers affect what form the writing takes.
- **Readers:** People who read definitions also do so for different reasons, which affect the type of definitions they seek. For example, one reader may find a term unclear but want only a brief definition. Another reader may find a term very confusing and want a lengthy analysis of it, including its etymology (its root meaning, where it comes from). A third reader may understand what the term means but want to learn how you will expand its meaning.
- **Topic:** For any definition, the topic is a term. But what terms might you focus on, and how does the term itself affect the form and style of the definition? That again depends on the writer's purpose and readers. For example, in "How 'Namaste' Flew Away from Us," Kumari Devarajan wants to clarify a culturally important word that has been taken over carelessly; she wants readers to use the term more respectfully and accurately.

## Principles of Definition Writing

Definition writing depends on the principles explained on this page and the next.

- **Examining a term's denotative (or literal) meaning, connotative (or suggested) meaning, and etymology (or historical meaning).** By studying one or more of these, you gain a foundational understanding of your topic and commonly find poignant details that lead to fresh insights. That's precisely what Mary Bruins was doing in "The Gullible Family."
- **Writing precise definitions.** As noted on the previous page, defining involves establishing the boundaries of a word or phrase—what belongs inside it and what lies outside it. In "The History of 'Coming Out'," scholar Abigail Saguy shows exactly how and when the boundaries of the phrase "coming out" changed.
- **Seeking accurate, authoritative sources.** For information on how to evaluate the credibility of a source, see chapter 20.

- **Using anecdotes, examples, illustrations and comparisons.** You use strategies such as these to engage readers and help them imagine a situation, visualize details, and discern subtle connotations. For example, in his essay "Dead Indians," Thomas King uses a multitude of examples, illustrations, and anecdotes to show how North American culture has made caricatures and stereotypes of Indigenous peoples.
- **Inserting transitions that lead into and out of definitions.** When composing a definition within a longer piece of writing, you typically insert a transition that introduces the definition and explains why it is relevant or needed. After the definition, you then insert another transition that leads readers back into the discussion that follows.
- **Avoiding logical fallacies.** Definitions are weakened by logical fallacies such as oversimplification, half-truths, ambiguity, and slanted language. Writers need to edit their definitions to correct any poor reasoning.

## Sample Definition Paragraph

The paragraph below is from a paper on the economic roots of various social and sexual abuses. As part of that discussion, the writer begins defining *human trafficking* in the paragraph below, explaining why the definition is needed and comparing it with related terms.

> Human trafficking, in particular, is a term that is difficult to define properly, but it must first be clarified if the problem itself is to be addressed. To begin, migration, human smuggling, and human trafficking are distinct but related phenomena, and incorrect definitions would put different groups of people in the wrong category, with potentially dire consequences. For example, the Trafficking Victims Prevention Act (TVPA), which came into law in 2000, requires the U.S. government to ensure that victims of trafficking are not jailed or "otherwise penalized solely for unlawful acts as a direct result of being trafficked" (U.S. Department of State, 2004), whereas illegal immigrants are still subject to deportation and criminal proceedings. The U.S. State Department recognizes the potentially "confusing" difference between smuggling and human trafficking, so it defines human smuggling as "the procurement or transport for profit of a person for illegal entry in a country" (2004). However, even if the smuggling involves "dangerous or degrading conditions," the act is still considered smuggling, not human trafficking, and so smuggling is considered an immigration matter, not necessarily a human rights issue (2004).

## Patterns for Definition Essays: Thesis Thinking

The central idea of your definition depends largely on your purpose and your main question. Are you aiming to clarify confusions about the term or perhaps to deepen understanding of a complex, unfamiliar concept? Do you wish to show the word or phrase's changing meaning over time, or to heighten the reader's awareness of the issues surrounding the term? Generally, let your purpose guide you.

### Sample Thesis

In this example, the writer signals with his thesis that his aim is to clarify the meaning and history of two closely related terms.

> Let me see if I can explain the original meaning and also how *daft* and *deft* came to part company.

**A Thesis Template:** If you're not sure where to begin with finding a thesis, you can use the structure of a formal definition. In this formula, you place the term within the larger class or grouping of terms to which it belongs; you then offer distinguishing features—that is, those elements of the term that separate it from those related terms in the class.

> Term = larger class + distinguishing features
>
> **Examples:** Here are a few from the *Oxford English Dictionary*.
>
> A virus is **an infective agent** that typically consists of a nucleic acid molecule in a protein coat, is too small to be seen by light microscopy, and is able to multiply only within the living cells of a host.
>
> A phobia **is an extreme or irrational** fear of or aversion to **something**.
>
> A gothic novel **is an English genre of fiction** popular in the 18th to early 19th centuries, characterized by an atmosphere of mystery and horror and having a pseudomedieval setting.

**From Weak to Strong:** In chapter 4 you learned about refining your thesis to make it stronger. You can do the same with the thesis of your definition essay.

> **Weak Thesis:** inaccurate, simplistic, opinionated, vague
>
> Marriage has always been between one man and one woman, and it always should be. *(historically inaccurate, legally incorrect)*
>
> **Good Thesis:** precise, accurate statement blending denotation, connotation, and etymology, as needed

> Marriage is essentially a personal union, a relationship typically between two adults made formal by a social and legal contract where, as spouses, they intimately share their lives in all aspects.

> ***Excellent Thesis:*** offers complexity, tension, or surprise that deepens the term

> While the traditional view of marriage has for centuries been characterized by a union between one man and one woman, both historical practices and contemporary changes in understandings of gender suggest that the institution is more flexible.

## Patterns for Definition Essays: Writing Moves

When it comes to the organization of your definition essay, what structures might help you develop your thesis effectively? Start by asking what organization follows naturally from your thesis. Then consider these options:

**Parse Your Formal Definition:** If your thesis is a formal definition of the term, you might develop your definition by expanding each element of that template: (1) the term's denotation and etymology; (2) the larger class or sphere to which the term belongs; and (3) the nature and meaning of the distinguishing features.

**Extend Your Definition to Bring the Term to Life:** A number of strategies can make the term alive for readers.

- Share a story about the term. Narratives relate the term to people's lives and experiences.
- Explain how the term has changed through time. The evolution of a word's meaning reveals much about cultural change.
- Connect the term to a living social context. Exploring how the term is used by different people in different places—as well as suggesting what's at stake with the word—suggests the word's relevance.

**Use a Writing Organizer to Expand the Term:** Figure 11.2 shows how you might elaborate your definition in a number of directions. Use the diagram to map out possible elements of your essay.

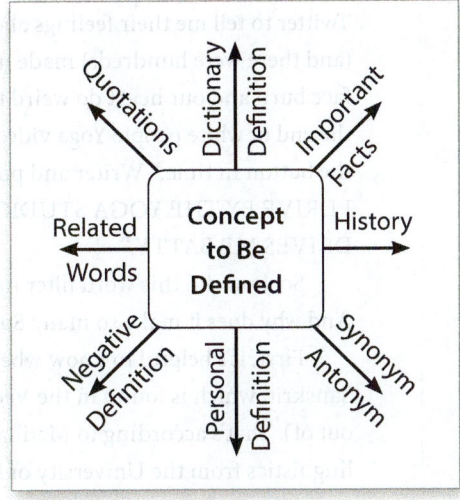

*fig. 11.2*

# Definition Essays: Learning Writers' Moves

To learn strategies for writing extended definitions, you can read other writers' definition essays with a writer's eye. By studying other authors' writing moves, you can try these moves yourself. Through reading, you also can find inspiration for topics for your own essays.

## Explaining a Misunderstood Term

Kumari Devarajan is a producer for *Code Switch* from National Public Radio. In this essay, she explains how *namaste*, coming from South Asian culture, has been adopted unthinkingly in Western culture.

---

### How 'Namaste' Flew Away from Us

1. It's often how you know yoga class is over: The teacher faces the class with their hands together in a bow and says, "Namaste." Maybe you bow and say it back.

2. But that's not the only place you'll encounter "namaste." In the years since yoga became commercially popular in the United States, the word has taken on a life of its own. *Namaste* has found its way onto T-shirts, welcome mats, mugs, socks, pencil cases, and tote bags.

3. And that's just the word on its own. Let's not forget the namaste puns and catchphrases: "Nama-stay in bed." "Namaslay." "Namaste, B****es."

4. Even if most Western Europeans and North Americans don't know anything else about South Asia, "they know about yoga, and they know about 'namaste,'" says Rumya Putcha. She's an assistant professor of women's studies and music at the University of Georgia.

5. But all that visibility isn't necessarily a good thing. I asked South Asians on Twitter to tell me their feelings about seeing *namaste* in these contexts. The responses (and there were hundreds) made it clear: For a lot of us, it makes our skin crawl, our face burn and our heart do weird things. One responder wrote, "I always mute it at the end of white people Yoga videos. I launch out of corpse pose like ants bit me to hit the button in time." Writer and podcaster Taz Ahmed said, "EVERY DAMN TIME I DRIVE BY THE YOGA STUDIO ON SUNSET THAT SAYS NAMASTE L.A. IT DRIVES ME BATTY."

6. So, how did this word filter into so many different pieces of American culture? And why does it make so many South Asians feel icky?

7. First, it's helpful to know where the word comes from. *Namaste* dates back to Old Sanskrit, which is found in the Vedas (the ancient texts that modern Hinduism grew out of). That's according to Madhav Deshpande, a professor emeritus of Sanskrit and linguistics from the University of Michigan. The oldest part of the Vedic literature comes from what is now Pakistan and the northwestern corner of India.

The first part of *namaste* comes from "namaha," a Sanskrit verb that originally meant "to bend." Deshpande says, "Bending is a sign of submission to authority or showing some respect to some superior entity." Over time, "namaha" went from meaning "to bend" to meaning "salutations" or "greetings."

The "te" in *namaste* means "to you," Deshpande says. So all together, *namaste* literally means "greetings to you." In the Vedas, *namaste* mostly occurs as a salutation to a divinity.

But the use and meaning have evolved. Today, among Hindi speakers throughout the world, *namaste* is a simple greeting to say hello. It's often used in more formal situations, like when addressing someone older or someone you don't know well. But that's all it means—hello.

A lot of words we use today have religious roots, but just like "adios," "inshallah" or "goodbye" (an abbreviation of "God be with ye"), it doesn't have to be that deep.

When it comes to yoga, it's a different story. The commercial yoga industry in the United States often uses *namaste* in a way that is almost completely divorced from its use in Hindi. Some yoga websites claim that *namaste* is "the belief that there is a Divine spark within each of us" or "The divine light in me bows to the divine light within you."

Yoga teachers all over the place teach these overblown interpretations of the word to try to ground their classes in a sense of authenticity, or even holiness. It helps that the word *namaste* comes from a language that is unfamiliar to many of the teachers and practitioners of yoga in the U.S. It's much easier to exaggerate the meaning of a word that sounds foreign.

With all of the faux gravity, it's easy to see how the commercial yoga industry flipped *namaste* into a catchphrase. Sporting *namaste* on a water bottle or tote bag lets people present an essence and a persona that they believe is a part of an "exotic" culture simply by . . . buying a tote bag.

Then come the jokes. The tendency to make a joke out of words from other languages—like "Nama-slay"—is very American, says Rumya Putcha. But of course, not everyone can be in on those jokes. Putcha says that deciding which languages get made fun of is one way society establishes which people and cultures are the norm and which are not. (Can you imagine Target selling tote bags and water bottles with a play on the word *hello*? Who's going to shell out big bucks for a *HELLO-M-G* yoga mat?)

And there are other consequences. When white English speakers fold words from other languages into their lexicon, they're often seen as cultured and worldly (and funny!). But for people of color, it's a totally different game. For example, after President Trump enacted the travel ban, Putcha says, her family became "hypervigilant" about speaking the language they normally spoke at home in public "for fear that it would raise suspicion" about their immigration status.

There's another reason South Asians may cringe when they see *namaste* everywhere—the experience of being namaste'd. It's the term I use for when a random stranger, usually white, says "namaste" to you for no discernible reason besides your appearance. A bunch of folks on Twitter brought it up.

In South Asia, *namaste* is mostly heard in Hindi-speaking areas. There are hundreds of other languages spoken in the region—as a Sri Lankan Tamil, *namaste* isn't really a word in my family's language. And yet, with brown skin and a name like Kumari, I'm no stranger to being namaste'ed. As Putcha points out, "racism isn't exactly geographically specific."

Being namaste'ed was one of the ways I learned what being South Asian was going to mean for my life. If folks were greeting me with a word that has no place in my family's heritage, then what other assumptions were they making?

*Namaste* has a meaning among Hindi speakers. But in the U.S., the word has been wrangled out of its context and tossed around to mean whatever people want it to. Sometimes that's something really heavy. Sometimes it's gibberish. But almost all of the time, it's just plain wrong.

## Reading for Better Writing

1. *Connections:* What has been your experience of the word *namaste*? Do you ever use it? When and why? As part of your South Asian culture? Or has it been doing yoga?
2. *Comprehension:* What did *namaste* mean originally, and what has it come to mean in Hindi? How is it used in an American context, and why is that meaning problematic?
3. *Writing Moves:*
   a. In her first five paragraphs, Devarajan puts the use of *namaste* in context. What does she do to bring the word to life? What's her theme or thesis about it?
   b. How do the questions in the sixth paragraph direct Devarajan's discussion?
   c. How does she explain the word's origin and what it now means for Hindi speakers?
   d. The rest of the essay explains misunderstandings and misuse of *namaste* in American culture. How does Devarajan describe and critique each misuse? How does the closing paragraph stress why the misuse matters?

**Your Project:** English is a living and dynamic language that has for centuries borrowed (or appropriated) words from other languages and cultures. Consider your own cultural heritage and background. What words has English borrowed from it, with what effects? Or, consider words that are important to a group you are part of (e.g., a religion, sport, hobby, or profession)—words that "outsiders" don't understand. What should they know?

# Examining the Changing Meaning of a Social Phrase

Abigail Saguy is a Professor of Sociology at UCLA. In this article that references her book, *Come Out, Come Out, Whoever You Are*, she outlines where "coming out" came from, how it has been used in gay culture over time, and how it's meaning has expanded into new territory. The piece originally appeared on *The Conversation* website.

## The History of "Coming Out": From Secret Gay Code to Popular Political Protest

You probably know what it means to "come out" as gay. You may even have heard the expression used in relation to other kinds of identity, such as being undocumented.

But do you know where the term comes from? Or that its meaning has changed over time?

In my new book, *Come Out, Come Out, Whoever You Are*, I explore the history of this term, from the earliest days of the gay rights movement, to today, when it has been adopted by other movements.

### Selective sharing

In the late 19th and early 20th century, gay subculture thrived in many large American cities.

Gay men spoke of "coming out" into gay society – borrowing the term from debutante society, where elite young women came out into high society. A 1931 news article in the *Baltimore Afro-American* referred to "the coming out of new debutantes into homosexual society." It was titled "1931 Debutantes Bow at Local 'Pansy' Ball."

The 1930s, '40s and '50s witnessed a growing backlash against this visible gay world. In response, gay life became more secretive.

The Mattachine Society, the earliest important organization of what was known as the homophile movement—a precursor of the gay rights movement—took its name from mysterious medieval figures in masks. In this context, coming out meant acknowledging one's sexual orientation to oneself and to other gay people. It did not mean revealing it to the world at large.

Such selective sharing relied on code phrases—such as "family," "a club member," "a friend of Dorothy's," "a friend of Mrs. King" or "gay"—that could be used in mixed company to designate someone as homosexual.

The term "gay" was originally borrowed from the slang of women prostitutes, when they used the word to refer to women in their profession. Of course, "gay" was ultimately "outed" when the gay rights movement adopted it following the Stonewall Rebellion in 1969.

## Out in public

Coming out took on a more political meaning after the 1969 Stonewall Rebellion, in which patrons of the Stonewall Inn in New York City fought back against a police raid. The rebellion included riots and a resistance that lasted for days. It was subsequently commemorated in an annual march known today as "gay pride."

At the first Gay Liberation March in New York City in June 1970, one of the organizers stated that "we'll never have the freedom and civil rights we deserve as human beings unless we stop hiding in closets and in the shelter of anonymity."

By this time, coming out was juxtaposed with being in the closet, conveying the shame associated with hiding. By the end of the 1960s, queer people who pretended to be heterosexual were said to be "in the closet" or labeled a "closet case" or, in the case of gay men, "closet queens."

By the 1970s, mainstream journalists were already using the term beyond sexual orientation—to speak of, for instance, "closet conservatives" and "closet gourmets."

## A rite of passage

By presenting coming out as a way to end internalized self-hatred and achieve a better life, the LGBTQ movement helped to encourage people to come out, despite associated risks. It also showed how coming out could be used to build solidarity and recruit other queer people.

For instance, in 1978, in his campaign to defeat a California initiative that would have banned gay teachers from working in state public schools, openly gay elected government official Harvey Milk urged people to "Come Out, Come Out, Wherever You Are."

Milk gambled that if queer people told their friends they were gay, Californians would realize that they had friends, coworkers and family members who were gay and —out of solidarity—would oppose the proposition. The campaign helped defeat the initiative.

In the 1980s, the gay and lesbian rights movement radicalized in response to the Christian right and AIDS epidemic. Activists used the mantra "Come Out, Come Out, Wherever You Are" to demand that people declare their homosexuality. The coming out narrative became a rite of passage, something to be shared with others, and the centerpiece of gay liberation movements.

**In your face**

In the 1990s, the radical organization Queer Nation took coming out to a new level.

Its members wore T-shirts in Day-Glo colors with slogans such as "PROMOTE HOMOSEXUALITY. GENERIC QUEER. FAGGOT. MILITANT DYKE." Wearing these T-shirts, they entered heterosexual bars in New York and San Francisco and staged "kiss-ins." They visited suburban shopping malls outside these same cities and chanted, "We're here, we're queer, we're fabulous—and we're not going shopping!" Through these tactics, they not only came out, but forced heterosexuals to acknowledge their presence.

The politics of coming out has helped make LGBTQ people more visible and better protected by law. As testimony of this shift, today, marriage equality is the law of the land, the popular TV comedy "Modern Family" features a gay couple and one of the leading candidates for the 2020 Democratic presidential ticket, Pete Buttigieg, is a gay man.

To be sure, homophobia and transphobia are still alive and well. Still, LGBTQ people have made clear strides in the past half-century and coming out politics has been part of their success.

**Going bigger**

The success of the LGBTQ movement has inspired other social movements—such as the fat acceptance movement and the undocumented youth movement, among others—to also "come out."

As I show in my new book, coming out has become what sociologists call a "master frame," a way of understanding the world that is elastic and inclusive enough for a wide range of social movements to use.

For example, just as Harvey Milk urged queer people to come out for "youngsters who are becoming scared," so too the undocumented immigrant youth movement has urged undocumented youth to "come out as undocumented and unafraid."

As one of the immigrant youth movement leaders quoted in my new book explained, Milk's speech had impressed upon her and her peers that, "If you don't come out nobody's gonna know that you're there. . . . They're gonna say or do whatever they want because nobody's standing up, and you're not standing up for yourself."

26  This campaign has been effective at convincing undocumented youth to be visible, which has been crucial for political mobilization.

27  The specific language of "coming out," which is so closely associated with LGBTQ rights, allows other social movements to liken their experience to that of LGBTQ people.

28  For instance, when fat liberation activist Marilyn Wann speaks about how she "came out" as fat, she is not just speaking about a turning point in her personal biography. By using the term "coming out," she implies that being fat is like being gay—and that, just as homophobia is morally wrong, so too is "fatphobia." In this context, coming out as fat means owning one's fatness and refusing to apologize for it.

29  As my book shows, the multiple meanings of coming out—including coming into community, cultivating self-love, and collectively organizing to promote equality and justice—offer a productive way for social movements to move forward.

## Reading for Better Writing

1. *Connections:* This essay identifies a number of movements for which "coming out" has been and is important, beginning with the LGBTQ community. Do you belong to one of these communities or know someone in them? What does "coming out" mean to you personally?
2. *Comprehension:* Saguy offers readers a sociological history lesson about "coming out." In your own words, what's the origin of the phrase, how did its meaning evolve in the twentieth century, and what does it mean today?
3. *Writing Moves:*
   a. Examine this essay's title and headings: How do they work? What do they offer readers?
   b. The essay's opening briefly identifies what most people know about the phrase "coming out." How is the rest of the essay a response to that common understanding?
   c. As a sociologist, Saguy is interested in "coming out" as a tool in society; in fact, in the last section of essay, she refers to it as a "master frame." How does this concept operate as a theme running through the history of "coming out"?

**Your Project:** "Coming out the closet" is a process—a choice some people make in terms of their private and public selves. What other significant processes do people go through? What big choices? Are there specific words and phrases attached to these changes? What is the history of those phrases?

"The History of 'Coming Out': From Secret Gay Code to Popular Political Protest" by Abigail C. Saguy. Originally published by theconversation.com.

## Defining Ethnic and Racial Attitudes

Born in California of Cherokee and Greek descent, Thomas King is an essayist, a fiction writer, and an emeritus English professor at the University of Guelph. He is one of Canada's best-known Indigenous intellectuals. In 2012, he published *The Inconvenient Indian: A Curious Account of Native People in North America*, from which the excerpt below is taken. "Dead Indians" comprises the opening to the third chapter, "Too Heavy to Lift."

### Dead Indians

1  Indians come in all sorts of social and historical configurations. North American popular culture is littered with savage, noble, and dying Indians, while in real life we have Dead Indians, Live Indians, and Legal Indians.

2  Dead Indians are, sometimes, just that. Dead Indians. But the Dead Indians I'm talking about are not the deceased sort. Nor are they all that inconvenient. They are the stereotypes and clichés that North America has conjured up out of experience and out of its collective imaginings and fears. North America has had a long association with Native people, but despite the history that the two groups have shared, North America no longer sees Indians. What it sees are war bonnets, beaded shirts, fringed deerskin dresses, loincloths, headbands, feathered lances, tomahawks, moccasins, face paint, and bone chokers. These bits of cultural debris—authentic and constructed—are what literary theorists like to call "signifiers," signs that create a "simulacrum," which Jean Baudrillard, the French sociologist and postmodern theorist, succinctly explained as something that "is never that which conceals the truth—it is the truth which conceals that there is none."

3  God, I love the French theorists. For those of us who are not French theorists but who know the difference between a motor home and a single-wide trailer, a simulacrum is something that represents something that never existed. Or, in other words, the only truth of the thing is the lie itself.

4  Dead Indians.

5  You can find Dead Indians everywhere. Rodeos, powwows, movies, television commercials. At the 1973 Academy Awards, when Sacheen Littlefeather (Yaqui-Apache-Pueblo) refused the Best Actor award on behalf of Marlon Brando, she did so dressed as a Dead Indian. When U.S. Senator Benjamin Nighthorse Campbell (Northern Cheyenne) and W. Richard West, Jr. (Cheyenne-Arapaho), the director of the American Indian Museum in New York, showed up for the 2004 opening ceremonies of the museum, they took the podium in Dead Indian leathers and

feathered headdresses. Phil Fontaine (Ojibway) was attired in the same manner when he stood on the floor of the House of Commons in 2008 to receive the Canadian government's apology for the abuses of residential schools.

I probably sound testy, and I suppose part of me is. But I shouldn't be. After all, Dead Indians are the only antiquity that North America has. Europe has Greece and Rome. China has the powerful dynasties. Russia has the Cossacks. South and Central America have the Aztecs, the Incas, and the Maya.

North America has Dead Indians.

This is why Littlefeather didn't show up in a Dior gown, and why West and Campbell and Fontaine didn't arrive at their respective events in Brioni suits, Canali dress shirts, Zegni ties, and Salvatore Ferragamo shoes. Whatever cultural significance they may have for Native peoples, full feather headdresses and beaded buckskins are, first and foremost, White North America's signifiers for Indian authenticity. Their visual value at ceremonies in Los Angeles or Ottawa is—as the credit card people say—priceless.

Whites have always been comfortable with Dead Indians. General Phil Sheridan, famous for inventing the scorched-earth tactics used in Sherman's "March to the Sea," is reputed to have said, "The only good Indian I ever saw was a dead one." Sheridan denied saying this, but Theodore Roosevelt filled in for him. In a speech in New York in 1886, some sixteen years before he became president of the United States, Roosevelt said, "I suppose I should be ashamed to say that I take the Western view of the Indian. I don't go so far as to think that the only good Indians are dead Indians, but I believe nine out of every ten are, and I shouldn't like to inquire too closely into the case of the tenth."

Which brings to mind that great scene in the 1994 film *Maverick*, in which Joseph, a Native con man played by the Oneida actor Graham Greene, spends his time pandering to the puerile whims of a rich Russian grand duke, played by Paul L. Smith. Smith is on a grand tour of the West and has become a bit bored with all the back-to-nature stuff. He has shot buffalo, lived with Indians, communed with nature, and is casting about for something new and exciting to do with his time. Greene, dressed up in standard Dead Indian garb, asks Smith if he would like to try his hand at the greatest Western thrill of all.

"What's the greatest Western thrill of all?" asks Smith.

"Kill Indians," says Greene.

"Kill Indians?" says Smith. "Is that legal?"

Sure, Greene assures him, "White man been doing it for years."

So Greene gets Mel Gibson to dress up like a Dead Indian, and the grand duke gets to shoot him. The greatest Western thrill of all? You bet.

And you don't necessarily have to head west to find Dead Indians. In one of Monty Python's skits, a gas official comes into a British household with a dead Indian slung over his shoulder. The Indian, who isn't quite dead, turns out to be part of the special deal the homeowner got when he bought a new stove. The free dead Indian was "in the very small print," says the gas man, "so as not to affect the sales."

On the other hand, if you like the West and are the outdoors type, you can run out to Wyoming and pedal your bicycle over Dead Indian Pass, spend the evening at Dead Indian campground, and in the morning cycle across Dead Indian Meadows on your way to Dead Indian Peak. If you happen to be in California, you can hike Dead Indian Canyon. And if you're an angler, you can fish Dead Indian Creek in Oregon or Dead Indian Lake in Oklahoma, though the U.S. Board on Geographic Names recently voted to rename it Dead Warrior Lake.

Sometimes you can only watch and marvel at the ways in which the Dead Indian has been turned into products: Red Chief Sugar, Calumet Baking Soda, the Atlanta Braves, Big Chief Jerky, Grey Owl Wild Rice, Red Man Tobacco, the Chicago Blackhawks, Mutual of Omaha, Winnebago Motor Homes, Big Chief Tablet, Indian motorcycles, the Washington Redskins, American Spirit cigarettes, Jeep Cherokee, the Cleveland Indians, and Tomahawk missiles.

Probably the most egregious example is Crazy Horse Malt Liquor, a drink that one reviewer enthusiastically described as "smooth, slightly fruity with an extremely clean, almost Zinfandel finish that holds together all the way to the dregs of the bottle. Personally we think the chief should be proud." That the Hornell Brewing Company would even think of turning the great Oglala leader into a bottle of booze should come as no surprise. Corporate North America had already spun the Ottawa leader Pontiac into a division of General Motors, the Apache into an attack helicopter, and the Cherokee into a line of clothing and accessories.

I once bought a pair of Cherokee underpants that I was going to send to my brother as a joke, but by the time I got them home and looked at them again, they had become more embarrassing than funny.

One of my favorite Dead Indian products is Land O' Lakes butter, which features an Indian Maiden in a buckskin dress on her knees holding a box of butter at bosom level. The wag who designed the box arranged it so that if you fold the box in a certain way, the Indian woman winds up *au naturel,* sporting naked breasts. Such a clever fellow.

Of course, all of this is simply a new spin on old notions. The medicine shows that toured the West in the eighteenth and early-nineteenth centuries used Aboriginal iconography and invention to sell Dead Indian elixirs and liniments, such as Kickapoo Indian Sagwa, a "blood, liver and stomach renovator," Dr. Morse's Indian Root Pills, Dr. Pierce's Golden Medical Discovery, featuring the caption "Used by the First Americans," White Beaver's Cough Cream, Ka-Ton-Ka, and Nez Perce Catarrh Remedy.

All of this pales by comparison with the contemporary entrepreneurs who have made a bull-market business out of Dead Indian culture and spirituality. Gone are the bogus potions and rubs that marked the earlier snake oil period. They have been replaced by books that illuminate an alternative Dead Indian reality, by workshops that promise an authentic Dead Indian experience, by naked therapy sessions in a sweat lodge or a tipi that guarantee to expand your consciousness and connect you to your "inner Dead Indian." Folks such as Lynn Andrews, Mary Summer Rains, Jamie Samms, Don Le Vie, Jr., and Mary Elizabeth Marlow, just to mention some of the more prominent New Age spiritual CEOs, have manufactured fictional Dead Indian entities—Agnes Whistling Elk, Ruby Plenty Chiefs, No Eyes, Iron Thunderhorse, Barking Tree, and Max the crystal skull—who supposedly taught them the secrets of Native spirituality. They have created Dead Indian narratives that are an impossible mix of Taoism, Buddhism, Druidism, science fiction, and general nonsense, tied together with Dead Indian ceremony and sinew to give their product provenance and validity, along with a patina of exoticism.

In the late nineteenth century, Kickapoo Indian Sagwa sold for fifty cents a bottle. Today's Indian snake oil is considerably more expensive. In her article "Plastic Shamans and Astroturf Sun Dances: New Age Commercialization of Native American Spirituality," Lisa Aldred makes note of someone called Singing Pipe Woman, in Springdale, Washington, who advertises a two-week retreat with a Husichol woman priced at $2,450. A quick trip to the Internet will turn up an outfit offering a one-week "Canyon Quest and Spiritual Warrior Training" course for $850 and an eight-night program called "Vision Quest," in the tradition of someone called Stalking Wolf, "a Lipan Apache elder" who has "removed all the differences" of the vision quest, "leaving only the simple, pure format that works for everyone." There is no fee for this workshop, though a $300-$350 donation is recommended. Stalking Wolf, by the way, was supposedly born in 1873, wandered the Americas in search of spiritual truths, and finally passed all his knowledge on to Tom Brown, Jr., a seven-year-old White boy whom he met in New Jersey. Evidently, Tom Brown, Jr., or his protégés, run the workshops, having turned Stalking Wolf's teachings into a Dead Indian franchise.

From the frequency with which Dead Indians appear in advertising, in the names of businesses, as icons for sports teams, as marketing devices for everything from cleaning products to underwear, and as stalking goats for New Age spiritual flimflam, you might think that Native people were a significant target for sales. We're not, of course. We don't buy this crap. At least not enough to support such a bustling market. But there's really no need to ask whom Dead Indians are aimed at, is there?

All of which brings us to Live Indians.

### Reading for Better Writing

1. *Connections:* What is your own relationship with Indigenous culture? How does King's exploration of "Dead Indians" complicate that relationship?
2. *Comprehension:* By the end of King's essay, what did the phrase "Dead Indians" come to mean to you? Point to specific passages that led to that conclusion.
3. *Writing Moves:*
   a. In paragraphs 1-4, King begins his exploration of "Dead Indians" by complicating the phrase: placing it beside other categories, "Live" and "Legal" Indians; offering a definition that goes beyond the literal; and introducing the concept of the simulacrum. Reread these paragraphs, and then explain how these complications work to deepen your understanding of "Dead Indians."
   b. Throughout this piece, King uses anecdotes and examples to illustrate his definition of "Dead Indians." What kinds of anecdotes and examples does he use? How does he present them? What does he make of them?
   c. How would you characterize King's writing style? Consider his tone of voice, his sentence patterns, even his paragraphing—locating specific examples. What does this style contribute to King's definition of "Dead Indians"?

**Your Project:** In a sense, Thomas King creates or re-defines the phrase "Dead Indians" to expose harmful cultural stereotypes. Think of other stereotypes that exist in society and the harm they do. Can you create a phrase or redefine one to expose the heart of a stereotype? Can you "take back" a term at the center of it?

From *The Inconvenient Indian* by Thomas King (Doubleday Canada, 2012). Copyright © 2012 Thomas King. With permission of the author.

"Chapter 3: Too Heavy to Lift" from THE INCONVENIENT INDIAN: A CURIOUS ACCOUNT OF NATIVE PEOPLE IN NORTH AMERICA by Thomas King, Copyright © 2012 Thomas King. Reprinted by permission of Anchor Canada/Doubleday Canada, a division of Penguin Random House Canada Limited. All rights reserved.

##  DIY: Craft Your Own Definition Essay

### Planning

1. **Select a topic.** Review your assignment for any topic requirements. The essays in this chapter may have given you an idea for a term to define. In addition, beneath headings like these, list words that you'd like to explore:

   - Words related to an art or sport
   - Words that are (or should be) in the news
   - Words that are overused, unused, or abused
   - Words that make you laugh or worry
   - Words that do (or don't) describe you

   **Tip:** The best topics are abstract nouns *(truth, individualism)*, complex terms *(code blue, dementia)*, culturally contentious words *(conservative, liberal)*, or words connected to a personal experience *(excellence, deft, daft)*.

2. **Identify what you know.** Write freely about the word, letting your writing go where it chooses. Explore both your personal and your academic connections with the word.

3. **Gather information.** To find information about the word's history, usage, and grammatical form, use strategies such as these:

   - **Consult a general dictionary**, preferably an unabridged dictionary; list both denotative (literal) and connotative (associated) meanings for the word.
   - **Consult specialized dictionaries** that define words from specific disciplines or occupations: music, literature, law, medicine, and so on.
   - If helpful, **interview experts** on your topic.
   - **Check reference resources** such as *Bartlett's Familiar Quotations* to see how famous speakers and writers have used the word.
   - **Research the word's etymology and usage** by consulting appropriate web sources such as dictionary.com and merriam-webster.com.
   - **Do a general search on the web** to see where the word pops up in titles of songs, books, or films; company names, products, and ads; nonprofit organizations' names, campaigns, and programs; and topics in the news.
   - **List synonyms** (words meaning the same—or nearly the same) and antonyms (words meaning the opposite).

4. **Compress what you know.** Based on your freewriting and research, try writing a formal, one-sentence definition. Remember this equation:

   **Equation:** Term = larger class + distinguishing characteristics

   **Examples:** Swedish pimple = fishing lure + silver surface, tubular body, three hooks
   melodrama = stage play + flat characters, contrived plot, moralistic theme
   Alzheimer's = dementia + increasing loss of memory, hygiene, social skills

5. **Get organized.** To organize the information that you have, and to identify details that you may want to add, fill out a writing organizer like Figure 11.2.

## Drafting

6. **Draft the essay.** Review your outline as needed to write the first draft. Draw upon the writing moves you learned in this chapter.
   - **Get the reader's attention and introduce the term.** If you are organizing the essay from general to specific, consider using an anecdote, an illustration, or a quotation to set the context. If you are organizing the essay from specific to general, consider including an interesting detail from the word's history or usage. When using a dictionary definition, avoid the dusty phrase "According to *Webster* . . ."
   - **Show your readers precisely what the word means.** Build the definition in paragraphs that address distinct aspects of the word: common definitions, etymology, usage by professional writers, and so on. Consider explaining what the word is *not* to draw distinctions and prevent confusion. Link paragraphs so that the essay unfolds the word's meaning layer by layer.
   - **Review your main point and close your essay.** You might, for example, conclude by encouraging readers to use—or not use—the word.

## Revising

7. **Improve the ideas, organization, and voice.** Ask a classmate or someone from your college's writing center to read your essay for the following:
   - \_\_\_\_ **Ideas:** Is each facet of the definition **clear**, showing precisely what the word does and does not mean? Is the definition **complete**, telling readers all that they need to know in order to understand and use the word?
   - \_\_\_\_ **Organization:** Does the **opening** identify the word and set the context for what follows? Are the **middle** paragraphs cohesive, each offering a unit of information? Does the **closing** wrap up the message and refocus on the word's core meaning?
   - \_\_\_\_ **Voice:** Is the voice informed, engaging, instructive, and respectful?

## Polishing

8. **Edit the essay by addressing these issues:**
   - \_\_\_\_ **Words:** The words are precise and clear.
   - \_\_\_\_ **Sentences:** The sentences are complete, varied in structure, and readable.
   - \_\_\_\_ **Correctness:** The copy includes no errors in spelling, usage, punctuation, grammar, or mechanics.
   - \_\_\_\_ **Design:** The page design is correctly formatted and attractive.

## Publishing

9. **Publish the essay.** Share your writing with interested readers, including friends, family, and classmates. Submit the essay to your instructor.

Modes of Writing

# Definition Essays: Applications

After you have finished your definition essay, consider how to apply what you have learned in the following situations.

1. **Wise Words:** Malcolm Bradbury said, "Culture is a way of coping with the world by defining it in detail." Based on your reading of the essays in this chapter and your writing of a definition essay, explore how Bradbury's statement makes sense of what definition does.
2. **Living Today:** New devices often spawn new terms (e.g., reality TV, eBooks, digital natives, smart phones) that re-define more traditional terms. Choose such a term and explore what the traditional term meant, what the new term means, how it evolved, and how the new device has affected current practices.
3. **Major Work:** Academic disciplines and the work or professions they lead to tend to have special terms that are at the core of what they're all about. (For example, in psychology it might be *mental illness*, *personality*, or *phobia*.) Consider your major: what are two or three of those terms? Choose one and research its meaning and importance.
4. **Public Texts:** Good writing uses words, sentences, and organization that the intended readers can readily understand. To test this principle, select a term used in your discipline (e.g., *fraction, sonnet, filibuster, quorum, carpet bagger, photosynthesis, osmosis, muscle spasm*). Then using the Internet, textbooks, or library resources, find two definitions of the term: the first for high school students and the second for college students. Compare and contrast the definitions.

## Learning-Objectives Checklist ✓

Have you achieved this chapter's learning objectives? Check your progress with the following items, revisiting topics in the chapter as needed. I have . . .

\_\_\_\_ determined what a definition essay is.
\_\_\_\_ practiced techniques of definition.
\_\_\_\_ developed a strong thesis for a definition essay.
\_\_\_\_ identified writing moves and strategies for shaping my definition writing.
\_\_\_\_ crafted a strong definition essay by drawing upon a range of writing moves.

# Chapter 12

# Analytical Writing: Classification

Have you ever been pigeonholed? *All Muslims are terrorists. Christians are nothing but Bible-thumping homophobes. Feminists—they're man-haters, every one of them. Illegals are criminals. Liberals (or conservatives) are the devil's spawn.* Hmm.

Pigeonholing is the process of forcing someone or something into a little box which it doesn't really fit. It's classification based on problematic categories, gross simplification, and stereotyping.

Why do classification, then? Done ethically, it helps you and your reader make sense of large or complex sets of people, places, things, concepts, activities, and more. It helps you sort items or members of your subject into distinguishable groups. When your classification scheme is nuanced and respectful, you can understand individuals in relation to the whole, different groups in relation to each other.

## Learning Objectives

By working through this chapter, you will be able to

- explain what a classification essay is and does.
- practice principles of classification.
- develop a strong thesis for a classification essay.
- identify writing moves and strategies for shaping classification writing.
- craft a strong classification essay by drawing upon a range of writing moves.

**Visually Speaking** What does Figure 12.1 suggest about the benefits and challenges of classifying things? How might using classification in writing be similar to warehousing products?

Baloncici / Shutterstock.com

fig. 12.1

## Meeting the Mode

What does effective, ethical classification look like, and what does it accomplish for the writer and the reader? In the essay below, Hillary Gammons examines a diverse bunch of college students in the weight room. Who does she see? Why are they there? These are the questions that guide her. As you read, activate your reading skills and keep these questions in mind.

### Why We Lift

I had heard rumors about it before I ever left for college, and once I moved into the dorm, I realized it was not just a rumor. I needed a way to combat the "freshman fifteen," that dreaded poundage resulting from a combination of late-night pizzas, care-package cookies, and cafeteria cheesecakes. So, my roommate and I headed to the university gym, where the weight-training rooms are filled with student "chain gangs" sweating and clanging their way through a series of mechanical monsters. As I looked around, it became obvious that people work out for quite different reasons. Health enthusiasts, toning devotees, athletes, and bodybuilders seem to be the main categories of those lifting weights.

Some students lift weights as part of an exercise program aimed at maintaining or improving health. They have heard how strong abdominals reduce lower-back problems. They have learned that improved flexibility can help to reduce tension buildup and prevent headaches and other problems related to prolonged periods of sitting or studying. They know that combining weights with aerobic exercise is an efficient way to lose weight. A person who exercises can lose weight while continuing to eat well because increased muscle mass burns more calories. Typical weight-lifting routines for health enthusiasts are around 20 minutes, three times a week.

The toners' routine is different because they want smoothly defined muscles. Not surprisingly, this group includes many young women. Lifting weights can target problem spots and help shape up the body. To develop solid arms, these people use dumbbells and a bench press. Other equipment focuses on achieving toned legs, abdominals, and buttocks. Toning workouts must be done more often than three times a week. I talked to a few young women who lift weights (after aerobic activity of some kind) for about 30 minutes, five times a week.

Athletes also lift weights. Volleyball, rowing, basketball, football—all these sports require weight training. It may seem obvious that a football player needs to be muscular and strong, but how do other athletes benefit from weight lifting? Muscles are a lot like brains: the more they are used, the more they can do. Strong muscles can increase a person's speed, flexibility, endurance, and coordination. Consider the competition required in various sports—different muscle groups matter more to different athletes. For example, while runners, especially sprinters, need bulging thighs for quick starts and speed, basketball players need powerful arms and shoulders for endless shots and passes. And while gymnasts want overall muscle strength for balance and coordination, football players develop large muscles for strength, speed, and agility. For all members of this group, weight lifting is a vital part of their training.

One last group that cannot be ignored are the people who lift weights to become as big and strong as possible. I worked out with a guy who is about 6 feet 2 inches and weighs more than 200 pounds. He bench-presses more than I weigh. In a room devoted to dumbbells and barbells (also known as free weights), bodybuilders roar bulk-boosting battle cries as they struggle to lift super heavy bars. After you spend only a short time in this grunt room, it is clear that the goal for bodybuilders is not simply to be healthy, toned, or strong. These lifters want muscles for both strength and show—muscles that lift and bulge. For this reason, many participants spend little time on aerobic activity and most of their time lifting very heavy weights that build bulk and strength. My partner works out for an hour or more, five days a week.

Not everyone fits neatly into these four categories. I work out to be healthy and toned, and find that I can benefit from lifting only three times a week. Weight lifting has become more and more popular among college students who appreciate exercise as a great stress reliever. And for me, the gym proves to be the best place to combat the dreaded "freshman fifteen."

## Converse with the Mode

So, what did a visit to the weight room teach you about classification? First, questions direct classification, guiding what you wish to sort out. Second, classification is systematic: it seeks to make sense of all the possibilities. Third, it is respectful, especially when focusing on people. To advance the conversation, explore these questions about "Why We Lift."

### Conversation Starters

1. Hillary separates the weight lifters into four groups: health enthusiasts, toners, athletes, and body builders. What strategies does she use to identify each group and distinguish it from the others?
2. Why do you think Hillary ordered the groups as she did, and how does she transition from one group to the next?
3. Because Hillary classifies people, she must do so respectfully and ethically. Does she? If yes, how so? If not, what problems do you notice?

**Moving On:** The author classifies a group of people with whom she is familiar. What groups do you know or belong to? Gamers? Social activists? Film buffs? To start your thinking about possible topics for a classification essay, brainstorm a list of these groups.

# Strategies for Writing Classification Essays

In classification writing, you create logical categories for grouping people, places, things, or concepts. Categorization makes sense of a body of information by showing how members of the group are both related and differentiated. Classification, then, can reveal something about the larger body structure of the whole, the nature of a particular category, or the distinctive features of one member of the larger body. Use the following strategies to classify effectively.

## The Rhetorical Situation

Consider the context in which you are using classification reasoning:

- **Purpose:** You might classify a body of information to explain its order, to clarify relationships, and to "locate" specific items within a larger structure. For example, in her essay, "Latin American Music: A Diverse and Unifying Force," Kathleen Marsh's purpose is to explain how the many types of Latin American music reflect Latinxs' cultural identity and impact social change.
- **Readers:** While your readership can vary, you can classify to illuminate the deeper order of a topic, either to enhance your readers' understanding or to support an argument. For example, Marsh's classification of Latin American music helps her readers understand the history and cultural impact of Latinxs' diverse music.
- **Topic:** Writers typically use classification with topics that include a complex body of individual items. For example, Marsh's topic is the nature and function of Latin American music—thousands of songs. To address the topic, she sorts the songs into four categories that clarify music's diverse roles in Latinx culture.

## Principles of Classification Writing

Classification writing depends on the principles that follow.

**Establishing clear criteria for grouping.** In order to classify, you need a basis or standard for categorizing items. This standard becomes the "common denominator" for the ordering scheme. For example, trees could be grouped as follows:

- **Size:** types of trees grouped by height categories
- **Geography:** trees common to different areas, zones, or elevations
- **Structure or composition:** division by leaf type (deciduous vs. coniferous)
- **Purpose:** windbreak trees, shade trees, flowering trees, fruit trees, etc.

**Creating a logical and orderly classification scheme.** These guidelines apply:
- As you sort items into groups, you should seek . . .

  - **consistency**—applying the same sorting criterion in the same way.
  - **exclusivity**—creating groups that are distinct and do not overlap.
  - **completeness**—fitting all elements from a larger body into the categories with no elements left over.

- To keep the classification structure manageable, writers usually limit the number of main categories to six.
- Subcategories distinguish the elements that comprise a category. To further distinguish elements within the whole, you can break subcategories into smaller groups. (See Figure 12.2.)
- When explaining the classification scheme, writers present the categories and subcategories in a logical order, selecting a sequence that will help readers digest the overall scheme and see connections and differences between categories.
- When classifying ideas or theoretical practices, writers might illustrate each. For example, in "Four Ways to Talk About Literature," John Van Rys identifies approaches to literary criticism. He then illustrates each one by describing how a critic using it might critique the poem, "My Last Duchess."

### Sample Classification Paragraph

The following paragraph is from the essay cited above. Note how Van Rys first describes the fourth approach to literary criticism, and then gives an example of each subgroup in it.

> The fourth approach to criticism applies ideas outside of literature to literary works. Because literature mirrors life, argue these critics, disciplines that explore human life can help us understand literature. Some critics, for example, apply psychological theories to literary works by exploring dreams, symbolic meanings, and motivation. Myth or archetype criticism uses insights from psychology, cultural anthropology, and classical studies to explore a text's universal appeal. Moral criticism, rooted in religious studies and ethics, explores the moral dilemmas literary works raise. Connecting literature and environmental studies, ecocriticism examines the nature-culture relationship expressed by literary texts, the importance of the natural world to them. Marxist, feminist, minority, and postcolonial criticism are, broadly speaking, sociological approaches to interpretation. While the Marxist examines the themes of class struggle, economic power, and social justice in texts, the feminist critic explores the just and unjust treatment of women as well as the effect of gender on language, reading, and the literary canon. The critic interested in race and ethnic identity explores similar issues, with the focus shifted to a specific cultural group, while the postcolonial critic examines the dynamics of colonialism found in literature of formerly colonized people.

## Patterns for Classification Essays: Thesis Thinking

As in "Why We Lift," the thesis for a classification essay can be patterned as an answer to the essential question you are asking about the subject.

> ***Example:*** In this example, the writer signals with his thesis that readers can approach discussing literary works from one of four angles.
>
> There are four main perspectives, or approaches, that readers can use to converse about literature.

**A Thesis Template:** If it helps, try this pattern for your thesis.

> To understand [question or issue about topic A], we can look at how it is divided into these categories: [group 1, group 2, group 3, etc.]
>
> *Example:* To understand how games and sports work to engage people who play and watch them, we can look at how these activities come in types: open-information, closed-information, and some combination of open and closed.

**From Weak to Strong:** Strive for an excellent thesis, aim for a good one, avoid a poor one.

> *Weak Thesis:* oversimplified, incomplete, binary thinking, "pigeonholing"
>
> There are only two kinds of marriages—good ones and bad ones.
>
> *Good Thesis:* establishes consistent, exclusive, and complete categories
>
> Historically, marriages have been formed through two types of ceremonies: civil or religious, or some combination of both. And such marriages have fallen into two broad categories: monogamous and polygamous.
>
> *Excellent Thesis:* offers complexity, nuance, depth, surprise
>
> For hundreds of years, marriage was understood in one form—a monogamous union between a man and a woman, legally binding; however, since the sexual revolution of the 1960s and 70s, new marital arrangements have emerged to challenge the traditional view: common law marriage, gay marriage, nonbinary relationships, polygamy, and open marriage.

## Patterns for Classification Essays: Writing Moves

A common method of organizing a classification essay is by breaking down the topic into main categories and treating each in turn. To plan your essay, you must ask what order of categories makes the most sense, and why. To help you map out this organization, try a line diagram (Figure 12.2) or a classification blueprint (Figure 12.3).

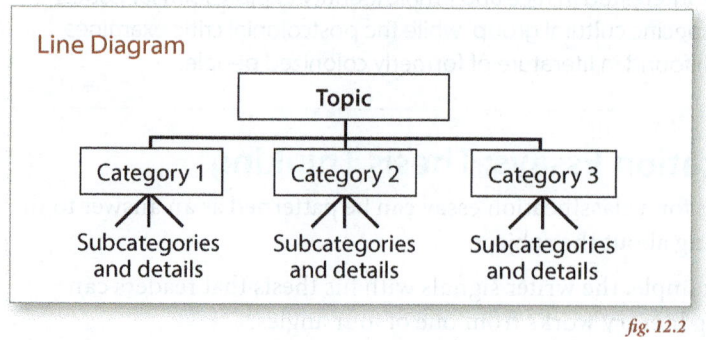

*fig. 12.2*

*fig. 12.3*

# Classification Essays: Learning Writers' Moves

To learn more writing moves for classification writing, read the essays that follow. The first uses classification to explore both the breadth and heart of Latin American music, the second to distinguish types of artificial intelligence so readers can understand this emerging knowledge, and the third to explain approaches to reading literature for students. By reading these essays, you'll also be able to add to the list of possible topics for your own essay.

## Analyzing Forms of Music

In the essay below, student writer Kathleen Marsh uses classification strategies to describe the nature of Latin American music and to explain how the music both reflects and affects Latin American culture.

### Latin American Music: A Diverse and Unifying Force

On September 20, 2009, Latin pop, rock, and salsa rhythms danced through the air in Havana's Plaza de la Revolución as more than one million people gathered to witness Paz Sin Fronteras II (Peace Without Borders II). These benefit concerts brought together performers from Cuba, Puerto Rico, Ecuador, and Venezuela. Juanes, a popular Colombian singer who headlined the concerts, explained the event's passion and power like this: "Music becomes an excuse to send a message that we're all here together building peace, that we are here as citizens and this is what we want, and we have to be heard" (Hispanic 17). His statement demonstrates Latinxs' belief that their music has the power to unify Latin American people, synthesize their cultural activities, and address their diverse needs. To understand how the music (which is as diverse as Latin America's people) can do this, it is helpful to sort the many forms of music into four major types and consider what each type contributes to Latin American society.

One type is indigenous music, a group of musical forms that connect the human and the spiritual. Archeological evidence indicates that indigenous musical cultures of the Americas began over 30,000 years ago. Over time the first instruments, which were stone and clay sound-producing objects, evolved into wind instruments such as flutes and windpipes. An example of indigenous music connecting the human and spiritual is found among Aymara-speaking musicians in the Lake Titicaca region of

Peru. The people of this region use music to mesh pre-Columbian agricultural rites with current Catholic practices. For instance, during feasts such as the annual Fiesta de la Candelaria (Candlemas Feast), celebrants use Sicus (panpipes), pincullos (vertical duct flutes), cajas (drums), chants, dances, and costumes—in combination with Catholic symbolism—to celebrate the gift of staple crops such as corn and potatoes (Indigenous 328, 330).

A second type, Iberian and Mestizo (mixed) folk music, enriches Latinxs' everyday lives in a variety of forms, including liturgical music, working songs, and mariachi tunes. For example, whereas the traditional Catholic mass featured organ music, more recent Catholic services such as the Nicaraguan Peasant Mass use the acoustic guitar along with the colorful sounds of the marimba, maracas, and melodies from popular festivals. As a result, worshipers find the music inviting and the passionate lyrics (which can cite issues of economic or political injustice) socially relevant.

"A second type, Iberian and Mestizo (mixed) folk music, enriches Latinxs' everyday lives in a variety of forms, including liturgical music, working songs, and mariachi tunes."

Another form of folk music known as tonadas (or tunes) are used as serenades and working songs. For example, in Venezuela, workers might whistle or sing tonadas while milking, plowing, or fishing (Tonadas): These vocal duets, which also can be accompanied by guitar, have pleasant harmonies, two main melodies, and faster tempos ("Iberian and mestizo folk music" 338, 341).

The mariachi band, a final form of folk music, adds festivity to Mexicans' many celebrations. With its six to eight violins, two trumpets, and a guitar, the band creates a vibrant, engaging sound. During birthdays or feast days, these bands commonly set up on streets and below windows where they awaken the residents above to the sounds of "Las Mañanitas," the traditional song for such days. Mariachis are also hired for baptisms, weddings, quinceañeras (the fifteenth birthday for a Mexican girl), patriotic holidays, and funerals (History of the Mariachi).

Afro-American music, the third type of Latin American music, infuses passion and power in its percussion-driven dances and complex rhythm structures. These songs and dances, performed throughout the Caribbean, function as an entertaining, unifying force among Latin people ("Afro-American" 345–46). The energy of Afro-American music is clear in genres such as the mambo and the rumba dances. The rumba, an Afro-Caribbean dance, is highly improvisational and exciting. The quinto (a high-pitched drum) establishes a dialogue with a solo voice and challenges the male dancer, while the tumbadora and palitos (sticks on woodblock) provide a contrast with regular, unchanging rhythm patterns.

The mambo, an Afro-Cuban dance, became popular in Havana, Cuba. In the 1940s, nightclubs throughout Latin America caught the energy of this fast tempo song and dance. Arsenio Rodríguez' "Bruca Managuá" exemplifies this form. Because of the song's sound and lyrics, many Black Cubans consider the piece to be an anthem of Afro-Cuban pride and resistance:

> I am Calabrí, black by birth/nation,
> Without freedom, I can't live,
> Too much abuse, the body is going to die.
> *(Oxford Encyclopedia for Latinos and Latinas in the United States.* 218)

Urban popular music, the fourth type of Latin American music, combines a dynamic sound with poignant appeals for social change, appeals that resonate with many listeners. The styles of this type of music include rock, heavy metal, punk, hip-hop, jazz, reggae, and R&B. During the September 20, 2009, Paz Sin Fronteras II concerts described earlier, urban popular music was common fare. As U.S. representative Jim McGovern observed, the message of the concerts was to "circumvent politics . . . using the medium of music to speak directly to young people, to change their way of thinking, and leave behind the old politics, hatred, prejudices, and national enmities that have locked too many people in patterns of conflict, violence, poverty, and despair. It is an attempt to break down barriers and ask people to join in common purpose" (Paz Sin Fronteras II). Popular urban musicians such as Juanes utilize music not only to entertain but also to unite Latinxs in a universal cause.

Passion and power permeate all of Latin America's music. The four major types of music—indigenous, Iberian and Mestizo folk, Afro-American, and popular urban—are as diverse as the people of Latin America, and each style serves a valued need or function in the everyday lives of Latinx people. As a result, those listening to Latin American music—whether it is an indigenous Peruvian chant, a Venezuelan farmer's whistled tune, a Cuban mambo drummer's vivacious beat, or the Bogotá rock concert's compelling rhythms—are hearing much more than music. They are hearing the passion and power of the Latin American people.

**Note:** The Works Cited page is not shown. For an example, see chapter 23.

## Reading for Better Writing

1. *Connections:* In her essay, Kathleen Marsh identifies four broad categories of Latin music, examining specific genres and songs within each group. How does Marsh's essay speak to your own musical tastes? If you were to categorize what you listen to and/or why, what would be revealed?
2. *Comprehension:* Review the opening in which Marsh introduces her topic, thesis, and choice to sort the music into four categories. What is the main point of her classification scheme for Latin American music? Describe her categories and what is distinctive about each.
3. *Writing Moves:*
    a. What strategies does Marsh use to distinguish the four types of music and the various forms within those groups? Are the strategies effective?
    b. Identify words with which she describes the tone and tenor of the music. Is the word choice helpful?
    c. Review the "Strategies for Writing Classification Essays" from earlier in this chapter, particularly the three guidelines for creating a logical classification scheme: consistency, exclusivity, and completeness. Then analyze Marsh's classification scheme and explain why it does or does not exemplify the three guidelines.
    d. In the last sentence, Marsh re-states and re-phrases the thesis. Is this sentence an effective closing?

**Your Project:** For your own writing, consider areas of culture similar to Latin American music. For example, you could categorize varieties of American music, or you could examine TV programs, video games, films, or fiction.

"Latin American Music: A Diverse and Unifying Force" by Kathleen Marsh. Used by permission of the author.

# Analyzing Artificial Intelligence

Arend Hintze is a professor at Michigan State University in the department of Integrative Biology and Computer Science and Engineering, where he does research into artificial intelligence (AI). In this article from *The Conversation*, he introduces current forms of AI and indicates where AI might be going in terms of new forms.

### Understanding the Four Types of AI: From Reactive Robots to Self-Aware Beings

1. The common, and recurring, view of the latest breakthroughs in artificial intelligence research is that sentient and intelligent machines are just on the horizon. Machines understand verbal commands, distinguish pictures, drive cars and play games better than we do. How much longer can it be before they walk among us?

2. The new White House report on artificial intelligence takes an appropriately skeptical view of that dream. It says the next 20 years likely won't see machines "exhibit broadly-applicable intelligence comparable to or exceeding that of humans," though it does go on to say that in the coming years, "machines will reach and exceed human performance on more and more tasks." But its assumptions about how those capabilities will develop missed some important points.

3. As an AI researcher, I'll admit it was nice to have my own field highlighted at the highest level of American government, but the report focused almost exclusively on what I call "the boring kind of AI." It dismissed in half a sentence my branch of AI research, into how evolution can help develop ever-improving AI systems, and how computational models can help us understand how our human intelligence evolved.

4. The report focuses on what might be called mainstream AI tools: machine learning and deep learning. These are the sorts of technologies that have been able to play "Jeopardy!" well, and beat human Go masters at the most complicated game ever invented. These current intelligent systems are able to handle huge amounts of data and make complex calculations very quickly. But they lack an element that will be key to building the sentient machines we picture having in the future.

5. We need to do more than teach machines to learn. We need to overcome the boundaries that define the four different types of artificial intelligence, the barriers that separate machines from us—and us from them.

### Type I AI: Reactive Machines

6. The most basic types of AI systems are purely reactive, and have the ability neither to form memories nor to use past experiences to inform current decisions.

Deep Blue, IBM's chess-playing supercomputer, which beat international grandmaster Garry Kasparov in the late 1990s, is the perfect example of this type of machine.

Deep Blue can identify the pieces on a chess board and know how each moves. It can make predictions about what moves might be next for it and its opponent. And it can choose the most optimal moves from among the possibilities.

But it doesn't have any concept of the past, nor any memory of what has happened before. Apart from a rarely used chess-specific rule against repeating the same move three times, Deep Blue ignores everything before the present moment. All it does is look at the pieces on the chess board as it stands right now, and choose from possible next moves.

This type of intelligence involves the computer perceiving the world directly and acting on what it sees. It doesn't rely on an internal concept of the world. In a seminal paper, AI researcher Rodney Brooks argued that we should only build machines like this. His main reason was that people are not very good at programming accurate simulated worlds for computers to use, what is called in AI scholarship a "representation" of the world.

The current intelligent machines we marvel at either have no such concept of the world, or have a very limited and specialized one for their particular duties. The innovation in Deep Blue's design was not to broaden the range of possible moves the computer considered. Rather, the developers found a way to narrow its view, to stop pursuing some potential future moves, based on how it rated their outcome. Without this ability, Deep Blue would have needed to be an even more powerful computer to actually beat Kasparov. Similarly, Google's AlphaGo, which has beaten top human Go experts, can't evaluate all potential future moves either. Its analysis method is more sophisticated than Deep Blue's, using a neural network to evaluate game developments.

These methods do improve the ability of AI systems to play specific games better, but they can't be easily changed or applied to other situations. These computerized imaginations have no concept of the wider world—meaning they can't function beyond the specific tasks they're assigned and are easily fooled.

They can't interactively participate in the world, the way we imagine AI systems one day might. Instead, these machines will behave exactly the same way every time they encounter the same situation. This can be very good for ensuring an AI system is trustworthy: You want your autonomous car to be a reliable driver. But it's bad if we want machines to truly engage with, and respond to, the world. These simplest AI systems won't ever be bored, or interested, or sad.

### Type II AI: Limited Memory

This Type II class contains machines that can look into the past. Self-driving cars do some of this already. For example, they observe other cars' speed and direction. That can't be done in just one moment, but rather requires identifying specific objects and monitoring them over time.

These observations are added to the self-driving cars' preprogrammed representations of the world, which also include lane markings, traffic lights and other important elements, like curves in the road. They're included when the car decides when to change lanes, to avoid cutting off another driver or being hit by a nearby car.

But these simple pieces of information about the past are only transient. They aren't saved as part of the car's library of experience it can learn from, the way human drivers compile experience over years behind the wheel.

So how can we build AI systems that build full representations, remember their experiences and learn how to handle new situations? Brooks was right in that it is very difficult to do this. My own research into methods inspired by Darwinian evolution can start to make up for human shortcomings by letting the machines build their own representations.

### Type III AI: Theory of Mind

We might stop here, and call this point the important divide between the machines we have and the machines we will build in the future. However, it is better to be more specific to discuss the types of representations machines need to form, and what they need to be about.

Machines in the next, more advanced, class not only form representations about the world, but also about other agents or entities in the world. In psychology, this is called "theory of mind"—the understanding that people, creatures and objects in the world can have thoughts and emotions that affect their own behavior.

This is crucial to how we humans formed societies, because they allowed us to have social interactions. Without understanding each other's motives and intentions, and without taking into account what somebody else knows either about me or the environment, working together is at best difficult, at worst impossible.

If AI systems are indeed ever to walk among us, they'll have to be able to understand that each of us has thoughts and feelings and expectations for how we'll be treated. And they'll have to adjust their behavior accordingly.

### Type IV AI: Self-Awareness

The final step of AI development is to build systems that can form representations about themselves. Ultimately, we AI researchers will have to not only understand consciousness, but build machines that have it.

This is, in a sense, an extension of the "theory of mind" possessed by Type III artificial intelligences. Consciousness is also called "self-awareness" for a reason. ("I want that item" is a very different statement from "I know I want that item.") Conscious beings are aware of themselves, know about their internal states, and are able to predict feelings of others. We assume someone honking behind us in traffic is angry or impatient, because that's how we feel when we honk at others. Without a theory of mind, we could not make those sorts of inferences.

While we are probably far from creating machines that are self-aware, we should focus our efforts toward understanding memory, learning, and the ability to base decisions on past experiences. This is an important step to understand human intelligence on its own. And it is crucial if we want to design or evolve machines that are more than exceptional at classifying what they see in front of them.

## Reading for Better Writing

1. *Connections:* Do you see artificial intelligence at work in your own life, or is it invisible? Do you see it as having great potential, great danger, or both?
2. *Comprehension:* What is AI? For each of the four types of AI, offer a brief definition in your own words. Using the article headings, your definitions might begin this way: "A reactive machine is one that . . . ."
3. *Writing Moves:*
   a. Hintze opens by describing the common view of AI and the view of a White House report on the topic. How does he present these, and how do they set up the direction he takes in the rest of his introduction?
   b. How is the fifth paragraph a kind of thesis paragraph?
   c. How would you characterize the order in which Hintze presents the four types of AI? Why does this order make sense?
   d. Within each category, what does Hintze do to make the complicated science of AI understandable for general readers?
   e. Re-read the closing paragraph. How does it relate to Hintze's thesis about AI?

**Your Project:** In the recent past, where else have you seen or experienced innovations? Think of broad fields such as entertainment, manufacturing, travel, food, education, and so on. Could you categorize the types of innovations in one of these?

"Understanding the four types of AI, from reactive robots to self-aware beings" by Arend Hintze of Michigan State University. Originally appeared at TheConversation.com.

## Approaches to Literary Criticism

In the following essay, Professor John Van Rys describes four schools of (or approaches to) literary criticism. He then illustrates each approach by describing how a critic using it might analyze Robert Browning's poem, "My Last Duchess."

### Four Ways to Talk About Literature

Have you ever been in a conversation in which you suddenly felt lost—out of the loop? Perhaps you feel that way in your literature class. You may think a poem or short story means one thing, and then your instructor suddenly pulls out the "hidden meaning." Joining the conversation about literature—in class or in an essay—may indeed seem daunting, but you can do it if you know what to look for and what to talk about. There are four main perspectives, or approaches, that you can use to converse about literature.

Text-centered approaches focus on the literary piece itself. Often called *formalist criticism*, such approaches claim that the structure of a work and the rules of its genre are crucial to its meaning. The formalist critic determines how various elements (plot, character, language, and so on) reinforce the meaning and unify the work. For example, the formalist may ask the following questions concerning Robert Browning's poem "My Last Duchess": How do the main elements in the poem—irony, symbolism, and verse form—help develop the main theme (deception)? How does Browning use the dramatic monologue genre in this poem?

Audience-centered approaches focus on the "transaction" between text and reader—the dynamic way the reader interacts with the text. Often called *rhetorical* or *reader-response criticism*, these approaches see the text not as an object to be analyzed, but as an activity that is different for each reader. A reader-response critic might ask these questions of "My Last Duchess": How does the reader become aware of the duke's true nature if it's never actually stated? Do men and women read the poem differently? Who were Browning's original readers?

Author-centered approaches focus on the origins of a text (the writer and the historical background). For example, an author-centered study examines the writer's life—showing connections, contrasts, and conflicts between their life and the writing. Broader historical studies explore social and intellectual currents, showing links between an author's work and the ideas, events, and institutions of that period.

Finally, the literary historian may make connections between the text in question and earlier and later literary works. The author-centered critic might ask these questions of "My Last Duchess": What were Browning's views of marriage, men and women, art, class, and wealth? As an institution, what was marriage like in Victorian England (Browning's era) or Renaissance Italy (the duke's era)? Who was the historical Duke of Ferrara?

The fourth approach to criticism applies ideas outside of literature to literary works. Because literature mirrors life, argue these critics, disciplines that explore human life can help us understand literature. Some critics, for example, apply psychological theories to literary works by exploring dreams, symbolic meanings, and motivation. Myth or archetype criticism uses insights from psychology, cultural anthropology, and classical studies to explore a text's universal appeal. Moral criticism, rooted in religious studies and ethics, explores the moral dilemmas literary works raise. Connecting literature and environmental studies, ecocriticism examines the nature-culture relationship expressed by literary texts, the importance of the natural world to them. Marxist, feminist, minority, and postcolonial criticism are, broadly speaking, sociological approaches to interpretation. While the Marxist examines the themes of class struggle, economic power, and social justice in texts, the feminist critic explores the just and unjust treatment of women as well as the effect of gender on language, reading, and the literary canon. The critic interested in race and ethnic identity explores similar issues, with the focus shifted to a specific cultural group, while the postcolonial critic examines the dynamics of colonialism found in literature of formerly colonized people.

Such ideological criticism might ask a wide variety of questions about "My Last Duchess": What does the poem reveal about the duke's psychological state and his personality? How does the reference to Neptune deepen the poem? What does the poem suggest about the nature of evil and injustice? In what ways are the duke's motives class-based and economic? How does the poem present the duke's power and the duchess's weakness? What is the status of women in this society?

If you look at the variety of questions critics might ask about "My Last Duchess," you see both the diversity of critical approaches and the common ground between them. In fact, interpretive methods actually share important characteristics: (1) a close attention to literary elements such as character, plot, symbolism, and metaphor; (2) a desire not to distort the work; and (3) a sincere concern for increasing interest in and understanding of a text. In actual practice, critics may develop a hybrid approach to criticism, one that matches their individual questions and concerns about a text. Now that you're familiar with some of the questions defining literary criticism, exercise your own curiosity (and join the ongoing literary dialogue) by discussing a text that genuinely interests you.

## Reading for Better Writing

1. *Connections:* How would you describe yourself as a reader? What types of writing do you enjoy, and how do you typically go about reading those works? How do your reading practices relate to the types of "conversation" described in this essay? Does this essay encourage you to change or broaden your reading habits in particular ways?

2. *Comprehension:* Briefly outline the four approaches to interpretation described in this essay—their focus, goals, and methods.

3. *Writing Moves:*
   a. In the opening paragraph, Van Rys creates a focus; he also establishes a tone and an approach to the topic. How would you characterize that tone and approach? What strategies does the writer use to engage readers?
   b. In introducing the four approaches to reading, Van Rys follows the same pattern with each. Describe that pattern and explain how it works to clarify each category.
   c. Van Rys uses a poem to illustrate the four critical approaches. How does the illustration clarify the discussion? Does the illustration work even if the reader hasn't read the poem?
   d. Examine the order in which the writer examines the four categories. What is the effect of following this specific order? Is there a particular logic or progression? How is the presentation of the fourth category different from the previous three?
   e. How does the closing paragraph enrich or complicate the discussion of the approaches? In what way do the introduction and conclusion frame the essay?

**Your Project:** Consider testing a critical approach more fully by analyzing some dimension of "My Last Duchess" by Robert Browning. (You can access the poem online by searching for the title and author.)

"Four Ways to Talk About Literature" by John Van Rys. Used by permission of the author.

#  DIY: Craft Your Own Classification Essay

## Planning

1. **Select a topic.** If your assignment does not specify or restrict your topic choice, review the project options listed at the end of each sample essay. For more topic ideas, write a few general headings like the academic headings in Figure 12.4; then list two or three related topics under each heading. Finally, pick a topic that is characterized by a larger set of items or members that can best be explained by ordering them into categories.

| Engineering | Biology | Social Work | Education |
|---|---|---|---|
| Machines | Whales | Child welfare | Learning styles |
| Bridges | Fruits | Organizations | Testing Methods |

*fig. 12.4*

2. **Look at the big picture.** Review the parameters of your assignment. Then start your preliminary research to get an overview of your topic. Review your purpose (to explain, persuade, inform, and so on), and consider which classification criteria will help you divide the subject's content into distinct, understandable categories.

3. **Choose and test your criteria.** Choose criteria for creating categories. Make sure they produce groups that are *consistent* (the same criteria are used throughout the sorting process), *exclusive* (groups are distinct—no member fits into more than one group), and *complete* (each member fits into a group with no member left over). Especially if your focus is groups of people, ensure that your categories are ethically sound— nuanced and respectful, no pigeonholing.

4. **Gather and organize information.** Gather information from reliable sources. To organize your information, take notes, possibly using a classification grid like the one shown in Figure 12.5. Set up the grid by listing the classification criteria down the left column and listing the groups in the top row of the columns. Then fill in the grid with appropriate details. (The grid in Figure 12.5 lists classification criteria and groups discussed in "Latin American Music: A Diverse and Unifying Force.")

| Classification Criteria | Group #1 | Group #2 | Group #3 | Group #4 |
|---|---|---|---|---|
| | Indigenous music | Iberian and Mestizo | Afro-American music | Urban popular music |
| Historical qualities/functions | • Trait #1<br>• Trait #2<br>• Trait #3 | • Trait #1<br>• Trait #2<br>• Trait #3 | • Trait #1<br>• Trait #2<br>• Trait #3 | • Trait #1<br>• Trait #2<br>• Trait #3 |

*fig. 12.5*

5. **Draft a thesis.** Draft a working thesis that states your topic and identifies your classification scheme. Include language introducing your criteria for classifying groups.

## Drafting

6. **Draft the essay.** Write your first draft, using the organization you planned in step four and writing moves you learned in this chapter.
    - **Opening:** Get the readers' attention, introduce the subject and thesis, and give your criteria for dividing the subject into categories.
    - **Middle:** Develop the thesis by discussing each category, explaining its traits, and showing how it is distinct from the other groups. For example, in the middle section of "Four Ways to Talk About Literature," Van Rys first shows the unique focus of each of the four approaches to literary criticism, and then illustrates each approach by applying it to the same poem, "My Last Duchess."
    - **Closing:** Reflect on and tie together the classification scheme. While the opening and middle of the essay separate the subject into distinct categories, the closing may bring the groups back together. For example, Van Rys closes by identifying characteristics that the four subgroups have in common.

## Revising

7. **Improve the ideas, organization, and voice.** Ask a classmate or someone from the writing center to read your essay, looking for the following:
    - ___ **Ideas:** Are the classification criteria logical and clear, resulting in categories that are consistent, exclusive, and complete? Do appropriate examples clarify the nature and function of each group? Do you avoid oversimplification and stereotypes? Do you acknowledge possible exceptions or changes to your criteria?
    - ___ **Organization:** Does the essay include (1) an engaging opening that introduces the subject, thesis, and classification criteria, (2) a well-organized middle that distinguishes groups, shows why each group is unique, and supports these claims with evidence, and (3) a unifying closing that restates the thesis and its relevance?
    - ___ **Voice:** Is the tone informed, respectful, and reasonable?

## Polishing

8. **Edit the essay.** Polish your writing by addressing these issues:
    - ___ **Words:** The words distinguishing classifications are defined clearly and used uniformly.
    - ___ **Sentences:** The sentences and paragraphs are complete, varied, and clear.
    - ___ **Correctness:** No usage, grammatical, or mechanical errors are present.

## Publishing

9. **Publish the essay** by sharing it with your instructor and classmates, publishing it on a website, or submitting it to a print or online journal.

# Classification Essays: Applications

After you have finished your classification essay, consider how to apply what you have learned in the following situations.

1. **Living Today:** Unscrupulous news sites and blogs published online often include articles based on an erroneous claim that a complex topic is "simply" a two-option issue. This type of claim, called either-or thinking, is a logical fallacy. Choose a complex topic and research the web to find such an either-or argument. Then find a piece that categorizes positions in a more nuanced way.
2. **Sports Talk:** Fully understanding a sport or game requires knowing how it is played, including the rules. Choose a sport or game that you enjoy, and create a classification scheme for different types of plays or moves. How does your scheme help you understand that sport or game?
3. **Social Situation:** Frequently, social sciences categorize people into generations. Here, for example, is a common scheme: (a) Generation Z/Boomlets, born after 2001; (b) Generation Y/Millennial, born between 1981 and 2000 (c) Generation X, born between 1965 and 1980, (d) Baby Boomers, born between 1946 and 1964, and (e) Mature/Silents, born between 1927 and 1945. Given your own experience, describe what characterizes each generation, consider what generation you belong to, and reflect on the strengths and limits of the generation concept.

## Learning-Objectives Checklist ✓

Have you achieved this chapter's learning objectives? Check your progress with the following items, revisiting topics in the chapter as needed. I have . . .

\_\_\_\_ determined what a classification essay is and does.
\_\_\_\_ practiced principles of classification, including those focused on its limits.
\_\_\_\_ developed a strong thesis for a classification essay.
\_\_\_\_ identified writing moves and strategies for shaping classification writing.
\_\_\_\_ crafted a strong classification essay by drawing upon a range of writing moves.

# Chapter 13

# Analytical Writing: Process

Have you ever followed a recipe that led to a delicious dish? Then you've been the beneficiary of good process writing. Have you ever cursed and swore as you attempted to assemble a piece of furniture by following confusing instructions? Sorry, but you've been the victim of poor process writing.

Process writing such as recipes and instructions guide readers step by step to complete a task. But process writing can focus as well on understanding a series of related events that unfold in time—which is essentially what a process is. As you'll see in this chapter, the world is filled with processes—natural, historical, and mechanical. Your goals as a process writer are to explain the nature of the process and map out its steps clearly and accurately.

This chapter, then, will help you do process analysis that benefits your reader—not the kind that gets you cussed out.

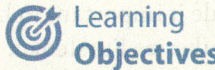

## Learning Objectives

By working through this chapter, you will be able to

- explain what a process essay is and what forms it might take.
- practice techniques for analyzing processes.
- develop a strong thesis for a process essay.
- identify writing moves and strategies for shaping process writing.
- craft a strong process essay by drawing upon a range of writing moves.

**Visually Speaking**  Figure 13.1 captures a moment in a process. What is the process, and what writing strategies would you use to explain how to do the process?

Tyler Olson / Shutterstock.com

fig. 13.1

# Meeting the Mode

What does process writing look like? One place to begin is with student writer Andrea Santiago's "American Lumpia: Filipino Egg Roll." Andrea wrote this essay for an assignment asking her to explain a recipe but also explore the history—the people, culture, and foods—that made it important to her. (The assignment was inspired, in part, by the food writings of Nina Mukerjee Furstenau, whose essay on yogurt appears later in this chapter.) As you read Andrea's essay, activate the reading strategies you learned in chapter 2, and consider these questions: What processes (related events unfolding in time) does Andrea present, and how does she present them?

### American Lumpia: Filipino Egg Roll

1. The San Francisco Bay area is my home—a center of diversity and culture in every way, especially food. Because we live in a large city near a port, finding food from my mother's home country, the Philippines, was never an obstacle.

2. My mother's go-to place for food from the Philippines was the International Market. There we could find anything Asian, including anything Filipino. My mother usually bought ingredients for lumpia, our family's personalized culinary specialty. She could buy the necessary items in bulk, especially the eggroll wrappers, which were hard to find in regular supermarkets. As we entered the International Market, we would see at eye-level the Hindu idols surrounded by fruit sacrifices. I always wondered why people would give inanimate objects perfectly good fruit. We would snake around the alcohol stand to the produce section, where we found vegetables Lola, my grandma from the Philippines, liked to put in soups. We also found the carrots and onions needed for our lumpia there. Nearer the back, we would watch the fresh fish and crabs swim in their tanks before picking up oyster sauce and water chestnuts from the canned food section. During our shopping excursions, my mother would often run into another Filipino and strike up a conversation in Tagalog, the national language of the Philippines. She always hoped that this person would be from her region so that they could speak with her in a Southern Philippines dialect. There was always a little disappointment when my mother found out that they were not from her island, but she would still be pleasant. Occasionally, walking down an aisle, we would see someone my mom knew, and the two women would stop for hours to get caught up with each other. Hours later, my mom might invite them [her family] to come over to our house for dinner and have some lumpia. She was seldom refused.

3. When I think of lumpia being made at my house, I hold these memories close: the sound of the food processor intertwined with the squish and squash of meat enfolding the remainder of the ingredients; the sight of my mother measuring each ingredient

with her experienced eyes; my Lola leaning over a large tub of ground pork and beef, using the force of her entire body and the strength of her hands to push the ingredients into the crevices of the meat; the melodic sounds of Mommy and Lola chattering back and forth in their dialect, discussing the welfare of my cousins, aunties, and uncles across the seas back home in the Philippine Islands. When Lola is ready to begin wrapping the meat, she asks me to slowly and carefully separate the thin eggroll wrappers from their stack. Once the meat and vegetables are wrapped just right, some of the lumpia will go into the freezer to be sold or given away and some will be set aside for our dinner that night.

To complete our meal, we would prepare rice in the ever-present rice cooker and our special sauce concoction to go with the lumpia and rice. I would be sent outside to grab the yellowest lemons I could find from the tree in the backyard, lifting my shirt to carry them back inside again. We would cut and squeeze the lemons and put an even proportion of soy sauce and lemon juice inside a shallow bowl. If the lemon tree was ever bare, we had to resort to vinegar, but it was never the same without the distinctive taste of the lemon zest dancing together with the other flavors in my mouth. When all was done, I would call my brothers and my dad to the table and we would all eat lumpia together.

Filipino lumpia finds its origins deep in Asia, with its roots traceable to China and Guam. Traditional lumpia is only a couple inches long and about half an inch in diameter. They are more wrapper than meat and very crunchy. When my mother moved here to America and married my father, she made lumpia the way that it was made in the Philippines. My father would always say, "Americans like meat! We should make lumpia fatter and longer." Slowly the lumpia began to grow longer, increasing from two inches to seven inches long. They also grew rounder, plumping from half an inch in diameter to one and a half inches. Mommy invented her own version of lumpia and named it "American lumpia." American lumpia became very popular in both church and community.

The Taylor family is known for our special American lumpia. Every year, my mother sells her lumpia to help raise money for summer camp for the children of my church. We make and freeze lumpia in mass quantities beforehand and then sell them by the dozen: $12 per dozen for packages of frozen and $15 per dozen for pre-fried. We set up a table in the foyer so people can smell the aroma as they walk in and out of church. Everybody we know loves them. They often consult with Mom since she knows how to cook them to the perfect crispness. This food has become part of our identity as a family. It has also helped connect us with our church family and community. American lumpia is a gift from my family's kitchen to the kitchen of those we love.

**Ingredients (estimated proportions):**

- 1 lb ground pork or beef
- 1 can water chestnuts
- 1 cup ground carrots
- ½ cup sliced green onions
- 3-5 eggs
- ¼ cup oyster sauce
- 2-3 Tbsps garlic
- 1-2 Tbsps ground pepper
- 1 package wrappers

**Directions:**

1. Grind chestnuts and carrots.
2. Chop green onions.
3. Mix all ingredients with meat of choice.
4. Wrap 1-2 Tbsps of meat for every wrapper.
5. Deep fry until golden brown.

*"American Lumpia: Filipino Egg Roll" by Andrea Santiago. Originally appeared in* Tasteful Diversity: Stories Our Foods Tell. *Used with permission.*

## Converse with the Mode

So, in what ways is Andrea's essay focused on processes? One answer is the recipe with which she ends her essay, but where else do we find them? If we go back to the beginning and walk through the essay, other processes emerge: taking trips to the market, making lumpia at home, tracing the origin of lumpia and how it came to be "American lumpia" in her family, and selling lumpia at church. Andrea's essay is process writing from start to finish.

### Conversation Starters

1. Look at the opening paragraph and the closing three sentences. In these, how does Andrea create a context for understanding American lumpia? What is she saying about food in general, and specifically about her family's lumpia?
2. If you look at the overall pattern of processes Andrea covers, what do you notice about the order? Is there a particular flow to it? Is that flow effective?
3. Examine one of the individual processes in Andrea's essay. How does the process unfold in time? What verbal signals help you follow along?

**Moving On:** Andrea focuses on the making of lumpia as a practical, familial, and cultural process. As a potential topic for your own process essay, consider foods that characterize your family and its story. Another option is to consider other cultural practices that seem at the heart of your life and your family's: travel, sports, music, religion, and so on.

# Strategies for Writing Process Essays

When you analyze a process, you aim to explain how something happens, works, is made, or is done. The process may be natural (a phenomenon that occurs in nature, including human nature), performative (mechanical, something people do), or historical/cultural (events in time and/or within communities or groups).

## The Rhetorical Situation

To put process writing in context, consider the situation that gives rise to it:

- **Purpose:** You write a process essay in order to analyze and explain how an event or other phenomenon transpires. To that end, you first offer an overview of the process and then explain how each step leads logically to the next, and how all the steps together complete the process. (If you want to help readers work through a process themselves, you write instructions—a recipe, for example.)
- **Readers:** In all process writing, the text should meet the needs of all its readers, including those who know the least about the topic. To do this, you should (1) include all the information that readers need, (2) use language that they understand, and (3) define unfamiliar or technical terms.
- **Topic:** In academic process writing, the topics are usually course-related phenomena that interest you and offer readers insight into the field of study. Topics addressed in professional publications should interest and educate their readers.

*Example:* In her blog post "Yogurt: Milk and Mayhem," Nina Mukerjee Furstenau explores her **topic**: the process by which yogurt is made. Her **purpose** with her **readers**—anyone who follows her blog—is to entertain them with the nature of the process, explain how the process works at the level of fermentation, and explore the cultural significance of this process around the globe. As a bonus, she offers her readers a recipe for an Indian Lassi Yogurt Drink.

## Principles of Process Writing

Analytical process writing should follow these principles:

**Being clear and complete.** Shape the analysis based on (1) how readers will use it, and (2) what they already know about it. Aim to deepen their current knowledge about how the process unfolds and what principles are at work.

**Offering an overview.** To understand individual parts of or moments in a process, readers generally need the big picture. Start, then, by explaining the process's essential principle, its goal, or its main product and/or result. That overview statement often serves as the thesis.
*Example:* When a cell functions abnormally, it can initiate a process that results in cancer.

**Making the process manageable.** A process essay unfolds effectively and clearly when the process is presented in manageable segments. First identify the process's major phases or stages (perhaps limiting these to three or four). Then break each stage into discrete steps or events, grouping actions in clear, logical ways.

**Making the process familiar.** To help readers understand the writing, use precise terms, well-chosen adjectives, and clear action verbs. Consider, as well, using comparisons for unfamiliar parts of the process, likening, for example, the growth of hair to the growth of grass. Finally, design graphics such as flowcharts, time lines, or sequential drawings that display the process. (See the sample flowchart in Figure 13.2.)

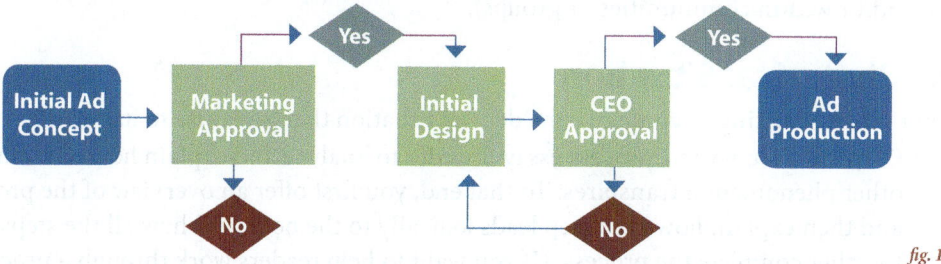

*fig. 13.2*

**Signaling temporal relationships.** Because process analysis is time related, readers need clear references to the order of events. Consider using terms such as *step, phase, stage*; transition words such as *first, second, next, finally*; or actual numbering systems (1, 2, 3).

### Sample Process Paragraph

In his essay "The Emancipation of Abe Lincoln," Eric Foner identifies stages in the development of Lincoln's support for the "Emancipation Proclamation." In the following paragraph, Foner describes a series of events included in one of these stages:

> In the summer of 1862, a combination of events propelled Lincoln in a new direction. Slavery was disintegrating in parts of the South as thousands of slaves ran away to Union lines. With the war a stalemate, more Northerners found themselves agreeing with the abolitionists, who had insisted from the outset that slavery must become a target. Enthusiasm for enlistment was waning in the North. The Army had long refused to accept black volunteers, but the reservoir of black manpower could no longer be ignored. In response, Congress moved ahead of Lincoln, abolishing slavery in the District of Columbia, authorizing the president to enroll blacks in the Army and freeing the slaves of pro-Confederate owners in areas under military control. Lincoln signed all these measures that summer.

## Patterns for Process Essays: Thesis Thinking

The thesis for your process writing can take many shapes, depending on whether you want your reader to do the process, understand the process, or put the process in a larger context (as Andrea Santiago did in "American Lumpia"). In the example below, the writer aims to explain how cancer cells multiply and affect the body.

> ***Example:*** When a cell begins to function abnormally, it can initiate a process that results in cancer.

**A Thesis Template:** Here is a possible pattern for your thesis.

> [Specific outcome of process] results from [name of process], a process that involves these main stages: [stage 1, stage 2, stage 3, etc.].
>
> *Example:* Cancer happens when body cells begin to function abnormally, a process that typically involves these phases: gene mutations of healthy cells, growth of a tumor, and spread of cancer through local invasion and/or metastasis.

**From Weak to Strong:** In chapter 4, you learned about refining your thesis to make it stronger. You can do the same with the thesis for your process essay.

> *Weak Thesis:* oversimplified or incorrect statement about the process
>
> Divorce is always messy, a disaster for everyone involved.
>
> *Good Thesis:* offers clarity about the meaning of the process and its overall shape
>
> Getting a divorce can be simple if both parties agree to it, more complicated, contentious, and drawn out if the couple disagree about important issues.
>
> *Excellent Thesis:* offers depth of understanding, contrast or tension, some surprise
>
> While getting legally divorced can be simple, recovering from the damage of a broken or failed relationship—especially when children are involved—can take a lifetime.

## Patterns for Process Essays: Writing Moves

The flowchart in Figure 13.2 offers a systematic way to organize the steps in a process. Another method would be the one you typically see with a recipe or a set of instructions: (1) a brief introduction with an overview of what the process will lead to and perhaps an estimate of how long it will take; (2) a list of ingredients or parts, tools and equipment; (3) numbered steps organized into manageable stages; and (4) diagrams, drawings, or photos, as needed.

If you wish to map out the process linearly, you might try a process analysis (Figure 13.3) or a timeline (Figure 13.4).

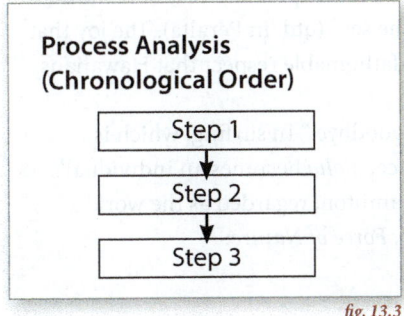

*fig. 13.3*

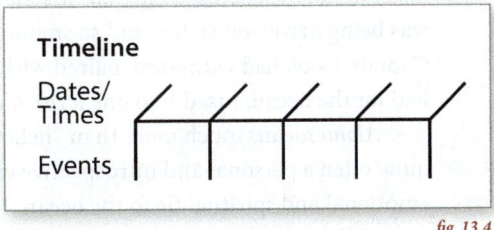

*fig. 13.4*

# Process Essays: Learning Writers' Moves

The readings that follow will show you more process-writing moves in action. The first essay examines the history of surfing. The second focuses on food culture—literally the bacterial culture that produces yogurt. And the third analyzes Abraham Lincoln's shifting response to slavery. Reading these essays may inspire potential topic ideas for your own process essay.

## Analyzing a Cultural Practice

In the following essay, student writer Tim Zekveld explores surfing culture—where it started and how it has developed into a global phenomenon.

### Chasing the Stoke

1   Surfing is much more than sliding down the face of a wave on a board. What began as a spiritual ritual in pre-modern Hawaii has transformed into a worldwide multi-billion dollar industry. This transformation has greatly affected the style of surfing and surf culture through innovation in board technology, ease of travel, and the sheer increase in the number of surfers around the globe. However, in many respects, surfing has stayed true to its Hawaiian roots through the idea of *aloha*—the concept and pursuit of a spiritual and soulful existence in relation to the ocean. Throughout all the changes to surfing and its culture, the stoke—or heartfelt excitement and reverence to each and every wave's curl—remains evident.

2   In Hawaii, surfing began as a joyous thanksgiving to the ocean for its providence and sustenance. Dating as far back as 800 AD, surfing was commonplace in Hawaiian society. Men, women, and children of every social status—from the commoner to the king—would surf regularly as a means of leisure and a form of ritual. When the ocean had provided food for their clan or had affected the people in a catastrophic way, Hawaiians would, while surfing the face of a wave, turn around and bow, wetting their head in the curl (Peralta). This ritual was a physical act meant to pay homage to the ocean, showing immense humility and reverence to their life force. Surfing on carved wooden boards measuring sixteen feet or longer and weighing well over a hundred pounds, the ancient Hawaiians would paddle into waves varying from three to thirty feet (Young 11). Captain James Cook, on viewing a Hawaiian surf in 1777, wrote, "I could not help concluding that this man felt the most supreme pleasure while he was being driven on so fast and so smoothly by the sea" (qtd. in Peralta). The joy that Captain Cook had witnessed, paired with the unfathomable respect that Hawaiians had for the ocean, fused into one term: *aloha*.

3   *Aloha* means much more than "hello" and "goodbye." In surfing, which is quite often a personal and introspective experience, *aloha* becomes an individual's emotional and spiritual tie to the ocean. Laird Hamilton, regarded as the world's greatest living surfer, speaks of aloha in his book, *Force of Nature*:

> There's a depth to "aloha" that isn't easily described because it encompasses an attitude toward life. It's a spirit of grace, generosity, peace—a kind of spiritual check-list of all that's good. *Aloha*'s literal meaning is "to breathe life." To have aloha means to share your life energy with others and with all that surrounds you. (175)

*Aloha* is a fluid concept. To have *aloha* means to live *aloha*. If surfing is a lifestyle, *aloha* underlies its virtues.

Surfing would undergo radical changes starting in the mid 1900s, though the adherence to *aloha* would remain the same. Surfing's rise in popularity was not immediate. The sport was originally brought overseas by a few Hawaiian champion swimmers in the 1920s who showed off their unique exercise to a few onlookers in California and Australia (Young 24). The spectacle enticed a handful of followers and by the early 1950s there were an estimated 5,000 surfers globally (26). However, the surfing world was about to change. Greg Noll, who began surfing in the 1940s, stated about the revolution, "Something went to hell in the late 50's. When the invention of the lightweight longboard came, something happened. It seemed that overnight, it went from 5,000 surfers, to 2 million" (qtd. in Peralta). Though advances in surfboard technology made it easier and more accessible for one to go surfing, it was the release of the Hollywood surf movie *Gidget* in 1959 that launched surfing into mainstream America. *Gidget* glorified the beach and surf life—honing in on Hawaiian *aloha* ideals. The media focused on the ease and relaxation that was paramount in Hawaiian culture. The widespread appearance of floral-print shirts, general beachwear, long hair for men, and surf jargon—words like radical, wipe-out, and hang-ten—were the result of the media's surf portrayal. The success of *Gidget* was followed by an explosion of Hollywood surf films. Riding the immense popular demand, the 1960s, often referred to as the post-*Gidget* era (Peralta), saw the rise of surf music, shops, movies, magazines, and clothing lines. The lifestyle that surfing appeared to encompass was pushed by the media and embraced by the public. Although the surf industry became focused on profits, the general idea of *aloha* survived.

The late 1960s brought the introduction of competitive surfing, propelled by advancements in board technology. Hollywood's portrayal of short board surfing created a demand for surfboards that were shorter, more aggressive, and highly maneuverable. Previously, boards were never shorter than eight feet. By the late 1960s, the most popular boards were anywhere from six to nine feet long. The newer, smaller boards featured three fins instead of the long boards' one. The introduction of rails—exaggerated lips on the bottom edges of the board—allowed the surfer to cut into a wave. Short boards changed the style of surfing completely. Long boards were maneuverable to a certain extent, capable of wide and slow turns. Short boards, on the other hand, could be ridden straight up the face of a wave, spun around on the lip, and then made to slide back down into the curl. This maneuver was labelled a cut-back and was soon followed by a myriad of other surf moves, with this novel style of surfing later referred to as shredding, as the surfing would appear to carve lines in the face of the wave. With the development of the short board, the first structured surf contests started in the late 1960s. These contests were originally without sponsors or prizes; instead, they were a way of settling egos (ASP History). By the early 1970s, however, newly developed surf-wear clothing companies such as Billabong, Quicksilver, and Volcom began sponsoring individual surfers and contest events. Individual contest prize money exceeded $10,000 per event, completely aside from the sponsor compensation (ASP History). As the number of surfing tournaments increased, careers in professional surfing became more and more possible. In 1984, the Association of Surfing Professionals formed—a world circuit boasting twenty contests worldwide.

While the world tournament scene was erupting, a separate stream of professional surfing was also developing. Stemming from Bruce Brown's monumental surfing documentary *Endless Summer* (1966), which followed several young surfers all over the world in their quest for the perfect wave, a large market for freelance surfing began. Brown had tapped into something with *Endless Summer*, a certain aura that surrounded the surfers he had captured on film. They were selfless surfers to whom the general surf population could easily relate. Documentaries, Hollywood films, surf magazines, and surf music began to focus on the alluring notions of the perfect wave and enjoyment surfing.

The past thirty years of surfing media has been dominated by the two streams—competitive and freelance. However, evidently individual surfers are not too concerned with the implications of professional competitive surfing. R.J. Farmer, in his psychoanalysis of surfers, found that when asked to rank their motivations to surf, not one surfer listed social motivation the highest; in fact, fifty percent of all those questioned ranked social motivation the lowest. It seems that surfers have discovered instinctively the concept of *aloha* and consider social benefits bestowed by surf media as secondary. Gerry Lopez, a surfer of nearly fifty years, states that "everyone who [surfs] understands immediately how great it is. It rocks your soul. You can never leave that feeling" (qtd. in Hamilton 189). Despite the evolution of surf culture, the root Hawaiian concept remains.

Two notable surfers from different sides of the surf world are Australia's Taj Burrows and Hawaii's Laird Hamilton. Taj is the world's leading competitive surfer. His bag of tricks includes intense late-fading cutbacks, "floaters" (riding on top of the breaking curl of the wave), and jaw-dropping aerials—lifting off the lip of the wave, spinning in the air, and landing back in the curl—all strung together into lines of unimaginable proportions. Taj is commonly referred to as "the evolution of surfing" or simply "the future." Kelly Slater, six-time ASP world champion, says of Burrows' surf style and skill, "It's going to take us a long time to really catch up to Taj's level. It's going to take the ASP judges a long time to comprehend what he's actually doing out there because he's truly somebody that doesn't compare to anybody else" (qtd. in Peralta). Though pulling in over six figures annually and travelling all over the globe, Taj is purely stoked about being in the water: "After touring for weeks, the first thing I do when I get home is go to the beach and surf. I'll be addicted to the curl until I die" (qtd. in Peralta). At the complete opposite end of the surfing spectrum is Laird Hamilton. Laird is regarded as the world's leading innovator in surf technology and big-wave riding. At the age of sixteen, Laird decided not to pursue the glory of competitive surfing. He has devoted his life to finding the biggest waves and being the best at surfing them. On riding big waves, Laird states, "You can't deny the spiritual world when you're staring into its eyes. I am continually humbled by the waves I surf" (Hamilton 146). In a relentless chase of the ultimate riding experience, Laird has pioneered tow-in surfing, allowing individuals to be towed by Jet-Ski into waves that were previously thought un-surfable. Laird will be searching for the Nirvana of surf until the day he dies.

Anyone who has jumped in the water and surfed in some capacity knows its undeniable draw. Rob August, one of the surfers from *Endless Summer*, says, "If you've surfed for any amount of time, you can't get it out of your mind. It is peace" (qtd. in Brown). It is apparent that no matter what size or type of board you have or what your skill level, the fever of surfing will catch you, just as it did the original Hawaiian surfers thousands of years ago. As long as there are waves, there will be people stoked to surf.

9

### Reading for Better Writing

1. *Connections:* Is surfing foreign or familiar to you? Did this essay deepen your understanding or appreciation of surfing? If yes, how so? If not, what was missing?
2. *Comprehension:* The essay locates the origin and meaning of surfing in *aloha*. What is the word's meaning, and how does its presence continue in modern surfing?
3. *Writing Moves:*
   a. How would you characterize the tone and style of this essay? Start, for example, by considering the word "stoke" in the title. What does it mean, and why does Zekveld use it? Is the style fitting for the topic? Why or why not?
   b. As a process essay, this piece relies upon chronology to trace the timeless yet changing nature of surfing. Scan the essay for references to time. What do they show about handling time in a process essay?
   c. One strategy used in the essay is to quote frequently from surfers themselves. What do these quotations add to the analysis of surfing culture?

**Your Project:** Tim Zekveld traces the origins of surfing. Are you curious about the origins of similar activities in your life? Where do they come from, and how have they developed through time? Add such activities to your list of possible topics for your process essay.

## Analyzing a Natural Process

Nina Mukerjee Furstenau is an award-winning food journalist and author who has written such books as *Biting Through the Skin: An Indian Kitchen in America's Heartland, Tasty! Mozambique,* and *Savor Missouri: River Hills Country Food and Wine.* (It was in part her writing, you remember, that inspired Andrea Santiago's "American Lumpia.") Furstenau has served in the Peace Corps, taught in The Missouri School of Journalism, and completed food nutrition projects in Ghana and Mozambique. She also writes a food blog, "A Likely Story," where this posting on yogurt first appeared.

### Yogurt: Milk & Mayhem

1   As Robin Sloan says in his delightful book, *Sourdough,* "I have come to believe that food is history of the deepest kind. Everything we eat tells a tale of ingenuity and creation, domination and injustice—and does so more vividly than any other artifact, any other medium."

2   I saw this in bacteria. It dawned on me as I glanced at a bowl of homemade yogurt, where deceptively calm fermentation was going on, that I had actually seen Sloan's type of war of the worlds many years ago on the windowsill of my grandmother's house in India. All seemed quiet with the whole milk in her bowl, but underneath the creamy white surface that was slowly thickening in the Bihari heat, there was mayhem.

3   In the cultures of milk, as Andrea S. Wiley says in her book of the same name (meaning the dairying communities in the world), fermentation is a process that produces lactic acid found in such sour foods as pickled cucumbers, kimchi, and yogurt, as well as alcoholic wine and beer.

4   To make these foods we love, as Sloan explains in *Sourdough,* it's a bloodbath. Vast cultures rise and fall, armies of bacteria convert carbohydrates into acids in what could be seen as a diabolical process: an organism converts (read eats) a carbohydrate, such as starch or a sugar, and transforms (read crushes) it into an alcohol or an acid.

5   Who knew metabolic process was so aggressive? In my kitchen, the cooling yogurt, which I greatly enjoy blended up with peaches in August, or maybe strawberries, or banana, seems so innocent.

6   I love the braided historical complexity of milk. Consider that it is one of two foods on the planet created just to be eaten. It could be debated if the other, honey, counts, as bees do not make it within themselves but use plant pollen[i]. Everything else, flora or fauna, has to be killed before it is consumed. Perhaps this is one reason

---

[i] Wiley, A. 2014. *Cultures of Milk: The Biology and Meaning of Dairy Products in the United States and India.* Cambridge, MA; Harvard University Press

milk is considered a "pure" food in India where its purity transports it to the realm of the sacred. If you consume milk or foods cooked with it, the sanctification rubs off.

If you think the culture of milk in the U.S. is vastly different in its story, think again of the biblical references to the land of "milk and honey," the lasting idea of its wholesomeness, iconic children's books with images of large and docile cows, the association with whiteness of milk and purity. It gets complicated, this connection between milk and purity. Even its physicality in India is fraught, as much milk there in fact comes from water buffalo, whose status is anything but sacred, but whose milk is much richer in butterfat and fetches a better return economically.[ii] While belief systems might seem curious at times, it is probably true that humans behave in ways that ultimately enhance, rather than diminish, our well-being.

And, sometimes those behaviors take on political, nation-building roles. Early cow protection laws in India, using the trope of the Hindu scared cow, served not only to generate more milk for citizenry ready to break free of colonizers and be better nourished, but showed resistance to both the British (and earlier Muslim) rulers and their predilection for beef,[iii] and who could only see the cow's main purpose as a source for meat or milk, leaving out dung and its uses valued for millennia in India.

Food is resistance, we've seen it time and again. A daily dose of what's good for you, and good for cultural imagination, too.

Through Wiley, I learned India ranks among the cultures of milk that include northern Europe and its subsequent populations in North America (looking at you, Wisconsin), Australia, and New Zealand, and nomadic populations of central Asia and East and West Africa. Even so, across India only an average of 20 percent of people can digest milk after weaning age. In the U.S., the average is closer 75% (National Dairy Council, 2012) with the average of European Americans at 90%, and African American, Native American, and Asian American at merely 10 to 25 percent, using a small sample test (NIH Consensus Development Conference, 2010).[iv]

Esteem for fresh milk has not meant uncomplicated digestion.

It's an unresolved mystery why this is. Humans are built to stop producing lactase at weaning. But across the world, after dairy animals were domesticated 8,000 years ago, the genetic mutation for lactase persistence that digests the milk sugar lactose throughout life grew.[v] But not in India.

I gaze at my slowly forming yogurt and consider that biology works both ways—we shift things around to make our environment more comfortable, changing the

---

[ii] Ibid.,15.
[iii] Ibid.,161.
[iv] Ibid., 12.
[v] Ibid., 10

ecology to suit us at times, and our environment reciprocates.

Fresh milk was mostly made into yogurt and ghee in India, and the process to make these removes almost all of the lactose from the end result, as well as increasing the life span of the milk. With yogurt, heating milk and letting it sit at warm temperatures encourages fermentation by bacteria such as *Lactobacillus* that converts lactose into lactic acid and yields the end result of yogurt. Depending on how long this process goes on, and the quantity of bacteria present (warriors all), most of the lactose will be removed. Butter made from the churning of these curds produces buttermilk to drink as a by-product, and in India, it is then heated and the remaining solids removed, forming ghee, also very low in lactase.

As I've mentioned in this blog before, the great sweet-making state of Bengal creates its oft-eaten specialties mostly from chhana, a soft cheese made by adding acid such as lemon or vinegar to heated milk and causing the milk curds to separate from the liquid whey. Again, lactose is reduced in this process by conveniently dissolving in the liquid whey that is drained off.

With these tasty products, little fresh milk was drunk in India and the population never had to develop a biological tolerance for digesting lactose as adults. For descendants of other dairying communities in the U.S. and elsewhere, fresh milk was a significant source of dairy and more lactase was necessary to digest it. Presto, the human body adapted.

Despite differing digestive lineages, India and the United States produce and consume the most milk in the world, and though thousands of years apart in milk history, they share milk mythology. It's mother love, it's nurturing, it's pure and protective and, in India, because of its status as a pure food, it supersedes many food codes that ground Hindu social interactions. Neat trick, that.

\*\*\*\*

India, with its ancient food-as-medicine focus, never neglected a food's effect *on the body*. Traditionally lassi was made with fresh homemade yogurt, salt, and cooling spices such as a small amount of roasted ground cumin to enhance its digestive properties. Even so, I never underestimate the basic, sweeter recipe below as an excellent cooler for hot summer days.

StockImageFactory.com/Shutterstock.com

**Basic Indian Lassi Yogurt Drink** 19

    1-3/4 cup plain yogurt
    6 cubes of ice, crushed
    1/2 cup chilled water
    2 teaspoons white sugar
    pinch salt

Mix all ingredients in a blender, or use a mixer or whisk for the best texture, and blend until frothy. 20

*Options:* add 1/4 teaspoon cardamom powder, or 1/2 teaspoon rose water, or a few strands of saffron to the basic mix. 21

*Mango lassi:* mix 1/2 cubed, ripe mango, 3 tablespoons sugar, 1/4 teaspoon cardamom powder, 3/4 cup yogurt, 3/4 cup chilled water and blend until frothy. If you add ice cubes, reduce the water by 1/4 cup, or to the thickness you prefer. 22

*Strawberry lassi:* mix 1 cup strawberries, 2 tablespoons sugar, 1 cup yogurt, 1/2 cup water and blend until frothy. If you add ice cubes, reduce the water by 1/4 cup, or to the thickness you prefer. 23

## Reading for Better Writing

1. *Connections:* What role does milk play in your life? What forms do you eat or drink, if any? Are you lactose tolerant or intolerant? How does that affect your life? How would you describe the larger "milk culture" you come from?
2. *Comprehension:* From reading this essay, what do you understand about how yogurt is made? And what do you understand about American culture's relationship with milk vs. Indian culture's history with milk?
3. *Writing Moves:*
   a. This essay is about yogurt: In the passages that are specifically about making yogurt, what strategies does Furstenau use to explain the process and bring it to life?
   b. This essay is about so much more than yogurt: If you consider the title, the opening paragraph, the ninth paragraph, and the closing paragraph—what is the larger process Furstenau is exploring? What's her theme or thesis?
   c. In paragraph 6, she says, "I love the braided historical complexity of milk." What strands of this braided complexity does she develop, using what strategies?

**Your Project:** This essay starts with the idea that "food is history of the deepest kind." What foods might have a curious and interesting history? Think of foods you love, foods you find weird, foods important for your city, state, or heritage. What's their story?

*"Yogurt: Milk and Mayhem" by Nina Furstenau. First appeared at ninafurstenau.com. Used with permission.*

## Analyzing a Policy

Eric Foner is a professor of history at Columbia University and the author of numerous publications, including *The Fiery Trial: Abraham Lincoln and American Slavery* and the essay that follows. He published the essay on December 31, 2012, one day before the 150th anniversary of Lincoln's signing of the "Emancipation Proclamation."

### The Emancipation of Abe Lincoln

ONE hundred and fifty years ago, on January 1, 1863, Abraham Lincoln presided over the annual White House New Year's reception. Late that afternoon, he retired to his study to sign the "Emancipation Proclamation." When he took up his pen, his hand was shaking from exhaustion. Briefly, he paused—"I do not want it to appear as if I hesitated," he remarked. Then Lincoln affixed a firm signature to the document.

Like all great historical transformations, emancipation was a process, not a single event. It arose from many causes and was the work of many individuals. It began at the outset of the Civil War, when slaves sought refuge behind Union lines. It did not end until December 1865, with the ratification of the 13th Amendment, which irrevocably abolished slavery throughout the nation.

But the Emancipation Proclamation was the crucial turning point in this story. In a sense, it embodied a double emancipation: for the slaves, since it ensured that if the Union emerged victorious, slavery would perish, and for Lincoln himself, for whom it marked the abandonment of his previous assumptions about how to abolish slavery and the role blacks would play in post-emancipation American life.

There is no reason to doubt the sincerity of Lincoln's statement in 1864 that he had always believed slavery to be wrong. During the first two years of the Civil War, despite insisting that the conflict's aim was preservation of the Union, he devoted considerable energy to a plan for ending slavery inherited from prewar years. Emancipation would be undertaken by state governments, with national financing. It would be gradual, owners would receive monetary compensation and emancipated slaves would be encouraged to find a homeland outside the United States—this last idea known as "colonization."

Lincoln's plan sought to win the cooperation of slave holders in ending slavery. As early as November 1861, he proposed it to political leaders in Delaware, one of the four border states (along with Kentucky, Maryland and Missouri) that remained in the Union. Delaware had only 1,800 slaves; the institution was peripheral to the state's economy. But Lincoln found that even there, slave holders did not wish to surrender their human property. Nonetheless, for most of 1862, he avidly promoted his plan to the border states and any Confederates who might be interested.

Lincoln also took his proposal to black Americans. In August 1862, he met with a group of black leaders from Washington. He seemed to blame the presence of blacks in America for the conflict: "but for your race among us there could not be war."

He issued a powerful indictment of slavery—"the greatest wrong inflicted on any people"—but added that, because of racism, blacks would never achieve equality in America. "It is better for us both, therefore, to be separated," he said. But most blacks refused to contemplate emigration from the land of their birth.

In the summer of 1862, a combination of events propelled Lincoln in a new direction. Slavery was disintegrating in parts of the South as thousands of slaves ran away to Union lines. With the war a stalemate, more Northerners found themselves agreeing with the abolitionists, who had insisted from the outset that slavery must become a target. Enthusiasm for enlistment was waning in the North. The Army had long refused to accept black volunteers, but the reservoir of black manpower could no longer be ignored. In response, Congress moved ahead of Lincoln, abolishing slavery in the District of Columbia, authorizing the president to enroll blacks in the Army and freeing the slaves of pro-Confederate owners in areas under military control. Lincoln signed all these measures that summer.

The hallmark of Lincoln's greatness was his combination of bedrock principle with open-mindedness and capacity for growth. That summer, with his preferred approach going nowhere, he moved in the direction of immediate emancipation. He first proposed this to his cabinet on July 22, but Secretary of State William H. Seward persuaded him to wait for a military victory, lest it seem an act of desperation.

Soon after the Union victory at Antietam in September, Lincoln issued the Preliminary Emancipation Proclamation, a warning to the Confederacy that if it did not lay down its arms by January 1, he would declare the slaves "forever free."

Lincoln did not immediately abandon his earlier plan. His annual message to Congress, released on Dec. 1, 1862, devoted a long passage to gradual, compensated abolition and colonization. But in the same document, without mentioning the impending proclamation, he indicated that a new approach was imperative: "The dogmas of the quiet past, are inadequate to the stormy present," he wrote. "We must disenthrall our selves, and then we shall save our country." Lincoln included himself in that "we." On Jan. 1, he proclaimed the freedom of the vast majority of the nation's slaves.

The Emancipation Proclamation is perhaps the most misunderstood of the documents that have shaped American history. Contrary to legend, Lincoln did not free the nearly four million slaves with a stroke of his pen. It had no bearing on slaves in the four border states, since they were not in rebellion. It also exempted certain parts of the Confederacy occupied by the Union. All told, it left perhaps 750,000 slaves in bondage. But the remaining 3.1 million, it declared, "are, and henceforward shall be free."

The proclamation did not end slavery in the United States on the day it was issued. Indeed, it could not even be enforced in most of the areas where it applied, which were under Confederate control. But it ensured the eventual death of slavery—assuming the

Union won the war. Were the Confederacy to emerge victorious, slavery, in one form or another, would undoubtedly have lasted a long time.

A military order, whose constitutional legitimacy rested on the president's war powers, the proclamation often disappoints those who read it. It is dull and legalistic; it contains no soaring language enunciating the rights of man. Only at the last minute, at the urging of Treasury Secretary Salmon P. Chase, an abolitionist, did Lincoln add a conclusion declaring the proclamation an "act of justice."

Nonetheless, the proclamation marked a dramatic transformation in the nature of the Civil War and in Lincoln's own approach to the problem of slavery. No longer did he seek the consent of slave holders. The proclamation was immediate, not gradual, contained no mention of compensation for owners, and made no reference to colonization.

In it, Lincoln addressed blacks directly, not as property subject to the will of others but as men and women whose loyalty the Union must earn. For the first time, he welcomed black soldiers into the Union Army; over the next two years some 200,000 black men would serve in the Army and Navy, playing a critical role in achieving Union victory. And Lincoln urged freed slaves to go to work for "reasonable wages"—in the United States. He never again mentioned colonization in public.

Having made the decision, Lincoln did not look back. In 1864, with casualties mounting, there was talk of a compromise peace. Some urged Lincoln to rescind the proclamation, in which case, they believed, the South could be persuaded to return to the Union. Lincoln refused. Were he to do so, he told one visitor, "I should be damned in time and eternity."

Wartime emancipation may have settled the fate of slavery, but it opened another vexing question: the role of former slaves in American life. Colonization had allowed its proponents to talk about abolition without having to confront this issue; after all, the black population would be gone. After January 1, 1863, Lincoln for the first time began to think seriously of the United States as a biracial society.

While not burdened with the visceral racism of many of his white contemporaries, Lincoln shared some of their prejudices. He had long seen blacks as an alien people who had been unjustly uprooted from their homeland and were entitled to freedom, but were not an intrinsic part of American society. During his Senate campaign in Illinois, in 1858, he had insisted that blacks should enjoy the same natural rights as whites (life, liberty and the pursuit of happiness), but he opposed granting them legal equality or the right to vote.

By the end of his life, Lincoln's outlook had changed dramatically. In his last public address, delivered in April 1865, he said that in reconstructing Louisiana, and by implication other Southern states, he would "prefer" that limited black suffrage be implemented. He singled out the "very intelligent" (educated free blacks) and "those who serve our cause as soldiers" as most worthy. Though hardly an unambiguous embrace of equality, this was the first time an American president had endorsed any political rights for blacks.

And then there was his magnificent second inaugural address of March 4, 1865, in which Lincoln ruminated on the deep meaning of the war. He now identified the institution of slavery—not the presence of blacks, as in 1862—as its fundamental cause. The war, he said, might well be a divine punishment for the evil of slavery. And God might will it to continue until all the wealth the slaves had created had been destroyed, and "until every drop of blood drawn with the lash, shall be paid by another drawn by the sword." Lincoln was reminding Americans that violence did not begin with the firing on Fort Sumter, S.C., in April 1861. What he called "this terrible war" had been preceded by 250 years of the terrible violence of slavery.

In essence, Lincoln asked the nation to confront unblinkingly the legacy of slavery. What were the requirements of justice in the face of this reality? What would be necessary to enable former slaves and their descendants to enjoy fully the pursuit of happiness? Lincoln did not live to provide an answer. A century and a half later, we have yet to do so.

### Reading for Better Writing

1. *Connections:* Reflect on someone who positively impacted your life. Then think about the people and events in this person's life that shaped the qualities that positively affected you. If you were to tell this person's story, what details would you include? Why?
2. *Comprehension:*
   a. Review Eric Foner's claim (in paragraph 2) that emancipation was a process, not a single event. What does he mean, and how does he support this claim?
   b. Identify a passage in which Foner analyzes how specific events caused a shift in Lincoln's thinking. How does this passage advance his thesis?
3. *Writing Moves:*
   a. Describe how Foner introduces his topic and thesis.
   b. Cite examples showing how he builds transitions that (a) link stages in the process and (b) link specific events within a stage.

**Your Project:** For your own writing, consider another historical character (e.g., Cesar Chavez, Malcolm X, Henry Standing Bear, Shirley Chisholm, or Eleanor Roosevelt) who sought to bring about significant social change. Then research the person's life and career so as to analyze the process by which this person became an important social activist.

From *The New York Times, January 1, 2013.* © 2013 The New York Times *All rights reserved. Used by permission and protected by the Copyright Laws of the United States. The printing, copying, redistribution, or retransmission of the Material without express written permission is prohibited.*

#  DIY: Craft Your Own Process Essay

## Planning

1. **Select a topic.** Begin by reviewing the project options listed at the end of each sample essay. To generate more topic ideas, review the following prompts.
   - A course-related process
   - A process in nature
   - A process in the news
   - A process that helps you get a job

2. **Review the process.** Use your knowledge of the topic to fill out an organizer like the one in Figure 13.5. List the subject at the top, each of the steps in chronological order, and the outcome at the bottom. For a complex process, break it down into stages or phases first; then outline the steps or events within each phase.

   > **Process Analysis**
   > **Subject:**
   > - Step #1
   > - Step #2
   > - Step #3
   > **Outcome:**
   >
   > *fig. 13.5*

3. **Research the process.** Find all the information that you need to fully understand the process yourself and to clearly explain it to your readers. To guide your research, you might list headings and related questions like these:
   - **Context:** When, where, how, and why does the process transpire? How is the context related to the nature of the process?
   - **Content:** What individual steps—or groups of steps—make up the process?
   - **Order:** In what order do the steps take place? Is the order important? Why?
   - **Connections:** What links steps to steps or links stages to stages and how?
   - **Causes:** What causes each individual step or event—or what causes the process as a whole? How can I distinguish between false causes and actual causes?
   - **Effects:** What is the outcome of each step or event—and what is the outcome of the whole process? What side effects are associated with the outcome?
   - **Materials:** What materials are used in the process and how do they affect it?
   - **History:** When did this process begin? How has it changed over time and why?
   - **Personnel:** Who is involved in the process? Why? How do they affect the process, and how does it affect them?
   - **Cost:** What is the financial cost? The emotional cost? The environmental cost?
   - **Impact:** How does the process affect my community, my friends, or me?

4. **Organize information.** Revise the organizer as needed. Then develop an outline, including steps listed in the organizer, as well as supporting details from your research.

## Drafting

5. **Write the first draft.** Using the writing moves that follow or others you've learned in this chapter, draft your essay.
   - **Opening:** Introduce the topic and give an overview of the process, possibly forecasting its main stages. Explain why the process is important.

- **Middle:** Clearly describe each step in the process, and link steps with transitions such as *first, second, next, finally,* and *while.* Explain the importance of each step, and how it is linked to other steps in the process. If the process is complex and has many steps, consider grouping them into 3-5 phases or stages. Describe the outcomes of steps and phases, as well as the overall outcome and relevance of the process. Depending on your purpose for writing, you might also analyze the causes and effects related to specific steps, or to the entire process.
- **Closing:** Summarize the process and restate key points as needed, such as why understanding the process has value. If appropriate, explain follow-up activity, such as how readers might learn more about the topic.

## Revising

6. **Improve the ideas, organization, and voice.** Evaluate the following:
   - ____ **Ideas:** Is the process presented as a unified phenomenon that includes a logical series of stages and steps? Are all claims clear, rational, and supported with reliable evidence? Are assertions regarding causes and effects relevant and explained fully? Does the writing avoid logical fallacies such as false cause, broad generalization, and false analogy? (See chapter 17 for more on these fallacies.)
   - ____ **Organization:** Does the essay include an opening that introduces the process, offers an overview, and states the thesis; a middle that describes stages and steps clearly and correctly; and a closing that unifies the essay?
   - ____ **Voice:** Is the tone informed, concerned, and objective? Are sensitive issues well researched, addressed respectfully, and shown to be relevant?

## Polishing

7. **Edit the essay.** Polish your writing by addressing the following:
   - ____ **Words:** The words are precise, clear, and correct. Technical terms are correct, used uniformly, and defined. Numbered steps begin with clear action verbs.
   - ____ **Sentences:** The sentences are smooth, varied in structure, and engaging.
   - ____ **Correctness:** The usage, grammar, punctuation, and spelling are correct.
   - ____ **Page Design:** The page design is attractive and features steps in the process. Essays are correctly formatted in MLA or APA style.

## Publishing

8. **Publish the essay** by offering it to instructors, students, and nonprofit agencies working with the process.

# Process Essays: Applications

Once you have finished your process essay, there may be more to think about. Consider how to apply what you have learned in the following situations.

1. **Living Today:** Think about a time or phase in your life during which your understanding of—or position on—an issue, event, or other topic changed. What was the process you went through? Was it smooth or rough, the outcome positive or negative? How would you divide the process into stages?
2. **Major Issue:** In what ways is your field of study focused on processes? Through reading and discussion, develop a list of such processes and consider why understanding these processes is central to mastering that field of knowledge.
3. **Public Texts:** Every day, we encounter process writing in the form of instructions—recipes, Google Map directions, assembly guidelines, game rules, and so on. Find and examine one such set of instructions. What strategies make instructions useful? What weaknesses make them frustrating for readers?
4. **Photo Op:** As shown with Figure 13.1 and Figure 13.2, visuals can be effective aids to explaining a process. Considering your own process essay, what photographs, charts, or other visuals would you include to clarify the process? Where and how would you position these in your writing?

## Learning-Objectives Checklist ✓

Have you achieved this chapter's learning objectives? Check your progress with the following items, revisiting topics in the chapter as needed. I have . . .

____ determined what a process essay is and what forms it might take.
____ practiced techniques for analyzing processes.
____ developed a strong thesis for a process essay.
____ identified writing moves and strategies for shaping process writing.
____ crafted a strong process essay by drawing upon a range of writing moves.

# Chapter 14

# Analytical Writing: Compare and Contrast

"You're comparing apples and oranges. Can't be done." This saying suggests that the things being compared are so different they're beyond comparison. The truth is, though, apples and oranges can be compared. They're both fruit; they belong to the same class or order of things. We can hold them up side by side and ask, "How are these similar? How are they different?" Looking for similarities is called *comparison*, whereas identifying differences is called *contrast*. Hence, *compare-contrast* analysis.

Examining similarities and/or differences reveals essential truths about things; we get deeper insights about what things have in common and what makes them unique. But a word of caution: compare-contrast analysis needs to be done ethically to avoid exaggeration and stereotypes. This chapter will help you compare apples and oranges while giving them the respect they deserve.

**Visually Speaking** What can you compare or contrast in Figure 14.1? What does the photo suggest about how comparing and contrasting can deepen your understanding of a topic?

## Learning Objectives

By working through this chapter, you will be able to

- explain what a compare-contrast essay is and what forms it might take.
- practice strategies for doing compare-contrast analysis.
- develop a strong thesis for a compare-contrast essay.
- identify writing moves for shaping compare-contrast writing.
- craft a strong compare-contrast essay by drawing upon a range of writing moves.

*Mazzzur / Shutterstock.com*

*fig. 14.1*

# Meeting the Mode

To become familiar with compare-contrast writing, read this essay by student writer Ariana King. Activate the reading strategies from chapter 2, and consider these questions: What is Ariana comparing? How does she present similarities? What does she do with differences?

### Modern Arranged Marriages

1. It's late Thursday night and I'm scrolling through YouTube videos when a new recommendation catches my eye. The show is called *Married at First Sight*, another one of Lifetime's reality television shows where a group of relationship experts match up a few hopefuls to be married—you guessed it—at first sight.

2. While I hate to admit that the show has me hooked, I didn't just watch it for the drama. In the back of my mind, I kept asking myself what this show teaches people about arranged marriages and how that representation is reflected in American culture. Mostly, I wondered why a show about arranged marriage would be such a spectacle now since arranged marriages have been around for ages.

3. Unlike the hopeless romantics who marry "for love" on the show, most arranged marriages up until the 1700s were made for family prestige, financial security, and social stability (Yandura, 2019).

4. Yet, it isn't surprising that each *Married at First Sight* star claims that "love" is their number one priority; 88 percent of Americans feel the same way according to a 2013 Pew Center poll (Fieger & Livingston, 2019). It's a big reason why arranged marriages, often thought of as loveless, are stigmatized.

5. Today, the majority of arranged marriages in America take place within immigrant communities, particularly ones that come from South Asia, Africa, the Middle East, and East Asia. They're often done to keep family tradition, but they are not as loveless as people make them out to be (Yandura, 2019).

6. Speaking as a first-generation Iraqi-American, Huda Al-Marashi penned a memoir about her own arranged marriage to fight misconceptions. She and her husband had known each other since childhood, and he had confessed his feelings for her long before they wed (Al-Marashi, 2018).

7. Unlike *Married at First Sight*, Al-Marashi writes that the vast majority of people do not marry a complete stranger. While they may meet their future spouse through dating apps or parental guidance, couples typically date before marriage (2018).

8. The benefits of arranged marriage also vary greatly from reality television to real life. Stars on Lifetime's hit series are merely offered the chance for a perfect match by experts. In real life, the parents, who have known their children all their lives, are often relied upon to help rationalize a situation in which their child has been blinded by love (Yandura, 2019).

9. The idea of arranged marriage is also appealing because each party knows the

other is looking for marriage; there is no "what are we" question (Yandura, 2019). Unfortunately, the same cannot be said for a reality television show.

Thus far, it is clear that modern arranged marriages differ greatly from the kinds seen on Lifetime television. However, both marriages often rely, in part, on quizzes and criteria found in dating apps in order to pair up. The show's stars trust expert evaluation—a human stand-in for computer algorithms—while the rise of matrimonial websites, particularly in the Indian diaspora, helps people find a potential partner (Batabyal, 2018).

This link of dating sites between arranged and non-arranged marriages gives Batabyal hope that the stigma in the United States against arranged marriage will diminish over time (Batabyal, 2018).

The reality of arranged marriages in America is not like reality television—surprise, surprise. But, that does not mean that the show presents no takeaways when it comes to American dating culture.

*Married at First Sight* reflects how prevalent dating apps and other "unconventional ways" to meet a partner have become, both on and off the show. It portrays the extensive trust in outside sources—the experts in this case—that is common in real-life arranged marriages as well. But most of all, it tells us just how much Americans prioritize love since that's the whole reason the participants embarked on this journey in the first place.

## Converse with the Mode

So, what did you notice about compare-contrast thinking in the essay? The main comparison is between the fantasy of arranged marriages portrayed on a reality TV show and the reality of what actual arranged marriages in North America entail. We might also say there's an implied comparison between such arranged marriages and the non-arranged marriages more typical in North America. Now look closer at the essay.

### Conversation Starters

1. Ariana begins by describing *Married at First Sight*. What does this accomplish? Why not just start by defining arranged marriage or giving a history of it?
2. How does Ariana present the truth about arranged marriages through contrast with the show? What resources does she draw upon to get at those truths?
3. In paragraph 10, Ariana takes a turn toward connections between the fantasy of the show and the reality of arranged marriages. How does she make those connections?

**Moving On:** As for topic ideas for your own compare-contrast essay, consider situations where a gap between fantasy and reality exists. It might be between another type of TV show and real life or between online celebrity personas and the reality of daily life.

"Modern Arranged Marriages" by Ariana King. Originally appeared in Moda Magazine. Reprinted with permission.

# Strategies for Writing Compare-Contrast Essays

Compare-contrast writing holds two or more things, phenomena, or concepts side by side—with comparison focusing on similarities, and contrast focusing on differences. When you hold up things side by side, you more clearly see their unique and shared traits. To learn techniques for your own compare-contrast essay, start with the principles that follow.

## The Rhetorical Situation

Consider the context in which you use compare-contrast reasoning:

- **Purpose.** You commonly compare and contrast subjects in order to explain how, why, and to what effect their distinguishing features make the subjects similar or different. Depending on your purpose, you may focus on the similarities between seemingly dissimilar things or on the differences between things that seem similar.
- **Readers.** When you use compare-contrast reasoning, you may have virtually any reader in mind—your instructor for an essay or potential clients for a marketing plan. Whatever the situation, you want your comparative analysis of the topic to enrich your readers' understanding of that topic.
- **Topic.** You can address a wide range of topics through comparison-contrast: people, events, phenomena, technologies, problems, products, stories, concepts, and so on.

*Example:* In "Beyond the Polite Smile," the writer's **topics** are the two communities of which she is a part: her Cantonese-speaking Chinese community in which her name is Pang Jing-Ling and her English-speaking community in which her name is Janice Pang. Her **purpose** is to help **readers** (her classmates and professor) understand how she is shaped by—and responds to—each group's customs, expectations, and opportunities. To that end, she compares and contrasts the traits of the two communities.

## Principles of Compare-Contrast Writing

Use the principles that follow to guide your own compare-contrast writing:

**Establishing a solid basis for comparison.** Comparable items are types of the same thing (e.g. two fruits, two rivers, two bodies of water, the atmosphere and oceans). Moreover, the subjects are of the same order—one cannot simply be an example of the other: e.g., all lakes and Lake Michigan. Whereas such a discussion would work as an example or illustration, the topics are not truly comparable.

**Developing criteria (standards, features, etc.) on which to base the comparison.** For example, a comparison of two characters in a play might focus on their backgrounds, their actions, their psychology, their fate, and so on. Similarly, as fruit, apples and oranges might be compared and contrasted based on their skin, flesh, juice, geographic origin, growing climate, and so on. Once you choose your criteria, you need to apply them consistently to the things you're comparing. A very useful tool for sorting out such features is the Venn Diagram (Figure 14.2). In the two circles, notice how what's shared between apples and oranges (their similarities) is placed in the overlap; then what's distinct about apples and oranges (their differences) is placed outside the overlap.

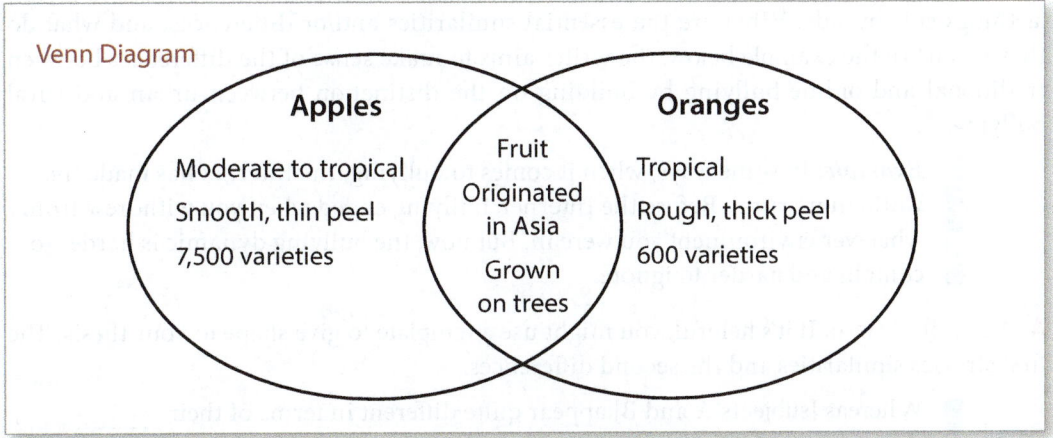

*fig. 14.2*

**Drawing conclusions that are ethical.** As with classification and "pigeonholing," compare-contrast thinking is vulnerable to logical fallacies and ethical pitfalls. As you compare things, aim to avoid exaggerating similarities and/or differences. Especially if you are comparing topics that involve people (those "human subjects" of your writing), don't fall into the traps of black-and-white thinking and overgeneralization. You want your comparisons to be nuanced, full, and fair.

**Considering how to use compare-contrast.** For example, compare-contrast may be . . .
- the framework for the entire essay, offering a compare-contrast thesis and structuring the discussion around appropriate points of comparison, or
- a strategy used in a paragraph or a section of an essay, comparing and contrasting details to illuminate an idea.

## Sample Compare-Contrast Paragraph

In her essay "How the Internet Has Changed Bullying," Maria Konnikova uses compare-contrast terms such as *more*, *before*, *but*, *harder*, and *as much as*.

> In some ways, when it comes to bullying, the Internet has made the world *more* rural. *Before* the Internet, bullying ended when you withdrew from whatever environment you were in. *But now*, the bullying dynamic is *harder to contain* and *harder to ignore*. If you're harassed on your Facebook page, all of your social circles know about it; as long as you have access to the network, a ceaseless stream of notifications leaves you vulnerable to victimhood. Bullying may not have become *more prevalent*—in fact, a recent review of international data suggests that its incidence has declined by *as much as* ten percent around the world. *But getting away* from it has become *more difficult*.

## Patterns for Compare-Contrast Essays: Thesis Thinking

The thesis for your compare-contrast essay offers your central observation as you look at things side by side. What are the essential similarities and/or differences, and what do they mean? In the example below, the writer aims to make sense of the differences between traditional and online bullying by building on the distinction between urban and rural bullying.

> *Example:* In some ways, when it comes to bullying, the Internet has made the world more rural. Before the Internet, bullying ended when you withdrew from whatever environment you were in. But now, the bullying dynamic is harder to contain and harder to ignore.

**A Thesis Template:** If it's helpful, you might use a template to give shape to your thesis. The first stresses similarities and the second differences.

> Whereas [subjects A and B] appear quite different in terms of their _____, they show important similarities in that _____.

> Whereas [subjects A and B] appear quite similar in terms of their _____, they are essentially different in that _____.

> *Example:* While *Zero Dark Thirty* and *Dunkirk* both dramatize historical events, *Zero*'s portrayal of events is more historically accurate than *Dunkirk*'s.

**From Weak to Strong:** In chapter 4, you learned about refining your thesis to make it stronger. You can do the same with the thesis for your compare-contrast essay. (**Caution:** We don't know if any of these ideas are true. We made them up!)

> *Weak Thesis:* obvious, shallow, or one-sided insight into the comparison
>
> Compared with a civil ceremony, a destination wedding is very expensive. It's a monumental waste of money, IMHO!

> *Good Thesis:* sound idea about the essential nature of similarities and/or differences
>
> While a destination wedding can be much more exotic and adventurous, a traditional religious ceremony—whatever the faith—creates a stronger sense of the communal importance and serious nature of marriage.

> *Excellent Thesis:* offers surprising, insightful thoughts about similarities and/or differences
>
> Compared with a civil ceremony or even a traditional wedding, destination weddings can be enormously expensive and crazily complicated to arrange. How can they possibly be worth it? It turns out, according to new research, that

> destination-wedding-couples are ten times more likely to stay married (possibly because they spend the rest of their lives paying for the wedding).

## Patterns for Compare-Contrast Essays: Writing Moves

The structure you create for your compare-contrast essay should grow naturally out of your thesis. If, for example, you are aiming to emphasize differences, you might begin with the apparent similarities (treating them briefly) and then dig into the differences at greater length, arranging those, perhaps, from simplest to most complex. You could use the reverse approach if your thesis stresses similarities. So, one of your choices has to do with the overall arrangement of similarities and differences, as well as the order in which you sequence specific points. As the compare-contrast blueprints show (Figure 14.3), you might also consider two other patterns:

- **Whole vs. whole**, also called the block method, discusses items separately, giving a strong overview of each. This pattern works well with short comparisons, as it requires readers to remember what they read about the first item in the first "block" after moving on to the second item in the second "block."
- **Point by point**, also called the ping-pong method, discusses items together, side by side so to speak, criterion by criterion back and forth (hence ping-pong). This pattern stresses fine distinctions, making sense for long, complex comparisons, especially in papers presenting numbers, charts, or statistics.

Whichever overall structure you choose, remember that the glue that holds it together are compare-contrast words such as more, less, similarly, in comparison, likewise, on the other hand, in contrast, however, still, and although. Additional glue is created by comparative form of adjectives: stronger, faster, higher, smarter, taller, smaller.

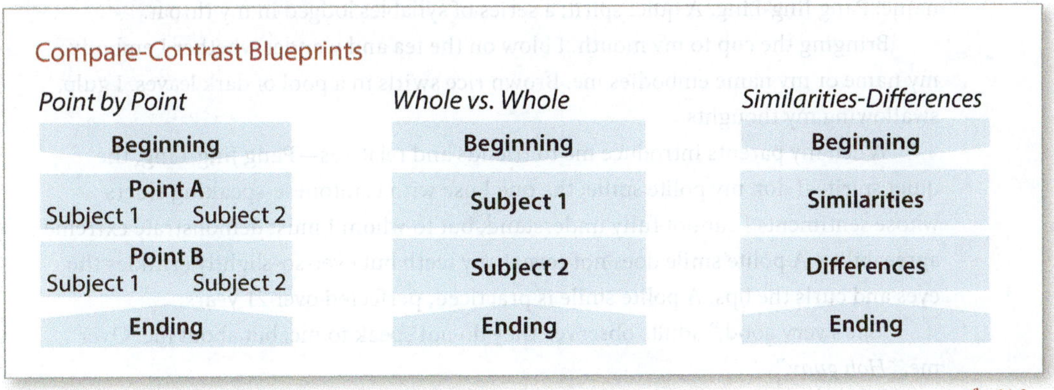

### Compare-Contrast Blueprints

| Point by Point | Whole vs. Whole | Similarities-Differences |
|---|---|---|
| Beginning | Beginning | Beginning |
| Point A — Subject 1 / Subject 2 | Subject 1 | Similarities |
| Point B — Subject 1 / Subject 2 | Subject 2 | Differences |
| Ending | Ending | Ending |

*fig. 14.3*

# Compare-Contrast Essays: Learning Writers' Moves

What do compare-contrast moves look like when writers use them in their essays? You can study these moves in the essays that follow. By reading these essays, you'll also be able to add to the list of possible topics for your own essay.

## Analyzing Two Cultures

Janice Pang, a student at the University of California at Davis, wrote the following essay, entered it in the school's annual writing contest, and was honored by having the paper published in *Prized Writing, 2014–2015*. In that text, she introduces her essay by saying, "My writing distills my views about language and identity into a narrative about culture, family, and personal growth." As you read Pang's essay, note how she uses compare-contrast thinking to clarify those views.

### Beyond the Polite Smile

1  "You were an easy baby."

2  Over tea, my mother tells me that I came out smiling. I had held my contented expression for three minutes until the doctor firmly patted my bottom, eliciting a shriek and an avalanche of tears. This, the doctor assured my parents, meant I was normal.

3  Over the ruckus of the restaurant—chopsticks clinking against porcelain, high-pitched howls of Cantonese—my mother coolly explains the origin of my Chinese name: Pang Jing-Ling. A quiet spirit; a series of syllables lodged in my throat.

4  Bringing the cup to my mouth, I blow on the tea and wonder whether I embody my name or my name embodies me. Brown rice swirls in a pool of dark leaves. I gulp, swallowing my thoughts.

5  When my parents introduce me to friends and relatives—Pang Jing-Ling, the quiet spirit—I don my polite smile; the one I use with Cantonese-speaking elders whose sentiments I cannot fully understand, but to whom I must demonstrate extreme agreeability. A polite smile does not reveal any teeth but ever-so-slightly crinkles the eyes and curls the lips. A polite smile is practiced, perfected over 21 years.

6  "She's very good," adults observe. They do not speak to me, but about me. Over me, "*Hoh guay.*"

7  I do not question the validity of their statements—that I'm quiet, that I'm shy. Rather, I accept them. Internalize them. Smile.

8  My parents speak Cantonese to scold me and to gossip with their friends, mouths shifting to accommodate native tongues. I know to listen.

9  In this language, I have never learned to respond or to speak for myself. I have,

however, become competent in obeying, in declining and thanking. Unable to translate more complex thoughts, I reduce Cantonese to a language of submission.

English, on the other hand, is a language I command. My public education taught me to stick with five-paragraph formats; to use semicolons sparingly; to write in complete sentences. After years of practicing these rules, I learned to break them.

With thoughts and the agency to voice them, I have the privilege of playing with syntax. I complicate sentences within dashes; I dismantle every subject, object, and verb.

In the spaces where I communicate in English—at work, in class, with friends—I wrangle hellish clients, I challenge problematic texts, I correct everyone's grammar. Anything but quiet, my voice refuses to be passive.

Understanding that I grew up with a repression of language, and a language of repression, I now have a greater appreciation for language that affirms. I use English to make sense of Cantonese, dissecting the language I have such trouble speaking beyond single syllables. I explore each character's meaning—its intricate shape and sound. Familiarizing my tongue with this language, I feel the corners of my polite smile relax.

## Reading for Better Writing

1. *Connections:* What practices (e.g., spoken languages, clothing styles, social etiquette, figures of speech, popular sports, forms of art) distinguish the culture of your community? Which of these do you appreciate, dislike, or identify with?
2. *Comprehension:*
   a. Pang titles her essay, "Beyond the Polite Smile." What does she mean by "beyond" and "polite"? What does the smile communicate to those whom she smiles at? What does it hide?
   b. Compare and contrast (a) her demeanor (and smile) when using the Cantonese language with (b) her demeanor (and smile) when using the English language.
   c. Explain what she means by, "I grew up with a repression of language, and a language of repression"?
3. *Writing Moves:*
   a. Pang uses precise terms to distinguish her two cultures. Cite examples and explain how her word choice works.
   b. Pang organizes her essay by first describing her Cantonese character and then contrasting it with her English character. What is the effect of using this subject-by-subject approach rather than the trait-by-trait structure?

**Your Project:** Consider comparing and contrasting the community in which you grew up and your current college community. How does being in each community affect your attitude, behavior, or self-concept?

"Beyond the Polite Smile" by Janice Pang. Originally appeared in Prized Writing. Reprinted by permission of the author.

## Analyzing Human Compassion

Marina Keegan (1989-2012) was an award-winning writer whose work was read on NPR and published in *The New York Times* and NewYorker.com. She accomplished all this and more before, just weeks after graduating from Yale University, a tragic car accident took her life. In this essay, by comparing and contrasting two distinct situations, Keegan analyzes what inspires human compassion.

### Why We Care About Whales

1. When the moon gets bored, it kills whales. Blue whales and fin whales and humpback, sperm, and orca whales: centrifugal forces don't discriminate.

2. With a hushed retreat, the moon pulls waters out from under fins and flippers, oscillating them backward and forward before they slip outward. At nighttime, the moon watches its work. Silver light traces the strips of lingering water, the jittery crabs, the lumps of tangled seaweed.

3. Slowly, awkwardly, the whales find their footing. They try to fight the waves, but they can't fight the moon. They can't fight the world's rotation or the bathymetry of oceans or the inevitability that sometimes things just don't work out.

4. More than two thousand cetaceans die from beaching every year. Occasionally they trap themselves in solitude, but whales are often beached in groups, huddled together in clusters and rows. Whales feel cohesion, a sense of community, of loyalty. The distress call of a lone whale is enough to prompt its entire pod to rush to its side—a gesture that lands them nose to nose in the same sand. It's a fatal symphony of echolocation, a siren call to the sympathetic.

5. The death is slow. As mammals of the Cetacea order, whales are conscious breathers. Inhalation is a choice, an occasional rise to the ocean's surface. Although their ancestors lived on land, constant oxygen exposure overwhelms today's creatures.

6. Beached whales become frantic, captives to their hyperventilation. Most die from dehydration. The salty air shrinks their oily pores, capturing their moisture. Deprived of the buoyancy water provides, whales can literally crush themselves to death. Some collapse before they dry out—their lungs suffocating under their massive bodies—or drown when high tides cover their blowholes, filling them slowly while they're too weak to move. The average whale can't last more than twenty-four hours on land.

7. In their final moments, they begin belching and erupting in violent thrashing. Finally, their jaws open slightly—not all the way, but just enough that the characteristic illusion of a perpetual smile disappears. This means it's over. I know this because I watched as twenty-three whale mouths unhinged. As twenty-three pairs of whale eyes glazed over.

I had woken up that morning to a triage center outside my window. Fifty or so pilot whales were lying along the stretch of beach in front of my house on Cape Cod, surrounded by frenzied neighbors and animal activists. The Coast Guard had arrived while I was still sleeping, and guardsmen were already using boats with giant nets in an attempt to pull the massive bodies back into the water. Volunteers hurried about in groups, digging trenches around the whales' heads to cool them off, placing wet towels on their skin, and forming assembly lines to pour buckets of water on them. The energy was nervous, confused, and palpably urgent.

Pilot whales are among the most populous of the marine mammals in the cetacean order. Fully grown males can measure up to twenty feet and weigh three tons, while females usually reach sixteen feet and 1.5 tons.

Their enormity was their problem. Unlike the three dolphins that had managed to strand themselves near our house the previous summer, fifty pilot whales were nearly impossible to maneuver. If unfavorable tidal currents and topography unite, the larger species may be trapped. Sandbars sneak up on them, and tides tie them back.

People are strange about animals. Especially large ones. Daily, on the docks of Wellfleet Harbor, thousands of fish are scaled, gutted, and seasoned with thyme and lemon. No one strokes their sides with water. No one cries when their jaws slip open.

Pilot whales are not an endangered species, yet people spend tens of thousands of dollars in rescue efforts, trucking the wounded to aquariums and in some places even airlifting them off beaches. Perhaps the whales' sheer immensity fosters sympathy. Perhaps the stories of Jonah or Moby Dick do the same. Or maybe it's that article we read last week about that whale in Australia understanding hand signals. Intelligence matters, doesn't it? Brain size is important, right? Those whales knew they were dying. They have some sort of language, some sort of emotion. They give birth, for God's sake! There aren't any pregnant fish in the Wellfleet nets. No communal understanding of their imminent fatality.

I worry sometimes that humans are afraid of helping humans. There's less risk associated with animals, less fear of failure, fear of getting too involved. In war movies, a thousand soldiers can die gruesomely, but when the horse is shot, the audience is heartbroken. It's the *My Dog Skip* effect. The *Homeward Bound* syndrome.

When we hear that the lady on the next street over has cancer, we don't see the entire town flock to her house. We push and shove wet whales all day, then walk home through town past homeless men curled up on benches—washed up like whales on the curbsides. Pulled outside by the moon and struggling for air among the sewers. They're suffocating too, but there's no town assembly line of food. No palpable urgency, no airlifting plane.

Fifty stranded whales are a tangible crisis with a visible solution. There's camaraderie in the process, a *Free Willy* fantasy, an image of Flipper in everyone's mind. There's nothing romantic about waking up a man on a park bench and making him walk to a shelter. Little self-righteous fulfillment comes from sending a check to Oxfam International.

Would there be such a commotion if a man washed up on the beach? Yes. But stranded humans don't roll in with the tide—they hide in the corners and the concrete houses and the plains of exotic countries we've never heard of, dying of diseases we can't pronounce.

In theory I can say that our resources should be concentrated on saving human lives, that our SAVE THE WHALES T-shirts should read SAVE THE STARVING ETHIOPIANS. Logically, it's an easy argument to make. Why do we spend so much time caring about animals? Yes, their welfare is important, but surely that of humans is more so.

Last year a nonprofit spent $10,000 transporting a whale to an aquarium in Florida, where it died only three days after arriving. That same $10,000 could have purchased hundreds of thousands of food rations. In theory, this is easy to say.

But when I was looking in the eye of a dying pilot whale at four in the morning, my thoughts were not so philosophical. Four hours until high tide. Keep his skin moist. Just three hours now. There wasn't time for logic. My rationality had slipped away with the ebbing dance of the waves.

I had helped all day. We had managed to save twenty-seven of the fifty whales, but twenty-three others were deemed too far up shore, too old, or already too close to death. That night, after most of the volunteers had gone home, I went back outside my bedroom to check on the whales.

It was mid-tide, and the up-shore seaward still crunched under my bare feet. The water was rising. The moonlight drifted down on the salt-caked battlefield, reflected in the tiny pools of water and half-shell oysters.

It was easy to spot the living whales. Their bodies, still moist, shone in the moonlight. I weaved between carcasses, kneeling down beside an old whale that was breathing deeply and far too rapidly for a healthy pilot.

I put my hands on his nose and placed my face in front of his visible eye. I knew he was going to die, and he knew he was going to die, and we both understood that there was nothing either of us could do about it.

Beached whales die on their sides, one eye pressed into the sand, the other facing up and forced to look at the moon, at the orb that pulled the water out from under its fins.

There's no echolocation on land. I imagine dying slowly next to my mother or a lover, helplessly unable to relay my parting message. I remember trying to convince myself that everything would be fine. But he wouldn't be fine. Just like the homeless man and the Ethiopian aren't fine.

Perhaps I should have been comforting one of them, placing my hands on their shoulders. Spending my time and my money and my life saving those who walked on two legs and spoke without echoes.

The moon pulled the waters forward and backward, then inward and around my ankles. Before I could find an answer, the whale's jaw unclenched, opening lightly around the edges.

## Reading for Better Writing

1. *Connections:* Have you witnessed a sick or injured animal struggle to live? Where did the event happen, when, and why? How did you respond at the time, and how does recalling the event now make you feel—especially in light of reading Keegan's essay?

2. *Comprehension:*
   a. Summarize Keegan's essay. What is her topic, how does she introduce it, and how does she entice us to care about it? What passages do you find most engaging?
   b. What is her thesis, and what does she compare and contrast in order to develop the thesis?
   c. Describe her attitude toward her topic and cite passages that convey this attitude.

3. *Writing Moves:*
   a. In the opening sentences, Keegan uses personification to describe the moon. What is the effect of beginning this way?
   b. For the first half of the essay (paragraphs 1-12), Keegan explores the human response to the beaching of whales. What techniques does she use to help readers understand this situation?
   c. At paragraph 13, Keegan turns from stranded whales to stranded people. What techniques does she use to compare and contrast the two situations?
   d. How do the opening and closing paragraphs frame Keegan's essay?

**Your Project:** Review your answer to question 1. Then consider writing an essay in which you compare and/or contrast your experience with Keegan's. Another option would be to consider other connections and distinctions between humans and animals.

Copyright Yale Daily News Publishing Company, Inc. All rights reserved. Reprinted with Permission.

## Analyzing Internet Bullying

As a contributor to *The New Yorker*, Maria Konnikova writes regularly about psychology and science. In the essay that follows, she uses compare-contrast thinking to analyze how and why bullying has changed during the last few decades. Konnikova's books include *Mastermind: How to Think Like Sherlock Holmes*, *The Confidence Game*, and *The Biggest Bluff*. (Her essay is from the October 21, 2015 edition of *The New Yorker*.)

### How the Internet Has Changed Bullying

This summer, *American Psychologist*, the official journal of the American Psychological Association, released a special issue on the topic of bullying and victimization. Bullying is, presumably, as old as humanity, but research into it is relatively young: in 1997, when Susan Swearer, one of the issue's two editors, first started studying the problem, she was one of the first researchers in the United States to do so. Back then, only four states had official statutes against bullying behavior, and the only existing longitudinal work had come out of Scandinavia, in the seventies. After Columbine, however, the landscape changed. The popular narrative at the time held that the shooters, Eric Harris and Dylan Klebold, had been bullied, and that idea—which has since been challenged—prompted a nationwide conversation about bullying, which researchers around the country began studying in earnest. This special issue marks one of the first attempts to systematically review what we've learned in the last two decades—and, especially, to explore whether and how the Internet has changed the bullying landscape.

In some ways, bullying research has affirmed what we already know. Bullying is the result of an unequal power dynamic—the strong attacking the weak. It can happen in different ways: through physical violence, verbal abuse (in person or online), or the management of relationships (spreading rumors, humiliation, and exclusion). It is usually prolonged (most bullies are repeat offenders) and widespread (a bully targets multiple victims). Longitudinal work shows that bullies and victims can switch places: there is an entire category of bully-victims—people who are victims in one set of circumstances and perpetrators in another. Finally, emerging research demonstrates that bullying follows us throughout life. Workplace and professional bullying is just as common as childhood bullying; often, it's just less obvious. (At work—one hopes—people don't steal your bicycle or give you a wedgie.)

To date, no one has systematically studied how different bullying settings affect bullying behavior—whether bullying in the Northeast differs from bullying in the Midwest, or whether bullying in certain cultures, neighborhoods, or professions comes with its own characteristics. What Swearer has noticed, however, in her nearly two decades of bullying research is a persistent—and seemingly fundamental—environmental distinction between urban and rural bullying. In urban and even mid-sized city environments, anonymity is possible. Even if you're bullied in school, you can have a supportive friend group at your local pickup basketball game. And there are multiple schools and multiple neighborhoods, which means you can float from one to the other, leaving bullying behind you in the process.

By contrast, in rural settings, "There aren't options," Swearer said, when we spoke earlier this month. "It's impossible to get away." The next school may be a hundred miles distant, so you are stuck where you are. What's more, everyone knows everyone. The problems of reporting a bully—or, if you are a bully, of becoming less of one—become much more intractable, because your reputation surrounds you, and behavioral patterns are harder to escape. "Your world becomes an isolated and small place," Swearer says. Isolation itself, she points out, can lead to a sense of helplessness and lack of control—feelings that are associated with some of the worst, most persistent psychological problems in any population, including bullying.

In some ways, when it comes to bullying, the Internet has made the world more rural. Before the Internet, bullying ended when you withdrew from whatever environment you were in. But now, the bullying dynamic is harder to contain and harder to ignore. If you're harassed on your Facebook page, all of your social circles know about it; as long as you have access to the network, a ceaseless stream of notifications leaves you vulnerable to victimhood. Bullying may not have become more prevalent—in fact, a recent review of international data suggests that its incidence has declined by as much as ten percent around the world. But getting away from it has become more difficult.

The inescapability of "cyberbullying" has huge consequences not just for children but also for adults. While workplace bullying is still a new field of study, adults seem to experience bullying just as much as kids do. A 2012 study from the University of Nottingham and the University of Sheffield, in the U.K., found that eight out of ten of the three hundred and twenty adults surveyed across three different universities had been victims of cyberbullying in the last six months; about a quarter reported feeling humiliated or ignored, or being the subject of online gossip, at least once a week. The effects of adult bullying can be just as severe, if not more so, than those of childhood bullying. While students can go to their teachers if they're being bullied, if you report your boss, you could be out of a job. And adult victims of cyberbullying tend to suffer higher levels of mental strain and lower job satisfaction than those subjected to more traditional forms of bullying. An undermining colleague can be put out of mind at the end of the day. But someone who persecutes you over email, social networks, or anonymous comments is far more difficult to avoid and dismiss.

Many forms of adult bullying are uncomfortably close to the sorts of shaming behaviors outlined by Jon Ronson in his recent book, *So You've Been Publicly Shamed*. Ronson documents the rise of cyberbrigades, which unite in virtual outrage, on Twitter, Reddit, or elsewhere online, to disparage someone's words or behavior. Participants often feel that their abusive actions flow from justified outrage—but all bullies think that their behavior is justified. "We know from moral disengagement work that all bullies feel morally justified in their actions," Swearer pointed out. Ask people why they bully, and they rarely say, "Because I can." They say, "Because I need to." Bullies believe they are teaching someone a lesson; they claim that their victims are, through their own actions or faults, asking for it, and that they need to be called out and corrected. "They say it's retaliatory. 'I just retaliated,'" Swearer said. "They build narratives of their behaviors." Many of the bullies Swearer has dealt with don't seem to have realized that what they did was bullying: they demonstrate "a lack of insight and self-awareness." Instead, they see themselves as righteous crusaders.

In children, it's possible to instill self-awareness about bullying through schoolwide interventions. Catherine Bradshaw, a psychologist and associate dean at the University of Virginia who studies bullying prevention, has found that the most effective approaches are multilayered and include training, behavior-modification guidelines, and systems for detailed data collection. (More, in other words, than a stray assembly or distributed book.) Unfortunately, the equivalent for adults can be hard to find. Many adult bullies hide behind the idea that bullying happens only among children. They conceive of themselves as adults who know better and are offering their hard-earned wisdom to others. The Internet makes that sort of certainty easier to attain: looking at their screens, adult bullies rarely see the impact of their words and actions. Instead, they comfortably bask in self-righteous glory. The U.K. study from 2012 found that online bystanders, too, are disengaged. Observing the actions of cyberbullies, they were less concerned than when they watched in-person bullying.

In short, the picture that's emerged suggests that the Internet has made bullying both harder to escape and harder to identify. It has also, perhaps, made bullies out of some of us who would otherwise not be. We are immersed in an online world in which consequences often go unseen—and that has made it easier to deceive ourselves about what we are doing. The first step to preventing bullying among adults, therefore, might be simple: introspection.

9

## Reading for Better Writing

1. *Connections:* Do you know anyone who has been a perpetrator or victim of cyberbullying? How did it start, how was it done, and what was the outcome?
2. *Comprehension:*
    a. Summarize paragraph 2 in which Konnikova describes bullying and offers examples.
    b. In paragraphs 3 and 4, she compares and contrasts urban bullying with rural bullying. How are they similar and different?
    c. In paragraph 5 Konnikova says, "In some ways, when it comes to bullying, the Internet has made the world more rural." What does she mean, and what does this claim suggest about the danger of cyberbullying?
    d. How is adult bullying similar to or different from adolescent or teen bullying?
3. *Writing Moves:*
    a. Konnikova compares in-person bullying to cyberbullying, urban bullying to rural bullying, and adolescent and teen bullying to adult bullying. How does she develop each of these comparisons? How does each advance her argument?
    b. She supports her claims by quoting authorities and citing research. Find two examples and explain how each one strengthens her argument.
    c. Review the last paragraph. How does it bring the essay to a close?

**Your Project:** Bullying is just one behavior that has been impacted by the digital revolution. Consider comparing and contrasting another behavior similarly impacted (e.g., reading, dating, researching, shopping, traveling).

*Maria Konnikova*, The New Yorker, *(c) Conde Nast*

#  DIY: Craft Your Own Compare-Contrast Essay

## Planning

1. **Select a topic.** Start by reviewing your assignment, noting any topic requirements or restrictions. Then review the project options listed at the end of each sample essay. To generate more topic ideas, list subjects that are similar and/or different in ways that you find interesting, perplexing, disgusting, infuriating, charming, or informing. Then choose two subjects whose comparison and/or contrast gives the reader some insight into who or what they are. *Note:* Make sure that the items have a solid *basis* for comparison. Comparable items are types of the same thing (e.g., two fruits, two rivers, two characters, two films, two mental illnesses, two theories).

2. **Get the big picture.** Using a computer or a paper and pen, create three columns as shown in Figure 14.4. Brainstorm a list of traits under each heading. Another option is to use a Venn Diagram, as shown in Figure 14.2.

| Features Peculiar to Subject #1 | Shared Features | Features Peculiar to Subject #2 |
|---|---|---|
| | | |

*fig. 14.4*

3. **Gather information.** Review your list of features, highlighting those that could provide insight into one or both subjects. Research the subjects, using hands-on analysis when possible. Consider writing your research notes in the three-column format shown in Figure 14.4.

4. **Draft a working thesis.** Write a sentence stating the core of what you learned about the subjects: what essential insight have you reached about the similarities and/or differences between the topics? If you're stuck, try using the thesis template from earlier in the chapter.

5. **Get organized.** Decide how to organize your essay, using the blueprints in Figure 14.3 if helpful. Generally, *subject by subject* works better for short, simple comparisons. *Trait by trait* works better for longer, more complex comparisons, in that you hold up the topics side by side, trait by trait. Consider, as well, the order in which you will discuss the topics and arrange the traits, choices that depend on what you want to feature and how you want to build and deepen the comparison.

## Drafting

6. **Write your first draft.** Review your outline and draft the paper drawing upon the writing moves you learned in this chapter.

**Subject-by-subject pattern:**
- **Opening:** Get readers' attention, introduce the subjects, and offer a thesis.
- **Middle:** Discuss the first subject, then analyze the second subject, discussing traits parallel to those you addressed with the first subject.
- **Conclusion:** Summarize similarities, differences, and implications.

**Trait-by-trait pattern:**
- **Opening:** Get readers' attention, introduce the subjects, and offer a thesis.
- **Middle:** Compare and/or contrast the two subjects trait by trait; include transitions that help readers look back and forth between the two subjects.
- **Conclusion:** Summarize the key relationships and note their significance.

## Revising

7. **Get feedback.** Ask someone to read your paper, looking for a clear thesis, an engaging introduction, a middle that compares and/or contrasts parallel traits in a logical order, and a unifying closing.

8. **Rework your draft.** Refer back to your assignment directions to make sure your writing meets the requirements. Based on feedback and your assignment, revise for the following issues:
   - \_\_\_\_ **Ideas:** The points made and conclusions drawn from comparing and contrasting provide insight into both subjects
   - \_\_\_\_ **Organization:** The structure, whether subject by subject or trait by trait, helps readers grasp the similarities and differences between the subjects
   - \_\_\_\_ **Voice:** The tone is informed, involved, and genuine

## Polishing

9. **Carefully edit and proofread your essay.** Look for the following issues:
   - \_\_\_\_ **Words** are precise, clear, and defined as needed.
   - \_\_\_\_ **Sentences** are clear, well reasoned, varied in structure, and smooth. Transitions and comparison terms clearly signal similarities and differences.
   - \_\_\_\_ **Correctness:** The writing is clean and properly formatted.
   - \_\_\_\_ **Page design** is attractive and follows MLA or APA guidelines.

## Publishing

10. **Publish your essay.** Share your writing by submitting it to your instructor, posting it on a website, sharing it with friends and family who might be interested in the topic, crafting a presentation or demonstration, or reshaping your comparison as a blog.

# Compare-Contrast Essays: Applications

After you have finished your compare-contrast essay, consider how to apply what you have learned in the following situations.

1. **Living Today:** In the workplace, people commonly use compare-contrast reasoning to complete tasks such as selecting employees, choosing materials and equipment, and designing marketing plans. Think about your current or future job and list ways in which sound compare-contrast reasoning will help you succeed.
2. **Career Plan:** Choose two or three occupations that interest you. Researching them as needed, compare and contrast their required training, social benefits, financial rewards, availability, required experience, and personal appeal. Consider using this information to write or update your career plan.
3. **Writing Reset:** Select a piece of your writing that could be improved. Then compare your writing with similar papers written by classmates or available on the Internet. Identify strategies for improving your ideas, organization, and voice.
4. **Cultural Insight:** Research two ethnic groups that interest you. Then use comparison and contrast to analyze their systems of government, religious practices, penal institutions, educational systems, or healthcare programs. Remember to make your comparisons ethical: your discussion of similarities and differences should be nuanced, full, and fair.
5. **Sports Talk:** Compare and contrast two coaches in the same sport, examining issues such as their philosophies of the game, personalities, experiences as players, win-loss records, coaching strategies, teams coached, awards, and titles.

## Learning-Objectives Checklist ✓

Have you achieved this chapter's learning objectives? Check your progress with the following items, revisiting topics in the chapter as needed. I have . . .
- \_\_\_\_ determined what a compare-contrast essay is and what forms it might take.
- \_\_\_\_ practiced strategies for comparing and contrasting things.
- \_\_\_\_ developed a strong thesis for a compare-contrast essay.
- \_\_\_\_ identified writing moves and strategies for shaping compare-contrast writing.
- \_\_\_\_ crafted a strong compare-contrast essay by drawing upon a range of writing moves.

# Chapter 15

# Analytical Writing: Cause and Effect

*Why is the sky blue, Daddy? How do birds fly, Mommy, and why oh why can't I?* These are the kinds of questions kids ask when they're curious about the world they find themselves in. Do you remember asking questions like these?

"Why" and "how" questions are at the heart of curiosity, which is at the center of cause-effect analysis. Such critical thinking looks at a phenomenon—an event, fact, or situation—and asks what created it: What forces (the causes) led to the phenomenon (the effect)? Or such thinking may look at the phenomenon itself as a cause and analyze its effects. In different ways, cause-effect thinking is central to education, science, business, civics, and the arts. It deepens understanding and, in turn, leads to wiser choices. That's what curiosity-driven cause-effect writing offers readers.

Did you leave behind such curiosity with your childhood? This chapter may help you regain it.

**Visually Speaking** Carefully study Figure 15.1. What cause-effect relationships are shown? What writing strategies could you use to analyze the phenomenon pictured?

##  Learning Objectives

By working through this chapter, you will be able to

- explain what a cause-effect essay is and what forms it might take.
- practice strategies for doing cause-effect analysis.
- develop a strong thesis for a cause-effect essay.
- identify writing moves for shaping cause-effect writing.
- craft a strong cause-effect essay by drawing upon a range of writing moves.

Strahil Dimitrov / Shutterstock.com

fig. 15.1

# Meeting the Mode

One way to get familiar with cause-effect thinking is to read cause-effect writing. In the essay below, student writer Sarah Hanley asks "why" and "how" about adrenaline highs and adrenaline junkies. As you read, activate the strategies you learned in chapter 2 and ask, "What good does it do for Sarah to analyze causes and effects? And does she do it well?"

### Adrenaline Junkies

What do you picture when you hear the phrase "adrenaline junkie"? Evel Knievel soaring through the air on a motorcycle? Tom Cruise rappelling down the side of a mountain? An excited retiree stuffing quarters in a slot machine? Actually, all three qualify as adrenaline junkies if they do the activities to get their adrenaline highs. But what, exactly, is an adrenaline high, what causes it, what are its effects, and are the effects positive?

Adrenaline (also called epinephrine) is a hormone linked to the two adrenal glands located on top of the kidneys. Each gland has two parts: the outer portion called the cortex, and the inner portion called the medulla. When a person experiences an unusual exertion or a crisis situation, their brain triggers the medullas, which release little packets of adrenaline into the bloodstream (Nathan). The rush of adrenaline in the blood leads to increased blood pressure, heart rate, sugar metabolism, oxygen intake, and muscle strength. All these phenomena cause an adrenaline high: feeling highly alert and very energetic (Scheuller 2).

However, while all healthy people experience adrenaline highs, different people need different levels of stimulus to trigger the highs. The level of stimulus that a person needs depends on the amount of protein in their medullas. In other words, the medullas release adrenaline through channels containing a certain protein. If the channels contain a large amount of the protein, they release adrenaline more easily than channels containing less protein. Therefore, a person with a higher level of protein in the channels of their medullas experiences an adrenaline release more easily than someone with a lower level of the protein (Scheuller 4).

To illustrate this difference, we'll call the people with a higher level of protein (and a more easily stimulated output of adrenaline) Type N, for nervous; the others we'll call Type C, for calm. Because Type N people release adrenaline more easily than Type C people do, Type Ns require a lesser stimulus to trigger an adrenaline release. For example, a Type N person may get an adrenaline high from finishing a research paper on time, whereas a Type C person will get a similar buzz when she parachutes from a plane at 10,000 feet!

While different people get their adrenaline highs differently, any person's highs can be channeled for healthy or harmful effects. For example, the Type N person who gets a rush from finishing the research project could do good work as a junkie research technician in a science lab. As long as he avoids becoming a workaholic, seeking the highs won't threaten his health, and the work may contribute to the overall welfare of society. Similarly, the Type C person who gets her highs by jumping out of airplanes could do good work as a junkie firefighter or a junkie brain surgeon. As long as she gets periodic relief from the tension, the highs won't hurt her health, and the work could help her community.

On the other hand, pursuing the wrong type of adrenaline high, or seeking too many highs, can be destructive. Examples of this kind of behavior include compulsive gambling, drug use, careless risk taking in sports, and win-at-all-costs business practices. Destructive pursuits have many high-cost results including bankruptcy, broken relationships, physical injury, drug addiction, and death (Lyons 3). 6

Because adrenaline highs can lead to positive results, maybe we waste time worrying about becoming adrenaline junkies. Instead, we should ask ourselves how to pursue those highs positively. In other words, the proteins, hormones, and chemical processes that produce adrenaline highs are, themselves, very good—and they can be used for good. In fact, someday we may figure out how to bottle the stuff and put it on the market! 7

*"Adrenaline Junkies" by Sarah Hanley. Used with permission.*

## Converse with the Mode

So, what good does Sarah's cause-effect analysis of adrenaline highs do? It explains how they happen, how they differ for different people, and how they might be both beneficial and harmful. Sarah does her analysis well by offering precise descriptions and illustrations grounded in sound research. Now look a little closer at the essay.

### Conversation Starters

1. Sarah begins by asking a series of questions. How do these introduce her analysis?
2. In paragraphs 2–4, Sarah explains the science behind adrenaline. How would you map out the cause-effect links based on her discussion of human physiology?
3. In paragraphs 5 and 6, Sarah contrasts the benefits and drawbacks of adrenaline highs. What does this discussion add to her cause-effect analysis?
4. How would you describe the closing? What does Sarah do to tie up her analysis?

**Moving On:** Sarah's essay focuses on the human body as a site of causes and effects. What other bodily functions and processes are you curious about? For your own cause-effect essay, consider harmful processes, such as vaping or using drugs. How and why are these harmful? How does addiction work? Or consider productive processes, such as how the brain learns to read and what reading offers the brain.

# Strategies for Writing Cause-Effect Essays

Cause-effect thinking can move in two directions. First, it can explore the effects of a particular event, action, or phenomenon—the logical results, actual or anticipated. Second, it can trace backward from a particular result to those forces that created the results—the causes. As you think through causes and effects, your challenge is to establish and explain solid cause-effect links, as discussed in the strategies below.

## The Rhetorical Situation

To put your cause-effect writing in context, consider the situation that gives rise to it:

- **Purpose.** You use cause-effect analysis to deepen your own and your readers' understanding of how specific forces work to bring about particular results. In college and the workplace, cause-effect logic operates in many forms of writing—from persuasive essays and lab reports to project proposals and market analyses. In each situation, you use cause-effect thinking to explain a phenomenon or to prove a point. (Note: Different academic disciplines have distinct standards for collecting and interpreting evidence to establish causes and effects.)
- **Readers.** The readers of your cause-effect writing may understand the topic at a basic level but want or need a deeper understanding of the forces operating within it. That new knowledge will help them make decisions about or take positions on the topic.
- **Topic.** Your cause-effect topics are phenomena—events, occurrences, developments, processes, problems, conditions, and so on—that need to be more fully explained in terms of their operating forces.

*Example:* In "The Rise of the New Groupthink," Susan Cain's **topic** is the trend in society toward collaboration and away from solitude. Her **purpose** is to show her **readers**—anyone impacted by this trend—that while collaboration is important for work, creative developments are more often rooted in focused time spent alone and uninterrupted.

## Principles of Cause-Effect Writing

Cause-effect writing about a phenomenon requires that you think critically and creatively about both causes and effects, and that you effectively and ethically reason about the links between them.

**Exploring causes:** A cause is essentially some force—a person, an event, a condition—that gave rise to the phenomenon. For many phenomena, causation can be complex:

- **What forces can be designated as primary or root causes?** These are the forces that appear most direct, that seem to make the largest contribution to the phenomenon.
- **What forces might be secondary or contributing causes?** While indirect, these forces may have played an important role in creating conditions for the phenomenon.
- **Which causes are immediate (near), and which are remote (distant)?** Contrasting proximity (perhaps both in space and time, perhaps in the chain of causes leading to the phenomenon) puts causation in a larger context.

*The Fishbone Diagram:* One tool for exploring causation is the Ishikawa Fishbone Diagram. Originally used in manufacturing processes to identify root causes of problems, the fishbone diagram can be used to map out complex causes of a particular effect. As shown in Figure 15.2, the diagram sets up the effect at the far right and then examines what may have contributed to the effect in a series of categories.

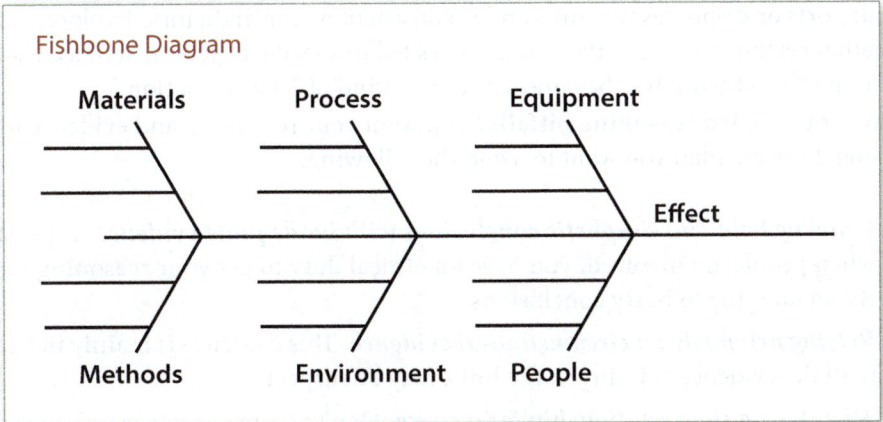

fig. 15.2

**Exploring effects:** As with causes, effects—changes that occur because of some causal force—can be complex:
- **What are the main or primary effects?** These are the most distinctive, the most direct and visible consequences of the forces at work.
- **What are secondary effects, outcomes that might also be called side-effects or ripple effects?** These indirect effects trace the sometimes unintended consequences of events, the way forces can have a wide and complicated impact.
- **Which effects are immediate, which long-term?** What is the seriousness or strength of each effect? These questions help you measure the nature and impact of effects.

*Reverse Fishbone Diagram:* To explore the full effects of a particular cause, you might try a reverse fishbone diagram (Figure 15.3). Put the cause at the far left, and then explore possible effects for each of the individual bones of the fish.

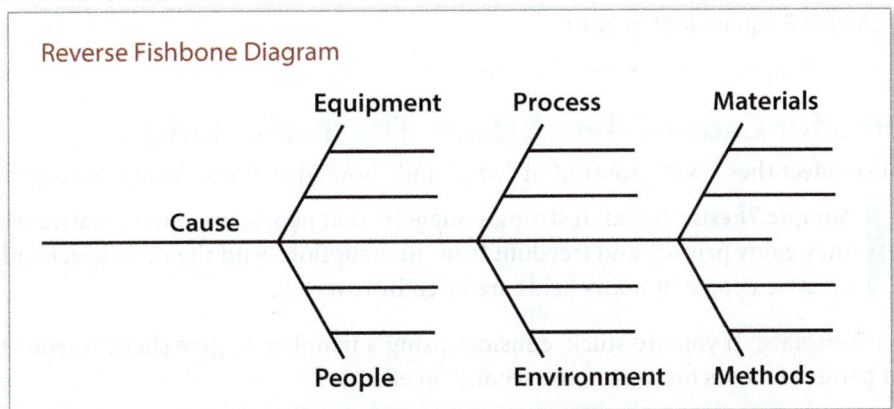

fig. 15.3

**Establishing reliable links:** While it's useful to think about causes and effects in isolation, you eventually need to examine the links between them. Ask these questions:
- **What's the evidence for links?** Evidence should be accurate, authoritative, close to the source, current, relevant, representative, and sufficient.
- **What reasoning makes sense of the evidence?** Examine the evidence to see whether it supports or disproves the links and is consistent or contradictory. Explore, too, whether certain aspects of the causal forces led to specific effects, as well as whether certain effects themselves became causes in a kind of "chain reaction."
- **Have you avoided reasoning pitfalls?** You want your reasoning and evidence to be strong. In particular, you want to avoid the following:

> *Drawing bold and simplistic conclusions with inadequate evidence.* Especially when people are involved, you have an ethical duty to get your reasoning right. Avoid jumping to hasty conclusions.
>
> *Relying primarily on circumstantial evidence.* This evidence is mainly indirect; if all the evidence is indirect, the links may be suspect.
>
> *Mistaking a time relationship for a cause.* Don't assume events were caused by preceding events.
>
> *Confusing associations with causes.* Don't assume that if two events occur at the same time that one causes the other.

### Sample Cause-Effect Paragraph

> The New Groupthink has overtaken our workplaces, our schools and our religious institutions. Anyone who has ever needed noise-cancelling headphones in her own office or marked an online calendar with a fake meeting in order to escape yet another real one knows what I'm talking about. Virtually all American workers now spend time on teams and some 70 percent inhabit open-plan offices, in which no one has "a room of one's own." During the last decades, the average amount of space allotted to each employee shrank 300 square feet, from 500 square feet in the 1970s to 200 square feet in 2010.

## Patterns for Cause-Effect Essays: Thesis Thinking

Your cause-effect thesis will grow out of "why" and "how" questions about your topic:

> **Sample Thesis:** Research strongly suggests that people are more creative when they enjoy privacy and freedom from interruption. And the most spectacularly creative people in many fields are often introverted.

**A Thesis Template:** If you are stuck, consider using a template to give shape to your thesis. The first pattern focuses on causes, the second on effects:

> *Focus on causes:* Based on a close examination of the forces at work, we can conclude that A and B are the fundamental causes of C.
>
> *Focus on effects:* Based on a close examination of the forces at work, we can conclude that the most important results of A have been X, Y, and Z.
>
> *Example:* When people around the globe watch Hollywood films [**cause**], they absorb a distorted vision of U.S. culture that fuels misunderstanding and, in fact, undermines the government's "war on terror" [**effects**].

**From Weak to Strong:** In chapter 4, you learned about refining your thesis to make it stronger. You can do the same with the thesis for your cause-effect essay. (*Warning:* These examples are for illustration. We aren't trained marriage counsellors!)

> *Weak Thesis:* obvious and simplistic analysis of causal forces; ethically questionable conclusion
>
> Having kids causes marriages to fall apart. Blame it on the kids.
>
> *Good Thesis:* logical cause-effect links rooted in sound reading of evidence
>
> If a marriage comes under strain in its early years, it's often a combination of four forces: child-rearing, career vs. home pressures, financial strains, and a stagnating sex life.
>
> *Excellent Thesis:* causal explanation with depth, surprising in what it reveals
>
> While a couple may divorce because of a wide range of troubles—infidelity, abuse, disagreements over parenting, and emotional distance—it turns out that the greatest reason by far is finances. That's right: it's about the money.

## Patterns for Cause-Effect Essays: Writing Moves

The structure you develop for your cause-effect essay should grow out of your thesis. In part, your thesis will determine the direction of your analysis: from an effect tracing back to its causes, or from a cause forward to its effects. Whichever structure you choose, also consider how you will arrange your points. You might, for example, arrange your discussion of causes from simplest to most complex, or from primary to secondary. You might arrange effects from immediate to distant, long-term consequences.

**Cause-Effect Blueprint**

| Cause-Focused | Effect-Focused |
|---|---|
| Beginning | Beginning |
| Effect(s) | Cause(s) |
| Cause | Effect |
| Cause | Effect |
| Cause | Effect |
| Ending | Ending |

*fig. 15.4*

To help you organize your cause-effect your essay, you might try either the fishbone diagram or its reverse. Another option would be one of the blueprints in Figure 15.4.

# Cause-Effect Essays: Learning Writers' Moves

How do writers shape cause-effect thinking in their essays? What do their writing moves look and sound like? You can learn some of these moves by studying the essays that follow. By reading these essays, you'll also add to the list of possible topics for your own essay.

## Analyzing Password Protection

Student writer Scott Reichelt wrote this essay for a course on writing in the science professions. Here, in language a nonscientist can understand, he explains the causes and effects at work in the rules established about two decades ago for computer passwords—that source of mild or extreme frustration for virtually all of us.

### 1$_Your_P@$$wOrd_Cl3v3r?

1   Like so many other tales of intrigue, the question of whether your password is truly clever begins deep within the labyrinthine bowels of the government bureaucracy. Here, we have an unassuming middle-management engineer—Bill Burr. In 2003 the National Institute of Standards and Technology (NIST) produced a document authored by Burr—"NIST Special Publication 800-63"—that has shaped passwords worldwide to this day. This document is the origin of ubiquitous password rules, now deeply entrenched in our collective consciousness, like "a minimum of eight characters," or "must include at least one capital letter," and the uninformative "cannot be in a dictionary." Even seemingly reasonable policies like "do not use the same password on multiple accounts" are laughably impractical in reality. These guidelines are so out of step with actual human behavior that they have, in practice, offered little to no increased security.

2   Bill Burr—since retired—admirably admitted to the world that his 2003 recommendation was incredibly misguided. "Much of what I did I now regret," Burr told *The Wall Street Journal*, in light of the countless millions he personally subjected to "guidelines" that are seemingly ripped straight from some deranged Orwellian oppression playbook. Burr concedes that the level of frustration stemming from the NIST guidelines he authored is not "commensurate with the overall value" they provide. Hundreds of man hours researching passwords simply concludes what most non-NIST bureaucrats know implicitly: creating a password in the modern era is a harrowing experience, which either results in some derivative of **mydogsname1!** Or that familiar process of recovering your account from a password as strong as it is impossible to remember—a process which of course cycles us back to making a brand-new password.

As tempting as it is to pin entirely on Bill Burr fifteen years of typing—and retyping *slowly*—these awkward strings, mathematicians and probability theory are squarely at the root of this problem. Key components for thinking about password strength in the language of probability are the length of the password, and how many characters there are to choose from. Users typically have a pool of 94 characters (52 letters, 32 symbols, and 10 numbers) available when constructing a password, and, fortunately, NIST has socially engineered people to interpret their recommended minimum of eight characters as "my password should be exactly eight characters." A particularly useful probability formula—raise the number of options to the power of the length—can quickly marshal these two components to give an idea of how many such passwords can be made, and consequently how hard it might be to randomly guess one. With 94 characters to choose from and our NIST-sanctioned 8-character length, we get $94^8$ possible passwords—that's 6,095,689,385,410,816, or roughly six quadrillion possibilities. NIST and the mathematicians would now like to think of password security as winning the lottery that is your Instagram account. When the NIST guidelines were written, this amount of complexity along with such a simplified view of hackers was thought to afford users centuries of protection from an attempt to crack their password. But Bill Burr miscalculated both the human capacity for subverting rules and the ability of hackers to exploit their understanding of human behavior.

These guidelines were meant to help you outfox an adversarial hacker; however, human beings, in practice, seem to rate actually *remembering* their passwords higher than achieving the cryptographically secure string of characters NIST intended. People unapologetically repudiate the spirit of those guidelines in order to achieve something usable; we trade in the potential for a true one-in-six quadrillion random snowflake of a password for a

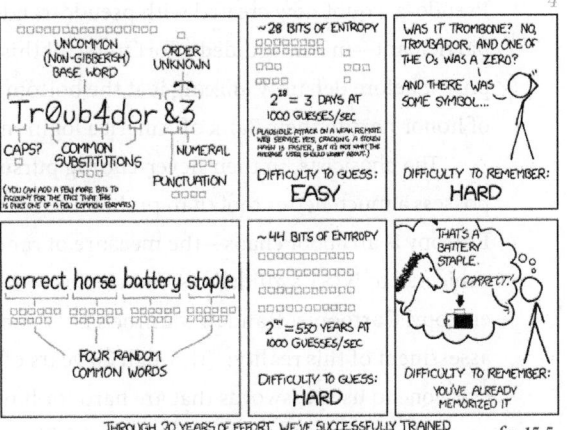

fig. 15.5

Comic courtesy of Randall Munroe at xkcd.com

banality that can be recalled. A 2011 study performed by students of Carnegie Mellon University along with Professor Lorrie Faith Cranor subjected 5,000 brave souls to the grueling process of both creating and remembering a password—for science. One participant eloquently captures our collective struggle, highlighting the predictable methods we all employ when faced with making a password under the watchful eye of our NIST overseers.

Our humble participant's first attempt at a password comes through as **cheese**. Something so viscerally memorable as creamy smoked Gouda meets exactly zero of the oppressive password requirements. The second attempt, **1cheese1**, gets closer, but lacks—the height of password pedanticism—a symbol. A dramatic change in direction, **12#$asdf**, makes attempt number three seem promising; but, alas, no capital letter. The devolution nearly complete, attempt number four—**12#$qwER**—is a cry for help, and, moreover, it fails the dictionary lookup. A tragic misnomer covertly referencing some esoteric computer science concept while masquerading as something so commonplace as *Merriam-Webster*—this is not that kind of dictionary. A better name might be a password blacklist, a repository of veritable clichés so woefully unclever they are no longer allowed to be passwords. Although **12#$qwER** may look like gibberish, **qwer** is just the first four letters of the top row of your keyboard, and **1234** is not magically subtle if you hold shift on 34 to achieve #$. The final attempt, with the old Missy Elliot "flip it and reverse it," gives us a winner with **43@!reWQ**. Pseudo-account now created with pseudo-random password. I imagine our beloved participant—in a misguided effort to recall this monstrosity later on—scrawls it on a post-it before defiantly affixing it at the bottom left corner of their monitor, a position of honor next to their Bank of America login information.

The physicists, in their never-ending pursuit to outperform mathematicians, possess a much better tool than probability for modeling password strength: entropy. Entropy is all about chaos—the measure of random disorder in a system. People subjected to NIST's guidelines find themselves with shockingly little password entropy. Cartoonist Randall Munroe's 2011 comic (see Figure 15.5) provides an apt assessment of this reality: "Through 20 years of effort, we have correctly trained everyone to use passwords that are hard for humans to remember, but easy for computers to guess." In her March 2013 TED talk, Carnegie Mellon professor Lorrie Cranor points out that "there is not actually a standard measure of [password] entropy," yet brutally effective modern password cracking algorithms abuse those formulaic—low entropy—password creation techniques we are all guilty of using.

Cranor created a quilt she calls "security blanket" (see Figure 15.6), which depicts the 1,000 most common passwords as a word cloud. This not-so-comforting blanket demonstrates how common these practices are.

fig. 15.6

"Security Blanket" courtesy of Lorrie Cranor

When large services have a security breach—like Yahoo's 2013 debacle resulting in three billion compromised accounts—your actual password should not be immediately known to hackers due to what is known as "hashing," or a hash function. Hash functions allow a service to store gibberish rather than your actual password on their servers to authenticate a login attempt. Sending your password through a series of hash functions transforms your p@$$wOrd into actual random nonsense, but the magic here is that every time you enter your p@$$wOrd, it hashes to the same exact nonsense. Hash functions can also not be reversed, thus when a service—say Yahoo—has a security breach, only gibberish is recovered initially, and hackers theoretically have to spend more than enough time hashing random strings of characters—playing the password lottery—for you to change your p@$$wOrd to something more secure (e.g., p@$$wOrd1). Thus, Yahoo has no idea what your actual password is, but authenticates your login using the knowledge that whatever you type into the password field on a login page exits their hash function as the precise gibberish they have stored on the server.

Dr. Mike Pound, a computer science research professor at the University of Nottingham, has a series of videos on the cat and mouse game of passwords. His July 2016 video, "Password Cracking Pound," demonstrates the terrifying efficiency with which a specialized computer and modern algorithms can crack passwords. Using only a naïve brute force attack, the specialized computer achieved an amazing 40 billion hashes-per-second; at this rate Pound can guess any targeted 8-character password in 42 hours or less by simply attempting every possible password until a match is found. Pound then demonstrates a tool (HashCat) performing a modern dictionary—any esoteric kind of dictionary—attack. Pound explains that a dictionary attack hashes a "list of commonly used passwords" first, and then "we manipulate them slightly, with rules, and we try them again." This technique models the iterative formulaic process people actually use when constructing passwords, allowing

Pound to go from one password cracked every 42 hours to thousands of passwords in a few minutes. The dictionary Pound uses is made up of actual users' passwords, accumulated through a long history of security breaches like what happened to Yahoo in 2013.

The art of designing cryptographically secure passwords may seem like a zero-sum game, but there are modern approaches to regain your edge over hackers. The model of using four random words (see Figure 15.5) is a simple but effective direction to take. If we assume a hacker knows you are using a password like this, we can apply our probability formula—raising the number of options to the power of the length—to see how secure this might be. Using a pool of just 10,000 words and choosing four at random, we get a massive $10,000^4$ (ten quadrillion) possible passwords. Dr. Pound recommends (if you're still worried) to have one word be "a bit weird," or even "just made up," and then "add a random symbol in the middle of one of those words." The likelihood that any known password-cracking approach will combine four random words in the correct order with the correct random symbol in the right position is as close to zero as we can reasonably hope. Now just make sure not to use the same password on multiple accounts, and you will have achieved NIST-approved nirvana. Or: just use a password manager and simplify your life.

9

## Reading for Better Writing

1. *Connections:* Do your computer passwords protect you sufficiently? How would you describe your level of care with them? Have you ever been hacked?
2. *Comprehension:* Summarize the NIST rules about passwords, as well as their failures. What alternative in the end does Reichelt offer?
3. *Writing Moves:*
   a. Reichelt opens his essay with the story of Bill Burr. What does this story accomplish? How is it a story of causes and effects?
   b. In paragraph 3, Reichelt describes probability theory as the "root of the problem." How does he proceed to explain this root cause?
   c. In paragraphs 4 and 5, Reichelt traces the actual effects of these rules. What strategy does he use to outline these? How does he make sense of the effects?
   d. The essay closes with an expert's explanation of the ease of hacking, along with his advice for beating hackers. What does this closing offer readers?
   e. This essay might be described as tracing a chain of causes and effects. How so?

**Your Project:** This essay examines the causal impacts surrounding computer passwords. What other technological developments have impacted your life? Might these be worthy of cause-effect analysis to understand their impact more fully?

"I$_YOur_P@$$wOrd_Cl3v3r?" by Scott Reichelt. Originally appeared in Prized Writing from UC-Davis. Used with permission.

## Analyzing the African American Experience of Baseball

Rob Ruck is a history professor at the University of Pittsburgh. With a focus on U.S. history and especially sports history, he's written extensively about baseball, particularly racial issues within the game. In this essay, published in February 2020 in *The Conversation*, he examines how during segregation African Americans established their own baseball institutions, and what happened to those after the game became integrated.

### On the 100th Anniversary of the Negro Leagues: A Look Back at What Was Lost

1   During the half century that baseball was divided by a color line, Black America created a sporting world of its own.

2   Black teams played on city sandlots and country fields, with the best barnstorming their way across the country and throughout the Caribbean.

3   A century ago, on Feb. 13, 1920, teams from eight cities formally created the Negro National League. Three decades of stellar play followed, as the league affirmed Black competence and grace on the field, while forging a collective identity that brought together Northern-born Blacks and their Southern brethren. And though Major League Baseball was segregated from the 1890s until 1947, these teams played countless interracial games in communities across the nation.

4   After World War II, Jackie Robinson hurdled baseball's racial divide. But while integration—baseball's great experiment—was a resounding success on the field, at the gates, and in changing racial attitudes, Negro League teams soon lost all of their stars and struggled to retain fans. The teams hung on for a bit, before eventually folding.

5   Years ago, when I worked on a documentary about the Negro Leagues, I was struck by how many of the interviewees looked back longingly on the leagues' heyday. While there was the understanding that integration needed to happen, there was also the recognition that something special was forever lost.

#### A League of Their Own

6   Given the injustices of the 1890s—sharecropping, lynchings, disenfranchisement, and the Supreme Court's sanctioning of segregation in Plessy v. Ferguson—exclusion from Major League Baseball was hardly the most grievous injury African Americans suffered. But it mattered. Their absence denied them the chance to participate in a very visible arena that helped European immigrants integrate into American culture.

7   While the sons of White immigrants—John McGraw, Honus Wagner, Joe DiMaggio—became major leaguers lionized by their nationalities, Black [people]

didn't have that opportunity. Most White [people] assumed that was because they weren't good enough. Their absence reinforced prevailing beliefs that African Americans were inherently inferior—athletically and intellectually—with weak abdominal muscles, little endurance, and prone to cracking under pressure.

The Negro Leagues gave Black ballplayers their own platform to prove otherwise. On Feb. 13, 1920, Chicago American Giants owner Rube Foster convened a meeting at the Paseo YMCA in Kansas City to organize the Negro National League. A Texas-born pitcher, Foster envisioned a Black alternative to the major leagues.

Northern Black communities were exploding in size, and Foster saw the league's potential. Teams like the American Giants and the Kansas City Monarchs regularly competed against White teams, drew large crowds and turned profits. Players enjoyed higher salaries than most Black workers, while Black newspapers trumpeted their exploits, as did some White papers.

Other leagues cropped up; the Negro National League was soon joined by the Negro American League and the Negro Southern League. Some years, the Negro National and Negro American Leagues played a Negro League World Series. The leagues also sent their best players to the East-West All-Star Classic, an annual exhibition game in Chicago.

But the Negro National League's ascent was stunted after Foster was exposed to a gas leak, nearly died, and suffered permanent brain damage. Absent his leadership and hammered by the Great Depression, the league disbanded in 1931.

## A Proving Ground

Gus Greenlee, who ran the popular lottery known as the numbers game, revived the league in Pittsburgh in 1933 after a sandlot club called the Crawfords, which included the young slugger Josh Gibson, approached him for support. He agreed to pay them salaries and reinforced their roster with the addition of flamethrower Satchel Paige.

Greenlee went on to build the finest Black-owned ballpark in the country, Greenlee Field, while headquartering the Negro National League on the floor above the Crawford Grill, his renowned jazz club in Pittsburgh's Hill District.

Pittsburgh soon became the mecca of Black baseball. Sitting along America's East-West rail lines, the city was a requisite stop for Black entertainers, leaders, and ball clubs, which traveled from cities as far away as Kansas City. Its two teams, the Homestead Grays and Pittsburgh Crawfords, won a dozen titles. Seven of the first 11 Negro Leaguers eventually inducted into the National Baseball Hall of Fame—stars like Cool Papa Bell, Oscar Charleston, Josh Gibson, Buck Leonard and Satchel Paige—played for one or both squads.

The sport, meanwhile, became a major source of Black pride.

"The very best," Pittsburgh-born author John Wideman noted, "not only competed among themselves and put on a good show, but [also] would go out and compete against their White contemporaries and beat the stuffing out of them."

Satchel Paige and the Crawfords famously defeated St. Louis Cardinals ace Dizzy Dean in an exhibition game in Cleveland—just two weeks after the Cardinals had won the 1934 World Series. Overall, Negro League teams won far more games against White squads than they lost.

"There was so much [negativity] living over [us] which we had no control [over]," Mal Goode, the first Black national network correspondent, recalled. "So anything you could hold on to from the standpoint of pride, it was there and it showed."

### Sacrificed on Integration's Altar

For Major League Baseball, no moment was more transformative than the arrival of Jackie Robinson, who, in 1947, paved the way for African Americans and darker-skinned Latinos to reshape the game.

But integration destroyed the Negro Leagues, plucking its young stars—Willie Mays, Henry Aaron, Roy Campanella, and Ernie Banks—who brought their fans with them. The big leagues never considered folding in some of the best Black teams, and its owners rejected the Negro National League owners' proposal to become a high minor league.

Like many Black papers, colleges, and businesses, the Negro National League paid a price for integration: extinction. The league ceased play after the 1948 season. Black owners, general managers, and managers soon disappeared, and it would be decades before a Black manager would get a chance to steer a major league ballclub.

Major League Baseball benefited from talent cultivated in the Negro Leagues and on the sandlots that sustained the sport, especially in inner cities. But when those leagues crumbled, prospective Black pros were relegated to minor league teams, often in inhospitable, southern cities. Many Negro League regulars simply hung up their cleats or played in the Caribbean.

The playwright August Wilson set his play, "Fences," which tells the story of an ex-Negro Leaguer who becomes a garbageman, in Pittsburgh.

"Baseball gave you a sense of belonging," Wilson said in a 1991 interview. At those Negro League games, he added, "The umpire ain't White. It's a Black umpire. The owner ain't White. Nobody's White. This is our thing ... and we have our everything—until integration, and then we don't have our nothing."

The story of African Americans in baseball has long been portrayed as a tale of their shameful segregation and redemptive integration. Segregation was certainly shameful, especially for a sport invested in its own rhetoric of democracy.

But for African Americans, integration was also painful. Although long overdue and an important catalyst for social change, it cost them control over their sporting lives.

It changed the meaning of the sport—what it symbolized and what it meant for their communities—and not necessarily for the better.

## Reading for Better Writing

1. *Connections:* Are you a baseball fan? Maybe a player? How would you describe your attitude toward the game? And what does it seem to stand for in American sports culture? Specifically, what's your sense of its connection to race relations?
2. *Comprehension:* During segregation, what was the African American experience of baseball all about? When did integration happen in baseball, and what were the results for African Americans?
3. *Writing Moves:*
    a. Ruck opens his essay with an historical overview. What does this accomplish? How does it set up the rest of his essay?
    b. In the sections "A League of Their Own" and "A Proving Ground," Ruck explains the rise of the Negro Leagues. What cause-effect forces does he identify, and how does he explain them?
    c. In the last section, "Sacrificed on Integration's Altar," Ruck explains the effects of integration on African Americans. How does he explain and support his conclusions?
    d. Segregation and integration are clearly ethically difficult topics in American culture. As he analyzes causes and effects, does Ruck approach the topic of segregation and integration in baseball fairly? If yes, how does he do so? If you believe he doesn't, where do you see problems?

**Your Project:** The history of race relations in the U.S. is an enormous topic. How has it been important in other sports, in education, in the workplace, in cities and rural areas, in religion, and so on? Consider how this issue has touched your life—whether positively, negatively, or both. Add these to your growing list of possible cause-effect topics.

"On the 100th anniversary of the Negro Leagues, a look back at what was lost" by Rob Ruck of the University of Pittsburgh. Originally published on February 13, 2020 at theconversation.com.

## Analyzing a Trend

Susan Cain is a Harvard-trained attorney, a businessperson, a negotiations consultant, and the author of a number of books and articles, including *Quiet: The Power of Introverts in a World That Can't Stop Talking*. In the following essay from *The New York Times*, she defines "New Groupthink" and analyzes its causes and effects.

### The Rise of the New Groupthink

1   Solitude is out of fashion. Our companies, our schools and our culture are in thrall to an idea I call the New Groupthink, which holds that creativity and achievement come from an oddly gregarious place. Most of us now work in teams, in offices without walls, for managers who prize people skills above all. Lone geniuses are out. Collaboration is in.

2   But there's a problem with this view. Research strongly suggests that people are more creative when they enjoy privacy and freedom from interruption. And the most spectacularly creative people in many fields are often introverted, according to studies by the psychologists Mihaly Csikszentmihalyi and Gregory Feist. They're extroverted enough to exchange and advance ideas, but see themselves as independent and individualistic. They're not joiners by nature.

3   One explanation for these findings is that introverts are comfortable working alone—and solitude is a catalyst to innovation. As the influential psychologist Hans Eysenck observed, introversion fosters creativity by "concentrating the mind on the tasks in hand, and preventing the dissipation of energy on social and sexual matters unrelated to work." In other words, a person sitting quietly under a tree in the backyard, while everyone else is clinking glasses on the patio, is more likely to have an apple land on his head. (Newton was one of the world's great introverts: William Wordsworth described him as "A mind for ever/ Voyaging through strange seas of Thought, alone.")

4   Solitude has long been associated with creativity and transcendence. "Without great solitude, no serious work is possible," Picasso said. A central narrative of many religions is the seeker—Moses, Jesus, Buddha—who goes off by himself and brings profound insights back to the community.

5   Culturally, we're often so dazzled by charisma that we overlook the quiet part of the creative process. Consider Apple. In the wake of Steve Jobs's death, we've seen a profusion of myths about the company's success. Most focus on Mr. Jobs's supernatural magnetism and tend to ignore the other crucial figure in Apple's creation: a kindly, introverted engineering wizard, Steve Wozniak, who toiled alone on a beloved invention, the personal computer.

Rewind to March 1975: Mr. Wozniak believes the world would be a better place if everyone had a user-friendly computer. This seems a distant dream—most computers are still the size of minivans, and many times as pricey. But Mr. Wozniak meets a simpatico band of engineers that call themselves the Homebrew Computer Club. The Homebrewers are excited about a primitive new machine called the Altair 8800. Mr. Wozniak is inspired, and immediately begins work on his own magical version of a computer. Three months later, he unveils his amazing creation for his friend, Steve Jobs. Mr. Wozniak wants to give his invention away free, but Mr. Jobs persuades him to cofound Apple Computer.

The story of Apple's origin speaks to the power of collaboration. Mr. Wozniak wouldn't have been catalyzed by the Altair but for the kindred spirits of Homebrew. And he'd never have started Apple without Mr. Jobs.

But it's also a story of solo spirit. If you look at how Mr. Wozniak got the work done—the sheer hard work of creating something from nothing—he did it alone. Late at night, all by himself.

Intentionally so. In his memoir, Mr. Wozniak offers this guidance to aspiring inventors: "Most inventors and engineers I've met are like me . . . they live in their heads. They're almost like artists. In fact, the very best of them are artists. And artists work best alone . . . I'm going to give you some advice that might be hard to take. That advice is: Work alone. . . . Not on a committee. Not on a team."

And yet. The New Groupthink has overtaken our workplaces, our schools and our religious institutions. Anyone who has ever needed noise-cancelling headphones in her own office or marked an online calendar with a fake meeting in order to escape yet another real one knows what I'm talking about. Virtually all American workers now spend time on teams and some 70 percent inhabit open-plan offices, in which no one has "a room of one's own." During the last decades, the average amount of space allotted to each employee shrank 300 square feet, from 500 square feet in the 1970s to 200 square feet in 2010.

Our schools have also been transformed by the New Groupthink. Today, elementary school classrooms are commonly arranged in pods of desks, the better to foster group learning. Even subjects like math and creative writing are often taught as committee projects. In one fourth-grade classroom I visited in New York City, students engaged in group work were forbidden to ask a question unless every member of the group had the very same question.

The New Groupthink also shapes some of our most influential religious institutions. Many mega-churches feature extracurricular groups organized around every conceivable activity, from parenting to skateboarding to real estate, and expect worshipers to join in. They also emphasize a theatrical style of worship—loving Jesus out loud, for all the congregation to see. "Often the role of a pastor seems closer to that of church cruise director than to the traditional roles of spiritual friend and counselor," said Adam McHugh, an evangelical pastor and author of *Introverts in the Church.*

13   Some teamwork is fine and offers a fun, stimulating, useful way to exchange ideas, manage information and build trust.

14   But it's one thing to associate with a group in which each member works autonomously on his piece of the puzzle; it's another to be corralled into endless meetings or conference calls conducted in offices that afford no respite from the noise and gaze of co-workers. Studies show that open-plan offices make workers hostile, insecure and distracted. They're also more likely to suffer from high blood pressure, stress, the flu and exhaustion. And people whose work is interrupted make 50 percent more mistakes and take twice as long to finish it.

15   Many introverts seem to know this instinctively, and resist being herded together. Backbone Entertainment, a video game development company in Emeryville, Calif., initially used an open-plan office, but found that its game developers, many of whom were introverts, were unhappy. "It was one big warehouse space, with just tables, no walls, and everyone could see each other," recalled Mike Mika, the former creative director. "We switched over to cubicles and were worried about it—you'd think in a creative environment that people would hate that. But it turns out they prefer having nooks and crannies they can hide away in and just be away from everybody."

16   Privacy also makes us productive. In a fascinating study known as the Coding War Games, consultants Tom DeMarco and Timothy Lister compared the work of more than 600 computer programmers at 92 companies. They found that people from the same companies performed at roughly the same level—but that there was an enormous performance gap between organizations. What distinguished programmers at the top-performing companies wasn't greater experience or better pay. It was how much privacy, personal workspace and freedom from interruption they enjoyed. Sixty-two percent of the best performers said their workspace was sufficiently private compared with only 19 percent of the worst performers. Seventy-six percent of the worst programmers but only 38 percent of the best said that they were often interrupted needlessly.

17   Solitude can even help us learn. According to research on expert performance by the psychologist Anders Ericsson, the best way to master a field is to work on the task that's most demanding for you personally. And often the best way to do this is alone. Only then, Mr. Ericsson told me, can you "go directly to the part that's challenging to

you. If you want to improve, you have to be the one who generates the move. Imagine a group class—you're the one generating the move only a small percentage of the time."

Conversely, brainstorming sessions are one of the worst possible ways to stimulate creativity. The brainchild of a charismatic advertising executive named Alex Osborn who believed that groups produced better ideas than individuals, workplace-brainstorming sessions came into vogue in the 1950s. "The quantitative results of group brainstorming are beyond question," Mr. Osborn wrote. "One group produced 45 suggestions for a home-appliance promotion, 56 ideas for a money-raising campaign, 124 ideas on how to sell more blankets."

But decades of research show that individuals almost always perform better than groups in both quality and quantity, and group performance gets worse as group size increases. The "evidence from science suggests that business people must be insane to use brainstorming groups," wrote the organizational psychologist Adrian Furnham. "If you have talented and motivated people, they should be encouraged to work alone when creativity or efficiency is the highest priority."

The reasons brainstorming fails are instructive for other forms of group work, too. People in groups tend to sit back and let others do the work; they instinctively mimic others' opinions and lose sight of their own; and, often succumb to peer pressure. The Emory University neuroscientist Gregory Berns found that when we take a stance different from the group's, we activate the amygdala, a small organ in the brain associated with the fear of rejection. Professor Berns calls this "the pain of independence."

The one important exception to this dismal record is electronic brainstorming, where large groups outperform individuals; and the larger the group the better. The protection of the screen mitigates many problems of group work. This is why the Internet has yielded such wondrous collective creations. Marcel Proust called reading a "miracle of communication in the midst of solitude," and that's what the Internet is, too. It's a place where we can be alone together—and this is precisely what gives it power.

My point is not that man is an island. Life is meaningless without love, trust and friendship.

And I'm not suggesting that we abolish teamwork. Indeed, recent studies suggest that influential academic work is increasingly conducted by teams rather than by individuals. (Although teams whose members collaborate remotely, from separate universities, appear to be the most influential of all.) The problems we face in science, economics and many other fields are more complex than ever before, and we'll need to stand on one another's shoulders if we can possibly hope to solve them.

But even if the problems are different, human nature remains the same. And most humans have two contradictory impulses: we love and need one another, yet we crave privacy and autonomy.

To harness the energy that fuels both these drives, we need to move beyond the New Groupthink and embrace a more nuanced approach to creativity and learning. Our offices should encourage casual, cafe-style interactions, but allow people to disappear into personalized, private spaces when they want to be alone. Our schools should teach children to work with others, but also to work on their own for sustained periods of time. And we must recognize that introverts like Steve Wozniak need extra quiet and privacy to do their best work.

Before Mr. Wozniak started Apple, he designed calculators at Hewlett-Packard, a job he loved partly because HP made it easy to chat with his colleagues. Every day at 10 a.m. and 2 p.m., management wheeled in doughnuts and coffee, and people could socialize and swap ideas. What distinguished these interactions was how low-key they were. For Mr. Wozniak, collaboration meant the ability to share a doughnut and a brainwave with his laid-back, poorly dressed colleagues—who minded not a whit when he disappeared into his cubicle to get the real work done.

## Reading for Better Writing

1. *Connections:* Was group work stressed in your grade school and high school? Were you seated in pods to encourage interaction with classmates? Is group work stressed in your college classes, and does it help or hinder your learning? Explain.
2. *Comprehension:*
    a. In your own words, state Susan Cain's thesis, paraphrase her definition of "New Groupthink," and summarize her primary argument.
    b. List four claims she makes about the causes and effects of New Groupthink.
    c. What does she say in paragraphs 11 and 12 regarding the effects of New Groupthink in schools and churches?
3. *Writing Moves:*
    a. Describe how Cain uses the Steve Wozniak anecdote. Is it effective? Why?
    b. When and how does she use researched evidence? How does that research support cause-effect reasoning?

**Your Project:** In her essay, Susan Cain analyzes a trend in society. What trends in society have you noticed? Which trends have impacted you in some way? Consider education, work, entertainment, technology, healthcare, sports, and more.

*From* The New York Times, *January 13, 2012 © 2012 The New York Times. All rights reserved. Used by permission and protected by the Copyright Laws of the United States. The printing, copying, redistribution, or retransmission of this Content without express written permission is prohibited.*

#  DIY: Craft Your Own Cause-Effect Essay

## Planning

1. **Select a topic.** Start by reviewing your assignment, noting any topic requirements or restrictions. Then revisit the project ideas at the end of each sample essay. You might also consider categories such as those listed below and brainstorm phenomena related to each category. From your brainstorming, choose a topic you really wish to understand more deeply.
   - **Society:** nurse, doctor, and engineer shortages; home-grown terrorists; elder and spouse abuse; shifting ethnic ratios; college student debt; super bugs; bitcoin use
   - **Environment:** decreasing bees, shale-oil pollution, noise pollution, lead-poisoned water, decreasing mines, increasing nuclear power plants, forest fires, earthquakes

2. **Narrow and research the topic.** State your topic and below it, list related causes and effects in two columns (see Figure 15.5). Another option is to do the fishbone diagram (Figure 15.2). Next, do preliminary research to expand your brainstorming and distinguish primary causes and effects from secondary ones. Revise your topic as needed to address only primary causes and/or effects that research links to a specific phenomenon.

   | Cause-effect Topic: _____ | |
   |---|---|
   | Causes (Because of) | Effects (this results) |
   | 1. _____ | 1. _____ |
   | 2. _____ | 2. _____ |
   | 3. _____ | 3. _____ |

   *fig. 15.5*

3. **Draft and test your thesis.** Based on your preliminary research, draft a working thesis (you may revise it later) that introduces the topic, along with the causes and/or effects you intend to discuss. Limit your argument to only those points you can prove.

4. **Gather and analyze information.** Research your topic, looking for clear evidence that links specific causes to specific effects. Make sure the evidence you collect is suited to your assignment. As you study the phenomenon, distinguish between primary and secondary causes (main and contributing), direct and indirect results, short-term and long-term effects, and so on. At the same time, test your analysis to avoid mistaking a coincidence for a cause-effect relationship. Use the list of logical fallacies in chapter 17 to weed out common errors in logic.

5. **Get organized.** Develop an outline that lays out your thesis and argument in a clear pattern. Use blueprints and writing organizers as needed. Under each main point asserting a cause-effect connection, list details from your research that support the connection. (See Figure 15.6.)

   | Thesis: _____ | | |
   |---|---|---|
   | Point #1 | Point #2 | Point #3 |
   | • Supporting details | • Supporting details | • Supporting details |
   | • Supporting details | • Supporting details | • Supporting details |

   *fig. 15.6*

## Drafting

6. **Use your outline to draft the essay.** Draft the essay's overall argument before you attempt to revise it, drawing on the writing moves you've learned for cause-effect reasoning. As you write, show how each specific cause led to each specific effect, citing examples as needed. Use transitional words to show cause-effect relationships:

   - accordingly
   - as a result
   - because
   - consequently
   - for this purpose
   - for this reason
   - hence
   - just as
   - since
   - so
   - such as
   - thereby
   - therefore
   - thus
   - to illustrate
   - whereas

## Revising

7. **Get feedback.** Ask a peer reviewer to read your essay for an engaging opening, a thoughtful cause-effect thesis, clear and convincing reasoning that links specific causes to specific effects, and a closing that deepens and extends the cause-effect analysis.

8. **Revise the essay.** Whether your essay presents causes, effects, or both, use the checklist below to trace and refine your argument. Also make sure the writing fits the assignment criteria.

   ____ **Ideas:** The essay explains the causes and/or effects of the topic in a clear, well-reasoned analysis. The analysis is supported by credible information and free of logical fallacies.

   ____ **Organization:** The structure helps clarify the cause-effect relationships through a well traced line of thinking, and the links between the main points, supporting points, and evidence are clear.

   ____ **Voice:** The tone is informed, reasonable, committed, and measured.

## Polishing

9. **Edit and proofread the essay for clarity and correctness.** Check for the following:

   ____ **Words:** The diction is precise and clear, and technical or scientific terms are defined. Causes are linked to effects with transitional words and phrases.

   ____ **Sentences:** Structures are clear, varied, and smooth.

   ____ **Correctness:** The grammar, punctuation, mechanics, usage, and spelling are correct.

   ____ **Design:** The format, layout, and typography fit the situation; any visuals used enhance the written analysis and clarify the paper's cause-effect reasoning.

## Publishing

10. **Publish your essay.** Share your writing by submitting it to your instructor, posting it on the class's or department's website, or turning it into a presentation.

# Cause-Effect Essays: Applications

Apply what you have learned about cause-effect writing by completing these activities.

1. **Career Plans:** How is cause-effect reasoning used in your discipline? Cite common applications and for each, explain who uses it, why, how, and to what end. If writing is involved, describe the document types, topics, likely writers, and readers. Finally, assess your ability to use cause-effect reasoning, and how you might hone those skills through course work, internships, or workplace experiences.
2. **Living Today:** In her essay, Susan Cain analyzes how the "New Groupthink" can limit the creative efforts of group members. Reflect on your own experiences working with groups. Did you ever witness the New Groupthink? If you did, describe its causes and effects, including how your role in the group supported or challenged the phenomenon.
3. **Sports Talk:** In his essay on the Negro Leagues, Rob Ruck analyzes the historical cause-effect forces at work in baseball. The history of changes in any sport may be understood in cause-effect terms. Consider sports you like playing or watching. Then choose one and do some research about how that sport has changed over time and/or is changing right now. What are the cause-effect forces at work?
4. **Public Texts:** In the public sphere, officials and experts are often called upon to explain phenomena and decisions, typically using cause-effect language. Especially in times of crisis, government officials, business leaders, scientists and other experts, and even cultural leaders are called upon by journalists and the public to explain what's going on and what needs to happen. Consider the COVID-19 crisis or an earlier time of troubles. Find a news article or video featuring an official addressing the crisis: how well does that person's cause-effect reasoning come through? What does it offer the public?

## Learning-Objectives Checklist ✓

Have you achieved this chapter's learning objectives? Check your progress with the following items, revisiting topics in the chapter as needed. I have . . .

____ determined what a cause-effect essay is and what forms it might take.
____ practiced strategies for analyzing causes and effects for phenomena.
____ developed a strong thesis for a cause-effect essay.
____ identified writing moves for shaping cause-effect writing.
____ crafted a strong cause-effect essay by drawing upon a range of writing moves.

# Chapter 16

# Reading Literature: A Case Study in Analysis

*What's your story, Bub? When she's on the court, she's poetry in motion. Hey! That's my line.* Sayings like these suggest that we experience life as story, poetry, drama. The reverse is also true: literature, as well-crafted writing, powerfully mirrors the life around us, including our own lives.

In college, you may read and analyze literature as part of your studies—and not just in English class. You might be asked to interpret a novel about the Vietnam War, provide insights into the gospel music created by African Americans, or review a bio pic about a politician. Whatever the case, your aim in a literary analysis is to offer a deep reading of the work, to illuminate some aspect of its form and meaning.

In this way, interpreting literature is a case study in analysis: you apply the modes of definition, classification, process, compare-contrast, and cause-effect thinking to the work. This chapter will help you use these modes to get at the literature-life relationship in the works you read.

**Visually Speaking** What does Figure 16.1 suggest about the relationship between art and life? Explain.

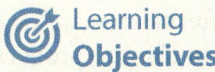

By working through this chapter, you will be able to

- analyze how the rhetorical situation informs literary analysis.
- implement principles for analyzing literature.
- develop a strong thesis for a literary-analysis essay.
- make effective moves for literary-analysis writing.
- craft a strong essay analyzing a poem, short story, play, or film.

*Lee Snider Photo Images / Shutterstock.com*

fig. 16.1

# Strategies for Analyzing Literature and the Arts

Analyzing the arts is something most of us do (at least informally) every day, whether we're reading reviews of concerts or albums, responding to paintings or photographs in public places, or assessing the value of a film or TV drama. However, this chapter will help you write a more formal, research-based analysis that is carefully articulated in well-crafted prose. To understand how to produce such analyses, start by considering the rhetorical situations that give rise to them and study the principles that guide such writing.

## The Rhetorical Situation

Consider the context in which you analyze literature and the arts:

- **Purpose:** In general, your aim is to describe the work's features, to explain how it impacts an audience, and to understand its essential qualities. However, if you're reviewing (rather than only analyzing) an artwork, focus more on its strengths and weaknesses. *Note:* Your instructors may direct specific ways to analyze works and present your ideas.
- **Readers:** In college, the primary readers for writing about the arts are fellow students and your instructors; outside of the classroom, you may write art news stories and reviews for community members interested in art events, art-related issues, or books.
- **Topic:** The topic might be one artwork (e.g., a sculpture, novel, or film), multiple works created by the same artist (e.g., a series of poems or paintings), a group performance (e.g., a play, an opera, or a symphony), an individual performance (e.g., a pianist, an actor, or a dancer), or critical approaches to an art.

*Example:* In "'Let Evening Come' An Invitation to the Inevitable," Sherry Mantel's primary readers are her professor and classmates. Her topic is the poem, "Let Evening Come" by Jane Kenyon, and her purpose is to explain what and how the poem communicates to her.

## Principles of Literary-Analysis Writing

Literary-analysis writing depends on the principles that follow.

**Understanding approaches to literary analysis.** You can interpret literary texts through different critical approaches or schools. Each school, with its specific foci and questions, offers a way of "conversing" about a text. The four basic approaches are as follows:

1. **Formalist criticism** focuses on the text itself, especially its structure and genre.
2. **Rhetorical criticism** is audience-centered, focused on the "transaction" between text and reader.
3. **Historical criticism** focuses on the historical context of the literary text, including its author.
4. **Ideological criticism** applies ideas outside of literature (e.g., psychology, mythology, feminism, postcolonialism, environmentalism) to literary texts.

To learn how writers from each school approach literary criticism, read John Van Rys's essay "Four Ways to Talk About Literature" in chapter 12.

**Drawing upon the analytical modes:** Because literary interpretations are a form of analytical writing, your thinking can draw upon one or more of these modes. Consider, for example, the kind of analytical questions you might ask of Shakespeare's *Hamlet*:

- **Definition:** What is the meaning of *hamartia*, or "tragic flaw," and how does this concept apply to Hamlet and his actions?
- **Classification:** *Hamlet* is a tragedy. But what kind of tragedy is it? What distinguishes this genre, and how has Shakespeare played with its conventions?
- **Process:** In the last act, what sequence of events leads to so many character deaths?
- **Compare-Contrast:** Laertes functions as a foil for Hamlet. (A *foil*'s qualities and behaviors contrast that of another character.) What comparisons or contrasts does the play draw between them, and what does it suggest through those comparisons?
- **Cause-Effect:** How can Ophelia's suicide be understood, and what does it lead to in the play? Why does Hamlet delay taking revenge against Claudius, and what are the consequences?

**Understanding literary terms that help you read and write about the arts.** The terms used to address specific art forms, such as the three examples below, help you read literature carefully and discuss your topic precisely. To refine your reading skills, learn how the literary elements that these terms identify shape or enrich a literary work. Then when reading a piece of literature, think about how these elements impact what you feel, see, and think.

- **Poetry:** You might describe word sounds with terms such as *assonance, consonance,* and *alliteration*; rhythmic effects with words such as *iambic* or *trochaic meter*; and figurative language with words such as *metaphor* and *simile*.
- **Fiction:** You might describe diction with terms such as *archaic, colloquial,* or *slang*; narrative method with phrases such as *first person* and *third person*; or genre with terms such as *satire* or *melodrama*.
- **Plays and films:** To describe characters, you might use terms such as *antagonist, protagonist,* or *tragic hero*; to discuss plots, words such as *exposition, rising action,* and *denouement*; or to describe a setting, phrases such as *stage picture, proscenium arch,* or *thrust stage*.

**Understanding primary and secondary research.** Your reading of a literary text—primary research—is usually the focus of your analyses. However, secondary research can serve many purposes, such as these:

- **Biographical research:** Learning about the author's life may enrich your analysis by helping you explore sources of inspiration, personal and literary influences, and modes of thought. You might gain such insights through learning about the author's childhood, cultural and ethnic background, education, writing apprenticeship, and relationships. Caution: You must be careful not to make simplistic connections between biographical details and literary texts (e.g., that the speaker of a poem or the narrator of a story is the author in a direct sense; that because the novelist grew up in the 1960s, the female characters are radical feminists; or that the author's intention must direct an interpretation of the text).

- **Research into historical and cultural context:** Such research illuminates the text by clarifying important contextual issues and historical details. These issues might be the historical realities surrounding the text's writing, its content, and its reception (past and present). Or the issues might be cultural concepts relevant to the text: class, economics, technology, religious institutions and practices, and so on.
- **Research into literary concepts:** This type of secondary research deepens your understanding of literary issues and techniques. For example, you might read about methods and theories of irony, or study the nature of tragedy with the aim of enriching your analysis of the text.
- **Research into theory:** Such research strengthens your understanding of the philosophical and ideological underpinnings of a particular literary school or theorist. Theoretical research—whether into reader-response theory, deconstruction, feminism, or the ideas of a particular theorist such as Mikhail Bakhtin—informs and directs your analysis of the literary text.
- **Research into scholarly interpretations:** In such research, you join the critical conversation about the text, a conversation that might have been going on for a few years, a few decades, or a few centuries. Many scholarly articles and books will likely offer interpretations of the text—ways of reading, analyzing, and understanding some aspect of the work, typically from a particular point of view. Reading these sources can strengthen your own interpretation in the following ways:

  - You can locate your own reading within the critical conversation, placing your interpretation in context.
  - You can refine your own reading through critical engagement, exploring why different readers interpret the text as they do (comparing their perspectives and values with your own).
  - You can create a critical survey early in your paper by reviewing the interpretive schools on the issues addressed and make space for your own reading.
  - Within your essay, you might use the critical comment of a scholar to (a) add expert support to your interpretive argument, (b) create a starting point for further reflection and analysis, or (c) present a claim with which your disagree.

**Focusing on Research Essentials:** In a literary analysis project, you should use secondary sources carefully and avoid these problems:

- **Substituting your own interpretation** of the text with the readings offered by secondary sources. If you find yourself continually talking about other people's interpretations or simply parroting their interpretations, you need to get back to your own interpretation in your own voice.
- **Limiting your secondary research** to opinions that you gather from Google searches (including sites such as Spark Notes and Cliff Notes). Instead, you should rely on sources in academic journals and scholarly books, which you can access through your library or library's website.

## Patterns for Literary-Analysis Essays: Thesis Thinking

The thesis is your personal discovery about the literary work turned into a statement to be shared with readers. It's an assertion, hypothesis, or key idea about the work's meaning—the deeper understanding you want to share with your readers, the answer to a significant question often asked by or implied in your assignment. This key idea grows out of your application of an analytical tool—a concept, principle, definition, etc.—to the literary work through a close reading. In the example below, the writer interprets a short story's ending in light of two events in the plot.

> *Example:* In Alice Munro's "Boys and Girls," the unnamed narrator's journey toward the ending where she is called "only a girl" by her father is explained by two key events: the shooting of the horse Mack, and the escape of the horse Flora.

**A Thesis Template:** Because your interpretation is a form of analysis, the thesis patterns in chapters 11-15 may prove useful. While it's impossible to say that a single pattern works for any literary analysis, here is a possibility you might try:

> In [title] by [author], [topic—specific aspect of the work] can best be understood as a combination of these elements: [element 1, element 2, element 3, etc.].

> *Example:* In Alice Munro's "Boys and Girls," the narrator's struggle with gender expectations can best be understood as a combination of forces: the cultural expectations of the time period, the dynamics within her farming family, and the biological and psychological changes she experiences growing up.

**From Weak to Strong:** In chapter 4, you learned about refining your thesis to make it stronger. You can do the same with the thesis for your literary-analysis essay.

> *Weak Thesis:* simply a statement of fact, a plot summary, or a "liked it / hated it" opinion

> Alice Munro's "An Ounce of Cure" is about a teenage girl who has a bad experience with alcohol.

> *Good Thesis:* demonstrates higher level thinking skills (analytical modes)

> In Alice Munro's "An Ounce of Cure," infatuation mars the narrator's judgment—with tragic-comic consequences for her life.

> *Excellent Thesis:* shows some intellectual complexity, risk, and tension

> While Alice Munro's "An Ounce of Cure" tells a simple story of infatuation leading to confusion and trouble, the story is more importantly about the "plots of life"—the way in which the narrator experiences life as a competing set of stories (romance, fairy tale, farce), none of which does justice to the complexity of real life.

## Patterns for Literary-Analysis Essays: Writing Moves

The writing moves you learned for the analytical modes will work well when applied to literary analysis. "Four Ways to Talk about Literature" in chapter 12 may also suggest specific writing moves. Consider the following moves as well:

- **Summarize when necessary:** In most literary-analyses, assume your reader has read the work—no need to summarize it when your main task is to illuminate something deeper about it. Sometimes, if the work itself is confusing and sorting out the plot might be helpful for your analysis, then use some brief, targeted summary. And if you are writing a review, your reader will expect some degree of summary.
- **Zero in on key passages:** Pay close attention to key lines or passages that support your thesis. Summarizing and paraphrasing works well, but interpreting specific quotations close up adds depth to your analysis.
- **Include a "literature review" in a research paper:** If your literary analysis is also a research paper, early in your paper you might review the various interpretations you found. This review prepares the reader for your specific interpretation. (See chapter 21 for more on literature reviews.)
- **Consider explication vs. parts analysis:** While your analysis may take shape organically, it might also be shaped according to one of two forms: (1) an explication that explores or "reads" the work from its beginning to its end, or (2) a parts analysis that makes sense of some aspect of the form-content relationship of the work by examining some or all of its elements. Figures 16.2 and 16.3 map out these options.

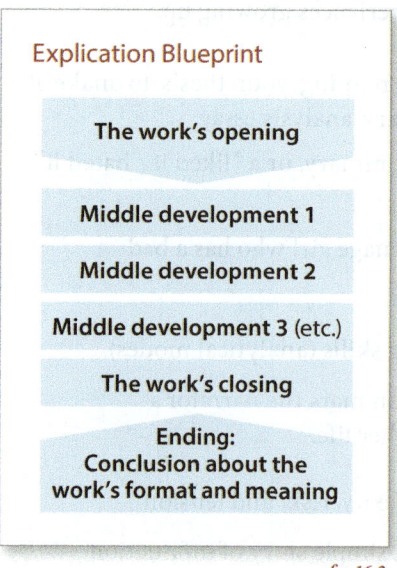

fig. 16.2

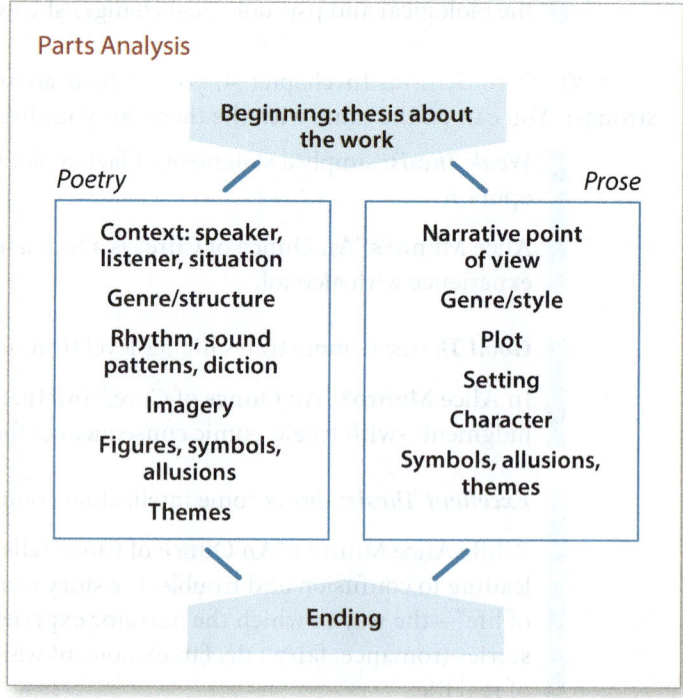

fig. 16.3

# Analyzing Literature: Learning Writers' Moves

To learn more about writing moves for literary analysis, you can study the essays that follow. You'll find an analysis of a poem by Jane Kenyon and a reading of a short story by Ernest Hemingway, as well as a film review. Reading these essays may also give you topic ideas for your own essay.

In the essay on the next two pages, student writer Sherry Mantel analyzes the form and meaning of the poem "Let Evening Come" by American poet Jane Kenyon.

## Analyzing a Poem

**Reading the poem:** Before you read the student writer's analysis, read the poem aloud to enjoy its sounds, rhythm, images, diction, and comparisons. Then read the piece again to grasp more fully how the poem is structured, what it expresses, and how its ideas might relate to your life. Finally, read Mantel's analysis and answer the questions that follow it.

### Let Evening Come

Let the light of late afternoon
shine through chinks in the barn, moving
up the bales as the sun moves down.

Let the crickets take up chafing
as a woman takes up her needles
and her yarn. Let evening come.

Let dew collect on the hoe abandoned
in long grass. Let the stars appear
and the moon disclose her silver horn.

Let the fox go back to its sandy den.
Let the wind die down. Let the shed
go black inside. Let evening come.

To the bottle in the ditch, to the scoop
in the oats, to air in the lung
let evening come.

Let it come, as it will, and don't
be afraid. God does not leave us
comfortless, so let evening come.

Jane Kenyon, "Let Evening Come" from *Collected Poems*. Copyright © 2005 by The Estate of Jane Kenyon. Reprinted with the permission of The Permissions Company, Inc. on behalf of Graywolf Press, Minneapolis, Minnesota, www.graywolfpress.org.

**Analysis of Kenyon's Poem:** In the essay below, student writer Sherry Mantel analyzes "Let Evening Come." Watch how she develops the essay by introducing the poem, describing how it unfolds, and then examining its structure, ideas, poetic devices, and theme.

## "Let Evening Come":
## An Invitation to the Inevitable

The work of American poet Jane Kenyon is influenced primarily by the circumstances and experiences of her own life. She writes carefully crafted, deceptively simple poems that connect both to her own life and to the lives of her readers. Growing out of her rural roots and her struggles with illness, Kenyon's poetry speaks in a still voice of the ordinary things in life in order to wrestle with issues of faith and mortality (Timmerman 163). One of these poems is "Let Evening Come." In this poem, the poet takes the reader on a journey into the night, but she points to hope in the face of that darkness.

That movement toward darkness is captured in the stanza form and in the progression of stanzas. Each three-line stanza offers a self-contained moment in the progress of transition from day to night. The first stanza positions the reader in a simple farm setting. Late afternoon fades into evening without the rumble of highways or the gleam of city lights to distract one's senses from nature, the peace emphasized by the alliteration of "l" in "Let the light of late afternoon." As the sun sinks lower on the horizon, light seeps through cracks in the barn wall, moving up the bales of hay. In the second stanza, the crickets get busy with their nighttime noises. Next, a forgotten farm hoe becomes covered with dew drops, and the silvery stars and moon appear in the sky. In the fourth stanza, complete blackness arrives as a fox returns to its empty den and the silent wind rests at close of day. The alliteration of "d" in "den" and "die down" gives a sinking, settling feeling (Timmerman 176). In the fifth stanza, a bottle and scoop keep still, untouched in their respective places, while sleep comes upon the human body. In the final stanza, Kenyon encourages readers to meet this emerging world of darkness without fear.

Within this stanza progression, the journey into the night is intensified by strong images, figures of speech, and symbols. The natural rhythm of work and rest on the farm is symbolized by the light that rises and falls in the first stanza (Timmerman 175). The simile comparing the crickets taking up their song to a woman picking up her knitting suggests a homespun energy and conviction. The moon revealing her "silver horn" implies that the moon does not instantly appear with brightness and beauty but rather reveals her majesty slowly as the night comes on. The den, the wind, and the shed in stanza four stress a kind of internal, hidden darkness. Then stanza five focuses on connected objects: the thoughtlessly discarded bottle resting in the ditch, oats and the scoop for feeding, human lungs and the air that fills them. Kenyon mentions the air in the lung after the bottle, ditch, scoop, and oats in order to picture humanity taking its position among the established natural rhythm of the farm (Harris 31).

The refrain, "let evening come," is a powerful part of the poem's journey toward darkness, though critics interpret the line differently. Judith Harris suggests that it symbolizes an acceptance of the inevitable: Darkness will envelop the world, and night will surely come, just as mortality will certainly take its toll in time. This acceptance, in turn, acts as a release from the confinement of one's pain and trials in life. Rather than wrestle with something that cannot be beaten or worry about things that must be left undone, Kenyon advises herself and her readers to let go (31). Night intrudes upon the work and events of the day, perhaps leaving them undone just as death might cut a life short and leave it seemingly unfinished.

By contrast, John Timmerman argues that "let" is used twelve times in a supplicatory, prayer-like manner (176). The final two lines, in turn, act as a benediction upon the supplications. The comfort of God is as inevitable as the evening, so cling to faith and hope and let evening come. Although the Comforter is mentioned only in the last two lines, that statement of faith encourages readers to find a spiritual comfort in spite of the coming of the night.

When asked how she came to write "Let Evening Come," Jane Kenyon replied that it was a redemptive poem given to her by the Holy Ghost. When there could be nothing—a great darkness and despair, there is a great mystery of love, kindness, and beauty (Moyers 238). In the poem's calm journey into the night, Kenyon confronts darkness and suffering with a certain enduring beauty and hope (Timmerman 161). Death will come, but there remains divine comfort. "Let Evening Come" encourages readers to release their grip on the temporary and pay attention to the Comforter who reveals Himself both day and night.

**Note:** The Works Cited page is not shown. For an example, see chapter 23.

## Reading for Better Writing

1. *Connections:* When you think of the evening, what images and associations come to mind? Can you recall a particularly memorable evening? What made it memorable, and how does it compare with the evening scene Kenyon describes?
2. *Comprehension:* What essential reading of Kenyon's poem does Mantel offer? What are the main elements of her reading?
3. *Writing Moves:*
   a. Review the opening and closing paragraphs. How do they create a framework for the writer's analysis of the poem?
   b. In her essay, Mantel refers to the poet's life and to ideas from secondary sources. What do these references add to her analysis of the poem?

**Your Project:** Has "Let Evening Come" inspired you to read more of Kenyon's poetry? Find another Kenyon poem and develop your own reading of it.

"'Let Evening Come' An Invitation to the Inevitable" by Sherry Mantel. Reprinted by permission of the author.

**A Poem to Analyze:** Now that you've read Jane Kenyon's "Let Evening Come" and Sherry Mantel's analysis of the poem, extend your poetry reading and interpretation skills by analyzing "The World Is Too Much With Us," a sonnet by William Wordsworth (1770–1850).

Wordsworth was a much-loved British poet and a founder of English Romanticism. Inspired by the natural world, he once wrote, "Nature never did betray the heart that loved her." He was born in the Lake District of England, which became a subject of much of his poetry. After taking a walking tour of Europe, he became a strong advocate for poetry written in the language of common people. He wrote the sonnet you will read below in response to the Industrial Revolution, which he scoffed at for ushering in an era of materialism. To get started on your analysis of the poem, do the following:

1. **Read the poem aloud.** Do this more than once, if helpful, paying attention to the rhythms and sounds at work. Online, find an audio reading of the poem, and compare the reading to yours.
2. **Work through the poem slowly,** line by line, to sort out what the speaker is saying.
3. **Through freewriting, explore your response to the poem**—the images it creates, the wisdom it shares, and anything else the poem prompts you to think about.
4. **Use the resources in this chapter** to develop your fuller interpretation of the poem. Consider comparing and contrasting Wordsworth's poem and Kenyon's.

### The World Is Too Much With Us

The world is too much with us; late and soon,
Getting and spending, we lay waste our powers;—
Little we see in Nature that is ours;
We have given our hearts away, a sordid boon!
This Sea that bares her bosom to the moon;
The winds that will be howling at all hours,
And are up-gathered now like sleeping flowers;
For this, for everything, we are out of tune;
It moves us not. Great God! I'd rather be
A Pagan suckled in a creed outworn;
So might I, standing on this pleasant lea,
Have glimpses that would make me less forlorn;
Have sight of Proteus rising from the sea;
Or hear old Triton blow his wreathèd horn.

—WILLIAM WORDSWORTH

*Included under permission of the public domain.*

## Analyzing a Short Story

Interpreting fiction—whether short stories or novels—requires careful attention to the text. When you read fiction, you should consider elements of story: plot, setting, character, theme, symbolism, and so on. You should also read the story in light of your questions about the narrative, the issues and puzzles you wish to understand more deeply.

In the essay that follows, student writer Julia Jansen interprets Ernest Hemingway's "A Clean, Well-Lighted Place." Study how she introduces the story, states her thesis, and then develops that idea through careful attention to the setting, the characters, and the dialogue. *Note:* Before you read Jansen's analysis, consider reading Hemingway's short story yourself, paying attention to the situation presented, the characters, and the dialogue. (To find the story online, simply complete a search for the title: "A Clean, Well-Lighted Place.")

---

### "A Clean, Well-Lighted Place": Emotional Darkness

Known for his dark perspective, Ernest Hemingway portrayed life as depressing in many of his literary works. One such story is "A Clean, Well-Lighted Place," set in a tidy, well-lit café where two waiters serve drinks to an elderly patron. Here, Hemingway symbolizes the loneliness and emptiness that reside within many ordinary people, particularly the elderly. The concept of nada and the contrast between dark and light demonstrate the emotional darkness that shrouds especially the story's two older characters. In this story, rich with terse dialogue and sharp detail, Hemingway relays his vision of a dark and depressing world that is softened only by patience, compassion, and dignity. This vision can be sensed in the symbolic use of light and dark, the debate between the younger and older waiters, and the inner conflicts of the two older characters. 1

Though quite short, "A Clean, Well-Lighted Place" uses light and dark imagery extensively to convey symbolically the characters' situation, especially the elderly patron's. When first mentioned, the elderly man is said to be sitting "in the shadow the leaves of the tree made against the electric light" (Hemingway 288). Though simple, this description reveals at least two details that are crucial to understanding the elderly man's loneliness; these details center on shade and electric light. Because there is electric light, one can assume the place is well-lit, which is also later revealed in the reflections of the older waiter, who says "it is well lighted" (290). Well-lighted, pleasant cafés are places where people can go to feel like they are part of a community even if they are alone (King). The pleasant, clean atmosphere creates a sense of order and happiness that the elderly man apparently values. Because he chooses to frequent a pleasant place of light, one might assume that he too is happy. However, this is not the case, as is evidenced by the second detail of the phrase describing the elderly man's sitting position: he is "in the shadow the leaves of the tree made against the electric light" (288). While there is light all over the café, the elderly man chooses to sit in the 2 only spot offering darkness. These images suggest that there is a darkness in his life, which is evident through the information one waiter reveals regarding the man: "Last week he tried to commit suicide" (288). The shade in which he sits reflects the dark emotional state in which he resides. The shade is a place where he can sit surrounded by light yet remain unseen by others, still in emotional and physical darkness (King). The light of the café may ward off the physical and emotional darkness of the early morning, but the electric light offers only a temporary release (Bassett).

Beyond the light and dark symbolism, Hemingway uses the dialogue between the younger and older waiters to deepen this vision of life. The younger waiter, increasingly frustrated that the old patron doesn't pay up and leave, wants to go home to his wife who waits for him in bed. In fact, at one point the young waiter says to the deaf old man "You should have killed yourself last week" (288). However, the older waiter recognizes the elderly patron's yearning for relief and sympathizes with the now-drunk man. For this reason, the older waiter defends the elderly patron's loitering against the younger waiter's wish to go home. The younger waiter believes the old man should "buy a bottle and drink at home," to which the older waiter responds, "Each night I am reluctant to close up because there may be some one who needs the café . . . You do not understand" (Hemingway 290). The contrast between the younger waiter's impatience with the old customer and the older waiter's empathy softens the story's dark vision by introducing compassion. After the young waiter goes home, the older waiter continues the conversation by himself, justifying why the elderly man should not have to drink alone at home or in a bar: "[One cannot] stand before a bar with dignity although that is all that is provided for these hours" (290). In contrast to the well-lighted café, bars and other places of the night are darker, louder, and more likely to draw in groups of people (King). In nearly every sense, the café is a preferred place for people who seek to ward off their loneliness and despair, to find some dignity in the darkness.

Hemingway's vision of human dignity in the face of life's darkness is deepened by the story's presentation of the struggles experienced by the elderly characters—the source of their suffering. With respect to the elderly patron, one waiter reflects that the unhappiness that drove the old man to attempt suicide was not caused by lack of financial means; he says the old man "has plenty of money" (288). Although he is cared for by a niece, the elderly patron has lost his wife. In his old age, this man seems to sense that hope and happiness are out of reach, and the only option is to retain his self-respect by drinking without spilling, responding to the young waiter's demeaning comments with politeness, and walking home "unsteadily but with dignity" (289). For his part, the older waiter is more explicit about the sources of his unhappiness. He says to the younger, "You have youth, confidence, and a job . . . you have everything" (290). By contrast, the older waiter has only a job. When both the elderly patron and the younger waiter are gone, the older waiter has no clean, well-lighted place to stay, so he turns to the last resort: a bar. He relates his desire for a more cheerful place when he says to the bartender, "The light is very bright and pleasant but the bar is unpolished" (291). His comment is not met with a reply, suggesting that even when he is with others, the older waiter is profoundly lonely. The older waiter demonstrates his sense of life's meaninglessness when referencing what he calls the nada, or the nothing. The narrator reflects, "What did he fear? It was not fear or dread. It was a nothing that he knew too well. It was all a nothing and a man was nothing too" (291). This sad outlook offers little sign of hope or redemption, which is made more obvious through the older waiter's version of the Lord's Prayer. The waiter replaces most of the words of the prayer with nada, saying, "Our nada who art in nada . . ." (291). This simple yet sad revelation reveals the waiter's hopelessness on a deeper level than before and shows that he views religion as a poor antidote to his loneliness (King). Some people turn to God in times of loneliness and desperation, but the older waiter and the elderly man seemingly cannot, finding temporary comfort only in the well-lighted café.

By portraying these struggles, Hemingway encourages readers to empathize with the two elderly characters. The inner conflicts that they experience are effectively revealed through the light and dark symbolism and through the contrasting perspectives of the young and old waiters. Though it may offer a depressing view of life, "A Clean, Well-Lighted Place" softens that vision with an emphasis on patience, compassion, and human dignity. While Hemingway portrays life as sad, he also suggests that a few clean, well-lighted places remain.

5

*Note:* The Works Cited page is not shown. For an example, see chapter 23.

### Reading for Better Writing

1. *Connections:* According to Jansen, Hemingway's story focuses on the need for a clean, well-lighted place within the world's darkness. What darkness do you see, feel, and experience in this world? Do you have your own clean, well-lighted place of refuge? Or do you see life as more "well-lit" than Hemingway's story suggests?
2. *Comprehension:* What essential interpretation of "A Clean, Well-Lighted Place" does Jansen's essay offer? What points does she offer in support of that interpretation?
3. *Writing Moves:*
   a. In part, Jansen's analysis focuses on the story's setting. How does she discuss the setting? What does she make of it?
   b. Jansen's analysis focuses primarily on the three central characters of the story: the old patron in the café, the younger waiter, and the older waiter. How does her analysis make sense of each character?

**Your Project:** For your own analysis, choose an engaging short story that includes a rich presentation of character, a story that challenges your vision and understanding of life.

## Analyzing a Film

During the last century, film has clearly become a dominant form of storytelling, entertainment, and art. As with analyzing poetry and fiction, interpreting film involves close attention to the medium and its various conventions and components—the camera work, acting, character development, cinematography, scene development, and more that constitute film's particular way of presenting images and narratives.

One form of film analysis is the film review. In the review below, Dr. James C. Schaap (who has written more than two dozen books, including nine novels and three collections of short stories) reviews *The Revenant*, especially director Iñárritu's treatment of the Hugh Glass tale, which Schaap compares to Frederick Manfred's approach to the same story in his novel *Lord Grizzly*. He begins the essay by calling attention to the image in Figure 16.4.

### *The Revenant*: A Brutal Masterpiece

*fig. 16.4*

H0nzaM/Shutterstock.com

1   I hope you'll agree that there is some beauty in this image, an elegance to what Emerson called "the frolic architecture" of snow, something dazzling in its loveliness. That having been said, no one would really want to be here. It's twenty below. Even a buffalo would move south.

2   *The Revenant* is a film-making masterpiece that's both beautiful and just plain awful to watch. Its sheer violence is matched only by the frightful deprivation Hugh Glass endures when he drags his bloody, broken self out of pure wilderness, a place, by the way, where the word *Disney* has absolutely no meaning. Alejandro G. Iñárritu's *The Revenant* is not for the faint of heart. Brace yourself. Its magnificence is as compelling as it is repellent.

3   Like Shakespeare, Iñárritu is working with materials long ago established, in this

case among the great sagas of the American West, the story of Hugh Glass, a dying trapper left on his own by companions who understand their own lives are in jeopardy if they wait to watch, mercifully, for their companion to die. They leave.

This story is pure rags-to-riches Americana in a way, because Hugh Glass is not dead, nor will he die. It's revenge that he breathes, revenge that gives him life. The story goes that Hugh Glass pulled himself up and away from death itself even though he had no bootstraps. Slowly, with pain that's just as unendurable to imagine as it is to witness, he returns to the fort in search of Fitzgerald, the man who left him behind.

In origin, the myth belongs to South Dakota. Glass was mauled by a she-bear somewhere near Lemmon, but eventually fought the elements, hand over hand, all the way back to Fort Kiowa, near Chamberlain, a 200-mile trek. Iñárritu chooses to set the story in the Canadian Rockies, which only makes the suffering more profound—and without a doubt more profoundly beautiful.

That's the material Iñárritu is bending and shaping in *The Revenant*, the myth many have repeated, retold, rewritten. Mostly, he's following Robert Punke's *The Revenant: A Novel of Revenge*.

The power of the original story—of the myth itself—is that at its climax it refuses to deliver what it promises all along. Call it what you will—retribution, spite, anger, hate—what gives Hugh Glass life is not simply a refusal to die but a gorging thirst for revenge that never happens. When he finds Fitzgerald, Glass doesn't kill him. That unforgettable end is what keeps the story alive.

If Hugh Glass had murdered the man who left him for dead, storytellers of the American West would not have retold the story that created the myth. Had Hugh Glass simply put a gun to Fitzgerald's temple, no one would have been surprised and the story wouldn't have been mythologized. That he doesn't is the shock that lifts the story into the level of what's unimaginable.

Frederick Manfred (1912-1994), a Western novelist of significant power, took a shot at the Hugh Glass story when he wrote *Lord Grizzly*, his rendition of the tale, published in 1954 and nominated for a National Book Award. *Lord Grizzly* has probably outsold all of the other Manfred novels combined. It's one of five he called his "Buckskin Man Tales," stories of the Northern Plains where he lived, a region he loved.

Fred Manfred's real name was Feike Feikema. He was born somewhere around Doon, Iowa. He loved his father but worshiped his mother, Alice Van Engen, a deeply religious woman born and reared in the Christian Reformed Church, who made sure her precocious oldest son got his education in Christian schools.

It is fair to say that his people, his tribe, the Dutch Reformed, "received him not," a rejection that sometimes pained him. Once upon a time, Manfred told me that he couldn't understand why it was that the men and women he grew up with had such faint toleration for his work, when the most famous novel he'd ever written was really all about forgiveness, the central thrust of orthodox Christianity. Manfred's problems with the community of his youth and childhood are a fascinating topic, but what's interesting about that statement in the shadow of *The Revenant* is his assessment of the Hugh Glass story: "it's all about forgiveness."

Iñárritu thinks so too, but he changes motivations, even hypes the revenge by giving Glass a son, Hawk, by way of a Native wife, a son who is with him because Glass's dearly beloved wife was murdered in a massacre. Iñárritu plays with the myth the way Shakespeare played with the story of *Hamlet, Prince of Denmark*.

Before the trek that made Glass famous, Fitzgerald murders Hawk in this new telling, which makes Glass's motivation in *The Revenant* something greater than revenge. His son's death reshapes the cause into a desire for justice in the American frontier, where there are no courts of law. If the score that needs to be settled is a matter of justice, then forgiveness is really of little importance, which makes Manfred's assessment of the shape of the Hugh Glass story irrelevant.

That's a shame. Whether or not Manfred is right is not the point. We're all free to alter the shape of the Hugh Glass story because it belongs to American mythology. But I think it's fair to point out that the reshaping which Iñárritu has given us in this simply incredible film does make the story more Hollywood and, if Manfred was right, less, well, divine.

There are distractions in this film, a film that will create untold dissertations in film schools, I'm sure. Iñárritu risks melodrama now and then, as if he can't stop himself. The horror and deprivation are so painfully acute that Iñárritu appears to think he has no limits to what he can show. At some moments near the end, the story gets a little heavy-handed, even preposterous. The horror of the story doesn't need this embellishment.

Another distraction is the amazement an audience can't help but feel about how on earth the movie was shot. Iñárritu was committed to natural light; therefore, frequently the crew could shoot only when the light was there—and *there*, in this case, is wilderness areas so remote you wonder if any other human beings have ever been even close. Reportedly, crew members quit in droves when they were forced to live in those conditions. When you watch this film, you have to stop once in a while and just shake your head at how it was done.

And then there is the myth itself. One of the reasons Shakespeare's audience found his *Hamlet* so interesting, or so say the scholars, is that his audience already knew the story; what interested them was how the playwright would tell it. I really loved watching this telling of the Hugh Glass story unfold, loved watching it play the myth itself.

*The Revenant* is not for everyone. The film spares nothing, soft-pedals nothing, refuses to restrain itself. It is a magnificent film that will, I'm sure, take home a number of major awards.

But *The Revenant* is not easy to watch. It's brutal and unceasing; it revels in beauty that's difficult to see. It's an amazing rendition of a grueling, bloody story we've already enjoyed for more than a century.

## Reading for Better Writing

1. *Connections:* If you have seen *The Revenant*, did it impact you as powerfully as Schaap describes its impact on him? If you haven't seen this film, can you point to another film that has impacted you in potent ways? Can you explain why?
2. *Comprehension:* What is Schaap's essential assessment of *The Revenant*? What are the main points that he uses in support of this assessment, and what does the essay teach about the larger context of the film's story?
3. *Writing Moves:*
    a. Schaap begins his review with a winter-scene photograph. What sense does this opening make? How does he connect the image and the film?
    b. Examine passages in which Schaap describes the film. What kind of language does he use? What do his descriptions add to the review?
    c. Schaap puts the film in context by referring to Shakespeare's *Hamlet* and Frederick Manfred's *Lord Grizzly*. What do such discussions add to Schaap's analysis of the film?
    d. How would you describe the tone of Schaap's review? Are there particular ways that he achieves balance in his assessment?

**Your Project:** For your own writing, find a film that is similarly based on a legend or a written text such as a novel that you have read. Like Schaap, review the film in light of its debt to the legend or a written narrative.

"The Revenant: A Brutal Masterpiece" by James C. Schaap. Used by permission of the author.

# Literary Terms

Your analysis of novels, poems, plays, and films will be deeper and more sophisticated if you understand the most common literary terms.

**Allusion** is a reference to a person, a place, or an event in history or literature.

**Analogy** is a comparison of two or more similar objects, suggesting that if they are alike in certain respects, they will probably be alike in other ways, too.

**Anecdote** is a short summary of an interesting or humorous, often biographical event.

**Antagonist** is the person or thing actively working against the protagonist, or hero.

**Climax** is the turning point, an intense moment characterized by a key event.

**Conflict** is the problem or struggle in a story that triggers the action. There are five basic types of conflict:

- **Person versus person:** One character in a story is in conflict with one or more of the other characters.
- **Person versus society:** A character is in conflict with some element of society: the school, the law, the accepted way of doing things, and so on.
- **Person versus self:** A character faces conflicting inner choices.
- **Person versus nature:** A character is in conflict with some natural happening: a snowstorm, an avalanche, the bitter cold, or any other element of nature.
- **Person versus fate:** A character must battle what seems to be an uncontrollable problem. Whenever the conflict is a strange or unbelievable coincidence, the conflict can be attributed to fate.

**Denouement** is the outcome of a play or story. See **Resolution**.

**Diction** is an author's choice of words based on their correctness or effectiveness.

- **Archaic** words are old-fashioned and no longer sound natural when used, such as "I believe thee not" for "I don't believe you."
- **Colloquialism** is an expression that is usually accepted in informal situations and certain locations, as in "He really grinds my beans."
- **Heightened language** uses vocabulary and sentence constructions unlike that of standard speech or writing, as in much poetry and poetic prose.
- **Profanity** is language that shows disrespect for someone or something regarded as holy or sacred.
- **Slang** is the everyday language used by group members among themselves.
- **Trite** expressions lack depth or originality, or are overworked or not worth mentioning in the first place.
- **Vulgarity** is language that is generally considered common, crude, gross, and, at times, offensive. It is sometimes used in fiction, plays, and films to add realism.

**Exposition** is the introductory section of a story or play. Typically, the setting, main characters, and themes are explained, and the action is initiated.

**Falling action** is the action of a play or story that follows the climax and shows the characters dealing with the climactic event or decision.

**Figure of speech** is a literary device used to create a special effect or to describe something in a fresh way. The most common types are *antithesis, hyperbole, metaphor, metonymy, personification, simile,* and *understatement*.

- **Antithesis** is an opposition, or contrast, of ideas.
  > "It was the best of times, it was the worst of times, it was the age of wisdom, it was the age of foolishness…"    — Charles Dickens, *A Tale of Two Cities*
- **Hyperbole** (hi-pur´ ba-lee) is an extreme exaggeration or overstatement.
  > "I have seen this river so wide it had only one bank."
  > —Mark Twain, *Life on the Mississippi*
- **Metaphor** is a comparison of two unlike things in which no word of comparison (*as* or *like*) is used: "Life is a banquet."
- **Metonymy** (ma-ton´a-mee) is the substituting of one term for another that is closely related to it, but not a literal restatement.
  > "Friends, Romans, countrymen, lend me your ears." (The request is for the attention of those assembled, not literally their ears.)
- **Personification** is a device in which the author speaks of or describes an animal, object, or idea as if it were a person: "The rock stubbornly refused to move."
- **Simile** is a comparison of two unlike things in which *like* or *as* is used.
  > "She stood in front of the altar, shaking like a freshly caught trout."
  > —Maya Angelou, *I Know Why the Caged Bird Sings*
- **Understatement** is stating an idea with restraint, often for humorous effect. Mark Twain described Aunt Polly as being "prejudiced against snakes." (Because she hated snakes, this way of saying so is *understatement*.)

**Genre** refers to a category or type of literature based on its style, form, and content. The mystery novel is a literary genre.

**Imagery** refers to words or phrases that a writer uses to appeal to the reader's senses.
> "The sky was dark and gloomy, the air was damp and raw…"
> —Charles Dickens, *The Pickwick Papers*

**Irony** is a deliberate discrepancy in meaning. There are three kinds of irony:
- **Dramatic irony**, in which the reader or the audience sees a character's mistakes or misunderstandings, but the character does not.
- **Verbal irony**, in which the writer says one thing and means another ("The best substitute for experience is being sixteen").
- **Irony of situation**, in which there is a great difference between the purpose of a particular action and the result.

**Mood** is the feeling that a piece of literature arouses in the reader: *happiness, sadness, peacefulness, anxiety,* and so forth.

**Paradox** is a statement that seems contrary to common sense yet may, in fact, be true: "The coach considered this a good loss."

**Plot** is the action or sequence of events in a story. It is usually a series of related incidents that build upon one another as the story develops. There are five basic elements in a plot line: *exposition, rising action, climax, falling action,* and *resolution.*

**Point of view** is the vantage point from which the story unfolds.

- In the **first-person** point of view, the story is told by one of the characters: "I stepped into the darkened room and felt myself go cold."
- In the **third-person** point of view, the story is told by someone outside the story: "He stepped into the darkened room and felt himself go cold."
- **Third-person narrations** can be *omniscient*, meaning that the narrator has access to the thoughts of all the characters, *limited*, meaning that the narrator focuses on the inner life of one central character, or *observational*, meaning that the narrator only reports on what people do and say.

**Protagonist** is the main character or hero of the story.

**Resolution** (or denouement) is the portion of the play or story in which the problem is solved. The resolution comes after the climax and falling action and is intended to bring the story to a satisfactory end.

**Rising action** is the series of conflicts or struggles that build a story or play toward a fulfilling climax.

**Satire** is a literary tone used to ridicule or make fun of human vice or weakness, often with the intent of correcting, or changing, the subject of the satiric attack.

**Setting** is the time and place in which the action of a literary work occurs.

**Structure** is the form or organization a writer uses for their literary work. A great number of possible forms are used regularly in literature: parable, fable, romance, satire, farce, slapstick, and so on.

**Style** refers to how the author uses words, phrases, and sentences to form their ideas. Style is also thought of as the qualities and characteristics that distinguish one writer's work from the work of others.

**Symbol** is a person, a place, a thing, or an event used to represent something else. For example, the dove is a symbol of peace.

**Theme** is the statement about life that a particular work shares with readers. In stories written for children, the theme is often spelled out clearly at the end. In more complex literature, the theme will often be more complex and will be implied, not stated.

**Tone** is the overall feeling, or effect, created by a writer's use of words. This feeling may be serious, mock-serious, humorous, satiric, and so on.

# Poetry Terms

**Alliteration** is the repetition of initial consonant sounds in words.
> "Our gang paces the pier like an old myth..."
> —Anne-Marie Oomen, "Runaway Warning"

**Assonance** is the repetition of vowel sounds without the repetition of consonants.
> "My words like silent rain drops fell..."     —Paul Simon, "Sounds of Silence"

**Blank verse** is an unrhymed form of poetry. Each line normally consists of ten syllables in which every other syllable, beginning with the second, is stressed. As blank verse is often used in very long poems, it may depart from the strict pattern from time to time.

**Consonance** is the repetition of consonant sounds. Although it is very similar to alliteration, consonance is not limited to the first letters of words:
> "...and high school girls with clear-skin smiles..."     —Janis Ian, "At Seventeen"

**Foot** is the smallest repeated pattern of stressed and unstressed syllables in a verse (see below).

- **Iambic:** an unstressed followed by a stressed syllable (re-peat´)
- **Anapestic:** two unstressed followed by a stressed syllable (in-ter-rupt´)
- **Trochaic:** a stressed followed by an unstressed syllable (old´-er)
- **Dactylic:** a stressed followed by two unstressed syllables (o´-pen-ly)
- **Spondaic:** two stressed syllables (heart´-break´)
- **Pyrrhic:** two unstressed syllables (Pyrrhic seldom appears by itself.)

**Onomatopoeia** is the use of a word whose sound suggests its meaning, as in *clang* or *buzz*.

**Refrain** is the repetition of a line or phrase of a poem at regular intervals, especially at the end of each stanza. A song's refrain may be called the *chorus*.

**Rhythm** is the ordered or free occurrences of sound in poetry. Ordered or regular rhythm is called meter. Free occurrence of sound is called *free verse*.

**Stanza** is a division of poetry named for the number of lines it contains:

- **Couplet:** two-line stanza
- **Triplet:** three-line stanza
- **Quatrain:** four-line stanza
- **Quintet:** five-line stanza
- **Sestet:** six-line stanza
- **Septet:** seven-line stanza
- **Octave:** eight-line stanza

**Verse** is a metric line of poetry. It is named according to the kind and number of feet composing it: *iambic pentameter, anapestic tetrameter,* and so on. (See **Foot**.)

- **Monometer:** one foot
- **Dimeter:** two feet
- **Trimeter:** three feet
- **Tetrameter:** four feet
- **Pentameter:** five feet
- **Hexameter:** six feet
- **Heptameter:** seven feet
- **Octometer:** eight feet

#  DIY: Craft Your Own Literary Analysis

## Planning

1. **Select a topic.** Choose a work of literature or another artwork with which you are familiar or about which you are willing to learn.

2. **Understand the work.** Read or experience it thoughtfully (two or three times, if possible), looking carefully at its content, form, and overall effect.
   - **For plays and films,** examine the plot, props, setting, characters, dialogue, lighting, costumes, sound effects, music, acting, and directing.
   - **For novels and short stories,** focus on point of view, plot, setting, characters, style, diction, symbols, and theme.
   - **For poems,** examine diction, tone, sound patterns, figures of speech (e.g., metaphors), symbolism, irony, structure, genre, and theme.
   - **For music,** focus on harmonic and rhythmic qualities, lyrics, and interpretation.

3. **Develop a focus and approach.** Take notes on what you experience, using the list above to guide you. Seek to understand the whole work before you analyze the parts. Select a dimension of the work as a focus, considering what approach to analyzing that element might work. (See "Four Ways to Talk About Literature" in chapter 12.)

4. **Organize your thoughts.** Review the notes that you took as you analyzed the work. What key insights has your analysis led you to see? Make a key insight your thesis, and then organize supporting points logically in an outline.

## Drafting

5. **Write the first draft.** Consider writing moves you learned earlier in the chapter, plus the strategies below.

    **Opening:** Use ideas like the following to gain your readers' attention, identify your topic, narrow the focus, and state your thesis:
    - Summarize your subject briefly. Include the title, the author or artist, and the literary form or performance.
        **Example:** Michael Ondaatje's poem "The Time Around Scars," a poem written in quasi-free verse, deals with scars, the stories they tell, and the people who can and cannot share these stories.
    - Start with a quotation from the work and then comment on its importance.
    - Open with a general statement about the artist's style or aesthetic process.
        **Example:** Flannery O'Connor's stories are filled with characters who are bizarre, freakish, devious, and sometimes even murderous.
    - Begin with a general statement about the plot or performance.
        **Example:** In Stephen Spielberg's movie *War of the Worlds*, Ray Ferrier and his two children flee from their New Jersey home in a stolen minivan.

- Assert your thesis. State the key insight about the work that your analysis has revealed—the insight your essay will seek to support.

**Middle:** Develop or support your focus by following this pattern:
- State the main points, relating them clearly to the focus of your essay.
- Support each main point with specific details or direct quotations.
- Explain how these details prove your point.

**Conclusion:** Tie key points together and assert your thesis or evaluation in a fresh way, leaving readers with a sense of the larger significance of your analysis.

## Revising

6. **Improve the ideas, organization, and voice.** Review your draft for its overall content and tone. Make sure the draft meets the parameters of the assignment. Ask a classmate or writing-center tutor for help, if appropriate.

   ___ **Ideas:** Does the essay show clear and deep insight into specific elements of the text, artwork, or performance? Is that insight effectively developed with specific references to the work itself?

   ___ **Organization:** Does the opening effectively engage the reader, introduce the text or artwork, and focus attention on an element or issue? Does the middle carefully work through a "reading" of the work? Does the conclusion reaffirm the insight into the work and expand the reader's understanding?

   ___ **Voice:** Does the tone convey a controlled, measured interest in the text or artwork? Is the analytical attitude confident but reasonable?

## Polishing

7. **Edit and proofread the essay by checking issues like these:**

   ___ **Words:** Language, especially terminology, is precise and clear.

   ___ **Sentences:** Constructions flow smoothly and are varied in length and structure; quotations are effectively integrated into sentence syntax.

   ___ **Correctness:** The copy includes no errors in spelling, usage, punctuation, grammar, or mechanics.

   ___ **Design:** The page design is correctly formatted and attractive; references are properly documented according to the required system (e.g., MLA).

## Publishing

8. **Publish your essay.** Submit your essay to your instructor, but consider other ways of sharing your insights about this work or artist—blogging, submitting a review to a periodical, or leading classmates in a discussion.

# Analyzing Literature: Applications

Once you have written your own analysis of a poem, story, or film, there may be more to think about. Consider how to apply what you have learned in the situations below.

1. **Living Today:** While traditional poetry and fiction continue to find audiences, the rise of different media has created new and different spaces for poetic language and for stories. Consider where and how you encounter poetry and story in your daily life. How do the analytical skills from this chapter help you engage these elements?
2. **Major Work:** As discussed in "Four Ways to Talk About Literature" in chapter 12, ideological criticism borrows concepts from other disciplines such as psychology, cultural studies, and environmental studies. In your discipline (if it isn't English), might various forms of literature enrich your study of the subject matter? How are close attention to language and an understanding of story relevant to your field of study?
3. **Art Crawl:** While this chapter focuses on poems and stories (with some attention to film), you might extend your literary analysis skills into other art forms. Explore the possibilities by completing one of these activities:
   a. Attend a concert with classmates. Afterward, discuss the style of the music, the performance of the singer or group, and the content of the lyrics. Note the age of the audience and discuss how and why it responded as it did. Finally, discuss whether you found the concert worthwhile.
   b. Visit an art gallery and examine an exhibit that engages you. Describe what you find appealing or intriguing and explain why. Also explain what value this exhibit might have for your community.

## Learning-Objectives Checklist ✓

Have you achieved this chapter's learning objectives? Check your progress with the following items, revisiting topics in the chapter as needed. I have . . .

\_\_\_\_ analyzed how my rhetorical situation informs literary analysis.
\_\_\_\_ implemented principles for analyzing literature.
\_\_\_\_ developed a strong thesis for my literary-analysis essay.
\_\_\_\_ made effective moves for literary-analysis writing.
\_\_\_\_ crafted a strong essay analyzing a poem, short story, play, or film.

# Chapter 17

# Persuasive Writing: Strategies for Argumentation

"I wasn't convinced." "I just didn't buy it." Maybe you've said something similar (or worse) while watching a political debate, viewing a TV ad, or discussing an issue in class or at work. You simply didn't find the argument logical or convincing.

College is a place where big issues get argued out—in class and out. To participate in that dialogue, you must be able to read and listen to others' arguments, analyze them, and build your own.

This chapter will help you do that. It explains what argumentation is and the different forms it can take. It shows you how to identify weak arguments, and how to construct strong ones. The next chapter then applies these concepts to your writing of a persuasive essay that takes a position, calls for action, and/or solves a problem.

**Visually Speaking** Carefully study Figure 17.1. What do you see in the foreground, the middle distance, and the background? What story do you imagine the photo is telling? In what ways is that story an argument?

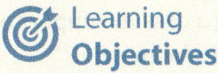

## Learning Objectives

By working through this chapter, you will be able to

- structure arguments according to common patterns.
- effectively engage opposing perspectives and alternatives.
- make appeals to *ethos*, *pathos*, and *logos*.
- develop three types of claims.
- support claims with convincing reasoning.
- support reasoning with various types of evidence.
- identify logical fallacies.

Spencer Platt / Staff

fig. 17.1

# Meeting the Mode

To get familiar with argumentation, it's helpful to start with a written argument. The essay below appeared in *Wired* magazine in 2020. Its author, Josh Wilbur, is a writer and editor based in New York City. To borrow a phrase from law, argument may be thought of as making a case in support of something. As you read, ask, "What case is Wilbur making, and how does he make it?"

## America Needs a Ministry of (Actual) Truth

1   Life in a nightmarish dystopia isn't all bad. For Winston Smith, the tragic everyman of George Orwell's *1984*, the "greatest pleasure in life" is his work at the Ministry of Truth, where lies are manufactured and truths tossed down memory holes. To help "correct" the historical record, Winston takes pride in inventing fake statistics, fake events, fake people, and even revises newspapers to include phantoms like Comrade Ogilvy, a made-up war hero. In essence, the MoT is a fake news factory.

2   In the real world of 2020, we're witnessing an inversion of the top-down fakery of *1984*. High-quality fakes are bubbling up as AI is increasingly democratized. Meanwhile, members of "the state," far from carrying out the efficient machinations imagined by Orwell, are themselves flummoxed by, and often the targets of, malicious fakes (like the "Drunk Pelosi" video). In a recent essay about the enduring relevance of *1984*, George Packer writes, "The Ministry of Truth is Facebook, Google, and cable news. We have met Big Brother and he is us." Any one of us can be a propagandist. What's more, the powers that be lack an effective regulatory mechanism for dealing with the next phase of the disinformation age, when indistinguishable fakes will flood the internet. While countless commentators have viewed *1984* as a black cauldron simmering with horrors to avoid, we may need to salvage the idea of a Ministry of Truth in order to preserve what's left of our shared reality.

3   Consider that our forgeries are already much better and far stranger than those of Big Brother. Right now, you can experience the pleasure of a well-done fake with only a click or a tap, no Winston Smith required. Visit the website This Person Does Not Exist, and refresh as many fictitious comrades as your heart desires. When the digital ghosts get too weird, you can marvel at a deepfake face swap: Behold, if you dare, Steve Buscemi as Jennifer Lawrence. Or you can fake yourself with FaceApp.

4   Fakery isn't always harmless. More than 90 percent of deepfakes are pornographic, much of it "revenge porn." Criminals have deployed deepfaked audio to impersonate CEOs. Synthetic content, experts warn, could be used to influence elections, sway financial markets, or trigger wars. Back in June 2019, House Democrat

Adam Schiff, a man permanently on the cusp of letting out a long, tired sigh, led a congressional hearing on deepfakes. All told, it was a gloomy affair.

That day, representatives learned that a "high school kid with a good graphics card can make this stuff." That the creators of malicious deepfakes (the bad guys) and those working to identify and intercept fake content (the good guys) are locked in an unending arms race. Hany Farid, an expert in digital forensics at UC Berkeley, has said, "We are outgunned. . . . The number of people working on the video-synthesis side, as opposed to the detector side, is 100 to 1." Finally, representatives learned of the tipping point of indistinguishability: In a few years, it will be impossible for the naked eye to distinguish a real video from a deepfake. The prospects are harrowing: perfect fakes, creatable by anyone, unleashed at scale and difficult to discern. It's no wonder that during the hearing Washington representative Denny Heck repeatedly quoted from Dante's *Inferno*: "Abandon hope all ye who enter here."

Putting aside such brash pessimism, what can be done? The platforms on which fake content appears (Facebook, Instagram, YouTube, Twitter) have taken some steps to combat disinformation. In a recent blog post, Facebook pledged to "remove misleading manipulated media" if "it is the product of artificial intelligence or machine learning that merges, replaces, or superimposes content onto a video, making it appear to be authentic." This is important, but detection is a serious challenge, and few trust Big Tech to fully self-regulate. Sure, there's a profusion of laws around identity theft and defamation that might dissuade creators of harmful fakes, but it's unclear who will enforce them or how.

As law professors Danielle Citron and Robert Chesney describe in their paper "Deepfakes: A Looming Challenge for Privacy, Democracy, and National Security," three federal agencies (the FCC, the FEC, and the FTC) could in theory regulate the dissemination of fake content, but "on close inspection, their potential roles appear quite limited." The FCC's jurisdiction is limited to radio and television. The FEC is concerned only with the electoral process. The FTC oversees "fake advertising," but deepfakes aren't typically hawking products or services.

So, what about a new federal agency? A central body tasked with combating disinformation, parsing fact from fiction and thereby ensuring Americans' collective sanity when the flood of fakes truly arrives: a Bureau of Information, a Department of Facts, a Ministry of . . . Truth!

Full circle, and we're back at dystopia. The idea might sound absurd, unimaginable even: Washington bureaucrats regulating reality itself, dictating to Americans what's true and what isn't.

Is it really so crazy? The EPA protects our environment, the FDA protects our bodies, the DHS protects our borders. In the era of indistinguishability, difficult choices will need to be made in order to protect our minds. When the fakes come for you and yours—when, for example, your adolescent child is deepfaked by an internet bully—you might want a Ministry of Truth that actually lives up to the name, that doesn't falsify but certifies the truth, that assertively stamps its authority atop fake videos: "This content is not real." American history includes no shortage of necessary (if at first uneasy) interventions, in which citizens trade some degree of individual autonomy for collective peace of mind: "FDA-approved" food and drugs; "MoT-approved" audio and video.

Obviously, a name change would be in order. Orwell's "Ministry" is something to think with and think against. Dorian Lynskey, author of *The Ministry of Truth: The Biography of George Orwell's 1984*, told me that "for Orwell, it's not the fact that the Ministry is a centralized agency that's problematic. The problem is that it lies." According to Lynskey, "the whole thrust of the novel is the horror of what happens if objective truth does not exist." When millions feel that horror close to home, people will want a regulatory force—no matter what it's called.

In practice, a new governmental entity could spearhead the application of technical solutions and industry standards, providing structure to what's currently a disorganized deepfake resistance of concerned lawyers and lawmakers, activists and technologists. On the tech side, efforts are being made in two areas: authentication on the front end (using "verified-at-capture" technology that proves the "provenance," or origin, of a particular piece of media) and forensic detection on the back end (using machine learning algorithms to identify, rather than create, deepfakes). Darpa is already pouring resources into detection efforts, as are Facebook and Google, but most observers agree that much more coordination between entities is needed. Witness, a nonprofit organization working at the intersection of human rights and media, recently published a report on media authentication entitled "Ticks or It Didn't Happen." The report imagines a world in which "every piece of media is expected to have a tick," like a checkmark, "signaling authenticity." Witness raises more than a dozen dilemmas with such a scenario while recognizing its potential eventuality. Good government could organize, enforce, and standardize authentication practices.

When it comes to technological solutions to the problem of malicious fakes, "there's no silver bullet," says Robert Chesney. I asked Chesney what a governmental response might look like, and he envisioned a "reasonably high-powered inter-agency task force or council or entity where all the relevant stake-holding federal entities—and hopefully state and local representation in some fashion—try to coordinate awareness of problems as they unfold." Relevant stakeholders might include the Department of Homeland Security, which has previously tackled digital threats with the creation of the Cybersecurity and Infrastructure Agency, as well as the FCC, FEC, and FTC.

Federal oversight wouldn't need to mean Orwell's ministry. Our hypothetical entity could function more like connective tissue than menacing monolith, putting private companies, governmental departments, non-profit organizations, and university researchers into close and regular contact. At a time when the Administration often behaves like a dystopian MoT, it would be important to "watch the watchmen" and create safeguards against political bias or factionalism. Authority would need to be distributed among relevant parties, lest any one group gain a monopoly on truth.

To envision this, imagine a scenario in which political candidates are being deepfaked en masse during an election year, with perfectly realistic video and audio sowing confusion about what's being said during town halls, rallies, debates, interviews. Social media platforms alert a centralized agency to the threat and share relevant data; researchers get to work on the tricky task of detection; regulators ensure that these videos are labeled as fake across all media platforms and work to encourage wider adoption of verified-at-capture technology. In this way, a governmental institution could serve as a referee and an arbiter with some legal backbone and regulatory teeth. Its purview would necessarily be limited to cases when the truth wasn't up for debate, when no "alternative facts" could be claimed. Did AOC say that she'd socialize American farming on January 24, 2024, in Des Moines, Iowa, or didn't she? There's only one answer.

Already, there are steps being taken in a regulatory direction. The DEEPFAKES Accountability Act was introduced in June but looks largely unenforceable. Congresswomen Anna G. Eshoo and Zoe Logfren have proposed establishing a "Digital Privacy Agency" to "enforce privacy protections and investigate abuses" within the online sphere. Eventually, some form of legislation addressing synthetic media will be passed: the technology is becoming too powerful for Washington to ignore.

In the meantime, Americans should "prepare, not panic," as Witness advises. No doubt, the next wave of fakes will be entertaining, surreal, and 100 percent meme-

> able; indistinguishable fakes will also generate confusion and further deepen our skepticism. Decisive action will be needed. Just as Winston Smith derives pleasure from crafting "delicate pieces of forgery," Americans in the 2020s should find gratification in identifying and stomping out fakeries. In doing so, we'd do well to remember that the message of *1984* isn't "fear the government." The message is to resist the notion that 2+2=5 before it's too late.

*Josh Wilbur, Wired (c) Conde Nast*

## Converse with the Mode

So, what case does Josh Wilbur make in this piece? Without proper oversight, he warns, deepfake technology may soon alter reality as we know it. A bold claim, isn't it? Yet, he grounds it with real examples of fakery and expert testimony. Next, he argues for an even bolder solution: a federal agency charged with parsing truth from fiction for the public. Seems a bit dystopian, doesn't it? Yet, Wilbur anticipates this reaction, too, responding to doubts with nuanced support and analysis. Now look a little closer at the essay.

### Conversation Starters

1. Wilbur opens his essay by referencing George Orwell's dystopian novel *1984*. Why does Wilbur introduce his argument in this way? What important distinctions does he make between the setting in *1984* and the real-world setting of 2020?
2. What specific problem does Wilbur address in his argument? What evidence does he introduce to highlight the urgency of the problem?
3. Wilbur explains current solutions to the problem in paragraphs 6 and 7 but also pokes holes in these ideas. How does highlighting the weaknesses of existing solutions strengthen his overall argument?
4. In paragraphs 8–16, Wilbur proposes his own solution: a new federal agency charged with combating disinformation. How does he support the viability of his solution? What part of his solution is most convincing to you, and why?
5. As you'll learn in this chapter, arguments involve making appeals. As you reflect on this essay, consider how Wilbur makes appeals to these:
   - *Ethos*—the **credibility** of himself and his argument.
   - *Pathos*—reaching out to the **emotions** of readers.
   - *Logos*—developing an argument that is **logically** sound.

**Moving On:** Wilbur raises awareness about a problem that he expects to worsen in the future. What concerns do you have about the future? What future issues might you address on your campus or in your community? Can you think of any outside-the-box solutions to the problems? Consider constructing your own argument on one of these topics.

# Structuring Arguments

The shape of an argument often emerges organically as you think about and research an issue. While you have a lot of freedom about how to shape arguments, two patterns have become popular methods of doing so: Toulmin and Rogerian. In what follows, you will find a brief introduction to each method. Use these introductions to guide your choices for specific arguments.

## Understand Toulmin Argumentation

Made popular by British philosopher Stephen Toulmin in his book *The Uses of Argument* (1958), this method lends structure to the way people naturally make arguments. Not exactly formal logic, this pattern offers a practical approach that allows you and your readers to wrestle over debatable issues through sound thinking. Toulmin's elements do not map out a strict sequence of elements, but you may draw upon the elements to unfold your thinking within a paragraph or for an entire essay. Many of these elements are addressed more fully later in this chapter, but here is an overview:

- **Claims** The debatable statements you aim to prove or support.
  > Planting trees is a practical step to fight climate change.

- **Qualifiers** Any limits you put on claims in order to make those claims more reasonable, precise, and honest.
  > *Although it is a small step*, planting trees is *one* practical way that *many* people can fight climate change.

- **Support** The reasoning that you offer to explain and defend the claim; the evidence that you use to back up the reasoning and thereby ground the claim (various forms of data, information, experience, narratives, authority, and so on).
  > According to the UN, "Deforestation causes 12-18 percent of the world's carbon emission, almost equal to all the $CO_2$ emissions from the global transport sector."

- **Warrants** The logical glue that holds together claims, reasons, and evidence; the assumptions, principles, and values (sometimes unstated), that lie behind your reasoning.
  > Stopping climate change is more important than the economic benefits of deforestation.

- **Backing** When warrants aren't shared or understood by readers, the special reasoning and evidence you offer to convince readers to accept those principles.
  > Recent research has determined that the 32 million acres of forest lost each year make a significant contribution to global warming.

- **Conditions of Rebuttal** Your anticipation of and response to possible objections; your sense of other perspectives and positions.
  > Economies dependent on deforestation can take a number of steps toward sustainable practices.

## Toulmin Patterns

The elements of Toulmin reasoning combine to give an argument its structure. What does that structure look like? Consider the following sentence pattern and writing organizer.

**Sentence Pattern:** If the components were placed in relationship to each other in sentence form, Toulmin reasoning might look like the statement below. A series of such statements added together could create a complete argument.

> Because of this **supporting point** (reasoning plus evidence), my fittingly **qualified claim** makes sense, especially when you consider this **warrant** (principle), which is **backed** by this evidence; while a particular objection might be made, additional reasoning **rebuts** it.

**A Writing Organizer:** The diagram in Figure 17.2 shows how a Toulmin argument with three points supporting the main claim might be structured. The map could be modified to reflect a different number of supporting points, as well as varied development in terms of reasoning, evidence, and warrants.

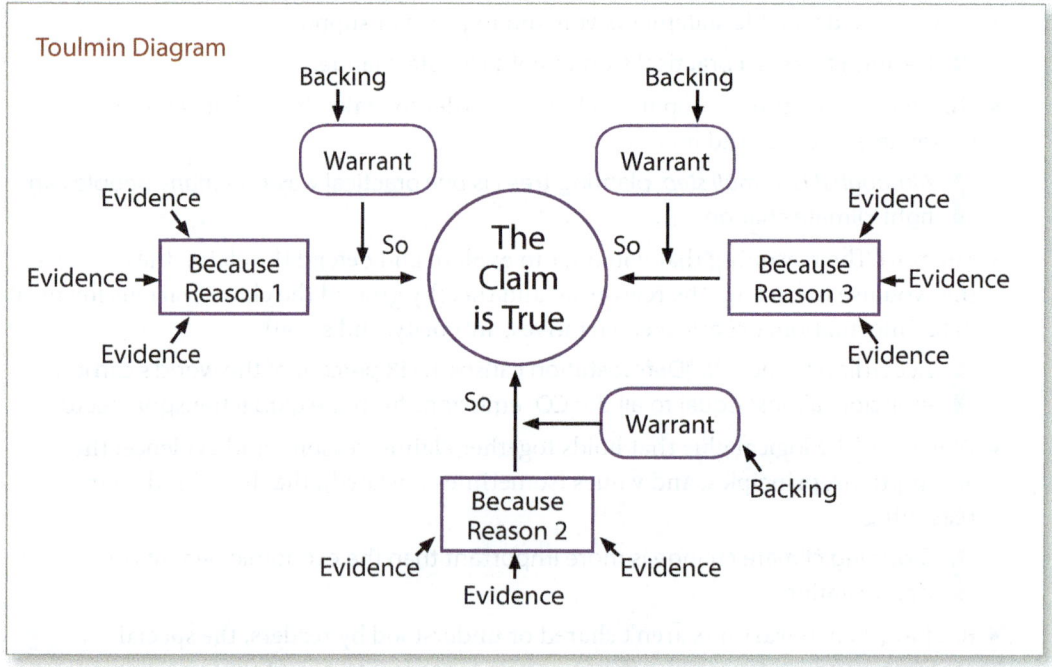

*fig. 17.2*

## Understand Rogerian Argumentation

While the Toulmin approach emphasizes proving a claim through reasoning and evidence (swaying the reader to your side), the Rogerian method aims at consensus building, connection, respect for differences, and collaboration. Borrowed from the therapeutic work of psychologist Carl Rogers, the pattern begins with the idea that disputes and differences cannot be resolved unless each disputant can fully, fairly, and sympathetically state the other's situation and position. The Rogerian approach, in other words, aims to offer an antidote to angry confrontation, divisiveness, and polarized thinking.

Making its way into rhetoric and composition, Rogers's psychological method has resulted in argumentative patterns that are sometimes called "invitational" in that they are grounded in careful listening with the aim of getting people to work together, disagreeing respectfully when agreement cannot be reached. This philosophy has led rhetoric scholars to develop a four-part Rogerian structure:

1. **Introduction:** As completely, richly, and fairly as possible, you describe the issue, disagreement, conflict, or problem—showing that you fully respect and understand the range of positions or alternatives available.
2. **Contexts:** Grounding the issue in a broader context or background, you explore situations in which different positions are valid and sensible.
3. **Writer's Position:** You then offer your perspective, stating a position but also explaining the conditions or circumstances under which this position is valid.
4. **Benefits to Opponent:** You explain to readers, who may hold a different position, how they would gain from agreeing with your position, making the position mutually beneficial.

## Rogerian Patterns

In Rogerian argumentation, you use similar components to those found in Toulmin reasoning, but it's less about the reasoning pattern and more about the approach and process. To arrive at the Rogerian invitational attitude, consider this process:

1. Given the polarized and contentious nature of the topic, think hard about where the differences lie and where there is common ground between opposites. What might opponents agree upon?
2. Study opponents fully. Extend them your understanding and empathy; aim to see the issue from their point of view. Why do they believe what they do, and in what ways are they right to do so?
3. Consider your position in light of the opposing perspective. How might opponents see your side? How can you make sense of it in a way they'll find acceptable? How might their accepting or at least respecting your position benefit them? Do you see a win-win pathway forward?

**Sentence Pattern:** If Rogerian thinking were mapped out in sentence form, here is what it might sound like—understanding that each element identified would need to be fleshed out.

> This issue is serious, divisive, and complex in several ways. Side A quite rightly looks at the issue this way; Side B quite rightly sees it this other way. Given these differences, there is nevertheless common ground, and my position is located there, at what is a sensible compromise. Here's what would be gained if together we accepted it.

**A Writing Organizer:** The four-part structure of introduction, context, writer's position, and benefits to opponent provides a clear blueprint for organizing a Rogerian argument; however, the organizer in Figure 17.3 offers a diagram in which you can map out your thinking visually. Note how it includes a Venn diagram, useful for comparing and contrasting sides.

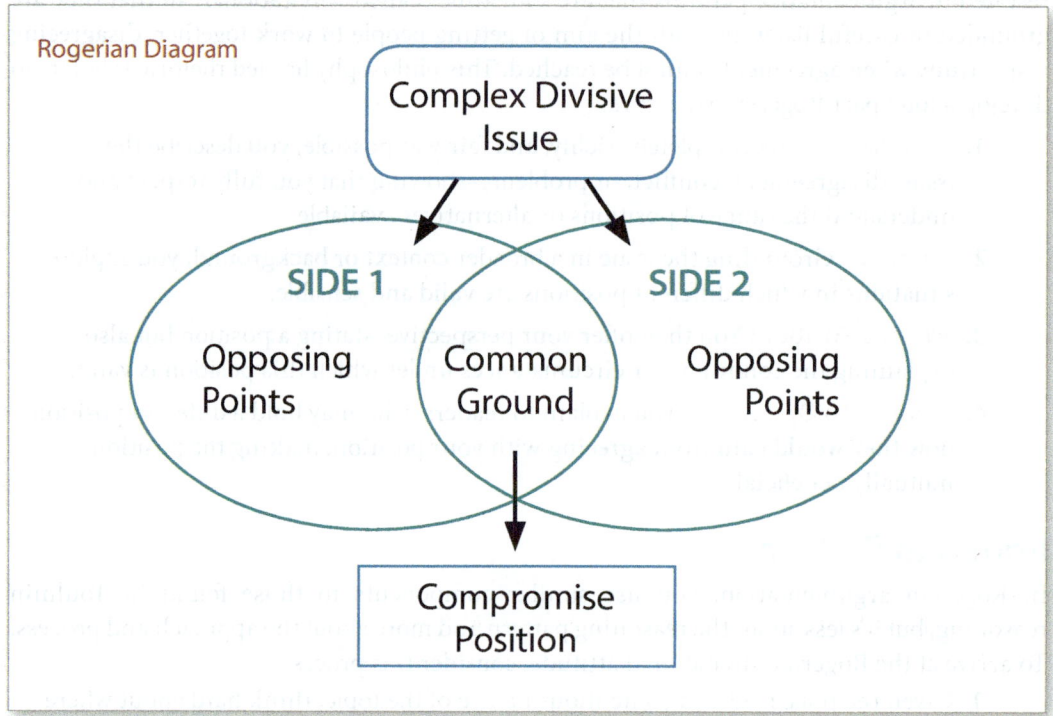

fig. 17.3

## Choose an Approach

While the Rogerian method is less common than the Toulmin method, both are good choices under the right circumstances. In fact, you should aim to learn how to use both approaches. To choose an approach or to perhaps develop your own hybrid structure for a particular project, consider these rhetorical issues:

- **Your Goal** Are you aiming to sway readers to your position, putting yourself out there as taking a strong stand? Or are you hoping to build bridges, arrive at consensus, or bring about reconciliation in a hurting situation?
- **Your Readers** Whom are you trying to reach with your argument? Are you seeking their respect for your position, even their adoption of it? Or are you aiming to build a collaborative relationship with specific readers, to enter a dialogue with them?
- **The Topic** Does the issue lend itself to one approach over the other? How charged is the topic, and what is at stake in the argument?
- **Your Beliefs and Style** What approach to argumentation feels natural to your own character and consistent with your values?

## Engaging the Opposition

A key element of any argument is engaging alternatives and opposing points of view. Whether you use the Toulmin or Rogerian approach, you should think of an argument as an intelligent, lively dialogue with readers. Anticipate their questions, concerns, objections, and counterarguments. Then follow these guidelines.

### Make Concessions

By offering concessions—recognizing points made by the other side—you acknowledge your argument's limits and the truth of other positions. Paradoxically, such concessions strengthen your overall argument by making it seem more credible. Concede your points graciously, using words such as the following:

| | | | |
|---|---|---|---|
| Admittedly | Granted | I agree that | I cannot argue with |
| It is true that | You're right | I accept | No doubt |
| Of course | I concede that | Perhaps | Certainly it's the case |

> While it is true that foot-and-mouth disease is not dangerous to humans, other animal diseases are.

### Develop Rebuttals

Even when you concede a point, you can often answer that objection by rebutting it. A good rebuttal is a small, tactful argument aimed at a weak spot in the opposing argument. Try these strategies:

1. **Point out the counterargument's limits** by putting the opposing point in a larger context. Show that the counterargument omits something important.
2. **Tell the other side of the story.** Offer an opposing interpretation of the evidence, or counter with stronger, more reliable, more convincing evidence.
3. **Address logical fallacies in the counterargument.** Check for faulty reasoning or emotional manipulation. For example, if the counterargument presents a half-truth, present "the rest of the story."

> It is true that Chernobyl occurred more than 30 years ago, so safety measures for nuclear reactors have been greatly improved. However, that single accident is still affecting millions of people exposed to the radiation.

### Consolidate Your Claim

After making concessions and rebutting objections, you may need to regroup. Restate your claim so carefully that the weight of your whole argument can rest on it.

> Although it is not ideal, burning fossil fuels is still a better option than nuclear power until renewable energy sources become more available.

Modes of Writing

# Arguing Through Appeals

For your argument to be persuasive, it must not only be logical, but also "feel right." It must treat readers as real people by appealing to their common sense, hopes, pride, and notion of right and wrong. How do you appeal to all these concerns? Do the following: (1) build credibility, (2) appeal to *pathos* by focusing on readers' values and needs, and (3) appeal to *logos* through sound reasoning.

## Appeal to *Ethos*

Sound arguments are rooted in *ethos*—a sense of the writer's character and credibility. As the connection between the words *ethos* and *ethics* suggests, a persuasive argument is so trustworthy that readers can change their minds painlessly. To build credibility, observe these rules:

- **Be thoroughly honest.** Demonstrate integrity toward the topic—don't falsify data, spin evidence, or ignore facts. Document your sources and cite them wherever appropriate. Moreover, use reputable, reliable sources; by doing so, you "borrow" the credibility of authorities.
- **Make realistic claims, projections, and promises.** Avoid emotionally charged statements, pie-in-the-sky forecasts, and undeliverable deals.
- **Develop and maintain trust.** From your first word to your last, develop trust—in your attitude toward the topic, your treatment of readers, and your respect for opposing viewpoints.

## Appeal to *Pathos*

When your argument seeks to connect with people emotionally, it appeals to *pathos*. When combined with appeals to *ethos* and *logos*, appeals to *pathos* can powerfully motivate readers to accept, believe, change, and/or act. But you want to avoid playing on readers' emotions. Instead, connect your argument with readers' needs and values. Follow these guidelines:

- **Know your real readers.** Who are they—peers, professors, or fellow citizens? What are their allegiances, their worries, their dreams?
- **Picture readers as resistant.** Accept that your readers, including those inclined to agree with you, need convincing. Think of them as alert, cautious, and demanding—but also interested.
- **Use appeals that match needs and values.** Your argument may support or challenge readers' needs and values. To understand those needs, study the table on the next page (Figure 17.4), which is based loosely on the thinking of psychologist Abraham Maslow. Maslow's hierarchy ranks people's needs on a scale from the most basic to the most complex. The table begins at the bottom with *having necessities* (a basic need) and ends at the top with *helping others* (a more complex need). For example, if you're arguing for more affordable housing for the elderly, you'd argue differently to legislators (whose focus is on *helping others*) than to the elderly who need the housing (whose focus is on *having necessities*).

- Use appeals that match the foremost needs and values of your readers.
- If appropriate, constructively challenge those needs and values.
- Whenever possible, phrase your appeals in positive terms.
- After analyzing your readers' needs, choose a persuasive theme for your argument—a positive benefit, advantage, or outcome that readers can expect if they accept your claim. Use this theme to help readers care about your claims.

| Reader needs . . . | Use persuasive appeals to . . . |
|---|---|
| **To make the world better by** helping others | values and social obligations |
| **To achieve by** being good at something, getting recognition | self-fulfillment, status, appreciation |
| **To belong by** being part of a group | group identity, acceptance |
| **To survive by** avoiding threats, having necessities | safety, security, physical needs |

*fig. 17.4*

## Appeal to *Logos*

Arguments stand or fall on their logical strength; for that reason, the rest of this chapter offers instruction in making sound claims, reasoning with and supporting those claims, and avoiding logical fallacies. However, your readers' acceptance of your logic is often affected more by the emotional appeal of your ideas and evidence. To avoid overly emotional appeals, follow these guidelines:

- **Engage readers positively.** Appeal to their better natures—to their sense of honor, justice, social commitment, altruism, and enlightened self-interest. Avoid appeals geared toward ignorance, prejudice, selfishness, or fear.
- **Use a fitting tone.** Use a tone that is appropriate for the topic, purpose, situation, and audience.
- **Aim to motivate, not manipulate, readers.** While you do want them to accept your viewpoint, it's not a win-at-all-costs situation. Avoid bullying, guilt-tripping, name calling, and exaggerated tugs on heartstrings.
- **Don't trash-talk the opposition.** Show tact, respect, and understanding. Focus on issues, not personalities.
- **Use arguments and evidence that readers can understand and appreciate.** If readers find your thinking too complex, too simple, or too strange, you've lost them.

**INSIGHT** Remember the adage: The best argument is so clear and convincing that it sounds like an explanation.

## Making and Qualifying Claims

An argument that appeals effectively to *ethos, pathos,* and *logos* centers on a claim—a debatable statement. That claim is the thesis, or key point you wish to explain and defend so well that readers agree with it. A strong claim has the following traits:

- **It's clearly arguable**—it can be vigorously debated.
- **It's defendable**—it can be supported with sufficient arguments and evidence.
- **It's responsible**—it takes an ethically sound position.
- **It's understandable**—it uses clear terms and defines key words.
- **It's interesting**—it is challenging and worth discussing, not bland and easily accepted.

### Distinguish Claims from Facts and Opinions

A claim is a conclusion drawn from logical thought and reliable evidence. A fact, in contrast, is a statement that can be checked for accuracy. An opinion is a personally held taste or attitude. A claim can be debated, but a fact or an opinion cannot. (Don't be fooled by the nonsensical notion of "alternative facts.")

> **Fact:** During the last three years, no major accident has occurred in a nuclear power plant in the U.S.
>
> **Opinion:** I think nuclear power plants are safe.
>
> **Claim:** Nuclear power and fossil fuels are two major methods of energy production, and nuclear power could be seen as the "greener" option. However, the risks of nuclear power far outweigh its benefits, making fossil fuels the safer and more environmentally friendly option.

*Note:* While the fact's accuracy can easily be checked, the opinion statement simply offers a personal feeling. Conversely, the claim states an idea that can be supported with reasoning and evidence.

### Distinguish Three Types of Claims

Truth, value, and policy—these types of claims are made in an argument. The differences among them are important because each type has a distinct goal.

- **Claims of truth** state that something is or is not the case. As a writer, you want readers to accept your claim as trustworthy.

    > The Arctic ice cap will melt completely during the summer as early as 2080.
    >
    > The cholesterol in eggs is not as dangerous as previously feared.
    >
    > **Comment:** Avoid statements that are (1) obviously true or (2) impossible to prove. Also, truth claims must be argued carefully because accepting them (or not) can have serious consequences.
    >
    > *Sample Essay:* "Is Marijuana as Safe as We Think?" (See chapter 18.)

- **Claims of value** state that something does or does not have worth. As a writer, you want readers to accept your judgment.

  > Volunteer reading tutors provide a valuable service.
  >
  > Many music videos fail to present positive images of women.
  >
  > **Comment:** Claims of value must be supported by referring to a known standard or by establishing an agreed-upon standard. To avoid bias, base your judgments on the known standard, not on your feelings.
  >
  > *Sample Essay:* "Reaction GIFs of Black People Are More Problematic Than You Think" (See chapter 18.)

- **Claims of policy** state that something ought or ought not to be done. As a writer, you want readers to approve your course of action.

  > Special taxes should be placed on gas-guzzling SUVs.
  >
  > The developer should not be allowed to fill in the pond where the endangered tiger salamander lives.
  >
  > **Comment:** Policy claims focus on action. To arrive at them, you must often first establish certain truths and values; thus an argument over policy may include both truth and value claims.
  >
  > *Sample Essay:* "Remedying an E-Waste Economy" (See chapter 18.)

## Develop a Supportable Claim

An effective claim balances confidence with common sense. Follow these tips:

- **Avoid all-or-nothing, extreme claims.** Propositions using words that are overly positive or negative—such as *all*, *best*, *never*, and *worst*—may be difficult to support. Statements that leave no room for exceptions are easy to attack.

  > **Extreme:** All people charged for a DUI should never be allowed to drive again.

- **Make a truly meaningful claim.** Avoid claims that are obvious, trivial, or unsupportable.

  > **Obvious:** Some people are against oil pipelines.
  >
  > **Trivial:** Oil pipelines are good at moving oil.
  >
  > **Unsupportable:** Building oil pipelines is immoral.

- **Use qualifiers to temper your claims.** Qualifiers are words or phrases that make claims more reasonable. Notice the difference between these two claims:

  > **Unqualified:** Star athletes take far too many academic shortcuts.
  >
  > **Qualified:** Some star athletes take improper academic shortcuts.

*Note:* The "qualified" claim is easier to defend because it narrows the focus and leaves room for exceptions. Use qualifier words or phrases like these:

| | | | |
|---|---|---|---|
| almost | if done correctly | maybe | tends to |
| before 2020 | in one case | might | typically |
| frequently | likely | probably some | usually |

# Supporting Your Claims

A claim stands or falls on its support. It's not the popular strength of your claim that matters, but rather the strength of your reasoning and evidence. To develop strong support, consider how to select and use evidence.

## Gather Evidence

Several types of evidence can support claims. To make good choices, review each type, as well as its strengths and weaknesses.

- **Observations and anecdotes** share what people (including you) have seen, heard, smelled, touched, tasted, and experienced. Such evidence offers an "eyewitness" perspective shaped by the observer's viewpoint, which can be powerful but may also prove narrow and subjective.

  > A generation ago, an American child could reasonably expect to grow up with their father. Today, an American child can reasonably expect not to.

- **Statistics** offer concrete numbers about a topic. Numbers don't "speak for themselves," however. They need to be interpreted and compared properly—not slanted or taken out of context. They also need to be up-to-date, relevant, and accurate.

  > Pennsylvania spends $30 million annually in deer-related costs.
  >
  > Wisconsin has an estimated annual loss of $37 million for crop damage alone.

- **Tests and experiments** provide hard data developed through the scientific method, data that must nevertheless be carefully studied and properly interpreted.

  > According to the two scientists, the rats with unlimited access to the functional running wheel ran each day and gradually increased the amount of running; in addition, they started to eat less.

- **Graphics** provide information in visual form—from simple tables to more complex charts, maps, drawings, and photographs. When poorly done, however, graphics can distort the truth.

- **Analogies** compare two things, creating clarity by drawing parallels. However, every analogy breaks down if pushed too far.

  > It is obvious today that America has defaulted on this promissory note insofar as her citizens of color are concerned. Instead of honoring this sacred obligation, America has given the Negro people a bad check; a check which has come back marked "insufficient funds." But we refuse to believe that the bank of justice is bankrupt.
  >
  > —Martin Luther King, Jr.

- **Expert testimony** offers insights from an authority on the topic. Such testimony always has limits: Experts don't know it all, and they work from distinct perspectives, which means that they can disagree.

  > One specialist opposed to drilling is David Klein, a professor at the Institute of Arctic Biology at the University of Alaska–Fairbanks. Klein argues that if the oil industry opens up the ANWR for drilling, the number of caribou will likely decrease because the calving locations will change.

- **Illustrations, examples, and demonstrations** support general claims with specific instances, making such statements seem concrete and observable. Of course, an example may not be your best support if it isn't familiar.

  > Think about how differently one can frame Rosa Parks' historic action. In prevailing myth, Parks—a holy innocent—acts almost on whim. . . . The real story is more empowering: It suggests that change is the product of deliberate, incremental action.

- **Analyses** examine parts of a topic through thought patterns—cause/effect, compare/contrast, classification, process, or definition. Such analysis helps make sense of a topic's complexity, but muddles the topic when poorly done.

  > If colorism lives underground, its effects are very real. Darker-skinned African-American defendants are more than twice as likely to receive the death penalty as lighter-skinned African-American defendants for crimes of equivalent seriousness. . . .

- **Predictions** offer insights into possible outcomes or consequences by forecasting what might happen under certain conditions. Like weather forecasting, predicting can be tricky. To be plausible, a prediction must be rooted in a logical analysis of present facts.

  > Fortunately, there is hope. Scientific research is already helping doctors do amazing things for people suffering with cancer. One treatment that has been used for some time is chemotherapy, or the use of chemicals to kill off all fast-growing cells, including cancer cells. . . . One of the newest and most promising treatments is gene therapy . . ."

## Use Evidence

Finding evidence is one thing; using it well is another. You want to reason with the evidence effectively, to use that evidence to advance and deepen your argument—to "thicken" it, so to speak. To marshal evidence in support of your claim, follow three guidelines:

1. **Go for quality and variety, not just quantity.** More evidence is not necessarily better. Instead, aim for sound evidence in different forms. Quality evidence is . . .
   - **accurate:** correct and verifiable in each detail.
   - **complete:** filled with pertinent facts.
   - **concrete:** filled with specifics.
   - **relevant:** clearly related to the claim.
   - **current:** reliably up-to-date.
   - **authoritative:** backed by expertise, training, and knowledge.
   - **appealing:** able to influence readers.

2. **Use inductive and deductive patterns of logic.** Depending on your purpose, use inductive or deductive reasoning.

   **Induction:** Inductive reasoning works from the particular toward general conclusions. In a persuasive essay using induction, look at facts first, find a pattern in them, and then lead the reader to your conclusion.

   > For example, in "America Needs a Ministry of (Actual) Truth" at the beginning of this chapter, Josh Wilbur first introduces specific incidents of public and private figures being victimized by deepfakes, before presenting his main argument: a call to create a federal agency in charge of combating disinformation (a solution to the problem he outlines from the beginning).

   **Deduction:** Deductive reasoning—the opposite of inductive reasoning—starts from accepted truths and applies them to a new situation so as to reach a conclusion about it. For deduction to be sound, be sure the starting principles or facts are true, the new situation is accurately described, and the application is logical.

   > For example, in the essay at the end of this chapter, "Executive Deception: Four Fallacies about Divestment, and One Big Mistake," philosopher Kathleen Dean Moore indicates at the start that university officials should address logically the issue of divesting their institutions' investments in fossil fuels. In her essay, she then outlines four ways their decisions approach the issue illogically—failing to follow this principle.

3. **Reason using valid warrants.** To make sense, claims and their supporting reasons must have a logical connection. That connection is called the *warrant*—the often unspoken thinking used to relate the reasoning to the claim. If warrants are good, arguments hold water; if warrants are faulty, then arguments break down. In other words, beware of faulty assumptions.

   Check the short argument outlined below. Which of the warrants seem reasonable and strong, and which seem weak? Where does the argument fail?

   > **Reasoning:** If current trends in water usage continue, the reservoir will be empty in two years.
   >
   > **Claim:** Therefore, Emeryville should immediately shut down its public swimming pools.

   **Unstated Warrants or Assumptions:**
   > It is not good for the reservoir to be empty.
   > The swimming pools draw significant amounts of water from the reservoir.
   > Emptying the pools would help raise the level of the reservoir.
   > No other action would better prevent the reservoir from emptying.
   > It is worse to have an empty reservoir than an empty swimming pool.

**INSIGHT** Because an argument is no stronger than its warrants, you must make sure that your reasoning clearly and logically supports your claims.

# Identifying Logical Fallacies

Fallacies are false arguments—that is, bits of fuzzy, dishonest, or incomplete thinking. They may crop up in your own thinking, in your opposition's thinking, or in such public "arguments" as ads, political appeals, and talk shows. Because fallacies may sway an unsuspecting audience, they are dangerously persuasive. By learning to recognize fallacies, however, you may identify them in opposing arguments and eliminate them from your own writing. In this section, logical fallacies are grouped according to how they falsify an argument. Afterward, the relevance of these fallacies is shown in an essay, "Executive Deception: Four Fallacies about Divestment, and One Big Mistake."

## Distorting the Issue

The following fallacies falsify an argument by twisting the logical framework.

- **Bare Assertion** The most basic way to distort an issue is to deny that it exists. This fallacy claims, "That's just how it is."

  > The private ownership of handguns is a constitutional right. (*Objection:* The claim shuts off discussion of the U.S. Constitution, the legal process of amending the Constitution, or the reasons for regulation.)

- **Begging the Question** Also known as circular reasoning, this fallacy arises from assuming in the basis of your argument the very point you need to prove.

  > We don't need a useless film series when students have computers and other devices. (*Objection:* There may be uses for a public film series that private video viewing can't provide. The word "useless" begs the question.)

- **Oversimplification** This fallacy reduces complexity to simplicity. Beware of phrases like "It's a simple question of." Serious issues are rarely simple.

  > Capital punishment is a simple question of protecting society.

- **Either/Or Thinking** Also known as black-and-white thinking, this fallacy reduces all options to two extremes. Frequently, it derives from a clear bias.

  > Either this community develops light-rail transportation or the community will not grow in the future. (*Objection:* The claim ignores the possibility that growth may occur through other means.)

- **Complex Question** Sometimes by phrasing a question a certain way, a person ignores or covers up a more basic question.

  > Why can't we bring down the prices that corrupt gas stations are charging? (*Objection:* This question ignores a more basic question—"Are gas stations really corrupt?")

- **Straw Man** In this fallacy, the writer argues against a claim that is easily refuted. Typically, such a claim exaggerates or misrepresents the opponents' position.

  > Those who oppose euthanasia must believe that individuals who are terminally ill deserve to suffer.

## Sabotaging the Argument

These fallacies falsify the argument by twisting it. They destroy reason and replace it with something hollow or misleading.

- **Red Herring** This strange term comes from the practice of dragging a stinky fish across a trail to throw tracking dogs off the scent. When a person puts forth a volatile idea that pulls readers away from the real issue, readers become distracted. Suppose the argument addresses drilling for oil in the Arctic National Wildlife Refuge (ANWR) of Alaska, and the writer begins with this statement:

  > In 1989, the infamous oil spill of the *Exxon Valdez* led to massive animal deaths and enormous environmental degradation of the coastline. (*Objection:* Introducing this notorious oil spill distracts from the real issue—how oil drilling will affect the ANWR.)

- **Misuse of Humor** Jokes, satire, and irony can lighten the mood and highlight a truth; when humor distracts or mocks, however, it undercuts the argument. What effect would the mocking tone of this statement have in an argument about tanning beds in health clubs?

  > People who use tanning beds will just turn into wrinkled old prunes or leathery sun-dried tomatoes!

- **Appeal to Pity** This fallacy engages in a misleading tug on the heartstrings. Instead of using a measured emotional appeal, an appeal to pity seeks to manipulate the audience into agreement.

  > Affirmative action policies ruined this young man's life. Because of them, he was denied admission to Centerville College.

- **Use of Threats** A simple but unethical way of sabotaging an argument is to threaten opponents. More often than not, a threat is merely implied: "If you don't accept my argument, you'll regret it."

  > If we don't immediately start drilling for oil in the ANWR, you will soon face hour-long lines at gas stations from New York to California.

- **Bandwagon Mentality** Someone implies that a claim cannot be true because a majority of people are opposed to it, or it must be true because a majority support it. (History shows that people in the minority have often had the better argument.) At its worst, such an appeal manipulates people's desire to belong or be accepted.

  > It's obvious to intelligent people that cockroaches live only in the apartments of dirty people. (*Objection:* Based on popular opinion, the claim appeals to a kind of prejudice and ignores scientific evidence about cockroaches.)

- **Appeal to Popular Sentiment** This fallacy consists of associating your position with something popularly loved: the American flag, baseball, apple pie. Appeals to popular sentiment sidestep thought to play on feelings.

  > Anyone who has seen *Bambi* could never condone hunting deer.

## Drawing Faulty Conclusions from the Evidence

This group of fallacies falsifies the argument by short-circuiting proper logic in favor of assumptions or faulty thinking.

- **Appeal to Ignorance** This fallacy suggests that because no one has proven a particular claim, it must be false; or, because no one has disproven a claim, it must be true. Appeals to ignorance unfairly shift the burden of proof onto someone else.

    > Flying saucers are real. No scientific explanation has ruled them out.

- **Hasty or Broad Generalization** Such a claim is based on too little evidence or allows no exceptions. In jumping to a conclusion, the writer may use intensifiers such as *all*, *every*, or *never*.

    > Today's voters spend too little time reading and too much time being taken in by 30-second sound bites. (*Objection:* Quite a few voters may, in fact, spend too little time reading about the issues, but it is unfair to suggest that this is true of everyone.)

- **False Cause** This well-known fallacy confuses sequence with causation: If *A* comes before *B*, *A* must have caused *B*. However, *A* may be one of several causes, or *A* and *B* may be only loosely related, or the connection between *A* and *B* may be entirely coincidental.

    > Since that new school opened, drug use among young people has skyrocketed. Better that the school had never been built.

- **Slippery Slope** This fallacy argues that a single step will start an unstoppable chain of events. While such a slide may occur, the prediction lacks evidence.

    > If we legalize marijuana, it's only a matter of time before hard drugs follow and America becomes a nation of junkies and addicts.

## Misusing Evidence

These fallacies falsify the argument by abusing or distorting the evidence.

- **Impressing with Numbers** In this case, the writer drowns readers in statistics and numbers that overwhelm them into agreement. In addition, the numbers haven't been properly interpreted.

    > At 35 ppm, CO levels factory-wide are only 10 ppm above the OSHA recommendation, which is 25 ppm. Clearly, that 10 ppm is insignificant in the big picture, and the occasional readings in some areas of between 40 and 80 ppm are aberrations that can safely be ignored. (*Objection:* The 10 ppm may be significant, and higher readings may indicate real danger.)

- **Half-Truths** A half-truth contains part of but not the whole truth. Because it leaves out "the rest of the story," it is both true and false simultaneously.

    > The new welfare bill is good because it will get people off the public dole. (*Objection:* This may be true, but the bill may also cause undue suffering for some truly needy individuals.)

- **Unreliable Testimonial** An appeal to authority has force only if the authority is qualified in the proper field. If they are not, the testimony is irrelevant. Note that fame is not the same thing as authority.

  > On her talk show, Alberta Magnus recently claimed that most pork sold in the United States is tainted. (*Objection:* Although Magnus may be an articulate talk show host, she is not an expert on food safety.)

- **Attack Against the Person** This fallacy, also called an "*ad hominem* attack," directs attention to a person's character, lifestyle, or beliefs rather than to the issue.

  > Would you accept the opinion of a candidate who experimented with drugs in college?

- **Hypothesis Contrary to Fact** This fallacy relies on "if only" thinking. It bases the claim on an assumption of what would have happened if something else had, or had not, happened. Being pure speculation, such a claim cannot be tested.

  > If only multiculturalists hadn't pushed through affirmative action, the United States would be a united nation.

- **False Analogy** Sometimes a person will argue that X is good (or bad) because it is like Y. Such an analogy may be valid, but it weakens the argument if the grounds for the comparison are vague or unrelated.

  > Don't bother voting in this election; it's a stinking quagmire. (*Objection:* Comparing the election to a "stinking quagmire" is unclear and exaggerated.)

## Misusing Language

Essentially, all logical fallacies misuse language. However, three fallacies falsify the argument particularly by the misleading use of words.

- **Obfuscation** This fallacy involves using fuzzy terms like *throughput* and *downlink* to muddy the issue. These words may make simple ideas sound more profound than they really are, or they may make false ideas sound true.

  > Through the fully functional developmental process of a streamlined target-refractory system, the U.S. military will successfully reprioritize its data throughputs. (*Objection:* What does this sentence mean?)

- **Ambiguity** Ambiguous statements can be interpreted in two or more opposite ways. Although ambiguity can result from unintentional careless thinking, writers sometimes use ambiguity to obscure a position.

  > Many women need to work to support their children through school, but they would be better off at home. (*Objection:* Does *they* refer to *children* or *women*? What does *better off* mean? These words and phrases can be interpreted in opposite ways.)

- **Slanted Language** By choosing words with strong positive or negative connotations, a writer can draw readers away from the true logic of the argument. Here is an example of three synonyms for the word stubborn that the philosopher Bertrand Russell once used to illustrate the bias in slanted language:

  > I am firm. You are obstinate. He is pigheaded.

## Identifying Fallacies in Others' Arguments

While it is important to identify and avoid fallacies in your own arguments, it is also valuable (though not necessarily appreciated) to point out logical errors in others' arguments. This is one strategy for engaging opposition within your own writing. In the following essay, Kathleen Dean Moore structures her whole essay around four logical fallacies in the arguments of university administrators who defend not divesting their university's finances of investments in fossil fuels. Moore is a distinguished professor emerita of philosophy at Oregon State University. She is the author or coeditor of several books, including *Great Tide Rising: Toward Clarity and Moral Courage in a Time of Planetary Change*. As you read her essay, examine how she explains and illustrates each fallacy, and note how each of her claims advances her thesis.

---

### Executive Deception: Four Fallacies About Divestment, and One Big Mistake

1   It pains this old logic professor to read university officials' arguments against divesting their institutions of investments in fossil fuels, not because their refusal to divest is wrong-headed, although I believe it is, but because their logic is so awful.

2   A sample of Ivy League universities' antidivestment statements offers a primer in the fallacies that students are warned against in Logic 101. Here are four:

3   **The ad hominem argument:** "I find a troubling inconsistency in the notion that, as an investor, we should boycott [the oil-and-gas industry, while we] are extensively relying on those companies' products and services," writes Drew Faust, president of Harvard University.

4   The assumption is that those who rely on fossil fuels do not have the moral authority to take a stand against them. This is an ad hominem (to the man) attack, which turns the focus from the argument itself to the person or institution making the argument. The attack might be fair if the university had freely chosen fossil fuels from an array of options. It did not. Over generations, fossil fuels have been built into the structure of our lives, our buildings, our cities. Big Oil works hard to perpetuate that dependency and to radically constrict choices, as it lobbies against renewable energies, influences the election of officials who will vote against alternative transportation, hires hacks to confuse the public about the scientific consensus on climate change, making sure that colleges (and all the rest of us) are forced to use fossil fuels. It's the ultimate triumph of the industry that even as it is externalizing its environmental costs, it is also externalizing its shame. And university officials making this argument haplessly cooperate to disempower their own moral voices and those of their students.

**The straw argument:** "Brown's holdings are much too small for divestiture to reduce corporate profits," writes Christina Paxson, president of Brown University.

Of course Brown's divestment, or anyone else's, will not cripple the fossil-fuel industry. The author and divestment leader Bill McKibben publicly affirms that it will not. Divestment isn't designed to destroy. It is designed to save, and what is imperiled here is the integrity of the university. A university has an overriding responsibility to advance the well-being of its students, which means that it is flat wrong to profit from industries that will devastate their future.

The Ivy League response is a classic straw argument, a cynical or careless misconstruing of the divestment argument. Instead of addressing the real issue of moral integrity, the president substitutes a scarecrow so flimsy that it might be made of straw. Easy enough to knock down the bogus argument, but the serious one remains.

**The false dichotomy:** "Yale will have its greatest impact in meeting the climate challenges through its core mission: research, scholarship, and education," claims the Yale Corporation Committee on Investor Responsibility.

Maybe so. But that doesn't mean that Yale should not study, educate, and at the same time divest from fossil fuels. Divest or educate? This is not a forced choice between alternatives. In fact, divestment may be a university's greatest opportunity for moral education, for instruction in the foundational moral imperative to let your values guide your decisions.

"Climate change is a grave threat to human welfare," the committee goes on to say. If so, then Yale should throw everything it's got at the threat. Research? Yes. Scholarship? Yes. Education? Beyond a doubt. Divestment? Absolutely, and anything else it can pull out of the hat. Addressing climate change is going to require the greatest exercise of the moral and technological imagination the world has ever seen. The future is no place for slackers.

**The hasty generalization.** "Logic and experience indicate that barring investments in [fossil fuels] would—especially for a large endowment reliant on sophisticated investment techniques, pooled funds, and broad diversification—come at a substantial economic cost." Harvard again.

It's sometimes logical to make predictions about the future on the basis of past experience, but only if you can assume that the future will resemble the past. When the future threatens to be staggeringly different from the past, reliance on experience is a hasty, often expensive mistake in reasoning.

Never before has life on the planet been so deeply threatened by a single energy technology—burning fossil fuels. And never before have there been so many alternative ways to generate energy. Never have the costs of alternatives fallen so rapidly.

It's a new world. Whether because of new technologies, new regulations, a global crisis of conscience, a global economy utterly devastated by climate change, or who knows what, the world will divest itself of the fossil-fuel economy, and probably sooner rather than later. The investors who quickly respond to a changing world have the best chance to prosper; the laggards will be left holding the bag.

And so we come to the big mistake: "The [university] endowment is a resource, not an instrument to impel social or political change." Harvard.

Oh, yes it is. By profiting from Big Oil, the university endowment casts a very public vote for short-term, short-sighted profit and against the victims of that business plan—future generations, plants and animals, the world's poor and displaced—and the university's own students. Shame.

## Reading for Better Writing

1. *Connections:* Where and how do you use fossil fuels in your own life? How would you characterize your dependence on them? Have you taken steps to lessen that dependence? On a different scale, does your college or university have a policy on divestment in fossil fuels? What rationale, if any, does your school offer for or against divestment?
2. *Comprehension:* For each of the four fallacies Moore discusses, restate the logical error and summarize how college administrators make the error.
3. *Writing Moves:*
    a. Moore both starts and ends her essay with some sharp statements. What is the effect of doing so? How do these statements frame her discussion, putting it in a larger context.
    b. For each fallacy, Moore quotes directly from administrators and then explains the fallacious reasoning in the quotation. What is the effect of this method and pattern?

**Your Project:** Fossil-fuel divestment is just one issue on which people are susceptible to thinking fallaciously. With what other contentious, difficult issues would people make logical errors? Consider choosing such a topic, researching what people think about it, and writing an exposé of the common fallacies people make.

"Executive Deception: Four Fallacies About Divestment, and One Big Mistake" by Kathleen Dean Moore. Originally appeared in The Chronicle for Higher Education. Reprinted by permission of the author.

# Strategies for Argumentation: Applications

Once you have finished learning and practicing strategies for argumentation, there may be more to think about. Consider how to apply what you have learned in the following situations.

1. **Photo Op:** The chapter's opening page contains a photograph of young environmentalists at a climate strike in New York City. One protestor holds up a sign that expresses a claim: "We Are Missing Our Lessons to Teach You One!"—a textual argument within a visual argument. Consider another controversial issue, and find or create an image that similarly makes a claim about that issue.

2. **Living Today:** What role does argument play in our daily lives and decisions? Reflect on an area of your life where you rely on arguments—consumer purchases, politics, sports, and so on. Examine the arguments that you make in that area of life, as well as the arguments that you listen to: Do they follow sound argumentation strategies?

3. **Public Texts:** Editorials in periodicals are often brief arguments. Find, read, and analyze an editorial on an issue that interests you:
   a. What approach does the editorial take—Toulmin, Rogerian, something else?
   b. How does the editorial present and address opposing points of view?
   c. In what ways does the editorial appeal to *ethos*? How does it build credibility?
   d. In its appeals to *pathos*, does the editorial connect with needs and values?
   e. What is the editorial's main claim? Is it a claim of truth, value, or policy?
   f. What arguments does the editorial offer to support that claim? Is the reasoning logical? Are the warrants behind the reasoning sound?
   g. What types of evidence does the writer provide to support their reasoning? Is the evidence valid, sufficient, current, and accurate?
   h. How would you characterize the overall success or failure of this argument?

## Learning-Objectives Checklist ✓

Have you achieved this chapter's learning objectives? Check your progress with the following items, revisiting topics in the chapter as needed. I have . . .

\_\_\_\_ identified different approaches to argumentation.
\_\_\_\_ practiced addressing alternatives and opposing perspectives.
\_\_\_\_ practiced appeals to *ethos, pathos,* and *logos.*
\_\_\_\_ analyzed the nature and effects of truth, value, and policy claims.
\_\_\_\_ revised arguments to correct these weaknesses: all-or-nothing claims, obvious claims, trivial assertions, and claims lacking needed qualifiers.
\_\_\_\_ analyzed the strengths and weaknesses of nine types of evidence.
\_\_\_\_ linked claims and their supporting reasons with valid warrants.
\_\_\_\_ corrected logical fallacies in others' arguments and in my own.
\_\_\_\_ written a brief argument that critiques a policy or practice or that reveals logical fallacies in a position.

# Chapter 18

# Persuasive Writing: Positions, Actions, and Solutions

"I changed my mind." Have you ever said this when you've reversed course on an earlier decision? It can sound a bit defensive, can't it—as if you've been accused of weak and waffly behavior. But a changed mind can be for the good. It can be a thinking and feeling mind, a growing mind.

Persuasive writing is about changing minds—both your writing mind and those minds reading your words. This change isn't easy, as we can be indifferent, resistant, or even outright opposed to clear thinking about complex, contentious issues. To move people—yourself included—your writing needs to overcome this defensiveness, this inertia.

In this chapter, you'll build on what you learned in chapter 17 about argumentation by applying that knowledge to three situations where persuasion is needed: taking a position, calling for action, and solving a problem. Prepare to change and be changed.

## Learning Objectives

By working through this chapter, you will be able to

- explain what a persuasive essay is and what forms it might take.
- practice strategies for persuasion.
- develop a strong thesis for a persuasive essay.
- identify specific moves for shaping persuasive writing.
- craft a convincing persuasive essay by drawing upon a range of writing moves.

**Visually Speaking**  Review Figure 18.1. What point or points does it make? What does it suggest about making arguments?

*Win McNamee / Staff*

fig. 18.1

# Meeting the Mode

To get familiar with persuasive writing, start with an essay that shows persuasion in action. In the essay below, student writer Dave DeHaan examines the gear and tackle of sport fishing. Why? With this relatively pleasant and harmless topic, what could possibly need to change? Consider the change Dave is calling for and how he goes about calling for it.

### Evening the Odds

A new breed of hunter dwells among North America's hidden waterways. Armed with a $100 rod and reel, $75 hip waders, and an array of lures ranging from glowing gadgets to old-fashioned worms, today's anglers have improved their arsenal well beyond the bent nail and old twine that Huck Finn used for jigging. But most modern anglers still carry one piece of equipment that is outdated: the barbed hook, which is still added to almost every lure produced commercially. This mechanism continues to plague the sport of fishing by damaging young fish stocks. Barbed hooks should be banned from lure fishing to protect fish that are not yet ready for anglers to keep.

A smooth (barbless) fishing hook is much easier to remove from a fish's mouth than a barbed hook. A smooth hook comes out cleanly, leaving only a small puncture, and giving anglers the opportunity to release undamaged fish. A properly set barbed hook, on the other hand, often inflicts serious injury to the jaw of the fish. While this is not a problem for the larger keepers, it does have serious consequences for smaller fish that should be released back into the waterway. Many of these small fish are kept because the anglers know that releasing them would be inhumane, while others are released with portions of their jaws missing, unable to feed properly. By improving the angler's chances of safely releasing unwanted fish, barbless hooks help to preserve our limited fish stocks.

Supporters of barbed fishing hooks say that banning the hooks would decrease the number of fish they are able to land. They claim that enjoyment of the sport would be limited by the increased difficulty of keeping fish on the line. They are at least partially correct: playing a fish is difficult without a barb. However, this does not have to limit the enjoyment of the sport.

When anglers stop to reflect on why they find fishing so enjoyable, most realize that what they love is the feel of a fish on the end of the line, not necessarily the weight of the fillets in their coolers. Fishing has undergone a slow evolution over the past century. While fishing used to be a way of putting food on the table, most of today's anglers do so only for the relaxation that it provides. The barbed hook was invented to increase the quantity of fish people could land so as to better feed their families. This need no longer exists, and so barbed hooks are no longer necessary.

According to some anglers who use smooth hooks, their lures perform better than barbed lures as long as they maintain a constant tension on the line. Smooth hooks can bite deeper than barbed hooks, actually providing a stronger hold on the fish.

> These anglers testify that switching from barbed hooks has not noticeably reduced the number of fish that they are able to land. In their experience, and in my own, enjoyment of the sport is actually heightened by adding another challenge to playing the fish (maintaining line tension).
>
> Some people have argued that replacing all of the barbed books in their tackle would be a costly operation. While this is certainly a concern, barbed hooks do not necessarily require replacement. With a simple set of pliers, the barbs on most conventional hooks can be bent down, providing a cost-free method of modifying one's existing tackle. These modified hooks are also much safer to use. While the possibility of snagging someone still remains with a smooth hook, the hook is much easier to remove from skin, clothing, and branches.
>
> The gradual evolution of fishing for food into fishing for sport has outdated the need for barbed hooks. Just as in any other sport, enjoyment comes from being able to achieve a goal despite considerable difficulty. If anglers chose their equipment solely on the quantity of fish they were able to land, we would all be fishing with dragnets. While everyone agrees that nets take the sport out of fishing, they must realize that barbed hooks do the same thing. Fishing with smooth hooks is a way of caring for and conserving our fish stocks while still maintaining the enjoyment of sport fishing for the angler.

*"Evening the Odds" by David DeHaan. Used with permission.*

## Converse with the Mode

So, what change is Dave calling for? By the end of the first paragraph, it's clear: barbed fishing hooks should be banned for sport fishing. The remainder of his essay is then an explanation and defense of this position, as well as an implied call for other anglers to willingly drop the barbed hook. Now look a little closer at the essay.

### Conversation Starters

1. How does Dave open his essay? How does he build toward his position statement at the end of the first paragraph?
2. Look at each body paragraph in order. In a sentence for each, describe what these paragraphs add to Dave's argument. How is each paragraph a persuasive move added to the one that comes before it?
3. What does the final paragraph achieve? What strategies make it persuasive?

**Moving On:** In the last paragraph, Dave begins one of his sentences with "Just as in any other sport…." Besides fishing, what other sports or leisure activities interest you? Do you see problems with the equipment or rules? What about the business side of that activity? Add such topics to your list of possibilities for your persuasive essay.

# Strategies for Persuasive Writing

Persuasive writing may take many forms: essays, editorials, position papers, proposals, to name a few. Whatever the form, such writing goes out on a limb by examining a controversy, a debatable issue, or a problem. Persuasive writing goes beyond careful analysis of the issue by asking questions like these: Why should we care? What should we believe? What can we do? To learn how to go out on a limb without breaking it, you need to understand the rhetorical situation behind your writing and follow the principles for taking a stand, calling for action, and solving a problem.

## The Rhetorical Situation

To construct an argument, you need to start by thinking about the purpose, the readers, and the specific topic of your writing.

- **Purpose:** You create persuasive papers to inform readers about the nature and relevance of a topic, to convince them to take a stand on it, and possibly to move them to take action. If the topic can be defined as a problem, your goal is to persuade readers of a solution. More limited goals might be to convince readers to care about the topic and to at least respect your argument.
- **Readers:** You may have a variety of readers: people opposed to the argument, uncertain what to think about the issue, or unaware that an issue exists. The audience may even be those who agree with your point of view but are looking for sensible reasons. You need to shape the content, organization, and tone of your arguments to effectively address such intended readers.
- **Topic:** The topics you address in argumentative writing are debatable issues about which informed people can reasonably disagree. Therefore, readers will learn more about a paper's topic by focusing not only on your position, call to action, or solution, but also on the reasoning that you use to develop the argument, including attention to alternatives.

**Example:** In "Is Marijuana as Safe as We Think?" Malcolm Gladwell's *purpose* is to ask and answer the question in the title, given the move to legalize cannabis in several states and in countries such as Canada. His goal is specifically to debate whether legalization strategies are wise. Although legalization has taken place, Gladwell sees the *topic* of cannabis use debatable because little research has been done on its effects. He wants his *readers*—the general public but perhaps more specifically policy-makers, public-health professionals, parents, and cannabis-users of all ages—to rethink the general attitude toward cannabis as a harmless drug.

## Principles: Taking a Stand

Writing that takes a position examines a controversial or debatable issue, and it then articulates and defends a specific stance on that issue. Effectively taking a position depends on the principles that follow.

**Researching, exploring, and respecting all available positions.** Before you can settle on a particular position, you need to openly and thoroughly examine all the options—getting inside different stances, objectively examining the reasoning and evidence, and weighing the pluses and minuses. Doing so helps you better determine where to stand and prepares you to speak to all the alternatives.

**Making a stance reasonable and measured.** A solid position must go beyond a pure opinion that is shouted shrilly. (Whereas your opinions may be uninformed and inherited, you *think* your way into a position.) You are certainly free to advance your position forcefully, but you also need to do so thoughtfully and respectfully: conceding points, addressing objections, and softening the stance (if necessary) with qualifiers. Essentially, you need to determine whether to advance your positions firmly or to seek a fair and reasonable compromise, working your way out of embattled and entrenched thinking. You can phrase such position statements as affirmations or as arguments against a claim:

- **Position statement:** *Barbed fishing hooks should be banned in favor of smooth hooks in order to protect fish stocks.*
- **Argument against a claim:** *Contrary to Breton's contention, violent video games do not make boys more violent in adulthood.*

**Rooting the position in sound analysis and reliable evidence.** You need to show how the evidence weighs in favor of your position—not verbal aggression, bluster, or the fervor of your feelings. The evidence needs to be sound, soundly reasoned with, and complete: You should not hide, ignore, or lightly dismiss evidence that does not support your position. In addition, your reasoning needs to be solid in these ways:

- **Built on an analytical foundation:** For a position to hold up, you may need to carefully *define* key terms in the debate or even the issue itself. Similarly, you may need to position the issue historically (*process* analysis), exploring how and why the issue arose. Finally, effective *compare-contrast* thinking makes sense of the range of possible positions on the issue.
- **Sensitive to logical fallacies:** Be aware of specific thinking errors within the debate, address them in opposing positions, and avoid them in you own stance. Avoid either-or thinking, a dualistic logic that reduces an issue to two polar opposite possibilities. Similarly, you need to avoid broad generalizations and oversimplification.
- **Recognizes possible change:** Because demographics, technology, cultures, and the economy change, you may wish to qualify your position. Point out how future changes could alter the situation, your findings, and your position.

## Principles: Calling for Action

Change is tough, so calling others to action in writing can be especially challenging. In this sense, call-to-action writing not only takes a position on an issue (encouraging readers to adopt or at least respect that position, as discussed above) but also presses readers to take the next logical step—translating that stance into concrete action or behavioral change. Persuading readers to act relies on writing principles like those that follow:

**Rooting the writing in sound reasoning.** Calls to action require trustworthy evidence and sound reasoning (*logos*). Because action is involved, you need to get it right. Especially important is cause-effect analysis—reasoning that can sort out the forces at work in an issue and predict the consequences of action. Similarly, call-to-action writing needs to avoid logical fallacies such as half-truths, unreliable testimonials, and false analogies.

**Building credibility through an encouraging but measured voice.** Your aim is to motivate, not manipulate. To that end, the tone in most call-to-action writing should communicate an objective urgency, though in some situations humor works well to deflate some tension and open a new perspective on the issue (*ethos*). Above all, the writing should never sound threatening or engage in guilt-tripping in order to prompt action. Not only is such an approach unethical, but it also tends to have an effect opposite to the one desired.

**Convincing readers to care about the issue.** Motivating readers to act begins with encouraging them to embrace the issue as their own (*pathos*). You do so by sharing compelling anecdotes and illustrations that put a human face on the issue, by correcting misunderstandings or commonly held views about the issue (often through the voices of respected experts), and by making sound appeals to shared needs and values. Through such strategies, you change readers' view of the issue.

**Motivating readers to undertake a doable action.** You must imagine points of resistance for readers—those thoughts and feelings that make them reluctant to act. With these realities in mind, determine what is a doable action, a concrete step or general change that is within reach for readers. Can you expect readers to stop using a word thoughtlessly or to donate to organizations that fight poverty? The doable action then becomes the theme and thesis of your writing, what it builds towards. Here are some examples of calls to doable action:

- *It's time for all consumers to learn more about where their food comes from and how it gets to their table.*
- *Sign the online petition and boycott Company X until it changes its unethical sourcing practices.*
- *Whatever your race, connect with the Black Lives Matter movement on your campus or in your community. Add your voice to the chorus calling for real racial reconciliation.*

## Principles: Proposing a Solution

Sometimes, the issue on which you take a position can be described as a *problem*, and the action you call for a *solution*. Explaining a problem flows naturally into arguing for a solution. As a problem-solution writer, your task is to convince the reader that the solution matches the problem. Doing so requires practicing a range of strategies.

**Rooting the argument in quality research.** A proposal stands or falls on the quality of both the reasoning and its support. You convince the reader of your credibility by using reliable sources for quality evidence ranging from the statistical to the historical, and by doing your homework concerning debates about the problem, its broader context, and past attempts at solutions.

**Thinking creatively.** Problem-solution thinking needs to be sound but also creative. Aim to be creative by thinking beyond what has already been done, by considering alternative perspectives on both the problem and possible solutions, and by bringing to bear on the problem ideas from other fields of knowledge. Proposal writing requires a willingness to challenge the status quo and a mind that is open to creative possibilities.

**Considering ethical issues.** Inherently, problem-solution writing involves an ethical dimension. It involves realizing that whereas some people may be harmed by the problem, other people may benefit from its existence. Such writing may seek common ground on some of life's most enduring challenges. It attempts to motivate readers to embrace a specific solution, a change that the writer stands behind and that might fail partly or wholly. You need to be aware of and speak to these ethical dimensions.

**Presenting Problems.** The first part of your proposal typically lays out the problem. The aim here is not only to convince readers that the problem exists but to persuade them to care about it enough to seek a solution. Laying out the problem involves strategies like these:

- **A measured approach:** Determine how deeply to treat and explain the problem based on what your audience needs and the level of seriousness inherent to the problem. The more unfamiliar the problem, the more serious it is, the more resistant the readers, the longer its history—the deeper you must go into presenting the problem in all its complexity, the more serious your tone.
- **Sound analysis:** Problems make sense when they are precisely defined (What is it?), vividly described (What does it look like?), explored as a narrative (What's the story?), explained as a process (When and how did it develop?), and/or probed for causes and effects (What brought about the problem? What are its consequences?).

**Arguing for Solutions.** When you turn from problems to solutions, you approach the heart of your writing—your thesis about what will end the problem or at least mitigate its harmful consequences. (The thesis thus often comes part-way through the essay, not at the beginning.) Arguing for a solution involves strategies like the ones that follow:

- **Criteria for a successful solution:** You establish a measurement for what a solution must accomplish, what it must look like.
- **Comparison of all options:** Using these criteria, you boldly explore all possible solutions, weighing and balancing them against each other in terms of how they attack root causes and bring about real benefits. In addition, you consider past attempts at solutions, to what degree these succeeded, and how they still fell short.
- **Support for the best solution (or a series of related solutions):** The best solution is neither superficial nor vague. Instead, you need to present a solution in precise and exact terms, addressing possible objections and explaining the positive outcomes that will result and the negative consequences that will be avoided.
- **Feasibility:** You need to show that your solution is workable, not just an empty wish. You do so by considering the resources required, mapping out how the solution should be implemented, and addressing any roadblocks to success.

**Sample Argumentative Paragraph**

In "The Rise of the New Groupthink," Susan Cain spends most of her essay exploring the dynamics at work in solitary and group work; however, toward the end she turns to the following argument:

> To harness the energy that fuels both these drives [our need for both others and privacy], we need to move beyond the New Groupthink and embrace a more nuanced approach to creativity and learning. Our offices should encourage casual, cafe-style interactions, but allow people to disappear into personalized, private spaces when they want to be alone. Our schools should teach children to work with others, but also to work on their own for sustained periods of time. And we must recognize that introverts like Steve Wozniak need extra quiet and privacy to do their best work.

## Patterns for Persuasive Essays: Thesis Thinking

Your thesis will grow out of your essential conclusions about the issue after you've studied all sides of it. Your thesis will describe the stand you're taking—a properly qualified claim of truth, value, or policy. Your thesis should be a manageable claim—something that can be fully and reasonably argued in your paper. This example focuses on a problem:

> *Sample Thesis:* Fatherlessness is the most harmful demographic trend of this generation. Yet, despite its scale and social consequences, fatherlessness is a problem that is frequently ignored or denied.

**Thesis Templates:** While your thesis will be shaped by the stand you wish to take, you might try one of the templates below, based upon the persuasive approach you've chosen.

> *Position Statement:* I believe this to be true about [topic]: [main claim].
>
> *Action Statement:* On the issue of [focused topic], I believe [main claim]; therefore, we must change by [recommended action].
>
> *Problem-Solution Statement:* Given that the problem is [its essential nature or cause], the best solution is to [specific fix matching that essential nature].
>
> *Example:* To combat the media's unrealistic and unattainable sense of beauty and to build self-esteem in young girls, the best approach is to strengthen mother-daughter relationships. [problem-solution]

**From Weak to Strong:** In chapter 4, you learned about refining your thesis to make it stronger. You can do the same with the thesis for your persuasive essay. (Caution: We don't know if any of these ideas are true. We made them up!)

> *Weak Thesis:* an opinion that can't be argued or a simple statement of fact
>
> I think pornography is disgusting (or the opposite).
>
> There's lots of pornography on the Internet.

> *Good Thesis:* offers a reasonable claim built on careful analysis
>
> Given the amount of pornography on the Internet, rates of pornography addiction among men, and the evidence of its impact on marriages, governments should fund research into technologies that truly curb online access for addicts, as well as passing laws that penalize noncompliant sites.

> *Excellent Thesis:* claim includes some intellectual risk, tension, surprise, and depth, while showing measure and attention to opposition
>
> While policy-makers and Internet companies should certainly continue to work on technologies and regulations that limit access to Internet pornography by porn addicts, we would be much further ahead if therapy for couples and sex education for young people addressed all elements of gender respect. After all, the root of the pornography problem is the objectification of human beings.

## Patterns for Persuasive Essays: Writing Moves

The Toulmin and Rogerian argumentation patterns in chapter 17 offer two distinct writing moves for constructing your persuasive essay. These may be particularly useful if your essay focuses on taking a position or calling for action. If your essay will focus on proposing a solution, then consider the blueprint in Figure 18.2 or writing organizer in Figure 18.3.

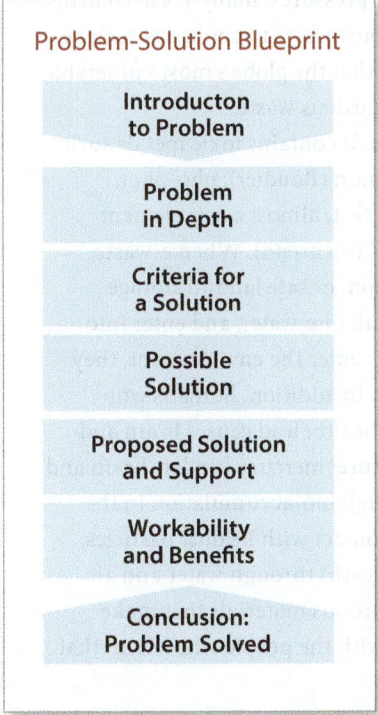

*fig. 18.2*

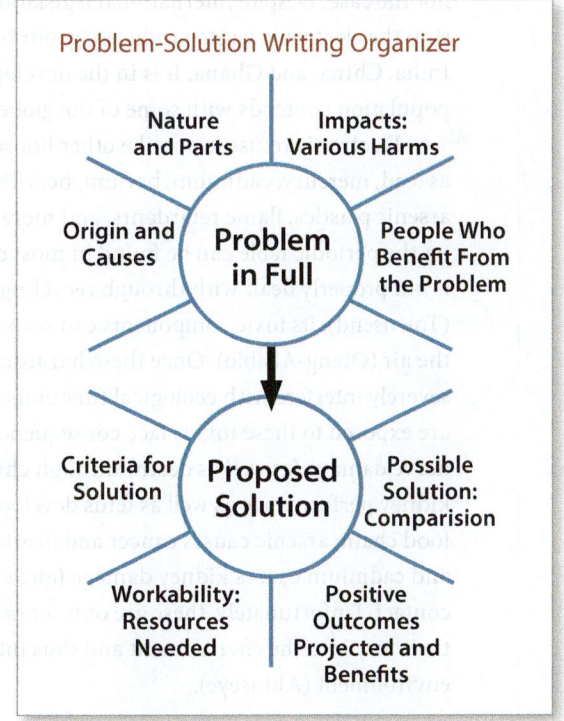

*fig. 18.3*

# Persuasive Essays: Learning Writers' Moves

To see persuasive-writing moves in action, study what the writers do in the following essays. While the first addresses the problem of electronic waste, the second argues that the reaction GIFs of African Americans on the Internet are problematic—a kind of digital blackface. The next pair of essays look at a contested word, *Latinx*, from opposite perspectives. In the final essay, Malcolm Gladwell calls for more caution in the legalization of marijuana.

## Solving the Problem of E-Waste

Student writer Rachel DeBruyn wrote the following essay out of a concern for the environment and for developing-world work conditions. As you read, consider how she presents both the problem of e-waste and her solution for it.

### Remedying an E-Waste Economy

1   Desktops, laptops, monitors, keyboards, iPhones, iPads . . . we buy them, use them, and wear them out. And then we recycle them. But are our electronics being recycled the way we think they are? We assume that a team of trained individuals meticulously disassembles our used electronics—referred to as e-waste—in a large recycling plant full of conveyer belts and safety equipment. Most often, however, this is not the case. Despite international legislation and state pressures, many Western firms ship the electronic waste produced by our homes and businesses to countries such as India, China, and Ghana. It is in the developing world that the globe's most vulnerable population contends with some of the globe's most hazardous waste.

2   Electronic refuse is not like other household waste. It contains toxic metals such as lead, mercury, cadmium, barium, beryllium, chromium (Boudier), phosphor, arsenic plastics, flame retardants, and more (Zhou). In fact, almost every element on the periodic table can be found in most electronics (Townsend). When e-waste is not properly dealt with through recycling, incineration, or safe landfill storage (Townsend), its toxic components can seep into soil, leak into water, and enter into the air (Oteng-Ababio). Once these hazardous elements enter the environment, they severely interfere with ecological functions (Akinseye). In addition, humans who are exposed to these toxins face consequences to their health: lead causes brain and nerve damage (as well as death) through chronic exposure; mercury hinders brain and kidney performance as well as fetus development through bio-accumulation in the food chain; arsenic causes cancer and death through contact with its dust particles; and cadmium causes kidney damage (and eventually death) through water and air contact. Unfortunately, these are only a few of the hazardous materials that make their way into the environment and thus into contact with the people who live in that environment (Akinseye).

Since many components of e-waste interfere with environmental functions and harm human health, proper disposal of electronics is crucial for the world's wellbeing. Nevertheless, despite the high ecological costs of improper e-waste disposal, the economic costs of proper recycling are also high. Rather than paying for the labor-intensive process and real estate costs associated with e-waste recycling, Western firms prefer shipping waste out of their countries (Boudier). By shipping out electronic refuse, the developed world pays neither the ecological nor the economic costs of its disposal. However, the only ones who can afford these costs are developed countries.

The electronic waste being shipped out of the West travels to countries with fragile, emerging economies. Neither adequate infrastructure nor knowledge exists in the developing world to properly handle or recycle these imports. Training and equipment are expensive, so developing countries send illegally imported e-waste to impoverished communities where unskilled workers, especially children, make a living by breaking down and selling its valuable components ("E-Waste from Antwerp to Ghana"). An observational study done in India found that with no knowledge of the most efficient ways to disassemble electronics, laborers beat, burn, and melt their materials using rudimentary tools and their bare hands. They expose themselves to a wide range of toxins through skin contact and by inhaling the smoke from burning (Zhou). Without an understanding of the toxicity of their materials, uninformed laborers also pollute their environment. Workers dump the used acid from acid baths (a popular metal extraction method), filled with residual toxins, into the sewage system that flows into nearby waterways (Boudier). Anything that is not sellable after the metal is extracted is sent to landfills. Landfills in countries like India are not suitable for hazardous material, so the toxic elements leach into the soil (Zhou). Without proper technology and knowledge, those who handle electronic refuse in developing countries cannot prevent the harm associated with e-waste disassembly.

International efforts have been made to halt the movement of electronic waste across state borders and into vulnerable countries. The most notable international regulatory system is the Basel Convention, which bans all cross-border movements of inoperative electronics. But due to inconsistency between individual state regulations, international control such as Basel is hard to maintain (Zhou). Developed countries easily circumvent any bans by claiming that the e-waste being shipped overseas is for second-hand use ("E-Waste Hell"). As a result of a severe lack of regulation in global ports, inspectors can prevent only a small fraction of waste from being shipped. In the Port of Antwerp, for example, four inspectors are responsible for monitoring the eight million containers that pass through the port each year ("E-waste from Antwerp to Ghana"). The quantity of electronic refuse being generated and transported is staggering. Greenpeace estimates that each year roughly 12 million tons of electronics are illegally shipped to Asia alone (Boudier). For developing countries receiving the vast quantities of e-waste, it is impossible to stop the flow.

How can we free the developing world from its role as "the industrial world's trash can" (Boudier)? The most obvious solution is to stop all shipments of electronic refuse to the developing world, thereby keeping hazardous waste out of communities that do not have the knowledge to process it. The flow of waste out of the industrial world could be slowed with improved regulations and increased policy maintenance. Yet the real solution to handling e-waste is not to keep it in the West. The issue is not that simple. Stopping the movement of waste to the developing world would mean cutting off a major source of its income. Entire communities have come to depend on earning a living by extracting and selling metals from electronics. A hierarchy of income generation has emerged around e-waste, beginning with shop-owners who find functioning electronics among the waste to sell, down to the children who pick over the shattered remains and trade what precious materials they can find ("E-Waste Hell"). If the West successfully strengthened its regulation against electronic waste exports, countless numbers of people would lose their means of livelihood.

If the West did, however, reduce its shipments of e-waste, it could be argued that those who depend on selling the components of electronics could find new forms of employment. Yet other sources of livelihood are not as profitable, and the surge of people seeking income would throw the entire labor force into stronger competition. Salvaging and selling the rare and valuable metals found in electronic waste is lucrative (Boudier). The industrial world needs rare metals (which are not found in abundance in nature) to continue producing electronics. Those who can salvage and recycle rare metals can sell them for an excellent price. For example, it is estimated that a forty-foot container of television sets can fetch up to 7,000 pounds in the markets of Ghana, and this is only the first level of the e-waste economic hierarchy ("Britain's E-waste Illegally Leaking"). Although laborers could find new forms of income if e-waste shipments ceased, there is a better solution.

Instead of ceasing e-waste exports and cutting off a major source of income in the world's poorest countries, the trade of e-waste must be fully legalized. Additionally, developing countries must be empowered to properly handle the waste they receive. The main problem for the developing world is that this otherwise profitable trade is causing health issues in its laborers and their communities. Ignorance of safety and a lack of proper protection prevent laborers from fully benefitting from their work. To encourage a safe, legal framework of e-waste disposal, training and technology must be provided as a part of pre-existing (or new) international aid efforts. If a system of proper hazardous material handling could be established and regulated, many people in the developing world would have jobs as sustainable as the influx of electronics.

If health threats are the major hindrance in the e-waste economy that has emerged, training and technology to prevent such harm make it possible for the West's trash to become the developing world's raw materials ("Mountains of E-Waste").

Continuing to send waste to the world's poorest countries is not an excuse to continue producing (or to produce more) waste. E-waste is an inevitable by-product of the Industrial Age, but we must keep in mind that the level of waste should be controlled. Our electronics should have the longest life possible before being properly and sustainably disassembled. Currently, our electronic trash is contributing to sickness and death in the developing world. The West unloads its hazardous waste on other countries to avoid the costs and consequences of dealing with it itself. To remedy the harm we are causing, we must empower workers to earn a living in a manner that does not harm their health.

The consequences of our actions, regardless of our ignorance towards them, are wreaking destruction in parts of the globe we may never see. Yet we are equally as responsible for our neighbors abroad as we are for our neighbors next door. In finding a solution to the problems we have caused, we must always seek the solution that best benefits those we have wronged. The developing world is suffering health consequences due to our e-waste, but they have also built an economy dependent on it. Instead of rushing to fix the problem the way we assume is best, we must consider carefully what the developing world needs most: a safe way to ensure financial security. In achieving this, we would not only remedy the suffering we have caused, but we would empower our neighbors to flourish.

## Reading for Better Writing

1. *Connections:* What role do various electronics play in your life? Can you list e-waste that you and your family have created over the years, and can you recall how you disposed of it? How has Rachel DeBruyn's essay raised your awareness of e-waste?
2. *Comprehension:* Starting with the opening paragraph, sketch or outline what DeBruyn's essay presents about the e-waste problem and its solution.
3. *Writing Moves:*
    a. In paragraphs 1–5, DeBruyn identifies and explains the problem: What does she do to encourage readers to both understand and own the problem?
    b. In the second section of her paper (paragraphs 6–10), DeBruyn explores possible solutions, identifies the solution she believes will work, and then supports that solution: What strategies does she use to support her solution?
    c. Review the first and last paragraphs: What strategies does DeBryun use?

**Your Project:** Consider other forms of waste: of time, of food, of talent, of water, of landscape, of life. What waste would you care to solve in your writing?

## Addressing a Racial Problem

Naomi Day is a software engineer who also writes speculative fiction and Afrofuturist work. In this essay from OneZero, a *Medium* publication, Day explains the problems with specific Internet images portraying African Americans, images that on the surface seem harmless.

### Reaction GIFs of Black People Are More Problematic Than You Think

The Internet is a portal to intercultural awareness. When discussing ramen versus pho, for example, all I have to do is pull out my phone and a quick Google search lets me know the noodle's country of origin, the differences in their broths, and their evolution over time. Now I know what I'm talking about in future discussions about either, and I'm less likely to make potentially harmful assumptions around the cultures from which these foods come.

On the other hand, technology also makes it much easier to borrow elements of other cultures. When we all live behind the relatively anonymous wall of the Internet, we have near-absolute power to display ourselves in whatever manner we like. I can pretend to be an Asian American man living in Wyoming if I want. (I'm not: I'm a Black woman living on the East Coast.)

One prominent problematic example of this is the use of digital blackface in GIFs. While using GIFs is not nearly as extreme as taking on a whole fake online identity, it represents a much more subversive way that cross-cultural blending from the Internet can reinforce negative stereotypes and make us less empathetic when it comes to other races.

### What is digital blackface?

Depending on whom you ask, digital blackface either refers to non-Black folks claiming Black identities online or to non-Black folks using Black people in GIFs or memes to convey their own thoughts or emotions.

Digital blackface takes its name from real-life blackface. The origins of this harmful tradition lie in mid-19th-century minstrel shows in which white performers darkened their faces and exaggerated their features in an attempt to look stereotypically "Black" while mimicking enslaved Africans in shows performed for primarily white audiences. This trend of putting on Black appearances and acting out insulting stereotypes went a long way toward cementing the damaging white vs. Black narrative that much of the United States is built on.

Digital blackface, while less obviously and intentionally harmful than 19th-century blackface, bears many similarities in the way it reduces Black people to stereotypes and enables non-Black people to use these stereotypes for their own amusement.

There is plenty of discussion on this topic, as the trend of non-Black people using often-exaggerated images of Black emotions or Black culture divorced from the original context to represent their own lives is not new. Ellen Jones in the *Guardian* wonders why reaction memes of Black people are becoming so popular online. Lauren Jackson in *Teen Vogue* lists a number of examples of Black folks in GIFs used for a wide range of emotional situations. Dr. Aaron Nyerges from the United States Studies Centre argues that the return of blackface in the digital era is a moment we should seize and use to avoid repeating the injustices of earlier years.

Technology is the vehicle that enables the rapid rise in this type of blackface. It allows for a faster and more widespread use of stereotypes in a more insidious and harder-to-fight manner than ever before. Digital blackface is frustrating and hurtful on an individual level. But to add injury to insult, digital blackface in GIFs helps reinforce an insidious dehumanization of Black people by adding a visual component to the concept of the single story.

GIFs help distill complex emotions or reactions into a single animated image. This reduction is common across the Internet: Twitter encourages brevity in words with its 280-character limit, and Instagram's focus on images means captions can be rendered entirely unnecessary if the user so desires. GIFs are useful when you're making a face in person or feeling a specific emotion but aren't quite sure how to translate it into text. They help ease the flat nature of words. Images are cross-cultural and often defy the bounds of language; all over the world sighted people process visual information in the same way.

GIFs can be useful digital replacements for our expressions when we communicate online. But they can also reduce the people in the images into a single representation that blocks nuanced understandings of the groups those people come from. Popular GIFs representing Black people abound, from the "think about it" reaction with a Black man tapping his head to the *That's So Raven* nervous chewing gum GIF to the "ain't nobody got time for that" sensation that is Sweet Brown.

Chimamanda Adichie gave a compelling TED Talk in 2009 on the danger of a single story. She discusses how everyone from her white college roommate to herself (a Nigerian writer) was guilty of reducing those they don't know to single stories based on incomplete narratives. As a child growing up, Adichie had a house boy (as is common in many Nigerian households). She had a mental image of him as being very poor, because that was all she had heard about his family. She was shocked to learn his family was also capable of making beautiful objects; she had simply never imagined another side to his life. The same was true for Adichie's white college roommate. She had the single story of catastrophe attached to Africans as a whole, and was astounded to learn Adichie knew how to speak English and use a stove.

One danger of non-Black people popularizing funny GIFs of Black people is that these images become the single stories for those who don't have other meaningful contact with Black folks. The exaggerated emotions often found in these GIFs become a form of entertainment, and the important contexts out of which they came are forgotten. Because of the rapid pace of technology, these single stories spread faster than ever before.

One problem with cross-cultural understanding is that if a person lives their life in a racially homogeneous region, they are unlikely to have significant interactions with someone of another race. If a white person has spent their entire life living in a white suburb, for example, the only experiences they may have had with Black folks might be with those who work in service positions in that suburb.

So is it not a good thing to have popularized images of Black folks, even if it does come in the form of digital blackface?

No. It's not a good thing.

Having more flat representations of Black people in images and GIFs does nothing to improve cross-cultural understanding. In my experience, it actually decreases the likelihood that people will extend compassion to other racial groups. If the most common image a non-Black person has of a Black person presents that person as humorous and nothing else, anger on a Black person then becomes more extreme. Sadness becomes more extreme; even joy becomes more extreme. Having access to these portrayals may make a non-Black person feel as though they "know" Black people, but using these in GIFs does nothing to actually increase anyone's cultural understanding of Black folks.

If anything, the false sense of awareness a person may gain from using these types of representations harms their ability to sympathize in reality and hurts cross-cultural understanding overall.

Take Sweet Brown, for example. The "ain't nobody got time for that" GIF comes from an interview with a local news station she did directly after evacuating from her apartment complex when it caught fire. This GIF is used for everything from homework, to cooking, to any number of day-to-day complaints. These are typically a far cry from the experience of Sweet Brown herself. This GIF inserts humor into the traumatizing experience of a Black woman watching her home burn. Its popularity displays a stark lack of understanding of the reality of her situation. As she says in an interview with Oklahoma TV station KJRH, she wasn't even trying to be funny.

But it's not all bad. There are also ways technology is being used to increase empathy between different groups of people that can close the gap that digital blackface in GIFs has helped open. Video games are one of the most obvious ways for technology to increase positive representations of racial diversity and help with increasing interracial empathy. My favorite games are those that help people step into cultures and experiences that are not their own.

The *Dungeons and Dragons*-like game *Ehdrigohr* is one such example. It's a nontraditional fantasy world that represents the concept of the different pace of American Indian time and assumes there are no colonizers. Playing this game is a cooperative experience that can teach important lessons about the Native experience.

The Afropunk sci-fantasy setting of *Swordsfall* is another example. It's a world of dark faces, in which gods live along humankind. The lore is made up of a world bible, *World Anvil*, a tabletop RPG coming in 2020, and upcoming novels. A structure like this, which will place RPG players in spaces where Black folks have advanced technology and exist in the beauty and power of a nation in which they are free and sovereign, inserts fundamental humanity back into technology's representation of Black people.

Virtual reality is another vehicle used to create an entirely immersive artificial space. I am seeing many new ways to simulate experiences common to specific racial groups (like police treatment of Black folks) for other racial groups to experience and understand.

Technology takes away borders and closes distance in some beautiful ways, but there are spaces where it's gone too far. The trend of blackface in GIF form is another way Black bodies are consumed by non-Black people in a harmful and stereotype-forming manner.

Digital blackface on its own doesn't seem like a huge deal, but it is part of a much larger trend currently sweeping the United States that dehumanizes Black folks and allows for horrifying treatment in hospitals, police encounters, and even domestic spaces. While technology has the capacity to be a powerful agent for change in all of these spaces, we need to ensure the efforts are not being undercut by insidiously negative examples such as digital blackface.

## Reading for Better Writing

1. *Connections:* GIFs, memes, funny videos, and more. These circulate the Internet freely. How much are they are part of your online experience? Do you think about where these come from and what they suggest?
2. *Comprehension:* What is digital blackface, according to Day? What forms does it take on the Internet, and why are those forms problematic?
3. *Writing Moves:*
    a. Day begins her essay by discussing the Internet and intercultural awareness. What point does she make, and how does it lead her to identify a problem?
    b. After this introduction, Day explains blackface. In paragraphs 4–10, how does she deepen and expand this discussion, particularly in terms of online activity?
    c. In paragraph 11, she introduces "the danger of a single story." How is this concept relevant to her argument?
    d. In the latter half of the essay, Day describes technologies being used to increase empathy between different groups. How does this discussion unfold?

**Your Project:** Day discusses the danger of reducing people to "one story," to flattened stereotypes or caricatures. Are you aware of other areas of life where groups of people are reduced in this way? What's the danger? Add these to your list of possible topics.

"Reaction GIFs of Black People Are More Problematic Than You Think" by Naomi Day. Originally appeared on the blog OneZero, a publication of Medium.com. Used by permission of the author.

## Debating *Latinx*

Chapter 7 discusses using fair language in your writing, including respect and equity concerning gender. Gender-related language preferences change through time, and a recent development has been the use of *Latinx* as a gender-neutral and non-binary alternative to *Latino* and *Latina*. Such changes generally involve some debate before the issue gets settled—at least temporarily. The next two essays explore the pros and cons of *Latinx*.

**Pro *Latinx*:** Katy Steinmetz writes for *Time*. In this article from 2018, she explains why *Latinx* is succeeding as a new cultural term and argues that it has staying power.

### Why 'Latinx' Is Succeeding While Other Gender-Neutral Terms Fail to Catch On

1. There are plenty of gender-neutral terms that people have tried to make a thing in American English. Take upstart pronouns like *xe* or *zir*, which have had champions for centuries and remain little-used. Consider "first-year student," which is gaining steam but has a long way to go before supplanting *freshman*. Or recall the discussions about genderless military titles, like "midshiperson," which have yet to leave port.

2. There have also been success stories, from *flight attendant* to *alum*. And it appears that the adjective *Latinx*—an alternative to Latino or Latina—is headed in that direction. Academic centers are adding the word to their titles. The term is becoming de rigueur among artists and politically active youth. Media outlets like NPR are using it without remark or explanation. Another sign that this word has staying power: dictionaries have recently taken the time to define it.

3. *Latinx (adj.): Relating to people of Latin American origin or descent (used as a gender-neutral or non-binary alternative to Latino or Latina)*

4. The word, which bubbled up from college campuses, has appeal on several levels.

5. For some, using *Latinx* can feel feminist. Cristina Mora, an associate professor of sociology at the University of California, Berkeley, says she first encountered it as a gender-neutral term that young people were using because they were "tired of reaffirming the patriarchy inherent in language." For example: In Spanish, a group of women is referred to as Latinas, while a group of men or a mixed group — even one that is mostly women—is a group of Latinos. Feminists might balk at this the same way they'd balk at using *he* as a default pronoun or referring to mixed groups as "guys" but never "gals." The subtext is the same: *It's a man's world, you ladies are just in it.*

6. *Latinx* gives people a way to avoid choosing a gender for a group or an unknown individual, much like using singular "they" avoids the choice between "he" or "she" in English. Both are gaining steam in a time when America is rethinking gender and whatever boundaries might come with it.

Mora notes that there have been other attempts to avoid this awkwardness in the past, like including both endings when writing about ethnicity (*Latino/a*) or writing the word as Latin@, because that symbol looks like the offspring of a feminine "a" and masculine "o." But using a slash is clunky. And while there has been criticism that it's not clear how to pronounce *Latinx*—many say "La-TEE-nex," like Kleenex—it's even less obvious how to utter "@."

The "x" also jibes with LGBTQ politics that have been permeating the culture. A growing number of young people reject the notion that everyone falls into the binary categories of male or female (just like a growing number refuse to identify as either totally gay or totally straight). People who describe themselves as non-binary might feel that neither box fits or that both do or that their feelings can change over time. "This is a generation that has emerged with different understandings about gender and sexuality," Mora says. And for some, the label *Latinx* "pushes against that idea that we should be gendered in the first place."

The letter X can refer to unknown locations or quantities and has a rebellious patina. "There's something visually arresting about the letter," says linguist Ben Zimmer. "It looks good on a poster announcing your group is meeting on campus." He says that the "x" helps the label immediately appear to be a political statement. Think Malcolm X, who used that letter as a way to buck a system in which many black Americans had ended up with the last names of slave owners. Zimmer also notes that the description has become popular enough to inspire imitation: Chicano is being recast as Chicanx; Filipina, as Filipinx.

Katherine Martin, head of Oxford's U.S. dictionaries, points out the similarity to the gender-neutral honorific Mx., which people can use instead of Mr. or Mrs. if they want to leave their gender undeclared. She says that, per their research, the word *Latinx* was thrust into the American consciousness after the horrific shooting at the Pulse nightclub in Orlando in 2016. It was a gathering spot where patrons were likely to have roots in both the LGBT community and Latin American culture, and the word cropped up time and again in the media coverage about what happened there. "That was the inflection point," Martin says.

While many view the label as inclusive, the word also has detractors. Ed Morales, a lecturer at Columbia University's Center for the Study of Ethnicity and Race, says that *Latinx* sounds futuristic—and while some consider that a good thing, others would prefer tradition. Critics have suggested that it sounds too American, erasing a Spanish language that needs to be preserved by immigrant communities. Others have said the word creates distance between Americans and people in Latin America who aren't using the term. "Some people just think it sounds odd, maybe forced," Morales says. And some conservatives see the label as just one more example of unnecessary political correctness.

There is a long history when it comes to political labels that have been adopted by—and forced upon—Americans with Latin American or Spanish roots. "No label has ever been perfect," says Mora, the Berkeley professor. People have objected to the word *Hispanic* because it has vestiges of colonialism, she says. People have objected to Latin American for sounding "too foreign," while Latino was "too vague."

The tussling over labels mirrors a complex history of attempting to politically unite people from disparate backgrounds under a single umbrella, finding common cause for Cubans, Mexicans and Puerto Ricans, for example. Mora suggests that some prominent immigrant rights groups may see a word like *Latinx* as a distraction in a time when they're still trying to "affirm that Latinos belong to the U.S."

Others see the rather mysterious-looking *Latinx* as the perfect label for a group that is hard to define. Morales may be biased, having decided to use the word in the title for his upcoming book about race and politics in the U.S. But he believes people will only see more of the word, one that his students have recently started wearing on T-shirts. "I see less and less resistance to it," he says, "and I think it may actually become standard."

## Reading for Better Writing

1. *Connections: Latino, Latina, Latinx.* Are you connected in particular ways to the community encompassed by these terms? What are the connotations of these words? What does the larger world of Latin America mean to you?
2. *Comprehension:* What are the signs that *Latinx* is gaining acceptance? For those who support *Latinx*, what is their reasoning?
3. *Writing Moves:*
    a. Steinmetz starts with an overview of gender-neutral terms that have failed to gain acceptance. How does this opening set up her discussion on *Latinx*?
    b. Paragraphs 4–10 outline support for *Latinx*. What forces does she describe as being behind the word, and how does she use experts to build this discussion?
    c. Steinmetz spends some time on the opposition in paragraphs 11–13. How does she address concerns over the term *Latinx*?
    d. As a journalist, Steinmetz takes a relatively neutral tone with respect to the debate. Does that add to the persuasiveness of her piece, or detract from it?

**Your Project:** This article is about language debates and cultural change. Are there other words and phrases that are especially contentious right now? What are the issues at play? What about cultural shifts you've witnessed, from small changes to seismic upheavals? Have these been productive or destructive? Add such topics to your project list.

From TIME.com. © 2018 TIME USA LLC. All rights reserved. Used under license.

**Con *Latinx*:** What does resistance to *Latinx* look and sound like? Kurly Tlapoyawa, who is Chicano/Nawa/Mazewalli in identity, is an archaeologist and filmmaker, as well as the founder of Chimalli Institute of Mesoamerican Arts. In this essay, he raises some objections to the use of *Latinx*.

### Can We Please Stop Using "Latinx"? Thanx

I recently came across a video about the Chicano Moratorium March of August 29, 1970. In case you've never heard of it, the march was a watershed moment in the Chicano Movement, in which the Los Angeles Police met a peaceful Chicana-Chicano-led protest against the Vietnam War with extreme violence. The ensuing police riot claimed three lives, most notably that of Journalist Ruben Salazar. It remains an important chapter in Chicana-Chicano history. Yet the video claims the Chicano Moratorium "sparked a movement in defense of *Latinx* lives."

Wait . . . what?

I have to admit, this bizarre rewriting of Chicana-Chicano history caught me by surprise. While it may be in vogue to adopt trendy terms like "Latinx" in an attempt to be more inclusive, this video in effect erases a part of history that many consider very important. I am not alone in feeling this way. The participants in the Chicano Moratorium most certainly did not identify as "Latinx," and no amount of historical revisionism is going to change that.

After watching the video, I had many questions. Why did its producers feel entitled to effectively erase an identity that so many fought to gain respect for? Why did they feel the need to retroactively assign an identity to people who had never adopted it? But mainly, I wondered why the promoters of the term "Latinx" felt the need to cling to such a Eurocentric/anti-indigenous identity in the first place.

The "x" in *Latinx* is an attempt to un-gender the term *Latino*, yet it still pays deference to a Eurocentric ideology that actively denies the indigenous and African heritage of the people it claims to represent. If one is serious about non-gendered terminology, why cling to a European language as the basis of one's identity? Why not simply adopt an indigenous term? Wouldn't this be more reflective of our cultural inheritance as native people?

Personally, I prefer to identify as *Mazewalli*, a term in the Nawatl language that means "indigenous person." Like many Mesoamerican languages, Nawatl is a non-gendered language. As an indigenous man who descends from the Nawa peoples of Puebla, I think it is far more powerful and meaningful to my identity if I use a term in the language of my ancestors.

Mexico is one of the most linguistically diverse nations on the planet, with 62 indigenous languages still being spoken. This means there are a multitude of authentic, culturally specific labels we can use to describe ourselves which better reflect who we are.

The very idea of a "Latin America" and "Latin" people comes from the French intellectual Michel Chevalier, who sought in the late 1800s to create an umbrella term that would unite colonial subjects under a generic "Latin" identity. In doing so, Chevalier hoped to assist Napoleon III in expanding the French empire. Chevalier hoped that if he could convince Mexicans to adopt a "Latin" view of themselves, they would be more inclined to align themselves with French interests. In 1968, John Leddy Phelan, in his "Pan-Latinism, French Intervention in Mexico, and the Genesis of the Idea of Latina America," explained Chevalier's intentions:

> In order to forestall such a dismal prospect, Chevalier had an emphatic answer. France must reassert in a vigorous fashion that hegemony over the Latin world which belonged to her since the time of Louis XIV. Chevalier exhorted, "Only she [France] can prevent this whole family [the Latin nations] from being engulfed in the double inundation of the Germans or the Anglo-Saxons and the Slavs. To France belongs the role of awakening the Latins from the lethargy in which they are now submerged in the two hemispheres, to raise them to the level of other nations and to put the Latins in a position where their influence can be felt in the rest of the world.

If Mexicans embraced the ideals of "Latinism," the French would now be their "Latin" brethren as opposed to the "Saxons" who also had interests in Mexico. As historian Thomas Holloway notes, "Napoleon III was particularly interested in using the concept to help justify his intrusion into Mexican politics that led to the imposition of Archduke Maximilian as Emperor of Mexico . . . "

Unfortunately, the idea found a home among Mexico's ruling elite. The notion that indigenous people would be "improved" by transforming them into *Latinos* was a central part of Jose Vasconcelos's idea of "La Raza Cosmica," a racial fantasy that promoted whiteness as the "door to the future" for indigenous Mexicans. In her book *Seeing Indians: A Study of Race, Nation, and Power in El Salvador,* author Virginia Q. Tilley breaks down the racism of "La Raza Cosmica" thusly:

> Vasconcelo's cosmic race concept had, however, little or nothing to do with Indians. Although citing the admixture of indigenous and black blood, he saw the true value of la Raza in its European Spanish and French—hence, "Latin"—cultural (racial) roots. In "La Raza Cosmica," his tone about Indians was indeed dismissive: those Indians not already "Spanishized" (españolizados) had "no other door to the future than the door of modern culture, nor any other future than the road already cleared by the latino civilization." His goal was to eliminate Indianness by turning Indians into "latino-mestizos" through cultural change, rather than truly to obviate and eliminate anti-Indian bias. Indeed, he believed that marginalizing — even eliminating — the indigenous peoples was essential to Latin America's international security and standing.

Knowing the origin of the term "Latino," I cannot bring myself to embrace it. No matter how you slice it, terms like "Latin," "Latino," "Latina," and "Latinx" represent a racist-colonialist mindset that actively erases people of indigenous and African origin. Why should we continue to promote a term that privileges whiteness at the expense of Brown and Black people? Sadly, in the race to be inclusive, a variety of alphabet-twisting terminology has emerged.

By appropriating and retrofitting the past for purposes of the present, those reframing the Chicano Movement to fit the "Latinx" worldview are creating a false narrative that reeks of Orwellianism and historical revisionism. Well-intentioned or not, this is dangerous. I think simply using the term *El Movimiento* would be a reasonable solution that both respects our history and serves as a gender inclusive term.

Now let me be clear, gender inclusivity is absolutely important, and deserves our full attention. But I don't think rewriting the identities of those who participated in historical events simply to appease current attitudes is the best way to do it. Some have begun to use the term "Chicanx" in order to ungender the term "Chicano." This term is far less problematic than "Latinx" ever will be, as it recognizes our roots as an Indigenous people. After all, it's not the "X" that is the cause for concern, it's the "Latin" part that denies our cultural inheritance.

I have noticed that, for some reason, the "Latinx" crowd appears openly hostile to the term "Chicanx." Which begs the question, is their issue with gendered language, or do they simply hate Chicana-Chicanos? 16

Here's my tip to the "Latinx" folks: Allow us to determine our own identities. 17

Just a suggestion . . . 18

## Reading for Better Writing

1. *Connections:* When is a word a mislabeling? Has there been a time in your life when you've felt mislabeled, when the way you think about yourself has been misrepresented by a word? Do you see others around you called something they are not? What's the result of such mislabeling?
2. *Comprehension:* What is the problem with *Latinx*, and why does Tlapoyawa prefer the terms *Chicano* and *Mazewalli* for himself?
3. *Writing Moves:*
    a. Tlapoyawa frames his argument about *Latinx* by discussing a film that bothered him in a specific way (paragraphs 1–5 and 15). How does the film discussion establish a focus for his argument and lead him to a solution?
    b. In the middle of his essay, he locates his trouble with *Latinx* not in the "x" but in the concept of Latin America. How does he develop this part of his argument? He uses two long quotations here, as well. What do they add?
    c. How does Tlapoyawa bring his essay to a persuasive close in the final paragraphs (15–18)?

**Your Project:** This essay aims to persuade readers that using a specific word is problematic because of its origins and purpose. Do you use words whose origins may be troubling? Words about race, gender, and ethnicity come to mind. But consider other areas of life. Does a word's origin matter in the present? This essay also focuses specifically on cultural identity. What debates about such identity are you aware of, perhaps even part of? Add these possibilities to your list of topics.

"Can We Please Stop Using 'Latinx'? Thanx." by Kurly Tlapoyawa. First appeared on the blog Human Parts from Medium.com. Used by permission of the author.

## Calling for Action on Cannabis

Malcolm Gladwell is the author of such popular books as *The Tipping Point, Blink, Outliers, What the Dog Saw, David and Goliath*, and most recently *Talking to Strangers*. Gladwell, who writes regularly for *The New Yorker* magazine, was born in England and grew up in Canada. In this *New Yorker* article, published in January 2019, Gladwell questions the wisdom of how cannabis legalization has taken place thus far and calls for greater caution by policy makers.

### Is Marijuana as Safe as We Think?

*Permitting pot is one thing; promoting its use is another.*

1  A few years ago, the National Academy of Medicine convened a panel of sixteen leading medical experts to analyze the scientific literature on cannabis. The report they prepared, which came out in January of 2017, runs to four hundred and sixty-eight pages. It contains no bombshells or surprises, which perhaps explains why it went largely unnoticed. It simply stated, over and over again, that a drug North Americans have become enthusiastic about remains a mystery.

2  For example, smoking pot is widely supposed to diminish the nausea associated with chemotherapy. But, the panel pointed out, "there are no good-quality randomized trials investigating this option." We have evidence for marijuana as a treatment for pain, but "very little is known about the efficacy, dose, routes of administration, or side effects of commonly used and commercially available cannabis products in the United States." The caveats continue. Is it good for epilepsy? "Insufficient evidence." Tourette's syndrome? Limited evidence. A.L.S., Huntington's, and Parkinson's? Insufficient evidence. Irritable-bowel syndrome? Insufficient evidence. Dementia and glaucoma? Probably not. Anxiety? Maybe. Depression? Probably not.

3  Then come Chapters 5 through 13, the heart of the report, which concern marijuana's potential risks. The haze of uncertainty continues. Does the use of cannabis increase the likelihood of fatal car accidents? Yes. By how much? Unclear. Does it affect motivation and cognition? Hard to say, but probably. Does it affect employment prospects? Probably. Will it impair academic achievement? Limited evidence. This goes on for pages.

4  We need proper studies, the panel concluded, on the health effects of cannabis on children and teen-agers and pregnant women and breast-feeding mothers and "older populations" and "heavy cannabis users"; in other words, on everyone except the college student who smokes a joint once a month. The panel also called

for investigation into "the pharmacokinetic and pharmacodynamic properties of cannabis, modes of delivery, different concentrations, in various populations, including the dose-response relationships of cannabis and THC or other cannabinoids."

Figuring out the "dose-response relationship" of a new compound is something a pharmaceutical company does from the start of trials in human subjects, as it prepares a new drug application for the F.D.A. Too little of a powerful drug means that it won't work. Too much means that it might do more harm than good. The amount of active ingredient in a pill and the metabolic path that the ingredient takes after it enters your body—these are things that drugmakers will have painstakingly mapped out before the product comes on the market, with a tractor-trailer full of supporting documentation.

> It's hard to study a substance that until very recently has been almost universally illegal.

With marijuana, apparently, we're still waiting for this information. It's hard to study a substance that until very recently has been almost universally illegal. And the few studies we do have were done mostly in the nineteen-eighties and nineties, when cannabis was not nearly as potent as it is now. Because of recent developments in plant breeding and growing techniques, the typical concentration of THC, the psychoactive ingredient in marijuana, has gone from the low single digits to more than twenty per cent—from a swig of near-beer to a tequila shot.

Are users smoking less, to compensate for the drug's new potency? Or simply getting more stoned, more quickly? Is high-potency cannabis more of a problem for younger users or for older ones? For some drugs, the dose-response curve is linear: twice the dose creates twice the effect. For other drugs, it's nonlinear: twice the dose can increase the effect tenfold, or hardly at all. Which is true for cannabis? It also matters, of course, how cannabis is consumed. It can be smoked, vaped, eaten, or applied to the skin. How are absorption patterns affected?

Last May, not long before Canada legalized the recreational use of marijuana, Beau Kilmer, a drug-policy expert with the RAND Corporation, testified before the Canadian Parliament. He warned that the fastest-growing segment of the legal market in Washington State was extracts for inhalation, and that the mean THC concentration for those products was more than sixty-five per cent. "We know little about the health consequences—risks and benefits—of many of the cannabis products likely to be sold in nonmedical markets," he said. Nor did we know how higher-potency products would affect THC consumption.

When it comes to cannabis, the best-case scenario is that we will muddle through, learning more about its true effects as we go along and adapting as needed—the way, say, the once extraordinarily lethal innovation of the automobile has been gradually tamed in the course of its history. For those curious about the worst-case scenario, Alex Berenson has written a short manifesto, "Tell Your Children: The Truth About Marijuana, Mental Illness, and Violence."

Berenson begins his book with an account of a conversation he had with his wife, a psychiatrist who specializes in treating mentally ill criminals. They were discussing one of the many grim cases that cross her desk—"the usual horror story, somebody who'd cut up his grandmother or set fire to his apartment." Then his wife said something like "Of course, he was high, been smoking pot his whole life."

Of course? I said.

Yeah, they all smoke.

Well . . . other things too, right?

Sometimes. But they all smoke.

Berenson used to be an investigative reporter for the *Times*, where he covered, among other things, health care and the pharmaceutical industry. Then he left the paper to write a popular series of thrillers. At the time of his conversation with his wife, he had the typical layman's view of cannabis, which is that it is largely benign. His wife's remark alarmed him, and he set out to educate himself. Berenson is constrained by the same problem the National Academy of Medicine faced—that, when it comes to marijuana, we really don't know very much. But he has a reporter's tenacity, a novelist's imagination, and an outsider's knack for asking intemperate questions. The result is disturbing.

The first of Berenson's questions concerns what has long been the most worrisome point about cannabis: its association with mental illness. Many people with serious psychiatric illness smoke lots of pot. The marijuana lobby typically responds to this fact by saying that pot-smoking is a response to mental illness, not the cause of it—that people with psychiatric issues use marijuana to self-medicate. That is only partly true. In some cases, heavy cannabis use does seem to cause mental illness. As the National Academy panel declared, in one of its few unequivocal conclusions, "Cannabis use is likely to increase the risk of developing schizophrenia and other psychoses; the higher the use, the greater the risk."

Berenson thinks that we are far too sanguine about this link. He wonders how large the risk is, and what might be behind it. In one of the most fascinating sections of "Tell Your Children," he sits down with Erik Messamore, a psychiatrist who specializes in neuropharmacology and in the treatment of schizophrenia. Messamore reports that, following the recent rise in marijuana use in the U.S. (it has almost doubled in the past two decades, not necessarily as the result of legal reforms), he has begun to see a new kind of patient: older, and not from the marginalized communities that his patients usually come from. These are otherwise stable middle-class professionals. Berenson writes, "A surprising number of them seemed to have used only cannabis and no other drugs before their breaks. The disease they'd developed looked like schizophrenia, but it had developed later—and their prognosis seemed to be worse. Their delusions and paranoia hardly responded to antipsychotics."

Messamore theorizes that THC may interfere with the brain's anti-inflammatory mechanisms, resulting in damage to nerve cells and blood vessels. Is this the reason, Berenson wonders, for the rising incidence of schizophrenia in the developed world, where cannabis use has also increased? In the northern parts of Finland, incidence of the disease has nearly doubled since 1993. In Denmark, cases have risen twenty-five per cent since 2000. In the United States, hospital emergency rooms have seen a fifty-per-cent increase in schizophrenia admissions since 2006. If you include cases where schizophrenia was a secondary diagnosis, annual admissions in the past decade have increased from 1.26 million to 2.1 million.

Berenson's second question derives from the first. The delusions and paranoia that often accompany psychoses can sometimes trigger violent behavior. If cannabis is implicated in a rise in psychoses, should we expect the increased use of marijuana to be accompanied by a rise in violent crime, as Berenson's wife suggested? Once again, there is no definitive answer, so Berenson has collected bits and pieces of evidence. For example, in a 2013 paper in the Journal of Interpersonal Violence, researchers looked at the results of a survey of more than twelve thousand American high-school students. The authors assumed that alcohol use among students would be a predictor of violent behavior, and that marijuana use would predict the opposite. In fact, those who used only marijuana were three times more likely to be physically aggressive than abstainers were; those who used only alcohol were 2.7 times more likely to be aggressive. Observational studies like these don't establish causation. But they invite the sort of research that could.

Berenson looks, too, at the early results from the state of Washington, which, in 2014, became the first U.S. jurisdiction to legalize recreational marijuana. Between

2013 and 2017, the state's aggravated-assault rate rose seventeen per cent, which was nearly twice the increase seen nationwide, and the murder rate rose forty-four per cent, which was more than twice the increase nationwide. We don't know that an increase in cannabis use was responsible for that surge in violence. Berenson, though, finds it strange that, at a time when Washington may have exposed its population to higher levels of what is widely assumed to be a calming substance, its citizens began turning on one another with increased aggression.

His third question is whether cannabis serves as a gateway drug. There are two possibilities. The first is that marijuana activates certain behavioral and neurological pathways that ease the onset of more serious addictions. The second possibility is that marijuana offers a safer alternative to other drugs: that if you start smoking pot to deal with chronic pain you never graduate to opioids.

Which is it? This is a very hard question to answer. We're only a decade or so into the widespread recreational use of high-potency marijuana. Maybe cannabis opens the door to other drugs, but only after prolonged use. Or maybe the low-potency marijuana of years past wasn't a gateway, but today's high-potency marijuana is. Methodologically, Berenson points out, the issue is complicated by the fact that the first wave of marijuana legalization took place on the West Coast, while the first serious wave of opioid addiction took place in the middle of the country. So, if all you do is eyeball the numbers, it looks as if opioid overdoses are lowest in cannabis states and highest in non-cannabis states.

Not surprisingly, the data we have are messy. Berenson, in his role as devil's advocate, emphasizes the research that sees cannabis as opening the door to opioid use. For example, two studies of identical twins—in the Netherlands and in Australia—show that, in cases where one twin used cannabis before the age of seventeen and the other didn't, the cannabis user was several times more likely to develop an addiction to opioids. Berenson also enlists a statistician at N.Y.U. to help him sort through state-level overdose data, and what he finds is not encouraging:

> Drug policy is always clearest at the fringes. Illegal opioids are at one end. They are dangerous. Manufacturers and distributors belong in prison, and users belong in drug-treatment programs. The cannabis industry would have us believe that its product, like coffee, belongs at the other end of the continuum.

"States where more people used cannabis tended to have more overdoses."

The National Academy panel is more judicious. Its conclusion is that we simply don't know enough, because there haven't been any "systematic" studies. But the panel's uncertainty is scarcely more reassuring than Berenson's alarmism. Seventy-two thousand Americans died in 2017 of drug overdoses. Should you embark on a pro-cannabis crusade without knowing whether it will add to or subtract from that number?

Drug policy is always clearest at the fringes. Illegal opioids are at one end. They are dangerous. Manufacturers and distributors belong in prison, and users belong in drug-treatment programs. The cannabis industry would have us believe that its product, like coffee, belongs at the other end of the continuum. "Flow Kana partners with independent multi-generational farmers who cultivate under full sun, sustainably, and in small batches," the promotional literature for one California cannabis brand reads. "Using only organic methods, these stewards of the land have spent their lives balancing a unique and harmonious relationship between the farm, the genetics and the terroir." But cannabis is not coffee. It's somewhere in the middle. The experience of most users is relatively benign and predictable; the experience of a few, at the margins, is not. Products or behaviors that have that kind of muddled risk profile are confusing, because it is very difficult for those in the benign middle to appreciate the experiences of those at the statistical tails. Low-frequency risks also take longer and are far harder to quantify, and the lesson of "Tell Your Children" and the National Academy report is that we aren't yet in a position to do so. For the moment, cannabis probably belongs in the category of substances that society permits but simultaneously discourages. Cigarettes are heavily taxed, and smoking is prohibited in most workplaces and public spaces. Alcohol can't be sold without a license and is kept out of the hands of children. Prescription drugs have rules about dosages, labels that describe their risks, and policies that govern their availability. The advice that seasoned potheads sometimes give new users—"start low and go slow"—is probably good advice for society as a whole, at least until we better understand what we are dealing with.

Late last year, the commissioner of the Food and Drug Administration, Scott Gottlieb, announced a federal crackdown on e-cigarettes. He had seen the data on soaring use among teen-agers, and, he said, "it shocked my conscience." He announced that the F.D.A. would ban many kinds of flavored e-cigarettes, which are especially popular with teens, and would restrict the retail outlets where e-cigarettes were available.

In the dozen years since e-cigarettes were introduced into the marketplace, they have attracted an enormous amount of attention. There are scores of studies and papers on the subject in the medical and legal literature, grappling with the questions raised by the new technology. Vaping is clearly popular among kids. Is it a gateway to traditional tobacco use? Some public-health experts worry that we're grooming a younger generation for a lifetime of dangerous addiction. Yet other people see e-cigarettes as a much safer alternative for adult smokers looking to satisfy their nicotine addiction. That's the British perspective. Last year, a Parliamentary committee recommended cutting taxes on e-cigarettes and allowing vaping in areas where it had previously been banned. Since e-cigarettes are as much as ninety-five per cent less harmful than regular cigarettes, the committee argued, why not promote them? Gottlieb said that he was splitting the difference between the two positions—giving adults "opportunities to transition to non-combustible products," while upholding the F.D.A.'s "solemn mandate to make nicotine products less accessible and less appealing to children." He was immediately criticized.

Among members of the public-health community, it is impossible to spend five minutes on the e-cigarette question without getting into an argument. And this is nicotine they are arguing about, a drug that has been exhaustively studied by generations of scientists. We don't worry that e-cigarettes increase the number of fatal car accidents, diminish motivation and cognition, or impair academic achievement. The drugs through the gateway that we worry about with e-cigarettes are Marlboros, not opioids. There are no enormous scientific question marks over nicotine's dosing and bio-availability. Yet we still proceed cautiously and carefully with nicotine, because it is a powerful drug, and when powerful drugs are consumed by lots of people in new and untested ways we have an obligation to try to figure out what will happen.

A week after Gottlieb announced his crackdown on e-cigarettes, on the ground that they are too enticing to children, Siegel visited the first recreational-marijuana facility in Massachusetts. Here is what he found on the menu, each offering laced with large amounts of a drug, THC, that no one knows much about:

    Strawberry-flavored chewy bites

    Large, citrus gummy bears

    Delectable Belgian dark chocolate bars

| | |
|---|---:|
| Assorted fruit-flavored chews | 34 |
| Assorted fruit-flavored cubes | 35 |
| Raspberry flavored confection | 36 |
| Raspberry flavored lozenges | 37 |
| Chewy, cocoa caramel bite-sized treats | 38 |
| Raspberry & watermelon flavored lozenges | 39 |
| Chocolate-chip brownies. | 40 |
| He concludes, "This is public health in 2018?" | 41 |

### Reading for Better Writing

1. *Connections:* Have you used marijuana? What about your circle of friends and acquaintances? How would you describe your attitude toward cannabis and cannabis culture?
2. *Comprehension:* In a nutshell, what are Gladwell's concerns about cannabis? What changes need to happen around legalization?
3. *Writing Moves:*
    a. At the beginning of his essay, Gladwell begins with an extended discussion of a report. What's the point of this discussion? How does it establish his concerns?
    b. Frequently, as in paragraph 7, Gladwell asks multiple questions. What does this questioning strategy accomplish in terms of persuasion?
    c. In the middle of his essay (paragraphs 9–23), Gladwell goes into great depth discussing the research of Alex Berenson. Why? What's Gladwell's purpose in doing this? What does it add to the persuasiveness of his piece?
    d. In the last section of his essay, Gladwell turns to the cannabis industry and to debates around e-cigarettes (paragraphs 24–28). What's the connection between the two? How does this discussion add to Gladwell's point that action is needed? What action does he seem to be calling for?

**Your Project:** Marijuana is one controversial substance among many. Consider other controversies about substances that people claim are or are not healthy (e.g., coffee). Expand your thinking to include habits, practices, and forms of activity. What's the truth about their health benefits or harm? Add these topics to your list.

From Malcolm Gladwell, "Is Marijuana as Safe as We Think?" *The New Yorker,* January 7, 2019. Reprinted with permission from the author.

#  DIY: Craft Your Own Persuasive Essay

Start your project by reviewing what you learned in chapter 17 about effective strategies for constructing arguments: following Toulmin and Rogerian approaches; engaging opposition; and appealing to *ethos, pathos,* and *logos.* Then follow the steps outlined below.

## Planning

1. **Select a debatable topic.** Begin by reviewing the project options listed at the end of each sample essay and the assignment guidelines outlined by your instructor. For more topic ideas, list issues about which you feel passionately, that impact your life, and/or that divide people. Think about problems that people face in different areas of life: at home or work, in society, in nature, in your academic discipline. Consider community problems, international issues, disaster-relief efforts, educational outreach programs, environmental clean-up efforts, social movements, or political campaigns. Then choose a topic that is debatable, significant, current, and manageable. Finally, test it: Is the issue real and serious?

2. **Identify and analyze your audience.** You could have a range of readers, from those opposed to your argument to those indifferent to it. Consider these questions:
   - What do readers know about the issue? What are their questions and concerns?
   - Why might they accept change or resist it? What position, action, or solution would they prefer?
   - What reasoning and evidence would convince them?
   - Which of their needs and values are clearly related to the issue?

3. **Narrow your focus and determine your purpose.** Should you focus on one aspect of the issue or all of it? Will your goal be to take a stance on the issue, persuade your readers to change, or to solve a problem? Let that goal guide your research and writing.

4. **Get inside the issue.** Start by taking stock of what you already know and believe about the topic. Where do your knowledge and attitudes come from? How does your thinking need to be tested, to grow? Then study the issue fully and carefully:
   - Research the issue or problem—its various causes and effects, its larger context and history, forecasts of where it's going, and so on. Immerse yourself in the topic, including the academic and social conversations about it.
   - Investigate all possible angles on the issue: different positions, possible actions, solutions. Think creatively about what's best and what's possible.
   - Set up "opposing viewpoints" columns in which you list arguments of those who advocate for different positions, solutions, and so on. Consider how attractive each might be to your readers.

5. **Develop a working thesis—your position, the action, or the solution.** By now, you may have sharpened or even radically changed your initial thinking on the topic. Before you organize and draft your essay, reflect on those changes. Then draft your thesis, drawing upon the examples and templates from this chapter.

6. **Organize your argument and support.** Review the Toulmin and Rogerian patterns from chapter 17, but consider as well a structure or flow that will be most convincing to your readers. Where might you begin? What background might they need? What sequence of claims would build an effective chain of reasoning? Where should you address alternatives, options, and opposition? How can you finish strong? Consider these options:

    - **Traditional Pattern:** Introduce the issue, state your main claim, support it, address and refute opposition, and restate your main claim.
    - **Blatant Confession:** Place your main claim in the very first sentence, and then run with it.
    - **Delayed Gratification:** Describe various positions on the topic, compare and contrast them, and then make your main claim and defend it.
    - **Changed Mind:** If research changed your mind, describe where you started and then explain how and why this change happened.
    - **Winning Over:** If readers will oppose your main claim, address their concerns by anticipating each objection and answering each question.

## Drafting

7. **Write your first draft.** Rough out your argument, drawing upon the writing moves you learned in this chapter. Work on the parts that follow, though not necessarily in this order:

    - **Opening:** Seize the reader's attention, possibly with a bold title—or raise concern for the issue with a dramatic story, a pointed example, a vivid picture, a thought-provoking question, or a personal confession. Supply background information that readers need to understand the issue or problem.
    - **Development:** Deepen, clarify, and support your main claim, using solid logic and reliable support. Address opposing views fairly as part of a clear, well-reasoned argument that helps readers understand and accept your position. Throughout, be mindful of readers' needs and values, as well as your own credibility and the credibility of your sources.
    - **Closing:** End on a lively, thoughtful note that stresses your commitment to your position, emphasizes the importance of the action called for, or encourages adoption of your solution.

## Revising

8. **Improve the ideas, organization, and voice.** Ask a classmate or someone from the college's writing center to read your position paper for the following:
   - \_\_\_\_ **Ideas:** Is the main claim clearly stated and effectively qualified and refined? Do the reasoning and support help the reader understand and appreciate the main claim?
   - \_\_\_\_ **Organization:** Does the opening effectively raise the issue? Does the middle offer a carefully sequenced development and defense of the claim? Does the closing successfully drive home the position, call to action, or solution?
   - \_\_\_\_ **Voice:** Is the voice thoughtful, measured, committed, and convincing?

## Polishing

9. **Edit and proofread the essay by addressing these issues:**
   - \_\_\_\_ **Words:** Language is precise, concrete, and lively—no jargon, clichés, or insults.
   - \_\_\_\_ **Sentences:** Constructions vary in length and flow smoothly. Syntax clearly and carefully conveys reasoning about the evidence.
   - \_\_\_\_ **Correctness:** The copy includes no errors in spelling, usage, punctuation, grammar, or mechanics.
   - \_\_\_\_ **Design:** The page design is correctly formatted and attractive, a compelling part of the argument; research is accurately documented according to the required system (e.g., MLA, APA).

## Publishing

10. **Publish your essay.** Submit your argumentative essay according to your instructor's requirements. In addition, seek a forum for stating your position, calling people to act, or presenting a solution—with peers in a discussion group or debate, with relatives, online on a blog, website, or other forum.

# Persuasive Essays: Applications

Once you have finished your persuasive essay, there may be more to think about. Consider how to apply what you have learned in the situations that follow.

1. **Wise Words:** One of Aesop's fables goes like this: "Passion is often more effectual than force." Is persuasive writing a form of passion? How is such passion different from force, perhaps even opposed to force?
2. **Photo Op:** Recall the photograph on this chapter's opening page. Find another photograph or a short video that similarly portrays the nature of persuasion in an interesting and insightful way. As an alternative, find a photograph or other graphic that could be incorporated into your own persuasive essay.
3. **Living Today:** Contemporary America is filled with issues that seem to have opposing poles but no middle ground: gun control, immigration, abortion, and the war on terror, to name just a few. Choose an issue like this, and then research news commentaries, editorials, blogs, and comment threads that characterize the opposing positions. Given what you have learned about persuasion, can you explain what is going on in these entrenched oppositions?
4. **Public Texts:** Persuasive writing can be found throughout the digital landscape: at sites sponsored by news organizations, political groups, businesses, and not-for-profits. Choose an organization that interests you, relates to your life, or perhaps even aggravates you. Then go to its website, and search for a page containing persuasion: a position, a call to action, or a solution to a problem. Assess how well the persuasion works.
5. **Major Work:** Consider your major and your future career. What is the focus of this field of study and this profession? Where and how will persuasion be part of what you do? Why will doing it well matter? Research these questions to get the answers you need.

## Learning-Objectives Checklist ✓

Have you achieved this chapter's learning objectives? Check your progress with the following items, revisiting topics in the chapter as needed. I have . . .

\_\_\_\_ determined what a persuasive essay is and what forms it might take.
\_\_\_\_ practiced strategies for persuasion.
\_\_\_\_ developed a strong thesis for my persuasive essay.
\_\_\_\_ identified specific moves for shaping persuasive writing.
\_\_\_\_ crafted a convincing persuasive essay by drawing upon a range of writing moves.

# III. Research and Writing

## Research and Writing

### 19 Planning Your Research
- Your Project: Writing a Research Proposal — 360
- Research: An Overview — 362
- Getting Focused — 364
- Understanding Primary, Secondary, and Tertiary Sources — 366
- Exploring Information Resources and Sites — 368
- Planning Keyword Searches — 370
- Building a Working Bibliography — 372
- Developing a Research Plan — 373
- Planning Your Research: Applications — 374

### 20 Doing Research
- Your Project: Creating an Annotated Bibliography — 376
- Working with Your Sources — 378
- Doing Primary Research — 390
- Doing Library Research — 399
- Doing Free-Web Research — 405
- Doing Research: Applications — 410

### 21 Practicing Research Ethics
- Your Project: Writing a Literature Review — 412
- Research Ethics: A Primer — 418
- Developing Credibility Through Source Use — 420
- Recognizing Plagiarism — 422
- Understanding Why Plagiarism Is Serious — 424
- Avoiding Plagiarism — 425
- Avoiding Other Source Abuses — 426
- Practicing Research Ethics: Applications — 428

### 22 Drafting Research Papers
- Papers with Documented Research: Quick Guide — 430
- Reviewing Your Findings — 431
- Considering Methods of Organization — 432
- Considering Drafting Strategies — 434
- Using Source Material in Your Writing — 436
- Sample Research Paper: A Humanities Essay — 440
- Sample Research Paper: Science IMRAD Report — 445
- Drafting a Research Paper: Applications — 452

### 23 MLA Style
- MLA Documentation: Quick Guide — 454
- Guidelines for In-Text Citations — 456
- Sample In-Text Citations — 458
- Guidelines for Works-Cited Entries — 464
- Sample Works-Cited Entries — 468
- MLA Format Guidelines — 475
- Sample MLA Paper — 479
- MLA Style: Applications — 490

### 24 APA Style
- APA Documentation: Quick Guide — 492
- Guidelines for In-Text Citations — 494
- Guidelines for APA References — 498
- Sample Reference Entries — 499
- APA Format Guidelines — 509
- Sample APA Paper — 510
- APA Style: Applications — 520

# Chapter 19

# Planning Your Research

At first glance, research might look like a dry-as-dust business carried out by obsessed scholars in dim libraries and mad scientists in cluttered laboratories. Research couldn't be further from the reality of your life.

But is it? Consider car tires. Before these were mounted an any vehicle you use, scientists researched which materials would resist wear and which adhesives would keep treads on steel belts. Sloppy research could cause blowouts; good research builds safe, dependable tires.

For you, the rewards of doing research projects can also be great—new insights into a subject that really interests you, a deepened understanding of your major or profession, reliable knowledge to share with others, and sharpened thinking skills. This chapter will help you plan such a project and prepare a research proposal.

**Visually Speaking** Figure 19.1 shows one form of research in action. Study the details. What does this image suggest about research? What other images would capture other dimensions of research today?

## Learning Objectives

By working through this chapter, you will be able to

- write a research proposal.
- identify the phases and steps in the research process.
- describe the qualities of ethical research.
- focus your project on a manageable topic, research question, and working thesis.
- distinguish primary, secondary, and tertiary sources of information.
- describe a range of information resources and sites.
- plan keyword searches for your project.
- build a working bibliography.
- plan your research project's methods, priorities, and timeline.

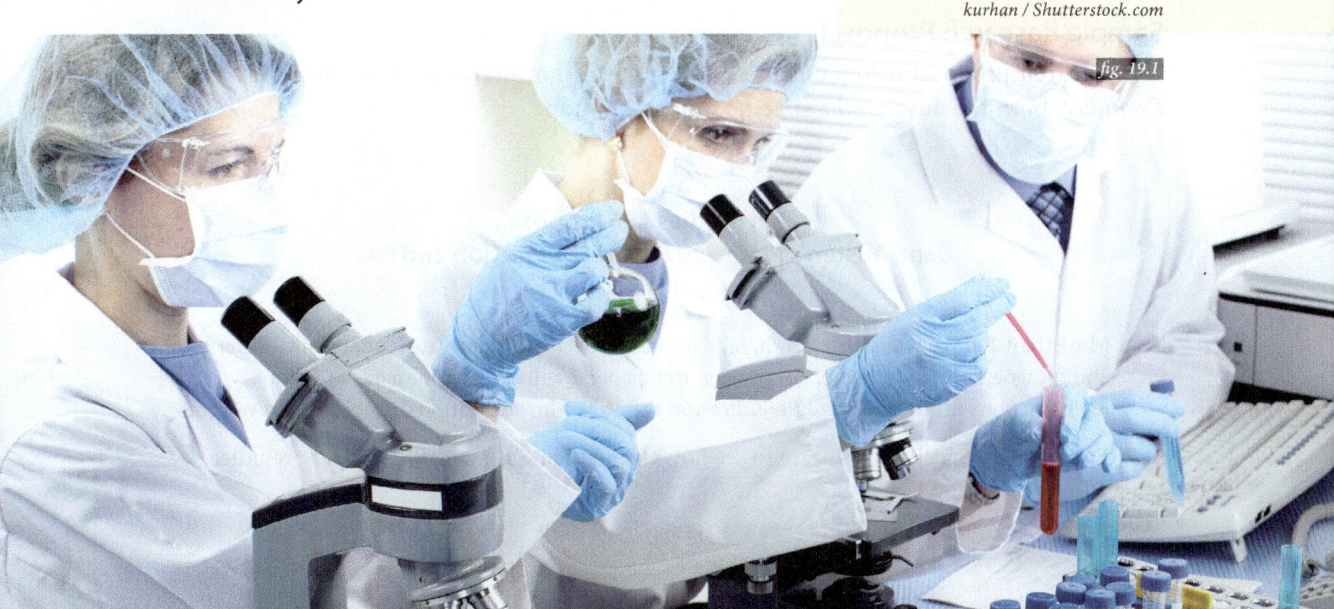

*kurhan / Shutterstock.com*

fig. 19.1

# Your Project: Writing a Research Proposal

Planning your project may lead naturally to your writing a research proposal. Such a proposal, which seeks to explain what you plan to research, why, and how, has several aims: (1) to show that the research is valid (makes good scholarly sense), (2) to argue that the research is valuable (will lead to significant knowledge), (3) to communicate your interest in the project, and (4) to demonstrate that your plan is workable within the constraints of the assignment—all in order to gain your instructor's feedback and approval. Note the parts modeled in the sample proposal. By the end of this chapter, you'll be able to put together your own.

## Understand the Parts of a Research Proposal

1. **Introduction:** In a brief paragraph, state your research idea, explaining why the topic is important and worth researching. Provide any background information that the instructor may need.
2. **Description:** Discuss your proposed research topic by identifying the central issue or concern about the topic, indicating the main question that you want to answer through research, listing secondary questions that relate to the main question, stating a working thesis or hypothesis in response to the main question, and explaining the research outcomes that you expect from the study.
3. **Plan (methods and procedures):** Explain how you expect to answer your questions and how you plan to research your topic. Include an explanation of your primary research (the "firsthand" investigation), a description of research tools you plan to use (e.g., reference works, lab equipment, survey software), methods of collecting and evaluating evidence, and a working bibliography indicating your initial survey of resources.
4. **Schedule:** List official assignment deadlines and deadlines you've set for yourself.
5. **Approval Request:** Ask for feedback and approval from your instructor.

### Sample Research Proposal

The research proposal below offers a student's plan for analyzing Jane Austen's *Pride and Prejudice*, both the novel and a specific film adaptation.

---

**Film Studies 201 Proposal:**
**Jane Austen's *Pride and Prejudice* as Fiction and Film**
Gwendolyn Mackenzie

More than 200 years after her death, Jane Austen's novels still captivate readers, filmmakers, and filmgoers—including me. For my research paper, I will explore one aspect of this phenomenon within *Pride and Prejudice* and the 2005 film adaptation directed by Joe Wright.

**Description:** Specifically, I want to see how the novel and film explore gender prejudice.

My main research question is, "What sense do these texts make of prejudice as it relates to relationships between men and women?" My working thesis is that the 2005 film portrayal of gender inequality in *Pride and Prejudice* highlights and intensifies the issue of gender inequality introduced in the novel.

This study of gender prejudice will allow me (1) to appreciate the treatment of this theme in fiction and in film, (2) to understand film adaptations more fully, and (3) to explain in a small way the Jane Austen phenomenon. As part of the project, I will write a 6-8 page paper.

**Plan:** My primary research will involve rereading the novel and reviewing the 2005 film adaptation. In terms of secondary research, I have done an initial search of our library's catalog and of EBSCOhost for books and articles. This is my working bibliography:

***Primary Sources***

Austen, Jane. *Pride and Prejudice: An Authoritative Text, Background and Sources, Criticism.* Edited by Donald J. Gray. Norton, 2001.

Wright, Joe, director. *Pride and Prejudice.* Universal Pictures, 2005.

***Secondary Sources***

Cartmell, Deborah, and Imelda Whelehan. *Adaptations: From Text to Screen, Screen to Text.* Routledge, 2004.

Crusie, Jennifer. *Flirting with* Pride and Prejudice*: Fresh Perspectives on the Original Chick-Lit Masterpiece.* BenBella, 2005.

Grandi, Roberta. "The Passion Translated: Literary and Cinematic Rhetoric in *Pride and Prejudice* (2005)." *Literature Film Quarterly*, vol. 36, no. 1, 2008, pp. 45-51.

Stovel, Nora Foster. "From Page to Screen: Dancing to the Altar in Recent Film Adaptations of Jane Austen's Novels." *Persuasions: The Jane Austen Journal*, 2006, pp. 185-198.

Sutherland, Kathryn. *Jane Austen's Textual Lives: From Aeschylus to Bollywood.* Oxford UP, 2007.

Todd, Janet M. *The Cambridge Introduction to Jane Austen*, 2nd ed. Cambridge UP, 2015.

**Schedule:** Here is my schedule for completing this project:
1. Finish rereading the novel and reviewing the film: November 14.
2. Complete secondary research: November 20.
3. Develop outline for paper: November 23.
4. Finish first draft of paper: November 30.
5. Revise, edit, and proofread paper: December 4.
6. Submit paper: December 6.

**Approval Request:** Dr. Rajan, I would appreciate your feedback on my proposed project, as well as your approval of my plan.

# Research: An Overview

A research project can be scary—so big, so much work, so many requirements, so much of your grade. You can succeed by taking it step-by-step and getting in the right frame of mind.

## The Research Process

As shown in Figure 19.2, the research process dovetails with the writing process you learned in Part I of *The College Writer*. In fact, research involves writing from start to finish. Whether your project is large or small, it maps out into three phases: planning your research, doing it, and writing it up in some form. Instruction on each phase is found in the chapters listed.

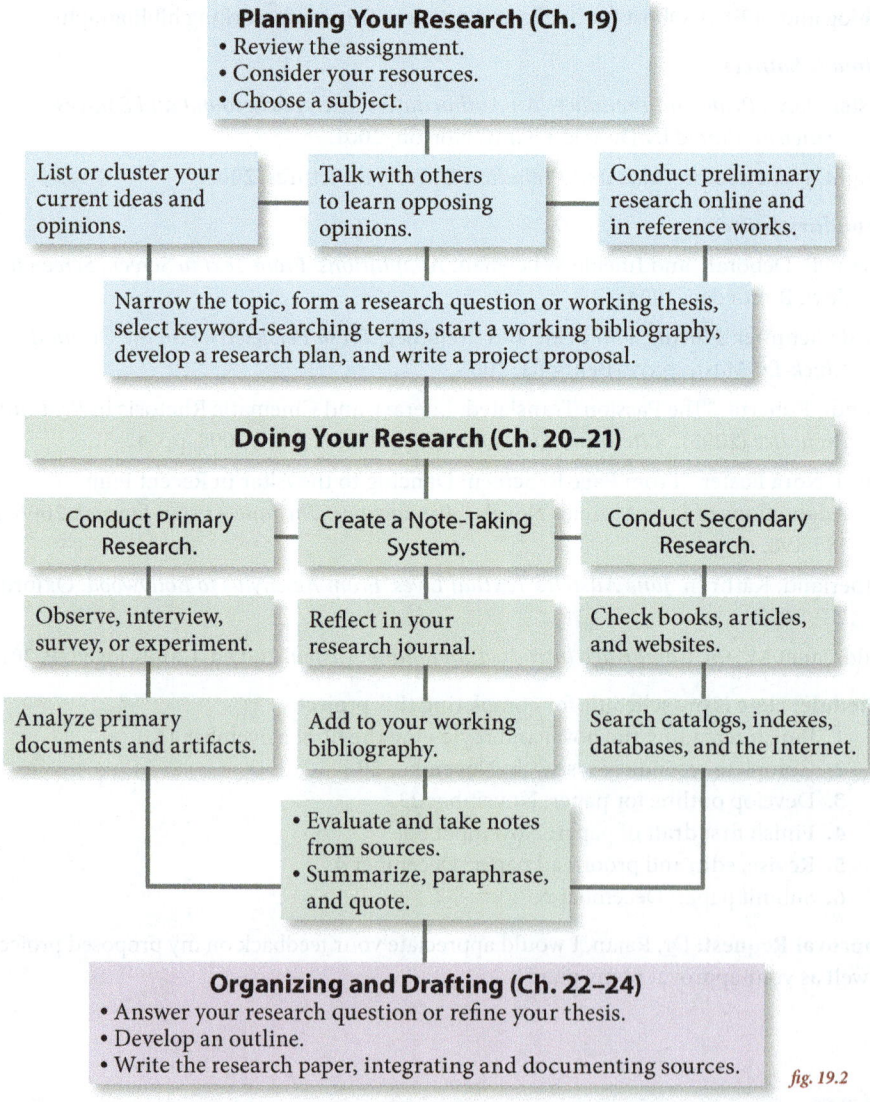

fig. 19.2

## The Research Frame of Mind

We seem to live in an age when truth, accuracy, and evidence are under fire. Conspiracy theories, junk science, misinformation, and "alternative facts" abound. Politicians yell "fake news" when they don't like the story, no matter how reliable the sources. While we'll look at this issue more fully in chapter 21, start every research project with a healthy frame of mind. In your project, you should ask important questions, look systematically for answers, and share your conclusions with readers. The work you do is focused on advancing understanding of the topic for yourself and for your reader. In other words, it's all about curiosity, discovery, and dialogue.

**Curiosity**

**Practices That Are Ethical:** When you commit to shedding light on your topic, you dispel darkness and confusion. However, because of the nature of information and the many challenges of working with it, conducting ethical research can be very complex and involved. Begin by committing to these principles of ethical research:

**Discovery**

- Do the research and write the paper yourself.
- Adhere to the research practices approved in your discipline.
- Follow school- and discipline-related guidelines for working with people, resources, and technology.
- Avoid one-sided research that ignores or conceals opposition.
- Present real, accurate data and results—not "fudged" or twisted facts.
- Distinguish between fact and opinion.
- Treat source material fairly in your writing, avoiding plagiarism and other abuses.

**Dialogue**

**Practices That Prevent Unintentional Plagiarism:**

- Maintain an accurate working bibliography.
- When taking notes, distinguish source material from your own thinking by using quotation marks, codes, and/or separate columns.
- When you draft your paper, transfer source material carefully by coding material that you integrate into your discussion, using quotation marks, double-checking your typing, or using copy and paste to ensure accuracy.
- Take time to do the project right—both research and writing. Avoid "all-nighters."

**Practices That Prevent Internet Plagiarism:** An especially thorny area related to unintentional plagiarism centers on the Internet. As with print sources, Internet sources must be properly credited; in other words, web material cannot simply be transferred to your paper without acknowledgement. So treat web sources like print sources. And if you copy and paste digital material in your notes or drafting, always track its origins with codes, abbreviations, or separate columns.

## Getting Focused

Early in your project you need to get focused by narrowing your topic, brainstorming research questions, and developing a working thesis. You can review chapter 1 to understand your assignment and select a topic. Then use the guidelines that follow to narrow your focus.

### Establish a Narrow, Manageable Topic

To do good research, you need an engaging, manageable topic. If you have a broad topic, narrow your focus to a specific feature or angle that allows for in-depth research. Try these strategies:

- **Read about your topic.** By consulting specialized reference works, explore background that directs you to subtopics.
- **Check the Internet.** What information is readily available? What subtopics might you explore further?
- **Search your library databases.** Scanning lists of articles will acquaint you with specific issues and details.
- **Freewrite to discover which aspect of the topic interests you most:** a local angle, a connection with a group of people, or a personal concern.

| Broad Topic | Manageable Focus |
|---|---|
| Homelessness | Homeless Families in Los Angeles |
| Bacteria and Viruses | Bacterial Resistance to Antibiotics |
| Alternative Energy Sources | Hydrogen Fuel-Cell Vehicles |

### Brainstorm Research Questions

Good research questions help you find meaningful information and ideas about your topic. Such questions sharpen your research goal, and the answers will become the focus of your writing. Brainstorm questions by following these guidelines:

**List both simple and substantial questions.** Basic questions aim for factual answers. More complex questions get at analysis, synthesis, and evaluation.

- **Question of fact:** How long did Kim Jong Il rule North Korea?
- **Question of interpretation:** How did Kim Jong Il maintain power?

**List main and secondary questions.** Ask a primary question about your topic—the main issue that you want to get at. Then brainstorm secondary questions that you need to research to answer your primary question.

- **Main Question:** Should consumers buy hydrogen fuel-cell cars?
- **Secondary Questions** *(Who, What, When, Where, Why, How)*: Who has developed hydrogen fuel-cell cars? What is a hydrogen fuel-cell car? When were these cars developed? Where are these cars currently used? Why are they being developed? How does one work?

### Testing Your Main Research Question

\_\_\_\_ Is the question so broad that I can't answer it in the project's time and page limits?

\_\_\_\_ Is the question so narrow that I won't be able to find sources?

\_\_\_\_ Is the question so simple that it will be too easy to answer?

\_\_\_\_ Will the question lead to significant sources and an intellectual challenge?

\_\_\_\_ Am I committed to answering this question? Does it interest me?

\_\_\_\_ Will the question and answers interest my readers?

## Develop a Working Thesis

A working thesis offers a preliminary answer to your main research question. As your initial perspective on the topic, a good working thesis keeps you focused during research, helping you decide whether to carefully read a particular book or just skim it, fully explore a website or quickly browse through it. Make your working thesis a statement that demands "Prove it!" Don't settle for a simple statement of fact about your topic; instead, choose a working thesis that seems debatable or that requires some explanation. Try this formula:

**Formula:**
*Working Thesis* = limited topic + tentative claim, statement, or hypothesis

**Examples:**
Digital communication technologies are rewiring our brains.

Downtown revitalization will have distinct economic, environmental, and social benefits.

Internet dating is weakening long-term relationships.

### Working Thesis Checklist

\_\_\_\_ Does my working thesis focus on a single, limited topic?

\_\_\_\_ Is my working thesis stated in a clear, direct sentence?

\_\_\_\_ Does my working thesis convey my initial perspective about the topic?

\_\_\_\_ Do I have access to enough good information to support this working thesis?

\_\_\_\_ Does my working thesis direct me to write a paper that meets all assignment requirements?

**INSIGHT** Your working thesis is written in sand, not stone. It may change as you research the topic because sources may push you in new directions. In fact, such change shows that you are engaging your sources and growing in your thinking.

# Understanding Primary, Secondary, and Tertiary Sources

Information sources for your project can be primary, secondary, or tertiary, depending on their nearness to your topic. With your college assignments, you will likely be expected to rely upon primary and secondary sources, not tertiary sources. As part of project planning, then, you need to understand the distinction between these types of sources.

## Primary Sources

A primary source is an original source, one that gives firsthand information on a topic: the source is close to the issue or question. This source (such as a person, a document, or an event) informs you directly about the topic, not through another person's explanation or interpretation. Common primary sources are observations, interviews, surveys, experiments, documents, and artifacts. Frequently, you generate the primary source yourself; sometimes, that primary information is available in published form.

> *Example:* For a project on Jane Austen's *Pride and Prejudice* in fiction and film, these sources would be primary: the text of the novel itself, the 2005 film adaptation of the novel, Jane Austen's letters, and an interview with a screen writer who adapts novels into films.
>
>  **Strengths of Primary Research:** Primary sources produce information precisely tailored to your research needs, giving you direct, hands-on access to your topic. If, for example, you were researching the impact of tornados on communities, interviews with survivors would provide information directly tailored to your project.
>
>  **Downsides of Primary Research:** Primary research can take a lot of time and many resources, as well as specialized skills (e.g., designing surveys and analyzing statistics). Primary sources may be limited to anecdotal accounts and not provide an overall survey of an issue or topic.

## Secondary Sources

Secondary sources present information one step removed from the origin: information has been collected, compiled, summarized, analyzed, synthesized, interpreted, and evaluated by someone studying primary sources and other secondary sources. Scholarly studies, journal articles, and documentaries are typical examples of such resources. Typically, you track down secondary resources in your library, through library databases, and on the free web.

> *Example:* For a project on Jane Austen's *Pride and Prejudice* in fiction and film, these sources would be secondary: books and articles by scholars on Austen and on film, literary biographies about Austen's life, and film reviews.

**Strengths of Secondary Research:** Good secondary sources—especially scholarly ones that have gone through a peer-review process—offer quality information in the form of expert perspectives on and analysis of your topic. As such, secondary sources can save you plenty of research labor while providing you with extensive data. In addition, secondary sources can help you see your topic from multiple angles through multiple perspectives; they can tell you the story of research done on your topic.

 **Downside of Secondary Research:** Because secondary research isn't written solely with your project in mind, you may need to do some digging to find relevant data. Moreover, the information that you do find may be filtered through the researcher's bias. In fact, the original research related through the secondary source may be faulty, a point suggesting that the quality of secondary sources can vary greatly. Finally, because knowledge about your topic can grow or change over time, secondary sources can become dated.

## Tertiary Sources

Some resources are tertiary—essentially reports of reports of research. That is, writers of tertiary sources are not reporting on the primary research they themselves have done but are compiling information based on their reading of secondary sources. Examples of tertiary sources would include some articles in popular magazines and entries in Wikipedia.

*Example:* For a project on Jane Austen's *Pride and Prejudice* in fiction and film, these sources would be tertiary: a Reddit exchange about a recent Austen biography or a Wikipedia entry on Austen.

 **Upside of Tertiary Research:** Tertiary sources are typically easy to find, easy to access, and easy to read. Note, for example, that an online search of a specific topic frequently lists a Wikipedia entry in the first ten items. Used cautiously, such tertiary sources can serve as one starting point for your research—to find basic facts that you'll likely have to verify elsewhere, some ideas for narrowing your topic, or some leads and links for further research.

 **Downside of Tertiary Research:** The main weakness of tertiary sources is their distance from the original research and information. Because the information and ideas have been passed along in this way, the possibility of error, distortion, gaps, and over-simplification of complex issues is greater than with primary and secondary sources. Generally, tertiary sources lack the reliability and depth necessary for college-level research projects.

 Whether a source is primary, secondary, or tertiary often depends on what your focused topic is. For example, if you were studying why power outages happen during heat waves, a newspaper editorial on the topic would be secondary. But if you were focusing on public attitudes towards outages, the editorial might prove primary. In other words, a given source is not always primary or always secondary: proximity depends on the research context.

# Exploring Information Resources and Sites

Today, it's tempting to believe that everything is on the Internet, that the web is all you need. But, believe it or not, the world of information is bigger even than the Internet. To do thorough but efficient research, creative but careful investigation, you need a larger sense of what types of resources are available for your project, as well as where you might find them or how you might create them. The tables below and on the next page give you that bigger picture. Consider the possibilities as you work on your project.

## Consider Different Information Resources

Examine the range of resources available: Which will give you the best information for your project? While one project (for example, a sociological report on airport behaviors) might require personal, direct sources, another project (for example, the effects of COVID-19 on the cruise ship industry) might depend on government reports, business publications, and journal articles. Generally, a well-rounded research paper relies on a range of quality resources; in particular, it avoids relying on insubstantial web information gathered through basic search engines. Figure 19.3 introduces some common information sources.

*fig. 19.3*

| Type of Resource | Examples |
| --- | --- |
| Personal, direct resources | Memories, diaries, journals, logs, experiments, tests, observations, interviews, surveys |
| Reference works (print and digital) | Dictionaries, thesauruses, encyclopedias, almanacs, yearbooks, atlases, directories, guides, handbooks, indexes, abstracts, catalogs, bibliographies |
| Books (print and digital) | Nonfiction, how-to, biographies, fiction, trade books, scholarly and scientific studies |
| Periodicals and news sources (print and digital) | Scholarly journals, newspapers, magazines; broadcast news and news magazines; online magazines, news sources, and discussion groups |
| Audiovisual, digital, social media, and multimedia resources | Graphics (tables, graphs, charts, maps, drawings, photos), audiotapes, music, videos, movies, web pages, online databases, podcasts, social-media posts, texts |
| Government publications (print and digital) | Guides, programs, forms, legislation, regulations, reports, records, statistics |
| Business and nonprofit publications (print and digital) | Correspondence, reports, newsletters, pamphlets, brochures, ads, catalogs, instructions, handbooks, manuals, policies and procedures, seminar and training materials |

## Consider Different Information Sites

Where do you go to find the resources that you need? "Just Google it" is a start, but consider the information "sites" listed in Figure 19.4, remembering that many resources may be available in different forms in different locations. For example, a scholarly journal article may be available in library holdings or in an electronic database. (See chapter 20 for tips for using electronic databases.)

*fig. 19.4*

| Information Location | Specific "Sites" |
| --- | --- |
| People | Experts (knowledge area, skill, occupation) <br> Population segments or individuals (with representative or unusual experiences) |
| Libraries | General: public, college, online <br> Specialized: legal, medical, government, business |
| Computer resources | Computers: software, disks <br> Networks: Internet and other online services (email, limited-access databases, discussion groups, websites, blogs, social networks, YouTube, image banks, wikis, podcast networks, streaming services) |
| Mass media | Radio (AM and FM) <br> Television (network, public, cable, satellite, Internet) <br> Print (newspapers, magazines, journals) |
| Testing, training, meeting, and observation sites | Plants, facilities, field sites, laboratories <br> Research centers, universities, think tanks <br> Conventions, conferences, seminars <br> Museums, galleries, historical sites |
| Municipal, state, and federal government offices | Elected officials, representatives <br> Offices and agencies, Government Printing Office <br> Websites (GPO, www.gpoaccess.gov) |
| Business and nonprofit publications | Computer databases, company files <br> Desktop reference materials <br> Bulletin boards (physical and electronic) <br> Company and department websites <br> Departments and offices <br> Associations, professional organizations <br> Consulting, training, and business information services |

# Planning Keyword Searches

Keyword searching will help you find information in electronic library catalogs, online databases that index periodical articles (for example, EBSCOhost or *Business Periodicals Index*), Internet resources, print books, and e-books. As part of your planning, develop a list of keywords to use in your quest for sources.

## Choose Keywords Carefully

Keywords give you "compass points" for navigating through a sea of information. That's why choosing the best keywords is crucial. Consider these tips:

1. **Brainstorm a list of possible keywords**—topics, titles, and names—based on your current knowledge and/or background reading.
2. **Consult the Library of Congress subject headings.** These headings, available in print or online at classificationweb.net (subscription) or at authorities.loc.gov (free), contain the keywords librarians use when classifying materials. For example, if you looked up *immigrants*, you would find the entry in Figure 19.5, indicating keywords to use and tips to follow (including that the topic may subdivide geographically), along with narrower, related, and broader terms. When conducting subject searches of catalogs and databases, these are the terms that will get you the best results.

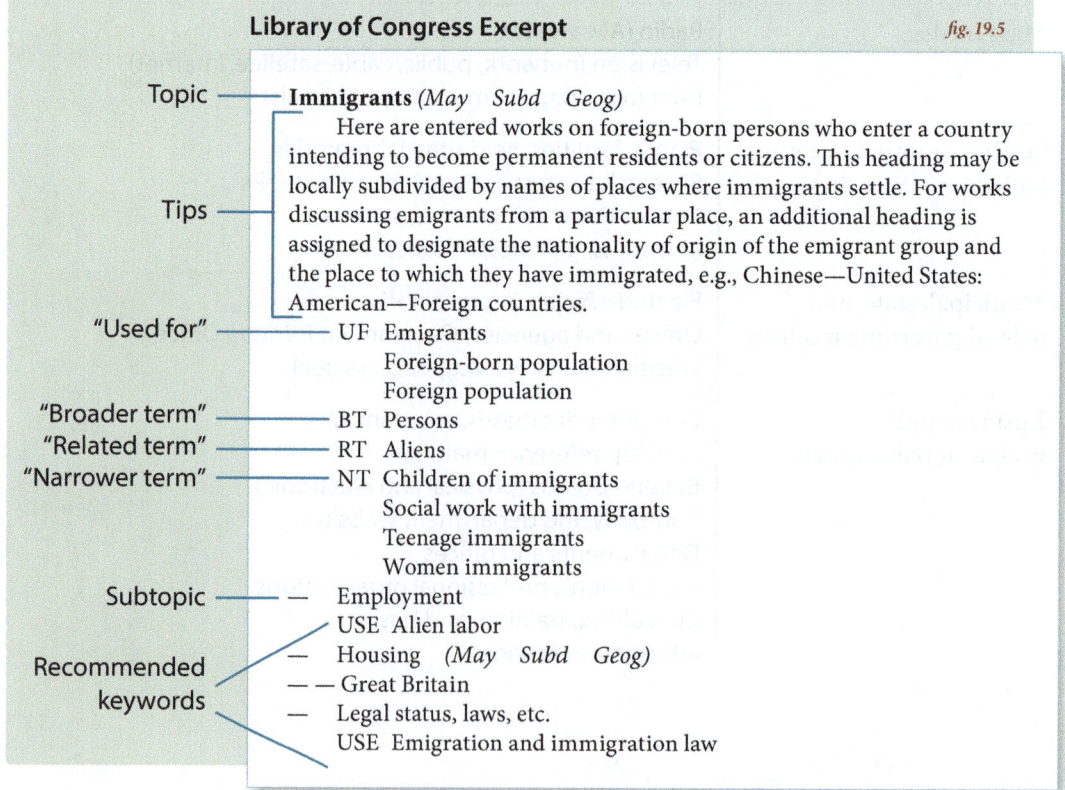

fig. 19.5

## Learn Keyword Strategies

The goal of a keyword search is to find quality sources. To discover the best resources available, learn these strategies which can be used with everything from Google to an e-book:

1. **Get to know the database or resource.** Look for answers to these questions:
   - What material does the database or resource contain? What time frames?
   - What are you searching—authors, titles, subjects, full text?
   - What are the search rules? How can you narrow the search?
2. **Use a shotgun approach at first.** Start with the most likely keyword. If you have no "hits," choose a related term. Once you get some hits, check the citations for clues regarding which words to use as you continue searching.
3. **Use Boolean operators to refine your search.** When you combine keywords with Boolean operators—such as those in Figure 19.6—you will obtain better results.

### Boolean Operators

*fig. 19.6*

| | | |
|---|---|---|
| **Narrowing a Search**<br>And, +, not, -<br>Use when one term gives you too many hits, especially irrelevant ones. | buffalo **and** bison *or* buffalo **+** bison<br><br>buffalo **not** water<br>**+**buffalo **–**water | Searches for citations containing both keywords<br><br>Searches for "buffalo" but not "water," so that you eliminate material on water buffalo |
| **Expanding a Search**<br>Or<br>Combine a term providing few hits with a related word | buffalo **or** bison | Searches for citations containing either term |
| **Specifying a Phrase**<br>Quotation marks<br>Indicate that you wish to search for the exact phrase enclosed | "reclamation project" | Searches for the exact phrase "reclamation project" |
| **Sequencing Operations**<br>Parentheses<br>Indicate that the operation should be performed before other operations in the search string | (buffalo or bison) and ranching | Searches first for citations containing either "buffalo" or "bison" before checking the resulting citations for "ranching" |
| **Finding Variations**<br>Wild card symbols<br>Depending on the database, symbols such as $, ?, or # can find variations of a word. | ethic#<br>ethic$ | Searches for terms like *ethics* and *ethical* |

# Building a Working Bibliography

A working bibliography lists sources you have used and intend to use. It helps you track your research, develop your final bibliography, and avoid plagiarism. Here's what to do:

## Select an Efficient Approach for Your Project

Choose an orderly method, such as one of the following:
- **Paper notebook:** Use a small, spiral-bound book to record sources.
- **Digital record:** Record source information digitally, either by capturing citation details from online searches or by recording bibliographic information using word-processing software, research software, or apps like Evernote. Screen shots and digital bookmarks can also help you save sources for future reference.

### Including Identifying Information for Sources

Record specific details for each kind of source you discover.
  a. **Books:** author, title and subtitle, publication details (place, publisher, date)
  b. **Periodicals:** author, article title, journal name, publication information (volume, number, date), page numbers
  c. **Online sources:** author (if available), document title, site sponsor, database name, publication or posting date, access date, other publication information, URL
  d. **Primary or field research:** date conducted, name and/or descriptive title of person interviewed, place observed, survey conducted, document analyzed

### Adding Locating Information

Because you may need to retrace your research footsteps, include details about your research path:
  a. **Books:** Include the Library of Congress or Dewey call number.
  b. **Articles:** Note where and how you accessed them (database, stacks, microfilm).
  c. **Web pages:** Record the complete URL (uniform resource locator) or the DOI (digital object identifier), not just the broader site address.
  d. **Field research:** Include contact information such as a telephone number or an email address, as well as locating information such as an address or GPS coordinates.

**INSIGHT** Consider recording bibliographic details in the format of the documentation system you are using—MLA (chapter 23) or APA (chapter 24), for example. Doing so now will save time later. In addition, some research software allows you to record bibliographic information and then format it according to a specific system.

**Note:** Maintaining a working bibliography will also help you build an annotated bibliography, a list of resources with your comments about how each resource relates to your topic. (See chapter 20 for an example.)

… | Chapter 19 | Planning Your Research

# Developing a Research Plan

It pays to plan your research. In fact, minutes spent planning research can save hours doing research. With your limited topic, main research question, and working thesis in front of you, plan your project more fully using the research tips below. When you're done, you should be ready to write a research proposal, as outlined at the beginning of this chapter.

## Choose Research Methods

Consider these questions: What do you already know about the topic? What do you need to know? Which resources will help you answer your research question? Which resources does the assignment require? Based on your answers, consider these methods:

- **Background research:** Do an initial search of the library catalog, journal databases, and the Internet to confirm that good resources on your topic exist. Use reference resources to find background information, definitions, basic facts, and statistics.
- **Primary research:** If it fits with your project, plan some primary research, whether interviews, surveys, observations, experiments, or analysis of documents or artifacts.
- **Library research:** Consider the range of books, journal articles, and other resources you need to find both in and through your college's library.
- **Free-web research:** Within the limits set by your assignment and by the nature of your project, what free-web resources would be both useful and reliable?

**Note:** See chapter 20 for in-depth instruction on each type of research.

## Get Organized to Do Research

An organized approach to research will save you time, help you work efficiently, and prevent frustration. Get organized by addressing these issues, some of which you can reference in your research proposal.

> **Priorities:** Consider how much research material is needed for the project, as well as what range of resources will give you quality information. What's specified in your assignment, and what's the weight of this project in the course?
>
> **Methods:** Consider the technologies you have available, and how to use them efficiently. In addition to a working bibliography, set up a note-taking system. Lastly, get familiar with the style and documentation system you are expected to use, such as MLA or APA.
>
> **Schedule:** Different projects involve different time frames. As a general guideline, spend about half your time on research, half on drafting, revising, and polishing. Work backward from the due date and establish interim deadlines for completing specific phases of the process, if your instructor hasn't set these in the assignment itself.

**INSIGHT** Gather more information than you could ever use in your paper. That richness gives you choices and allows you to sift for crucial information.

## Planning Your Research: Applications

Once you have used the instruction in this chapter to plan your project and write a research proposal, there may be more to think about. Consider how to apply what you've learned in the situations below.

1. **Wise Words:** Speaking metaphorically, Alexander Graham Bell once advised, "Leave the beaten track behind occasionally and dive into the woods. Every time you do you will be certain to find something you have never seen before." How might this advice apply to doing research?
2. **Photo Op:** The opening page of the chapter offers a photo of researchers at work. Find another photo or take one yourself that captures some other dimension of research.
3. **Major Work:** This chapter offers instruction on planning any research project. Now consider your major or one in which you are interested. How are planning elements treated specifically in that discipline? What is its research "frame of mind"? What questions does it ask? What forms of primary and secondary research does it practice? What research sites does it value? What research plans does it put together?
4. **Career Plan:** When you consider your future profession, does it involve research of some kind? Develop a research plan for answering this question. Then implement your plan to discover the answers.
5. **Living Today:** Most days, we have many opportunities to "Google it" when we have a simple question. When it comes to the bigger issues in our lives (e.g., what college to attend), we need to go a little deeper and farther. Think about a big choice you have faced or are facing. How might the research planning strategies in this chapter be helpful in this situation?

## Learning-Objectives Checklist ✓

Have you achieved this chapter's learning objectives? Check your progress with the items below, revisiting topics in the chapter as needed. I have . . .

\_\_\_\_ written a research proposal that effectively explains the purpose, methods, and benefits of my project, as well as offering a timeline and working bibliography.
\_\_\_\_ applied the phases and steps in the research process to my own project.
\_\_\_\_ described the qualities of ethical research as they apply to my project.
\_\_\_\_ focused my project on a manageable topic, research question, and working thesis.
\_\_\_\_ distinguished primary, secondary, and tertiary sources of information.
\_\_\_\_ described a range of information resources and sites that might relate to my focus.
\_\_\_\_ planned keyword searches for my project.
\_\_\_\_ started a working bibliography.
\_\_\_\_ planned the methods, priorities, and timelines I hope to follow in my project.

Chapter 20

# Doing Research

A colleague jokingly told us that we might replace this chapter with "Just Google it!" Perhaps he was commenting on the power of Google, or maybe on our reliance on the Internet giant. Either way, doing research for college projects requires that you go beyond Google.

Today, in fact, research is both easy and difficult. It's easy because research technology is powerful, and we have many research methods available at our fingertips. But it's difficult because that technology and those methods give us access to so much information—the good, bad, and ugly.

This chapter will help you do quality, college-level research. First, it will show you how to build an annotated bibliography—an important step to writing a full research paper. Then it will show you how to evaluate sources—crucial in a world of information overload. Finally, it will help you do primary, library, and free-web research.

**Visually Speaking** "Libraries are research centers." Think about this statement in light of Figure 20.1, and relate this idea to your own experience of research, inside and outside of libraries.

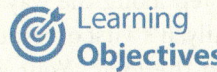

## Learning Objectives

By working through this chapter, you will be able to

- produce an annotated bibliography.
- engage sources through effective note-taking.
- evaluate your sources for quality and reliability.
- do primary research that fits your project.
- do library research that produces promising books, reference resources, and journal articles.
- do free-web research that leads to quality resources.

Jens Goepfert / Shutterstock.com

fig. 20.1

# Your Project: Creating an Annotated Bibliography

Your research project may include producing an annotated bibliography either as the goal or as a step along the way showing your instructor that your research is proceeding well. Essentially, it's a list of resources you've found, with your comments about how each resource relates to the topic. Your aim is to show that you've done a clear survey of the available resources, and have carefully reviewed and reflected on the sources with your project in mind. The instruction in this chapter will give you the tools you need to write a strong annotated bibliography, one that follows the guidelines below.

## The Elements of an Annotated Bibliography

An annotated bibliography may include a brief description of your topic, a list of issues or questions you're exploring, and a working thesis. In that sense, such a bibliography grows out of the research proposal you wrote. With respect to the annotated bibliography itself, each individual entry contains two types of information:

1. **Bibliographical information:** This information should be formatted according to the style required by the assignment (e.g., MLA works-cited entries, APA references entries).
2. **The annotation:** Indented .5 inches in APA but 1 inch in MLA, this statement, which ranges from a brief phrase to a whole paragraph, should provide information specified by the instructor, such as the following:
   - a description of the source.
   - a summary of the source's content.
   - an assessment of the source's value for your specific project.
   - a review of the source's perspective.
   - an evaluation of the source's quality.

## Sample Annotated Bibliography

This sample bibliography provides examples of annotated sources for a student's project on Alice Munro's collection of short stories, *Runaway*. Notice how the annotations focus on describing the sources and estimating their possible usefulness for the student's project—a literary analysis essay. (This sample follows MLA citation style.)

---

**Project on Alice Munro's *Runaway*: An Annotated Bibliography**

**Topic and Focus:** In my major paper, I plan to examine the role of female passion in selected stories from Alice Munro's 2005 collection, *Runaway*. My focus will be on passion as a double concern: (a) part of the narrative technique that Munro uses to tell stories, and (b) part of the experience of her characters.

**Working Bibliography of Resources:**

Beran, Carol L. "The Pursuit of Happiness: A Study of Alice Munro's Fiction." *The Social Science Journal*, vol. 37, no. 3, 2000, pp. 329–45.

    As its title suggests, this article focuses on happiness as a theme in Munro's fiction. Beran uses the story "White Dump" from *The Progress of Love*, but her analysis should prove relevant for an exploration of passion in *Runaway*.

Duffy, Dennis. "'That Rubbish About Love': Alice Munro's 'Love of a Good Woman' and Indeterminacy." *Eureka Studies in Teaching Short Fiction*, vol. 6, no. 2, spring 2006, pp. 36–41.

    While Duffy looks at an earlier story from Munro, he does focus on the complex way Munro treats love in her fiction, making this a useful article for my study.

Duncan, Isla. *Alice Munro's Narrative Art*. Palgrave Macmillan, 2011.

    This study examines Munro's narrative method and art, with some focus on intimacy, testimony, and memory. The book shows some attention to *Runaway*, especially the story "Passion," which will be one of the key stories I examine.

Howells, Coral Ann. *Alice Munro*. Manchester UP, 1998. Contemporary World Writers.

    This scholarly study offers a good introduction to Munro's work, analyzing her fiction book by book up to *Open Secrets*. Because of its publication date, Howells's study does not directly discuss *Runaway*, but this scholar's ideas should apply to these later stories.

May, Charles E. "The Short Story's Way of Meaning: Alice Munro's 'Passion.'" *Narrative*, vol. 20, no. 2, May 2012, pp. 172–82.

    This article should prove very useful to my project, as May gives an analysis of the story "Passion" from *Runaway*. Although he focuses on the issue of what distinguishes short story from novel, his close reading of this story should help me understand the narrative method more deeply.

Munro, Alice. *Runaway*. Knopf, 2004.

    This is the primary source for my project on passion in Munro's fiction. While the story "Passion" will be central to my analysis, the trilogy of stories about Juliet ("Chance," "Soon," and "Silence") should also connect well with this theme.

Raabe, David. "Living on Masculine Standard Time: Alice Munro's Conflicted Women." *Eureka Studies in Teaching Short Fiction*, vol. 6, no. 2, spring 2006, pp. 42–48.

    Raabe looks at the troubled relationships between men and women in Munro's fiction, a topic central to my project. Moreover, one of the key examples he looks at is the title story from *Runaway*.

# Working with Your Sources

To prepare to do primary, library, and free-web research, you need to consider techniques for working with the sources you find. Start with the critical reading and viewing strategies that were introduced in chapters 2 and 3. Then use the instruction below and on the following pages to help you engage your sources, take notes on them, and evaluate their quality and reliability.

## Engage Your Sources

Engaged reading is the opposite of passive reading—treating all sources equally, swallowing whole what's in the material, or looking only for information that supports your opinion. Full engagement means practicing these strategies:

**Test each source to see if it's worth reading.** When reviewing a source citation, study titles, descriptions, lengths, and publication dates. Ask these questions:

- How closely related to my topic is this source?
- Is this source too basic, overly complex, or just right?
- What could this source add to my overall balance of sources?

If you were writing about the International Space Station, for example, you might find a ten-page article in *Scientific American* more valuable and insightful than a brief news article on a specific event onboard or a *Star Trek* fan's blog on the topic.

**INSIGHT** Don't reject a source simply because it disagrees with your perspective. Good research engages rather than ignores opposing points of view.

**Skim sources before reading in-depth.** Consider marking key pages or passages with sticky notes, tabs, digital bookmarks, or highlights.

- Review the author's biography, the preface, and/or the introduction to discover the perspective, approach, scope, and research methods.
- Using your keywords, review any outline, abstract, table of contents, index, or home page to get a sense of coverage.

**Read with an open but not an empty mind.** Carry on a dialogue with the source, asking questions like "Why?" and "So what?"

- Note the purpose and audience. Was the piece written to inform or persuade? Is it aimed at the public, specialists, supporters, or opponents?
- Read to understand the source: What's clear and what's confusing?
- Relate the source to your research question: How does the source affirm or challenge your ideas? Synthesize what you read with what you know.
- Record your reactions to it—what it makes you think, feel, believe.
- Consider how you might use this source in your writing—key facts, important ideas, opposing perspectives, or examples.
- Check footnotes, references, appendices, and links for leads on other sources.

## Choose a Note-Taking System

A good note-taking system should help you do the following:
- Avoid unintentional plagiarism by developing accurate records, distinguishing among sources, and separating source material from your own ideas.
- Work efficiently at gathering what you need for the project.
- Work flexibly with a wide range of resources—primary and secondary, print and digital, verbal and visual.
- Engage sources through creative and critical reflection.
- Record summaries, paraphrases, and quotations correctly.
- Be accurate and complete so that you need not reread sources.
- Efficiently develop your paper's outline and first draft.

Four note-taking systems are outlined on the pages that follow. Choose the system that works best for your project, or combine elements to develop your own.

**System 1: Paper or digital note cards.** Using paper note cards is the traditional method of note taking; however, note-taking software is now available with most word-processing programs and special programs like Zotero, Evernote, and OneNote. Here's how a note-card system works:

1. Establish one set of cards for your bibliography.
2. On a second set of cards, take notes on sources (see Figure 20.2):
   - Record one point from one source per card.
   - Clarify the source: List the author's last name, a shortened title, or a code from the matching bibliography card. Include a page number.
   - Provide a topic or heading: Called a "slug," the topic helps you categorize and order information.
   - Label the note as a summary, paraphrase, or quotation of the original.
   - Distinguish between the source's information and your own thoughts.

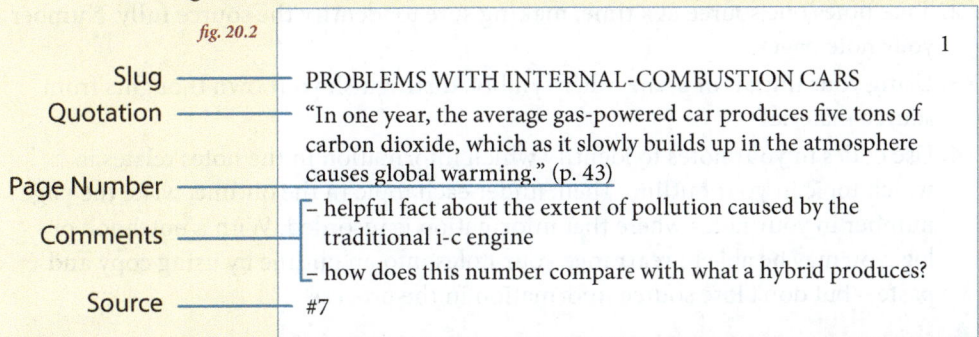

fig. 20.2

Slug — PROBLEMS WITH INTERNAL-COMBUSTION CARS
Quotation — "In one year, the average gas-powered car produces five tons of carbon dioxide, which as it slowly builds up in the atmosphere causes global warming." (p. 43)
Page Number
Comments — – helpful fact about the extent of pollution caused by the traditional i-c engine
– how does this number compare with what a hybrid produces?
Source — #7

**Upside:** Note cards are highly systematic, helping you categorize material and organize it for an outline and a first draft.

**Downside:** The method can be initially tedious and time-consuming.

**System 2: Copy (or save) and annotate.** The copy-and-annotate method involves working with photocopies, print versions, or digital texts of sources:

1. Selectively print, save, and/or photocopy important sources. Copy carefully, making sure you have full pages, including the page numbers.
2. As needed, add identifying information on the copy—author, publication details, and date. Each page should be easy to identify and trace. When working with books, simply copy the title and copyright pages and keep them with the rest of your notes.
3. As you read, mark up the copy and highlight key statements. In the margins or digital file, record your ideas:
   - Ask questions. Insert a "?" in the margin, or write out the question.
   - Make connections. Draw arrows to link ideas, or make notes like "see page 36."
   - Add asides. Record what you think and feel while reading.
   - Define terms. Note important words that you need to understand.
   - Create a marginal index. Write keywords to identify themes and main parts.

**Upside:** Copying, printing, and/or saving helps you record sources accurately; annotating encourages careful reading and thinking.

**Downside:** Organizing material for drafting is inconvenient; when done poorly, annotating and highlighting involve skimming, not critical thinking.

**System 3: The digital notebook or research log.** The digital notebook or research log method involves taking notes on a computer or on sheets of paper. Here's how it works:

1. Establish a central location for your notes—a notebook, a file folder, a binder, or a digital folder.
2. Take notes one source at a time, making sure to identify the source fully. Number your note pages.
3. Using your initials or some other symbol, distinguish your own thoughts from source material.
4. Use codes in your notes to identify which information in the notes relates to which topic in your outline. Then, under each topic in the outline, write the page number in your notes where that information is recorded. With a notebook or log, you may be able to rearrange your notes into an outline by using copy and paste—but don't lose source information in the process!

**Upside:** Taking notes feels natural without being overly systematic.

**Downside:** Outlining and drafting may require time-consuming paper shuffling.

**System 4: The double-entry notebook.** The double-entry notebook involves parallel note taking—notes from sources beside your own brainstorming, reaction, and reflection. Using a notebook or the columns feature of your word-processing program, do the following:

1. Divide pages in half vertically.
2. In the left column, record bibliographic information and take notes on sources.
3. In the right column, write your responses. Think about what the source is saying, why the point is important, whether you agree with it, and how the point relates to other ideas and other sources. See Figure 20.3 for an example.

⬆ **Upside:** This method creates accurate source records while encouraging thoughtful responses; also, it can be done on a computer.

⬇ **Downside:** Organizing material for drafting may be a challenge.

fig. 20.3

| | |
|---|---|
| Cudworth, Erika. <u>Environment and Society</u>. Routledge Introductions to Environment Series. Routledge, 2003. | |
| Ch. 6 "Society, 'Culture' and 'Nature'— Human Relations with Animals" | I've actually had a fair bit of personal experience with animals—the horses, ducks, chickens, dogs, and cats on our hobby farm. Will this chapter make trouble for my thinking? |
| chapter looks at how social scientists have understood historically the relationship between people and animals (158) | |
| the word <u>animal</u> is itself a problem when we remember that people too are animals but the distinction is often sharply made by people themselves (159) | Yes, what really are the connections and differences between people and animals? Is it a different level of intelligence? Is there something more basic or fundamental? Are we afraid to see ourselves as animals, as creatures? |
| "In everyday life, people interact with animals continually." (159)–author gives many common examples | Many examples—pets, food, TV programs, zoos—apply to me. Hadn't thought about how much my life is integrated with animal life! What does that integration look like? What does it mean for me, for the animals? |

## Summarizing, Paraphrasing, and Quoting Source Material

As you work with sources, you must decide what to put in your notes and how to record it—as a summary, a paraphrase, or a quotation. Use these guidelines:

- How relevant is the passage to your research question or working thesis?
- How strong and important is the information offered?
- How unique or memorable is the thinking or phrasing?

The more relevant, the stronger, and the more memorable the material is, the more likely you should note it. The passage below comes from an article on GM's development of fuel-cell technology. Review the passage; study how the researcher summarizes, paraphrases, and quotes from the source; and then practice these same strategies as you take notes on sources.

From Burns, L. D., McCormick, J. B., and Borroni-Bird, C. E. "Vehicle of Change." *Scientific American 287*(4), 64-73.

> When Karl Benz rolled his Patent Motorcar out of the barn in 1886, he literally set the wheels of change in motion. The advent of the automobile led to dramatic alterations in people's way of life as well as the global economy—transformations that no one expected at the time. The ever-increasing availability of economical personal transportation remade the world into a more accessible place while spawning a complex industrial infrastructure that shaped modern society.
>
> Now another revolution could be sparked by automotive technology: one fueled by hydrogen rather than petroleum. Fuel cells—which cleave hydrogen atoms into protons and electrons that drive electric motors while emitting nothing worse than water vapor—could make the automobile much more environmentally friendly. Not only could cars become cleaner, they could also become safer, more comfortable, more personalized—and even perhaps less expensive. Further, these fuel-cell vehicles could be instrumental in motivating a shift toward a "greener" energy economy based on hydrogen. As that occurs, energy use and production could change significantly. Thus, hydrogen fuel-cell cars and trucks could help ensure a future in which personal mobility—the freedom to travel independently—could be sustained indefinitely, without compromising the environment or depleting the earth's natural resources.
>
> A confluence of factors makes the big change seem increasingly likely. For one, the petroleum-fueled internal-combustion engine (ICE), as highly refined, reliable and economical as it is, is finally reaching its limits. Despite steady improvements, today's ICE vehicles are only 20 to 25 percent efficient in converting the energy content of fuels into drive-wheel power. And although the U.S. auto industry has cut exhaust emissions substantially since the unregulated 1960s—hydrocarbons dropped by 99 percent, carbon monoxide by 96 percent and nitrogen oxides by 95 percent—the continued production of carbon dioxide causes concern because of its potential to change the planet's climate.

## Summarize useful passages:

Summarizing condenses in your own words the main points in a passage. Summarize when the source provides relevant ideas and information on your topic.

1. **Reread the passage,** jotting down a few key words.
2. **State the main point in your own words.** Add key supporting points, leaving out examples, details, and long explanations. Be objective: Don't include your reactions.
3. **Check your summary against the original,** making sure that you use quotation marks around any exact phrases you borrow.

## Sample Summary:

> While the introduction of the car in the late nineteenth century has led to dramatic changes in society and world economics, another dramatic change is now taking place in the shift from gas engines to hydrogen technologies. Fuel cells may make the car "greener," and perhaps even safer, cheaper, and more comfortable. These automotive changes will affect the energy industry by making it more environmentally friendly; as a result, people will continue to enjoy mobility while transportation moves to renewable energy. One factor leading to this technological shift is that the internal-combustion engine has reached the limits of its efficiency, potential, and development—while remaining problematic with respect to emissions, climate change, and health.

## Paraphrase key passages:

Paraphrasing involves putting a passage from the source into your own words—keeping the content but phrasing it in your own voice and style, so to speak. Typically, you would paraphrase a passage that contains important points, explanations, or arguments but that is not phrased memorably or clearly. The passage might be primarily factual, making direct quotation unnecessary, or the passage might be technical, dense, and complex, requiring that you put it in plainer terms. To paraphrase effectively, follow these steps:

1. **Review the passage** to make sure that you have the gist of the whole.
2. **Go through the passage carefully,** sentence by sentence, doing the following:
   - State the ideas in your own words, substituting terms and defining words as needed.
   - Rework the sentence patterns, as needed—changing syntax, combining clauses, and so on—so that the passage takes on your voice.
   - If you do borrow phrases directly, put them in quotation marks.
3. **Check your paraphrase against the original:** Is the meaning accurate and complete? Have you fairly "translated" the source into your own wording and voice?

## Sample Paraphrase of the Second Paragraph in the Passage:

> Automobile technology may lead to another radical economic and social change through the shift from gasoline to hydrogen fuel. By breaking hydrogen into protons and electrons so that the electrons run an electric motor with only the by-product of water vapor, fuel cells could make the car a "green" machine. But this technology could also increase the automobile's safety, comfort, personal tailoring, and affordability. Moreover, this shift to fuel-cell engines in automobiles could lead to drastic, environmentally friendly changes in the broader energy industry, one that will be now tied to hydrogen rather than fossil fuels. The result from this shift will be radical changes in the way we use and produce energy. In other words, the shift to hydrogen-powered vehicles could promise to maintain society's valued mobility, while the clean technology would preserve the environment and its natural resources.

## Quote crucial phrases, sentences, and passages:

Quoting records statements or phrases in the original source word for word. Quote nuggets only—statements that are well phrased or authoritative:

1. **Note the quotation's context**—how it fits in the author's discussion.
2. **Copy the passage word for word,** enclosing it in quotation marks and checking its accuracy.
3. **If you omit words, note that omission with an ellipsis (. . .).** If you change any word for grammatical reasons, put changes in brackets—[ ].

## Sample Quotation:

> "[H]ydrogen fuel-cell cars and trucks could help ensure a future in which personal mobility . . . could be sustained indefinitely, without compromising the environment or depleting the earth's natural resources."

*Note:* This sentence captures the authors' main claim about the benefits and future of fuel-cell technology.

**INSIGHT** Whether you are summarizing, paraphrasing, or quoting, aim to be true to the source by respecting the context and spirit of the original. Avoid shifting the focus or ripping material out of its context and forcing it into your own. For example, in the sample passage the authors discuss the limits of the internal-combustion engine. If you were to claim that these authors are arguing that the internal-combustion engine was an enormous engineering and environmental mistake, you would be twisting their comments to serve your own writing agenda.

## Rate Source Reliability and Depth

You should judge each source on its own merit. Generally, however, types of sources can be rated for depth and reliability, as shown in Figure 20.4, based on their authorship, length, topic treatment, documentation, publication method, review process, distance from primary sources, allegiances, stability, and so on. Figure 20.4 will help you do the following:

1. target sources that fit your project's goals,
2. assess the approximate quality of the sources you're gathering, and
3. build a strong bibliography that readers will respect.

*fig. 20.4*

**Deep, Reliable, Credible Sources**

- **Scholarly Books and Scholarly Articles:** largely based on careful research; written by experts for experts; address topics in depth; involve peer review and careful editing; offer stable discussion of topic

- **Trade Books and Articles in Quality, Specialized Magazines:** largely based on careful research; written by experts for educated general audience. **Sample periodicals:** *The Atlantic, Scientific American, Nature, Orion*

- **Government Resources:** books, reports, web pages, guides, statistics developed by experts at government agencies; provided as service to citizens; relatively objective. **Sample source:** EPA "Climate Change" website

- **Reviewed Official Online Documents:** Internet resources posted by legitimate institutions—colleges and universities, research institutes, service organizations; although offering a particular perspective, these sources tend to be balanced.

- **Reference Works and Textbooks:** provide general and specialized information; carefully researched, reviewed, and edited; lack depth for focused research (e.g., general encyclopedia entry).

- **News and Topical Stories from Quality Sources:** provide current affairs coverage (print and online), introduction-level articles of interest to general public; may lack depth and length. **Sample sources:** *the Washington Post, the Wall Street Journal, Time, Psychology Today,* NPR's *All Things Considered*

- **Popular Magazine Stories:** short, introductory articles often distant from primary sources and without documentation; heavy advertising. **Sample sources:** *Glamour, Seventeen, Reader's Digest*

- **Business and Nonprofit Publications:** pamphlets, reports, news releases, brochures, manuals; range from informative to sales-focused.

- **Blog Posts, Social Media Posts, Podcast Discussions:** highly open, fluid, undocumented, untested exchanges and publications; unstable resource.

**Shallow, Unreliable, Not Credible Sources**

- **Unregulated Web Material:** personal sites, joke sites, chat rooms, special-interest sites, Reddit pages, advertising and junk email (spam); no review process, little accountability, biased presentation.

- **Tabloid Articles (Print and Web):** contain exaggerated and untrue stories written to titillate and exploit. **Sample source:** *National Enquirer*

## Evaluate Each Source

As you work with a source, you need to test its reliability. The benchmark criteria that follow apply to both print and online sources; note, however, the additional tests offered on the next page for free-web sources.

- ___ **Assignment fit:** Start by asking whether the source meets the guidelines and restrictions of your assignment.
- ___ **Credible author:** An expert is an authority—someone who has mastered a subject area. Is the author an expert on this topic? What are the person's credentials, and can you confirm them? For example, an automotive engineer could be an expert on hydrogen fuel-cell technology, whereas a celebrity on Twitter would not.
- ___ **Reliable publication:** Has the source been published by a scholarly press, a peer-reviewed professional journal, a quality trade-book publisher, or a trusted news source? Did you find this resource through a reliable search tool (for example, a library catalog or database)?
- ___ **Unbiased discussion:** While all sources come from a specific perspective and represent specific commitments, a biased source may be pushing an agenda in an unfair, unbalanced, or incomplete manner. Watch for bias toward a certain region, country, political party, industry, gender, race, ethnic group, or religion. Be alert to connections among authors, financial backers, and the points of view shared. For example, if an author has functioned as a consultant to or a lobbyist for a particular industry or group (oil, animal rights), the person's allegiances may lead to a biased presentation of an issue.
- ___ **Current information:** A five-year-old book on computers may be outdated, but a forty-year-old book on Abraham Lincoln could still be the best source. Given what you need, is this source's discussion up-to-date?
- ___ **Accurate information:** Bad research design, poor reporting, and sloppy documentation can lead to inaccurate information. Check the source for factual errors, statistical flaws, and conclusions that don't add up.
- ___ **Full, logical support:** Is the discussion of the topic reasonable, balanced, and complete? Are claims backed up with quality evidence? Does the source avoid faulty assumptions, twisted statistical analysis, logical fallacies, and unfair persuasion tactics?
- ___ **Quality writing and design:** Is the source well written? Is it free of sarcasm, derogatory terms, clichés, catch phrases, mindless slogans, grammar slips, and spelling errors? Generally, poor writing correlates with sloppy thinking.
- ___ **Positive relationship with other sources:** Does the source disagree with other sources? If yes, is the disagreement about the facts themselves or about how to interpret the facts? Which source seems more credible?

## Test Free-Web Sources

For sources you get off the Internet, the same evaluation criteria from the previous page apply. However, your close inspection becomes even more important with free-web resources. While the Internet has a wealth of information, much of it isn't suitable for college-level research projects. Check the criteria below and the examples on the next page for guidance.

- **Assignment fit:** Before engaging free-web sources, make sure your assignment allows them. If they are allowed, abide by any restrictions.
- **Credible author:** Is an author indicated? If so, are the author's credentials noted and contact information offered?
- **Reliable publication:** Who posted this page or resource? What type of site is it? Make sure sites are sponsored by legitimate, recognizable organizations: government agencies, nonprofit groups, and educational institutions. Check "About Us" pages to learn the credentials and stability of the site.
- **Unbiased discussion:** Is the resource one-sided? Is it pushing a cause, product, service, or belief? How do advertising and special interests affect the site? Look for obvious bias.
- **Current information:** One strength of the Internet is that information can be up-to-date. But check when the resource was originally posted and last updated. Are links live or dead?
- **Accurate information:** Is the site rich or poor in information? Does it have substance, or is it mostly fluff? Can you trace and confirm sources by following links, conducting your own search, or doing some fact-checking?
- **Full, logical support:** Does the logic pass the smell test? Is the reasoning sensible? Is it well-supported with data, links to supporting data, and some form of bibliographic references? Or is the thinking filled with leaps and fallacies?
- **Quality writing and design:** Are words neutral or loaded, emotionally charged? Are pages well designed—with clear rather than flashy, distracting elements? Avoid sites that show sloppy editing and poor design; at the same time, don't be fooled by flash that covers lack of content.
- **Positive relationship with other sources:** Is the site's information logically consistent with print sources? Do other reputable sites offer links to this site?

**INSIGHT** Engage and evaluate visual resources as thoroughly as verbal materials. For example, ask yourself what tables, graphs, and photos really "say":

- Is the graphic informative or merely decorative?
- Does the graphic create a valid or manipulative central idea? For example, does the image seek to bypass logic by appealing to sexual impulses or to crude stereotypes?
- What does the graphic include and exclude in terms of information?
- Is the graphic well designed and easy to understand, or is it cluttered and distorted?
- Is a reliable source provided?

## Sample Evaluations

**Assignment Restrictions**
- The site shown in Figure 20.5 would be appropriate for most assignments about the life and work of William Faulkner, as long as free-web sources are allowed.

**Author/ Organization**
- This site is sponsored by the University of Mississippi, a scholarly source for information, and the article's author, Dr. John B. Padgett, is an authority on Faulkner.

**Balance or Bias**
- The site clearly extols Faulkner as a great writer but does not shy from showing his shortcomings. The claims are fair and amply supported, without logical fallacies.

**Quality of Information**
- The website is current, often updated, and information-rich. It is also connected to many other Faulkner resources available on the web.

**Quality of Writing and Design**
- The site includes easy navigation, readable text, informative headings, helpful photos, and strong links. The text is well written and well edited.

*fig. 20.5*

*Courtesy of Dr. John B. Padgett/Brevard College*

- As a blog, the site shown in Figure 20.6 would not be appropriate for an assignment about the life and work of William Faulkner. A site such as this should be recognized as reflective only of the writer's opinion, not of reliable information or fact.

- There is no author or organization listed for this website. The domain name—myviewsonliterature.wordpress.com—shows that this is a personal opinion blog. Its lack of connection to other websites shows it represents an isolated opinion.

- This blog post shows a strong bias against William Faulkner. The few facts cited inadequately support the writer's main point, and logical fallacies are apparent. The tone of the post is unscholarly, with inflammatory language.

- Though this website is frequently updated, the blog post does not represent current scholarship about William Faulkner. The website is information-poor and is not backed up by any reputable print or online sources.

- The site has an amateurish design and numerous errors, including the persistent misspelling of William Faulkner's name. The writing is slipshod, and the editing is poor.

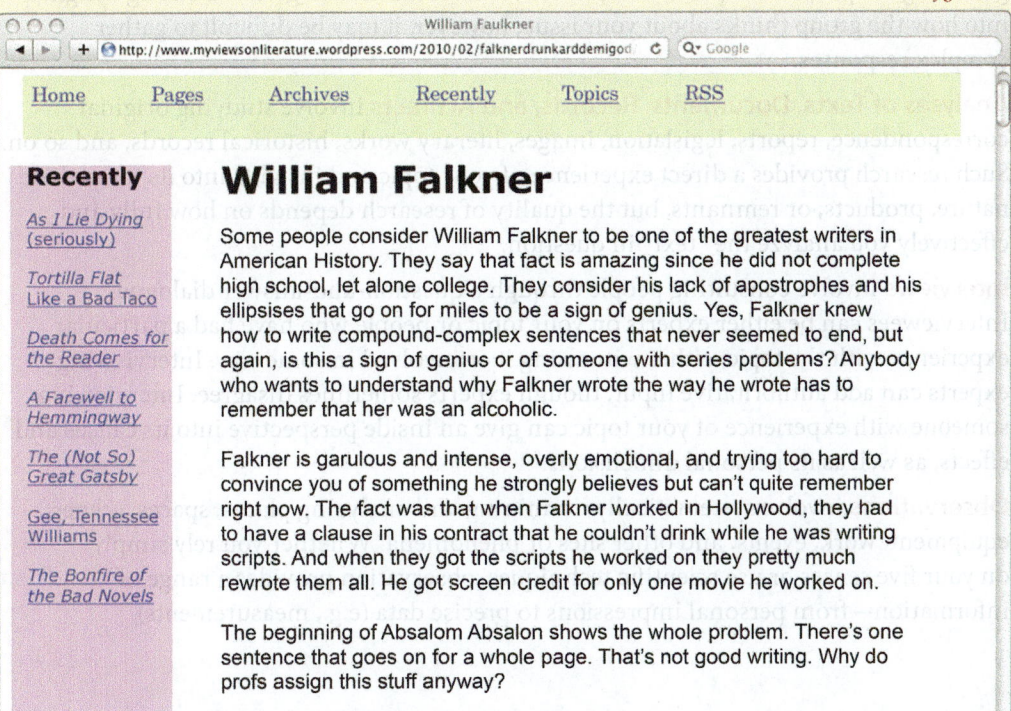

*fig. 20.6*

# Doing Primary Research

Your sources can be primary, secondary, or tertiary. Doing primary research is particularly hands-on and requires careful planning. To do truly useful primary research, you need to choose methods that will gather information directly related to your main research question and learn the proper methods of doing such research. To start your planning, consider these factors:

- **The assignment:** Does the assignment dictate a particular form of primary research?
- **The field of study:** Does the course's subject matter point you towards particularly valued methods of primary research?
- **The topic:** How might your understanding of the topic deepen with information gathered through a particular method?
- **The timing:** How much time do you have for doing primary research?
- **The audience:** What forms of primary research will your readers expect, respect, or value?

## Methods of Primary Research

After considering the factors above, review the methods below and choose those that make sense for your project.

- **Surveys and Questionnaires** gather information from representative groups of people as responses you can review, tabulate, and analyze, most often statistically. Whether gathering simple facts or personal opinions, such research can give you strong insights into how the group thinks about your issue; however, it may be difficult to gather complex responses.

- **Analyses of Texts, Documents, Records, and Artifacts** involve studying original correspondence, reports, legislation, images, literary works, historical records, and so on. Such research provides a direct experience of your topic and insights into its immediate nature, products, or remnants, but the quality of research depends on how fully and effectively you analyze the "text" in question.

- **Interviews** involve consulting people through a question-and-answer dialogue. Interviewees can be either experts on your topic or people who have had a particular experience with the topic, either witnessing it or involved in some way. Interviewing experts can add authoritative input, though experts sometimes disagree. Interviewing someone with experience of your topic can give an inside perspective into its causes and effects, as well as its personal dimensions.

- **Observations** involve systematically examining and analyzing places, spaces, scenes, equipment, work, events, and other sites or phenomena. Whether you rely simply on your five senses or use scientific techniques, observation provides a range of information—from personal impressions to precise data (e.g., measurements).

- **Experiments** test hypotheses—predictions about why things are as they are or happen as they do—so as to arrive at conclusions that can be tentatively accepted, related to other knowledge, and acted upon. Such testing often explains cause-effect relationships for varied natural, social, or psychological phenomena, offering a degree of scientific certainty about the forces at work in your topic.

## Principles for Doing Primary Research

Whatever primary research you choose to do, you should conduct that research in a systematic, careful manner in order to generate valid, reliable primary information and ideas. Here are some principles common to doing any method of primary research:

1. **Locate a reliable source.** Make sure, in other words, that the person, place, group, document, or image is the real thing—an authoritative, representative, respected source of information. Whether you find your source in a print publication (e.g., a version of a Shakespeare play published by a scholarly press), on the Internet (e.g., a piece of legislation), in an archive or museum (e.g., a sculpture), through personal contact (e.g., a home visit), or through exploration (e.g., a ravine in your city)—make sure that the source matches your research need and has the right "weight" for your project.

2. **Aim for objectivity.** You should approach most primary research with an objective frame of mind: remain open to the evidence that arises by keeping your wishes in check; otherwise, your research will be slanted and your readers will recognize the biases in your thinking.

3. **Get ready through background research.** That is, don't go cold into your primary research. Do your homework first—learning the key concepts and perspectives on your topic, the theories debated, and the knowledge that has already been built by others. That way, your primary research will grow out of some foundational thinking and be driven by a specific purpose and specific questions.

4. **Use the right tools.** Each method of primary research requires tools—physical tools (e.g., field notebook, instruments), software (e.g., survey software, spreadsheet software), or analytical tools (e.g., the ability to sort out causes and effects). Make sure that you have reliable tools and are using them effectively.

5. **Gather and work with data carefully.** Primary information is only as good as the care with which it is gathered, interpreted, and presented. Keep accurate, complete records of your research; in some projects, you may even have to include such records and "raw data" in an appendix. Above all, work ethically with your data by avoiding errors, gaps, and omissions, and by not fudging your data or doctoring graphics.

 If your research involves working with people, typically called "human subjects," strive to (1) do no harm, whether psychological, social, or financial, and (2) respect individual autonomy—participants' rights, dignity, and privacy, for example. Check if your school has a research-ethics committee that reviews, approves, and oversees such research by students.

## Conduct Surveys

One source of primary information that you can use for research projects is a survey or questionnaire. Surveys can collect facts and opinions from a wide range of people about virtually any topic. To get valid information, follow these guidelines:

1. **Find a focus.**
   - Limit the purpose of your survey.
   - Target a specific audience.
2. **Ask clear questions.**
   - Phrase questions so they can be easily understood.
   - Use words that are objective (not biased or slanted).
3. **Match your questions to your purpose.**
   - Closed questions give respondents easy-answer options, and the answers are easy to tabulate. Such questions can provide two choices (*yes* or *no*, *true* or *false*), multiple choices, a rating scale (*poor  1  2  3  excellent*), or a blank to fill.
   - Open-ended questions bring in a wide variety of responses and more complex information, but they take time to complete, and the answers can be difficult to summarize.
4. **Organize your survey so that it's easy to complete.**
   - In the introduction, state who you are and why you need the information. Explain how to complete the survey and when, where, and how to return it.
   - Guide readers by providing numbers, instructions, and headings.
   - Begin with basic questions and end with any complex, open-ended questions that are necessary. Move in a logical order from one topic to the next.
5. **Test your survey before using it.**
   - Ask a friend or classmate to read your survey and help you revise it, if necessary, before printing or posting it.
   - Try out your survey with a small test group. If the test group seems to misunderstand or misinterpret a question, then revise it.
6. **Conduct your survey.**
   - Distribute the survey to a clearly defined group that won't prejudice the sampling (random or cross section).
   - Get responses from a sample of your target group (10 percent at minimum).
   - Tabulate responses carefully and objectively.

*Note:* To develop statistically valid results, you may need expert help. Check with your instructor. In addition, consider online survey tools such as SurveyMonkey or Google Forms.

## Sample Survey

> ### Confidential Survey
>
> My name is Cho Lang, and I'm conducting research about the use of training supplements. I'd like to hear from you, Alfred University's athletes. Please answer the questions below by circling or writing out your responses. Return your survey to me, care of the Dept. of Psychology, through campus mail by Friday, April 5. Your responses will remain confidential.
>
> 1. What is your gender?
>
> 2. Circle your year.
>    **Freshman   Sophomore   Junior   Senior**
>
> 3. List the sports that you play.
>
>
>
> 4. Are you presently using a training supplement?
>    **Yes   No**
>
>    *Note:* If you circled "no," you may turn in your survey at this point.
>
> 5. Describe your supplement use (type, amount, and frequency).
>
>
>
> 6. Who supervises your use of this training supplement?
>    **Coach   Trainer   Self   Others**
>
> 7. How long have you used it?
>    **Less than 1 month   1–12 months   12+ months**
>
> 8. How many pounds have you gained while using this supplement?
>
> 9. How much has your athletic performance improved?
>    **None   1   2   3   4   5   Greatly**
>
> 10. Circle any side effects you've experienced.
>     **Dehydration   Nausea   Diarrhea**

*The introduction includes the essential information about the survey.*

*The survey begins with clear, basic questions.*

*The survey asks an open-ended question.*

*The survey covers the topic thoroughly.*

## Analyze Texts, Documents, Records, and Artifacts

An original document or record is one that relates directly to the event, issue, object, or phenomenon you are researching. Examining original documents and artifacts can involve studying letters, email exchanges, Tweets, case notes, literary texts, blog posts, sales records, legislation, and material objects such as tools, sculptures, buildings, and tombs. As you analyze such documents and records, you examine evidence in an effort to understand a topic, arrive at a coherent conclusion about it, and support that judgment. How do you work with such diverse documents, records, and artifacts? Here are some guidelines:

### Choose evidence close to your topic:

Which texts, documents, records, and artifacts originated from or grew out of the topic you are researching? The closer to the topic, the more primary the source. Select materials that are directly related to your research questions and/or working thesis.

> *Example:* If you were studying English labor riots of the 1830s, you could investigate these primary sources:
> - To identify the rioters, names from police reports or union membership lists
> - To understand what rioters were demanding, copies of speeches given at demonstrations
> - To learn the political response to the riots, political speeches or legislation
> - To get at the attitudes of people from that time, newspaper reports, works of art, or novels from the period
> - To find people's personal stories and private opinions related to the riots, personal letters, diaries, family albums, gravestones, and funeral eulogies

### Put the document or artifact in context:

So that the material takes on meaning, clarify its external and internal natures. First, consider its external context—the five W's and H: What exactly is it? Who made it, when, where, why, and how? Second, consider its internal nature—what the document means, based on what it can and cannot show you: What does the language mean or refer to? What is the document's structure? What are the artifact's composition and style?

> *Example:* If you were examining Mary Wollstonecraft's *A Vindication of the Rights of Woman* in a history or women's studies course, you would consider the following:
> - **External Context:** who Mary Wollstonecraft was; when and why she wrote *A Vindication* and under what conditions; for whom she wrote it and their response; the type of document it is
> - **Internal Context:** Wollstonecraft's essential argument and evidence; the nature of her views, their relationship to her times, and their relevance today

### Frame your examination with questions:

To make sense of the text, document, record, or artifact, understand what you are looking for and why. List the secondary questions that you want to answer in relation to the main question behind your research project.

> *Example:* To study the legislative background behind the development of cleaner cars, such as the hybrid-fuel vehicle, you could access various documents on the Clean Air Act of 1990 (for example, *The Plain English Guide to the Clean Air Act*, an EPA publication). As you study this legislation, you could frame your reading with these additional questions:
> - What are the requirements of the Clean Air Act?
> - What legislation followed the Clean Air Act?
> - Specifically, how do those requirements affect automotive technology?
> - Which research projects will likely influence these requirements?
> - Are schedules for change or deadlines written into the Clean Air Act?

### Draw coherent conclusions about meaning:

Make sense of the source in relation to your research questions. What connections does it reveal? What important developments? What cause/effect relationships? What themes?

> *Example:* A study of the Clean Air Act might lead you to conclusions regarding how environmental legislation relates to the development of hybrid technology—for example, that the United States must produce cleaner cars if it hopes to gain improved air quality.

**INSIGHT** Studying primary documents and artifacts is central to many disciplines—history, literature, theology, philosophy, political studies, and archaeology, for example. Good analysis depends on asking research questions appropriate for the discipline. With the English labor riots of the 1830s again as an example, here's what three disciplines might ask:

- **Political science:** What role did political theories, structures, and processes play in the riots—both in causing and in responding to them?
- **Art:** How were the concerns of the rioters embodied in the new "realist" style of the mid-1800s? Did artists sympathize with and address an alienated working-class audience? How did art comment on the social structures of the time?
- **Sociology:** What type and quality of education did most workers have in the 1830s? How did that education affect their economic status and employment opportunities? Did issues related to the riots prompt changes in the English educational system? What changes and why?

With these examples in mind, consider your own major: What questions would this discipline ask of the English labor riots, of Mary Wollstonecraft's *A Vindication of the Rights of Woman,* or of the Clean Air Act of 1990 and its related legislation?

## Conduct Interviews

The purpose of an interview is simple: To get information, you talk with someone who has significant experience or someone who is an expert on your topic. Use the guidelines below whenever you conduct an interview.

1. **Before the interview,** research the topic and the person you are planning to interview.
   - Arrange the interview in a thoughtful way. Explain to the interviewee your purpose and the topics to be covered.
   - Think about the specific ideas you want to cover in the interview and write questions for each. Addressing the 5 W's and H (*Who? What? Where? When? Why?* and *How?*) is important for good coverage.
   - Organize your questions in a logical order so the interview moves smoothly from one subject to the next.
   - Write the questions on the left side of a page. Leave room for quotations, information, and impressions on the right side.

2. **During the interview,** try to relax so that your conversation is natural and sincere.
   - Provide some background information about yourself, your project, and your plans for using the interview information.
   - Use recording equipment only with the interviewee's permission.
   - Jot down key facts and quotations.
   - Listen actively. Show that you're listening through your body language—eye contact, nods, smiles. Pay attention not only to what the person says, but also to how it is said.
   - Be flexible. If the person looks puzzled by a question, rephrase it. If the discussion gets off track, redirect it. Based on the interviewee's responses, ask follow-up questions, and don't limit yourself to your planned questions only.
   - End positively. Conclude by asking if the person wants to add, clarify, or emphasize anything. (Note: Important points may come up late in the interview.) Thank the person, gather your notes and equipment, and part with a handshake.

3. **After the interview,** do the appropriate follow-up work.
   - As soon as possible, review your notes. Fill in responses you remember but couldn't record at the time.
   - Analyze the results. Study the information, insights, and quotations you gathered. What do they reveal about the topic? How does the interview confirm, complement, or contradict other sources on the topic? What has the interview added to your understanding?
   - Thank the interviewee with a note, an email, a text, or a phone call.
   - If necessary, ask the interviewee to check whether your information and quotations are accurate, and/or send an email asking the interviewee if there is anything they would like to add or change.
   - Offer to send the interviewee a copy of your writing.

## Sample interview note-taking sheet:

Below, note how the researcher sets up questions for an interview with an automotive engineer regarding hybrid technology. The interviewer begins with identifying information for future reference, and then moves from a basic "connecting" question into the technology's principles, strengths, challenges, and future. On the right, he leaves room (approximately half the sheet) for taking notes.

**Interview with Jessica Madison, automotive engineer for Future Fuel Corporation** (email jmadison@futurefuel.com; phone 555-555-5555) January 22, 2021: 2:30 p.m.

*Notes, quotations, observations:*

**Preliminaries:** thanks/appreciation; introduction of myself; background, purpose, hoped-for outcome of research (report on hybrids' environmental potential)

**Initial Question**
1. Please tell me about your research into hybrid technology. When and how did you become interested? What discoveries have you made?

**Hybrid Technology: Principles**
2. How does hybrid technology actually work? What's the principle behind the hybrid vehicle?
3. How is the hybrid engine different from the traditional internal-combustion engine?

**Strengths and Challenges**
4. What are the strengths of hybrid vehicles?
5. What are some of the challenges of hybrids? Some of the weaknesses?

**The Future/Viability**
6. Where is hybrid technology going? What's the next generation of clean-car technology?
7. What are the benefits or drawbacks of society investing in hybrids? Why should the average person care about hybrid technologies?
8. Would you like to add or clarify anything about hybrid technologies?

**Closing:** final thank you, offer a follow-up

## Make Observations

Observation places you at a site directly related to your topic. Whether you are examining people's behavior, natural phenomena, or a location's features, observation can gather subjective impressions, sensory data, various recordings, or concrete measurements. To observe effectively, follow the guidelines below:

### Prepare to observe:

1. **Know your goal.** Do you need to understand a place or a process? Solve a problem? Answer a question? What kind of information do you want to gather?
2. **Consider possible perspectives and vantage points.** Should you observe the site passively or interact with it? Should you simply record data or also include impressions? Should you observe from one position or several?
3. **Plan your observation.** Preparation involves both academic and practical issues: doing sufficient background research; listing questions to answer; seeking permission to observe, if needed; taking safety precautions; considering timing issues; and gathering observation tools.

### Conduct your observations:

1. **Be flexible but focused.** Follow your plan, but be open to surprises. Pay attention to the big picture (the context, time frame, and surroundings), but focus on your observational goal by filtering out unnecessary details.
2. **Identify your position.** Where are you in the site? What is your angle? More broadly, what is your personal and/or cultural stance here?
3. **Take notes on specific details and impressions.** While being careful not to miss too much, jot down data for later review—conditions, appearances, actions, events, and so on. If appropriate, focus on your five senses: sight, sound, smell, touch, and taste.
4. **Gather other forms of evidence.** Take measurements, record images and sound, gather samples, interview people, study event programs, get brochures.

### Make sense of your observations:

1. **Complete and review your notes and evidence.** As soon as possible, flesh out your notes a bit more fully—while your memory is still good. Then examine closely everything that you have written, recorded, and collected, looking for patterns and themes.
2. **List your conclusions.** Describe what has been clarified about your topic through the observation.
3. **Relate your observations to your other research.** Explore how your observations confirm, contradict, complement, or build on other sources of information.

# Doing Library Research

The library's door—both physical and digital—is your gateway to information. Inside, the college library holds a wide range of research resources, from books to periodicals, from information specialists to digital databases.

To improve your ability to succeed at all your research assignments, become familiar with your college library system. Take advantage of tours and orientation sessions to learn its physical layout, resources, and services. Check your library's website for policies, tutorials, and research tools. The college library offers a variety of resources for your research projects.

**Librarians and media specialists:** These library specialists are information experts:
- They manage the library's materials and guide you to resources.
- They help you perform online searches.

**Collections:** The library collects, houses, and provides access to a variety of materials:
- **Books and digital materials**—print books, ebooks, and more.
- **Periodicals**—journals, magazines, and newspapers (print, microform, pdf, and html)
- **Reference materials**—directories, indexes, handbooks, encyclopedias, and almanacs (print and digital)
- **Special collections**—government publications, historical documents, archival materials, and original artifacts

**Research tools:** The library contains many tools that direct you to materials:
- The online catalog allows you to search everything in the library.
- Subscription databases (Lexis-Nexis, EBSCOhost, Gale, ProQuest Direct) point you to abstracts and full-text articles.
- Internet access connects you with other library catalogs and online references.

**Special services:** Special services may also help you to complete research:
- Interlibrary loan allows you to obtain books and articles not available in your library or online.
- "Hold" allows you to request a book that is currently signed out.
- "Reserve" materials give you access to materials recommended by your instructors or heavily in demand.
- The reference desk can help you find information quickly, point you to the right resources, and help you with a search.
- Photocopiers, scanners, and presentation software help you perform and share your research.

*Cross-Curricular Connection:* As you advance in your field of study, become especially familiar with the reference holdings, journals, book stacks, and web resources related to your major.

## Search the Catalog

Library materials are catalogued so they are easy to find. In most college libraries, books, videos, and other holdings are catalogued in an electronic database (see Figure 20.7). To find material, use book titles, author names, and related keyword searching.

**Sample Electronic Catalog**

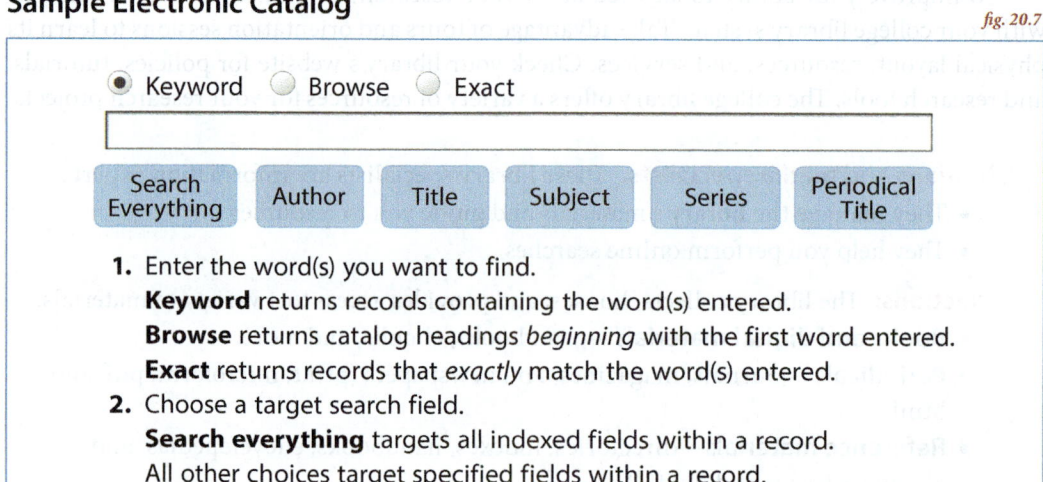

*fig. 20.7*

When you find a citation for a book or other resource, the result will provide some or all of the information in Figure 20.8. Use that information to determine whether the resource is worth exploring further and to figure out other avenues of research. Note that a number of items appearing in blue, underlined type provide links to related books and other resources in the catalog.

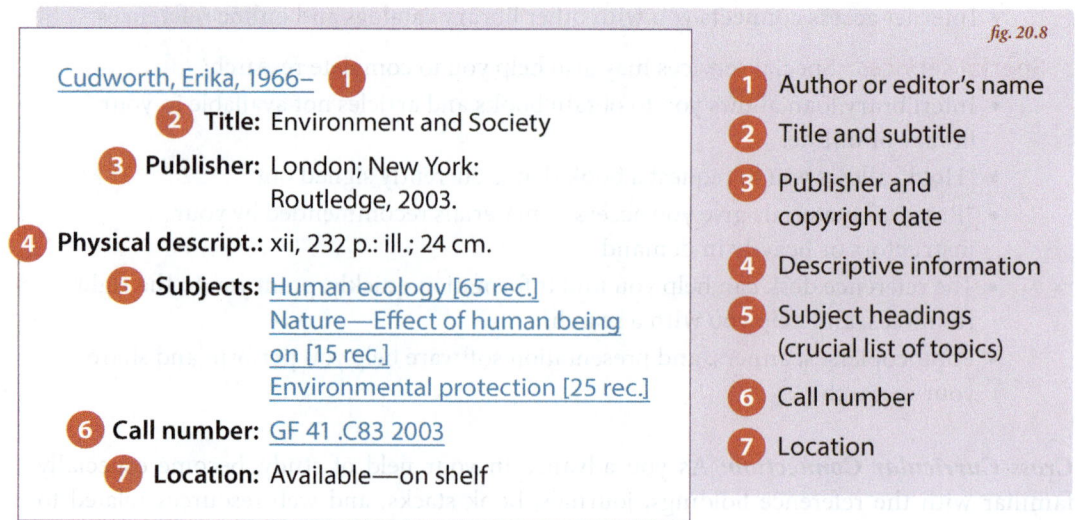

*fig. 20.8*

## Locate Resources by Call Numbers

Library of Congress (LC) call numbers combine letters and numbers to specify a resource's broad subject area, topic, and authorship or title. Finding a book, journal, or other item involves combining both the alphabetical and the numerical order. Here is a sample call number for *Arctic Refuge: A Vanishing Wilderness?*:

### VIDEO QH84.1.A72 1990

subject area (QH) topic number (84) subtopic number (1) cutter number (A72)

To find this resource in the library, first note the tab VIDEO. Although not part of the call number, this locator may send you to a specific area of the library. Once there, follow the parts of the call number one at a time:

1. Find the library section on natural history containing videos with the "QH" designation.
2. Follow the numbers until you reach "84."
3. Within the "84" items, find those with the subtopic "1."
4. Use the cutter "A72" to locate the resource alphabetically with "A," and numerically with "72."

*Note:* In the LC system, pay careful attention to the arrangement of subject area letters, topic numbers, and subtopic numbers: Q98 comes before QH84; QH84 before QH8245; QH84.A72 before QH84.1.A72.

## Classification Systems

The LC classification system combines letters and numbers. The Dewey decimal system, which is used in some libraries, uses numbers only. Figure 20.9 shows a list of the subject classes for both the LC and Dewey systems.

### The Library of Congress and Dewey Decimal Systems

*fig. 20.9*

| LC Category | | Dewey Decimal | LC Category | | Dewey Decimal |
|---|---|---|---|---|---|
| A | General Works | 000–999 | K | Law | 340–349 |
| B | Philosophy | 100–199 | L | Education | 370–379 |
|   | Psychology | 150–159 | M | Music | 780–789 |
|   | Religion | 200–299 | N | Fine Arts | 700–799 |
| C | History: Auxiliary Sciences | 910–929 | P | Language Literature | 800–899 400–499 |
| D | History: General and Old World | 930–999 | Q | Science | 500–599 |
| E–F | History of the Americas | 970–979 | R | Medicine | 610–619 |
| G | Geography | 910–919 | S | Agriculture | 630–639 |
|   | Anthropology | 571–573 | T | Technology | 600–699 |
|   | Recreation | 700–799 | U | Military Science | 355–359, 623 |
| H | Social Sciences | 300–399 | V | Naval Science | 359, 623 |
| J | Political Science | 320–329 | Z | Bibliography and Library Science | 010–019 020–029 |

## Work with the Books You Find

Your college library contains a whole range of books for you to use. Unfortunately, for many research projects you simply don't have time to read an entire book, and rarely do the entire contents relate to your topic. Instead, use the strategies outlined below to approach each book systematically.

1. **Identify the book type.** Trade books are typically written for a broad public and published by for-profit presses. Often written by experts, such books can be filled with reliable, useful information for a lay audience, though quality, depth, and reliability can vary. Example: *Flirting with* Pride & Prejudice: *Fresh Perspectives on the Original Chick-Lit Masterpiece.* By comparison, scholarly books are typically written for a specialized audience and college-level students. Published by university presses and other respected scholarly presses, such studies typically provide advanced research findings. Example: *Jane Austen on Screen* (Cambridge University Press).

2. **Check out front and back information.** The title and copyright pages give the book's full title and subtitle; the author's name; and publication information, including publication date and Library of Congress subject headings. The back may contain a note on the author's credentials and other publications.

3. **Scan the table of contents.** Examine the contents page to see what the book covers and how it is organized. Ask yourself which chapters are relevant to your project.

4. **Using key words, search the index.** Check the index for coverage and page locations of the topics most closely related to your project. Are there plenty of pages, or just a few? A scattered mention of key words likely represents more superficial coverage than concentrated, in-depth coverage.

5. **Skim the preface, foreword, or introduction.** The opening materials will often indicate the book's perspective, explain its origin, and preview its contents.

6. **Check appendices, glossaries, or bibliographies.** These special sections may be a good source of tables, graphics, definitions, statistics, and clues for further research.

7. **Carefully read appropriate chapters and sections.** Think through the material you've read and take good notes. Follow references to authors and other works to do further research on the topic. Study footnotes and endnotes for insights and leads to additional resources.

Consider these options for working productively with books:
- When you find a helpful book, browse nearby shelves for more books.
- To confirm a book's quality, check the Internet or a periodical database for a review.
- If your library subscribes to an e-book service such as netLibrary, you have access to thousands of books in digital form. You can conduct electronic searches, browse or check out promising books, and read them online.

## Consult Reference Resources

Reference works, whether print or digital, are information-rich resources that can give you an overview of your topic, supply basic facts, share common knowledge about your topic, and offer ideas for focusing and furthering your research. While some reference resources are available on the free web, your library offers you excellent access to reference resources in both print and digital formats. Consider options like those below.

**Check reference works that supply information:**

- **Encyclopedias** supply facts and overviews for topics arranged alphabetically. General encyclopedias cover many fields of knowledge: *Encyclopedia Britannica* (online version). Specialized encyclopedias focus on a single topic: *Encyclopedia of American Film Comedy*.
- **Almanacs, yearbooks, and statistical resources,** normally published annually or posted regularly, contain diverse facts. For example, the www.census.gov website provides data on population, geography, politics, employment, business, science, industry, and more.
- **Vocabulary resources** supply information on languages. General dictionaries, such as *The American Heritage College Dictionary,* supply definitions and histories for a whole range of words. Specialized dictionaries define words common to a field, topic, or group: *The New Harvard Dictionary of Music*. Bilingual dictionaries translate words from one language to another.
- **Biographical resources** supply information about people. General biographies cover a broad range of people. Other biographies focus on people from a specific group. *Examples: Who's Who in America, World Artists 1980–1990.*
- **Directories** supply contact information for people, groups, and organizations. *Examples: USPS ZIP Code Lookup and Address Information* (online).

**Check reference works that are research tools:**

- **Guides and handbooks** help readers explore specific topics: *The Handbook of North American Indians, A Guide to Prairie Fauna*.
- **Indexes** point you to useful resources. Whether general or specialized, such indexes are available online in databases your library subscribes to.
- **Bibliographies** list resources on a specific topic. A good, current bibliography can be used as an example when you compile your own bibliography on a topic.
- **Abstracts**, like indexes, direct you to articles on a particular topic. But abstracts also summarize those materials so you learn whether a resource is relevant before you invest time in locating and reading it. Such abstracts are typically incorporated into many online subscription databases.

## Find Articles Via Databases

Periodicals are publications or broadcasts produced at regular intervals (daily, weekly, monthly, quarterly). Although some periodicals are broad in their subject matter and audience, as a rule they focus on a narrow range of topics geared toward a particular audience.

- **Daily newspapers** provide up-to-date information on current events, opinions, and trends—from politics to natural disasters *(Wall Street Journal, USA Today)*.
- **Weekly and monthly magazines** generally provide more in-depth information on a wide range of topics *(Time, Newsweek, 60 Minutes)*.
- **Journals**, generally published quarterly, provide specialized scholarly information for a narrowly focused audience *(English Journal)*.

With thousands of periodicals available, how do you find helpful articles? Learn (a) which search tools your library offers, (b) which periodicals it has available in which forms, and (c) how to gain access to those periodicals.

1. **Search your library's online databases:** Using keyword search techniques and instruction offered by your library, check general or subject-specific databases for articles on your topic. Most databases include tools such as limiters and expanders to help you narrow your search.
2. **Generate a citation list of promising articles:** Your search should generate lists of citations, brief descriptions of articles flagged through keywords in titles, subject terms, and abstracts (summaries). Study citations to determine the relevance of articles to your project. "Capture" the identifying details of promising ones.
3. **Find and retrieve the full text of the article:** The full article may be available digitally through a link to a pdf or an html file. From there, you can read, print, save, or email it to yourself. If the article is available only in print, follow your library's procedure for retrieving articles or ordering them using interlibrary loan. Figure 20.10 shows the type of information supplied for a source retrieved from a database.

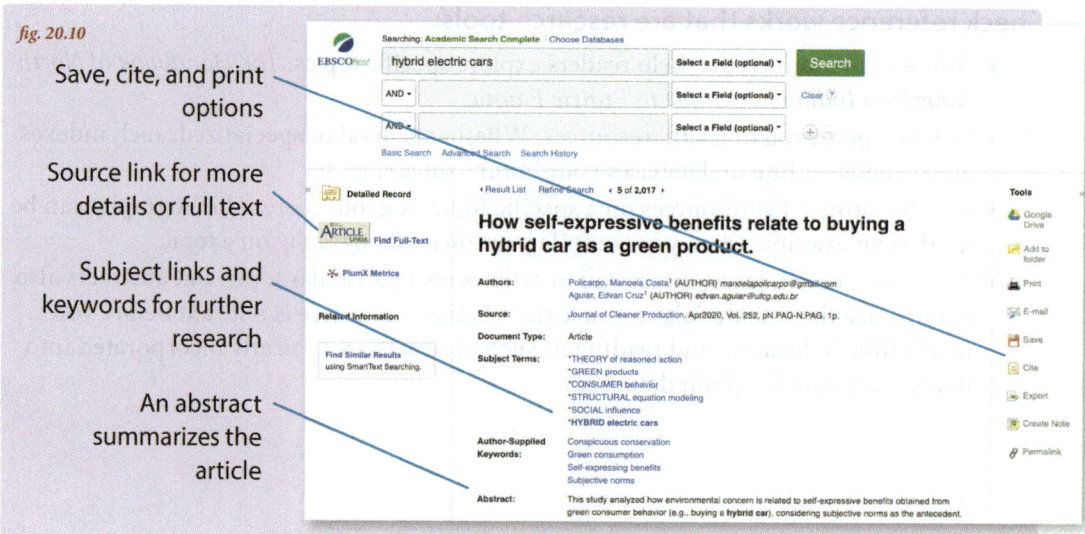

*fig. 20.10*

Save, cite, and print options

Source link for more details or full text

Subject links and keywords for further research

An abstract summarizes the article

*Image courtesy of EBSCO Publishing*

# Doing Free-Web Research

Here, we're back to the phrase we started with: "Just Google it!" But what exactly does this advice mean, and what's involved? How do you "Google it" effectively? The instruction below and on the following pages will help.

## Using Search and Metasearch

Search and metasearch engines provide quick and powerful access to much of the content of the web. They are invaluable tools for researchers. This page gives tips for getting the most out of your searches, and the next two pages look at online searching in depth.

1. **Select effective keywords:** Keywords are words or phrases that the search engine looks for across the web. The more specific a keyword or phrase is, the more tightly a search will be focused. Here are a set of keywords for the research topic of "games used to simulate real-world scenarios":

   | General → Specific | Keyword | Explanation |
   |---|---|---|
   | General | game | This general term will produce a very unfocused list of millions of websites, ranging from stores selling games to recipes for cooking game. |
   | | simulation | This more-specific term will narrow the search considerably, but will show off-topic sites such as suppliers of simulated wood products. |
   | | simulation game | This set of keywords is much more specific, but the engine will also find sites using both words but not in combination. |
   | Specific | "simulation game" | The quotation marks around this search will turn up only sites that use the exact phrase "simulation game." |

2. **Use Boolean operators:** In addition to using quotation marks, you can use words and symbols to make your search specific.

   | | |
   |---|---|
   | game and war | *and* indicates sites with both terms |
   | game + war | + indicates sites with both terms |
   | game not war | *not* indicates sites with the first term but not the second |
   | game – war | – indicates sites with the first term but not the second |
   | game or simulation | *or* indicates sites with either term |

3. **Act on search results:** Survey the results and act on them.
   - Read the name of the site and determine how the term is used.
   - Review the domain and extension to decide if you will click it.
   - Look for information and links.

## Use Search Engines Effectively

Like millions of people, you probably "Google it" when you have a question. But how should you use search engines for college research projects? A search engine automatically scours a large amount of web material using keywords and commands that you submit. In that respect, the search is only as productive as the terms you use, the quality of the search program, and the amount and areas of the Web that the engine searches. When you use search engines, be aware of the issues below, and use the tips on the following page to work around the limitations discussed.

- **Web Coverage:** Even though the largest search engines search billions of online resources, those pages represent just a portion of the web—as little as 20 percent. The point to keep in mind is that any given search engine is not searching the entire web for you and may be focusing on particular kinds of pages and documents. Moreover, a given engine may not be searching each resource in its entirety but only certain portions (e.g., citations) or up to a certain size of the document.

- **Resource Ranking:** A search engine returns results in a ranking of resources based on complex mathematical algorithms—a weighing of a variety of criteria that differ from one engine to the next. One criterion used is the number of times your keywords appear in a given resource. A second criterion might be the number and type of links to a given page—a measure, in other words, of the site's importance or popularity on the web. A third criterion relates to your search history: Given sites that you have looked at in the past, what types of sites do you prefer? Algorithms answer this question by *personalizing* your search, potentially creating what Eli Pariser calls a "filter bubble"—results restricted to your interests and biases.

  One more point: Businesses and other organizations work very hard to make sure that their pages get ranked near the top of searches; some companies hire consultants to help achieve this result or even try to fool the programs. In other words, what you are getting in your search is not necessarily an objective listing of the most relevant and reliable resources for an academic research project.

- **Search Habits:** Using search engines is complicated not just by algorithms but by the habits of users themselves. Studies suggest, for example, that very few users look past the first three hits returned by a search; in fact, only one percent of searchers go past the first ten hits. (You can understand, then, why some organizations work so hard to get into that top-ten list for specific keyword searches.) Moreover, very few users go on to refine their search after the initial results, supposedly satisfied with what they have found, although studies also suggest that few users can effectively evaluate the returned resources in terms of their quality, authority, objectivity, and timeliness (currency of information). The implications for your college research projects are clear: Such search habits rarely lead to quality resources that you can use in an academic project.

Given how search engines work, what practices should you follow in using them for an academic research project? Obviously, start by following the assignment's restrictions about using free-web resources. But here are four additional guidelines:

1. **Restrict search-engine use to specific purposes.** Generally, a search engine is useful for college research projects in these circumstances:
    - You need general information about your topic.
    - You have a very narrow topic in mind or an exact question you need answered.
    - You have a highly specific word or phrase to use in your search.
    - You want a large number of results.
    - You are looking for a specific type of Internet file.
    - You have the time to sort the material for reliability.

2. **Learn to do advanced searches.** Basic searches tend to lead to basic results. Most search engines actually allow you to do quite complex searches through advanced-search screens. With these, you can employ Boolean logic to a degree, use limiters and expanders, and refine your results in other ways. Study the search engine's help pages for instructions on how to benefit from these advanced-searching techniques.

3. **Approach results with suspicion.** Given the wide-ranging quality and reliability of material on the free web, it is imperative that you evaluate resources that you find through search engines.

4. **Use search engines that seem to give you more quality results.** Conduct the same search using a variety of search engines and compare the results. While you generally want to choose search engines that cover a large portion of the web, offer quality indexing, and give you high-powered search capabilities, you also want to consider a search-engine's information focus: try out search engines whose goals seem more obviously focused on academics. Consider, for example, Google Scholar. While it indexes just a small portion of all published articles, Google Scholar can help you build citations from a variety of sources, citations you can then find in your library's subscription databases. Moreover, it ranks articles by weighing the full text, the author, the publication, and frequency of citation in other sources. (See example search results from Google Scholar in Figure 20.11.)

fig. 20.11

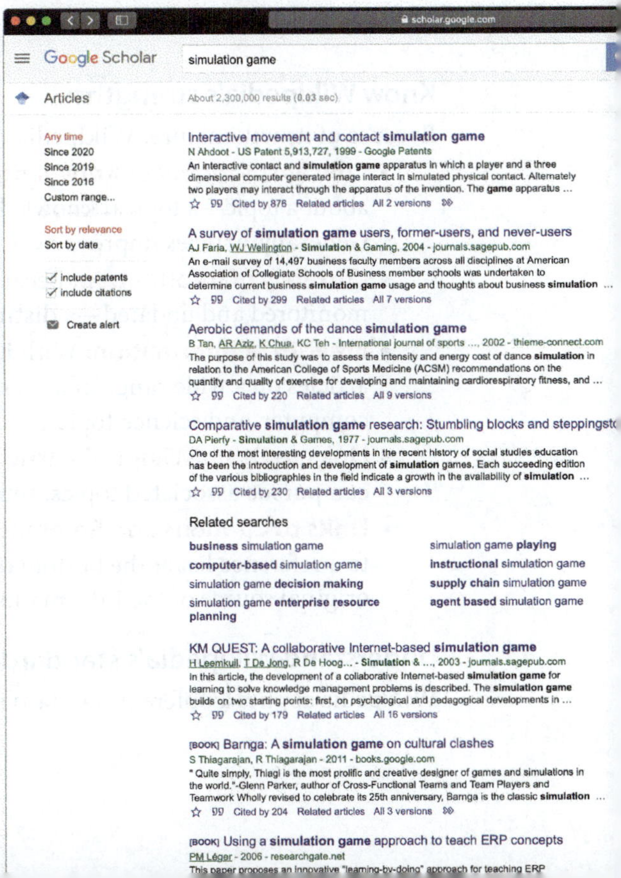

©2020 Google LLC, used with permission. Google and the Google logo are registered trademarks of Google LLC.

## Understanding the Uses and Limits of Wikipedia

You likely recognize Figure 20.12—an entry from Wikipedia. From Wikipedia's beginning in 2001 to today, a large population of volunteer writers and editors has made it a frequently trafficked site. But is Wikipedia acceptable for college-level research? Put simply, Wikipedia remains a controversial resource for academic research.

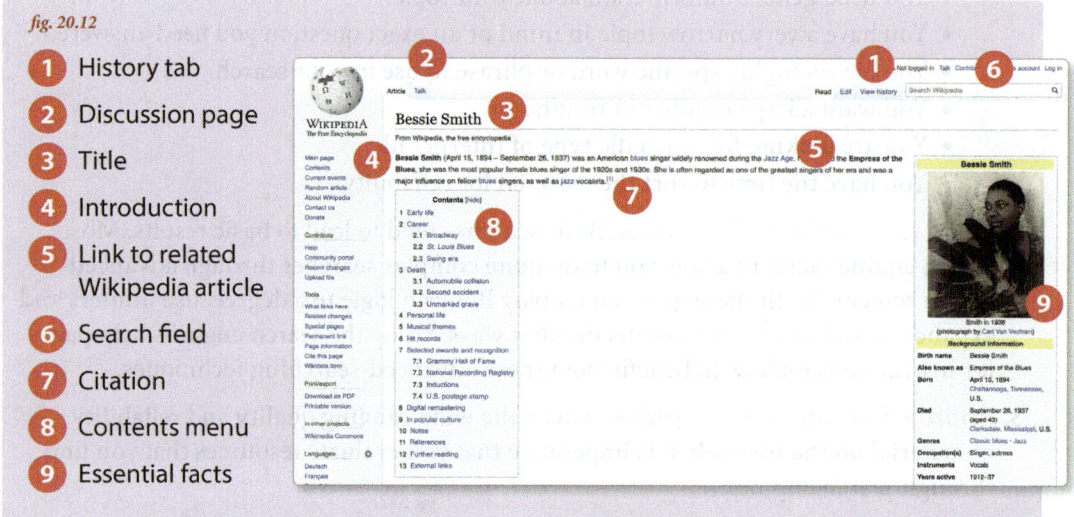

*fig. 20.12*

1. History tab
2. Discussion page
3. Title
4. Introduction
5. Link to related Wikipedia article
6. Search field
7. Citation
8. Contents menu
9. Essential facts

*Image courtesy of Wikipedia*

### Know Wikipedia's strengths:

Because of its wiki nature, Wikipedia offers researchers a number of advantages.

- **Consensus Model of Knowledge:** Articles represent a collaborative agreement about a topic—a topical knowledge base that is fair and fairly comprehensive. Generally, articles improve over time, offering "open-source" knowledge.
- **Currency of Information:** Because they are web-based, articles are regularly monitored and updated—a distinct advantage over print encyclopedias.
- **Breadth of Information:** With its size and global community, Wikipedia offers articles on a wide range of topics—especially strong in pop culture, current events, computer, and science topics.
- **Links to Other Wikipedia Articles:** Articles are linked throughout so that readers can pursue associated topics, sources, recommended reading, and related categories.
- **Links to Citations and References:** Articles include citation links, which direct you to a reference list at the bottom of the page. Each reference in the list links to the original source of the information. This trail helps you to evaluate the content.

### Understand Wikipedia's standards for truth:

Wikipedia applies a different standard of truth than more traditional sources of information.

To learn more about Wikipedia's standard of truth, read Simson L. Garfinkle's revealing article, "Wikipedia and the Meaning of *Truth*" (available through a web search).

**Know Wikipedia's weaknesses:**

In some ways, Wikipedia's strengths are closely related to its weaknesses for college-level research. Consider these issues:

- **Popularity Model of Knowledge:** The dynamics of popularity can lead to bias, imbalance, and errors. In some ways, this approach minimizes the value of training, education, and expertise while promoting a kind of democracy of knowledge.
- **Anonymity of Authorship:** Wikipedia allows contributors to remain anonymous. Researchers thus have little way of checking credentials and credibility.
- **Variable Quality of Content:** While many well-established articles are quite stable, balanced, and comprehensive, other articles can be partial, driven by a biased perspective, erroneous, and poorly sourced.
- **Variable Coverage:** Wikipedia's strength in some content areas is matched by gaps and incompleteness in other content areas.
- **Vulnerability to Vandalism:** Wikipedia has a number of processes in place to limit people from harming articles with misinformation, with the result that most vandalism is corrected within hours, but some errors have persisted for months.
- **Tertiary Nature of Information:** For most research projects, Wikipedia articles function as tertiary sources—reports of reports of research. As such, Wikipedia articles are not substantial enough for academic projects.

**Use Wikipedia cautiously:**

Based on Wikipedia's strengths and weaknesses, follow these guidelines:

1. **Respect your assignment.** Instructors may give you varied instruction about using Wikipedia. Respect their guidelines.
2. **Verify Wikipedia information.** If you use information from Wikipedia, also use other more traditional sources to verify that information.
3. **Use Wikipedia as a semi-authoritative reference source.** Generally, the more academic your research assignment, the less you should rely on Wikipedia articles, which are essentially sources of basic and background information.
4. **Use Wikipedia as one starting point.** From a Wikipedia article, you can learn what is considered "open-source" knowledge on your topic, gather ideas for developing a topic, find links to related topics and other resources, and begin to build a bibliography.
5. **Study individual articles to get a sense of their reliability.** When you find a Wikipedia article relevant to your research project, check the article for quality and stability. Use the evaluation criteria, but also check the article's history, its discussion page, any tags or icons indicating the article's state, and the "what links here" link in the toolbox at the left of the screen.

Research and Writing

# Doing Research: Applications

Once you have studied the research methods in this chapter, you might apply what you have learned through a number of activities.

1. **Wise Words:** Wernher von Braun once said, "Basic research is what I am doing when I don't know what I am doing." In what sense does all research involve figuring out what you are doing?
2. **Research Map:** Think about a research project that you have done or are doing now. How might primary research and library research (scholarly books and journals) strengthen your writing? Why not do all your research on the free web?
3. **Information Orientation:** Working with your library's website and its orientation tools, identify where you can physically and/or digitally locate books, reference resources, and journals. Then explore your library's handouts and website for information about Internet research. What services, support, and access does the library provide?
4. **Photo Op:** The photo on the opening page of this chapter shows the interior of a library. Now that you've studied this chapter, what other image might capture for you something about doing research? Find or take such a photo.
5. **Living Today:** Brainstorm issues related to food production, consumption, or culture. Choosing one issue, use your library's tools to find and evaluate print books and periodical articles. Then do a web search of the topic, comparing the results.
6. **Public Texts:** Using the variety of methods outlined in this chapter, work with classmates to search the Internet for information on a controversial topic, event, person, or place. Analyze and evaluate the range of web information you find.

## Learning-Objectives Checklist ✓

Have you achieved this chapter's learning objectives? Check your progress with the items below, revisiting topics in the chapter as needed. I have . . .

\_\_\_\_ produced an annotated bibliography.
\_\_\_\_ engaged sources through effective note-taking.
\_\_\_\_ evaluated my sources for quality and reliability.
\_\_\_\_ completed primary research that fits my project.
\_\_\_\_ completed library research that produced promising books, reference resources, and journal articles.
\_\_\_\_ completed free-web research that led to quality resources.

# Chapter 21

# Practicing Research Ethics

"That's incredible!" is normally a positive exclamation of amazement. But maybe it's an exclamation that you do not want to hear about your research writing, if "incredible" means "unbelievable." If your paper is unbelievable, your credibility as a researcher and a writer is seriously damaged.

Obviously, you want to draft a strong, well-documented paper—a credible discussion of your carefully researched topic. But ethical research goes further. It goes beyond avoiding plagiarism to treating sources fairly and representing them accurately. It aims to counter misinformation and misunderstanding, or at least to do no harm by not adding to them.

This chapter will help you cultivate ethical research habits. While it will help you understand and avoid plagiarism, it first teaches you to write a literature review that treats sources fully and fairly, as well as some essential principles to follow in all your research writing.

 **Learning Objectives**

By working through this chapter, you will be able to

- produce a literature review.
- explain ethical principles to follow in your research writing.
- differentiate between poor and effective uses of sources in your writing.
- recognize plagiarism.
- explain why plagiarism is a serious academic offense.
- prevent plagiarism within your own writing.
- avoid other source abuses in your writing.

**Visually Speaking** Copying—what's wrong with it? Using Figure 21.1 as a starting point, reflect on the nature of copying as an issue in life and in research.

*Jay Clint / Shutterstock.com*

*fig. 21.1*

# Your Project: Writing a Literature Review

The literature review builds on the research proposal and the annotated bibliography by taking the next step: guiding readers through the published studies on your topic. In fact, a research proposal may actually require a full literature review, not simply a working or annotated bibliography. And in a full research paper, you may offer a literature review early in the essay (sometimes called a survey of the literature), before moving into your main discussion.

In such a review, you describe key qualities in each source, but you also synthesize these articles, books, and other documents by doing some or all of the following:

- Pointing out similarities and differences between the sources.
- Noting writers' research strategies, methods, or perspectives.
- Showing connections between the works, including how studies build on each other.
- Identifying traits (such as gaps) in the overall collection of studies.
- Giving readers an overall review of the quality of the source.

As a result, you and your readers gain a valuable overview of the topic, including scholars' treatment of it, the status of these studies, and the questions or issues needing more study.

Writing a literature review, then, offers you excellent practice at treating sources carefully, fully, and fairly—in short, ethically.

## Guidelines for Writing a Literature Review

You start by narrowing your topic and using the research strategies outlined in the previous two chapters. Then follow these steps:

**Select the studies for your review:** Choose promising studies and preview their contents by doing the following:

- Reading the titles, headings, abstracts, openings, and closings, and by scanning the rest.
- Assessing which studies would together show the span of research on your topic.
- Looking for elements that will help you distinguish the studies, organize your presentation of them, and unify the paper.
- Choosing the number of studies needed to address your topic and to fulfill your assignment.

**Choose your focus:** Based on your assignment and writing purpose, decide how to approach your topic. Are you expected to look at the theories at work, the methods used, the purposes, and/or the history of research on the topic? Or is your review mainly about understanding the topic? Knowing the focus will guide you forward.

**Read and analyze the studies:** Read each study carefully, noting its date, research site, and participants, along with the writer's description of the topic, initial hypothesis, research methods and procedures, and ultimate findings. Focus especially on qualities cited in your assignment. Compare and contrast these elements to assess how the studies are related.

**Develop a thesis:** What's your core observation about these studies? What do they reveal about the topic, the research on it, and your specific focus? That's your thesis.

**Organize and draft your review:** Most literature reviews have these parts:
- **Opening:** Introduce the topic and cite the literature on it to indicate the purpose of your review. Offer your thesis about the studies.
- **Middle:** Briefly describe each study, especially its experiments, methodology, findings, and impact on current thinking about the topic. Cite details and quotations as needed, but mainly summarize the research. Describe what distinguishes studies from each other, and analyze strengths and weaknesses. If helpful, group similar types of studies thematically, or order studies chronologically.
- **Closing:** Briefly re-state your thesis, note unanswered questions, and recommend issues needing further research. List the reviewed literature in a bibliography.

## Sample Literature Review

Student writer Kadee Rowe completed the following literature review using APA documentation as part of a research proposal for a sociology class. The proposal and its literature review led to a larger project in which Kadee studied the lives of Haitian women.

---

**Assertiveness Use and Abuse Experience of Haitian Women:**
**A Literature Review**

In recent decades, movements aiming to empower women and to reduce the levels of abuse women are experiencing have grown in popularity. While many issues still exist, women within North America have gained a legally equal status to that of men and have obtained more power and influence in regards to ensuring their rights are met. However, global studies show that the abuse of women is still largely accepted and practiced within many cultures (Cohen, 2006, p. 261; Gage & Hutchinson, 2006). One way to address abuse is by empowering women through the provision of assertiveness training programs. While it is theoretically likely that assisting women in assertively recognizing and fighting against abuse will successfully reduce the levels of abuse they are subject to, minimal research has been performed on the topic and results have been inconclusive thus far.

The following literature review will evaluate some of the studies completed to determine the effectiveness of assertiveness training, ways to provide culturally competent practice, and the way in which both of those factors interact with the abuse experiences of women. Within North America, studies have found that assertiveness training programs are an effective way to reduce the levels of abuse experienced by women (Ellis & Nichols, 1979; Jansen & Myers-Abell, 1981; Simpson Rowe, Jouriles,

McDonald, Platt & Gomez, 2012). Early research on the provision of assertiveness training for physically abused women demonstrated through self-reports that participants implemented behavior changes and felt the program was beneficial in assisting with their life situations (Jansen & Myers-Abell, 1981, p. 165). Many years later, Simpson Rowe et al. (2012) also determined that women who participated in their Dating Assertiveness Training Experience program were at a lower risk for sexual victimization. They also found that women who had received the assertiveness training were more likely to respond assertively when experiencing victimization. However, risk for victimization did not decline for women who had been sexually victimized prior to participation in the assertiveness training (Simpson Rowe et al., 2012, p. 216). This suggests that assertiveness training may be more beneficial at reducing rates of abuse if provided to girls/women at a young age in order to decrease the risk of initial victimization. A major limitation of this study is that the sample consisted of mostly university women pursuing psychology majors at a private college. The study also took place in the USA and no details on the ethnicity of participants were provided (Simpson Rowe et al., 2012, p. 212). These limitations make it difficult to generalize results to a wider community or determine any cultural impacts. Simpson Rowe et al. (2012) themselves recognized that "attitudes towards assertive behavior and comfort with behaving assertively differ across racial and ethnic groups, so it is unclear if our findings apply to more diverse samples" (p. 217). In addition, the study examined only the impacts of assertiveness on sexual abuse, not accounting for how assertiveness skills may have affected the various other forms of abuse that women often encounter.

Culture is an essential concept to consider when implementing assertiveness programs. Studies specifically relating assertiveness training to abuse levels within diverse cultures are limited (Dwairy, 2004; Wood & Mallinckrodt, 1990). Dwairy (2004) recognized that western individualistic cultures and collective-authoritarian cultures view assertiveness very differently (p. 428). While western cultures are based around the individual's right to expression and freedom of choice, collective-authoritarian cultures often view assertive behavior as rude and selfish. Authoritarian cultures, such as that present within Haiti, value obedience and respect over meeting individual needs (Dwairy, 2004, p. 428).

More studies are available which discuss experiences of abuse for women in diverse cultures (Ahn & Gilbert, 1992; Cohen, 2006; Gage & Hutchinson, 2006). Cohen (2006) discussed the different status of women within developing and developed countries. Cohen (2006) determined that "[e]xploitation and abuse of women, including outright violence, are acceptable in countries where women have an inferior social status by customary or formal laws" (p. 261). Gage and Hutchinson (2006) recognized that one of the struggles of addressing sexual violence within Haiti is the poor judicial system (p. 22). Even if women's rights are formally recognized within laws, the systems are unjust (due to corruptions stemming from normative or customary laws). Research of various cultures has supported conclusions that males are more likely to become aggressive and violent when they believe they are superior to females (Gage & Hutchinson, 2006). Similar to Dwairy (2004), Cohen (2006) recognized that even the women living in developing countries (which are often collective-authoritarian) have accepted women's inferior status and norms of submission. Some women even agreed that violence is acceptable when women disobey male authorities (Cohen, 2006, p. 261). Gage and Hutchinson (2006) found a strong association between "wife's approval of wife beating and the prevalence of sexual violence" (p. 18). Unfortunately, this association alone does not show that helping women recognize that they are being wrongfully abused (which is one of the aims of assertiveness training) will by itself help reduce abuse. In fact, it was Haitian women who approved of wife beating under any circumstance that reported the lowest levels of sexual violence (Gage & Hutchinson, 2006, p. 18). This is likely because they do not recognize abuse as such and therefore do not report it. However, the study also reported that Haitian women who believed violence against wives was only justified in some circumstances did experience higher levels of sexual violence than women who believed use of violence was never justified (Gage & Hutchinson, 2006, p. 21). This finding may provide support for the use of assertiveness training to reduce abuse levels and therefore supports further research on this topic.

Overall, the research done by Cohen (2006) and Gage and Hutchinson (2006) presents inconclusive results as to the potential effects assertiveness training may have on abuse levels in diverse cultural situations. Once again, the research is limited since it only measured experiences of sexual abuse. Many challenges in regards to the research process have also been identified. For example, if women do not recognize abuse, researchers and service providers will experience challenges in recruiting women to participate within research studies/agency programs. Difficulties in regards to obtaining accurate reports on abuse experiences presents another obstacle.

In his research, Dwairy (2004) recognized that teaching and encouraging minority members (i.e. children and women) of authoritarian cultures to be assertive could actually provoke abuse such as physical punishment (which at times is even fatal) and abandonment (p. 428-431). Again, while a western perspective recognizes these behaviors as explicit forms of abuse, those within traditional authoritarian cultures may not experience any sense of wrong-doing or guilt when a man physically punishes a woman for opposing him. Ahn and Gilbert (1992) recognized that while it is essential that social workers are aware of and respectful towards the cultural beliefs of clients in respect to definitions of abuse, it is also important to recognize that "to observe that cultural differences exist is not necessarily a justification for accepting all sorts of behavior" (p. 424). When doing research and providing social services, one can neither disqualify the importance of respecting culture, nor accept all cultural norms as just. While it is important to respect culture, abuse is unacceptable no matter if legal or cultural norms forbid or support it. In order to mitigate these risks of abuse, Dwairy (2004) identified the necessity of introducing culturally and situationally appropriate levels of assertiveness and ensuring that individuals receiving the training have appropriate personal strength and familial support to participate (p. 430). However, the challenge is that it is the women who are part of strict authoritarian families (rather than those with familial support) who are most likely being abused and in need of assistance. These are important ethical challenges and considerations to recognize when pursuing further research.

It is worthwhile to note that although Dwairy (2004), Ahn and Gilbert (1992), and Cohen (2006) all produced results that were peer-reviewed, based on reliable cultural knowledge, and in correspondence with the conclusions of other studies, none of them actually empirically tested the effects of assertiveness training on abuse rates in any particular culture. Therefore, further research is necessary to determine the effects of assertiveness training on abuse within authoritarian cultures, and on the extent of and ways to mitigate the ethical risks which exist when providing any type of assertiveness training programs for women who are members of strict traditional cultures and families.

### References

Ahn, H. N., & Gilbert, N. (1992). Cultural diversity and sexual abuse prevention. *Social Service Review, 66*(3), 410-427. https://doi.org/10.1086/603930

Cohen, M. F. (2006). The condition of women in developing and developed countries. *Independent Review, 11*(2), 261. Retrieved August 11, 2020, from www.jstor.org/stable/24562227

Dwairy, M. (2004). Culturally sensitive education: Adapting self-oriented assertiveness training to collective minorities. *Journal Of Social Issues, 60*(2), 423-436. https://doi.org/j.0022-4537.2004.00114.x

Ellis, E. M., & Nichols, M. P. (1979). A comparative study of feminist and traditional group assertiveness training with women. *Psychotherapy: Theory, Research & Practice, 16*(4), 467-474. https://doi.org/0.1037/h0088374

Gage, A. J., & Hutchinson, P. L. (2006). Power, control, and intimate partner sexual violence in Haiti. *Archives Of Sexual Behavior, 35*(1), 11-24. https://doi.org/10.1007/s10508-006-8991-0

Jansen, M. A., & Myers-Abell, J. (1981). Assertive training for battered women: A pilot program. *Social Work, 26*(2), 164-165. https://doi.org/10.1093/sw/26.2.164

Simpson Rowe, L., Jouriles, E. N., McDonald, R., Platt, C. G., & Gomez, G. S. (2012). Enhancing women's resistance to sexual coercion: A randomized controlled trial of the DATE program. *Journal Of American College Health, 60*(3), 211-218. https://doi.org/10.1080/07448481.2011.587068

Wood, P. S., & Mallinckrodt, B. (1990). Culturally sensitive assertiveness training for ethnic minority clients. *Professional Psychology: Research And Practice, 21*(1), 5-11. https://doi.org/10.1037/0735-7028.21.1.5

## Reading for Better Writing

1. *Connections:* Kadee discusses a difficult topic in this review—assertiveness and abuse. Would you describe yourself as assertive? Why or why not? Has your life been touched by abuse in some way? If yes, with what effects?
2. *Comprehension:* What is Kadee's essential theme about the research on assertiveness training and abuse of women? What specific strands in the research lead her to that conclusion?
3. *Writing Moves:*
    a. What does the opening paragraph do to establish the focus of Kadee's review?
    b. As the review unfolds, how does Kadee make it manageable? How does she organize all the information she has? Look specifically at paragraph divisions.
    c. At the sentence level, what style techniques does Kadee use to discuss sources?
    d. What does Kadee do to treat her sources ethically?
    e. How does the last paragraph bring the review to a close?

**Your Project:** Kadee's literature review tackles research on a complex and troubling topic in sociology. Consider your own major. What are complex and troubling topics in your field? What might you learn from a literature review on one of those topics?

# Research Ethics: A Primer

When it comes to the wise and fair treatment of information, we live in complicated times. Consider both your participation in the larger information culture and your specific responsibilities in your research writing.

## Participation in Information Culture

We are all citizens of a larger information culture—a world of stories, news, studies, social media posts, blogs, documentaries, advertising campaigns, politics, and more. What should citizenship look like? We might start with the Golden Rule and how it applies to this world: Do unto others as you would have them do unto you. It begins with respect, tolerance, and neighborliness in the spaces where information gets shared, discussed, and debated.

Consider a difficult and controversial topic such as the COVID-19 pandemic. What would a healthy information culture look like? Here are some principles:

**Seek out, rely on, and share ethically-sourced information:** Learn where information comes from. It's easy to passively rely on social media as a source, as it often feeds us what we want to hear—a lot of it junk-food information. Instead, become a more active information consumer—seeking out trustworthy, respected, ethically-produced sources. These typically come from organizations that have the well-being of individuals and society, as well as advancing knowledge, as part of their mission: government agencies, universities, nonprofits, media entities with high standards and moderate leanings. They're not perfect, but they do what's humanly possible to share information people can count on.

> *Example:* To get reliable information on COVID-19, you would go to a source such as the CDC—the Centers for Disease Control and Prevention, a government agency whose mission is "Saving Lives, Protecting People." Be suspicious of resources such as the video, "Plandemic: The Hidden Agenda Behind COVID-19"—produced by a well-known conspiracy theorist, featuring a discredited scientist from the National Cancer Institute, and spread on social media.

**Avoid misinformation:** Put simply, don't believe it, create it, or share it. Of course, you need to recognize misinformation when you see it. Develop your nose for falsehood, a healthy suspicion, so that you can practice the smell test: Does something seem too good to be true? Too crazy? Too connected to the source's self-interest? Bottom line: Never call a lie the truth, the truth a lie. When you hear phrases such as "That's just your opinion" or "It's all relative" or "These are just alternative facts," don't accept them: While it's sometimes difficult to get at, truth exists. If you need help knowing whether something is misinformation, turn to fact-checking organizations (e.g., FactCheck.org and PolitiFact), as well as reliable sources that might confirm or counter the information in question.

> *Example:* To test the truth-content of the video "Plandemic," a quick Google search will take you to reputable news articles and a Wikipedia entry that explain the falsehoods and errors in the film.

**Resist confirmation bias:** We all want our current beliefs, theories, and understandings to be true. Sometimes, that makes us rush to accept information that confirms them or to reject information that calls them into question. In a sense, we let the tail (our belief) wag the dog (the information). Step back and examine your own motives and desires. We all quite rightly have beliefs and values that guide our thinking, but those beliefs should be open to evidence. Moreover, we should exercise some humility about our beliefs and what we claim to be true: Misguided and aggressive certainty often adds to the polarization of ideas and people.

> *Example:* If we are distrustful of China, we are more likely to accept claims that the Chinese government was behind COVID-19—and that the virus should really be called the CCP (Chinese Communist Party) Virus, even if there's no reliable evidence for this claim.

## Your Research-Writing Responsibilities

When it comes to your specific research projects, the guidelines above apply. In addition, follow the basic advice below, which leads into the discussion of plagiarism and other source abuses in the rest of this chapter.

**Be honest, accurate, and measured:** To the best of your ability, offer a true picture of the facts, a fair analysis of the evidence, and arguments so clear they sound like explanations.

**Show respect to your reader, the topic, and opposing viewpoints:** Here, the Golden Rule applies in the very words you use. While your views on your topic may be strong, you owe your readers and those with perspectives different from yours the basic courtesy of a fair and full treatment of the topic. Especially when your research involves or is about people, often called "human subjects," the standard of respect is high. That respect extends to the use of inclusive language, recommended by both the MLA and the APA. See pages 105–107 for guidelines on fair language.

**Establish your credentials by showing you have done careful research:** Put simply, evidence of extensive research and proper treatment of quality sources within your writing helps readers trust you and your thinking.

**Write the paper yourself:** Take full ownership of your thinking, research, and writing—no outsourcing, ever.

> **INSIGHT** Economically, society includes "haves" and "have nots" (and people in between). The same is true of information: There are those who have plenty of it and the benefits that go with it, and those who have little to none. When you see ways to correct this inequity, promote them. Fight for information democracy in your communities. Everyone deserves access to quality information. Might we call it a human right? Perhaps that could be the subject of a research project.

# Developing Credibility Through Source Use

Your credibility—how fully readers trust and believe you—is partly rooted in how well you treat your sources. While abuses such as distorting a source's ideas damage your credibility, good practices enhance it. Contrast the passages that follow.

## Writing with Poor Use of Sources

A poor paper might read like a recitation of unconnected facts, unsupported opinions, or undigested quotations. It may contain contradictory information or illogical conclusions. A source's ideas may be distorted or taken out of context. At its worst, poor source use involves plagiarism.

> *The writing offers weak generalizations in several spots.*
>
> It goes without saying that cell phone usage has really increased a lot, from the beginning of the cell phone's history until now. How many people still don't have a cell—basically, no one! The advantages of cell phones are obvious, but has anyone really thought about the downside of this technological innovation? For example, there's "rinxiety," where people believe that their cell phones are ringing but they're not. Two-thirds of cell users have reported this feeling, which some experts believe to be a rewiring of the nervous system similar to phantom limb pain, while other experts thinks it's about the pitch of cell rings. It's not good.
>
> *Material from sources is clearly borrowed but not referenced through in-text citation.*
>
> *A passage from an online source is copy-and-pasted into the paper without credit.*
>
> But the most serious problem with cell phones is without a doubt driving while talking or texting. Due to the increasing complexity of mobile phones –often more like mobile computers in their available uses– it has introduced additional difficulties for law enforcement officials in being able to tell one usage from another as drivers use their devices. This is more apparent in those countries who ban both hand-held and hands-free usage, rather than those who have banned hand-held use only, as officials cannot easily tell which function of the mobile phone is being used simply by visually looking at the driver. This can mean that drivers may be stopped for using their device illegally on a phone call, when in fact they were not; instead using the device for a legal purpose such as the phones' incorporated controls for car stereo or satnav usage – either as part of the cars' own device or directly on the mobile phone itself.
>
> *The writer uses a visual without indicating the source or effectively discussing its meaning.*
>
> The question arises, is the cell phone even being used as a phone? And are these other uses legitimate or just gimmicks? This chart makes the point.

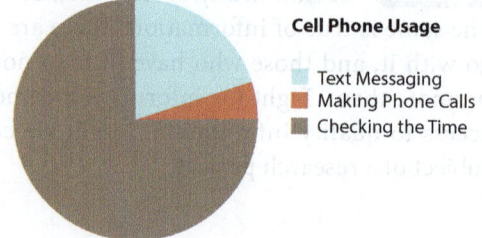

## Writing with Strong Use of Sources

A strong paper centers on the writer's ideas—ideas advanced through thoughtful engagement with and crediting of sources. It offers logical analysis or a persuasive argument built on reliable information from quality sources that have been treated with intellectual respect. Note these features at work in the excerpt below from student writer Brandon Jorritsma's essay on cell-phone dependency.

> *Facts and ideas are credited through in-text citations, which are linked to full source information on a works-cited page.*
>
> *The writer builds on and reasons with source material.*
>
> *Direct quotations from sources are indicated with quotation marks.*
>
> *A case study from a source makes a concept concrete through cause-effect reasoning.*

This dependency on cells is reflected in the phenomenon that has come to be termed "rinxiety." Frequent cell phone users are reporting numerous instances of either hearing their phones ring or feeling them vibrate, even if their phones are not around. Two thirds of cell phone users in a recent survey report having experienced this phenomenon ("Phantom Ringing"), which is thought by some to be a rewiring of the nervous system similar to phantom limb pain (Lynch). Others theorize that rinxiety is a result of the pitch of typical cell rings being similar to elements of commonplace sounds, such as running water, music, traffic, and television (Lynch, Goodman). Regardless of the particular explanation, the experience of rinxiety is more common among young, frequent users of cell phones, which seems to indicate a constant expectation of calls ("Phantom Ringing"). This expectation is damaging to relationships because someone expecting a phone call, email, or text to arrive at any moment is not mentally present in other interactions they may be involved in. We've all experienced being around someone who was waiting for a phone call. How much more distracted would that person be if they subconsciously expected a phone call every hour of the day?

The corollary of constantly expecting incoming cell communication is the constant impulse to send out messages. Fifty-two percent of respondents to an informal survey at CSU, Fresno, admitted to being "preoccupied with the next time they could text message," and forty-six percent of students "reported irritability when unable to use their cell phones" (Lui). In a study of an international sample of cell phone users, some respondents recounted how they felt anxiety if they forgot to take their phone out of the house with them (Jarvenpaa 12). Even when the phone was not anywhere near them, they couldn't escape its demands on their attention. The phone has transformed from being an object of utility to being one of psychological necessity, which constantly demands attention from its user regardless of its proximity or restrictions on its use. Lauren Hawn, a student at Pennsylvania State University, reports that when she is near her cell, she does the following: "I seem to look at it a lot and check the time [on the phone's digital display] even when I don't need to" (qtd. in Lynch). Hawn does not consciously think that there is a phone call or text message . . . .

"Weak Signals: How Cellular Phones Inhibit Communication" by Brandon Jorritsma. Reprinted by permission of the author.

# Recognizing Plagiarism

The road to plagiarism may be paved with the best intentions—or the worst. Either way, the result is still a serious academic offense. As you write your research paper, do everything you can to stay off that road! Start by studying your school's and your instructor's guidelines on plagiarism and other academic offenses. Then study the following pages.

## What Is Plagiarism?

Plagiarism is using someone else's words, ideas, or images (what's called intellectual property) so they appear to be your own. When you plagiarize, you use source material—whether published in print or online—without acknowledging the source. In this sense, plagiarism refers to a range of thefts:

- Submitting a paper you didn't write yourself.
- Pasting large chunks of a source into your paper and passing it off as your own work.
- Using summaries, paraphrases, or quotations without documentation.
- Using the exact phrasing of a source without quotation marks.
- Mixing up source material and your own ideas—failing to distinguish between the two.

 Plagiarism refers to more than "word theft." Because plagiarism is really about failing to credit ideas and information, the rules also apply to visual images, tables, graphs, charts, maps, music, videos, and so on.

## What Does Plagiarism Look Like?

Plagiarism refers to a range of source abuses. What exactly do these violations look like? Read the passage below, and then review the five types of plagiarism that follow, noting how each example misuses the source.

> The passage below is from page 87 of "Some Stories Have to Be Told by Me: A Literary History of Alice Munro," by Marcela Valdes, published in the *Virginia Quarterly Review*, vol. 82, no. 3, 2006.
>
> What makes Munro's characters so enthralling is their inconsistency; like real people, at one moment they declare they will cover the house in new siding, at the next, they vomit on their way to the hospital. They fight against and seek refuge in the people they love. The technique that Munro has forged to get at such contradictions is a sort of pointillism, the setting of one bright scene against another, with little regard for chronology.

## Submitting Another Writer's Paper

The most blatant plagiarism is taking an entire piece of writing and claiming it as your own work. Examples:

- Downloading, reformatting, and submitting an article as your own work
- Buying a paper from a "paper mill" or taking a "free" paper off the Internet
- Turning in another student's work as your own (also known as "Falstaffing")

## Using Copy and Paste

It is unethical to take chunks of material from another source and splice them into your paper without acknowledgment. In the example below, the writer pastes in a sentence from the original article (boldfaced red text) without using quotation marks or a citation. Even if the writer changed some words, it would still be plagiarism.

> Life typically unfolds mysteriously for Munro's characters, with unexplained events and choices. **Like real people, at one moment they declare they will cover the house in new siding, at the next, they vomit on their way to the hospital.**

*Note:* Highlighting or color-coding source information that you copy and paste in an early draft will remind you to return to and revise it ethically.

## Failing to Cite a Source

Borrowed material must be documented. Even if you use information accurately and fairly, don't neglect to cite the source. Below, the writer correctly summarizes the passage's idea but offers no citation.

> For the reader, the characters in Munro's stories are interesting because they are so changeable. Munro shows these changes by using a method of placing scenes side by side for contrast, without worrying about the chronological connections.

## Neglecting Necessary Quotation Marks

Whether it's a paragraph or a phrase, if you use the exact wording of a source, that material must be enclosed in quotation marks. In the example below, the writer cites the source but doesn't use quotation marks around a phrase taken from the original (boldfaced red text).

> What makes Munro's characters so typically human is that they **fight against and seek refuge in the people they love** (Valdes 87).

## Confusing Borrowed Material with Your Own Ideas

Through carelessness (often in note taking), you may confuse source material with your own thinking. Below, the writer indicates that he borrowed material in the first sentence, but fails to indicate that he also borrowed the next sentence.

> As Marcela Valdes explains, "[w]hat makes Munro's characters so enthralling is their inconsistency" (87). **To achieve this sense of inconsistency, Munro places brightly lit scenes beside each other in a kind of pointillist technique.**

 Just as it's easy to plagiarize using the Internet, it's also easy for your professors to recognize and track down plagiarism using Internet tools, such as Turnitin.com.

# Understanding Why Plagiarism Is Serious

Perhaps the answer is obvious. But some people operate with the notion that material on the Internet is "free" and, therefore, fairly used in research writing. After all, a lot of stuff on the web doesn't even list an author, so what's the harm? Here's some food for thought:

## Academic Dishonesty

At its heart, plagiarism is cheating—stealing intellectual property and passing it off as one's own work. Colleges take such dishonesty seriously. Plagiarism, whether intentional or unintentional, will likely be punished in one or more ways:

- A failing grade for the assignment
- A failing grade for the course
- A note on your academic transcript (often seen by potential employers) that failure resulted from academic dishonesty
- Expulsion from college

## Theft from the Academic Community

The research paper represents your dialogue with other members of the academic community—classmates, the instructor, others in your major, others who have researched the topics, and so on. When you plagiarize, you short-circuit the dialogue:

- You gain an unfair advantage over your classmates who follow the rules and earn their grades.
- You disrespect other writers, researchers, and scholars.
- You disrespect your readers by passing off others' ideas as your own.
- You insult your instructor, a person whose respect you need.
- You harm your college by risking its reputation and its academic integrity.

## Present and Future Harm

Because research projects help you master course-related concepts and writing skills, plagiarism robs you of an opportunity to learn. Moreover, you rob yourself of your integrity and reputation. After all, as a student you are seeking to build your credibility within the broader academic community, your major, and your future profession.

In addition, research projects often train you for your future work in terms of research, thinking, and writing skills—skills that you will need to succeed in the workplace. If you do not learn the skills now, you will enter the workplace without them—a situation that your employer will, at some point, find out.

 One tool to deter plagiarism is Turnitin.com. Students submit their papers for comparison against millions of web pages and other student papers. Students and instructors get reports about originality and matching text.

# Avoiding Plagiarism

Preventing plagiarism begins the moment you get an assignment. Essentially, prevention requires your commitment and diligence throughout the project. Follow these tips:

1. **Resist temptation.** With the Internet, plagiarism is a mouse click away. Avoid last-minute all-nighters that make you desperate; start research projects early. *Note:* It's better to ask for an extension or accept a penalty for lateness than to plagiarize.

2. **Play by the rules.** Become familiar with your college's definition, guidelines, and policies regarding plagiarism so that you don't unknowingly violate them. When in doubt, ask your instructor for clarification.

3. **Take orderly, accurate notes.** From the start, carefully keep track of source material and distinguish it from your own thinking. Specifically, do the following:
   - Maintain an accurate working bibliography.
   - Adopt an effective note-taking system.
   - Accurately summarize, paraphrase, and quote sources.

4. **Document borrowed material.** Credit information that you have summarized, paraphrased, or quoted from any source, whether that information is statistics, facts, graphics, phrases, or ideas. Readers can then see what's borrowed and what's yours, understand your support, and do their own follow-up research.

   > **Common Knowledge Exception:** Common knowledge is information that is generally known to readers or easily found in several sources, particularly reference works—birth dates, achievements, milestones, etc. For example, *the U.S. entered World War II after the bombing of Pearl Harbor* is widely known. Such knowledge need not be cited. However, when you go beyond common knowledge into research findings, interpretations of the facts, theories, explanations, claims, arguments, and graphics, you must document the source. Study the examples below, but whenever you are in doubt, document.
   >
   > *Examples:*
   > - The fact that automakers are developing hybrid-electric cars is common knowledge, whereas the details of GM's AUTOnomy project are not.
   > - The fact that Shakespeare wrote *Hamlet* is common knowledge, whereas the details of his sources are not.

5. **Work carefully with source material in your paper.** See chapters 22–24 for more on integrating and documenting sources, but here, briefly, are your responsibilities:
   - Distinguish borrowed material from your own thinking by signaling where source material begins and ends.
   - Indicate the source's origin with an attributive phrase and a citation.
   - Provide full source information in a works-cited or references page.

# Avoiding Other Source Abuses

Plagiarism, though the most serious offense, is not the only source abuse to avoid when writing a paper with documented research. Consider these additional pitfalls.

## Sample Source Abuses

### Using Sources Inaccurately

When you get a quotation wrong, botch a summary, paraphrase poorly, or misstate a statistic, you misrepresent the original. In this quotation, the writer carelessly uses several wrong words that change the meaning, as well as adding two words that are not in the original.

> As Marcela Valdes explains, "[w]hat makes Munro's characters so appalling is their consistency.... They fight against and seek refuse in the people they say they love" (87).

### Using Source Material Out of Context

By ripping a statement out of its context and forcing it into yours, you can make a source seem to say something that it didn't really say. This writer uses part of a statement to say the opposite of the original.

> According to Marcela Valdes, while Munro's characters are interesting, Munro's weakness as a fiction writer is that she shows "little regard for chronology" (87).

### Overusing Source Material

When your paper reads like a string of references, especially quotations, your own thinking disappears. The writer below takes the source passage, chops it up, and splices it together.

> Anyone who has read her stories knows that "[w]hat makes Munro's characters so enthralling is their inconsistency." That is to say, "like real people, at one moment they declare they will cover the house in new siding, at the next, they vomit on their way to the hospital." Moreover, "[t]hey fight against and seek refuge in the people they love." This method "that Munro has forged to get at such contradictions is a sort of pointillism," meaning "the setting of one bright scene against another, with little regard for chronology" (Valdes 87).

### "Plunking" Quotations

When you "plunk" or "drop" quotations into your paper without preparing the reader for them and clearly transitioning out of them, the discussion becomes choppy and disconnected. The writer below interrupts the flow of ideas with a quotation "out of the blue." In addition, the quotation hangs at the end of a paragraph with no follow-up.

> Typically, characters such as Del Jordan, Louisa Doud, and Almeda Roth experience a crisis through contact with particular men. "They fight against and seek refuge in the people they love" (Valdes 87).

### Using "Blanket" Citations

Your reader shouldn't have to guess where borrowed material begins and ends. For example, if you place a parenthetical citation at the end of a paragraph, does that citation cover the whole paragraph or just the final sentence?

### Relying Too Heavily on One Source

If your writing is dominated by one source, readers may doubt the depth and integrity of your research. Instead, your writing should show your reliance on a balanced diversity of sources.

### Failing to Match In-Text Citations to Bibliographic Entries

All in-text citations must clearly refer to accurate entries in the works-cited, references, or endnotes page. Mismatching occurs in the following circumstances:
- An in-text citation refers to a source that is not listed in the bibliography.
- A bibliographic resource is never actually referenced anywhere in the paper.

## Related Academic Offenses

Beyond plagiarism and related source abuses, steer clear of these academic offenses:

**Double-dipping:** When you submit one paper in two different classes or otherwise turn in a paper you have turned in before without permission from both instructors, you take double credit for one project.

**Falstaffing:** This practice refers to a particular type of plagiarism in which one student submits another student's work. Know that you are guilty of Falstaffing if you let another student submit your paper.

**Copyright violations:** When you copy, distribute, and/or post in whole or in part any intellectual property without permission from or payment to the copyright holder, you commit a copyright infringement, especially when you profit from this use. To avoid copyright violations in your research projects, do the following:
- **Observe fair use guidelines:** Quote small portions of a document for limited purposes, such as education or research. Avoid copying large portions for your own gain.
- **Understand what's in the public domain:** You need not obtain permission to copy and use public domain materials—primarily documents created by the government, but also some material posted on the Internet as part of the "copy left" movement.
- **Observe intellectual property and copyright laws:** First, know your college's policies on copying documents. Second, realize that copyright protects the expression of ideas in a range of materials—writings, videos, songs, photographs, drawings, computer software, and so on. Always obtain permission to copy and distribute copyrighted materials.
- **Avoid changing a source** (e.g., a photo) without permission of the creator or copyright holder.

# Practicing Research Ethics: Applications

Now that you have learned strategies to do ethical research, there may be more to consider. Apply your knowledge through the following activities:

1. **Photo Op:** The image on the chapter's opening page focuses on the concept of copying. Consider another key idea in this chapter and find or develop an image that suggests the concept.
2. **Living Today:** In the wider world, what happens when research is shoddy, involves deception, or contains plagiarized material? Research a story of unethical research, misinformation, alternative facts, and/or plagiarism. What were the circumstances, the nature of the offense, and the consequences? Write a literature review of the resources on this story.
3. **Public Texts:** Find three articles on the same topic, articles from different media (e.g., a news source, a magazine, a blog). How does each writer attempt to establish and build credibility? How well does each succeed?
4. **School Policy:** Research your school's academic-integrity policies. How does your school define plagiarism, and how does it address the problem in its policies and procedures? Similarly, explore your school's use or lack of use of Turnitin.com: What role does this program play in academic life where you are?
5. **Major Work:** What does credibility mean in your discipline? What ethical practices for treating sources are emphasized in your major? Research these questions by interviewing professors, examining publications in the field, and studying ethics statements from professional organizations (e.g., MLA, APA).

## Learning-Objectives Checklist ✓

Have you achieved this chapter's learning objectives? Check your progress with the items below, revisiting topics in the chapter as needed. I have . . .

\_\_\_\_ written a literature review that offers a fair and insightful summary of research on my topic.
\_\_\_\_ explained ethical principles to follow in my research writing.
\_\_\_\_ differentiated between writing that uses sources poorly and writing that uses sources effectively.
\_\_\_\_ recognized the various forms that plagiarism might take.
\_\_\_\_ explained the seriousness of plagiarism as a form of academic dishonesty that harms the academic community, as well as my own integrity now and in the future.
\_\_\_\_ prevented plagiarism in my own writing, following strategies that include knowing the difference between material that must be credited and material that is common knowledge.
\_\_\_\_ avoided other source abuses, from inaccurate use of a source to mismatched in-text citations and bibliographic entries, in my writing.
\_\_\_\_ avoided academic offenses such as double dipping, Falstaffing, and copyright violations.

# Chapter 22

# Drafting Research Papers

This is it. You've planned and conducted your research. You've wrestled with your sources to make sense of them, and of what they reveal about your topic. You've explored what it means to research ethically. Now it's time to explore in writing what you've learned—and to share it with readers.

When you write a research paper, you enter a larger conversation about your topic. Because you are seeking to add your voice to the conversation, the paper should center on your own ideas while thoughtfully engaging with the ideas of others.

This chapter explains how to make the shift from researching your topic to writing about it, focuses on effective and conscientious use of sources in your writing, and helps you write a first draft of your paper. So, have all your research notes and materials handy. You'll put them to good use as you walk through the instruction in this chapter.

## Learning Objectives

By working through this chapter, you will be able to

- identify the key qualities of a research paper.
- examine your research findings so as to deepen your thinking on a topic.
- strengthen your working thesis.
- organize your writing with your research findings in mind.
- draft your essay so as to respect, smoothly integrate, and effectively document source material.
- compare and contrast research-writing practices in the humanities and the sciences.

**Visually Speaking** Scales like the one shown in Figure 22.1 weigh and balance things. In what ways does drafting research-based writing involve mental versions of these activities?

vetre / Shutterstock.com

fig. 22.1

# Papers with Documented Research: Quick Guide

To get ready to write a full research paper, you may have written a project proposal (chapter 19), an annotated bibliography (chapter 20), and/or a literature review (chapter 21). That writing has prepared you well to write your research paper. You've been asking questions and looking systematically for answers so as to deepen your understanding of your topic.

The research paper gives you a chance to further explore, discover, and deepen your answers to these questions, and then to share them with readers—whether in the form of an essay, like the ones in Part II of *The College Writer*, or a report, like those you write in natural science and social science courses. In fact, you'll find instruction on both these forms of research writing, a humanities essay and an IMRAD report, in this chapter.

To get there, start with the quick guide below offering you a picture of the research paper, followed by the instruction on reviewing your findings, organizing your paper, and drafting it while integrating source material effectively.

- **Starting Point:** Your assignment usually relates to a key course concept, so consider what your instructor wants you to learn and how your project will be evaluated. As you plan your paper, look for an angle that makes the writing relevant for you.

- **Purpose:** The project requires you to show the results of your research. Your main goal is to discover the complex truth about a topic and clarify that discovery for others in an informative and compelling way.

- **Form:** The traditional research paper is a fairly long essay (5 to 15 pages) complete with a thesis, supporting paragraphs, integrated sources, and careful documentation. However, you may be asked to shape your research into a field report, a presentation, or a multimodal project.

- **Audience:** Traditionally, research writing addresses "the academic community," a group made up mainly of instructors and students. However, your actual audience may be more specific: addicted smokers, all Floridians, fellow immigrants, and so on.

- **Voice:** The tone is usually formal or semiformal, but check your instructor's expectations. In any research writing, maintain a thoughtful, confidently measured tone. After all, your research has made you somewhat of an authority on the topic.

- **Point of View:** Generally, research writers avoid the pronouns "I" and "you" in an effort to remain properly objective and academic sounding. Unfortunately, this practice can result in an overuse of both the pronoun "one" and the passive voice. Some instructors encourage students to connect research with experience, meaning that you may use the pronouns "I" and "you" occasionally. Be careful, however, to keep the focus where it belongs—on the topic. Bottom line: Follow your instructor's requirements concerning pronoun use.

**INSIGHT** The best research writing centers on your ideas—ideas you develop through thoughtful engagement with sources. In poor research papers, the sources dominate, and the writer's perspective disappears.

# Reviewing Your Findings

To transition from research to writing, from exploring your topic to sharing discoveries, take time to review your findings. Going over your notes will stimulate both your thinking and your planning. What have you found? Helpful background? Principles, theories, and expert reasoning? Examples and case studies? Concrete facts? Consider all this as you use the strategies below.

## Deepen Your Thinking on the Topic

During note-taking, you focused on making sense of what individual sources said about your topic. Now, take these steps to deepen and expand your thinking:

- **Identify key discoveries.** What central ideas and new facts have you learned through research? What conclusions have you reached, and why?
- **Identify connections between sources.** How are your sources related to each other? Do they share similar points of view and similar conclusions? Do some sources build on other sources? Which one was published first, second, third, etc.?
- **Identify differences between sources.** In what ways and on what issues do sources disagree? Why? What sense do you make of the differences?
- **Identify limits and gaps.** What issues do your sources not cover? For what questions have you not found answers? How are these gaps important for your project?

## Sharpen Your Working Thesis

Review your working thesis. Given the research that you have completed, does this thesis stand up? It is possible, of course, that your research has led you to a conclusion quite different from your original working thesis. If so, rewrite your thesis accordingly. However, you might also retain your original thesis but strengthen it by using these strategies:

1. **Use richer, clearer terms.** Test your working thesis for vague, broad, or inappropriate terms or concepts. Replace them with terms that have rich meanings, are respected in discussions of your topic, and refine your original thinking.
2. **Introduce qualifying terms where needed.** With qualifying terms such as "normally," "often," and "usually," as well as with phrases that limit the reach of your thesis, you are paradoxically strengthening your thesis by making it more reasonable.
3. **Stress your idea through opposition.** You can deepen your working thesis by adding an opposing thought (usually phrased in a dependent clause).

   > **Original Working Thesis:** In Alice Munro's "An Ounce of Cure," infatuation messes with the narrator's head so her life gets turned upside down.
   >
   > **Revised Working Thesis:** While Alice Munro's "An Ounce of Cure" tells a simple story of infatuation leading to confusion and trouble, the story is more importantly about the "plots of life"—the ways in which the narrator experiences life as a competing set of stories (romance, fairy tale, farce), none of which does justice to the complexity of real life.

# Considering Methods of Organization

Before drafting, explore which methods of organization would work well for your paper. For help, see chapter 4, "Planning Your Piece." The discussion on this page and the next will help you make choices, but start by avoiding these simplistic patterns:

- The five-paragraph essay: Popularly known as the high school hamburger, this structure is too basic and limiting for most college research papers.
- Information regurgitation: Generally, college-level research requires analytical thinking about information, not just the presentation of data.
- A series of source summaries: Your paper should not be structured simply as a summary of one source after another.

## Organizational Practices That Consider Sources

Because the writing you are doing is research based, you want to factor your sources into your thinking about organization. Here are some ideas that may work with your project.

### Consider Where to Position Primary and Secondary Sources

Different writing projects require different approaches to using, balancing, and integrating primary and secondary sources. Where and how should you work in primary sources—interview material, survey data, textual analysis, observation results? Where and how should you bring in secondary sources—scholarly books, journal articles, and the like? ***Example:*** In a literary analysis, you may rely on primary textual analysis of a novel throughout your paper but support that analysis with secondary-source information from biographical research.

### Order Your Writing Around Key Sources

While you shouldn't organize your whole paper as a series of source summaries, sometimes your writing can take direction specifically from source material. Consider these options:

- **Make one of your key points a response to a specific source.** Did a particular source stand out as especially supportive of or especially contrary to your own thinking? Shape part of your paper as an affirmation or rebuttal of the source.
- **Structure your paper around a dialogue with sources.** Do your sources offer multiple, divergent, or even contradictory perspectives on your topic? If they do, consider organizing your paper around a dialogue with these sources.

### Map Out Relationships Between Sources and Ideas

Having reviewed your findings and sharpened your working thesis, consider how your sources support that thesis. To visualize your options, create a diagram, map, or flowchart that shows where particular sources speak to particular points.

### Put Your Discussion in Context

Often, the early part of your paper will involve establishing a context for exploring your topic. Consider, then, tapping your sources to present necessary background, explain key terms, describe the big picture, or establish a theoretical framework for your discussion.

## Traditional Organizational Patterns

Organizing your paper into an opening, middle, and closing can involve a variety of strategies. The traditional patterns below offer sound methods for developing your thinking. Each choice offers a basic structure for your paper, but several patterns may be useful within your paper's body. As indicated, full instruction for many of these patterns can be found elsewhere in this book.

- **Analysis** clarifies how something works by breaking the object or phenomenon into parts or phases and then showing how they work together. See chapters 11–15.

- **Argumentation** asserts and supports a main claim with supporting claims, logical reasoning about each claim, and concrete evidence to back up the reasoning. This pattern also includes acknowledging and countering any opposition, as well as reasserting the main claim (perhaps in a modified form). See chapters 17 and 18.

- **Cause-effect** can (1) explore the factors that led to an event or phenomenon, (2) explore the consequences of an event or phenomenon, or (3) do both. See chapter 15.

- **Chronological order** arranges items in a temporal sequence (order of events, steps in a process).

- **Classification** places items within categories. Each category is characterized by what the items share with each other and by what makes them different from items in the other categories. See chapter 12.

- **Comparison-contrast** examines two or more items for similarities, differences, or both. Such a study typically holds the items side by side, comparing or contrasting traits point by point. See chapter 14.

- **Definition** clarifies a term's meaning through appropriate strategies: explaining the term's origin and history, offering examples and illustrations, elaborating key concepts at the heart of the term, and so on. See chapter 11.

- **Description** orders details in terms of spatial relationships, sounds, components, color, form, texture, and so on.

- **Evaluation** measures the strength or quality of something against particular standards, standards that are already accepted or that are established prior to the evaluation.

- **Order of importance** arranges items from most to least important, or least to most.

- **Partitioning** breaks down an object, a space, or a location into ordered parts, or a process into steps or phases.

- **Problem-solution** describes a problem, explores its causes and effects, surveys possible solutions, proposes the best one, and defends it as desirable and doable. This pattern may also involve explaining how to implement the solution. See chapters 17 and 18.

- **Question-answer** moves back and forth from questions to answers in a sequence that logically clarifies a topic.

# Considering Drafting Strategies

With research writing, developing the first draft involves exploring your own thinking in relation to the ideas and information that you have discovered through research. Your goal is to develop and support your ideas—referring to and properly crediting sources, but not being dominated by them. Such drafting requires both creativity and care: the creativity to see connections and to trace lines of thinking, and the care to respect ideas and information that you are borrowing from sources. Consider the tips below.

## Choose a Drafting Method

Before starting your draft, choose a drafting method that makes sense for your project (its complexity, formality, etc.) and your writing style. Here are two options:

### Writing Systematically

1. Develop a detailed outline, including supporting evidence.
2. Arrange all your research notes in the precise order of your outline.
3. Write methodically, following your thesis, outline, and notes. However, be open to taking your writing in an interesting direction and modifying your outline as you write.
4. Cite sources as you draft.

### Writing Freely

1. Review your working thesis and notes. Then set them aside.
2. If you need to, jot down a brief outline or basic list.
3. Write away—get all your research-based thinking down without stressing about details and flow.
4. Going back to your notes, develop your draft further and carefully integrate and cite research material.

## Respect Your Sources While Drafting

Research writing involves handling your sources with care, including during the first draft. While drafting, try to have source material at your fingertips so that you can integrate summaries, paraphrases, and quotations without disrupting the flow and energy of your drafting. Moreover, take care not to overwhelm your draft with source material. As you draft, keep the focus on your own ideas:

- **Avoid strings of references and chunks of source material** without your discussion, explanation, or interpretation in between.
- **Don't offer entire paragraphs of material from a source** (whether paraphrased or quoted) with a single in-text citation at the end: when you do so, your thinking disappears.
- **Be careful not to overload your draft with complex information** and dense data lacking explanation.
- **Resist the urge to copy-and-paste big chunks from sources.** Even if you document the sources, your paper will quickly become a patchwork of source material with a few stitches (your slim contribution) holding the paper together.

## Reason with the Evidence

Your paper presents the weight of your research findings in the light of your best thinking. Here you support your thesis with a line of reasoning that is carefully thought out and backed up by evidence. That line of reasoning is typically carried by well-developed paragraphs. A typical body paragraph starts with a topic sentence that makes a point in support of your thesis, then elaborates that point with careful reasoning and detailed evidence, and finishes with a concluding sentence that reiterates and advances the idea. For more on paragraphing, see chapter 5.

**Sample Body Paragraph Showing Reasoning with Evidence:**

**Topic Sentence:** idea elaborating and supporting thesis

**Development of idea through reasoning**

**Support of idea through reference to evidence from source material**

**Concluding statement of idea**

> Finally, Fairtrade consumers can misjudge producers. Whereas Fairtrade has been rightly criticized for inadvertently spreading a sort of neo-colonial attitude, consider, for instance, the problem of quality control that was explored earlier: that Fairtrade does not press producers to develop high-quality products. "Companies such as Green & Black's," on the other hand, "say they aid farmers more by helping them to improve quality and go organic rather than just guaranteeing a price" (Beattie 34). The Fairtrade model ensures that producers will never be able to grow beyond the need for a fixed minimum, while alternate models seek to empower producers. It is not hard to see which paradigm is rife with paternalistic, colonialist implications. Getting consumers in the right frame of mind is not an irrelevant need. As Ian Hussey puts it, "decolonization is not just a material process, but also a mental one" (17). Fair trade, he says, "serves to reinforce racist and colonial distinctions between the poor Global South farmer and the benevolent Global North consumer" (15). In the long run, this mindset is destructive in that it denigrates Fairtrade producers as charity cases rather than potential partners.

As your writing unfolds, make sure that your thinking is sound. To that end, consider these points:

- **Supporting Ideas:** Your topic sentence is essentially a claim—an idea that explains or argues a point. Clearly and logically tie your claim to your thesis.
- **Reasons:** These sentences develop and deepen the claim in the topic sentence. However, reasoning also functions to explain the evidence when you present it. Just remember that the evidence does not generally speak for itself: You will likely have to introduce it to your reader, who is seeing it for the first time.
- **Evidence:** This material is foundational to your thinking—the facts, statistics, quotations, artifacts, illustrations, case studies, and more that you have gathered through research. Always choose evidence that clarifies and convinces, and aim for providing a level of detail that makes your discussion concrete, clear, and convincing.

## Using Source Material in Your Writing

After you've found good sources and taken good notes on them, you want to use that research effectively in your writing. Specifically, you want to show (1) what information you are borrowing and (2) where you got it. By doing so, you create credibility. This section shows you how to develop credibility by integrating and documenting sources so as to avoid plagiarism and other abuses (see chapter 21). *Note:* For a full treatment of documentation, see chapter 23 (MLA) and chapter 24 (APA).

### Integrate Source Material Carefully

Source material—whether a summary, a paraphrase, or a quotation—should be integrated smoothly into your discussion. Follow these strategies:

#### The Right Reasons

Focus on what you want to say, not on all the source material you've collected. Use sources to do the following:

- **Deepen and develop your point** with the reasoning offered by a source.
- **Support your point and your thinking** about it with evidence—with facts, statistics, details, and so on.
- **Give credibility to your point** with an expert's supporting statement.
- **Bring your point to life** with an example, an observation, a case study, an anecdote, or an illustration.
- **Address a counterargument** or an alternative.

#### Quotation Restraint

In most research documents, restrict your quoting to nuggets:

- **Key statements by authorities** (e.g., the main point that a respected Shakespeare scholar makes about the role of Ophelia in *Hamlet*)
- **Well-phrased claims and conclusions** (e.g., a powerful conclusion by an ethicist about the problem with the media's coverage of cloning debates and technological developments)
- **Passages where careful word-by-word analysis and interpretation** are important to your argument (e.g., an excerpt from a speech made by a politician about the International Space Station—a passage that requires a careful analysis for the between-the-lines message)

Quotations, especially long ones, must pull their weight, so generally paraphrase or summarize source material instead.

> **Primary Document Exception:** When a primary text (a novel, a piece of legislation, a speech) is a key piece of evidence or the actual focus of your project, careful analysis of quoted excerpts is required.

## Smooth Integration

When you use quotations, work them into your writing as smoothly as possible. To do so, you need to pay attention to style, punctuation, and syntax.

Use enough of the quotation to make your point without changing the meaning of the original. Use quotation marks around key phrases taken from the source.

> Ogden, Williams, and Larson also conclude that the hydrogen fuel-cell vehicle is "a strong candidate for becoming the Car of the Future," given the trend toward "tighter environmental constraints" and the "intense efforts underway" by automakers to develop commercially viable versions of such vehicles (25).

Integrate all sources thoughtfully. Fold source material into your discussion by relating it to your own thinking. Let your ideas guide the way, not your sources, by using this pattern:

1. **State and explain your idea,** creating a context for the source.
2. **Identify and introduce the source,** linking it to your discussion.
3. **Summarize, paraphrase, or quote the source,** providing a citation in an appropriate spot.
4. **Use the source by explaining, expanding, or refuting it.**
5. **When appropriate, refer back to a source** to further develop the ideas it contains.

**Sample Passage:** Note the integration of sources in the following paragraph.

| | |
|---|---|
| Writer's ideas | The motivation and urgency to create and improve hybrid-electric technology comes from a range of complex forces. Some of these forces are economic, others environmental, and still others social. |
| Attributive phrase | In "Societal Lifestyle Costs of Cars with Alternative Fuels/Engines," Joan Ogden, Robert Williams, and Eric Larson argue |
| Paraphrase, quotation, or summary | that "[c]ontinued reliance on current transportation fuels and technologies poses serious oil supply insecurity, climate change, and urban air pollution risks" |
| Citation | (7). |
| Commentary | Because of the nonrenewable nature of fossil fuels as well as their negative side effects, the transportation industry is confronted with making the most radical changes since the introduction of the internal-combustion automobile more than 100 years ago. |
| Conclusion | Hybrid-electric vehicles are one response to this pressure. |

## Effectively Document Your Sources

Just as you need to integrate source material carefully into your writing, so you must also carefully document where that source material comes from. Readers should recognize which material is yours and which material is not.

### Identify Clearly Where Source Material Begins

Your discussion must offer a smooth transition to source material. Follow these guidelines:

- For first reference to a source, use an attributive statement that indicates some of the following: author's name and credentials, title of the source, nature of the study or research, and helpful background.

  > **Joan Ogden, Robert Williams, and Eric Larson, members of the Princeton Environmental Institute, explain** that modest improvements in energy efficiency and emissions reductions will not be enough over the next century because of anticipated transportation increases (7).

- For subsequent references to a source, use a simplified attributive phrase, such as the author's last name or a shortened version of the title.

  > **Ogden, Williams, and Larson go on to argue** that "[e]ffectively addressing environmental and oil supply concerns will probably require radical changes in automotive engine/fuel technologies" (7).

- In some situations, such as providing straightforward facts, simply skip the attributive phrase. The parenthetical citation supplies sufficient attribution.

  > Various types of transportation are by far the main consumers of oil (three fourths of world oil imports); moreover, these same technologies are responsible for one fourth of all greenhouse gas sources (Ogden, Williams, and Larson 7).

- The verb you use to introduce source material is key. Use fitting verbs, such as those in the table below—verbs indicating that the source informs, analyzes, or argues. Normally, use the present tense. Use the past tense only to stress the "pastness" of a source.

  > In their 2004 study, "Societal Lifecycle Costs of Cars with Alternative Fuels/Engines," Ogden, Williams, and Larson **present** a method for comparing and contrasting alternatives to internal-combustion engines. Earlier, these authors **made** preliminary steps . . .

### Verbs for Signal Phrases

| | | | | |
|---|---|---|---|---|
| accepts | considers | explains | rejects | contrasts |
| contradicts | highlights | reminds | adds | insists |
| identifies | responds | affirms | criticizes | shows |
| shares | argues | declares | interprets | believes |
| asserts | defends | lists | states | describes |
| denies | maintains | stresses | cautions | points out |
| outlines | suggests | claims | disagrees | urges |
| supports | compares | discusses | praises | confirms |
| concludes | emphasizes | proposes | verifies | |
| enumerates | refutes | warns | acknowledges | |

## Indicate Where Source Material Ends

Closing quotation marks and a citation, as shown below, indicate the end of a source quotation. Generally, place the citation immediately after any quotation, paraphrase, or summary. However, you may also place the citation early in the sentence or at the end if the parenthetical note is obviously obtrusive. When you discuss several details from a page in a source, use an attributive phrase at the beginning of your discussion and a single citation at the end.

> As the "Lifestyle Costs" study concludes, when greenhouse gases, air pollution, and oil insecurity are factored into the analysis, alternative-fuel vehicles "offer lower LCCs than typical new cars" (Ogden, Williams, and Larson 25).

## Set Off Longer Quotations

If a quotation is longer than four typed lines, set it off from the main text. Generally, introduce the quotation with a complete sentence and a colon. Indent the quotation a half inch (five spaces) and double-space it, but don't put quotation marks around it. Put the citation outside the final punctuation mark.

> Toward the end of the study, Ogden, Williams, and Larson argue that changes to the fuel-delivery system must be factored into planning:
>
>> In charting a course to the Car of the Future, societal LCC comparisons should be complemented by considerations of fuel infrastructure requirements. Because fuel infrastructure changes are costly, the number of major changes made over time should be minimized. The bifurcated strategy advanced here—of focusing on the H2 FCV for the long term and advanced liquid hydrocarbon-fueled ICEVs and ICE/HEVs for the near term—would reduce the number of such infrastructure changes to one (an eventual shift to H2). (25)

## Mark Changes to Quotations

You may shorten or change a quotation so that it fits smoothly into your sentence—but don't alter the original meaning. Use an ellipsis to indicate that you have omitted words from the original. An ellipsis is three periods with spaces between them (. . .).

> In their projections of where fuel-cell vehicles are heading, Ogden, Williams, and Larson discuss GM's AUTOnomy vehicle, with its "radical redesign of the entire car. . . . In these cars, steering, braking, and other vehicle systems are controlled electronically rather than mechanically" (24).

Use square brackets to indicate a clarification or to change a pronoun or verb tense or to switch around uppercase and lowercase.

> As Ogden, Williams, and Larson explain, "[e]ven if such barriers [the high cost of fuel cells and the lack of an H2 fuel infrastructure] can be overcome, decades would be required before this embryonic technology could make major contributions in reducing the major externalities that characterize today's cars" (25).

To indicate a spelling error or typographical error in the original source, add [sic] immediately after the error.

# Sample Research Paper: A Humanities Essay

The humanities study aspects of human experience, as well as the ideas that grow out of that experience. Student writer Lucas Koomans does that in the humanities essay below: He explores the impact of a new surveillance technology on people's privacy and security. As you read Lucas's essay, explore how it is rooted in research and how he reasons with that research. Note: The sample essay shows source documentation according to the MLA style. However, the paper does not show MLA format rules (heading, margins, spacing, etc.). Those details are addressed in chapter 23.

## Chipping Away at Our Privacy?

Ever since English novelist George Orwell explored possible threats to privacy in his dystopian novel *1984* (published in 1949), many people have responded by condemning advances in technology, particularly in surveillance. However, the dangers with these privacy threats are not the technology itself, but rather what its capabilities are, who controls it, and how it is used. These issues deserve special attention as they relate to *1984*, which describes how people's privacy is threatened when their every movement is monitored and every thought controlled by Big Brother, the representation of government in the novel. This monitoring is accomplished through two-way cameras known as "telescreens" and by "thoughtpolice." Though many examples of privacy breaches are evident in the novel (e.g. encouragement of spying on others), the main concern is Big Brother's use of telescreens and thoughtpolice to destroy citizens' privacy and to maintain control over them. Today, the VeriChip could represent a similar threat to personal privacy. To understand why this surveillance technology might be labeled Orwellian, it's helpful to explore the VeriChip's capabilities, uses, and potential abuses. While misuse of the device could be destructive, effective public policy guidelines and regulations could help ensure that the VeriChip remains a useful technology.

What exactly is the VeriChip? It is a "glass-encapsulated RFID [radio frequency identification] microchip designed for implantation in the human body" (Albrecht

1). Similar in size to a grain of rice, the device "holds an identification number, an electromagnetic coil for transmitting data, and a turning capacitor" (Barnea 1). Importantly, these RFID tags "do not contain an internal source of power, but instead receive transmission power from an interrogating reader"; as a result, they have "short read ranges" of approximately thirty feet (Halamka et al 603). The interrogating reader is a device that activates the information in the chip; at all other times, the chip is passive in that it does not transmit information. Although it is unknown how many people use the VeriChip today, the VeriChip corporation stated in 2007 that "several thousand people throughout the world have been implanted with its product" (Albrecht 1).

    On the positive side, the VeriChip offers many useful services, including "identification of medical patients, physical access control, contactless retail payment, and even the tracing of kidnapping victims" (Halamka et al 1). The VeriChip's main function is to serve as an identification device for human beings. For example, in the healthcare industry, hospitals use this chip to track patients and maintain their medical records. Ann Marburger, Jim Coon, Kevin Fleck, and Treva Kremer explain how areas in the healthcare industry such as trauma centers, nursing homes, and physicians' offices are "main areas where VeriChips [are used]" (5). With patients bearing the VeriChip, doctors and nurses can have access to "implanted medical device identification [and] emergency access to patient-supplied health information" (6). The VeriChip is also useful as an identification device when patients' identities are "difficult to establish," if they happen to be "incapacitated or disoriented" (6). With the VeriChip, doctors and nurses are able to identify patients, access their medical records, and treat individuals effectively. In addition, the VeriChip provides medical personnel enhanced control. For example, in private facilities, it "permits automated identification of individuals and tracking of their movements in buildings" (Halamka et al 2). Lastly, the VeriChip is capable of tracking lost patients at a hospital or even kidnapped victims. In brief, as these examples illustrate, the VeriChip has proven to be what it was originally designed to be—an effective identification device that benefits the bearer by offering their trusted contacts ready access to the user's personal information.

Unfortunately, this ready-access feature also makes the personal information recorded on the VeriChip vulnerable to exploitation. The danger exists if the VeriChip's nature were to shift from identification to authentication. Identification means "the action or process of identifying someone or something"; by contrast, authentication means "the process of determining whether someone or something is, in fact, who or what it is declared to be" (Halamka et al 602). Whereas identification is passive, authentication is active; for that reason, authentication makes users vulnerable to attack and abuse. This danger is illustrated by the story of a man whose thumb was severed by attackers so that they could use it to steal his Mercedes, a car whose starting mechanism required fingerprint recognition (Kent 1). Because the VeriChip as an authentication device would be like a fingerprint, this example indicates one reason that the VeriChip should not be used for authentication purposes: to physically protect the bearers of the chip. Similarly, the user's private information could become more vulnerable if the VeriChip were to become an active rather than a passive device. In addition, if the read range on these chips grows larger than its current distance of roughly thirty feet, the chips' information also becomes less secure. And if people are capable of accessing personal information from VeriChip users, what can be done with such information becomes troubling. The VeriChip itself "contains only a unique 16 digit identification number," something similar to an American's social security number. That number "can be used to look up a record in a database" (Albrecht 1). Abusing that record would begin with sharing it with others, a common privacy concern today, and would expand from there.

For these reasons, use of the VeriChip must be guided by sound policies and regulations. The VeriChip must remain an identification device that receives its power only from "an interrogating reader" (Halamka et al 603). The chip must continue to be designed with no internal source of power and a short reading range. Moreover, the VeriChip must also be equipped with a privacy protection plan (604). Emily Stewart, a policy analyst at the Health Privacy Project, argues that "to protect patient privacy, the devices should reveal only vital medical information, like blood type and allergic reactions, needed for healthcare workers to do their jobs" (qtd. in "FDA Approves" 1). Stewart agrees that to do their jobs, healthcare workers need access to some information from VeriChip bearers; however, such access becomes a concern when other information is accessible and the user's privacy is not protected in the process. In "Microchip Implants for Humans as Unique Identifiers: A Case Study on VeriChip," the authors ask readers to consider what it means for technology "to be embedded beneath the skin in a perfectly healthy human being for the purposes of 'easy' identification" (Michael et al 1). These authors believe that people should consider this question when implanting VeriChips, and when developing policies and regulations for devices such as these.

In *1984*, Orwell still speaks to the modern world by warning humans how privacy is fragile, particularly because of surveillance technology. As a surveillance technology, the VeriChip may seem to be an Orwellian device for Big Brother. However, it was designed to be a technology that benefits humans, and it can remain so if it is used in accordance with its original purpose: to identify people. If the VeriChip is used for authentication, it becomes Orwellian and puts users in danger of having their privacy invaded and their lives threatened. For this reason, designers must develop a privacy-protection plan for the chip to prevent people from exploiting users' privacy. Ensuring that the VeriChip has no internal source of power is a start, but that is not enough to protect VeriChip users from being exploited. More safeguards are needed to keep the VeriChip a beneficial piece of technology.

*"Chipping Away at Our Privacy?" by Lucas Koomans. Reprinted by permission of the author.*

## Works Cited

Albrecht, Katherine. "Microchip Implants: Answers to Frequently Asked Questions." *CASPIAN Consumer Privacy*, 2008, www.antichips.com/faq/.

Barnea, Sivan. "VeriChip." *TechTarget*, contributed by Margaret Rouse, Sept. 2005, internetofthingsagenda.techtarget.com/definition/VeriChip.

"FDA Approves Computer Chip for Humans." *NBC News*, 13 Oct. 2004, nbcnews.com/id/6237364/ns/health-health_care/t/fda-approves-computer-chip-humans/#.V2gnYaIk3T8.

Halamka, J, et al. "The Security Implications of Verichip Cloning." *Journal of the American Medical Informatics Association*, vol. 13, no. 6, 2006, pp. 601-07.

Kent, Jonathan. "Malaysia Car Thieves Steal Finger." *BBC News*, 31 Mar. 2005, news.bbc.co.uk/2/hi/world/asiapacific/4396831.stm.

Marburger, Ann, et al. *VeriChip: Implantable RFID for the Health Industry*, 7 June 2005, docplayer.net/12920605-Verichip-implantable-rfid-for-the-health-industry-ann-marburger-jim-coon-kevin-fleck-treva-kremer.html.

Michael, Katina, et al. "Microchip implants for humans as unique identifiers: a case study on VeriChip." *Conference on Ethics, Technology, and Identity*, edited by N. Manders-Huits, Delft U of Technology, 2008, pp. 81-84.

Orwell, George. *1984*. Plume, 1983.

## Reading for Better Writing

1. *Connections:* How has your own privacy been impacted by technology? In a digital age, how do you maintain your privacy—if at all?
2. *Comprehension:* Summarize the VeriChip's nature, its benefits, its potential dangers, and policies to safeguard its use.
3. *Writing Moves:*
   a. In paragraphs 3 and 4, Lucas seeks to balance the benefits and dangers of the VeriChip. What strategies does he use to present each?
   b. Writers of humanities essays aim to understand more deeply human experience and humanity's place in the world. Where and how does this essay present such big ideas?
   c. Review the essay's sources as listed in the Works Cited, but also as they are referred to and used in the paper itself. What does this review suggest to you about the nature of research in the humanities?

**Your Project:** What other technologies—current or historical—have challenged and changed humanity's sense of itself? Choose a technology, consider its impact on your own life, research it carefully, and write about its effects on humans, past or present.

# Chapter 22 | Drafting Research Papers

# Sample Research Paper: Science IMRAD Report

A common form of research writing in the natural and social sciences is the experiment report, often called the IMRAD report because of its structure: an *introduction* establishing the problem, a *methods* section detailing experimental procedures, a *results* section providing the data, and a *discussion* that interprets the data. This structure is rooted in the scientific method, a procedure by which experiments are set up to test hypotheses about why things happen.

In the report below, student writers Dana Kleckner, Brittany Korver, Nicolette Storm, and Adam Verhoef share the results of an experiment in which they tested a hypothesis about the impact of an invasive plant species, Eastern Red Cedar, on Midwestern native species. Note: The sample essay shows source documentation according to the APA style. However, the paper does not show in detail APA format rules (margins, spacing, etc.). Those details are addressed in chapter 24. Note, as well, that documentation in the natural sciences often follows CSE format. For more information, check councilscienceeditors.org.

## The Effects of the Eastern Red Cedar on Seedlings and Implications for Allelopathy

### Abstract

The Eastern Red Cedar *(Juniperus virginiana)* is an invasive species that threatens native tall-grass prairies in much of the Midwest (Norris et al., 2001). In an effort to learn more about its invasive characteristics, we decided to test for possible allelopathic properties. Allelopathy refers to the growth inhibition of one species by another species releasing toxins from its tissues (Simberloff, 1995). In this study, the germination and survival of black-eyed Susans *(Rudbeckia hirta)* and poppies *(Papaver orientale)* were examined. Seeds were planted in soil gathered from under three eastern red cedar trees at Oak Grove State Park (Northwestern Iowa) and in soil from three non-cedar locations at this park. Germination and survival of the seedlings in controlled conditions were documented over thirty-two days. We found no significant difference between germination and survival proportions of the two seed types between the cedar and non-cedar soil. This led us to conclude that the eastern red cedar does not negatively affect the germination and survival of the selected seed types.

### Introduction

Several factors can give a plant dominance in an area. One of these factors is the production of allelopathic chemicals. Allelopathy is the secretion of chemicals by one plant that suppresses the growth of other nearby plants (Simberloff, 1995).

This phenomenon reduces competition for limited resources. One possible method of allelopathy is the secreting of chemicals through the roots, directly into the soil. The chemicals can also be stored in the leaves, flowers, fruits, and seeds, releasing chemicals into the soil as they decompose (Norris, Blair, & Johnson, 2007). These allelopathic properties are present in several invasive species, such as the Japanese Red Pine (Node et al., 2003).

The object in this experiment was to test for allelopathic capabilities of the eastern red cedar *(Juniperus virginiana)*. The eastern red cedar is a pioneer invader in the Midwest, quickly populating disturbed land (Norris et al., 2001). This invasion is problematic in certain areas of the Midwest, as it often changes the native ecology of the area it invades, namely tall-grass prairies (Norris et al., 2001). In the effort to preserve native ecosystems, a correct understanding of the characteristics of invaders is useful. The knowledge of the allelopathic properties of this species could assist in preservation efforts.

We predicted that eastern red cedars are allelopathic and that the soil around cedar trees would have a negative effect on the germination and lifespan of other plants. We hypothesized that seeds planted in cedar soil would germinate at a lower frequency and have shorter life spans than those planted in non-cedar soil under the same conditions.

## Methods

The experiment took place from March 19 to April 20, 2009, in the Northwestern College biology lab. Our professors collected soil from Oak Grove State Park near Hawarden, Iowa, several months in advance. They gathered soil from three different locations under three different cedars trees and from three nearby non-cedar locations. They placed the soils under sun lamps to dry, and then stored the soil in plastic ziplock bags.

To prepare for this experiment, two rows of evenly spaced holes were drilled into 18 potting trays for drainage. Each tray was labeled with the soil's location number and the soil type (cedar or non-cedar). From each specified location, soil was measured out equally and placed into the trays. In an effort to make the growing conditions realistic, any foreign plant roots, stems, etc. were left in the soil.

Black-eyed Susans *(Rudbeckia hirta)* and poppies *(Papaver orientale)* were chosen because of their equal planting depth and equal time for seed germination. Two rows were planted in each tray with 10 evenly spaced black-eyed Susan seeds on one side and ten evenly spaced poppy seeds on the other side (both were planted according to the directions on the packages).

On March 19, each tray was placed approximately 35cm. under sun lamps that ran on a 12hrs. on/12hrs. off cycle. Each day, the trays were watered and rotated so that they received an equal amount of light and warmth. When a seed germinated, the date and the plant location in the tray were documented. If the plant died, the date of the death was recorded. Any foreign species that grew were left so as not to disturb the soil. On April 20, thirty-two days later, the data were compiled. The number of each species that germinated at each location and the number of days each plant survived were recorded.

Using Microsoft Excel, we first ran ANOVAs to see if there were any significant differences in germination rates among the three cedar soil sites or any significant difference in germination rates among the non-cedar sites. Then we ran paired t-tests on germination for each seed type between the cedar and non-cedar soils. To compare the percentage of surviving seedlings between cedar and non-cedar soils, we ran an ANOVA for each seed type.

**Results**

We found no significant differences related to location in germination of black-eyed Susan seeds (ANOVA: F=2.71, F-crit=5.14, df=8, p-value=0.14) (Fig.1) or poppy seeds (ANOVA: F=0.37, F-crit=5.14, df=8, p-value=0.7) (Fig. 1) among the three cedar sites. We also found that there were no significant differences related to location in the germination of black-eyed Susans (ANOVA: F=1.63, F-crit=5.14, df=8, p-value=0.27) (Fig. 2) or poppies (ANOVA: F=0.31, F-crit=5.14, df=8, p-value=0.74) (Fig. 2) among the three non-cedar sites. Knowing that there were no significant differences in germination among the sites, we condensed the data into four different groups: black-eyed Susan cedar, black-eyed Susan non-cedar, poppy cedar, and poppy non-cedar.

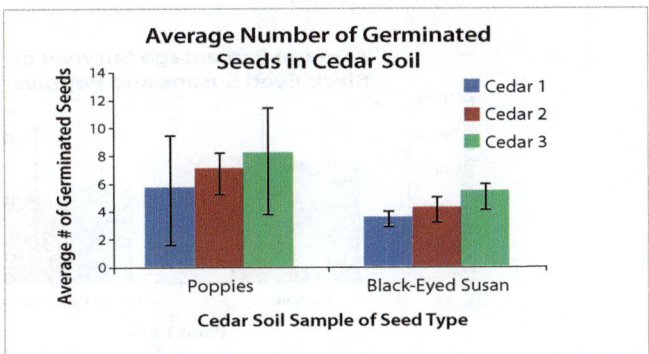

*Figure 1.* There is no significant difference in seed germination among the three cedar soils for poppies (p=.7) or black-eyed Susans (p=.14). Bars represent standard deviation.

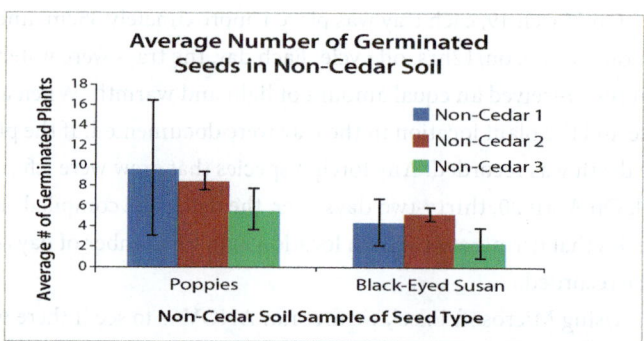

*Figure 2.* There is no significant difference in seed germination among the three non-cedar soils for poppies (p=.74) or black-eyed Susans (p=.27). Bars represent standard deviation.

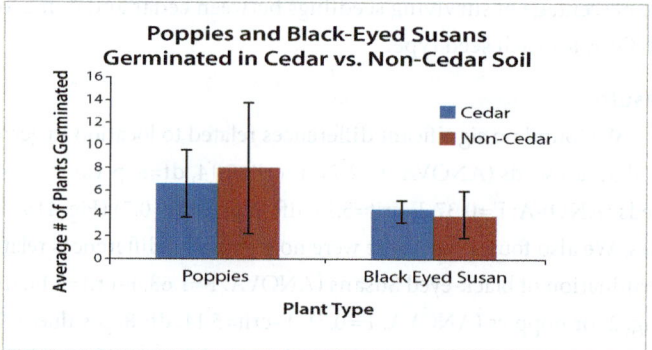

*Figure 3.* There is no significant difference in germination between cedar and non-cedar soil for poppies (p=.48) or black-eyed Susans (p=.77). Bars represent standard deviation.

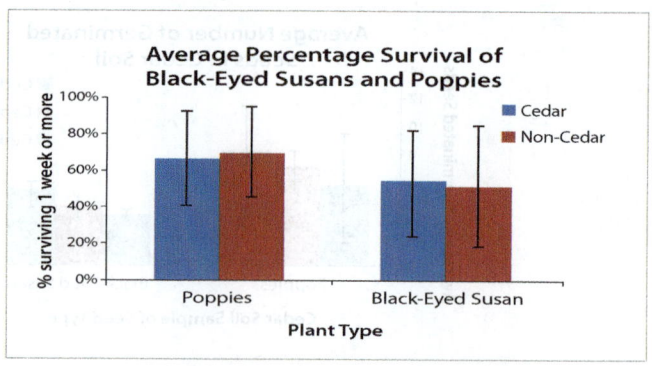

*Figure 4.* There is no significant difference in seedling survival between cedar and non-cedar soil for poppies (p=.82) or black-eyed Susans (p=.92). Bars represent standard deviation.

The two paired t-tests comparing seed germination in cedar soil versus non-cedar soil showed no significant differences in black-eyed Susan germination between the two soil types (t=0.31, p=0.77) (Fig.3) or in poppy germination between the two soil types (t=-0.78, p=0.46) (Fig.3).

When comparing survivorship of the two seedling types in each soil, we defined surviving plants as those that lived for seven days or more. We ran ANOVAs and found that there was no significant difference between the proportion of seedlings that survived in cedar versus non-cedar soil for black-eyed Susans (ANOVA: F=0.01, F-crit=4.49, df=1, p=0.92) (Fig. 4) or for poppies (ANOVA: F=0.06, F-crit=4.49, df=1, p=0.82) (Fig. 4).

## Discussion

In this experiment, we sought to discover whether eastern red cedar soil is allelopathic. We predicted that cedar soil was allelopathic and hypothesized that if our prediction were correct, seeds planted in non-cedar soil would show higher germination and higher survival. We tested for significant differences in soil sites, germination of the two seeds types between soil types, and survival percentages of the seed types between soil types. None of these tests yielded a significant difference.

If the black-eyed Susans and poppies are good representatives of typically affected plants, then eastern red cedar soil appears not to reduce germination or survival. For those concerned with protecting native ecosystems from these invaders, the implications seem positive. An allelopathic invader would produce more damage than a non-allelopathic invader not only in the secretion of chemicals, but also in those chemicals remaining to harm desirable native species even if that invader is removed (Medley & Krisko, 2007).

However, even if cedars do not release allelopathic chemicals, a study conducted in the tall grass prairies of Kansas found that the eastern red cedar increased the amount of above-ground biomass and surface-litter nitrogen pools that are linked to the conversion of grassland to forest (Norris et al., 2007). Though this is not allelopathy, the invasive eastern red cedar still changes the composition of the soil in a manner that could affect the growth of other plants (Norris et al., 2007).

Also, though the cedar soil appeared not to be allelopathic in our study, we are hesitant to make an assessment of the eastern red cedar's affect on other plant types. Several factors may have confounded our non-allelopathic conclusion. The cedar's chemical may simply not be allelopathic to the types of plants we chose (Medley & Krisko, 2007). We purchased the seeds at a local Bomgaars store, and these seeds are domesticated strains. Domesticated strains may be more resistant to allelopathic chemicals and selected for high germination (Node et al., 2003). If allelopathic chemicals are present, the chemicals may have been affected by the storage period and drying process and consequently have a different effect on seedlings (Norris et al., 2001).

Though we doubt that chemicals affected the outcome of our study, we had several slight complications. In one of our planting boxes, more than ten poppies germinated. This was likely due to accidentally planting more than ten of the tiny seeds. In our statistics, we chose to count them all because excessive seeds were likely accidentally planted in other boxes as well. A recording complication occurred when some poppies germinated outside of their row in their container. The species type of some of the small seedlings was hard to distinguish as they were mixed together.

If we repeated this experiment, we would change both materials and methods. We would grow separate seed types in separate containers so there would be no confusion as to the species. We would also be more attentive to the seeds during the planting process, so none would stick together and distort our data. To see if the drying process was a factor, in addition to planting in dried soil, we would plant in freshly gathered soil. Finally, we would use plant species that are actually threatened by possible cedar allelopathy instead of species to which this possibility is irrelevant in real life. A native tall grass may react much differently to cedar soil and would provide more interesting and relevant application.

"The Effects of the Eastern Red Cedar on Seedlings and Implications for Allelopathy" by Dana Kleckner, Brittany Korver, Nicolette Storm, and Adam Verhoef

## References

Medley, K., & Krisko, B. (2007). Physical site conditions and land use history as factors influencing the conservation of regrowth forests in a southwest Ohio nature reserve. *Natural Areas Journal, 27*(1), 31-40. https://doi.org/10.3375/0885-8608(2007)27[31:PSCALU]2.0.CO;2

Node, M., Tomita-Yokotani, K., Suzuki, T., Kosemura, S., Hirata, H., Hirata, K., Nawamaki, T., Yamamura, S., & Hasegawa, K. (2003). Allelopathy of pinecone in Japanese red pine tree *(Pinus densiflora Sieb. et Zucc.). Weed Biology & Management, 3*(2), 111-116. https://doi.org/10.1046/j.1445-6664.2003.00092.x

Norris, M. D., Blair, J.M., Johnson, L. C., & McKane, R. B. (2001). Assessing changes in biomass, productivity, and C and N stores following *Juniperus virginiana* forest expansion into tallgrass prairie. *Canadian Journal of Forest Research, 31*(11), 1940. https://doi.org/10.1139/cjfr-31-11-1940

Norris, M. D., Blair, J. M., & Johnson, L. C. (2007). Altered ecosystem nitrogen dynamics as a consequence of land cover change in tallgrass prairie. *American Midland Naturalist, 158*(2), 432-445. https://doi.org/10.1674/0003-0031

Simberloff, D. (1995). Introduced species. In *Encyclopedia of environmental biology* (pp. 323-336). Academic Press.

## Reading for Better Writing

1. *Connections:* This IMRAD report studies the possible impacts of an invasive species. Where you live or go to school, what invasive species—plant or animal—have impacted the environment? What have those impacts been? Can you sense or imagine how your own experience of this place has been shaped by this invasion?
2. *Comprehension:* The abstract in paragraph 1 summarizes the report. Choose one statement from the abstract and elaborate your understanding of it in more detail.
3. *Writing Moves:*
   a. The IMRAD structure—introduction, methods, results, and discussion—reflects a pattern of scientific thinking. How would you characterize that pattern? What are the key principles behind it and features of it, based upon your reading?
   b. Select any one of the IMRAD parts in the report and study the writing strategies used in that section. What practices do the writers follow? What do those practices accomplish in dealing with the subject matter?

**Your Project:** If you have the time and resources, you might consider conducting an experiment related to an invasive species in your local environment. However, if that is not possible, consider writing a literature review—a survey and synthesis of the scientific studies that have been conducted and published about that invasive species.

# Drafting a Research Paper: Applications

Once you have used the instruction in this chapter to write a research paper, there may be more to think about. Consider these applications:

1. **Photo Op:** The opening of this chapter includes an image of a scale to suggest the weighing and balancing of researched material that goes into drafting research writing. Based on the key concepts covered in this chapter, what other image might capture the head work involved?
2. **Public Texts:** This chapter focuses on deepening your thinking through reflecting on sources and reasoning well with documented evidence. While news stories, web pages from organizations, and speeches by prominent figures are not identical to research papers, we do have expectations that such statements be rooted in sound research. Look closely at a news story, a web page from a nonprofit or business, or a speech by a politician or celebrity: How would you evaluate the use of reasoning and evidence?
3. **Writing Reset:** Review a research paper that you wrote in the past. Does that paper follow the principles for using, integrating, and documenting source material, as outlined in this chapter? How might you improve the treatment of sources in your paper?
4. **Major Work:** Compare and contrast the humanities essay and the IMRAD report from this chapter. What similarities do they share with respect to research and research writing? What differences stand out? What do these similarities and differences suggest about research writing in your own field of study?

## Learning-Objectives Checklist ✓

Have you achieved this chapter's learning objectives? Check your progress with the following items, revisiting topics in the chapter as needed. I have . . .

- ____ identified the key qualities of a research paper.
- ____ carefully examined my research findings so as to deepen my thinking on the topic and imagine my paper.
- ____ strengthened my working thesis in light of my research.
- ____ organized my thinking by considering what I discovered through research, along with traditional methods of organization.
- ____ drafted my paper either systematically or freely, but have focused on respecting my sources and reasoning with the evidence.
- ____ smoothly integrated source material into my writing.
- ____ carefully documented all source material in my paper.
- ____ compared research-writing practices in a humanities essay and a sciences IMRAD report.

# Chapter 23

# MLA Style

In writing research papers, it is commonly said, "You are commanded to borrow but forbidden to steal." To borrow ideas while avoiding plagiarism, you must not only mention the sources you borrow from but also document them completely and accurately. You must follow the documentation principles for papers written in your area of study.

If you are composing a research paper in the humanities, your instructor will most likely require you to follow the conventions established in the style manual of the Modern Language Association (MLA). This chapter provides you with overarching guidelines, detailed explanations, and helpful examples for citing sources in MLA format. You can find MLA guidelines for inclusive language on pages 105–107.

**Visually Speaking** Library shelves organize a vast amount of knowledge (Figure 23.1). In what sense does a system such as MLA style make sense of and order knowledge in research writing?

## Learning Objectives

By working through this chapter, you will be able to

- implement MLA guidelines for documenting sources.
- produce research writing that adheres to MLA guidelines for formatting.
- evaluate MLA practices at work in a sample student research paper.

Amy Johansson / Shutterstock.com

*fig. 23.1*

# MLA Documentation: Quick Guide

The MLA system aims, above all, to make documentation clear and useful to readers. To do so, the system involves two parts: (1) an in-text citation within your paper when you use a source and (2) a matching bibliographic entry at the end of your paper. Note these features:

- **It's minimalist.** In your paper, you provide the least amount of information needed for your reader to identify the source in the works-cited list.
- **It uses signal phrases and parenthetical references** to set off source material from your own thinking and discussion. A signal phrase names the author and places the material in context (e.g., "As Margaret Atwood argues in *Survival*").
- **It's smooth, unobtrusive, flexible, and orderly.** While in-text citations keep the paper readable, alphabetized entries in the works-cited list make locating source details easy. Moreover, instead of requiring writers to follow unique, "correct" formats for several different source types, MLA style offers a basic pattern that researchers can follow, allowing them to make judgements about what to include.

You can see these features at work in the example below. "Anna Hutchens" and "(449)" tell the reader the following things:

- The borrowed material came from a source written by Anna Hutchens.
- The specific material can be found on page 449 of the source.
- Full source details are in the works-cited list under the author's last name.

1. **In-Text Citation in Body of Paper**

   > As Anna Hutchens puts it, there is an "absence of a policy framework and institutional mechanisms that promote women's empowerment as a rights-based rather than a culture-based issue" (449).

2. **Matching Works-Cited Entry at End of Paper**

   > Hutchens, Anna. "Empowering Women Through Fair Trade? Lessons from Asia." *Third World Quarterly*, vol. 31, no. 3, 2010, pp. 449–67. *EBSCOhost*, doi:10.1080/01436597.2010.488477.

## In-Text Citation: The Basics

In MLA, in-text citations typically follow these guidelines:

1. Refer to the author (plus the work's title, if helpful) and a page number (if available) by using one of these methods:

   **Last name and page number in parentheses:**
   — last name only in citation
   > Fair trade is not necessary for consumers to "exercise a moral choice" with their money (Chandler 256).
   — no "p." for "page"
   — no comma between name and page number

   **Name cited in sentence, page number in parentheses:**
   — full name in first reference
   > As Paul Chandler admits, fair trade is not necessary for consumers to "exercise a moral choice" with their money (256).
   — page number only in citation

2. Present and punctuate citations according to these rules:
   - Place the parenthetical reference after the source material.
   - Within the parentheses, normally give the author's last name only.
   - Do not put a comma between the author's last name and the page reference.
   - Cite the page number as a numeral, not a word.
   - Don't use *p.*, *pp.*, or *page(s)* before the page number(s).
   - Place any sentence punctuation after the closed parenthesis.

   **fyi** For many of these rules, exceptions exist. For example, many electronic sources have no stated authors and/or no pagination.

## Works Cited: Nine Core Elements

Essentially, all works-cited entries are built out of nine core elements typically shared across different sources. Here is a sample entry and an overview of the nine elements. Note: not all entries must contain all nine elements. (The example does not include a *version* or *number*.)

[1] Beckerman, Bernard. [2] "The Uses and Management of the Elizabethan Stage." [3] *The Third Globe: Symposium for the Reconstruction of the Globe Playhouse, Wayne State University, 1979,* [4] edited by C. Walter Hodges, S. Schoenbaum, and Leonard Leone, [7] Wayne State UP, [8] 1981, [9] pp. 151–63.

1. **Author:** The person, people, or organization that created the source; or the person whose work on the source you choose to emphasize.
2. **Title of Source:** The full title of the specific source you are using—a whole book, an essay or other text within a book, an article in a periodical or reference work, a specific web page, a film, an episode of a television show, and so on.
3. **Title of Container:** The larger source that contains or holds the source you are using—possibly a book, a journal or magazine, a database, or a website. Note: stand-alone sources have no containers.
4. **Contributors:** People whose contribution may be noteworthy—editors, translators, performers, and so on.
5. **Version:** When there is more than one version of a source (e.g., revised or numbered editions), a description of the version used.
6. **Number:** An indication of how the source fits into a sequence—volume and issue numbers for journals, season and episode numbers for televisions shows.
7. **Publisher:** The organization that produces or sponsors the source, responsible for delivering it—a book publisher, a production company, a website host.
8. **Publication Date:** When the source was made available to the public.
9. **Location:** Where a source was and can be found—page numbers within print sources, DOI (digital object identifier) or URL (uniform resource locator) for online sources, the site for a lecture or performance.

# Guidelines for In-Text Citations

The *MLA Handbook*, Ninth Edition (2021), suggests giving credit for your sources of information in the body of your research paper. One way to do so is by indicating the author and/or title in the text of your essay, and then putting a page reference in parentheses after the summary, paraphrase, or quotation, as needed. The simplest way to do so is to insert the appropriate information (usually the author and page number) in parentheses after the words or ideas taken from the source.

To avoid disrupting your writing, place citations where a pause would naturally occur (usually at the end of a sentence but sometimes within a sentence, before internal punctuation such as a comma or semicolon). These in-text citations (often called "parenthetical references") refer to sources listed on the "Works Cited" page at the end of your paper. Essentially, <u>each in-text citation must clearly point to a source in your works cited, and every source in the works-cited list must be referred to at least once within your paper.</u>

## Citations for Regular Sources

As you integrate citations into your paper, follow the guidelines below, referring to the sample citation as needed.

### Sample In-Text Citation

> As James Cuno, director of the Harvard University Art Museums, points out, the public, which subsidizes museums either directly through donations or indirectly via their status as tax-free nonprofit organizations, expects them to "carry out their duties professionally on its behalf" (164).

- **Make sure each in-text citation clearly points to an entry in your list of works cited.** The identifying information provided (usually the author's last name) must be the word or words by which the entry is alphabetized in that list.

- **Keep citations brief, and integrate them smoothly** into your writing.

- **When paraphrasing or summarizing rather than quoting, make it clear where your borrowing begins and ends.** Use stylistic cues to distinguish the source's thoughts ("Kalmbach points out . . . ," "Some critics argue . . .") from your own ("I believe . . . ," "It seems obvious, however").

- **When using a shortened title of a work, begin with the word by which the work is alphabetized** in your list of works cited (e.g., "Egyptian, Classical," not "Middle Eastern Art," for "Egyptian, Classical, and Middle Eastern Art").

- **For inclusive page numbers larger than ninety-nine, give only the last two digits of the second number** (346–48, not 346–348).

- **When including a parenthetical citation at the end of a sentence, place it <u>before</u> the end punctuation.** (Citations for long, indented quotations are an exception.)

> Historian Kim Christensen cautions that historic house museums often fall into a trap of formulaic, apolitical, and object-centered interpretations of the past (155).

## Citations for Sources Without Traditional Authorship and/or Pagination

Today many sources, especially digital ones, have no stated authors and/or no pagination. For such sources, use these in-text citation strategies:

### Source Without a Stated Author

In a signal phrase or in the parenthetical reference, identify the source as precisely as possible by indicating the sponsoring agency, the type of document, or the title (shortened in the parenthetical reference to the initial phrase).

> While the Brooklyn Museum may be best known for the recent controversy over the Sensation exhibition, the museum does contain a strong collection of contemporary if less controversial art, "ranging from representational to abstract to conceptual" ("Contemporary Art").

### Source with No Pagination

If no pagination exists within the document, use paragraph numbers (with the abbreviation *par.*), if the document provides them. If the document includes neither page nor paragraph numbers, cite the entire work. Do not create your own numbering system.

> The Museum's *Art of the Americas* collection includes extensive holdings of works by the aboriginal peoples of North, Central, and South America, many of these gathered by archaeologist Herbert Spinden during at least seven expeditions between 1929 and 1950 (*Art of the Americas*, par. 3).

Because parenthetical notations are used to signal the end of an attribution, sources with no pagination or paragraph numbers offer a special challenge. When no parenthetical notation is possible, signal a shift back to your own discussion with a source-reflective statement indicating your thinking about the source.

> ... indicated by his recording the audio tour of the exhibit, his supporting the show financially, and his promoting *Sensation* at his website. As Welland's discussion of David Bowie's participation suggests, the controversy over the Brooklyn Museum of Art's *Sensation* exhibit ...

**INSIGHT** Stable pagination for many digital resources is available when you use the ".pdf" rather than the ".html" version of the source. For instruction on smoothly integrating source material into your paper, see chapter 22.

# Sample In-Text Citations

The following entries illustrate the most common in-text citations.

### One Author: A Complete Work

You do not need a parenthetical citation if you identify the author in your text. (See the first entry below.) However, you must give the author's last name in a parenthetical citation if it is not mentioned in the text. (See the second entry.) When a source is listed in your works-cited page with an editor, a translator, a speaker, or an artist instead of the author, use that person's name in your citation.

**With Author in Text:** (This is the preferred way of citing a complete work.)

> In *No Need for Hunger*, Robert Spitzer recommends that the U.S. government develop a new foreign policy to help Third World countries overcome poverty and hunger.

**Without Author in Text:**

> *No Need for Hunger* recommends that the U.S. government develop a new foreign policy to help Third World countries overcome poverty and hunger (Spitzer).

**Note:** Do not offer page numbers when citing complete works, articles in alphabetized encyclopedias, one-page articles, and unpaginated sources.

### One Author: Part of a Work

List the necessary page numbers in parentheses if you borrow words or ideas from a particular source. Leave a space between the author's last name and the page reference. No abbreviation or punctuation is needed.

**With Author in Text:**

> Bullough writes that genetic engineering was dubbed "eugenics" by a cousin of Darwin's, Sir Francis Galton, in 1885 (5).

**Without Author in Text:**

> Genetic engineering was dubbed "eugenics" by a cousin of Darwin's, Sir Francis Galton, in 1885 (Bullough 5).

### A Work by Two Authors

Give the last names of both authors in the same order that they appear in the works-cited section. (The correct order of the authors' names can be found on the title page of the book.)

> Students learned more than a full year's Spanish in ten days using the complete supermemory method (Ostrander and Schroeder 51).

### A Work by Three or More Authors
Give the first author's last name as it appears in the works-cited section followed by *et al.* (meaning "and others").

> Communication on the job is more than talking; it is "inseparable from your total behavior" (Culligan et al. 111).

*Note:* You may instead choose to list all of the authors' last names.

### Two or More Works by the Same Author(s)
In addition to the author's last name(s) and page number(s), include a shortened version of the work's title when you cite two or more works by the same author(s).

**With Author in Text:**

> Wallerstein and Blakeslee claim that divorce creates an enduring identity for children of the marriage (*Unexpected Legacy* 62).

**Without Author in Text:**

> They are intensely lonely despite active social lives (Wallerstein and Blakeslee, *Second Chances* 51).

*Note:* When including both author(s) and title in a parenthetical reference, separate them with a comma, as shown above, but do not put a comma between the title and the page number.

### Works by Authors with the Same Last Name
When citing different sources by authors with the same last name, it is best to use the authors' full names in the text to avoid confusion. However, if circumstances call for parenthetical references, add each author's first initial. If first initials are the same, use each author's full name.

> Some critics think *Titus Andronicus* too abysmally melodramatic to be a work of Shakespeare (A. Parker 73). Others suggest that Shakespeare meant it as black comedy (D. Parker 486).

### A Work Authored by an Agency, a Committee, or an Organization
If a book or other work was created by an organization such as an agency, a committee, a studio, or a task force, it is said to have a corporate author. If the corporate name is long, include it in the text (rather than in parentheses) to avoid disrupting the flow of your writing. After the full name has been used at least once, use a shortened form of the name (including common abbreviations such as *Dept.*) in subsequent references. For example, *Task Force* may be used for *Task Force on Education for Economic Growth*.

> The thesis of the Task Force's report is that economic success depends on our ability to improve large-scale education and training as quickly as possible (113–14).

### An Anonymous Work

When there is no author listed, give the title or a shortened version of the title as it appears in the works-cited section.

> Statistics indicate that drinking water can make up 20 percent of a person's total exposure to lead (*Information* 572).

### Two or More Works Included in One Citation

To cite multiple works within a single parenthetical reference, separate the references with a semicolon.

> In Medieval Europe, Latin translations of the works of Rhazes, a Persian scholar, were a primary source of medical knowledge (Albala 22; Lewis 266).

### A Series of Citations from a Single Work

If no confusion is possible, it is not necessary to name a source repeatedly when making multiple parenthetical references to that source in a single paragraph. If all references are to the same page, identify that page in a parenthetical note after the last reference. If the references are to different pages within the same work, you need identify the work only once, and then use a parenthetical note with page number alone for the subsequent references.

> Domesticating science meant not only spreading scientific knowledge, but also promoting it as a topic of public conversation (Heilbron 2). One way to enhance its charm was by depicting cherubic putti as "angelic research assistants" in book illustrations (5).

### A Work Referred to in Another Work

If you must cite an indirect source—that is, information in a source that is quoted from another source—use the abbreviation *qtd. in* (quoted in) before the indirect source in your reference, unless it is clear from your prose that the source is secondhand.

> Paton improved the conditions in Diepkloof (a prison) by "removing all the more obvious aids to detention. The dormitories [were] open at night: the great barred gate [was] gone" (qtd. in Callan xviii).

### A Work Without Page Numbers or Other Markers

If a work has no page numbers, paragraph numbers, or other markers included, treat it as you would a complete work. This is commonly the case with some digital resources, for example. Do not count pages or paragraphs to create reference numbers of your own.

> Antibiotics become ineffective against such organisms through two natural processes: first, genetic mutation; and second, the subsequent transfer of this mutated genetic material to other organisms (Davies).

## A Work in an Anthology or a Collection

When citing the entirety of a work that is part of an anthology or a collection, if it is identified by author in your list of works cited, treat the citation as you would for any other complete work.

> In "The Canadian Postmodern," Linda Hutcheon offers a clear analysis of the self-reflexive nature of contemporary Canadian fiction.

Similarly, if you are citing particular pages of such a work, follow the directions for citing part of a work.

> According to Hutcheon, "postmodernism seems to designate cultural practices that are fundamentally self-reflexive, in other words, art that is self-consciously artifice" (18).

## An Item from a Reference Work

An entry from a reference work such as an encyclopedia or a dictionary should be cited similarly to a work from an anthology or a collection (see above). For a dictionary definition, include the abbreviation *def.* followed by the particular entry designation.

> This message becomes a juggernaut in the truest sense, a belief that "elicits blind devotion or sacrifice" ("Juggernaut," def. 1).

*Note:* While many such entries are identified only by title (as above), some reference works include an author's name for each entry (as below). Others may identify the entry author by initials, with a list of full names elsewhere in the work.

> The decisions of the International Court of Justice are "based on principles of international law and cannot be appealed" (Pranger).

## A Part of a Multivolume Work

When citing only one volume of a multivolume work, if you identify the volume number in the works-cited list, there is no need to include it in your in-text citation. However, if you cite more than one volume of a work, each in-text reference must identify the appropriate volume. Give the volume number followed by page number, separated by a colon and a space.

> "A human being asleep," says Spengler, ". . . is leading only a plantlike existence" (2: 4).

When citing a whole volume, however, either identify the volume number in parentheses with the abbreviation *vol.* (using a comma to separate it from the author's name) or use the full word *volume* in your text.

> The land of Wisconsin has shaped its many inhabitants more significantly than they ever shaped that land (Stephens, vol. 1).

### A One-Page Work

Cite a one-page work just as you would a complete work.

> As Samantha Adams argues in her editorial, it is time for NASA "to fully reevaluate the possibility of a manned mission to Mars."

### A Sacred Text or Famous Literary Work

Sacred texts and famous literary works are published in many different editions. For that reason, it is helpful to identify sections, parts, chapters, and such instead of or in addition to page numbers. If using page numbers, list them first, followed by a semicolon and then an abbreviation for the type of division and the division number.

> The more important a person's role in society—the more apparent power an individual has—the more that person is a slave to the forces of history (Tolstoy 690; bk. 9, ch. 1).

Books of the Bible and other well-known literary works may be abbreviated, if no confusion is possible. The first reference should indicate the edition being used; subsequent references need supply only the abbreviated citation.

> "A generation goes, and a generation comes, but the earth remains forever" (*The New Oxford Annotated Bible*, Eccles. 1.4).

> As Shakespeare's famous Danish prince observes, "One may smile, and smile, and be a villain" (Ham. 1.5.104).

### Quoting Prose

To cite prose from fiction (novels, short stories), list more than the page number if the work is available in several editions. Give the page reference first, and then add a chapter, section, or book number in abbreviated form after a semicolon.

> In *The House of the Spirits*, Isabel Allende describes Marcos, "dressed in mechanic's overalls, with huge racer's goggles" (13; ch. 1).

When you are quoting any sort of prose that takes more than four typed lines, indent each line of the quotation a half inch (five spaces) and double-space it; do not add quotation marks. In this case, you put the parenthetical citation (the pages and chapter numbers) outside the end punctuation mark of the quotation itself.

> Allende describes the flying machine that Marcos has assembled:
>
> > The contraption lay with its stomach on terra firma, heavy and sluggish and looking more like a wounded duck than like one of those newfangled airplanes they were starting to produce in the United States. There was nothing in its appearance to suggest that it could move, much less take flight across the snowy peaks. (12; ch. 1)

## Quoting Verse

Do not use page numbers when referencing classic verse plays and poems. Instead, cite them by division (act, scene, canto, book, part) and line, using Arabic numerals for the various divisions unless your instructor prefers Roman numerals. Use periods to separate the various numbers.

> In the first act, Hamlet comments, "How weary, stale, flat and unprofitable, / Seem to me all the uses of this world" (1.2.133–34).

*Note:* A slash, with a space on each side, shows where each line of verse ends and a new one begins. If a short poem's lines are numbered in the edition you are using, you may cite the poem using lines only, not page number. Use the word *line* or *lines* in your first reference and numbers only in additional references. If a short poem's lines are not numbered in the edition, simply cite the whole work; do not count lines yourself.

> At the beginning of the sestet in Robert Frost's "Design," the speaker asks this pointed question: "What had that flower to do with being white, / The wayside blue and innocent heal-all?" (lines 9–10).

Verse quotations of more than three lines should be indented one inch and double-spaced. Do not add quotation marks. Each line of the poem or play begins a new line of the quotation; do not run the lines together. If a line or lines of poetry are dropped from the quotation, ellipses that extend the width of the stanza should be used to indicate the omission.

> Bin Ramke's poem "A Little Ovid Late in the Day" tells of reading by the last light of a summer day:
>
> > [T]ales of incest, corruption,
> > any big, mythic vice
> > against the color of the sun,
> > the sweetness of the time of day—
> > I know the story,
> > it is the light I care about. (3–8)

Alina Poronik / Shutterstock.com

# Guidelines for Works-Cited Entries

The works-cited section lists only those sources that you have cited in your paper. For guidelines on formatting your works-cited list, see "MLA Format Guidelines" later in this chapter. In what follows, you will first find a template for works-cited entries, showing the essential pattern to follow. After the template, you will find guidelines for constructing any entry by drawing upon the nine core elements of source identification and arranging those elements in the order listed.

## Works-Cited Template

Every works-cited entry will include some or all of nine elements, formatted and punctuated in the manner indicated.

> Author. Title of Source [normally italicized or in quotation marks]. *Title of Container*, Contributors, Version, Number, Publisher, Publication Date, Location.

## Works-Cited Components

The following table provides you with guidelines for presenting each of the nine main components of works-cited entries. Review both the instructions and examples to understand the logic of each element.

**1. The Author** is the person, people, or organization that created the source. Note that for online sources, pseudonyms and handles may be used. In general, omit titles and degrees from names, but present the name accurately from the source. Follow the author with a period.

- **One author:** Invert the author's name (last name, first name).
- **Two authors:** Follow the order given in the source. Invert the first author's name, but put the second in traditional order. Separate the authors' names with a comma.
- **Three or more authors:** Name only the first author listed, followed by *et al.* (meaning *and others*).
- **Other contributors:** If appropriate, you may put another contributor in this first position to emphasize the focus in your writing: an editor, a director, a performer, and so on. Spell out the role after the name and a comma.

Jacob, Mira.

King, Martin Luther, Jr.

@PiradorUSA.

Environmental Protection Agency.

Pratchett, Terry, and Neil Gaiman.

Raabe, William A., et al.

Dunham, Lena, performer.

**2. The Title of the Source** is the full title of the specific source you are using—a whole book, an essay or other text within a book, an article within a periodical, a specific web page, a film, an episode of a television show, and so on. Typically, titles of longer works and stand-alone works are italicized (see item 28.86 in chapter 28); titles of shorter works and those within longer works are placed within quotation marks (see item 28.74 in chapter 28); untitled sections of a work are neither italicized nor put in quotation marks. Follow standard capitalization practices, and separate a main title and a subtitle with a colon and a space. Conclude the full title with a period.

*Design for How People Learn.*

*Selma.*

"The Yellow Wallpaper."

"The One with Phoebe's Wedding."

Introduction.

**3. The Title of the Container** refers to the name of a larger whole that may contain or hold the specific source you are using. Information about containers is key for readers seeking to understand and/or find your source. The container may be a book containing an essay or short story, a journal or magazine issue containing a specific article, a television series containing an episode, a website containing a specific web page or posting. Sometimes, a container may be nested inside a larger container. For example, an article may be contained in a journal that is itself contained within the database you used to access the article. In this case, your entry would list information for both containers, in order, with as much information from core elements 3-9 as you have for each container. Note that stand-alone sources have no container, so you would not list one in the entry. Italicize the title of a container; normally follow the title with a comma, as the entry supplies more information (elements 4-9) about the container.

*The New Yorker,*

*African American Review,*

*The Concise Anthology of American Literature,*

*Game of Thrones,*

*EBSCOhost,*

*Netflix,*

*ACLS Humanities E-book,*

*Fairtrade International*

Sergey Mironov / Shutterstock.com

**4. Contributors** are those people whose contribution is important to your use of the source or whose identity is valuable information for your readers. Introduce each name that you include in the entry with a description of the role. If a contributor follows element 2 (title of the source, punctuated with a period), capitalize the description; if listed after element 3 (title of container, punctuated with a comma), do not capitalize the description. Separate multiple roles with commas. Note that in scholarly books, editors and translators play important roles and should generally be included in the entry.

. Translated by David McLoghlin,

, adapted by Anne Carson,

. Directed by Mira Nair, performance by Naseeruddin Shah.

**5. The Version** refers to the form of the source you used, when there is more than one version available. Such a version may indicate a revised, expanded, updated, or numbered edition; or it may be a descriptive phrase. Use the abbreviations *ed.* (edition) and *rev.* (revised), but spell out other words; use ordinal numbers with arabic numerals for numbered editions. Write the edition description all lowercase, unless it is a proper noun phrase, which would be capitalized.

rev. ed.,

6th ed.,

e-book ed.,

director's cut,

Authorized King James Version,

**6. The Number** indicates how the source fits into a sequence: volume and issue numbers for journals, volume number for a book in a numbered multivolume set, season and episode numbers for television shows, comic book numbers, and so on. Use abbreviations *vol.* (volume) and *no.* (issue), but spell out other descriptors, such as *episode*. Lowercase all words and use numerals; follow each number with a comma.

vol. 24, no. 2,

season 6, episode 11,

no. 77,

**7. The Publisher** is the organization that produces or sponsors the source, making it available to readers or viewers. These organizations include book publishers, production companies, website hosts (e.g., museums, libraries, businesses), and blog networks. If a source has more than one publisher, separate them with a slash (/). Omit the publisher's name for a periodical, a work published by an author, a website whose name is essentially the same as the organization, or a website such as YouTube that isn't involved in producing the source (but is essentially a container). The publication city is not required. Spell out most names, but omit initial articles (*a, an, the*) and corporate words (*Inc., Corp.*). Abbreviate *University* (U) and *Press* (P).

Vintage Books,

U of Virginia Library / Museum of Design,

Melville House,

Rutgers UP,

U of Michigan P,

Cengage Learning,

**8. The Publication Date** indicates when the source was made available to the public through publishing, republishing, updating, releasing, broadcasting, or performing. In some cases, the source may indicate more than one date (e.g., an original copyright date of a book's first edition, a print publication date for an online source, an original broadcast date for a television episode). When this happens, cite the date most meaningful to your use and discussion of the source; as a general rule for books, however, give the most recent date offered by the book's title or copyright page.

2017,

Jan.-Feb. 2014,

10 May 2020, 9:30 p.m.,

**9. The Location** indicates where a source was and can be found. For some sources, this detail typically includes page numbers, listed in numerals after the abbreviation *p.* (for a single page) or *pp.* (for multiple pages). For periodical articles printed on non-consecutive pages, use a plus sign (+) after the numeral for the first page. For online sources, provide a DOI (digital object identifier), if available, as a link beginning with https://doi.org/. If a DOI is not available, use a direct URL (uniform resource locater), ideally a permalink. Do not use angle brackets or include prefixes such as http://.

p. 45.

pp. 185–89.

p. 13+

https://doi.org/10.1002/cplx.21590.

milkdelivers.org/about

Guthrie Theater, Minneapolis.

## Supplemental Elements

Most details that you need to include in a works-cited entry will fit in core elements 1–9. Occasionally, it may be helpful or necessary to include one or more of the following details:

- **Date of original publication:** If the original publication date of a republished source is important to know, supply it right after the source's title.
- **Date of access:** If you believe that an online source might change or disappear (especially if the source itself provides no publication or posting date), supply the date you accessed it in this format: Accessed 26 April 2020. Place the access date at the end of the citation, after the location.
- **Publication city:** If the publisher is unfamiliar, if the version of the text is unexpected, or if a book was published before 1900, consider adding the publication city before the publisher's name, separated by a comma.
- **Type of work:** If the source's format is unclear from the rest of the entry, clarify the medium with a term such as *Transcript, Lecture,* or *Address*, placed at the end of the entry.
- **Name of series:** If a book is part of a publishing series, consider adding the name of the series (capitalized, but not in italics or quotation marks) and the book's number within the series (if applicable) at the end of the entry.
- **Prior publication information:** If the source was previously published in another form and that information is useful to your readers, add an "Originally published" statement at the end of the entry, supplying full publication details.

# Sample Works-Cited Entries

Knowing the nine core elements of any works-cited entry should prove sufficient for building your works-cited list. You may find it useful, however, to develop your entries by following sample entries such as those that follow.

## Books

### A Print Book

Crawford, Margo Natalie. *What Is African American Literature?* Wiley-Blackwell, 2020.

### A Book from an Online Database

Note that the first date in the entry, placed after the title, refers to the original publication date. The second date indicates when the book was published online.

Wells, H. G. *The Invisible Man: A Grotesque Romance.* 1897. *Bartleby.com*, 2000, bartleby.com/1003/.

### An E-Reader Version of a Book (App or on Device)

Cadhain, Máirtín Ó. *The Dirty Dust.* Translated by Alan Titley, Kindle ed., Yale UP, 2015.

### A Book by Two Authors

Naifeh, Steven, and Gregory White Smith. *Van Gogh: The Life.* Random House, 2011.

### A Book by Three or More Authors

Baron, Cynthia, et al. *Appetites and Anxieties: Food, Film, and the Politics of Representation.* Wayne State UP, 2014.

### A Work Authored by an Agency, a Committee, or an Organization

Exxon Mobil Corporation. *Great Plains 2000.* Publications International, 2001.

### An Anonymous Book

*Chase's Calendar of Events 2002.* Contemporary, 2002.

### A Complete Anthology, Collection, or Conference Proceedings

King, Lovalerie, and Shirley Moody-Turner, editors. *Contemporary African American Literature: The Living Canon.* Indiana UP, 2013.

### A Single Work from an Anthology, Collection, or Conference Proceedings

Díaz, Junot. "Aurora." *The Ecco Anthology of Contemporary American Short Fiction*, edited by Joyce Carol Oates and Christopher R. Beha, Harper Perennial, 2008, pp. 213–26.

### Two or More Works from an Anthology, Collection, or Conference Proceedings

To avoid unnecessary repetition when citing two or more entries from a larger collection, you may cite the collection once with complete publication information (see Rothfield, below). The individual entries (see Becker and Cuno, below) can then be cross-referenced by listing the author, title of the piece, editor of the collection, and page numbers.

> Becker, Carol. "The Brooklyn Controversy: A View from the Bridge." Rothfield, pp. 15–21.

> Cuno, James. "Sensation and the Ethics of Funding Exhibitions." Rothfield, pp. 162–70.

> Rothfield, Lawrence, editor. *Unsettling Sensation: Arts-Policy Lessons from the Brooklyn Museum of Art Controversy.* Rutgers UP, 2001. Rutgers Series on the Public Life of the Arts.

### One Volume of a Multivolume Work

> Kennedy, David M., and Lizabeth Cohen. *The American Pageant: Since 1865,* 15th ed., vol. 2, Wadsworth, 2012.

### An Introduction, a Preface, a Foreword, or an Afterword

Start with the author of the part, followed by the type of the part, with no quotation marks or italics. If the part has a distinct title, that title can go in quotation marks after the author's name. Follow the book's title with the book's author, publication details, and page numbers for the part, as shown in the examples below.

> Barry, Anne. Afterword. *Making Room for Students,* by Celia Oyler, Teachers College, 1996, pp. 139–40.

> Atwood, Margaret. Introduction. *Alice Munro's Best: Selected Stories,* by Alice Munro, McClelland and Stewart, 2006, pp. vii-xviii.

### A Book with a Title within Its Title

If the book's title contains within it a title normally in quotation marks, keep the quotation marks and italicize the entire title. If the title contains within it another title that is normally italicized, do not italicize that title within the entry's title.

> Stuckey-French, Elizabeth. *"The First Paper Girl in Red Oak, Iowa" and Other Stories.* Doubleday, 2000.

> Beckwith, Charles E., editor. *Twentieth Century Interpretations of* A Tale of Two Cities: A Collection of Critical Essays. Prentice Hall, 1972.

## Periodical Articles

### A Print Journal Article
Give the original publication date after the title.

> Milatovic-Ovadia, Maja. "Shakespeare's Fools: A Piece in a Peacebuilding Mosaic." *Critical Survey*, vol. 31, no. 4, winter 2019, pp. 29–41.

### An Online Journal Article from a Database
This entry shows how to nest a container within a container. The article is contained within the journal (container 1), which is contained within the EBSCOhost database (container 2).

> Pavlovic, R. Y., and A. M. Pavlovic. "Dostoevsky and Psychoanalysis: Psychiatry in 19th-Century Literature." *The British Journal of Psychiatry*, vol. 200, no. 3, 2012, p. 181. *EBSCOhost*, https://doi.org/10.1192/bjp.bp.111.093823.

### A Print Magazine Article

> Khazan, Olga. "Being Black in America Can Be Hazardous to Your Health." *The Atlantic*, July/Aug. 2018, pp. 74–84.

### An Online Magazine Article
The first example that follows is from the free web; the second is from a database, which functions as the second container in the entry.

> Kay, Jonathan. "Uber v. Taxi." *The Walrus*, Aug. 2015, thewalrus.ca/uber-v-taxi/.

> Wood, Graeme. "Prison Without Walls." *The Atlantic*, Sept. 2010, pp. 86–96. *EBSCOhost*, eds.b.ebscohost.com.libproxy.redeemer.ca:2048/eds/detail/detail?sid=e2ff81a2-0421-4fa2-a646-86b4230f9119%40sessionmgr105&vid=7&hid=119&bdata=JnNpdGU9ZWRzLWxpdmU%3d#AN=53442640&db=rch.

### A Print Newspaper Article

> Simon, Lizzie. "The Art of Obsession." *The Wall Street Journal*, 19 Mar. 2012, pp. A24+.

### An Online Newspaper Article
The first example that follows is from the free web; the second is from a database, which functions as the second container in the entry.

> Turow-Paul, Eve, and Sophie Egan. "Eating Our Way to a Healthier Planet." *The Washington Post*, 15 May 2020, www.washingtonpost.com/climate-solutions/2020/05/15/eating-our-way-healthier-planet/?arc404=true.

> "Outsider Candidates Generating Buzz." *The Toronto Star*, 19 Mar. 2016, p. A16. *LexisNexis Academic*, www.lexisnexis.com.proxy.wexler.hunter.cuny.edu/ Inacui2api/api/version1/getDocCui?1ni=5JBB-WWG1-DY91-K4PR&csi =237924&hl=t&hv=t&hnsd=f&hns=t&hgn=t&oc=00240&perma=true.

### A Review

> Buskey, Megan. "A Wealth of Insight." Review of *When I Was a Child I Read Books*, by Marilynne Robinson. *Wilson Quarterly*, vol. 36, no. 2, 2012, pp. 98–99.

### An Editorial or Letter to the Editor

> Sory, Forrest. Letter. *Milwaukee Journal Sentinel*, July 2001, p. 10.

### An Article with a Title or Quotation Within Its Title

When an article title contains within it a title of a longer work (e.g., a novel or a film), italicize that title. If the article title contains within it a quotation or the title of a shorter work (e.g., a poem or a short story), then place that quotation or title within single quotation marks.

> Petit, Susan. "Field of Deferred Dreams: Baseball and Historical Amnesia in Marilynne Robinson's *Gilead* and *Home*." *MELUS*, vol. 37, no. 4, 2012, pp. 119–37.

> Melczarek, Nick. "Narrative Motivation in Faulkner's 'A Rose for Emily.'" *Explicator*, vol. 67, no. 4, 2009, pp. 237–43.

## Interviews and Personal Correspondence

### A Printed Interview

Begin with the name of the person interviewed if they are the person whom you are quoting. If the interview is untitled, use *Interview* (no italics) after the interviewee's name. Follow the title or description with a comma, *by*, and the interviewer's name.

> Robinson, Marilynne. "Marilynne Robinson: The Art of Fiction No. 198," by Sarah Fay. *Paris Review*, no. 186, 2008, pp. 37–66.

### A Personal Interview by You (the Author)

Place the name of the person you interviewed in the author position.

> Jackson, Sha-Mena. Personal Interview. 7 Aug. 2020.

### A Letter, Memo, Email, or Text

For correspondence of this nature, put the writer in the author position; use the subject line, if available, as the title; and offer a *Received by* statement for the recipient. If helpful, add the medium at the end of the entry.

> Thomas, Bob. "Re: Research Plan." Received by author, 10 Jan. 2021. Email.

## Multimedia Works

### A Web Page or Blog Post

> Wise, Hannah. "An American Mystery: Who or What Is Killing All These Bald Eagles?" *The Scoop Blog*, Dallas Morning News, 28 Mar. 2016, 4:31 p.m., thescoopblog. dallasnews.com/2016/03/an-american-mystery-who-or-what-is-killing-bald-eagles.html/.

### A Podcast or Video Podcast

> "Does This Phone Make Me Look Human?" *Still Processing*, from *The New York Times*, 7 May 2020, www.nytimes.com/2020/05/07/podcasts/still-processing-internet-vulnerability-sondheim-parks-recreation.html.

### A Tweet or Similar Social Media Post

Untitled sources typically use a generic descriptive term in place of the title. For quite short posts, such as tweets, you may reproduce the entire post enclosed in quotation marks as the title. Indicate not only the date of posting but the time as well.

> Newkirk, Tom [@Tom_Newkirk]. "The essay is a perpetual motion machine--not a fixed form. It can always open for more. Montaigne taught us that." *Twitter*, 12 Dec. 2019, 03:57 p.m., twitter.com/Tom_Newkirk/status/1205245295505874946.

### An Episode or Program (App, Streaming Service)

> "Cops Redesign." *Portlandia*, directed by Jonathan Krisel, performances by Fred Armisen and Carrie Brownstein, season 2, episode 5, IFC, 3 Feb. 2012. *Netflix*, www.netflix.com/watch/70236274.

### A Transcript of a Broadcast

> Lehrer, Jim. "Character Above All." *Online NewsHour*, National Public Radio, 29 May 1996, www.pbs.org/newshour/spc/character/transcript/. Transcript.

### A Recording (Music, Film, Etc.)

> Beyoncé. "Flawless." *Beyoncé*, performance by Chimamanda Ngozi Adichie, Columbia Records, 12 Aug. 2014.

> *Lincoln*. Directed by Steven Spielberg, performances by Daniel Day-Lewis and Sally Field, Dreamworks, 2012.

### An Artwork

When referring to the work of art itself (not a reproduction of it in print or online), include the medium. Place the date of creation immediately after the title.

> da Vinci, Leonardo. *Mona Lisa*. 1517, oil on canvas. Louvre Museum, Paris.

### A Cartoon or Comic Strip

> Chast, Roz. "Ed Revere, Spam Courier." Cartoon. *The New Yorker*, 22 Apr. 2013, p. 67.

### A Map or Chart

> *West Virginia State Map*. Folded ed. Rand McNally, 2011.

### A Public Speech, Address, Lecture, or Performance

> Gopnik, Adam. "Radical Winter." CBC Massey Lectures, 12 Oct. 2011, Dalhousie Arts Centre, Halifax, Nova Scotia. Address.

> *Twelfth Night*. 8 Feb. 2020, Wurtele Thrust Stage, Guthrie Theater, Minneapolis. Performance.

### An Advertisement

> "Apple Watch—Dance." Advertisement. *YouTube*, 21 Oct. 2015, www.youtube.com/user/Apple?v=fHE5WDO515Y.

## Government Publications, Reference Works, and Other Documents

### A Document from a Government Agency

When a government agency is the author of a document, start with the name of the government; then follow with any organizational units, moving from larger to smaller, separating each unit with a comma.

> United States, Department of Labor, Office of Disability Employment Policy. "Self-Employment for Artists with Disabilities." *Job Accommodation Network*, 17 Mar. 2015, askjan.org/media/occind.htm.

### An Item from Congress

For U.S. congressional publications (reports, bills, etc.), you may include additional details about the session and the chamber, as well as publication type and number.

> United States, Congress, House, House Administration Committee. National POW/MIA Remembrance Act of 2015. Congress.gov, www.congress.gov/congressional-report/114th-congress/house-report/410/1. 114th Congress, 2nd session, House Report 114–410.

### An Item from a Print Reference Source

> Lum, P. Andrea. "Computed Tomography." *World Book*, 2000 edition.

> "Macaroni." Def. 2b. *The American Heritage College Dictionary,* 4th edition, 2007.

### An Item from an Online or Digital Reference Source

> Hutchinson, George. "Harlem Renaissance." *Encyclopedia Britannica*, 8 Jan. 2016, www.britannica.com/event/Harlem-Renaissance-American-literature-and-art.

### A Sacred Text

The Bible and other such sacred texts are treated as anonymous books. Documentation should read exactly as it is printed on the title page.

> *The Jerusalem Bible*. Doubleday, 1966.

### An Unpublished Manuscript or Historical Document

> "The Work-for-All-Plan." 1933. Mildred Hicks Papers. Manuscript, Archives, and Rare Book Library, Emory U. *Online Manuscript Resources in Southern Women's History*, pid.emory.edu/ark:/25593/8zfd6.

---

#### Two or More Works by the Same Author

When your works-cited list includes two or more works by the same author, list the items alphabetically according to the titles. (Ignore *a*, *an*, or *the* if it is the first word in a title.) For second and subsequent items, substitute the author's name with three hyphens.

> McCluhan, Marshall. *Counterblast*. Harcourt, 1969.

> ---. *The Gutenberg Galaxy: The Making of Typographic Man*. U of Toronto P, 1962.

# MLA Format Guidelines

The most recent editions of the *MLA Handbook*, the eighth and ninth, have become less explicit about paper format than past editions, partially because media and formats for research-based writing continue to expand. For traditional research papers, however, we recommend following accepted formatting guidelines. These are detailed in Figures 23.2–23.4 and on the following pages, as well as in the sample MLA paper at the end of this chapter.

## MLA Format at a Glance

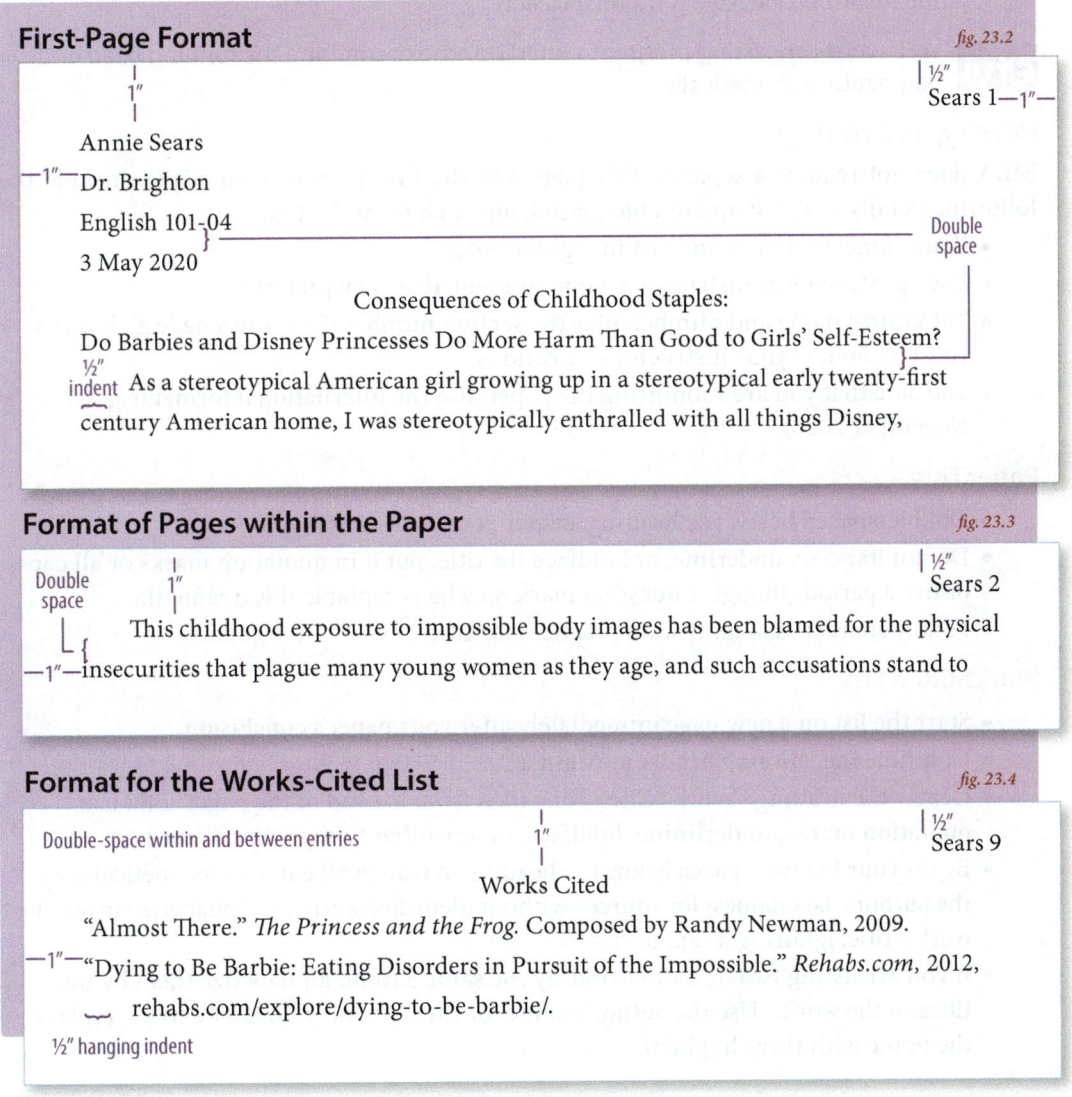

*fig. 23.2* First-Page Format

*fig. 23.3* Format of Pages within the Paper

*fig. 23.4* Format for the Works-Cited List

## Whole-Paper Format and Printing Issues

The instructions that follow explain how to set up the parts of a traditional academic paper and print it for submission. Page references are to the sample MLA paper later in this chapter.

### Running Head and Pagination

- Number pages consecutively in the upper-right corner, one-half inch from the top and flush with the right margin (1 inch from the edge of the page).
- Use numerals only—without *p., page, #,* or any other symbol.
- Include your last name on each page typed one space before the page number. (Your name identifies the page if it's misplaced.)

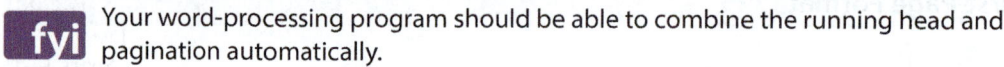
Your word-processing program should be able to combine the running head and pagination automatically.

### Heading on First Page

MLA does not require a separate title page. On the first page of your paper, include the following details flush left and double spaced, one inch from the top:
- Your name, both first and last in regular order
- Your professor's or instructor's name (presented as they prefer)
- The course name and number, plus the section number if appropriate (e.g., History 100-05). Follow your instructor's directions.
- The date that you are submitting the paper: use the international format (e.g., 11 November 2020).

### Paper Title

- Double-spaced below the heading, center your paper's title.
- Do not italicize, underline, or boldface the title; put it in quotation marks or all caps; or use a period (though a question mark may be acceptable if warranted).
- Follow standard capitalization practices for titles.

### Works-Cited List

- Start the list on a new page immediately after your paper's conclusion.
- Continue the running head and pagination.
- Center the heading "Works Cited" one inch from the top of the page; don't use quotation marks, underlining, boldface, or any other typographical markers.
- Begin your list two spaces below the heading. Arrange all entries alphabetically by the authors' last names; for sources without identified authors, alphabetize using the work's title, ignoring *a, an,* or *the.*
- If you are listing two or more works by the same author, alphabetize them by the titles of the works. Use the author's name for the first entry; in later entries, replace the name with three hyphens.

- Start each entry flush left; indent second and subsequent lines for specific entries one-half inch. Use your word-processing program's hanging indent feature.
- Double-space within and between all entries, and follow standard rules for capitalization, italics, quotation marks, and punctuation.
- Do not repeat the "Works Cited" heading if your list runs longer than one page.

**Paper, Printing, and Binding**
- Print on standard 8.5-by 11-inch paper.
- Use quality 20 pound bond paper. Avoid both thin, erasable paper and heavy card stock. Similarly, use only standard white or off-white paper—no neons, pastels, letterheads, or scents.
- Use a laser or inkjet printer to create a crisp, clean copy; avoid using nearly empty print cartridges.
- Avoid submitting a paper with handwritten corrections; however, if you must make a change, make a caret symbol (^), put a single clean line through words that must be dropped, and write additions above the line.
- As a first choice, use a paperclip. A single staple in the upper left corner may be acceptable. Avoid fancy covers or bindings, and never simply fold over the corners.
- Print your essay single-sided unless instructed otherwise.

## Typographical Issues

**Typeface:** Choose a standard serif typeface like Times New Roman. (Serif type, for example, the type you're reading, has finishes on each letter, as opposed to sans serif, like this.) Avoid unusual, hard-to-read typefaces.

**Type Size:** Use a readable type size, preferably 12 points, throughout the paper.

**Type Styles** (underlining, italics, bold, etc.):
- Use italics (not underlining) for titles of resources and individual words requiring this feature. An exception may be an online publication or posting; consult your instructor.
- Avoid using boldface, yellow highlighting, all caps, and so on.

rangizzz / Shutterstock.com

## Page-Layout Issues

### Spacing

- **Margins:** Set margins top and bottom, left and right at one inch, with the exception of the running head (one-half inch from top).
- **Line Spacing:** Double-space the entire paper—including the heading and works-cited entries, as well as tables, captions, and inset quotations.
- **Line Justification:** Use left justified throughout, except for the running head (right justified) and the title and works-cited heading (both centered). Leave the right margin ragged.
- **Word Hyphenation:** Avoid hyphenating words at the end of lines.
- **Spacing after Punctuation:** Use one space after most forms of punctuation, including end punctuation—but not before or after a dash or a hyphen.
- **Paragraph Indenting:** Indent all paragraphs one-half inch.

### Longer (Inset) Quotations

- Indent one half inch any verse quotations longer than three lines and prose quotations longer than four typed lines.
- Use no quotation marks, and place the parenthetical citation after the closing punctuation.
- With a verse quotation, make each line of the poem or play a new line; do not run the lines together. Follow the indenting and spacing in the verse itself.
- To quote two or more paragraphs, indent the first line of each paragraph one-quarter inch in addition to the half inch for the whole passage. However, if the first sentence quoted does not begin a paragraph in the source, do not make the additional indent. Indent only the first lines of subsequent paragraphs.

### Tables and Illustrations

Position tables, illustrations, and other visuals near your discussion of them—ideally, immediately after your first reference to the graphic, whether pasted in after a paragraph or positioned on a separate following page. Observe these rules:

- **Tables:** Identify all tables using "Table," an Arabic numeral, and a caption (descriptive title). Both the identifying headings and captions should be flush left, appropriately capitalized. Provide source information and explanatory notes below the table. Identify notes with superscript lowercase letters, not numerals. Double-space throughout the table.
- **Illustrations:** Number and label other visuals (graphs, charts, drawings, photos, maps, etc.) using "Figure" or "Fig.," an Arabic numeral (followed by a period), and a title or caption one space after the period—all flush left below the illustration, along with source information and notes.

### Formatting Non-Print Media

The ninth edition of the *MLA Handbook* offers guidelines like those on the previous pages for the traditional research paper and its formatting, while acknowledging that today research writing may be published in many formats shared both in print and digitally. Whatever the format, however, when projects rely on research, they should still document their sources. In any research-based document, your goals should be to credit sources you relied upon and provide source details that allow readers to find those resources themselves. The MLA offers the following tips for different media:

- **Slide Presentations:** when using programs such as PowerPoint, include brief citations for borrowed material (quotations, paraphrases, images, etc.) on each slide. Then add a works-cited list at the end of your presentation. Consider, as well, including your works cited in any handout you share.
- **Videos:** Integrate acknowledgements and brief text overlays (e.g., title of a borrowed clip); offer full documentation in closing credits.
- **Web Pages and Postings:** Integrate links to online sources that you reference within your document, but also provide a works-cited list at the end of your project.

**INSIGHT** If traditional works-cited format and spacing are not possible or desirable, use other spacing techniques, typographical features, or color to separate and feature entries for easy reading.

## Sample MLA Paper

Student writer Annie Sears wrote "Consequences of Childhood Staples" as a research paper for her composition class. In her paper, starting on the next page, she explores whether toys such as Barbie and characters such as Disney princesses harm or benefit girls as they grow up, documenting her research using MLA style. Strictly speaking, MLA format does not require or even recommend a title page or an outline. You can use Sears's paper in three ways:

1. To study how a well-written, major research paper develops careful thinking, builds a discussion, and orders supporting points and evidence.
2. To examine how source summaries, paraphrases, and quotations are carefully integrated into the writer's discussion to advance her thinking—a full-length example of the strategies addressed in chapter 22.
3. To see in detail the format and documentation practices of MLA style, practices that allow the writer to share a professional-looking paper that fairly respects sources used.

# Sample Paper: Format, In-Text Citation, and Works-Cited List

Note that a traditional research paper is double-spaced throughout.

> **The writer's last name and page number are placed in the upper right corner of every page.**

> **No separate title page is required. The heading identifies the writer, the professor, the course, and the date—in the order and format shown, flush left.**

> **The title, indicating the paper's topic and theme, is centered, in regular typeface and type size—no special effects such as boldface.**

> **From the start, in-text citations indicate borrowed material: summaries, paraphrases, and quotations.**

Sears 1

Annie Sears

Dr. Brighton

English 101-04

3 May 2020

Consequences of Childhood Staples:
Do Barbies and Disney Princesses Do More Harm Than Good to Girls' Self-Esteem?

As a stereotypical American girl growing up in a stereotypical early twenty-first century American home, I was stereotypically enthralled with all things Disney, especially where the princesses were concerned. I owned dozens of dresses, ranging from Cinderella's pale blue to Belle's vibrant yellow, from Aurora's modest neckline to Jasmine's belly-baring attire. I would watch the same films repeatedly, never growing weary of Snow White's humming or Ariel's "Part of Your World." I would imitate Cinderella in my chores or Belle in my bedtime stories. The magic I experienced as a child, the enchantment with the princesses who brought me innocent delight and taught me essential life lessons will forever linger. The same is true for millions of girls who had similar, Disney-focused childhood fixations.

Other girls, however, chose as their stereotypical childhood staple Barbie, the portable doll with brushable hair and hundreds of changeable outfits. Barbie has held many vocations, ranging from stay-at-home mom to astronaut, from professional basketball player to schoolteacher: a Barbie doll exists to appeal to every aspiring child, making her a universal role model over the years. In fact, Mattel released the first Barbie doll in 1959 (Do Rozario 38). Her sales reached a peak toward the end of the twentieth century, when "available in 150 countries, Barbie [sold] at the rate of two per second . . . racking up more than $1.9 billion a year" (Meyer). Those sales statistics are so remarkable that, "if you placed head to foot every doll ever sold, Barbie . . . would circle the globe 72 times" (Meyer). However, it was also at the height of her popularity that worldwide organizations began to attack Barbie: ridiculously thin, disproportionate, and, therefore, an unhealthy standard of beauty for all girls.

In 1992, researchers at a hospital in Helsinki released Barbie's first criticism: "If Barbie were real, she'd be too thin to menstruate" (Meyer). Since then, many studies have been done on the never-aging doll's body-type. (See figure 1 contrasting Barbie's body proportions with an average woman's.) As stated in "Ken and Barbie at Life Size," Barbie's bust, which to scale would be 32 inches, is only 4 inches smaller than the average woman's (Norton et al. 291). However, her waist, a mere 16 inches, is *half* that of the average. Barbie's 29-inch hips are significantly smaller than the average 37-38 inches. Just as her 7-inch bicep and 6-inch forearm are much thinner than the average 11-inch bicep and 10-inch forearm, her 16-inch thighs and 11-inch calf are much thinner than the average 22-inch thigh and 15-inch calf. Her 3.5-inch wrist (half of the average value) would prevent all moderate lifting; in turn, her US size 3 feet would

Figure 1. A computer-generated woman with Barbie's proportions is compared to a woman with average proportions ("Dying to Be Barbie")

render walking impossible. In addition, her two-times-too-tall, six-inches-too-thin neck wouldn't be able to bolster the weight of her slightly enlarged head, just as her half-sized waist would not allow room for more than half a liver and a few inches of intestine (291). Ultimately, Barbie would not exist; she could not sustain life.

Barbie is not only unrealistic; she is also highly sexualized, sporting a hip to waist ratio of 0.56: her waist circumference is exactly 56 percent of her hip circumference. In contrast, a healthy woman's hip to waist ratio is closer to 0.80. Barbie's bust-to-waist ratio (2.0) is almost twice that of a healthy woman's (Norton et al. 291).

This childhood exposure to impossible body images has been blamed for the physical insecurities that plague many young women as they age, and such accusations stand to reason. However, recent studies have proven that such effects may not be as drastic as accusers insist. In 2006, a research team led by Helga Dittmar, a psychology professor at the University of Sussex, took 162 five-to-eight-year-old girls and divided them into three groups. The first group, serving as a control, was not exposed to any dolls during playtime. The second was exposed only to Barbie dolls, while the third was exposed only to Emme dolls: a US size 16 doll designed to combat Barbie's unrealistic body shape (286–87). After an allotted amount of playtime, these girls were asked to honestly complete a body-image survey.

Overall, the girls who had played with the Barbie dolls were more prone to desire thinner, curvier body shapes while the other two groups were more satisfied with their current state. Nonetheless, primarily the younger girls (ages five and six) were susceptible to Barbie's self-depreciating effects; the majority of the older girls (ages seven and eight) were content with their body shapes (290). Thus, the data gathered from this experiment supports a twofold conclusion: Barbie does indeed have an effect on girls' self-esteem, but this effect lessens with age. Girls are able to recognize Barbie as a flawed role model.

Another study, instead involving older, middle-school-aged girls, yielded similar results. In 2004, Tara Kuther and Erin McDonald, psychology professors at Western Connecticut State University, took twenty sixth-grade girls from a typical Connecticut middle school (primarily White, middle-class students) and had them participate in a weekly support group, discussing honest views on Barbie dolls, self-esteem, and correlations between the two. Each girl had played with Barbie as a child, but the manner of play differed from girl to girl (41).

Some girls engaged in "torture play" (42-43), in which Barbie was manipulated, shaved, painted, thrown out windows, flushed down toilets, and so on for pure enjoyment; girls admitted that this type of play usually occurred when boys were around, in an attempt to impress them. Interestingly, though, one child openly stated that this type of play occurred solely with Barbie, not with other dolls, "because she is the only one that is perfect" (43). Even at a young age, when children are not cognizant of significant gender issues, they resent the body type placed before them, demanded of them. More important than any sort of resentment, though, is the fact that the child recognized Barbie's unrealistic standard of perfection. These children were not unlike those from the 2006 study: aware of Barbie's physical abnormalities.

Other girls in Kuther and McDonald's study admitted to "anger play" (43), in which Barbie was thrown against the wall or abused repeatedly after an argument with parents, siblings, or classmates. One child explained, "I did [those things] to Barbie and said that [whoever I was angry at] got it back, but I would never really do that to a person" (43). In this case, Barbie play seems to be a healthy outlet for the inevitable emotions precipitated by social interactions; children are able to release their pent-up anger without causing harm to friends and family members. Therefore, children are able to ignore Barbie's unrealistic attributes and instead use her.

Sears 4

Lastly, all children involved in Kuther and McDonald's study engaged in "imaginative play" (42), wherein Barbie would go to prom, have a family, seek adventure in outer space, and more. These girls would often reenact the same scenarios over and over, as if writing and perfecting a script. Kuther and McDonald explain, "Toys present messages about gender, adult roles, and values that children internalize" (39). Through repetitively enacting scenes with their dolls, children begin to understand how to interact with other people, what different roles exist within a culture, and what roles and interactions they long to emulate. It is precisely through imaginative play that these sorts of ideas become concrete, a part of each child's identity.

Thus, it would appear that Barbie's influence, though it may seem negative initially, proves positive: she helps children release strong emotions and internalize concepts pertaining to societal values, all without affecting self-esteem too detrimentally. In fact, one eighth-grade student responded eloquently when asked about Barbie-related experiences: "I think Barbie was a good role model for girls, even though she was fake. She was pretty, lovable, and could do any profession. Even though she was kind of anorexic, Barbie gave girls the chance to imagine things and to be anything they wanted to" (Kuther and McDonald 47-48).

Regarding Kuther and McDonald's research, if all three types of common Barbie play prove healthy, and if each type of activity is essential to a child's development in regard to societal understanding, social interaction, and identity formation, then shouldn't attacks on Barbie's body shape be muted? Regarding Dittmar's study, if, as they age, children realize that Barbie's image is unattainable, shouldn't the same attacks become even further irrelevant? Barbie's effect on young girls proves more beneficial than detrimental.

The ongoing allegations about Barbie have recently shifted to another childhood staple: my personal favorite, the Disney princess. In May 2013, when Disney decided to make Merida an official princess, including her on princess merchandising and the princess web page, she was redesigned for her coronation. The results sparked public outrage. Signatories of an online petition argued that the beloved Pixar princess, who refuses marriage, rides bareback through Medieval Scottish forests, and sports red, untamed hair to match her fiery personality, had been redesigned to mask her strongest characteristics: Merida proved "thinner with a bigger bust, more revealing

> **Ellipses indicate an omission from the original source; a shortened title in parentheses, with no page number, indicates a one-page source or one without pagination that also has no author.**

dress, a face full of makeup, less wild hair, and . . . a sassy sash" in lieu of her "signature bow and arrows" ("PR Nightmare"). The free spirit who offered hope to anyone waiting for or uninterested in marriage, capturing hearts with her contrast to former princesses, was gone. At least 200,000 people who signed a Change.org petition wanted her back. Once the petition reached such great popularity, Disney did indeed replace sexualized-Merida with carefree-Merida on the princess homepage ("PR Nightmare").

While the extent of Merida's sexual nature in the new design may have been too much, the changes did not warrant such a large outcry. In her essay on the function of Disney princesses, Rebecca Anne Do Rozario, a professor at Monash University, explains Disney's design philosophy this way:

> **A quotation longer than four typed lines is inset—indented 5 spaces (about a half inch) and double-spaced throughout; end punctuation is placed before the parenthetical citation.**

> The princess has always thus been rendered in the cinematic trends occurring at her original release. Disney actually maintains her contemporaneity in its dual aspects: maintaining the original design, while successfully renewing its appeal by re-rendering her in new releases, marketing, and merchandising. Disney does not precisely erase her original quality, so much as create continuity between that quality and her contemporary audiences. (36-37)

Snow White, the original Disney princess, is a prime example. The technology used to produce *Snow White and the Seven Dwarfs* is long outdated; thus, Snow White needed to be redesigned so that her animation was cohesive with that of the newer princesses (Do Rozario 37). When this change happened, there were no petitions, no discontented fans. Yet, when Merida's computer animation was altered to match the simpler animation of her fellow princesses, many people were upset. It seems that the effective attacks on Barbie's body have made an impact on American society; the concept that media sources are entirely to blame for personal insecurities has permeated popular thinking. Therefore, even the Disney princesses, who are redesigned for practical purposes, are subject to unjust criticism.

Because Barbie's body shape is so drastically unreal, it is difficult to argue that her effects on children are solely beneficial; some of the false ideas girls have about their own bodies are rooted in the images ingrained in their minds while growing up, and, despite all of the positive impacts she does make, Barbie undoubtedly plays a role in a child's negative self-image development. The same, however, is not true of Disney princesses. These young heroines' negative impacts are practically nonexistent in light of all the good they do for a child's development, beginning with the fact that a princess is a "relevant anachronism over centuries, through revolutions, wars, and globalization. Some have sought to reveal her beauty as a stereotype, her good nature as submissiveness, but still she prevails" (Do Rozario 34). The princess is a timeless classic, a character that never ages, never loses popularity, and perfectly represents the cultural aspects of her story's historical time period.

However, the princess represents not only the society her story takes place in but also the society her movie was released into. Snow White, yet again, offers a perfect example. *Snow White and the Seven Dwarfs*, released in 1937, opens with Snow White as a formal princess, living in the castle with her jealous stepmother; in this scene, Snow White is still a "1920's starlet with a flapper's haircut, rosebud mouth, and high-pitched warble" (Do Rozario 38). When the queen attempts to kill Snow White, forcing her to flee into the woods, the 1920s beauty finds herself in poverty, a Great Depression of sorts. She lives with the working-class dwarves, cooks and cleans and engages in all activities not suited for a princess or the glamour of the Roaring Twenties. At the end of the film, though, she is restored from her peasant state, rescued by her prince; similarly, America came out of the Great Depression, rescued by the president (39). Snow White exemplifies not only the women of her medieval day and age but also the women who survived the Great Depression: willing to help, able to overcome, and lady-like through all adverse circumstances.

The second Disney princess offers no less a complete example. Princess Aurora from *Sleeping Beauty*, released in 1959, is a "prototype Baby Boomer. She wanders barefoot in the woods and is uninterested in the affairs of kings, devastated when she learns she is a princess and will not be able to make her date with the boy she met in the woods" (Do Rozario 38). Like other young people of her era, the Baby Boomer generation, Princess Aurora resents responsibility and the nagging of her parents. Prince Phillip, her male counterpart, goes as far as to ridicule his father, the king: "Father, you're living in the past. This is the fourteenth century!" (qtd. in Do Rozario 38). These young royals exemplify the dominant character traits of 1950s-1960s youth.

Similarly, *The Little Mermaid*, released in 1989, features Princess Ariel: a rebellious young girl, dissatisfied with the customs of her people and the constraints of her own body. Ariel's father, naturally, wishes her to fall in love with a merman and live happily, as Sebastian's song boasts, "under the sea," but Ariel's heart lies elsewhere. She "[wants] to be where the people are," to "[walk] around on those—what do they call 'em?—feet" ("Part"). This desire for a world beyond her own runs so deep that Princess Ariel falls in love with a two-legged, land-loving man.

Ariel's unruly nature is similar to that of other media icons of her day: Sandy from *Grease* (1978) and Baby from *Dirty Dancing* (1987). Just as Sandy falls in love with a bad boy, of sorts, Ariel goes for the unattainable Erik; neither girl's father approves of her romance. Just as Ariel is "sick of swimming, ready to stand," Baby feels awkward, dissatisfied with her developing body ("Part"; Do Rozario 50). Additionally, both girls mimic Busby Berkeley's burlesque dance moves (Do Rozario 48), and Ariel and Ursula both dance somewhat suggestively during "Poor Unfortunate Souls"; Ursula even advises, "Don't underestimate the power of body language" (qtd. in Do Rozario 49). The same lesson is applied in both *Grease* and *Dirty Dancing*, highly successful teen-movie-musicals. These similarities simply reinforce the parallels between Ariel and the young women of the world *The Little Mermaid* was released into.

Furthermore, each early princess living within a patriarchal society was incredibly dependent upon her prince. Neither Snow White nor Sleeping Beauty could reawaken from eternal sleep, nor could Ariel speak without true love's kiss. Cinderella was powerless to escape her stepmother's tyranny until her prince identified her foot. Belle was literally the Beast's prisoner. Jasmine could only claim her throne through marriage to a prince, but, much like Ariel, she fell in love with an unsuitable, forbidden "street rat." Each early princess does not have a functioning story without a prince to complete the picture.

The later princesses, however, initially live independently of flirtation; their romance enhances the story rather than serving as the primary focus. Pocahontas (1995), though she falls in love with a White man, teaches him more about "things [he] never knew [he] never knew" and, ultimately, saves her tribe before giving up romance to remain with her family ("Colors"). Mulan (1998) pretends to be a man to protect her father and eventually saves all of China before dating General Shang. Tiana (2009) places her restaurant before love, belittling the concept while singing, "That's just gonna have to wait a while. I ain't got time for messin' around, and that's not my style" ("Almost There"). Merida (2011) refuses marriage entirely; instead, her story chronicles a conflict with her mother. Also more family-focused, Anna's relationship with Hans in *Frozen* (2013) proves an act, whereas her relationship with her sister, fellow princess Elsa, proves true. As time progresses, each princess becomes more and more independent of her prince—resulting in nonexistent princes in the most recent princess films.

This shift into more independent, family-focused, feminist princesses runs parallel to the progression of feminism within America. As stated in the Pew Research Center's study "Breadwinner Moms," the number of American families with children under eighteen years of age utilizing both maternal and paternal income to provide for their family increased from twenty-five percent in 1960 to sixty-five percent in 2011. In addition, nearly fifty percent of all college degrees are earned by women, resulting in nearly fifty percent of America's workforce being composed of women (Wang). American feminism has advanced toward gender equality quickly over the last fifty years, and the Disney Princesses have clearly joined the movement.

If each princess is a representation of the culture her movie was released into, then she must teach young viewers about the society they were born into, about how to behave and interact within that cultural context; therefore, a princess's influence on children is primarily beneficial, enabling each child to develop their own societal identity. Any sort of visual presentation or animation alteration becomes irrelevant in light of the learning potential each princess's story exemplifies.

All childhood fixations have great impact on children's development, including their body-image-related self-esteem, personal identity, and concept of social interactions. For American girls, the most significant toys are likely Barbie and Disney princesses. These characters have received a great deal of criticism for the influence they have on girls' body-image-related self-esteem, but the benefits of these childhood fascinations far outweigh any negative effects that may come later in life. Barbie's body image is skewed, but even at a young age, children are able to recognize her impossibility; therefore, her encouragement of childhood aspirations holds more weight than her body shape. Disney princesses undergo constant redesign, but their stories ultimately reflect the society their movie was released into; therefore, children are able to better understand their world and, in turn, themselves through princess obsession. Ultimately, the childhood staples that permeate current American culture do much more good than harm for upcoming generations. Disney princesses—and even Barbie!—should be shown immense gratitude for the impact they have on child development.

## Works Cited

"Almost There." *The Princess and the Frog.* Composed by Randy Newman, 2009.

"Colors of the Wind." *Pocahontas.* Written by Stephen Schwartz, composed by Alan Menken, 1995.

Dittmar, Helga, et al. "Does Barbie Make Girls Want to be Thin? The Effect of Experimental Exposure to Images of Dolls on the Body Image of 5-to-8-Year-Old Girls." *Developmental Psychology,* vol. 42, no.2, March 2006, pp. 283–92. *ProQuest,* https://doi.org/10.1037/0012-1649.42.2.283.

Do Rozario, Rebecca-Anne C. "The Princess and the Magic Kingdom: Beyond Nostalgia, the Function of the Disney Princess." *Women's Studies in Communication,* vol. 27, no. 1, spring 2004, pp. 34–59. *ProQuest,* https://doi.org/10.1080/07491409.2004.10162465.

"Dying to Be Barbie: Eating Disorders in Pursuit of the Impossible." *Rehabs.com,* 2012, rehabs.com/explore/dying-to-be-barbie/.

Kuther, Tara L., and Erin McDonald. "Early Adolescents' Experiences with and Views of Barbie." *Adolescence,* vol. 39, no. 153, spring 2004, pp. 39–51. *ProQuest,* proxy1.aims.edu:2080/docview/195942979/BF73B52E053E4F19PQ/3?accountid=35907.

Meyer, Michele. "Barbie Hits 40." *Parenting,* vol. 13, no. 2, March 1999, p. 31. *ProQuest,* proxy1.aims.edu:2080/docview/203323009/92A6745C7C404442PQ/1?accountid=35907.

Norton, Kevin I., et al. "Ken and Barbie at Life Size." *Sex Roles: A Journal of Research,* vol. 34, no. 3-4, Feb. 1996, pp. 287–94.

"Part of Your World." *The Little Mermaid.* Written and composed by Alan Menken and Howard Ashman, 1989.

"PR Nightmare for Disney Princess." *Advertising Age,* vol. 84, no. 20 (2013), p. 5. *ProQuest,* proxy1.aims.edu:2080/docview/1354351849/F7D80244F83B43D9PQ/1?accountid= 35907.

Wang, Wendy, et al. "Breadwinner Moms: Mothers Are the Sole or Primary Provider in Four-in-Ten Households with Children; Public Conflicted about the Growing Trend." *Pew Research Center,* 29 May 2013, pewsocialtrends.org/2013/05/29/breadwinner-moms/.

## Reading for Better Writing

1. *Connections:* In her essay, Annie Sears examines the effects of childhood toys and entertainment on girls. No matter what gender you identify as, how do you relate to Sears's discussion? What toys and activities engaged you as a child? What influence have those had on who you are as an adult?
2. *Comprehension:* Sears's essay offers an extended discussion of both Barbies and Disney princesses. Condense that discussion by developing your own one-paragraph summary of the essay.
3. *Writing Moves:*
    a. In her argument, what types of evidence does Sears use? Where has she gotten her evidence? Are her sources reliable? Does she have a balanced range of sources?
    b. How does Sears distinguish her own thinking from source material? Why are these strategies necessary?

**Your Project:** In addition to toys and movie characters, many childhood influences shape us into the adults we become: environment (e.g., urban vs. rural), religious institutions, friendships, sports and leisure activities, family dynamics, and so on. For your own paper, consider researching and writing about a particular influence that matters to you.

Annie Sears "Consequences of Childhood Staples: Do Barbies and Disney Princesses Do More Harm Than Good to Girls' Self-Esteem?" Used by permission of the author.

Figure 1 on page 481 from Rehabs.com. Rehabs.com is a website designed to provide individuals and families with helpful tools and resources to make informed decisions about addiction treatment.

# MLA Style: Applications

Once you have used the instruction in this chapter to format and document your paper according to MLA style, extend what you have learned by doing the following activities:

1. **System Check:** The MLA style involves many guidelines and rules about documentation. To make some sense of these rules, answer these questions: What is the essential logic of the MLA system? In other words, what does the MLA hope to accomplish with these rules?
2. **Works-Cited Practice:** Create MLA works-cited entries for the following publications:
   a. An article in the summer 2009 issue (volume 34, no. 2) of the periodical *MELUS*, by Joni Adamson and Scott Slovic: "The Shoulders We Stand On: An Introduction to Ethnicity and Ecocriticism" (pages 5–24)
   b. Ernest Hemingway's novel *A Farewell to Arms*, published in 1986 by Collier Books
   c. The web page "Vaccines for Children Program (VFC)," part of the Vaccines and Immunizations section of the Centers for Disease Control and Prevention (CDC) website, sponsored by the U.S. government's Department of Health and Human Services. No author or publication date is listed. The site was last accessed June 3, 2020, at www.cdc.gov/vaccines/programs/vfc/index.html.

## Learning-Objectives Checklist ✓

Have you achieved this chapter's learning objectives? Check your progress with the following items, revisiting topics in the chapter as needed. I have . . .

____ gained an overview of the MLA system of documentation—the basic logic of in-text citations in relation to works-cited entries.

____ applied rules of in-text citation, whether for regular sources or for sources without traditional authorship and/or pagination.

____ developed a works-cited list that is properly formatted and that correctly and fully identifies sources, whether books, journal articles, or other resources.

____ correctly implemented MLA format guidelines for whole-paper issues (e.g., header, heading on the first page, pagination), typography, and page layout.

____ examined MLA style at work in "Consequences of Childhood Staples" by Annie Sears, learning how the system is practiced concretely in a research-based argumentative essay.

# Chapter 24

# APA Style

Those who write papers in the social sciences—psychology, sociology, political science, and education, for example—usually follow the research-writing guidelines established by the American Psychological Association (APA). This chapter summarizes these guidelines and helps you use APA format and documentation.

APA format is similar to MLA format in two ways: Both require (1) parenthetical citations within the text and (2) a final listing of all references cited in the paper. But in the social sciences, the date of publication is often much more crucial than it is in the humanities, so the date is highlighted in in-text citations. APA format also requires a title page and an abstract. Like the MLA, the APA has guidelines for inclusive language; you can find these on pages 105–107.

**Visually Speaking** Figure 24.1 suggests something about humans and their societies. Consider the possibilities, and explore what social-science research and research writing in particular seek to contribute to an understanding of people and the societies they build.

## Learning Objectives

By working through this chapter, you will be able to

- implement APA guidelines for documenting sources.
- produce research writing that adheres to APA guidelines for format.
- identify APA practices at work in a sample student research report.

*Scott Norsworthy / Shutterstock.com*

*fig. 24.1*

# APA Documentation: Quick Guide

The APA system involves two parts: (1) an in-text citation within your paper when you use a source and (2) a matching bibliographic entry at the end of your paper. Note these features of the APA author-date system:

- **It uses signal phrases and parenthetical references** to set off source material from your own thinking and discussion. A signal phrase names the author and places the material in context (e.g., "As Jung described it, the collective unconscious . . .").
- **It's date-sensitive.** Because the publication dates of resources are especially important in social-science research, the publication year is included in the parenthetical reference and after the authors' names in the reference entry.
- **It's smooth, unobtrusive, and orderly.** APA in-text citations identify borrowed material while keeping the paper readable. Moreover, alphabetized reference entries at the end of the paper make locating source details easy.

You can see these features at work in the example below. The parenthetical material "Pascopella, 2011, p. 32" tells the reader these things:

- The borrowed material came from a source authored by Pascopella.
- The source was published in 2011.
- The specific material can be found on page 32 of the source.
- Full source details are in the reference list under the surname Pascopella.

1. **In-Text Citation in Body of Paper**

   In newcomer programs, "separate, relatively self-contained educational interventions" (Pascopella, 2011, p. 32) are implemented to meet the academic and transitional needs of recent immigrants before they enter mainstream English Language Development.

2. **Matching Reference Entry at End of Paper**

   Pascopella, A. (2011). Successful strategies for English language learners. *District Administration, 47*(2), 29-44.

## In-Text Citation: The Basics

Follow these basic rules for in-text citation.

1. Refer to the author(s) and date of publication by using one of these methods:

   **Last name(s), publication date in parentheses:**

   ELLs normally spend just three years in 30-minute "pull-out" English language development programs (Calderón et al., 2011).

   **Last name(s) cited in text with publication date in parentheses:**

   In "Key Issues for Teaching English Learners in Academic Classrooms," Carrier (2005) explained that it takes an average of one to three years to reach conversational proficiency in a second language, but five to seven years to reach academic proficiency.

2. Present and punctuate citations according to these rules:
   - Keep authors and publication dates as close together as possible in the sentence.
   - Separate the author's last name, the date, and any locating detail with commas.
   - If referencing part of a source, use an appropriate abbreviation: *p.* (page), *para.* (paragraph)—but do not abbreviate *chapter*.

*Note:* When citing previous research, use past tense or present perfect tense—Smith (2003) found *or* Smith (2003) has found.

## References: The Basics

Complete coverage of reference issues is offered later in this chapter. Here, however, are templates for the most common entries:

**Template for Book:**

> Author's Last Name, Initials. (Publication Year). *Title of book*. Publisher. [Other publication details are integrated as needed.]
>
> Pandya, J. Z. (2011). *Overtested: How high-stakes accountability fails English Language Learners*. Teachers College Press.

— author's name, followed by period
— publication year in parentheses, followed by period
— exact and full title in italics, first word and proper nouns capitalized, followed by period
— publisher name from title page, followed by period

**Template for Periodical Article:**

> Author's Last Name, Initials. (Publication Year). Title of article. *Journal Title, volume*(issue), page numbers. [Other publication details are integrated as needed. For online periodical articles, add the digital object identifier.]
>
> Slama, R. B. (2012). A longitudinal analysis of academic English proficiency outcomes for adolescent English Language Learners in the United States. *Journal of Educational Psychology, 104*(2), 265-285. https://doi.org/10.1037/a0025861

— author's name, followed by period
— article title, no quotation marks, first word and proper nouns capitalized
— journal title and volume number italicized
— page numbers followed by period
— DOI presented as hyperlink

**Template for Online Document:**

> Author's Last Name, Initials. (Publication Date). *Title of work* OR Title of entry. DOI (digital object identifier) or URL
>
> U.S. Department of Education. (2013, January). *Projection of education statistics to 2021*. http://nces.ed.gov/programs/projections/projections2021/

— author's name, followed by period
— publication date in parentheses, followed by period
— document title
— URL presented as hyperlink

# Guidelines for In-Text Citations

## The Form of an Entry

The APA documentation style is sometimes called the "author-date" system because both the author and the date of the publication must be mentioned in the text when citing a source. Both might appear in the flow of the sentence, like this:

> Children in India are being trafficked for adoption, organ transplants, and labor such as prostitution, according to a 2021 article by Nilanjana Ray.

If either name or date does not appear in the text, it must be mentioned within parentheses at the most convenient place, like this:

> According to an article by Nilanjana Ray (2021), children in India . . .
>
> According to a recent article (Ray, 2021), children in India . . .

## Points to Remember

1. When paraphrasing rather than quoting, make it clear where your borrowing begins and ends. Use stylistic cues to distinguish the source's thoughts ("Sacks points out . . . ," "Some critics argue . . .") from your own ("I believe . . . ," "It seems obvious, however . . .").
2. When using a shortened title of a work, begin with the word by which the work is alphabetized in your references list (for example, for "Measurement of Stress in Fasting Man," use "Measurement of Stress," not "Fasting Man").
3. When including a parenthetical citation at the end of a sentence, place it *before* the end punctuation: (Sacks, 2009).

## Sample In-Text Citations

### One Author: A Complete Work

The correct form for a parenthetical reference to a single source by a single author is parenthesis, last name, comma, space, year of publication, parenthesis. Also note that final punctuation should be placed outside the parentheses.

> . . . in this way, the public began to connect certain childhood vaccinations with an autism epidemic (Baker, 2020).

### One Author: Part of a Work

When you cite a specific part of a source, give the page number, chapter, or section, using the appropriate abbreviations (p. or pp. or sec.). Always give the page number for a direct quotation.

> . . . while a variety of political and scientific forces were at work in the developing crisis, it was parents who pressed the case "that autism had become epidemic and that vaccines were its cause" (Baker, 2020, p. 251).

## One Author: Several Publications in the Same Year

If the same author has published two or more articles in the same year, avoid confusion by placing a small letter *a* after the first work listed in the references list, *b* after the next one, and so on. Determine the order alphabetically by title.

**Parenthetical Citation:**

> Reefs harbor life forms heretofore unknown (Milius, 2001a, 2001b).

**References**:

> Milius, D. (2001a). Another world hides inside coral reefs. *Science News, 160*(16), 244.
>
> Milius, D. (2001b). Unknown squids—with elbows—tease science. *Science News, 160*(24), 390.

## Works by Authors with the Same Last Name

When citing different sources by authors with the same last name, add the authors' initials to avoid confusion, even if the publication dates are different.

> While J. D. Wallace (2011) argued that privatizing social security would benefit only the wealthiest citizens, others such as E. S. Wallace (2013) supported greater control for individuals.

## Multiple Authors

If a source has two authors, include both names in the in-text citation, separated by an ampersand when enclosed in parentheses.

> Love changes not just who we are, but who we can become, as well (Lewis & Lannon, 2021).

For works with three or more authors, use only the name of the first author followed by "et al.," like this:

> These discoveries lead to the hypothesis that love actually alters the brain's structure (Lewis et al., 2019).

*Note:* If doing so would create confusion because you have two or more sources with the same first author, then use as many names as needed to distinguish these sources.

## A Work with No Author Indicated

If your source lists no author, treat the first few words of the title (capitalized normally) as you would an author's last name. A title of an article or a chapter belongs in quotation marks; the titles of books or reports should be italicized:

> . . . including a guide to low-stress postures ("How to Do It," 2021).

## A Work Authored by an Agency, a Committee, or Other Organization

Treat the name of the group as if it were the last name of the author. If the name is long and easily abbreviated, provide the abbreviation in square brackets. Use the abbreviation without brackets in subsequent references, as follows:

### First Text Citation:

> A problem for many veterans continues to be heightened sensitivity to noise (National Institute of Mental Health [NIMH], 2020).

### Subsequent Citations:

> In addition, veterans suffering from PTSD continue to have difficulty discussing their experiences (NIMH, 2020).

## A Work Referred to in Another Work

If you need to cite a source that you have found referred to in another source (a "secondary" source), mention the original source in your text. Then, in your parenthetical citation, cite the secondary source, using the words "as cited in."

> ... theorem given by Ullman (as cited in Hoffman, 2018).

*Note:* In your references list at the end of the paper, you would write out a full citation for Hoffman (not Ullman).

## Two or More Works in a Parenthetical Reference

Sometimes it is necessary to lump several citations into one parenthetical reference. In that case, cite the sources as you usually would, separating the citations with semicolons. Place the citations in alphabetical order, just as they would be ordered in the references list.

> Others report near-death experiences (Rommer, 2016; Sabom, 2020).

## A Work in an Anthology

When citing an article or a chapter in an anthology or a collection, use the authors' names for the specific article, not the names of the anthology's editors. (Similarly, the article should be listed by its authors' names in the references section.)

> Phonological changes can be understood from a variationist perspective (Guy, 2005).

## A Digital or Other Internet Source

As with print sources, cite a digital source by the author (or by shortened title if the author is unknown) and the publication date (not the date you accessed the source).

> One study compared and contrasted the use of web and touch screen transaction log files in a hospital setting (Nicholas, Huntington, & Williams, 2019).

## A Website

Whenever possible, cite a website by its author and posting date. In addition, refer to a specific page or document rather than to a home page or a menu page. If you are referring to a specific part of a web page that does not have page numbers, direct your reader, if possible, with a section heading and a paragraph number.

> According to the National Multiple Sclerosis Society (2020, "Complexities" section, para. 2), understanding of MS could not begin until scientists began to research nerve transmission in the 1920s.

## A Sacred Text or Famous Literary Work

Sacred texts and famous literary works are published in many different editions. For that reason, the original date of publication may be unavailable or not pertinent. In these cases, use your edition's year of translation (for example, *trans.* 2003) or indicate your edition's year of publication (2003 *version*). When you are referring to specific sections of the work, it is best to identify parts, chapters, or other divisions instead of your version's page numbers.

> An interesting literary case of such dysfunctional family behavior can be found in Franz Kafka's *The Metamorphosis,* where it becomes the commandment of family duty for Gregor's parents and sister to swallow their disgust and endure him (trans. 1972, part 3).

Books of the Bible and other well-known literary works may be abbreviated.

> "Generations come and generations go, but the earth remains forever" (*The New International Version Study Bible,* 1985 version, Eccles. 1.4).

## Personal Communications

If you do personal research, you may have to cite personal communications that have provided you with some of your knowledge. Personal communications may include personal letters, phone calls, emails, and so forth. Because they are not published in a permanent form, APA style does not place them among the citations in your references list. Instead, cite them only in the text of your paper in parentheses, like this:

> ... according to M. T. Cann (personal communication, April 1, 2016).
>
> ... by today (M. T. Cann, personal communication, April 1, 2016).

## Traditional Knowledge and Oral Traditions of Indigenous People

If your research involves gleaning wisdom from interaction with an Indigenous person, you would cite this source one of two ways. When you have recorded the interaction (e.g., an audio or video file), follow the guidelines for citing that form of medium. When the interaction was not recorded, offer a modified form of the personal communications citation: add to the person's name their Indigenous group or nation, their location, and other relevant details.

> ... their traditional laws (Gary Naziel, Wet'suwet'en hereditary subchief in territory west of Prince George, British Columbia, personal communication, May 2020).

## Guidelines for APA References

The references section lists all the sources you have cited in your text (with the exception of personal communications such as phone calls and emails). Begin your references list on a new page after the last page of your paper. Number each references page, continuing the numbering from the text. Then format your references list by following the guidelines that follow. (See also the references page at the end of sample paper later in this chapter .)

1. Type the page number in the upper-right corner, approximately one-half inch from the top of the page.

2. Center the title, *References,* approximately one inch from the top; then double-space before the first entry.

3. Begin each entry flush with the left margin. If the entry runs more than one line, indent additional lines approximately one-half inch (five to seven spaces) using a hanging indent.

4. Adhere to the following conventions about spacing, capitalization, and italics:
   - Double-space between all lines on the references page.
   - Use one space following each word and punctuation mark.
   - With book and article titles, capitalize only the first letter of the title (and subtitle) and proper nouns. (Note that this practice differs from the presentation of titles in the body of the essay.) **Example:** The results of the first world war: An economic review
   - Use italics for titles of books and periodicals, not underlining.

5. List each entry alphabetically by the last name of the author, or, if no author is given, by the title (disregarding *A, An,* or *The*). For works with multiple authors, use the first author listed in the publication.

6. Follow these conventions with respect to abbreviations:
   - With authors' names, generally shorten first and middle names to initials, leaving a space after the period. For a work with more than one author, use an ampersand (&) before the last author's name.
   - Spell out "Press" in full, but for other publishing information, use the abbreviations in Figure 24.2.

| | |
|---|---|
| Comp. . . . . . . . . . . . . . . .compiler, compiled, compiled by | Pt. . . . . . . . . . . . . . . . . . . . . . . . . . . . . . . . . . . . . . . Part |
| Ed. . . . . . . . . . . . . . . . . . . . . . . . . . . . . . . . . editor(s) | Sec. (sect.). . . . . . . . . . . . . . . . . . . . . . . section(s) |
| N.d. . . . . . . . . . . . . . . . . . . . . . . . . . . no date given | 2nd ed. . . . . . . . . . . . . . . . . . . . Second edition |
| N.p. . . . . . . . . . . . . . . . .no place of publication, no publisher given | Suppl. . . . . . . . . . . . . . . . . . . . . . . . . . Supplement |
| p., pp. . . . . . . .page(s) (if necessary for clarity) | Tech. Rep. . . . . . . . . . . . . . . .Technical Report |
| | Trans. (tr.) . . . . . . . . . . . translator, translation |

*fig. 24.2*

# Sample Reference Entries

The following pages offer detailed instructions and sample entries for specific types of sources. These samples are divided into print books and other documents; print periodical articles; online sources, including articles and ebooks from databases; and other sources, including primary, personal, and multimedia.

## Books and Other Documents

The general form for a book or brochure entry is this:

> Author, A. (year). *Title*. Publisher.

The entries that follow illustrate the information needed to cite books, sections of a book, brochures, and government publications.

### A Book by One Author

> Horstmann, A. (2015). *Building Noah's ark for migrants, refugees, and religious communities*. Palgrave Macmillan.

### A Book by Two or More Authors

List up to twenty authors by last name and first initial, separating them by commas, with an ampersand (&) before the last.

> Hooyman, N., & Kramer, B. (2006). *Living through loss: Interventions across the life span*. New York, NY: Columbia University Press.

For twenty-one or more authors, list the first nineteen followed by an ellipsis, and then the last.

### An Anonymous Book

If an author is listed as "Anonymous," treat it as the author's name. Otherwise, follow this format:

> *Publication manual of the American Psychological Association* (7th ed.). (2020). American Psychological Association.

### A Chapter from a Book

List the chapter title after the date of publication, followed by a period or appropriate end punctuation. Use *In* before the book title, and follow the book title with the inclusive page numbers of the chapter.

> Tattersall, I. (2002). How did we achieve humanity? In *The monkey in the mirror* (pp. 138–168). Harcourt.

## A Single Work from an Anthology

Start with information about the individual work, followed by details about the collection in which it appears, including the page span. For editors' names in the middle of an entry, follow the usual order: initial first, surname last. Note the placement of Eds. in parentheses.

> Guy, G. R. (2005). Variationist approaches to phonological change. In B. D. Joseph & R. D. Janda (Eds.), *The handbook of historical linguistics* (pp. 369–400). Blackwell.

## One Volume of a Multivolume Edited Work

Indicate the volume in parentheses after the work's title.

> Salzman, J., Smith, D. L., & West, C. (Eds.). (1996). *Encyclopedia of African-American culture and history* (Vol. 4). Simon & Schuster Macmillan.

## A Separately Titled Volume in a Multivolume Work

> The Associated Press. (1995). *Twentieth-century America: Vol. 8. The crisis of national confidence: 1974–1980*. Grolier Educational Corp.

*Note:* When a work is part of a larger series or collection, as with this example, make a two-part title with the series and the particular volume you are citing.

## An Edited Work, One in a Series

Start the entry with the work's author, publication date, and title. Then follow with publication details about the series.

> Marshall, P. G. (2002). The impact of the cold war on Asia. In T. O'Neill (Ed.), *World history by era: Vol. 9. The nuclear age* (pp. 162–166). Greenhaven Press.

## A Group Author as Publisher

When the author is also the publisher, simply put Author in the spot where you would list the publisher's name.

> Amnesty International. (2007). *Maze of injustice: The failure to protect indigenous women from sexual violence in the USA*. Author.

*Note:* If the publication is a brochure, identify it as such in brackets after the title.

## An Edition Other Than the First

> Baylis, J., Smith, S., & Owens, P. (2011). *The globalization of world politics: An introduction to international relations* (5th ed.). Oxford University Press.

## Two or More Books by the Same Author

When you are listing multiple works by the same author, arrange them by the year of publication, earliest first.

> Sacks, O. (1995). *An anthropologist on Mars: Seven paradoxical tales.* Alfred A. Knopf.

> Sacks, O. (2015). *On the move: A life.* Alfred A. Knopf.

## An English Translation

> Setha, R. (1998). *Unarmed* (R. Narasimhan, Trans.). Macmillan. (Original work published 1995).

*Note:* If you use the original work, cite the original version; the non-English title is followed by its English translation, not italicized, in square brackets.

## An Article in a Reference Book

Start the entry with the author of the article, if identified. If no author is listed, begin the entry with the title of the article.

> Lewer, N. (1999). Non-lethal weapons. In *World encyclopedia of peace* (pp. 279–280). Pergamon Press.

## A Reprint, Different Form

> Albanov, V. (2000). *In the land of white death: An epic story of survival in the Siberian Arctic.* Modern Library. (Original work published 1917).

*Note:* This work was originally published in Russia in 1917; the 2000 reprint is the first English version. If you are citing a reprint from another source, the parentheses would contain "Reprinted from Title, pp. xx–xx, by A. Author, year, Publisher."

## A Technical or Research Report

> Taylor, B. G., Fitzgerald, N., Hunt, D., Reardon, J. A., & Brownstein, H. H. (2001). *ADAM preliminary 2000 findings on drug use and drug markets: Adult male arrestees.* National Institute of Justice.

## A Government Publication

Generally, refer to the government agency as the author. When possible, provide an identification number for the document after the title in parentheses.

> National Institute on Drug Abuse. (2000). *Inhalant abuse* (NIH Publication No. 00–3818). National Clearinghouse on Alcohol and Drug Information.

For reports obtained from the U.S. Government Printing Office, list location and publisher as "Government Printing Office."

## Print Periodical Articles

The general form for a periodical entry is this:

> Author, A. (year). Article title. *Periodical Title, volume number*(issue number), page numbers.

If the periodical does not use volume and issue numbers, include some other designation with the year, such as a date, a month, or a season. The entries that follow illustrate the information and arrangement needed to cite most types of print periodicals.

### An Article in a Scholarly Journal

> Dunn, E. C. (2016). Refugee protection and resettlement problems. *Science, 352*(6287), 772-773.

 Pay attention to the features of this basic reference to a scholarly journal:

1. Provide the authors' last names and initials, as for a book reference. List up to twenty authors. If the article has twenty-one or more authors, list the first nineteen, then an ellipsis [...], followed by the last author's name.
2. Place the year of publication in parentheses, followed by a period.
3. Format the article's title in lowercase, except for the first word of the main title and of a subtitle and except for proper nouns, acronyms, or initialisms; do not italicize the article title or place it in quotation marks.
4. Capitalize the first and all main words in the journal title; italicize it.
5. Italicize the volume number but not the issue number; place the issue in parentheses, without a space after the volume number.
6. Provide inclusive page numbers, without "pp." or "pages."

### An Abstract of a Scholarly Article (from a Secondary Source)

When referencing an abstract published separately from an article, provide publication details of the article followed by information about where the abstract was published.

> Shlipak, M. G., Simon, J. A., Grady, O., Lin, F., Wenger, N. K., & Furberg, C. D. (2001, September). Renal insufficiency and cardiovascular events in postmenopausal women with coronary heart disease. *Journal of the American College of Cardiology, 38*(3), 705–711. Abstract obtained from *Geriatrics, 2001, 56*(12). (Abstract No. 5645351.)

## A Review

To reference a book review or a review of another medium (film, exhibit, and so on), indicate the review and the medium in brackets, along with the title of the work being reviewed by the author listed.

> Hutcheon, L., & Hutcheon, M. (2008). Tuning into the mind. [Review of the book *Musicophilia: Tales of music and the brain*, by O. Sacks]. *Canadian Medical Association Journal, 178*(4), 441.

## A Magazine Article

> Pincott, J. (2016, May-June). Acting a fool: Why is female intelligence a turnoff for some men—even those who profess otherwise? *Psychology Today, 49*(3), 35, 39.

*Note:* If the article is unsigned, begin the entry with the title of the article.

> Tomatoes target toughest cancer. (2002, February). *Prevention, 54*(2), 53.

## A Newspaper Article

For newspaper articles, include the full publication date, year first followed by a comma, the month (spelled out) and the day. Identify the article's location in the newspaper using page numbers and section letters, as appropriate. If the article is a letter to the editor, identify it as such in brackets following the title. For newspapers, use *p.* or *pp.* before the page numbers; if the article is not on continuous pages, give all the page numbers, separated by commas.

> Schmitt, E., & Shanker, T. (2008, March 18). U.S. adapts cold-war idea to fight terrorists. *The New York Times*, pp. 1A, 14A–15A.

> Knaub, M. (2013, August 12). Area men recall their time as 'braceros.' *Yuma Times*, pp. 1A, 5A.

## A Newsletter Article

Newsletter article entries are similar to newspaper article entries; only a volume number is added.

> Teaching mainstreamed special education students. (2002, February). *The Council Chronicle,* 11, pp. 6–8.

## Online Sources

When it comes to references for online sources, follow these guidelines:

1. **Whenever possible, use the final version of a digital resource.** Typically, this is called the archival copy or the version of record, as opposed to a prepublished version. Right now, that final version is likely the same as the printed version of an article, though there is some movement toward the online publication being the final version (complete with additional data, graphics, and so on).

2. **In the reference entry for a digital source, start with the same elements in the same order as for print or other fixed-media resources** (author, title, and so on). Then add the most reliable electronic retrieval information that will (a) clarify what version of the source you used and (b) help your reader find the source him- or herself. Determine what you need to include based on these guidelines:

    - **Whenever possible, use the digital document's digital object identifier (DOI).** More and more, electronic publishers are using this registration code for the content of journal articles and other documents so that the document can be located on the Internet, even if the URL changes. The DOI will usually be published at the beginning of the article or be available in the article's citation.

        > Author, A. A. (year). Title of article. *Title of Periodical, volume number*(issue number), pages. DOI code

    - **If a DOI is not available for the digital document,** give the complete URL (without a period at the end). Generally, a database name is no longer needed, except for hard-to-find documents and those accessed through subscription-only databases. Use the home- or menu-page URL for subscription-only databases and online reference works.

        > Author, A. A. (year). Title of article. *Title of Periodical, volume number*(issue number), pages. URL

    - **If the content of the document is stable** (e.g., archival copy or copy of record with DOI), do not include a retrieval date in your reference entry. However, if the content is likely to change or be updated, as is the case with a lot of the material on the free web, then offer a retrieval date. This would be the case with open-web material with no fixed publication date, edition, or version, or material that is prepublished (in preparation, in press).

        > Author, A. A. (year). *Title of document.* Retrieved date from website: URL

    - **Insert DOIs and URLs in your reference entries as live links, if possible.** Do not add a period after the URL, as that may interfere with the link.

## A Journal Article with DOI

> Grinker, R. R. (2015). Reframing the science and anthropology of autism. *Culture, Medicine and Psychiatry, 39*(2), 345-350. https://doi.org/10.1007/s11013-015-9444-9

*Note:* Because the DOI references the final version of the article, the retrieval date, URL, and database name are not needed. If the online article is a preprint version, add "Advance online publication" and your retrieval date before the DOI.

## A Journal Article Without DOI

> Bell, J. B., & Nye, E. C. (2007). Specific symptoms predict suicidal ideation in Vietnam combat veterans with post-traumatic stress disorder. *Military Medicine, 172*(11), 1144–1147. http://www.ebscohost.com

*Note:* Because this article has no DOI, the complete URL is provided for the subscription database search service. If you retrieved the article from the open web, you would supply the exact URL. If the version of the article you access is in press and you have retrieved it from the author's personal or institutional website, place "in press" in parentheses after the author's name and add a retrieval date before the URL.

## A Newspaper Article

> Zernike, K. (2016, June 28). A sea of charter schools in Detroit leaves students adrift. *The New York Times.* https://www.nytimes.com/2016/06/29/us/for-detroits-children-more-school-choice-but-not-better-schools.html

## An Article in an Online Magazine (Ezine) not Published in Print

> Grossman, A. (2016, April 5). Why didn't you tell me that I love you? Asexuality, polymorphous perversity, and the liberation of the cinematic clown. *Bright Lights Film Journal.* http://brightlightsfilm.com/didnt-tell-love-chaplin-tati-keaton-lloyd-langdon-silent-comedy-asexuality-polymorphous-perversity-liberation-cinematic-clown/#.V3Kkxalk3T8p

## A Book Review

> Shapiro, K. (2007). Mystic chords. [Review of the book *Musicophilia: Tales of music and the brain,* by O. Sacks]. *Commentary, 124*(5), 73–77. http://web.ebscohost.com

## An Ebook

> Kafka, F. (2002). *Metamorphosis.* D. Wylie (Trans.). http://www.gutenberg.org/etext/5200

## Material from an Online Reference Work

> Agonism. (2008). In *Encyclopaedia Britannica*. http://search.eb.com

*Note:* See chapter 20 for more on using Wikipedia for research projects.

## Online Course Material

> Rodriguez, N. Unit 3, *Lecture 3: Sociological Theories of Deviance*. http://www.uh.edu/~nestor/lecturenotes/unit3lecture3.html

## A Workplace Document or Other "Gray Literature"

"Gray Literature" refers to informative documents (e.g., brochures, fact sheets, white papers) produced by government agencies, corporations, and nonprofit groups. If possible, give a document number or identify the type of document in brackets.

> Foehr, U. G. (2006). *Media multitasking among American youth: Prevalence, predictors and pairings* (Publication No. 7592). Kaiser Family Foundation. http://www.kff.org/entmedia/upload/7592.pdf

## Undated Content on Website

> National Institute of Allergy and Infectious Diseases. (n.d.). *Antimicrobial (drug) resistance*. http://www3.niaid.nih.gov/topics/AntimicrobialResistance/default.htm

## A Podcast Episode

> Vogt, P., & Goldman, A. (Hosts). (2020, March 5). The case of the missing hit (No. 158) [Audio podcast episode]. In *Reply all*. Gimlet media. https://gimletmedia.com/shows/reply-all/o2h8bx/158-the-case-of-the-missing-hit

## Message on a Newsgroup, an Online Forum, or a Discussion Group

> [ManaSyn]. (2020, May 23). *Solar farm in Portugal*. [Online forum post]. Reddit. https://www.reddit.com/r/RenewableEnergy/comments/gp8zvr/solar_farm_in_portugal/

*Note:* When the legal name of the poster is unknown, begin with the username in brackets, as shown above.

## A Blog Post

> Paine, N., & Thomson-DeVeaux, A. (2020, June 23). What economists fear most during this recovery. *FiveThirtyEight, ABC News*. https://fivethirtyeight.com/features/what-economists-fear-most-during-this-recovery/

### A Tweet

> Hannah-Jones, N. [@nhannahjones] (2019, August 14). *The #1619Project published today and it is my profound hope that it will reframe . . . the way we understand our nation* [Tweet]. Twitter. https://twitter.com/nhannahjones/status/1161655165767884801?s=20

### Online Lecture Notes and Presentation Slides

> Kemper, T. (2020, March 14). *Multimodal storytelling* [PowerPoint slides]. SlideShare. https://slideshare.net/UMSLFYC2020/multimedia-storytelling-FYC-Spring-1

### YouTube, Ted Talk, or other Streaming Video

> Talhouk, S. (2012, December). *Don't kill your language* [Video]. TED. https://www.ted.com/talks/suzanne_talhouk_don_t_kill_your_language

## Other Sources (Primary, Personal, and Multimedia)

Cite audiovisual media sources and electronic sources as follows.

### A Television or Radio Episode

Indicate the episode by writers and directors, if possible. Then follow with the airing date, the episode title, and the type of series in brackets. Add the producer(s) as you would the editors(s) of a print medium, and complete the entry with details about the series itself.

> Morgan, P. (Writer), & Jarrold, J. (Director). (2016, November 4). Act of god (Season 1, Episode 4) [TV series episode]. In A. Eaton (Producer), *The Crown*. Netflix.

### An Audio Recording

Begin the entry with the speaker's or writer's name, not the producer. Indicate the type of recording in brackets.

> Kim, E. (Author, speaker). (2000). *Ten thousand sorrows* [Album]. Random House.

### A Music Recording

Give the name and function of the originators or primary contributors. Indicate the recording medium in brackets immediately following the title.

> ARS Femina Ensemble. (Performers). (1998). *Musica de la puebla de Los Angeles: Music by women of baroque Mexico, Cuba, & Europe* [Album]. Nannerl Recordings.

### A Film

Give the name and function of the director, producer, or both.

> Lee, A. (Director). (2012). *Life of Pi* [Motion picture]. Twentieth-Century Fox.

### A Published Interview, Titled, No Author

Start the entry with the interview's title, followed by publication details.

> Stephen Harper: The Report interview. (2002, January 7). *The Report* (Alberta, BC), 29, 10–11.

### A Published Interview, Titled, Single Author

Start the entry with the interviewee's name, followed by the date and the title. Place the interviewer's name in brackets before other publication details.

> Fussman, C. (2002, January). What I've learned. [Interview by Robert McNamara.] Esquire, 137, 85.

### An Unpublished Paper Presented at a Meeting

Indicate when the paper was presented, at what meeting, in what location.

> Sifferd, K., & Hirstein, W. (2012, June). *On the criminal culpability of successful and unsuccessful psychopaths*. Paper presented at the meeting of the Society for Philosophy and Psychology, Boulder, CO.

### An Unpublished Doctoral Dissertation

Place the dissertation's title in italics, even though the work is unpublished. Indicate the school at which the writer completed the dissertation.

> Roberts, W. (2001). *Crime amidst suburban wealth* (Unpublished doctoral dissertation). Bowling Green State University, Bowling Green, OH.

# APA Format Guidelines

To submit a polished academic paper in APA format, follow the rules below and refer to the sample APA paper, beginning on the next page. These rules apply to student papers.

- **Title Page:** On the first page, type your paper's title three or four lines from the top, boldface and centered. Capitalize major words. Four lines down, type these elements on separate lines, double-spaced, in regular type, and centered: your name and that of any co-authors; your department and school name; the course name; your instructor's name as presented on course materials; and the due date for the assignment. In the top right corner, put the page number. (For student papers, a running head is not required.)

- **Abstract:** On the second page, include an abstract—a 150- to 250-word paragraph summarizing your paper. Place the title *Abstract* (no italics) approximately one inch from the top of the page and center it. The number 2 should appear at the top right corner of the page.

- **Body:** Format the body (which begins on the third page) as follows:
    - **Margins:** Leave a one-inch margin on all four sides of each page (one and one-half inches on the left if the paper will be bound). Do not justify lines, but rather leave a ragged right margin and do not break words at the ends of lines.
    - **Line Spacing:** Double-space your entire paper, unless your instructor allows single spacing for tables and figures.
    - **Page Numbers:** Place the page number flush right at the top of each page.
    - **Headings:** Like an outline, headings show the organization of your paper and the importance of each topic. All topics of equal importance should have headings of the same level, or style. Figure 24.3 shows the levels of headings used in APA papers.

> Level 1:    **Centered, Boldface, Uppercase and Lowercase Heading**
> Level 2:  **Flush Left, Boldface, Uppercase and Lowercase Side Heading**
> Level 3:    **Indented, boldface, lowercase paragraph heading ending with a period.**
> Level 4:    ***Indented, boldface, italicized, lowercase paragraph heading with a period.***
> Level 5:    *Indented, italicized, lowercase paragraph heading with a period.*
>
> **Example:**
>
> > **Teaching K-12 English Language Learners in the Mainstream Classroom**
> > **The English Language Learner Landscape**
> > > **Myths and misconceptions.**
> > > ***Myth 1: Exposure will lead to learning.***
> > > *The need for explicit morphological instruction.*
>
> *fig. 24.3*

- **Appendix:** Tables and figures (graphs, charts, maps, etc.) already appear on separate pages following the reference list. If necessary, one or more appendices may also supplement your text, following any tables or figures.

# Sample APA Paper

In her Writing in Psychology and Human Development course, Julia Sweigert wrote the following report on siblings of children with autism. Inspired by her own experience as the sibling of a sister with Down syndrome and by interactions with other siblings of children with disabilities, Julia researched this topic with the goal of advancing family support in a household where a sibling has autism. You can use Julia's paper in three ways:

1. To study how a well-written research paper uses a range of resources to build a discussion or line of reasoning that answers a research question.
2. To examine how sources are used and integrated into social-sciences research writing.
3. To see in detail the format and documentation practices of APA style.

*Note:* Often, a social-sciences research paper takes the form of an experiment report. For an example of such a report, see chapter 22.

## Sample Title Page

Note that APA format requires that the paper be double-spaced throughout, with a one-inch margin on all sides.

> Insert the page number in the top right corner.

> Full title, author(s), department, school name, course number and name, instructor name, and due date are centered on the page, typed in uppercase and lowercase as shown.

**The Silent Sibling:**
**How Current Autism Intervention Neglects Typically-Developing Siblings**

Julia Sweigert

University Writing Program, University of California, Davis

UWP 102H: Writing in Psychology and Human Development

Dr. Wrye Sententia

April 17, 2015

## Sample Abstract

The abstract summarizes the paper's central issue, its main conclusion, the key reasoning and evidence presented, and the study's significance.

### Abstract

This paper explores the experience of siblings of individuals with autism and the failure of current systems to understand and support that experience. With current rates of autism, more and more siblings are playing an instrumental role in the care and support of their affected brothers and sisters, including as playmates, translators, and caregivers. However, current research and services rarely provide opportunities for siblings to participate in the conversation on autism. To achieve a better understanding of autism spectrum disorders and to create more effective intervention and treatment programs, the sibling experience should be heard. Siblings need the opportunity to voice their stories and to reach out for help as they face the unique realities of providing long-term care for brothers and sisters with autism.

***Note:*** The *APA Style Guide*, 7th edition, contains extensive guidelines for writing with bias-free language, including attention to race and ethnicity, gender, sexual orientation, age, disability, socioeconomic status, and intersectionality. For help with these guidelines in your writing, see chapter 7 or visit the APA website at **apastyle.apa.org/style-grammar-guidelines/bias-free-language**.

## The Silent Sibling:
### How Current Autism Intervention Neglects Typically Developing Siblings

The Centers for Disease Control and Prevention (2014) recently reported that 1 in 68 children is diagnosed with an autism spectrum disorder. Autism spectrum disorders, or ASD, include a variety of developmental disabilities characterized by communication deficits and repetitive interests or behaviors. Because American families average approximately two children per family (U.S. Census Bureau, 2013), the reported autism rate means that about 1 in 68 children is also growing up as the sibling to someone with autism spectrum disorder. From a young age, these typically-developing siblings experience firsthand the full impact of autism, as they help their parents with the extensive care required of some people with this disability. Yet, siblings rarely receive any external help as they endure the challenges and responsibilities that autism can bring to a family. Despite the growing number of autism research and treatment centers in the United States, very few of these organizations offer programs geared towards siblings. By neglecting the siblings, current autism intervention services leave these children isolated and struggling to process their unique experiences, a situation that can be detrimental later in life as siblings prepare to take on the increasing responsibilities of caregiving for their brothers and sisters with autism.

### What Makes a Sibling?

In the disabilities community, siblings include any typically developing children in the family of a person with autism or other physical and developmental disabilities. Siblings can be young children living at home or older adults with children of their own. Because autism can affect individuals across many different regions, cultures, and socioeconomic groups, siblings come from various backgrounds as well. Regardless of these differences, siblings share many common experiences and emotional struggles. Research has found that most siblings report some level of frustration, embarrassment, and isolation as a result of their situation (Orsmond & Seltzer, 2007b). These shared experiences result from the stress brought on by disabilities themselves, as well as a failure on the part of disability treatment centers to provide intervention services just for siblings.

While siblings can have brothers or sisters with a number of different disabilities, the recently reported rise in autism rates (Centers for Disease Control and Prevention [CDC], 2014) coupled with the unique and diverse behavioral profiles seen in individuals with autism makes siblings of children with autism an important group in need of support. In order to be diagnosed with autism spectrum disorder, a child must show two key behavioral traits: a deficit in social communication and interactions, and some form of restricted, repetitive behaviors and interests (American Psychiatric Association [APA], 2013). Commonly, children with autism meet the diagnostic criteria with behaviors that include limited to absent verbal communication, increased sensory sensitivity, a strong preference for predictable schedules, and compulsive actions, such as hand-flapping or full-body rocking. Day-to-day experiences that conflict with these behaviors can often trigger a sort of "fight or flight" response from people with autism; they may become aggressive or attempt to escape the situation. Additionally, as a result of these pervasive behavioral deficits, people with autism might have very limited ability to self-care, including both the personal hygiene and life skills that allow for independent living. The complexities and magnitudes of these behaviors associated with autism transform the sibling relationship.

Siblings of people with autism grow up experiencing life in a manner distinctly different from members of a neurotypical sibling pair. Children diagnosed with the disability can be very dependent on family members for care and behavioral mediation. While most of this caregiving burden falls on parents, siblings take on a significant portion of the responsibility too. On a daily basis, siblings help feed their affected brothers or sisters, supervise them in public settings, and help to interpret their limited communication. Because of their close proximity, siblings can also become the target of aggression when the child with autism is upset or over-stimulated (Orsmond & Seltzer, 2007b). Thus, on a daily basis, these siblings become caregivers and emotional buffers, a distinct difference when compared to the playmate relationship of typical sibling pairs.

## Why Do Siblings Matter?

Siblings witness most things that their families go through as a result of the disability and serve as life-long friends and caregivers. In addition to dealing with typical autism behaviors and providing personal care, siblings know their brothers and sisters intimately, including what they like, what they dislike, how to annoy them, and how to make them smile. Thus, the sibling perspective is an invaluable and underappreciated one that can enhance our understanding of disabilities such as autism.

**Siblings Are Playmates**

Siblings of children with autism spend a significant portion of their day interacting directly with their affected brother or sister. For example, researchers conducting in-home observations found that siblings, age 2-12, spend as much as 40 minutes of every hour in shared activities with the child with autism (Orsmond & Seltzer, 2007b). The siblings' frequent and close proximity commonly enables them to understand the wants and needs of the child with autism better than the child's caregiving adults, including parents and teachers. As one 13-year-old sibling said, "I can understand my brother—a lot of other people don't—even my dad doesn't always understand him—then he's asking me: what does he mean? And I always know what my brother means" (Moyson & Roeyers, 2012, p. 93). While parents pay close attention to the care and therapies a child with autism needs, many siblings better understand what their brother or sister wants and needs. Siblings' perspective on the disability may differ significantly from their parents' perspective, as these children do not yet have to bear the added stress of being primary caregivers. Sibling perspectives could supplement parent and therapist perspectives in autism intervention to create a more accurate picture of how autistic behavior transpires at home.

**Siblings Become Caregivers**

As parents age and their ability to provide care declines, the sibling transitions from companion to caregiver. In addition to normal aging, parents of people with intellectual and developmental disabilities, including autism, experience significantly more health problems by their early sixties (Seltzer et al., 2011), which can interfere with their ability to provide care to their dependent child. Consequently, during this time parents must find an alternate living situation for their child. A longitudinal study of parents found that between their mid-fifties and mid-sixties, approximately 20% of parents saw their children with intellectual and developmental disabilities move out of the parents' home into a different residential living situation (Seltzer et al., 2011). As parents experience a diminishing ability to provide care for their children with autism, the adult siblings begin to take on a greater caregiving and support role.

Siblings may simultaneously have to offer additional support for both their brother or sister with autism and for their aging parents; in addition, as they enter adulthood, these siblings commonly have careers and families of their own.

Such siblings increasingly take on the responsibilities of their affected brother or sister's well-being (Burke, et al., 2012). While typical sibling pairs may develop close friendships as they move into adulthood, siblings of people with autism must adjust their future to include the realities of providing care and making decisions regarding their brother or sister. In some instances, the person with autism is moved into a residential facility, but the siblings still provide significant emotional support (Orsmond & Seltser, 2007a). Thus, siblings play an important and lifelong role in maintaining a stable and enriching environment for their brothers and sisters with autism.

### When Are Siblings Absent?

Autism takes center-stage in the life of these siblings; even so, siblings are often left out of the research and services aimed at improving autism outcomes. For example, as parents take their child with autism to a number of behavior therapies and life skills classes each week, siblings are often lost in the shuffle. During the various appointments, neurotypical siblings play in the waiting room or spend the afternoon at a friend or relative's house. This accidental exclusion can leave the siblings uninformed. They might have a basic understanding of what autism looks like because they see it daily at home, but they miss the opportunity to learn fully how autism affects people, and why their brother or sister has such distinct behaviors. Additionally, because young siblings do not get to see the interventions in action, they may not understand the benefits of constant therapy and fail to see all the hard work that goes into little moments of progress seen in the children with autism.

### Sibling Absence in Research

Research into the effects of autism on families relies primarily on assessments of the affected child and reports made by the parents, with minimal to no input from school-age siblings. For example, D. E. Gray (2002) conducted a longitudinal study of families having a child diagnosed with autism, but only surveyed the parents from each family. While he did give some attention to the topic of autism's impact on other children in the family, he based these results entirely on parental reports, without providing the siblings an opportunity to share their perspectives. Thus, his conclusions about the sibling experience came only from parents inferring what their other children might be experiencing, a filtering that introduces significant bias to the results. More recently, researchers have begun to consider the sibling's perspective but often rely on retrospective accounts by adult siblings (Arnold, et al., 2012), rather than allowing younger siblings to report for themselves. By omitting narratives made directly by school-age siblings, current research does not adequately present or address the needs of neurotypically developing children.

**Sibling Absence in Support Services**

Because therapy providers base autism interventions on current research findings, the absence of young siblings in research leads to a lack of services geared specifically toward their needs. Children with autism receive intervention services to improve behavioral problems and develop life skills, while parents have access to support groups that help them to endure the challenges of raising a child with autism. Siblings have begun expressing a need for help in coping with their unique experiences. In 2012, to more thoroughly assess the needs of siblings, researchers conducted a survey of adult siblings of people with developmental disabilities. Over half of these individuals cited the need for better sibling inclusion, both with services geared directly towards sibling support and also with a definition of "family" that includes the neurotypical siblings, in addition to the parents and child with autism (Arnold et al., 2012). Siblings need a safe space to process their experiences and work through challenges, away from their parents and brother or sister.

**Sibling Absence in Awareness**

While they have a general idea of the day-to-day needs of their brother or sister with autism, siblings do not necessarily know the full scope of autism across the lifetime and may not be aware of the services and programs available to support individuals with autism (Arnold et al., 2012). As children, siblings might have a general idea of the services their brother or sister is receiving, but they are uninformed regarding the process involved in procuring such services. This lack of information can become problematic. As siblings mature and begin to take on an instrumental role in supporting their loved one with autism, they must quickly learn to navigate the complicated system of accessing the necessary autism-support programs. The failure to involve siblings earlier in the therapy process can lead to a more stressful transition of care-giving responsibilities as the siblings enter adulthood.

## What Do Siblings Need?

The emotional impact of autism on siblings' lives raises the question of how such emotions, particularly the stresses and isolation, can be better mediated during the earlier years to produce more favorable outcomes. Support groups are being developed that allow siblings a forum to share their stories and connect with people who share those experiences. The efficacy of these programs has not been fully confirmed, but preliminary analysis of participant outcomes in one such program showed a positive and persistent effect on the well-being of siblings (Conway & Meyer, 2008).

Unfortunately, such programs are not widespread and need to be made more readily accessible. Sibshop, one such sibling support program that is starting to gain momentum, has only 57 programs within the United States listed in their online database (Sibling Support Project, 2015), meaning that many states have only one such program available to families in need. Incorporating sibling-support programs into currently existing autism intervention services could quickly increase availability and access. For example, Easter Seals already provides a variety of services and resources to individuals with autism and their parents (Easter Seals, 2014) and could serve as excellent facilitators for sibling-support therapy. These organizations already see the families of autism frequently and could partner with Sibshop to connect siblings and form a support network. By providing these new programs, service providers can engage the siblings more effectively in the autism treatments and also allow them to gain a better understanding of their sibling experiences and identity.

## Conclusion

School-age siblings hold a unique position in the discussion of autism treatment and intervention. While therapies frequently address the needs of the diagnosed child and of parents, these intervention programs often overlook the siblings. These typically developing children have their own unique set of needs and play a significant role in providing care and company to their brother or sister with autism. Siblings experience frequent frustrations and isolation, which can lead to significant stress later in adulthood as they transition into becoming the primary caregivers for their brothers and sisters with autism. By developing programs that meet the emotional and peer needs of siblings, service providers can create a more holistic family-based approach to autism and move towards improved outcomes for people with autism and their entire family.

## References

American Psychiatric Association. (2013). *Diagnostic and statistical manual of mental disorders*. 5th ed. Author.

Arnold, C., Heller, T., & Kramer, J. (2012). Support needs of siblings of people with developmental disabilities. *Intellectual and Developmental Disabilities, 50*(5), 373-382.

Burke, M., Taylor, J., Urbano, R., & Hodapp, R. (2012). Predictors of future caregiving by adult siblings of individuals with intellectual and developmental disabilities. *Journal on Intellectual and Developmental Disabilities, 117*(1), 33-47.

Centers for Disease Control and Prevention. (2014). Prevalence of autism spectrum disorder among children aged 8 years. *MMWR Surveillance Summaries Publication, 63*(2), 1-21.

Conway, S. & Meyer, D. (2008). Developing support for siblings of young people with disabilities. *Support for Learning, 23*(3), 113-117. https://doi.org/10.1111/j.1467-9604.2008.00381.x

Easter Seals Inc. (2014). *Autism Spectrum Disorder Services*. http://www.easterseals.com/our-programs/autism-services/

Gray, D. E. (2002). Ten years on: A longitudinal study of families of children with autism. *Journal of Intellectual and Developmental Disability, 27*(3), 215-222. https://doi.org/10.1080/1366825021000008639

Moyson, T. & Roeyers, H. (2012). "The overall quality of my life as a sibling is all right, but of course it could always be better." Quality of life of siblings of children with intellectual disability: the siblings' perspective. *Journal of Intellectual Disability Research, 56*(1), 87-101. https://doi.org/10.1111/j.1365-2788.2011.01393.x

Orsmond, G. & Seltzer, M. (2007a). Siblings of individuals with autism or Down syndrome: effects on adult lives. *Journal of Intellectual Disability Research, 51*(9), 682-696. https://doi.org/10.1111/j.1365-2788.2007.00954.x

Orsmond, G. & Seltzer, M. (2007b). Siblings of individuals with autism spectrum disorder across the lifetime. *Mental Retardation & Developmental Disabilities Research Review, 13*, 313-320.

Seltzer, M., Floyd, F., Song, J., Greenberg, J., & Hong, J. (2011). Midlife and aging parents of adults with intellectual and developmental disabilities: Impacts of lifelong parenting. *American Journal on Intellectual and Developmental Disabilities, 116*(6), 479-499.

Sibling Support Project. (2015). *Sibshops*. https://www.siblingsupport.org/about-sibshops

U.S. Census Bureau. (2013). FM-3: Average number of own children under 18, for families with children under 18. *Current Population Survey*. https://www.census.gov/hhes/families/data/families.html

## Reading for Better Writing

1. *Connections:* In your extended family and acquaintances, do you know people with autism or another disability? How would you describe their experience and the experience of their family?
2. *Comprehension:* What did you learn from Julia's paper about the experiences and needs of siblings of autistic children? List all the points that you can remember.
3. *Writing Moves:*
   a. Julia uses questions as headings to organize her paper. What is the effect of using questions? How do the questions create a logical structure or flow for the paper?
   b. Study Julia's list of sources and her use of those sources within her paper. How would you characterize the research she has done? How does she use sources within her own writing, while also distinguishing source material from her own thinking?

**Your Project:** What sibling issues interest you? The phenomenon of only-children? Brother-sister dynamics? Birth order of siblings? Twins? Grandparent-grandchild relationships? The impact of divorce on sibling relationships? The impact of culture, gender identity, and/or race on sibling dynamics? Consider a phenomenon like these for your own research and writing.

"The Silent Sibling: How Current Autism Intervention Neglects Typically-Developing Siblings" by Julia Sweigert. Originally appeared in the University of California-Davis' Prized Writing. Used by permission of the author.

# APA Style: Applications

Once you have used the instruction in this chapter to format and document your paper according to APA style, extend what you have learned by doing the following activities:

1. **System Check:** To make sense of APA guidelines and rules, answer these questions: What is the essential logic of the APA system? How does this logic reflect research practices and values in the Social Sciences?
2. **Reference Practice:** Create references list entries in correct APA style for the following sources:
   - An article in the summer 2009 issue (volume 34, no. 2) of the periodical *MELUS*, by Joni Adamson and Scott Slovic: "The Shoulders We Stand On: An Introduction to Ethnicity and Ecocriticism" (pages 5–24)
   - The book *The Playful World: How Technology Is Transforming Our Imagination,* by Mark Pesce, published in 2000 by Ballantine Books
   - The web page "Vaccines for Children Program (VFC)," part of the Vaccines and Immunizations section of the Centers for Disease Control and Prevention (CDC) website, sponsored by the U.S. government's Department of Health and Human Services. No author or publication date is listed. The URL is http://www.cdc.gov/vaccines/programs/vfc/index.html.

## Learning-Objectives Checklist ✓

Have you achieved this chapter's learning objectives? Check your progress with the following items, revisiting topics in the chapter as needed. I have . . .

\_\_\_\_ gained an overview of the APA system of documentation—the basic logic of in-text citations in relation to reference entries.

\_\_\_\_ applied rules of in-text citation for a whole range of sources.

\_\_\_\_ developed a references list that is properly formatted and that correctly and fully identifies sources, whether books or journal articles or online documents.

\_\_\_\_ correctly implemented APA format guidelines (e.g., title page, abstract, pagination, heading system, references page).

\_\_\_\_ examined APA style at work in Julia Sweigert's "The Silent Sibling: How Current Autism Intervention Neglects Typically-Developing Siblings," learning how the system is practiced effectively in her paper.

# IV. Handbook

## 25 Understanding Grammar

| | |
|---|---|
| Noun | 523 |
| *Exercises* | 526 |
| Pronoun | 527 |
| *Exercises* | 531 |
| Verb | 532 |
| *Exercises* | 538 |
| Adjective | 539 |
| Adverb | 540 |
| Preposition | 541 |
| Conjunction | 542 |
| Interjection | 542 |
| *Exercises* | 543 |

## 26 Constructing Sentences

| | |
|---|---|
| Using Subjects and Predicates | 545 |
| *Exercises* | 548 |
| Using Phrases | 549 |
| Using Clauses | 551 |
| Using Sentence Variety | 552 |
| *Exercises* | 554 |

## 27 Avoiding Sentence Errors

| | |
|---|---|
| Subject–Verb Agreement | 555 |
| Pronoun–Antecedent Agreement | 559 |
| *Exercises* | 560 |
| Shifts in Sentence Construction | 561 |
| Fragments, Comma Splices, and Run-Ons | 562 |
| *Exercises* | 564 |
| Misplaced and Dangling Modifiers | 565 |
| Ambiguous Wording | 566 |
| *Exercises* | 567 |
| Nonstandard Language | 568 |
| *Exercises* | 569 |
| Avoiding Sentence Problems Review | 570 |

## 28 Marking Punctuation

| | |
|---|---|
| Period | 571 |
| Ellipsis | 572 |
| Question Mark | 573 |
| *Exercises* | 574 |
| Comma | 575 |
| *Exercises* | 580 |
| Semicolon | 581 |
| Colon | 582 |
| Hyphen | 583 |
| Dash | 585 |
| *Exercises* | 586 |
| Quotation Marks | 587 |
| Italics (Underlining) | 589 |
| Parentheses | 590 |
| Diagonal | 590 |
| Brackets | 591 |
| Exclamation Point | 591 |
| Apostrophe | 592 |
| *Exercises* | 594 |

## 29 Checking Mechanics

| | |
|---|---|
| Capitalization | 595 |
| *Exercises* | 599 |
| Plurals | 600 |
| Numbers | 602 |
| *Exercises* | 604 |
| Abbreviations | 605 |
| Acronyms and Initialisms | 607 |
| *Exercises* | 608 |
| Basic Spelling Rules | 609 |
| Commonly Misspelled Words | 610 |
| Steps to Becoming a Better Speller | 615 |
| *Exercises* | 616 |

## 30 Using the Right Word

| | |
|---|---|
| *Exercises* | 620 |
| *Exercises* | 624 |
| *Exercises* | 628 |
| *Exercises* | 632 |

## 31 Multilingual and ESL Guidelines

| | |
|---|---|
| Five Parts of Speech | 633 |
| Noun | 633 |
| *Exercises* | 636 |
| Verb | 637 |
| *Exercises* | 643 |
| Adjective | 644 |
| Adverb | 645 |
| Preposition | 646 |
| *Exercises* | 647 |
| Understanding Sentence Basics | 648 |
| Sentence Problems | 649 |
| *Exercises* | 651 |
| Numbers, Word Parts, and Idioms | 652 |
| *Exercises* | 654 |
| *Exercises* | 658 |

### Handbook: Mixed Review

| | |
|---|---|
| *Exercises* | 659 |
| *Exercises* | 660 |
| *Exercises* | 661 |
| *Exercises* | 662 |
| *Exercises* | 663 |
| *Exercises* | 664 |

# Chapter 25

# Understanding Grammar

**Grammar** is the study of the structure and features of the language, consisting of rules and standards that are followed to produce clear, acceptable writing and speaking. **Parts of speech** refers to the eight different categories that indicate how words are used in the English language—as *nouns, pronouns, verbs, adjectives, adverbs, prepositions, conjunctions,* or *interjections*.

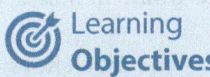

**Learning Objectives**

By working through this chapter, you will be able to
- understand the role of nouns.
- understand the role of pronouns.
- understand the role of verbs.
- understand the role of adjectives.
- understand the role of adverbs.
- understand the role of prepositions.
- understand the role of conjunctions.
- understand the role of interjections.

## 25.01 Noun

A **noun** is a word that names something: a person, a place, a thing, or an idea.

Toni Morrison/author  *Parasite*/film
UC-Davis/university  *Red at the Bone*/book
Renaissance/era  liberty/idea

**ESL Note:** See 31.03–31.04 for information on count and noncount nouns.

## 25.02 Classes of Nouns

All nouns are either proper nouns or common nouns. Nouns may also be classified as *individual* or *collective,* or *concrete* or *abstract*.

### 25.03 Proper Nouns

A **proper noun,** which is always capitalized, names a specific person, place, thing, or idea.

**Rembrandt, Bertrand Russell** (people)
**Albuquerque, Tower of London** (places)
***The Night Watch,* Rosetta Stone** (things)
**New Deal, Christianity** (ideas)

### 25.04 Common Nouns

A **common noun** is a general name for a person, a place, a thing, or an idea. Common nouns are not capitalized.

**optimist, instructor** (people)  **cafeteria, park** (places)
**computer, chair** (things)  **freedom, love** (ideas)

### 25.05 Collective Nouns

A **collective noun** names a group or a unit.

> family     audience     crowd     committee     team     class

### 25.06 Concrete Nouns

A **concrete noun** names a thing that is tangible (can be seen, touched, heard, smelled, or tasted).

> child     The Black Keys     gym     village     microwave oven     pizza

### 25.07 Abstract Nouns

An **abstract noun** names an idea, a condition, or a feeling—in other words, something that cannot be seen, touched, heard, smelled, or tasted.

> beauty     Jungian psychology     anxiety     agoraphobia     trust

## 25.08 Forms of Nouns

Nouns are grouped according to their *number, gender,* and *case*.

### 25.09 Number of Nouns

**Number** indicates whether a noun is singular or plural.

A singular noun refers to one person, place, thing, or idea.

> student     laboratory     lecture     note     grade     result

A plural noun refers to more than one person, place, thing, or idea.

> students     laboratories     lectures     notes     grades     results

### 25.10 Gender of Nouns

**Gender** indicates whether a noun is masculine, feminine, neuter, or indefinite.

**Masculine:**
> father     king     brother     men     colt     rooster

**Feminine:**
> mother     queen     sister     women     filly     hen

**Neuter** (without sex):
> notebook     monitor     car     printer

**Indefinite or common** (masculine or feminine):
> professor     customer     children     doctor     people

### 25.11 Case of Nouns

The **case** of a noun tells what role the noun plays in a sentence. There are three cases: *nominative, possessive,* and *objective.*

A noun in the **nominative case** is used as a subject. The subject of a sentence tells who or what the sentence is about.

> **Dean Henning** manages the College of Arts and Communication.

**Note:** A noun is also in the nominative case when it is used as a predicate noun (or predicate nominative). A predicate noun follows a linking verb, usually a form of the *be* verb (such as *am, is, are, was, were, be, being, been*), and repeats or renames the subject.

> Ms. Yokum is the **person** to talk to about the college's impact in our community.

A noun in the **possessive case** shows possession or ownership. In this form, it acts as an adjective.

> Our **president's** willingness to discuss concerns with students has boosted campus morale.

A noun in the **objective case** serves as an object of the preposition, a direct object, an indirect object, or an object complement.

> To survive, institutions of higher **learning** sometimes cut **budgets** in spite of **protests** from **students** and **instructors**. (*Learning* is the object of the preposition *of, budgets* is the direct object of the verb *cut, protests* is the object of the preposition *in spite of,* and *students* and *instructors* are the objects of the preposition *from*.)

## 25.12 A Closer Look
### Direct and Indirect Objects

A **direct object** is a noun (or pronoun) that identifies what or who receives the action of the verb.

> Budget cutbacks reduced class **choices**. (*Choices* is the direct object of the active verb *reduced*.)

An **indirect object** is a noun (or pronoun) that identifies the person *to whom* or *for whom* something is done, or the thing *to which* or *for which* something is done. An indirect object is always accompanied by a direct object.

> Recent budget cuts have given **students** fewer class choices. (*Choices* is the direct object of *have given*; *students* is the indirect object.)

**ESL Note:** Not every transitive verb is followed by *both* a direct object and an indirect object. Both can, however, follow *give, send, show, tell, teach, find, sell, ask, offer, pay, pass,* and *hand.*

# Handbook

 **Grammar Exercises:**

## Nouns

### A. Classes of Nouns

Identify the class of the underlined noun in each sentence. Mark all classes that apply.

1. Jenna used a <u>pencil</u> to sketch a design for the new recreational center.
   - a. proper noun
   - b. common noun
   - c. concrete noun
2. My <u>team</u> won a regional debate championship.
   - a. collective noun
   - b. common noun
   - c. abstract noun
3. The end of the movie left me with deep <u>disappointment</u>.
   - a. common noun
   - b. concrete noun
   - c. abstract noun
4. Tomorrow night I'm going to the <u>Yankees</u> game.
   - a. proper noun
   - b. abstract noun
   - c. common noun
5. Can someone buy me a <u>soda</u> at the store?
   - a. collective noun
   - b. concrete noun
   - c. abstract noun
6. I'm trying to work up the <u>motivation</u> to go to the gym.
   - a. proper noun
   - b. common noun
   - c. abstract noun

### B. Case of Nouns

For each sentence identify the case of the underlined noun.

1. Social media have changed the way we receive <u>news</u>.
   - a. nominative case
   - b. possessive case
   - c. objective case
2. <u>The Weeknd</u> sings R&B music.
   - a. nominative case
   - b. possessive case
   - c. objective case
3. <u>Justin's</u> favorite restaurant is on LaGrange Avenue.
   - a. nominative case
   - b. possessive case
   - c. objective case

### C. Gender of Nouns

Write down the feminine nouns from the list below.

desk   writer   princess   child   pilot   tree   waitress

## 25.13 Pronoun

A **pronoun** is a word that is used in place of a noun.

Miguel was the most interesting 10-year-old **I** ever taught. **He** was a good thinker and thus a good writer. **I** remember **his** paragraph about the cowboy hat **he** received from **his** grandparents. **It** was "too new looking." The brim was not rolled properly. But the hat's imperfections were not the main idea in Miguel's writing. No, the main idea was how **he** was fixing the hat **himself** by wearing it when **he** showered.

## 25.14 Antecedents

An **antecedent** is the noun or pronoun that the pronoun refers to or replaces. Most pronouns have antecedents, but not all do. (See 25.20.)

As the wellness **counselor** checked *her* chart, several **students** *who* were waiting *their* turns shifted uncomfortably. (*Counselor* is the antecedent of *her*; *students* is the antecedent of *who* and *their*.)

**Note:** Each pronoun must agree with its antecedent in number, person, and gender.

### 25.15 Classes of Pronouns

**Personal**

I, me, my, mine / we, us, our, ours / you, your, yours
they, them, their, theirs / he, him, his, she, her, hers, it, its

**Reflexive and Intensive**

myself, yourself, himself, herself, itself, ourselves, yourselves, themselves

**Relative**

who, whose, whom, which, that

**Indefinite**

| all | anything | everybody | most | no one | some |
| another | both | everyone | much | nothing | somebody |
| any | each | everything | neither | one | someone |
| anybody | each one | few | nobody | other | something |
| anyone | either | many | none | several | such |

**Interrogative**

who, whose, whom, which, what

**Demonstrative**

this, that, these, those

**Reciprocal**

each other, one another

## 25.16 Classes of Pronouns

There are several classes of pronouns: *personal, reflexive and intensive, relative, indefinite, interrogative,* and *demonstrative.*

### 25.17 Personal Pronouns

A **personal pronoun** refers to a specific person or thing.

*Marge* started **her** car; **she** drove the antique *convertible* to Monterey, where **she** hoped to sell **it** at an auction.

### 25.18 Reflexive and Intensive Pronouns

A **reflexive pronoun** is formed by adding *-self* or *-selves* to a personal pronoun. A reflexive pronoun can act as a direct object or an indirect object of a verb, an object of a preposition, or a predicate nominative.

Charles loves **himself**. (direct object of *loves*)

Charles gives **himself** A's for fashion sense. (indirect object of *gives*)

Charles smiles at **himself** in store windows. (object of preposition *at*)

Charles can be **himself** anywhere. (predicate nominative)

An **intensive pronoun** intensifies, or emphasizes, the noun or pronoun it refers to.

Leo **himself** taught his children to invest their lives in others.

The lesson was sometimes painful—but they learned it **themselves**.

### 25.19 Relative Pronouns

A **relative pronoun** relates an adjective dependent (relative) clause to the noun or pronoun it modifies. (The noun is italicized in each example below; the relative pronoun is in bold.)

*Freshmen* **who** believe they have a lot to learn are absolutely right.

Just navigating this *campus,* **which** is huge, can be challenging.

Make sure you know when to use the relative pronouns *who* or *whom* and *that* or *which.* (See 28.27 and the word pairs in chapter 30.)

### 25.20 Indefinite Pronouns

An **indefinite pronoun** refers to unnamed or unknown people, places, or things.

**Everyone** seemed amused when I was searching for my classroom in the student center. (The antecedent of *everyone* is unnamed.)

**Nothing** is more unnerving than rushing at the last minute into the wrong room for the wrong class. (The antecedent of *nothing* is unknown.)

Most indefinite pronouns are singular, so when they are used as subjects, they should have singular verbs. (See 27.13.)

## 25.21 Interrogative Pronouns

An **interrogative pronoun** asks a question.

So **which** will it be—renting an apartment or staying in the dorms?

**Note:** When an interrogative pronoun modifies a noun, it functions as an adjective.

## 25.22 Demonstrative Pronouns

A **demonstrative pronoun** points out people, places, or things.

We advise **this:** Bring along as many maps and schedules as you need.
**Those** are useful tools. **That** is the solution.

**Note:** When a demonstrative pronoun modifies a noun, it functions as an adjective.

## 25.23 Forms of Personal Pronouns

The **form** of a personal pronoun indicates its *number* (singular or plural), its *person* (first, second, or third), its *case* (nominative, possessive, or objective), and its *gender* (masculine, feminine, neuter, or indefinite).

## 25.24 Number of Pronouns

A **personal pronoun** is either singular *(I, you, he, she, it)* or plural *(we, you, they)*.

**He** should have a budget and stick to it. (singular)

**We** can help new students learn about budgeting. (plural)

**Note:** For a discussion of singular *they*, see page 107.

## 25.25 Person of Pronouns

The **person** of a pronoun indicates whether the person is speaking (first person), is spoken to (second person), or is spoken about (third person).

**First person** is used to name the speaker(s).

I know **I** need to handle **my** stress in a healthful way, especially during exam week; **my** usual chips-and-doughnuts binge isn't helping. (singular)

**We** all decided to bike to the tennis court. (plural)

**Second person** is used to name the person(s) spoken to.

Maria, **you** grab the rackets, okay? (singular)

John and Bijah, would **you** find the water bottles? (plural)

**Third person** is used to name the person(s) or thing(s) spoken about.

Today's students are interested in wellness issues. **They** are concerned about **their** health, fitness, and nutrition. (plural)

Mina practices yoga and feels **she** is calmer for **her** choice. (singular)

One of the advantages of regular exercise is that **it** raises one's energy level. (singular)

# Handbook

## 25.26 Case of Pronouns

The **case** of each pronoun tells what role it plays in a sentence. There are three cases: *nominative, possessive,* and *objective.*

A pronoun in the **nominative case** is used as a subject. The following are nominative forms: *I, you, he, she, it, we, they.*

> **He** found the missing phone charger under his bed.
>
> My friend and **I** went biking. (not *me*)

A pronoun is also in the nominative case when it is used as a predicate nominative, following a linking verb *(am, is, are, was, were, seems)* and renaming the subject.

> It was **he** who discovered electricity. (not *him*)

A pronoun in the **possessive case** shows possession or ownership: *my, mine, our, ours, his, her, hers, their, theirs, its, your, yours.* A possessive pronoun before a noun acts as an adjective: *your* coat.

> That coat is **hers**.     This coat is **mine**.     **Your** coat is lost.

A pronoun in the **objective case** can be used as the direct object, indirect object, object of a preposition, or object complement: *me, you, him, her, it, us, them.*

> Professor Adler hired **her**. (*Her* is the direct object of the verb *hired*.)
>
> He showed Mary and **me** the language lab. (*Me* is the indirect object of the verb *showed*.)
>
> He introduced the three of **us**—Mary, Shavonn, and **me**—to the faculty.
> (*Us* is the object of the preposition *of*; *me* is part of the appositive renaming *us*.)

## 25.27 Gender of Pronouns

The **gender** of a pronoun indicates whether the pronoun is masculine, feminine, neuter, or indefinite. For a discussion of gender-neutral pronouns, see page 107.

**Masculine:**
he, him, his

**Feminine:**
she, her, hers

**Neuter** (without gender):
it, its

**Indefinite** (masculine or feminine):
they, them, their

## 25.28 Number, Person, and Case of Personal Pronouns

|  | Nominative Case | Possessive Case | Objective Case |
|---|---|---|---|
| **First Person Singular** | I | my, mine | me |
| **Second Person Singular** | you | your, yours | you |
| **Third Person Singular** | he, she, it | his, her, hers, its | him, her, it |
| **First Person Plural** | we | our, ours | us |
| **Second Person Plural** | you | your, yours | you |
| **Third Person Plural** | they | their, theirs | them |

# Grammar Exercises: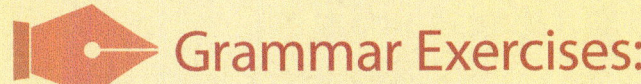

## Pronouns

### A. Classes of Pronouns

Identify the class of the underlined pronoun in each sentence.

1. Krunal asked <u>himself</u> if he should reprioritize his responsibilities.
   a. personal    b. reflexive    c. relative
2. <u>Who</u> is coming to the rally?
   a. demonstrative    b. relative    c. interrogative
3. <u>That</u> is quite possibly the most worthless product I've ever used.
   a. demonstrative    b. reflexive    c. interrogative
4. Victoria washed <u>her</u> car on the way home from work.
   a. personal    b. intensive    c. indefinite
5. <u>Some</u> of the burgers were undercooked.
   a. personal    b. intensive    c. indefinite
6. The new fitness center, <u>which</u> is awesome, is open until 10:00 p.m.
   a. personal    b. relative    c. reflexive

### B. Person of Pronouns

For each sentence, indicate whether the underlined pronoun is written in the first, second, or third person.

1. Russell is excited for <u>his</u> new opportunity at the sailing club.
   a. first person    b. second person    c. third person
2. Hey Britney, can <u>you</u> pass me the salt and pepper?
   a. first person    b. second person    c. third person
3. I was hoping I could make the start of the play, but <u>my</u> class schedule interfered with my plans.
   a. first person    b. second person    c. third person

### C. Case of Pronouns

Write down the objective-case pronouns from the list below.

his    me    your    us    he    they    them    him

## 25.29 Verb

A **verb** shows action *(pondered, grins)*, links words *(is, seemed)*, or accompanies another action verb as an auxiliary or helping verb *(can, does)*.

> Harry **honked** the horn. (shows action)
> Harry **is** impatient. (links words)
> Harry **was** honking the truck's horn. (accompanies the verb *honking*)

## 25.30 Classes of Verbs

Verbs are classified as *action, auxiliary (helping),* or *linking (state of being).*

### 25.31 Action Verbs: Transitive and Intransitive

As its name implies, an **action verb** shows action. Some action verbs are *transitive*; others are *intransitive*. (The term *action* does not always refer to a physical activity.)

> Rain **splashed** the windshield. (transitive verb)
> Josie **drove** off the road. (intransitive verb)

**Transitive verbs** have direct objects that receive the action.

> The health care industry **employs** more than 7 million **workers** in the United States. (*Workers* is the direct object of the action verb *employs*.)

**Intransitive verbs** communicate action that is complete in itself. They do not need an object to receive the action.

> My new college roommate **smiles** and **laughs** a lot.

> **Note:** Some verbs can be either transitive or intransitive.
> Professor Hull **teaches** physiology and microbiology. (transitive)
> She **teaches** well. (intransitive)

### 25.32 Auxiliary (Helping) Verbs

**Auxiliary verbs** (helping verbs) help to form some of the *tenses* (25.40), the *mood* (25.46), and the *voice* (25.44) of the main verb. In the following example, the auxiliary verbs are in **bold**, and the main verbs are in *italics*.

> I *believe*, I **have** always *believed*, and I **will** always *believe* in private enterprise as the backbone of economic well-being in America. —Franklin D. Roosevelt

#### 25.33 Common Auxiliary Verbs

| am | been | could | does | have | might | should | will |
|----|------|-------|------|------|-------|--------|------|
| are | being | did | had | is | must | was | would |
| be | can | do | has | may | shall | were | |

> **ESL Note:** "Be" auxiliary verbs are always followed by either a verb ending in *ing* or a past participle. Also see "Common Modal Auxiliary Verbs" (31.19).

## 25.34 Linking (State of Being) Verbs

A **linking verb** is a special form of intransitive verb that links the subject of a sentence to a noun, a pronoun, or an adjective in the predicate.

The streets **are** flooded. (adjective)    The streets **are** rivers! (noun)

### 25.35 Common Linking Verbs

am  are  be  become  been  being  is  was  were

### 25.36 Additional Linking Verbs

appear  feel  look  seem  sound  grow  remain  smell  taste

**Note:** The verbs listed as "additional linking verbs" above function as linking verbs when they do not show actual action. An adjective usually follows these linking verbs.

The thunder **sounded** ominous. (adjective)
My little brother **grew** frightened. (adjective)

**Note:** When these same words are used as action verbs, an adverb or a direct object may follow them.

I **looked** carefully at him. (adverb)
My little brother **grew** corn for a science project. (direct object)

## 25.37 Forms of Verbs

A verb's **form** differs depending on its *number* (singular, plural), *person* (first, second, third), *tense* (present, past, future, present perfect, past perfect, future perfect), *voice* (active, passive), and *mood* (indicative, imperative, subjunctive).

### 25.38 Number of a Verb

**Number** indicates whether a verb is singular or plural. The verb and its subject both must be singular, or they both must be plural. (See "Subject–Verb Agreement," 27.01–27.15.)

My college **enrolls** high schoolers in summer programs. (singular)
Many colleges **enroll** high schoolers in summer courses. (plural)

### 25.39 Person of a Verb

**Person** indicates whether the subject of the verb is *first, second,* or *third person*. The verb and its subject must be in the same person. Verbs usually have a different form only in **third person singular of the present tense**.

|  | First Person | Second Person | Third Person |
|---|---|---|---|
| **Singular** | I think | you think | he/she/it thinks |
| **Plural** | we think | you think | they think |

## 25.40 Tense of a Verb

**Tense** indicates the time of an action or state of being. There are three basic tenses (*past*, *present*, and *future*) and three verbal aspects (*progressive*, *perfect*, and *perfect progressive*).

## 25.41 Present Tense

**Present tense** expresses action happening at the present time or regularly.

> In the United States, a majority of workers **hold** service jobs.

**Present progressive tense** also expresses action that is happening continually, in an ongoing fashion at the present time, but it is formed by combining *am*, *are*, or *is* and the present participle (ending in *ing*) of the main verb.

> More restaurants than ever before **are partnering** with food-delivery apps.

**Present perfect tense** expresses action that began in the past and has recently been completed or that continues up to the present time.

> My sister **has taken** four years of swimming lessons.

**Present perfect progressive tense** also expresses an action that began in the past but stresses the continuing nature of the action. Like the present progressive tense, it is formed by combining auxiliary verbs (*have been* or *has been*) and present participles.

> She **has been taking** them since she was six years old.

## 25.42 Past Tense

**Past tense** expresses action that was completed at a particular time in the past.

> A hundred years ago, more than 75 percent of laborers **worked** in agriculture.

**Past progressive tense** expresses past action that continued over an interval of time. It is formed by combining *was* or *were* with the present participle of the main verb.

> A century ago, my great-grandparents **were farming**.

**Past perfect tense** expresses an action in the past that was completed at a specific time before another past action occurred.

> By the time we sat down for dinner, my cousins **had eaten** all the olives.

**Past perfect progressive tense** expresses a past action but stresses the continuing nature of the action. It is formed by using *had been* along with the present participle.

> They **had been eating** the olives all afternoon.

## 25.43 Future Tense

**Future tense** expresses action that will take place in the future.

> Next summer I **will work** as a lifeguard.

**Future progressive tense** expresses an action that will be continuous in the future.

> I **will be working** for the park district at North Beach.

**Future perfect tense** expresses future action that will be completed by a specific time.

> By 10:00 p.m., I **will have completed** my research project.

**Future perfect progressive tense** also expresses future action that will be completed by a specific time but (as with other perfect progressive tenses) stresses the action's continuous nature. It is formed using *will have been* along with the present participle.

> I **will have been researching** the project for three weeks by the time it's due.

### 25.44 Voice of a Verb

**Voice** indicates whether the subject is acting or being acted upon.

**Active voice** indicates that the subject of the verb is performing the action.

> People **update** their resumés on a regular basis. (The subject, *People*, is acting; *resumés* is the direct object.)

**Passive voice** indicates that the subject of the verb is being acted upon or is receiving the action. A passive verb is formed by combining a *be* verb with a past participle.

> Your resumé **should be updated** on a regular basis. (The subject, *resumé*, is receiving the action.)

---

#### 25.45 Using Active Voice

Generally, use active voice rather than passive voice for more direct, energetic writing. To change your passive sentences to active ones, do the following: First, find the noun that is doing the action and make it the subject. Then find the word that had been the subject and use it as the direct object.

> **Passive:** The winning goal **was scored** by Eva. (The subject, *goal*, is not acting.)
> **Active:** Eva **scored** the winning goal. (The subject, *Eva*, is acting.)

---

**Note:** When you want to emphasize the receiver more than the doer—or when the doer is unknown—use the passive voice. (Much technical and scientific writing regularly uses the passive voice.)

### 25.46 Mood of a Verb

The mood of a verb expresses the tone or attitude with which a statement is made.

**Indicative mood,** the most common, states a fact or asks a question.

> **Can** any theme **capture** the essence of the complex 1960s culture? President John F. Kennedy's directive [stated below] **represents** one ideal popular during that decade.

**Imperative mood** gives a command. (The subject of an imperative sentence is *you*, which is usually understood and not stated in the sentence.)

> **Ask** not what your country can do for you—**ask** what you can do for your country.
> —John F. Kennedy

**Subjunctive mood** expresses a wish, an impossibility or unlikely condition, a necessity, or a motion in a formal business meeting. The subjunctive mood is often used with *if* or *that*. The verb forms below create an atypical subject–verb agreement, forming the subjunctive mood.

> If I **were** rich, I would travel for the rest of my life. (a wish)
>
> If each of your brain cells **were** one person, there would be enough people to populate 25 planets. (an impossibility)
>
> The English Department requires that every student **pass** a proficiency test. I move that the motion **be adopted**. (a necessity)

## 25.47 Verbals

A **verbal** is a word that is made from a verb, but it functions as a noun, an adjective, or an adverb. There are three types of verbals: *gerunds, infinitives,* and *participles*.

### 25.48 Gerunds

A **gerund** ends in *ing* and is used as a noun.

**Waking** each morning is the first challenge. (subject)
I start **moving** at about seven o'clock. (direct object)
I work at **jump-starting** my weary system. (object of the preposition)
As Woody Allen once said, "Eighty percent of life is **showing up**." (predicate nominative)

### 25.49 Infinitives

An **infinitive** is *to* and the base form of the verb. The infinitive may be used as a noun, an adjective, or an adverb.

**To succeed** is not easy. (noun)
That is the most important thing **to remember**. (adjective)
Students are wise **to work** hard. (adverb)

**ESL Note:** It can be difficult to know whether a gerund or an infinitive should follow a verb. It's helpful to become familiar with lists of specific verbs that can be followed by one but not the other. (See 31.15–31.18.)

### 25.50 Participles

A **present participle** ends in *ing* and functions as an adjective. A **past participle** ends in *ed* (or another past tense form) and also functions as an adjective.

The **studying** students were annoyed by the **partying** ones.
The students **playing** loud music were **annoying**.

(These participles function as adjectives: *studying* students and *partying* students. Notice, however, that *playing* has a direct object: *music*. All three types of verbals may have direct objects. See 26.18.)

### 25.51 Using Verbals

Make sure that you use verbals correctly; look carefully at the examples below.

**Verbal:** **Diving** is a popular Olympic sport.
(*Diving* is a gerund used as a subject.)
**Diving** gracefully, the Olympian hoped to get high marks.
(*Diving* is a participle modifying *Olympian*.)
**Verb:** The next competitor was **diving** in the practice pool.
(Here, *diving* is a verb, not a verbal.)

# Chapter 25 | Understanding Grammar

## 25.52 Irregular Verbs

Irregular verbs can often be confusing. That's because the past tense and past participle of irregular verbs are formed by changing the word itself, not merely by adding *d* or *ed*. The following list contains the most troublesome irregular verbs.

### 25.53 Common Irregular Verbs and Their Principal Parts

| Present Tense | Past Tense | Past Participle | Present Tense | Past Tense | Past Participle | Present Tense | Past Tense | Past Participle |
|---|---|---|---|---|---|---|---|---|
| am, be | was, were | been | fly | flew | flown | see | saw | seen |
| arise | arose | arisen | forget | forgot | forgotten, forgot | set | set | set |
| awake | awoke, awaked | awoken, awaked | freeze | froze | frozen | shake | shook | shaken |
| beat | beat | beaten | get | got | gotten | shine (light) | shone | shone |
| become | became | become | give | gave | given | shine (polish) | shined | shined |
| begin | began | begun | go | went | gone | show | showed | shown |
| bite | bit | bitten, bit | grow | grew | grown | shrink | shrank | shrunk |
| blow | blew | blown | hang (execute) | hanged | hanged | sing | sang | sung |
| break | broke | broken | hang (suspend) | hung | hung | sink | sank | sunk |
| bring | brought | brought | have | had | had | sit | sat | sat |
| build | built | built | hear | heard | heard | sleep | slept | slept |
| burn | burnt, burned | burnt, burned | hide | hid | hidden | speak | spoke | spoken |
| burst | burst | burst | hit | hit | hit | spend | spent | spent |
| buy | bought | bought | keep | kept | kept | spring | sprang | sprung |
| catch | caught | caught | know | knew | known | stand | stood | stood |
| choose | chose | chosen | lay | laid | laid | steal | stole | stolen |
| come | came | come | lead | led | led | strike | struck | struck, stricken |
| cost | cost | cost | leave | left | left | strive | strove | striven |
| cut | cut | cut | lend | lent | lent | swear | swore | sworn |
| dig | dug | dug | let | let | let | swim | swam | swum |
| dive | dived, dove | dived | lie (deceive) | lied | lied | swing | swung | swung |
| do | did | done | lie (recline) | lay | lain | take | took | taken |
| draw | drew | drawn | make | made | made | teach | taught | taught |
| dream | dreamed, dreamt | dreamed, dreamt | mean | meant | meant | tear | tore | torn |
| drink | drank | drunk | meet | met | met | tell | told | told |
| drive | drove | driven | pay | paid | paid | think | thought | thought |
| eat | ate | eaten | prove | proved | proved, proven | throw | threw | thrown |
| fall | fell | fallen | put | put | put | wake | woke, waked | woken, waked |
| feel | felt | felt | read | read | read | wear | wore | worn |
| fight | fought | fought | ride | rode | ridden | weave | wove | woven |
| find | found | found | ring | rang | rung | wind | wound | wound |
| flee | fled | fled | rise | rose | risen | wring | wrung | wrung |
| | | | run | ran | run | write | wrote | written |

# Grammar Exercises:

## Verbs

### A. Classes of Verbs

Identify the class of the underlined verb in each sentence.

1. Shawn <u>sprinted</u> back to his apartment to retrieve his laptop.
   - a. action verb
   - b. auxiliary verb
   - c. linking verb
2. The streets <u>were</u> teeming with partygoers.
   - a. action verb
   - b. auxiliary verb
   - c. linking verb
3. Niki's gaze <u>remained</u> fixed on the ice-cream cone.
   - a. action verb
   - b. auxiliary verb
   - c. linking verb
4. I think I <u>should</u> take time to study the new material.
   - a. action verb
   - b. auxiliary verb
   - c. linking verb

### B. Forms of Verbs

For each sentence, identify the tense of the underlined verb.

1. Before we even got to the concert, the band <u>had played</u> my favorite song.
   - a. past tense
   - b. past progressive tense
   - c. past perfect tense
2. On Sunday I <u>will finish</u> my manuscript.
   - a. future tense
   - b. future progressive tense
   - c. future perfect tense
3. The mechanics <u>have been working</u> for ten straight hours.
   - a. present progressive tense
   - b. present perfect tense
   - c. past progressive tense
4. Yesterday at this time I <u>was relaxing</u> on the beach.
   - a. past tense
   - b. past progressive tense
   - c. past perfect tense

### C. Irregular Verbs

Write the past tense of the following irregular verbs.

1. buy
2. prove
3. swim
4. lead
5. pay
6. lay
7. wear
8. fly
9. give
10. sleep

## 25.54 Adjective

An **adjective** describes or modifies a noun or pronoun. The articles *a*, *an*, and *the* are adjectives.

> Advertising is **a big** and **powerful** industry. (*A*, *big*, and *powerful* modify the noun *industry*.)

Numbers are also adjectives.

> **Fifty-three** relatives came to my party.

**Note:** Many demonstrative, indefinite, and interrogative forms may be used as either adjectives or pronouns (*that*, *these*, *many*, *some*, *whose*, and so on). These words are adjectives if they come before a noun and modify it; they are pronouns if they stand alone.

> **Some** advertisements are less than truthful. (*Some* modifies *advertisements* and is an adjective.)
>
> **Many** cause us to chuckle at their outrageous claims. (*Many* stands alone; it is a pronoun and replaces the noun *advertisements*.)

### 25.55 Proper Adjectives

**Proper adjectives** are created from proper nouns and are capitalized.

> **English** has been influenced by advertising slogans. (proper noun)
>
> The **English** language is constantly changing. (proper adjective)

### 25.56 Predicate Adjectives

A **predicate adjective** follows a form of the *be* verb (or other linking verb) and describes the subject.

> At its best, advertising is **useful**; at its worst, **deceptive**. (*Useful* and *deceptive* modify the noun *advertising*.)

### 25.57 Forms of Adjectives

Adjectives have three forms: *positive*, *comparative*, and *superlative*.

The **positive form** is the adjective in its regular form. It describes a noun or a pronoun without comparing it to anyone or anything else.

> Joysport walking shoes are **strong** and **comfortable**.

The **comparative form** (*-er*, *more*, or *less*) compares two things. (*More* and *less* are used generally with adjectives of two or more syllables.)

> Air soles make Mile Eaters **stronger** and **more comfortable** than Joysports.

The **superlative form** (*-est*, *most*, or *least*) compares three or more things. (*Most* and *least* are used most often with adjectives of two or more syllables.)

> My old Canvas Wonders are the **strongest**, **most comfortable** shoes of all!

**ESL Note:** Two or more adjectives before a noun should have a certain order when they do not modify the noun equally. (See 28.18.)

Handbook

## 25.58 Adverb

An **adverb** describes or modifies a verb, an adjective, another adverb, or a whole sentence. An adverb answers questions such as *how, when, where, why, how often,* or *how much.*

The temperature fell **sharply**. (*Sharply* modifies the verb *fell*.)

The temperature was **quite** low. (*Quite* modifies the adjective *low*.)

The temperature dropped **very quickly**. (*Very* modifies the adverb *quickly,* which modifies the verb *dropped*.)

**Unfortunately**, the temperature stayed cool. (*Unfortunately* modifies the whole sentence.)

## 25.59 Types of Adverbs

Adverbs can be grouped in four ways: *time, place, manner,* and *degree.*

**Time** (These adverbs tell *when, how often,* and *how long.*)

**today, yesterday    daily, weekly    briefly, eternally**

**Place** (These adverbs tell *where, to where,* and *from where.*)

**here, there    nearby, beyond    backward, forward**

**Manner** (These adverbs often end in *ly* and tell *how* something is done.)

**precisely    regularly    regally    smoothly    well**

**Degree** (These adverbs tell *how much* or *how little.*)

**substantially    greatly    entirely    partly    too**

## 25.60 Forms of Adverbs

Adverbs have three forms: *positive, comparative,* and *superlative.*

The **positive form** is the adverb in its regular form. It describes a verb, an adjective, or another adverb without comparing it to anyone or anything else.

With Joysport shoes, you'll walk **fast**. They support your feet **well**.

The **comparative form** (*-er, more,* or *less*) compares two things. (*More* and *less* are used generally with adverbs of two or more syllables.)

Wear Jockos instead of Joysports, and you'll walk **faster**. Jockos' special soles support your feet **better** than the Joysports do.

The **superlative form** (*-est, most,* or *least*) compares three or more things. (*Most* and *least* are used most often with adverbs of two or more syllables.)

Really, I walk **fastest** wearing my old Canvas Wonders. They seem to support my feet, my knees, and my wallet **best** of all.

### 25.61 Regular Adverbs

| positive | comparative | superlative |
|---|---|---|
| fast | faster | fastest |
| effectively | more effectively | most effectively |

### 25.62 Irregular Adverbs

| positive | comparative | superlative |
|---|---|---|
| well | better | best |
| badly | worse | worst |

## 25.63 Preposition

A **preposition** is a word (or group of words) that shows the relationship between its object (a noun or pronoun following the preposition) and another word in the sentence.

> **Regarding** your reasons **for** going **to** college, do they all hinge **on** getting a good job **after** graduation? (In this sentence, *reasons, going, college, getting,* and *graduation* are objects of their preceding prepositions *regarding, for, to, on,* and *after*.)

### 25.64 Prepositional Phrases

A **prepositional phrase** includes the preposition, the object of the preposition, and the modifiers of the object. A prepositional phrase may function as an adverb or an adjective.

> A broader knowledge **of the world** is one benefit **of higher education**. (The two phrases function as adjectives modifying the nouns *knowledge* and *benefit* respectively.)
>
> He placed the flower **in the window**. (The phrase functions as an adverb modifying the verb *placed*.)

### 25.65 Prepositions

| | | | | |
|---|---|---|---|---|
| aboard | back of | excepting | notwithstanding | save |
| about | because of | for | of | since |
| above | before | from | off | subsequent to |
| according to | behind | from among | on | through |
| across | below | from between | on account of | throughout |
| across from | beneath | from under | on behalf of | 'til |
| after | beside | in | onto | to |
| against | besides | in addition to | on top of | together with |
| along | between | in behalf of | opposite | toward |
| alongside | beyond | in front of | out | under |
| alongside of | by | in place of | out of | underneath |
| along with | by means of | in regard to | outside | until |
| amid | concerning | inside | outside of | unto |
| among | considering | inside of | over | up |
| apart from | despite | in spite of | over to | upon |
| around | down | instead of | owing to | up to |
| as far as | down from | into | past | with |
| aside from | during | like | prior to | within |
| at | except | near | regarding | without |
| away from | except for | near to | round | |

**ESL Note:** Prepositions often pair up with a verb and become part of an idiom, a slang expression, or a two-word verb. (See 31.20 and 31.50.)

## 25.66 Conjunction

A **conjunction** connects individual words or groups of words.

    **When** we came back to Paris, it was clear **and** cold **and** lovely.

                                                    —Ernest Hemingway

### 25.67 Coordinating Conjunctions

**Coordinating conjunctions** usually connect a word to a word, a phrase to a phrase, or a clause to a clause. The words, phrases, or clauses joined by a coordinating conjunction are equal in importance or are of the same type.

    Civilization is a race between education **and** catastrophe.

                                                    —H. G. Wells

### 25.68 Correlative Conjunctions

**Correlative conjunctions** are a type of coordinating conjunction used in pairs.

    There are two inadvisable ways to think: **either** believe everything **or** doubt everything.

### 25.69 Subordinating Conjunctions

**Subordinating conjunctions** connect two clauses that are not equally important. A subordinating conjunction connects a dependent clause to an independent clause. The conjunction is part of the dependent clause.

    Experience is the worst teacher; it gives the test **before** it presents the lesson. (The clause *before it presents the lesson* is dependent. It connects to the independent clause *it gives the test*.)

#### 25.70 Conjunctions

| | |
|---|---|
| **Coordinating:** | and, but, or, nor, for, so, yet |
| **Correlative:** | either, or; neither, nor; not only, but (but also); both, and; whether, or |
| **Subordinating:** | after, although, as, as if, as long as, because, before, even though, if, in order that, provided that, since, so that, though, unless, until, when, whenever, where, while |

**Note:** Relative pronouns (25.19) can also connect clauses.

## 25.71 Interjection

An **interjection** communicates strong emotion or surprise (*oh, ouch, hey,* and so on). Punctuation (often a comma or an exclamation point) is used to set off an interjection.

    **Hey! Wait! Well,** so much for catching the bus.

# Grammar Exercises:

## Adjectives, Adverbs, Prepositions, Conjunctions, and Interjections

### A. Forms of Adjectives

Write the correct form (positive, comparative, or superlative) of the adjective shown in parentheses for each sentence.

1. I ate the _____ chicken wings I had ever tasted in my life. (*spicy*)
2. The Wi-Fi connection at the coffeehouse is _____ than the connection at the library. (*fast*)
3. Arizona is known for its _____ and dry climate. (*hot*)
4. Online shopping is _____ than mall shopping. (*efficient*)

### B. Types of Adverbs

Indicate whether the adverb reveals time, place, manner, or degree.

1. completely
2. smartly
3. easily
4. briefly
5. everywhere
6. tomorrow

### C. Conjunctions

Create a three-column table and label the columns "Coordinating," "Subordinating," and "Correlative." Then sort out the conjunctions below into their appropriate columns.

| | | |
|---|---|---|
| after | even though | so that |
| although | for | that |
| and | if | though |
| as | in order that | unless |
| as if | neither/nor | until |
| as long as | nor | when |
| because | not only/but also | whenever |
| before | or | where |
| both/and | provided that | while |
| but | since | yet |
| either/or | so | |

## 25.72 A Closer Look
### Parts of Speech

**Noun**  A **noun** is a word that names something: a person, a place, a thing, or an idea.

grandmother/person  *The Avengers*/film
Loyola/university  Industrial Revolution/era
*Fresh Off the Boat*/book  independence/idea

**Pronoun**  A **pronoun** is a word used in place of a noun.

| I | my | that | themselves | which |
| it | ours | they | everybody | you |

**Verb**  A **verb** is a word that expresses action, links words, or acts as an auxiliary verb to the main verb.

| are | break | drag | fly | run | sit | was |
| bite | catch | eat | is | see | tear | were |

**Adjective**  An **adjective** describes or modifies a noun or pronoun. (The articles *a*, *an*, and *the* are adjectives.)

**The carbonated** drink went down easily on **that hot, dry** day.
(*The* and *carbonated* modify *drink*; *that*, *hot*, and *dry* modify *day*.)

**Adverb**  An **adverb** describes or modifies a verb, an adjective, another adverb, or a whole sentence. An adverb generally answers questions such as *how*, *when*, *where*, *how often*, or *how much*.

| greatly | precisely | regularly | there |
| here | today | partly | quickly |
| slowly | yesterday | nearly | loudly |

**Preposition**  A **preposition** is a word (or group of words) that shows the relationship between its object (a noun or pronoun that follows the preposition) and another word in the sentence. Prepositions introduce prepositional phrases, which are modifiers.

across  for  with  out  to  of

**Conjunction**  A **conjunction** connects individual words or groups of words.

and  because  but  for  or  since  so  yet

**Interjection**  An **interjection** is a word that communicates strong emotion or surprise. Punctuation (often a comma or an exclamation point) is used to set off an interjection from the rest of the sentence.

**Stop! No! What,** am I invisible?

Chapter 26

# Constructing Sentences

A **sentence** is made up of at least a subject (sometimes understood) and a verb and expresses a complete thought. Sentences can make statements, ask questions, give commands, or express feelings.

> The Wi-Fi is spotty.
> Are you driving?
> Run! (The subject "you" is understood.)
> I feel upset.

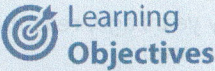

**Learning Objectives**

By working through this chapter, you will be able to

- use subjects and predicates to form sentences.
- use phrases effectively.
- use clauses effectively.
- vary your sentence structure.

## 26.01 Using Subjects and Predicates

Sentences have two main parts: a **subject** and a **predicate**.

> Technology frustrates many people.

**Note:** In the sentence above, *technology* is the subject—the sentence talks about technology. *Frustrates many people* is the complete predicate—it tells what the subject is doing.

## 26.02 The Subject

The **subject** names the person or thing either performing the action, receiving the action, or being described or renamed. The subject is most often a noun or a pronoun.

> **Technology** is an integral part of almost every business.
> **Manufacturers** need technology to compete in the world market.
> **They** could not go far without it.

A verbal phrase or a noun dependent clause may also function as a subject.

> **To survive without technology** is difficult. (infinitive phrase)
> **Connecting through social media** is easy. (gerund phrase)
> **That the information age would arrive** was inevitable. (noun dependent clause)

**Note:** To determine the subject of a sentence, ask yourself *who* or *what* performs or receives the action or is described. In most sentences, the subject comes before the verb; however, in many questions and some other instances, that order is reversed. (See 26.32, 26.33, 27.04, and 31.35.)

**ESL Note:** Some languages permit the omission of a subject in a sentence; English does not. A subject must be included in every sentence. (The only exception is an "understood subject," which is discussed at 26.06.)

## 26.03 Simple Subject

A **simple subject** is the subject without the words that describe or modify it.

> Thirty years ago, reasonably well-trained **mechanics** could fix any car on the road.

## 26.04 Complete Subject

A **complete subject** is the simple subject *and* the words that describe or modify it.

> Thirty years ago, **reasonably well-trained mechanics** could fix any car on the road.

## 26.05 Compound Subject

A **compound subject** is composed of two or more simple subjects joined by a conjunction and sharing the same predicate(s).

> Today, **mechanics** and **technicians** would need to master a half million manual pages to fix every car on the road.

> **Dealerships** and their service **departments** must sometimes explain that situation to the customers.

## 26.06 Understood Subject

Sometimes a subject is **understood**. This means it is not stated in the sentence, but a reader clearly understands what the subject is. An understood subject occurs in a command (imperative sentence). (See 26.33.)

> **(You)** Park on this side of the street. (The subject *you* is understood.)

> Put your phone on the charger.

## 26.07 Delayed Subject

In sentences that begin with *There is, There was,* or *Here is,* the subject follows the verb.

> There are 70,000 **fans** in the stadium. (The subject is *fans; are* is the verb. *There* is an expletive, an empty word.)

> Here is a **problem** for stadium security. (*Problem* is the subject. *Here* is an adverb.)

The subject is also delayed in questions.

> Where was the **event**? (*Event* is the subject.)

> Was **Beyoncé** playing? (*Beyoncé* is the subject.)

## 26.08 Common Sentence Patterns

Working together, subjects and predicates make sentences. But what are the most common patterns that subject-predicate combinations take? See 31.35 for five basic patterns of simple sentences:

- Subject + Verb
- Subject + Verb + Direct Object
- Subject + Verb + Indirect Object + Direct Object
- Subject + Verb + Direct Object + Object Complement
- Subject + Linking Verb + Predicate Nominative (or Predicate Adjective)

## 26.09 The Predicate (Verb)

The **predicate**, which contains the verb, is the part of the sentence that either tells what the subject is doing, tells what is being done to the subject, or describes or renames the subject.

Students **need technical skills as well as basic academic skills**.

## 26.10 Simple Predicate

A **simple predicate** is the complete verb without the words that describe or modify it. (The complete verb can consist of more that one word.)

Today's workplace **requires** employees to have a range of skills.

## 26.11 Complete Predicate

A **complete predicate** is the verb, all the words that modify or explain it, and any objects or complements.

Today's workplace **requires employees to have a range of skills**.

## 26.12 Compound Predicate

A **compound predicate** is composed of two or more verbs, all the words that modify or explain them, and any objects or complements.

Engineers **analyze problems** and **calculate solutions**.

## 26.13 Direct Object

A **direct object** is the part of the predicate that receives the action of an active transitive verb. A direct object makes the meaning of the verb complete.

Marcos visited several **campuses**. (The direct object *campuses* receives the action of the verb *visited* by answering the question "Marcos visited what?")

> **Note:** A direct object may be compound.

A counselor explained the academic **programs** and the application **process**.

## 26.14 Indirect Object

An **indirect object** is the word(s) that tells *to whom/to what* or *for whom/for what* something is done. A sentence must have a direct object before it can have an indirect object.

I showed our **children** my new school.

Use these questions to find an indirect object:

- What is the verb?    *showed*
- *Showed* what?    *school* (direct object)
- *Showed school* to whom?    *children* (indirect object)

I wrote **them** a note.

> **Note:** An indirect object may be compound.

I gave the **instructor** and a few **classmates** my email address.

 # Constructing Sentences Exercises:

## Subjects and Predicates

### A. Subjects

1. Write the complete subject of each numbered sentence in the following paragraph. Then underline the simple subjects. (You will find one compound subject.)

   (1) Every modern war seems to have its own terrible illness for soldiers. (2) In World War I, blistered skin and ravaged lungs resulted from exposure to mustard gas. (3) World War II saw the problem of "shell shock." (4) Agent Orange was blamed for causing cancer in Vietnam War veterans. (5) The Gulf War saw the rise of "post-traumatic stress disorder." (6) And many veterans of combat in Iraq and Iran return with "mild traumatic brain injury" due to improvised explosive devices.

2. Create your own sentence with an understood subject.
3. Create your own sentence with a delayed subject.

### B. Predicates

1. Write the complete predicate of each numbered sentence in the following paragraph. Then underline the simple predicates. (You will find one compound predicate.)

   (1) Women today have more than one choice for professional assistance with childbirth. (2) The obstetrician of your parents' era is trained to diagnose abnormalities and is prepared to deal with emergencies. (3) Today's midwife practitioner, on the other hand, is focused upon normal deliveries. (4) This makes the two occupations quite complementary.

2. List the direct objects in the numbered sentences of the following paragraph. If a sentence also includes an indirect object, list that in parentheses after the direct object.

   (1) Different situations bring you happiness. (2) Various pursuits deliver satisfaction. (3) And many agree that parents pass along their values and goals to their children. (4) So your own offspring will also receive this intangible inheritance.

## Chapter 26 | Constructing Sentences

### 26.15 Using Phrases

A **phrase** is a group of related words that functions as a single part of speech. A phrase lacks a subject, a predicate, or both. There are three phrases in the following sentence:

**Examples of technology can be found in ancient civilizations.**

**of technology**
(prepositional phrase that functions as an adjective; no subject or predicate)

**can be found**
(verb phrase—all of the words of the verb; no subject)

**in ancient civilizations**
(prepositional phrase that functions as an adverb; no subject or predicate)

### 26.16 Types of Phrases

There are several types of phrases: *verb, verbal, prepositional, appositive,* and *absolute.*

### 26.17 Verb Phrase

A **verb phrase** consists of a main verb and its helping verbs.

Students, worried about exams, **have camped** at the library all week.

### 26.18 Verbal Phrase

A **verbal phrase** is a phrase that expands on one of the three types of verbals: *gerund, infinitive,* or *participle*. (See Figure 26.1 on the next page.)

A **gerund phrase** consists of a gerund and its modifiers and objects. The whole phrase functions as a noun. (See 25.48.)

**Becoming a marine biologist** is Rashanda's dream. (The gerund phrase is used as the subject of the sentence.)

She has acquainted herself with the various methods for **collecting sea-life samples**. (The gerund phrase is the object of the preposition *for*.)

An **infinitive phrase** consists of an infinitive and its modifiers and objects. The whole phrase functions as a noun, an adjective, or an adverb. (See 25.49.)

**To dream** is the first step in any endeavor. (The infinitive phrase functions as a noun used as the subject.)

Remember **to make a plan to realize your dream**. (The infinitive phrase *to make a plan* functions as a noun used as a direct object; *to realize your dream* functions as an adjective modifying plan.)

Finally, apply all of your talents and skills **to achieve your goals**. (The infinitive phrase functions as an adverb modifying *apply*.)

A **participial phrase** consists of a present or past participle (a verb form ending in *ing* or *ed*) and its modifiers. The phrase functions as an adjective. (See 25.50.)

**Doing poorly in biology**, Theo signed up for a tutor. (The participial phrase modifies the noun *Theo*.)

Some students **frustrated by difficult course work** don't seek help. (The participial phrase modifies the noun *students*.)

### 26.19 Functions of Verbal Phrases

*fig. 26.1*

|  | Noun | Adjective | Adverb |
|---|---|---|---|
| Gerund | ■ | | |
| Infinitive | ■ | ■ | ■ |
| Participial | | ■ | |

### 26.20 Prepositional Phrase

A **prepositional phrase** is a group of words beginning with a preposition and ending with its object, a noun or a pronoun. Prepositional phrases are used mainly as adjectives and adverbs. See 25.65 for a list of prepositions.

> Denying the existence **of exam week** hasn't worked **for anyone** yet.
> (The prepositional phrase *of exam week* is used as an adjective modifying the noun *existence*; *for anyone* is used as an adverb modifying the verb *has worked*.)

> Test days still dawn and GPAs still plummet **for the unprepared student**.
> (The prepositional phrase *for the unprepared student* is used as an adverb modifying the verbs *dawn* and *plummet*.)

**ESL Note:** Do not mistake the following adverbs for nouns and incorrectly use them as objects of prepositions: *here, there, everywhere*.

### 26.21 Appositive Phrase

An **appositive phrase**, which follows a noun or a pronoun and renames it, consists of a noun and its modifiers. An appositive adds new information about the noun or pronoun it follows.

> The Olympic-size pool, **a prized addition to the physical education building,** gets plenty of use. (The appositive phrase renames *pool*.)

### 26.22 Absolute Phrase

An **absolute phrase** consists of a noun and a participle (plus the participle's object, if there is one, and any modifiers). It usually modifies the entire sentence.

> **Their enthusiasm sometimes waning,** the students who cannot swim are required to take lessons. (The noun *enthusiasm* is modified by the present participle *waning*; the entire phrase modifies *students*.)

 Phrases can add valuable information to sentences, but some phrases add nothing but "fat" to your writing.

## 26.23 Using Clauses

A **clause** is a group of related words that has both a subject and a verb.

### 26.24 Independent/Dependent Clauses

An **independent clause** contains at least one subject and one verb, presents a complete thought, and can stand alone as a sentence; a **dependent clause** (also called a subordinate clause) does not present a complete thought and cannot stand alone (make sense) as a sentence.

> Though airplanes are twentieth-century inventions (dependent clause), people have always dreamed of flying (independent clause).

### 26.25 Types of Clauses

There are three basic types of dependent, or subordinate, clauses: *adverb*, *adjective*, and *noun*. These dependent clauses are combined with independent clauses to form complex and compound-complex sentences.

### 26.26 Adverb Clause

An **adverb clause** is used like an adverb to modify a verb, an adjective, or an adverb. All adverb clauses begin with subordinating conjunctions. (See 25.69.)

> **Because Orville won a coin toss**, he got to fly the power-driven air machine first. (The adverb clause modifies the verb *got*.)

### 26.27 Adjective Clause

An **adjective clause** is used like an adjective to modify a noun or a pronoun. Adjective clauses begin with relative pronouns *(which, that, who)*. (See 25.19.)

> The men **who invented the first airplane** were brothers, Orville and Wilbur Wright. (The adjective clause modifies the noun *men*. *Who* is the subject of the adjective clause.)
>
> The first flight, **which took place December 17, 1903,** was made by Orville. (The adjective clause modifies the noun *flight*. *Which* is the subject of the adjective clause.)

### 26.28 Noun Clause

A **noun clause** is used in place of a noun. Noun clauses can appear as subjects, as direct or indirect objects, as predicate nominatives, or as objects of prepositions. Noun clauses can also play a role in the independent clause. They are introduced by subordinating words such as *what*, *that*, *when*, *why*, *how*, *whatever*, *who*, *whom*, *whoever*, and *whomever*.

> He wants to know **what made modern aviation possible**. (The noun clause functions as the object of the infinitive.)
>
> **Whoever invents an airplane with vertical takeoff ability** will be a hero. (The noun clause functions as the subject.)

> **Note:** If you can replace a whole clause with the pronoun *something* or *someone*, it is a noun clause.

## 26.29 Using Sentence Variety

A sentence can be classified according to the kind of statement it makes and according to the way it is constructed.

## 26.30 Kinds of Sentences

Sentences can make five basic kinds of statements: *declarative, interrogative, imperative, exclamatory,* or *conditional.*

### 26.31 Declarative Sentence

**Declarative sentences** make statements. They tell us something about a person, a place, a thing, or an idea.

> In 1955, Rosa Parks refused to follow segregation rules on a bus in Montgomery, Alabama.

### 26.32 Interrogative Sentence

**Interrogative sentences** ask questions.

> Do you think Ms. Parks knew she was making history?
>
> Would you have had the courage to do what she did?

### 26.33 Imperative Sentence

**Imperative sentences** give commands. They often contain an understood subject (*you*). (See 26.06.)

> Read chapters 6 through 10 for tomorrow.

**ESL Note:** Imperative sentences with an understood subject are the only sentences in which it is acceptable to have no subject stated.

### 26.34 Exclamatory Sentence

**Exclamatory sentences** communicate strong emotion or surprise. They are punctuated with exclamation points.

> I simply can't keep up with these long reading assignments!
>
> Oh my gosh, you scared me!

### 26.35 Conditional Sentence

**Conditional sentences** express two circumstances. One of the circumstances depends on the other circumstance. The words *if, when,* or *unless* are often used in the dependent clause in conditional sentences.

> **If** you practice a few study-reading techniques, college reading loads will be manageable.
>
> **When** I manage my time, it seems I have more of it.
>
> Don't ask me to help you **unless** you are willing to do the reading first.

## 26.36 Structure of Sentences

A sentence may be *simple, compound, complex,* or *compound-complex,* depending on how the independent and dependent clauses are combined.

### 26.37 Simple Sentence

A **simple sentence** contains one independent clause. The independent clause may have compound subjects and verbs, and it may also contain phrases.

My **back aches**.
(single subject: *back*; single verb: *aches*)

My **teeth** and my **eyes hurt**.
(compound subject: *teeth* and *eyes*; single verb: *hurt*)

My **memory** and my **logic come** and **go**.
(compound subject: *memory* and *logic*; compound verb: *come* and *go*)

I **must need a vacation**.
(single subject: *I*; single verb: *must need*; direct object: *vacation*)

### 26.38 Compound Sentence

A **compound sentence** consists of two independent clauses. The clauses must be joined by a semicolon, by a comma and a coordinating conjunction (*and, but, or, nor, so, for, yet*), or by a semicolon followed by a conjunctive adverb (*besides, however, instead, meanwhile, then, therefore*) and a comma.

I had eight hours of sleep, **so** why am I so exhausted?

I take good care of myself**;** I get enough sleep.

I still feel fatigued**; therefore,** I must need more exercise.

### 26.39 Complex Sentence

A **complex sentence** contains one independent clause (in bold) and one or more dependent clauses (underlined).

<u>When I can,</u> **I get eight hours of sleep.** (dependent clause; independent clause)

<u>When I get up on time,</u> and <u>if someone hasn't used up all the milk,</u> **I eat breakfast.** (two dependent clauses; independent clause)

When the dependent clause comes before the independent clause, use a comma.

### 26.40 Compound-Complex Sentence

A **compound-complex sentence** contains two or more independent clauses (in bold type) and one or more dependent clauses (underlined).

<u>If I'm not in a hurry,</u> **I take leisurely walks,** and **I try to spot some wildlife.**
(dependent clause; two independent clauses)

**I saw a hawk** <u>when I was walking,</u> and **other smaller birds were chasing it.**
(independent clause; dependent clause; independent clause)

 **Constructing Sentences Exercises:**

# Phrases, Clauses, and Sentence Variety

## A. Phrases and Clauses

Identify the numbered phrases (gerund, infinitive, participial, prepositional, appositive, or absolute), and clauses (adverb, adjective, or noun). Note that not every type is represented.

The marionette, (1) <u>a type of puppet manipulated by strings or rods</u>, has been around for millennia. Stringed puppets have been found in Egyptian tombs from around 2000 B.C. Greek philosophers such as Xenophon wrote about these articulated puppets as early as 422 B.C. (2) <u>To control their marionettes</u>, the ancient Romans used rods from above, and Italy retains a strong tradition of articulated puppetry from these Roman roots. (3) <u>Employed in religious performances during ancient times</u>, marionettes found similar use in morality plays during the Renaissance. Most likely, the term "marionette" originated as a diminutive form (4) <u>of the Virgin Mary's name</u> in these plays. Starting in the eighteenth century, entire operas were performed by marionettes in theaters such as the Salzburg Marionette Theatre in Austria, (5) <u>which continues performances to this day</u>. Of course, marionettes have also starred in television and film, and (6) <u>since puppetry is still a valued storytelling art</u>, chances are you've seen them perform at your local grade school.

## B. Sentence Variety

Identify each sentence in the following paragraph by kind (declarative, interrogative, imperative, exclamatory, or conditional).

(1) Do you realize how far personal computers have come since their early days? (2) Understand that the first examples were marketed to scientists and researchers. (3) After that came kits for hobbyists to build and program their own machines. (4) The introduction of the microprocessor chip allowed PCs to proliferate after 1975. (5) If blinkenlights.com is correct, the HP 9830, originally sold in 1972, qualifies as the very first personal computer, being a fully built desktop machine with a keyboard and display. (6) Other people argue that the Commodore PET in 1977 better suited that designation because it was commercially available to everyone. (7) In any case, the popular Apple II and the IBM-PC then solidified the personal computer's role in business and at home.

# Chapter 27

# Avoiding Sentence Errors

## 27.01 Subject–Verb Agreement

The subject and verb of any clause must agree in both *person* and *number*. Person indicates whether the subject of the verb is *first*, *second*, or *third person*. Number indicates whether the subject and verb are *singular* or *plural*. (See 25.38 and 25.39.)

|  | Singular | Plural |
|---|---|---|
| First Person | I think | we think |
| Second Person | you think | you think |
| Third Person | he/she/it thinks | they think |

### Learning Objectives

By working through this chapter, you will be able to

- maintain subject-verb agreement.
- establish pronoun-antecedent agreement.
- recognize improper shifts in sentence construction.
- avoid fragments, comma splices, and run-ons.
- identify misplaced and dangling modifiers.
- recognize ambiguous wording.
- identify nonstandard language.

## 27.02 Agreement in Number

A verb must agree in number (singular or plural) with its subject.

> The **student was** rewarded for her hard work. (Both the subject *student* and the verb *was* are singular; they agree in number.)

**Note:** Watch out for phrases that come between the subject and the verb; they do not alter the number of the subject. Such phrases may begin with words like *in addition to*, *as well as*, or *together with*.

> The **instructor**, as well as the students, **is** expected to attend the orientation. (*Instructor*, not *students*, is the subject.)

## 27.03 Compound Subjects

**Compound subjects** connected with *and* usually require a plural verb.

> **Dedication and creativity are** trademarks of successful students.

**Note:** If a compound subject joined by *and* is thought of as a unit, use a singular verb.

> **Bacon and eggs is** on the menu. (a single dish)
> **Bacon and eggs are** on the menu. (separate menu items)

(Also see 27.06 and 27.07.)

## 27.04 Delayed Subjects

**Delayed subjects** occur when the verb comes *before* the subject in a sentence. In these inverted sentences, the true (delayed) subject must still agree with the verb.

> There **are** many nontraditional **students** on our campus.
> Here **is** the **syllabus** you need.
> (*Students* and *syllabus* are the subjects of these sentences, not the adverbs *there* and *here*.)

**Note:** Using an inverted sentence, on occasion, will lend variety to your writing style. Simply remember to make the delayed subjects agree with the verbs.

> However, included among the list's topmost items **was** "revise research paper."
> (Because the true subject here is singular—one item—the singular verb *was* is correct.)

## 27.05 Titles as Subjects

When the subject of a sentence is the title of a work of art, literature, or music, the verb should be singular. This is also true of a word (or phrase) being used as a word (or phrase).

> ***Lyrical Ballads* was** published in 1798 by two of England's greatest poets, Wordsworth and Coleridge. (Even though the title of the book, *Lyrical Ballads,* is plural in form, it is still a single title being used as the subject, correctly taking the singular verb *was*.)
>
> **"Over-the-counter drugs" is** a phrase that means nonprescription medications. (Even though the phrase is plural in form, it is still a single phrase being used as the subject, correctly taking the singular verb *is*.)

## 27.06 Singular Subjects with *Or* or *Nor*

**Singular subjects** joined by *or* or *nor* take a singular verb.

> Neither a **textbook** nor a **notebook is required** for this class.

**Note:** When the subject nearer a present-tense verb is the singular pronoun *I* or *you*, the correct singular verb does not end in *s*.

> Neither **Marcus** nor **I feel** (not *feels*) right about this.
> Either **Rosa** or **you have** (not *has*) to take notes for me.
> Either **you** or **Rosa has** to take notes for me.

## 27.07 Singular/Plural Subjects

When one of the subjects joined by *or* or *nor* is singular and one is plural, the verb must agree with the subject nearer the verb.

> Neither the **professor** nor her **students were** in the lab. (The plural subject *students* is nearer the verb; therefore, the plural verb *were* agrees with *students*.)
>
> Neither the **students** nor the **professor was** in the lab. (The singular subject *professor* is nearer the verb; therefore, the singular verb *was* is used to agree with *professor*.)

## 27.08 Collective Nouns

Generally, **collective nouns** (*faculty, pair, crew, assembly, congress, species, crowd, army, team, committee,* and so on) take a singular verb. However, if you want to emphasize differences among individuals in the group or are referring to the group as individuals, you may use a plural verb.

> My lab **team takes** its work very seriously. (*Team* refers to the group as a unit; it requires a singular verb, *takes*.)
>
> The **team assume** separate responsibilities for each study they undertake. (In this example, *team* refers to individuals within the group; it requires a plural verb, *assume*.)

> **Note:** Collective nouns such as (the) *police, poor, elderly,* and *young* use plural verbs.
>
> The **police direct** traffic here between 7:00 and 9:00 a.m.

## 27.09 Plural Nouns with Singular Meaning

Some nouns that are plural in form but singular in meaning take a singular verb: *measles, news, mathematics, economics, robotics,* and so on.

> **Economics is** sometimes called "the dismal science."
>
> The economic **news is** not very good.

> **Note:** The most common exceptions are *scissors, trousers, tidings,* and *pliers*.
>
> The **scissors are** missing again.
>
> **Are** these **trousers** prewashed?

## 27.10 With Linking Verbs

When a sentence contains a linking verb (usually a form of *be*)—and a noun or pronoun comes before and after that verb—the verb must agree with the subject, not the predicate nominative (the noun or pronoun coming after the verb).

> The cause of his problem **was** poor study habits. (*Cause* requires a singular verb, even though the predicate nominative, *habits*, is plural.)
>
> His poor study habits **were** the cause of his problem. (*Habits* requires a plural verb, even though the predicate nominative, *cause*, is singular.)

## 27.11 Nouns Showing Measurement, Time, and Money

Mathematical phrases and phrases that name a period of time, a unit of measurement, or an amount of money take a singular verb.

> Three and three **is** six.
>
> Eight pages **is** a long paper on this topic.
>
> In my opinion, three dollars **is** a high price for a cup of coffee.

### 27.12 Relative Pronouns

When a **relative pronoun** (*who, which, that*) is used as the subject of a dependent clause, the pronoun's antecedent determines the number of the verb. (The *antecedent* is the word to which the pronoun refers.)

> This is one of the **books that are** required for English class.
> (The relative pronoun *that* requires the plural verb *are* because its antecedent is *books*, not the word *one*. To test this type of sentence for agreement, read the *of* phrase first: *Of the books that are . . .* )

> **Note:** Generally, the antecedent is the nearest noun or pronoun to the relative pronoun and is often the object of a preposition. Sometimes, however, the antecedent is not the nearest noun or pronoun, especially in sentences with the phrase "the only one of."

> Dr. Graciosa wondered why Claire was the only **one** of her students **who was** not attending lectures regularly. (In this case, the addition of the modifiers *the only* changes the meaning of the sentence. The antecedent of *who* is *one*, not *students*. Only one student was not attending.)

### 27.13 Indefinite Pronoun with Singular Verb

Many indefinite pronouns (*someone, somebody, something; anyone, anybody, anything; no one, nobody, nothing; everyone, everybody, everything; each, either, neither, one, this*) serving as subjects require a singular verb.

> **Everybody is** welcome to attend the chancellor's reception.
> **No one was** sent an invitation.

> **Note:** Although it may seem to indicate more than one, *each* is a singular pronoun and requires a singular verb. Do not be confused by words or phrases that come between the indefinite pronoun and the verb.

> **Each** of the new students **is** (not *are*) **encouraged** to attend the reception.

### 27.14 Indefinite Pronoun with Plural Verb

Some indefinite pronouns (*both, few, many, most,* and *several*) are plural; they require a plural verb.

> **Few are** offered the opportunity to study abroad.
> **Most take** advantage of opportunities closer to home.

### 27.15 Indefinite Pronoun or Quantity Word with Singular/Plural Verb

Some indefinite pronouns or quantity words (*all, any, most, part, half, none,* and *some*) may be either singular or plural, depending on the nouns they refer to. Look inside the prepositional phrase to see what the antecedent is.

> **Some** of the students **were** missing. (*Students*, the noun that *some* refers to, is plural; therefore, the pronoun *some* is considered plural, and the plural verb *were* is used to agree with it.)
> **Most** of the lecture **was** over by the time we arrived. (Because *lecture* is singular, *most* is also singular, requiring the singular verb *was*.)

## Chapter 27 | Avoiding Sentence Errors

### 27.16 Pronoun–Antecedent Agreement

A pronoun must agree in number, person, and gender (sex) with its *antecedent*. The antecedent is the word to which the pronoun refers.

**Note:** Singular *they* is an exception; see page 107.

**Darrell** brought **his** laptop to the technology center. (The pronoun *his* refers to the antecedent **Darrell**. Both the pronoun and its antecedent are singular, third person, and masculine; therefore, the pronoun is said to agree with its antecedent.)

### 27.17 Singular Pronoun

Use a singular pronoun to refer to such antecedents as *each, either, neither, one, anyone, anybody, everyone, everybody, somebody, another, nobody,* and *a person*.

**Each** of the maintenance vehicles has **their** doors locked at night. (Incorrect)

**Each** of the maintenance vehicles has **its** doors locked at night. (Correct: Both *Each* and *its* are singular.)

To make singular indefinite pronouns—like *each* and *somebody*—agree in gender, grammar books used to suggest using *his or her* alternating with *her or his*. This solution, though, is clunky and can be taken as sexist and gender binary. The *Chicago Manual of Style*, the *Modern Language Association*, and other major style guides now allow third-person plural pronouns (*they, them, their*) to refer to singular indefinite pronouns when gender is indeterminate.

**Somebody** left **their** vehicle unlocked.

**Note:** When a singular indefinite pronoun refers to a person of any gender, rewriting the sentence using a plural form avoids sexism and wordy constructions.

**Original Sentence:** Every employee must turn in **his or her** time card.

**Plural Replacement:** All employees must turn in **their** time cards.

### 27.18 Plural Pronoun

When the antecedent is plural, use a plural pronoun.

**People** must learn to wait **their** turn patiently.

### 27.19 Two or More Antecedents

When two or more antecedents are joined by *and,* they are considered plural.

**Tomas** and **Jamal** are finishing **their** assignments.

When two or more singular antecedents are joined by *or* or *nor,* they are considered singular.

**Connie** or **Shavonn** left **her** headset in the library.

**Note:** If one of the antecedents identifies as masculine and one feminine, likewise one pronoun should be masculine and one should be feminine. (If the gender is indeterminate or if a person identifies as gender binary, use the singular *their.*)

Is **Ahmad** or **Phyllis** bringing **his or her** laptop computer?

**Note:** If one of the antecedents joined by *or* or *nor* is singular and one is plural, the pronoun is made to agree with the nearer antecedent.

Neither **Ravi** nor **his friends** want to spend **their** time studying.

# Avoiding Sentence Errors Exercises:

# Agreement

### A. Subject-Verb Agreement

Correct the agreement errors in the following paragraph by writing down the line number and any incorrect verb, crossed out, with the correct form beside it.

There is in beautiful Barcelona, Spain, many surprises to be found. *1*
Barcelona, Spain's second-largest city, and Madrid, the country's capital, *2*
has a traditional rivalry. At one time, the population of Barcelona *3*
were forbidden to speak the city's native tongue, Catalan, by a royal *4*
decree from Madrid. Today, however, neither Spanish nor Catalan are *5*
discriminated against in the region. One of the sites that belongs on *6*
every tour, the outlandish cathedral La Sagrada Familia ("The Sacred *7*
Family"), was designed by Antoni Gaudi. People using the word "gaudy" *8*
actually have Gaudi's name on his tongue. A series of thirteenth- to *9*
fifteenth-century palaces now house the Museo Picasso, which display *10*
a history of Picasso's work and his many years living in Barcelona. *Les* *11*
*Demoiselles d'Avignon,* or *The Young Ladies of Avignon,* are one example *12*
of a painting inspired by his time in Barcelona. Whether you prefer *13*
cobblestone streets with centuries-old buildings or asphalt streets with *14*
modern shops and taverns, each are found in Barcelona. At night, every *15*
one of the streets seem to have a festive air, reflecting the vivacity of *16*
Spanish culture. *17*

### B. Pronoun-Antecedent and Subject-Verb Agreement

Provide the correct pronoun or verb for each blank in the following sentences. Use the directions or choices in parentheses.

1. Some people _____ math with an abacus. (*do/does*)

2. This counting device has been used for thousands of years, and _____ is still very popular in Eastern nations. (pronoun for "device")

3. The earliest examples _____ employed between 2700 and 2300 B.C. in Sumer. (*was/were*)

4. As recently as the 1990s, school children in the Soviet Union were taught to use _____. (pronoun for "examples" in the previous sentence)

5. Pocket-sized abacuses _____ still popular in Japan, despite the availability of portable calculators. (*is/are*)

6. Expert abacus users _____ able to add, subtract, multiply, divide, and even calculate square roots and cube roots very quickly. (*is/are*)

Chapter 27 | Avoiding Sentence Errors

## 27.20 Shifts in Sentence Construction

A shift is an improper change in structure midway through a sentence. The following examples will help you identify and fix several different kinds of shifts.

### 27.21 Shift in Person

**Shift in person** is mixing first, second, or third person within a sentence.

*Shift:* **One** may get spring fever unless **you** live in California or Florida. (The sentence shifts from third person, *one*, to second person, *you*.)

*Corrected:* **You** may get spring fever unless **you** live in California or Florida. (Stays in second person)

*Corrected:* **People** may get spring fever unless **they** live in California or Florida. (*People*, a third person plural noun, requires a third person plural pronoun, *they*.)

### 27.22 Shift in Tense

**Shift in tense** is using more than one tense in a sentence when only one is needed.

*Shift:* Sheila **looked** at nine apartments in one weekend before she **had chosen** one. (Tense shifts from past to past perfect for no reason.)

*Corrected:* Sheila **looked** at nine apartments in one weekend before she **chose** one. (Tense stays in past.)

### 27.23 Shift in Voice

**Shift in voice** is mixing active with passive voice. Usually, a sentence beginning in active voice should remain so to the end.

*Shift:* As you look (active voice) for just the right place, many interesting apartments **will probably be seen.** (passive voice)

*Corrected:* As you look (active voice) for just the right place, **you will probably see** (active voice) many interesting apartments.

### 27.24 Unparallel Construction

**Unparallel construction** occurs when the kind of words or phrases being used shifts or changes in the middle of a sentence.

*Shift:* In my hometown, people pass the time shooting pool, doing yard work, and at softball games. (Sentence shifts from a series of general phrases, *shooting pool* and *doing yard work*, to the prepositional phrase *at softball games*.)

*Parallel:* In my hometown, people pass the time **shooting pool, doing yard work, and playing softball.** (Now all three activities are gerund phrases—they are consistent, or parallel.)

## 27.25 Fragments, Comma Splices, and Run-Ons

Except in a few special situations, you should use complete sentences when you write. By definition, a complete sentence expresses a complete thought. However, a sentence may actually contain several ideas, not just one. The trick is getting those ideas to work together to form a clear, interesting sentence that expresses your exact meaning. Among the most common sentence errors that writers make are fragments, comma splices, and run-ons.

### 27.26 Fragments

A **fragment** is a phrase or dependent clause used as a sentence. It is not a sentence, however, because a phrase lacks a subject, a verb, or some other essential part, and a dependent clause must be connected to an independent clause to complete its meaning.

*Fragment:* Pete gunned the engine. Forgetting that the boat was hooked to the truck. (This is a sentence followed by a fragment. This error can be corrected by combining the fragment with the sentence.)

*Corrected:* Pete gunned the engine, forgetting that the boat was hooked to the truck.

*Fragment:* Even though my best friend had a little boy last year. (This clause does not convey a complete thought. We need to know what is happening despite the birth of the little boy.)

*Corrected:* Even though my best friend had a little boy last year, **I do not comprehend the full meaning of "motherhood."**

### 27.27 Comma Splices

A **comma splice** is a mistake made when two independent clauses are connected ("spliced") with only a comma. The comma is not enough: A period, semicolon, or conjunction is needed.

*Splice:* People say that being a stay-at-home parent is an important job, their actions tell a different story.

*Corrected:* People say that being a stay-at-home parent is an important job, **but** their actions tell a different story. (The coordinating conjunction *but*, added after the comma, corrects the splice.)

*Corrected:* People say that being a stay-at-home parent is an important job; their actions tell a different story. (A semicolon—rather than just a comma—makes the sentence correct.)

*Corrected:* People say that being a stay-at-home parent is an important job; however, their actions tell a different story. (A semicolon and a conjunction—or conjunctive adverb—also make the sentence correct.)

*Corrected:* People say that being a stay-at-home parent is an important job. **Their** actions tell a different story. (A period creates two sentences and corrects the splice.)

Chapter 27 | Avoiding Sentence Errors

### 27.28 Run-Ons

A run-on sentence is actually two sentences (two independent clauses) joined without adequate punctuation or a connecting word.

*Run-on:* The Alamo holds a special place in American history it was the site of an important battle between the United States and Mexico.

*Corrected:* The Alamo holds a special place in American history **because** it was the site of an important battle between the United States and Mexico. (A subordinating conjunction is added to fix the run-on by making the second clause dependent.)

*Run-on:* Antonio de Santa Anna, the president of Mexico who once held a funeral for his amputated leg, is the same Santa Anna who stormed the Alamo he led his troops to victory over the Texan rebels defending that fort. Two famous American frontiersmen died they were James Bowie and Davy Crockett. Santa Anna enjoyed fame, power, and respect among his followers. He died in 1876 he was poor, blind, and ignored.

*Corrected:* Antonio de Santa Anna, the president of Mexico who once held a funeral for his amputated leg, is the same Santa Anna who stormed the Alamo. He led his troops to victory over the Texan rebels defending that fort. Two famous American frontiersmen were killed in the battle; they were James Bowie and Davy Crockett. Santa Anna enjoyed fame, power, and respect among his followers. When he died in 1876, he was poor, blind, and ignored.

The writer corrected the run-on sentences in the paragraph above by adding punctuation and making one sentence a dependent clause. While doing so, the writer also made a few changes to improve the ideas. The writer makes further improvements in the paragraph below by revising one sentence and by combining two sets of short sentences into one stronger sentence.

*Improved:* Antonio de Santa Anna, the president of Mexico who once held a funeral for his amputated leg, is the same Santa Anna who stormed the Alamo. He led his troops to victory over Texan rebels defending that fort. Two famous American frontiersmen, **James Bowie and Davy Crockett, were killed in the battle**. Santa Anna enjoyed fame, power, and respect among his followers; **but when** he died in 1876, he was poor, blind, and ignored.

**fyi** Once you make a correction, you may see an opportunity to add, cut, or improve something else. Correcting and editing sentences can be frustrating at times, but with practice, these processes can become some of the more enjoyable parts of the writing process.

 **Avoiding Sentence Errors Exercises:**

# Shifts in Construction, Fragments, Comma Splices, and Run-Ons

## A. Identifying Errors

Identify the type of sentence error illustrated by each example below. If the error is a shift in construction, tell which type. (See 27.20.)

1. Much music in the Western world is based upon a "diatonic scale" of seven notes, five half steps separate all but two notes in a complete diatonic scale.
2. A quick look at the piano keyboard to understand this scale.
3. From C to B, for example, you can count seven white keys and five black keys, and one can see that each black key is a half step between the white keys on either side.
4. There is no black key between E and F, nor between B and C, so these notes were understood to be only a half step apart.
5. One advantage of this arrangement of black and white keys is that pianists can easily tell the difference between notes as they touch the keyboard imagine if there were nothing but white keys all a half step apart!

## B. Correcting Errors

In the following paragraph, locate each sentence error (fragment, comma splice, run-on, and unparallel construction). Identify each with the sentence number and name of the error. Then write the sentence correctly.

(1) When you're listening to jazz, you're hearing a uniquely American style of music. (2) From the American South, a fusion of African and European traditions. (3) As Art Blakely, an originator of bebop drumming, is quoted saying, "No America, no jazz." (4) The earliest jazz bands emerged in New Orleans around the turn of the twentieth century here Black gospel music and Latin American brass met, and Dixieland was spawned in the 1910s. (5) During the 1920s, many popular and influential jazz musicians found their way to Chicago clubs, recordings in the Windy City began to spread the sound to other parts of the country. (6) New York City also played an important role in jazz history by adding piano, incorporating jazz into swing music, and through sales of jazz records. (7) During the late 1920s and the 1930s, local jazz bands formed all around the country, establishing the style firmly in American culture.

## 27.29 Misplaced and Dangling Modifiers

Writing is thinking. Before you can write clearly, you must think clearly. Nothing is more frustrating for the reader than having to reread writing just to understand its basic meaning. Look carefully at the common errors that follow. Then use this section as a checklist when you revise. Always avoid leaving misplaced or dangling modifiers in your finished work.

### 27.30 Misplaced Modifiers

**Misplaced modifiers** are descriptive words or phrases so separated from what they are describing that the reader is confused.

*Misplaced:* The neighbor's dog has nearly been barking nonstop for two hours. (*Nearly* been barking?)

*Corrected:* The neighbor's dog has been barking nonstop **for nearly two hours**. (Watch your placement of *only, just, nearly, barely,* and so on.)

*Misplaced:* The commercial advertised an assortment of combs for active people with unbreakable teeth. (*People* with unbreakable teeth?)

*Corrected:* For active people, the commercial advertised an assortment of combs with unbreakable teeth. (*Combs* with unbreakable teeth)

*Misplaced:* The pool staff gave large beach towels to the students marked with chlorine-resistant ID numbers. (*Students* marked with chlorine-resistant ID numbers?)

*Corrected:* The pool staff gave the students large beach towels marked with chlorine-resistant ID numbers. (*Towels* marked with chlorine-resistant ID numbers)

### 27.31 Dangling Modifiers

**Dangling modifiers** are descriptive phrases that tell about a subject that isn't stated in the sentence. These often occur as participial phrases containing *ing* or *ed* words.

*Dangling:* After standing in line all afternoon, the manager informed us that all the tickets had been sold. (It sounds as if the manager has been *standing in line all afternoon*.)

*Corrected:* **After we had stood in line all afternoon,** the manager informed us that all the tickets had been sold.

*Dangling:* After living in the house for one month, the electrician recommended we update all the wiring. (It sounds as if the electrician has been *living in the house*.)

*Corrected:* After living in the house for one month, **we hired an electrician, who recommended that we update all the wiring.**

## 27.32 Ambiguous Wording

Sloppy sentences confuse readers. No one should have to wonder, "What does this writer mean?" When you revise and edit, check for indefinite pronoun references, incomplete comparisons, and unclear wording.

### 27.33 Indefinite Pronoun References

An **indefinite reference** is a problem caused by careless use of pronouns. There must always be a word or phrase nearby (its antecedent) that a pronoun clearly replaces.

*Indefinite:* When Tonya attempted to put her dictionary on the shelf, it fell to the floor. (The pronoun *it* could refer to either the dictionary or the shelf since both are singular nouns.)

*Corrected:* When Tonya attempted to put her dictionary on the shelf, **the shelf** fell to the floor.

*Indefinite:* Juanita reminded Kerri that she needed to print a copy of her resumé before going to her interview. (Who *needed to print a copy of her resumé*—Juanita or Kerri?)

*Corrected:* Juanita reminded Kerri **to print a copy of her resumé before going to her interview.**

### 27.34 Incomplete Comparisons

**Incomplete comparisons**—leaving out words that show exactly what is being compared to what—can confuse readers.

*Incomplete:* After completing our lab experiment, we concluded that helium is lighter. (*Lighter* than what?)

*Corrected:* After completing our lab experiment, we concluded that helium is lighter **than oxygen.**

### 27.35 Unclear Wording

One type of ambiguous writing is wording that has two or more possible meanings due to an unclear reference to something elsewhere in the sentence.

*Unclear:* I couldn't believe that my sister bought a cat with all those allergy problems. (Who has the *allergy problem*s—the cat or the sister?)

*Corrected:* I couldn't believe that my sister, **who is very allergic, bought a cat.**

*Unclear:* Dao intended to wash the car when he finished his homework, but he never did. (It is unclear which he *never did*—wash the car or finish his homework.)

*Corrected:* Dao intended to wash the car when he finished his homework, **but he never did manage to wash the car.**

 Avoiding Sentence Errors Exercises:

# Misplaced and Dangling Modifiers and Ambiguous Wording

## A. Correcting Sentences

Rewrite the following sentences to correct misplaced and dangling modifiers and ambiguous wording.

1. When it touched down on the moon in 1969, the onboard guidance computer of the *Apollo 11's Eagle* lander contained less than 80 kilobytes of memory.
2. Most smart phones today at least hold 80 gigabytes of memory.
3. That's equivalent to 80 million *Apollo 11* computers roughly in one device.
4. Imagine using your phone to land 80 million *Apollo* craft at the same time in your bedroom.
5. Of course, you couldn't see all the lunar-lander controls at once because of their tiny screens.
6. After spending almost a day on the moon's surface, NASA had the crew launch back into orbit and return to Earth.
7. The *Eagle's* journey to the moon had made it a sensation around the world.
8. The crew were all heroes, but they certainly liked the Earth better.
9. Today the Science Museum in London displays a lunar-lander replica for visitors in full size.
10. When seeing the display, you will notice the lunar-lander replica is smaller.

## B. Correcting Errors in Context

Locate a misplaced modifier and several indefinite-pronoun-reference errors in the following paragraph. For each error, write the sentence number, identify the error type, and rewrite the sentences correctly.

(1) One famous Russian joke lampoons the *nouveau-riche* Russians, known as "New Russians," by comparing cars. (2) In this joke, unexpectedly, a New Russian and an old man wake up in an emergency room. (3) The New Russian asks the old man how he ended up there. (4) The old man replies, "I put my war-trophy Messerschmitt jet engine on my old Zaporozhets car to make it go faster. (5) But after a couple of miles I lost control and crashed into a tree. (6) How about you?" (7) He answers that when an old Zaporozhets passed his new Ferrari on the highway, he thought it had stalled. (8) So he opened the door and stepped out.

## 27.36 Nonstandard Language

**Nonstandard language** is language that does not conform to the standards set by schools, media, and public institutions. It is often acceptable in everyday conversation and in fictional writing but seldom is used in formal speech or other forms of writing.

### 27.37 Colloquial Language

**Colloquial language** is wording used in informal conversation that is unacceptable in formal writing.

*Colloquial:* Hey, slow up! Cal wants to go with.

*Standard:* **Hey, wait!** Cal wants to go with **us**.

### 27.38 Double Preposition

The use of certain **double prepositions**—*off of, off to, from off*—is unacceptable.

*Double Preposition:* Pick up the dirty clothes from off the floor.

*Standard:* Pick up the dirty clothes **from the floor**.

### 27.39 Substitution

Avoid substituting *and* for *to*.

*Substitution:* Try and get to class on time.

*Standard:* **Try to** get to class on time.

Avoid substituting *of* for *have* when combining with *could, would, should,* or *might*.

*Substitution:* I should of studied for that exam.

*Standard:* **I should have** studied for that exam.

### 27.40 Double Negative

A **double negative** is a sentence that contains two negative words used to express a single negative idea. Double negatives are unacceptable in academic writing.

*Double Negative:* After paying for essentials, I haven't got no money left.

*Standard:* **I haven't got** any money left. / **I have no** money left.

*Note:* Because a double negative makes a positive statement, "I haven't got no money left" means "I have money left."

### 27.41 Slang

Avoid the use of **slang** or any "in" words in formal writing.

*Slang:* The way the stadium roof opened was bananas.

*Standard:* The way the stadium roof opened **was remarkable**.

# Avoiding Sentence Errors Exercises:

## Nonstandard Language

### A. Correcting Sentences

Identify the type of error exhibited in each sentence below (colloquialism, double preposition, substitution, double negative, or slang). Then correct it.

1. Would you of guessed that soccer is the world's most popular sport?
2. The word "soccer" is Oxford slang for "association," 'cause officially the game is "Association Football."
3. Most countries call soccer "football"; they haven't no interested in American football.
4. The World Cup is a wicked awesome competition played every four years.
5. Soccer rules were set up in England in 1863, and they haven't hardly changed since then.
6. The point of the game is to try and kick the ball into the other team's goal area.
7. Normally play continues until someone commits a foul or kicks a ball off of the field.
8. Most players aren't not allowed to touch the ball with their hands.
9. If you've ever watched soccer, though, you might of seen the goalie engage the ball that way.
10. The other players don't have no official titles.
11. Most times, though, there are forwards, defenders, and midfielders.
12. According to the rules, games needn't never go into overtime; they can end in a tie.
13. But some games can just keep agoin' in overtime till somebody scores.
14. Unlike in 2018, the U.S. team did pretty good for itself in the 2010 World Cup.
15. Some folks say that Europeans feel closer to us since our team rocked big time and stayed in the competition so long.
16. I wonder what they would of thought if the U.S. had won!
17. Personally, though, I was rooting for Spain from the get go.
18. If you're interested, it doesn't hardly take much equipment to play soccer.
19. All's you really need's a ball and maybe some markers for the goals.
20. Well, you also gotta have two teams with eleven players each.

### B. Correcting Your Own Writing

Write freely about a sport or hobby you find interesting. Imagine describing that sport or hobby to someone unfamiliar with it, or simply explain your own interest in it. When you have finished, review your writing for nonstandard language and make any necessary corrections.

## 27.42 Avoiding Sentence Problems Review

**Does every subject agree with its verb?** (See 27.01–27.15.)
- In person and number?
- When a word or phrase comes between the subject and the verb?
- When the subject is delayed?
- When the subject is a title?
- When a compound subject is connected with *or*?
- When the subject is a collective noun (*faculty, team,* or *crowd*)?
- When the subject is a relative pronoun (*who, which, that*)?
- When the subject is an indefinite pronoun (*everyone, anybody,* or *many*)?

**Does every pronoun agree with its antecedent?** (See 27.16–27.19.)
- When the pronoun is a singular indefinite pronoun such as *each, either,* or *another*?
- When two antecedents are joined with *and*?
- When two antecedents are joined with *or*?

**Did you unintentionally create inappropriate shifts?** (See 27.20–27.24.)
- In person?
- In tense?
- From active voice to passive voice?
- In an unparallel construction?

**Are all your sentences complete?** (See 27.25–25.28.)
- Have you used sentence fragments?
- Are some sentences "spliced" or run together?

**Did you use any misplaced modifiers or ambiguous wording?** (See 27.29–27.35.)
- Have you used misplaced or dangling modifiers?
- Have you used incomplete comparisons or indefinite references?

**Did you use any nonstandard language?** (See 27.36–27.41.)
- Have you used slang or colloquial language?
- Have you used double negatives or double prepositions?

# Chapter 28

# Marking Punctuation

## 28.01 Period

### 28.02 After Sentences

Use a **period** to end a sentence that makes a statement, requests something, or gives a mild command.

**Statement:** Many jobs require a college degree.

**Request:** Please read the instructions carefully.

**Mild command:** If your topic sentence isn't clear, rewrite it.

**Indirect question:** The professor asked if we had completed the test.

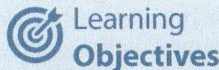
**Learning Objectives**

By working through this chapter, you will be able to

- recognize when and where to use different types of punctuation: periods, ellipses, question marks, commas, semicolons, colons, hyphens, dashes, and quotation marks.
- distinguish the various roles of different punctuation marks.

**Note:** It is not necessary to place a period after a statement that has parentheses around it and is part of another sentence.

Think about joining a club **(the student affairs office has a list of organizations)** for fun and for leadership experience.

### 28.03 After Initials and Abbreviations

Use a period after an initial, after some abbreviations, and between a Bible chapter and verse.

| Mr. | Mrs. | Dr. | John 3.16 | i.e. | Booker T. Washington |
| Sr. | U.S. | p.m. | Rev. 21.3 | e.g. | Sen. Elizabeth Warren |

Use no periods after academic degrees (e.g., *BA, PhD, MD*), acronyms (e.g., *radar, CARE, NASA*), and initialisms (e.g., *CIA, DVD, ROTC*). See also "Abbreviations" (29.32) and "Acronyms and Initialisms" (29.33).

When an abbreviation is the last word in a sentence, use only one period at the end of the sentence.

Mikhail promptly locked the door at 10:00 p.m.

### 28.04 As Decimal Points

Use a period as a decimal point.

The government spends approximately **$15.5** million each year just to process student loan forms.

## 28.05 Ellipsis

### 28.06 To Show Omitted Words

Use an **ellipsis** (three periods) to show that one or more words have been omitted in a quotation. Also leave one space before and after each period.

> **(Original)** We the people of the United States, in order to form a more perfect Union, establish justice, insure domestic tranquility, provide for the common defense, promote the general welfare, and secure the blessings of liberty to ourselves and our posterity, do ordain and establish this Constitution for the United States of America.
> —Preamble, U.S. Constitution

> **(Quotation)** "We the people . . . in order to form a more perfect Union . . . establish this Constitution for the United States of America."

> **Note:** Omit internal punctuation (a comma, a semicolon, a colon, or a dash) on either side of the ellipsis marks unless it is needed for clarity.

### 28.07 To Use After Sentences

If words from a quotation are omitted at the end of a sentence, place the ellipsis after the period or other end punctuation.

> **(Quotation)** "Five score years ago, a great American, in whose symbolic shadow we stand, signed the Emancipation Proclamation. . . . But one hundred years later, we must face the tragic fact that the Negro is still not free."
> —Martin Luther King, Jr., "I Have a Dream"

The first word of a sentence following a period and an ellipsis may be capitalized, even though it was not capitalized in the original.

> **(Quotation)** "Five score years ago, a great American . . . signed the Emancipation Proclamation. . . . One hundred years later, . . . the Negro is still not free."

> **Note:** If the quoted material forms a complete sentence (even if it was not in the original), use a period, then an ellipsis.

> **(Original)** I am tired; my heart is sick and sad. From where the sun now stands I will fight no more forever.
> —Chief Joseph of the Nez Percé

> **(Quotation)** "I am tired. . . . I will fight no more forever."

### 28.08 To Show Pauses

Use an ellipsis to indicate a pause or to show unfinished thoughts.

> Listen . . . did you hear that?

> I can't figure out . . . this number doesn't . . . just how do I apply the equation in this case?

## 28.09 Question Mark

### 28.10 After Direct Questions

Use a **question mark** at the end of a direct question.

> What can I know? What ought I to do? What may I hope?
> —Immanuel Kant

> Since when do you have to agree with people to defend them from injustice?
> —Lillian Hellman

### 28.11 Not After Indirect Questions

No question mark is needed after an indirect question.

> After listening to Edgar sing, Mr. Noteworthy asked him if he had ever had formal voice training.

**Note:** When a single-word question like *how*, *when*, or *why* is woven into the flow of a sentence, capitalization and special punctuation are not usually required.

> The questions we need to address at our next board meeting are not *why* or *whether*, but *how* and *when*.

### 28.12 After Quotations That Are Questions

When a question ends with a quotation that is also a question, use only one question mark, and place it within the quotation marks. (Also see 28.77.)

> Do you often ask yourself, "What should I be?"

### 28.13 To Show Uncertainty

Use a question mark within parentheses to show uncertainty about a word or phrase within a sentence.

> This July will be the fifty-second(?) anniversary of the first moon walk.

**Note:** Do *not* use a question mark in this manner for formal writing.

### 28.14 For Questions in Parentheses or Dashes

A question within parentheses—or a question set off by dashes—is punctuated with a question mark unless the sentence ends with a question mark.

> You must consult your handbook **(what choice do you have?)** when you need to know a punctuation rule.

> Should I use your charge card (you have one, don't you), or should I pay cash?

> Maybe somewhere in the pasts of these humbled people, there were cases of bad mothering or absent fathering or emotional neglect—**what family surviving the '50s was exempt?**—but I couldn't believe these human errors brought the physical changes in Frank.
> —Mary Kay Blakely, *Wake Me When It's Over*

# Punctuation Exercises:

## Periods, Ellipses, Question Marks

### A. End Punctuation

Indicate the correct form of end punctuation for each sentence—a period or a question mark.

1. Have you heard of the Ring of Fire
2. It is a volcanically active area
3. The Ring of Fire circles the Pacific
4. How many people has it killed
5. Over 300,000 died from one tsunami
6. Where did the tsunami take place
7. The tsunami ravaged India
8. An earthquake rocked Chile
9. The Ring of Fire is restless
10. How can we predict its catastrophes

### B. Ellipses

Shorten each sentence by removing the bold words and inserting an ellipsis.

1. "Now we are engaged in a great civil war, testing whether that nation, **or any nation so conceived and so dedicated,** can long endure."
2. "We have come to dedicate a portion of that field, as a final resting place for those who here gave their lives **that that nation might live.**"
3. "But, in a larger sense, we can not dedicate—**we can not consecrate—we can not hallow—**this ground."
4. "The brave men, **living and dead,** who struggled here, have consecrated it**, far above our poor power to add or detract.**"
5. "The world will little note, **nor long remember** what we say here, but it can never forget what they did here."

### C. Punctuation Practice

Indicate where periods and question marks are needed in the following paragraph by writing the word and the mark after it, and by writing any initials or abbreviations correctly.

    Music is the universal language At least that's what people say But have you ever noticed how hard it is to get people to agree on music Play a song by BB King, and some people will be in heaven and others in dread Why would that be Dr Jim Fredericks indicates that the reason may be music's power to reach to our very hearts "Music is intensely personal, and the type of music that makes one person excited and happy may make another person very uncomfortable" Jill Davis, PhD, disagrees She says music is primarily cultural What does music do except make us feel "at home" or feel like a stranger When music alienates us, we dislike it, but when it makes us feel welcome, we like it So, what music makes you feel at home

## 28.15 Comma

### 28.16 Between Independent Clauses

Use a **comma** between independent clauses that are joined by a coordinating conjunction (*and, but, or, nor, for, yet, so*). (See 26.38.)

> Heath Ledger completed his brilliant portrayal as the Joker in *The Dark Knight,* **but** he died before the film was released.

**Note:** Do not confuse a compound verb with a compound sentence.

> Ledger's Joker became instantly iconic and won him the Oscar for best supporting actor. (compound verb)
>
> His death resulted from the abuse of prescription drugs, but it was ruled an accident. (compound sentence)

### 28.17 Between Items in a Series

Use commas to separate individual words, phrases, or clauses in a series. (A series contains at least three items.)

> Many college students must balance studying with **taking care of a family, working a job, getting exercise,** and **finding time to relax.**

**Note:** Do *not* use commas when all the items in a series are connected with *or, nor,* or *and.*

> Hmm . . . should I study **or** do laundry **or** go out?

### 28.18 To Separate Adjectives

Use commas to separate adjectives that *equally* modify the same noun. Notice in the examples below that no comma separates the last adjective from the noun.

> You should exercise regularly and follow a **sensible, healthful** diet.
>
> A good diet is one that includes lots of **high-protein, low-fat** foods.

---

#### 28.19 To Determine Equal Modifiers

To determine whether the adjectives in a sentence modify a noun *equally,* use these two tests.

1. Reverse the order of the adjectives; if the sentence is clear, the adjectives modify equally. (In the example below, *hot* and *crowded* can be reversed, and the sentence is still clear; *short* and *coffee* cannot.)

   > Matt was tired of working in the **hot, crowded** lab and decided to take a **short coffee** break.

2. Insert *and* between the adjectives; if the sentence reads well, use a comma when *and* is omitted. (The word *and* can be inserted between *hot* and *crowded,* but *and* does not make sense between *short* and *coffee.*)

### 28.20 To Set Off Nonrestrictive Appositives

A specific kind of explanatory word or phrase called an **appositive** identifies or renames a preceding noun or pronoun.

Albert Einstein, **the famous mathematician and physicist,** developed the theory of relativity.

**Note:** Do *not* use commas with *restrictive appositives*. A restrictive appositive is essential to the basic meaning of the sentence.

The famous mathematician and physicist **Albert Einstein** developed the theory of relativity.

### 28.21 To Set Off Adverb Dependent Clauses

Use a comma after most introductory dependent clauses functioning as adverbs.

**Although Charlemagne was a great patron of learning,** he never learned to write properly. (adverb dependent clause)

You may use a comma if the adverb dependent clause following the independent clause is not essential. Adverb clauses beginning with *even though, although, while,* or another conjunction expressing a contrast are usually not needed to complete the meaning of a sentence.

Charlemagne never learned to write properly, **even though he continued to practice.**

**Note:** A comma is *not* used if the dependent clause following the independent clause is needed to complete the meaning of the sentence.

Maybe Charlemagne didn't learn **because he had an empire to run.**

### 28.22 After Introductory Phrases

Use a comma after introductory phrases.

**In spite of his practicing,** Charlemagne's handwriting remained poor.

**Note:** A comma is usually omitted if the phrase follows an independent clause.

Charlemagne's handwriting remained poor **in spite of his practicing.**

**Also Note:** You may omit the comma after a short (four or fewer words) introductory phrase unless it is needed to ensure clarity.

**At 6:00 a.m.** he would rise and practice his penmanship.

### 28.23 To Set Off Transitional Expressions

Use a comma to set off conjunctive adverbs and transitional phrases. (See 28.42–28.43.)

Handwriting is not, **as a matter of fact,** easy to improve upon later in life; **however,** it can be done if you are determined enough.

**Note:** If a transitional expression blends smoothly with the rest of the sentence, it does not need to be set off. *Example:* If you are in fact coming, I'll see you there.

## 28.24 A Closer Look
## Nonrestrictive and Restrictive Clauses and Phrases

### 28.25 Use Commas with Nonrestrictive Clauses and Phrases

Use commas to enclose **nonrestrictive** (unnecessary) phrases or dependent (adjective) clauses. A nonrestrictive phrase or dependent clause adds information that is not necessary to the basic meaning of the sentence. For example, if the clause or phrase (in **boldface**) were left out of the two examples below, the meaning of the sentences would remain clear. Therefore, commas are used to set off the nonrestrictive information.

> The locker rooms in Swain Hall, **which were painted and updated last summer**, give professors a place to shower. (nonrestrictive clause)
>
> Work-study programs, **offered on many campuses,** give students the opportunity to earn tuition money. (nonrestrictive phrase)

### 28.26 Don't Use Commas with Restrictive Clauses and Phrases

Do *not* use commas to set off **restrictive** (necessary) adjective clauses and phrases. A restrictive clause or phrase adds information that the reader needs to understand the sentence. For example, if the adjective clause and phrase (in **boldface**) were dropped from the examples below, the meaning would be unclear.

> Only the professors **who run at noon** use the locker rooms in Swain Hall to shower. (restrictive clause)
>
> Using tuition money **earned through work-study programs** is the only way some students can afford to go to college. (restrictive phrase)

### 28.27 Using "That" or "Which"

Use *that* to introduce restrictive (necessary) adjective clauses; use *which* to introduce nonrestrictive (unnecessary) adjective clauses. When the two words are used in this way, the reader can quickly distinguish the necessary information from the unnecessary.

> Campus jobs **that are funded by the university** are awarded to students only. (restrictive)
>
> The cafeteria, **which is run by an independent contractor**, can hire nonstudents. (nonrestrictive)

**Note:** Clauses beginning with *who* can be either restrictive or nonrestrictive.

> Students **who pay for their own education** are highly motivated. (restrictive)
>
> The admissions counselor, **who has studied student records,** said that many returning students earn high GPAs in spite of demanding family obligations. (nonrestrictive)

### 28.28 To Set Off Items in Addresses and Dates

Use commas to set off items in an address and the year in a date.

> Send your letter to **1600 Pennsylvania Avenue, Washington, DC 20006,** before **January 1, 2020,** or send an email to president@whitehouse.gov.

> **Note:** No comma is placed between the state and ZIP code. Also, no comma separates the items if only the month and year are given: January 2020.

### 28.29 To Separate Numbers

Use commas to separate a series of numbers to distinguish hundreds, thousands, millions, and so on.

> Do you know how to write the amount **$2,025** on a check?
>
> 25,000     973,240     18,620,197

### 28.30 To Set Off the Speaker from Dialogue

Use commas to set off the words of the speaker from the rest of the sentence.

> **"Never be afraid to ask for help,"** advised Ms. Kane.
>
> **"With the evidence that we now have,"** Professor Thom said, **"many scientists believe there is life on Mars."**

### 28.31 To Separate the Person Named in Direct Address

Use a comma to separate a noun of direct address from the rest of the sentence.

> **Jamie,** would you please stop whistling while I'm trying to work?

### 28.32 Before Tags

Use a comma before tags, which are short statements or questions at the ends of sentences.

> You studied for the test**, right?**

### 28.33 To Separate Interjections

Use a comma to separate a mild interjection from the rest of the sentence.

> **Okay,** so now what do I do?

> **Note:** Exclamation points are used after strong interjections: Wow! You're kidding!

### 28.34 To Set Off Interruptions

Use commas to set off a word, phrase, or clause that interrupts the movement of a sentence. Such expressions usually can be identified through the following tests: (1) They may be omitted without changing the meaning of a sentence; and (2) they may be placed nearly anywhere in the sentence without changing its meaning.

> For me, **well,** it was just a good job gone!     —Langston Hughes, "A Good Job Gone"
>
> Lela, **as a general rule,** always comes to class ready for a pop quiz.

## 28.35 To Enclose Explanatory Words

Use commas to enclose an explanatory word or phrase.

> Time management, **according to many professionals,** is such an important skill that it should be taught in college.

## 28.36 To Separate Contrasted Elements

Use commas to separate contrasted elements within a sentence.

> We work to become, **not to acquire.** —Eugene Delacroix
>
> Where all think alike, **no one thinks very much.** —Walter Lippmann

## 28.37 To Enclose Titles or Initials

Use commas to enclose a title or initials and given names that follow a surname.

> Until Martin, **Sr.,** was 15, he never had more than three months of schooling in any one year.
> —Ed Clayton, *Martin Luther King: The Peaceful Warrior*
>
> The genealogical files included the names Sanders, **L. H.,** and Sanders, **Lucy Hale.**

**Note:** Some style manuals no longer require commas around titles.

## 28.38 For Clarity or Emphasis

Use a comma for clarity or for emphasis. There will be times when none of the traditional rules call for a comma, but you will need to use one to prevent misreading or to emphasize an important idea.

> What she does, does matter to us. (clarity)
>
> It may be those who do most, dream most. (emphasis) —Stephen Leacock

---

### 28.39 Avoid Overusing Commas

The commas (in red) below are used incorrectly. Do *not* use a comma between the subject and its verb or the verb and its object.

> Current periodicals on the subject of psychology**,** are available at nearly all bookstores.
>
> I think she should read**,** *Psychology Today.*

Do *not* use a comma before an indirect quotation.

> My roommate said**,** that she doesn't understand the notes I took.

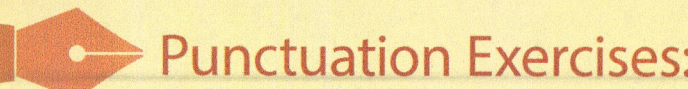

# Punctuation Exercises:

## Commas

### A. Basic Comma Use

Indicate correct comma placement in each sentence below. Some sentences have multiple commas.

1. To succeed in college you need focus dedication and hard work.
2. A compatible amiable roommate helps and you will want access to a computer.
3. To keep your sanity a balanced workable schedule is also a must.
4. You should consult with family friends and counselors about course schedules.
5. Between classes jobs and the social scene many students are stretched.
6. College prepares people for life and one way is by teaching them to juggle priorities.
7. Students also must afford books supplies and food.
8. A manageable realistic budget keeps money matters in order.
9. Students should work hard think deeply and enjoy their time in college.
10. With goals such as these students can get the most out of college.

### B. Restrictive and Nonrestrictive Clauses and Phrases

For each sentence, indicate correct comma placement. If a sentence needs no commas, write "correct."

1. Author Lauren Beukes who lives in South Africa wrote *Moxyland*.
2. *Moxyland* a dystopian thriller focuses on a world overrun by governmental and corporate domination of technology.
3. Gareth L. Powell who is an author in his own right said the book "gives us a dystopia to rival *1984*."
4. Another reviewer said *Moxyland* is a book that changed science fiction.
5. Lauren Beukes an avid user of social media released a *Moxyland* soundtrack and a plush doll which gave two-thirds of its proceeds to a women's charity.

### C. Advanced Comma Use

For each sentence, indicate correct comma placement.

1. I live at 3415 West Kane Drive Chicago Illinois.
2. Jamar where do you live?
3. All right who turned out the lights?
4. If you think I turned them out well you're mistaken.
5. I sure would like to receive a check for $5000.

## 28.40 Semicolon

### 28.41 To Join Two Independent Clauses

Use a **semicolon** to join two or more closely related independent clauses that are not connected with a coordinating conjunction. In other words, each of the clauses could stand alone as a separate sentence.

> I was thrown out of college for cheating on the metaphysics exam; I looked into the soul of the boy next to me.
>
> —Woody Allen

### 28.42 Before Conjunctive Adverbs

Use a semicolon before a conjunctive adverb when the word clarifies the relationship between two independent clauses in a compound sentence. A comma often follows the conjunctive adverb. Common conjunctive adverbs include *also, besides, however, instead, meanwhile, then,* and *therefore.*

> Many college freshmen are on their own for the first time; **however,** others are already independent and even have families.

### 28.43 Before Transitional Phrases

Use a semicolon before a transitional phrase when the phrase clarifies the relationship between two independent clauses in a compound sentence. A comma usually follows the transitional phrase.

> Pablo was born in the Andes; **as a result,** he loves mountains.

#### 28.44 Transitional Phrases

| | | | |
|---|---|---|---|
| after all | at the same time | in addition | in the first place |
| as a matter of fact | even so | in conclusion | on the contrary |
| as a result | for example | in fact | on the other hand |
| at any rate | for instance | in other words | |

### 28.45 To Separate Independent Clauses Containing Commas

Use a semicolon to separate independent clauses that contain internal commas, even when the independent clauses are connected by a coordinating conjunction.

> Your laptop, bike, and other valuables are expensive to replace; so include these items in your homeowner's insurance policy and remember to use the locks on your door, bike, and storage area.

### 28.46 To Separate Items in a Series That Contains Commas

Use a semicolon to separate items in a series that already contain commas.

> My favorite foods are pizza with pepperoni, onions, and olives; peanut butter and banana sandwiches; and salad with bacon, peppers, and onions.

## 28.47 Colon

### 28.48 After Salutations

Use a **colon** after the salutation of a business letter.

> Dear Mr. Spielberg:    Dear Professor Higgins:    Dear Members:

### 28.49 Between Numbers Indicating Time or Ratios

Use a colon between the hours, minutes, and seconds of a number indicating time.

> 8:30 p.m.    9:45 a.m.    10:24:55

Use a colon between two numbers in a ratio.

> The ratio of computers to students is 1:20. (one to twenty)

### 28.50 For Emphasis

Use a colon to emphasize a word, a phrase, a clause, or a sentence that explains or adds impact to the main clause.

> **I have one goal for myself**: to become the first person in my family to graduate from college.

### 28.51 To Distinguish Parts of Publications

Use a colon between a title and a subtitle and between a volume and a page.

> *Ron Brown: An Uncommon Life*    *Britannica* 4: 211

### 28.52 To Introduce Quotations

Use a colon to introduce a quotation following a complete sentence.

> **John Locke is credited with this prescription for a good life:** "A sound mind in a sound body."

> **Lou Gottlieb, however, offered this version:** "A sound mind or a sound body—take your pick."

### 28.53 To Introduce a List

Use a colon to introduce a list following a complete sentence.

> **A college student needs a number of things to succeed:** basic skills, creativity, and determination.

---

#### 28.54 Avoid Colon Errors

Do *not* use a colon between a verb and its object or complement.

> Dave likes: comfortable space and time to think. **(Incorrect)**

> Dave likes two things: comfortable space and time to think. **(Correct)**

## 28.55 Hyphen

### 28.56 In Compound Words

Use a **hyphen** to make some compound words.

great-great-grandfather (noun)   starry-eyed (adjective)
mother-in-law (noun)   three-year-old (adjective)

Writers sometimes combine words in new and unexpected ways. Such combinations are usually hyphenated.

And they pried pieces of **baked-too-fast** sunshine cake from the roofs of their mouths and looked once more into the boy's eyes.

—Toni Morrison, *Song of Solomon*

**Note:** Consult a dictionary to find how it lists a particular compound word. Some compound words (*living room*) do not use a hyphen and are written separately. Some are written solid (*bedroom*). Some do not use a hyphen when the word is a noun (*ice cream*) but do use a hyphen when it is a verb or an adjective (*ice-cream sundae*).

### 28.57 To Join Letters and Words

Use a hyphen to join a capital letter or a lowercase letter to a noun or a participle.

T-shirt   U-turn   V-shaped   x-ray

### 28.58 To Join Words in Compound Numbers

Use a hyphen to join the words in compound numbers from twenty-one to ninety-nine when it is necessary to write them out. (See 29.27.)

**Forty-two** people found seats in the cramped classroom.

### 28.59 Between Numbers in Fractions

Use a hyphen between the numerator and the denominator of a fraction, but not when one or both of these elements are already hyphenated.

four-tenths   five-sixteenths   seven thirty-seconds (7/32)

### 28.60 In a Special Series

Use a hyphen when two or more words have a common element that is omitted in all but the last term.

We have cedar posts in **four-**, **six-**, and **eight-**inch widths.

### 28.61 To Create New Words

Use a hyphen to form new words beginning with the prefixes *self, ex, all,* and *half.* Also use a hyphen to join any prefix to a proper noun, a proper adjective, or the official name of an office.

post-Depression   mid-May   ex-mayor

## 28.62 To Prevent Confusion

Use a hyphen with prefixes or suffixes to avoid confusion or awkward spelling.

**re-cover** (not *recover*) the sofa    **shell-like** (not *shelllike*) shape

## 28.63 To Join Numbers

Use a hyphen to join numbers indicating a range, a score, or a vote.

Students study **30-40** hours a week.    The final score was **84-82**.

## 28.64 To Divide Words

Use a hyphen to divide a word between syllables at the end of a line of print.

### 28.65 Guidelines for Word Division

1. Leave enough of the word at the end of the line to identify the word.
2. Never divide a one-syllable word: **rained, skills, through**.
3. Avoid dividing a word of five or fewer letters: **paper, study, July**.
4. Never divide a one-letter syllable from the rest of the word: **omit-ted**, not **o-mitted**.
5. Always divide a compound word between its basic units: **sister-in-law**, not **sis-ter-in-law**.
6. Never divide abbreviations or contractions: **shouldn't**, not **should-n't**.
7. When a vowel is a syllable by itself, divide the word after the vowel: **epi-sode**, not **ep-isode**.
8. Avoid dividing a numeral: **1,000,000**, not **1,000,-000**.
9. Avoid dividing the last word in a paragraph.
10. Never divide the last word in more than two lines in a row.
11. Check a dictionary for acceptable word divisions.

## 28.66 To Form Adjectives

Use a hyphen to join two or more words that serve as a single-thought adjective before a noun.

In real life I am a large, **big-boned** woman with rough, **man-working** hands.
—Alice Walker, "Everyday Use"

Most single-thought adjectives are not hyphenated when they come after the noun. (Check the dictionary to be sure.)

In real life, I am large and **big boned**.

**Note:** When the first of these words is an adverb ending in *ly*, do not use a hyphen. Also, do not use a hyphen when a number or a letter is the final element in a single-thought adjective.

fresh**ly** painted barn    grade **A** milk (letter is the final element)

## 28.67 Dash

### 28.68 To Set Off Nonessential Elements

Use a **dash** to set off nonessential elements—explanations, examples, or definitions—when you want to emphasize them.

> Near the semester's end—**and this is not always due to poor planning**—some students may find themselves in academic trouble.
>
> The term *caveat emptor*—**let the buyer beware**—is especially appropriate to Internet shopping.

**Note:** A dash is indicated by two hyphens--with no spacing before or after--in typewriter-generated material and in handwritten material. Don't use a single hyphen when a dash (two hyphens) is required.

### 28.69 To Set Off an Introductory Series

Use a dash to set off an introductory series from the clause that explains the series.

> **Cereal, coffee, and Instagram**—without these I can't get going in the morning.

### 28.70 To Show Missing Text

Use a dash to show that words or letters are missing.

> Mr. — won't let us marry.
>
> —Alice Walker, *The Color Purple*

### 28.71 To Show Interrupted Speech

Use a dash (or an ellipsis) to show interrupted or faltering speech in dialogue. (Also see 28.08.)

> Well, I—**ah**—had this terrible case of the flu, **and**—**then**—**ah**—**the** library closed because of that flash flood, **and**—**well**—**the** high humidity jammed my printer.
>
> —Excuse No. 101

> "If you *think* you can—"
> "Oh, I *know*—"
> "Don't interrupt!"

### 28.72 For Emphasis

Use a dash in place of a colon to introduce or to emphasize a word, a series, a phrase, or a clause.

> **Jogging**—that's what he lives for.
>
> **Life is like a grindstone**—whether it grinds you down or polishes you up depends on what you're made of.
>
> **This is how the world moves**—not like an arrow, but a boomerang.
>
> —Ralph Ellison

# Punctuation Exercises:

## Semicolons, Colons, Hyphens, and Dashes

### A. Semicolons and Colons

Indicate correct placement of semicolons or colons in each sentence.
1. Aaron Copland revolutionized music Leonard Bernstein called him "Moses."
2. Copland wrote ballets such as *Appalachian Spring*, *Billy the Kid*, and *Rodeo* music for films such as *Our Town* and *The Red Pony* and symphonies such as the *Organ Symphony*, the *Short Symphony*, and his *Third Symphony*.
3. Copland also founded ASCAP the American Society of Composers, Authors, and Publishers.
4. ASCAP made it possible to be a composer it set up royalty standards.
5. Copland was trained in Paris despite that fact, he was all-American.
6. Copland is well known for one piece "Fanfare for the Common Man."
7. Unlike Bernstein, Copland wrote slowly he composed at the piano.
8. At first, Copland composed atonal music he changed his style during the Great Depression.
9. In the '50s, Copland and Bernstein ran up against an antagonist McCarthy.
10. Copland showed the way for young composers he was a kind of "Moses."

### B. Hyphens

For each item, insert hyphens correctly. If an item needs no hyphen, write "correct."

1. forty five
2. midMarch
3. nine thirty seconds
4. father in law
5. recreate (meaning "to create again")
6. a 36 38 score
7. hard working people
8. grade A meat
9. U shaped valley
10. two year old

### C. Dashes

For each sentence, indicate correct dash placement.
1. The expression *carpe diem* seize the day was written on the classroom wall.
2. "Faith, hope, and love these three, but the greatest of these is love."
3. He stuttered, "I um well wanted to ask you on a date."
4. Performing before a live audience that's what I love.
5. I will caution you this is what I tell everyone don't give up your dreams.

## 28.73 Quotation Marks

### 28.74 To Punctuate Titles

Use **quotation marks** to punctuate some titles (typically subsections of a larger work). (Also see 28.86.)

"Two Friends" (short story)
"New Car Designs" (newspaper article)
"Truth Hurts" (song)
"Multiculturalism and the Language Battle" (lecture title)
"The New Admissions Game" (magazine article)
"Reflections on Advertising" (chapter in a book)
"Casino Night" (television episode from *The Office*)
"Annabel Lee" (short poem)

### 28.75 For Special Words

Use quotation marks (1) to show that a word is being discussed as a word, (2) to indicate that a word or phrase is directly quoted, (3) to indicate that a word is slang, or (4) to point out that a word is being used in a humorous or ironic way.

1. A commentary on the times is that the word **"honesty"** is now preceded by **"old-fashioned."**
2. She said she was **"incensed."**
3. I drank a Dixie and ate bar peanuts and asked the bartender where I could hear **"chanky-chank,"** as Cajuns call their music. —William Least Heat-Moon, *Blue Highways*
4. In an attempt to be popular, he works very hard at being **"cute."**

**Note:** A word used as a word can also be set off with italics.

### 28.76 Placement of Periods or Commas

Always place periods and commas inside quotation marks.

"Dr. Slaughter wants you to have liquids, Will," Mama said anxiously. "He said not to give you any solid food tonight." —Olive Ann Burns, *Cold Sassy Tree*

### 28.77 Placement of Exclamation Points or Question Marks

Place an exclamation point or a question mark inside quotation marks when it punctuates both the main sentence and the quotation *or* just the quotation; place it outside when it punctuates the main sentence.

Do you often ask yourself, "What should I be?"

I almost croaked when he asked, "That won't be a problem, will it?"

Did he really say, "Finish this by tomorrow"?

### 28.78 Placement of Semicolons or Colons

Always place semicolons or colons outside quotation marks.

I just read "Computers and Creativity"; I now have some different ideas about the role of computers in the arts.

## 28.79 A Closer Look
### Marking Quoted Material

#### 28.80 For Direct Quotations

Use quotation marks before and after a direct quotation—a person's exact words.

> Sitting in my one-room apartment, I remember Mom saying, **"Don't go to the party with him."**

**Note:** Do *not* use quotation marks for *indirect* quotations.

> I remember Mom saying **that I should not date him.** (These are not the speaker's exact words.)

#### 28.81 For Quoted Passages

Use quotation marks before and after a quoted passage. Any word that is not part of the original quotation must be placed inside brackets.

> **(Original)** First of all, it must accept responsibility for providing shelter for the homeless.
>
> **(Quotation)** "First of all, it **[the federal government]** must accept responsibility for providing shelter for the homeless."

**Note:** If you quote only part of the original passage, be sure to construct a sentence that is both accurate and grammatically correct.

> The report goes on to say that the federal government **"must accept responsibility for providing shelter for the homeless."**

#### 28.82 For Long Quotations

If more than one paragraph is quoted, quotation marks are placed before each paragraph and at the end of the last paragraph (**Example A**). Quotations that are five or more lines (MLA style) or forty words or more (APA style) are usually set off from the text by indenting one-half inch from the left margin (a style called "block form"). Do not use quotation marks before or after a block-form quotation (**Example B**), except in cases where quotation marks appear in the original passage (**Example C**).

| Example A | Example B | Example C |
|---|---|---|
| " _____ | _____ . | _____ . |
| _____ . | _____ | _____ |
| " _____ | _____ . | " _____ " |
| _____ ." | | |

#### 28.83 For Quoting Quotations

Use single quotation marks to punctuate quoted material within a quotation.

> "I was lucky," said Jane. "The proctor announced, **'Put your pencils down,'** just as I was filling in the last answer."

## 28.84 Italics (Underlining)

### 28.85 In Handwritten and Printed Material

**Italics** is a printer's term for a style of type that is slightly slanted. In this sentence, the word *happiness* is printed in italics. In material that is handwritten or typed on a machine that cannot print in italics, underline each word or letter that should be in italics.

In <u>The Road to Memphis,</u> racism is a contagious disease.
(typed or handwritten)

Mildred Taylor's *The Road to Memphis* exposes racism. (printed)

### 28.86 In Titles

Use italics to indicate the titles of magazines, newspapers, books, pamphlets, full-length plays, films, videos, radio and television shows, book-length poems, ballets, operas, lengthy musical compositions, albums, paintings and sculptures, legal cases, websites, and the names of ships and aircraft. (Also see 28.74.)

| | |
|---|---|
| *The Week* (magazine) | *The New York Times* (newspaper) |
| *The Lost Symbol* (book) | *Yankee Tavern* (play) |
| *Enola Gay* (airplane) | *Purple Rain* (album) |
| *ACLU v. State of Ohio* (legal case) | *Billy the Kid* (ballet) |
| *Get Out* (film) | *The Thinker* (sculpture) |
| *Arrested Development* (television show) | *The Ringer* (website) |
| *College Loans* (pamphlet) | |

When one title appears within another title, punctuate as follows:

**I read an article entitled "The Making of *Up*."** (title of movie in an article title)

**He wants to watch *Inside* The New York Times *on PBS tonight.*** (title of newspaper in title of TV program)

### 28.87 For Key Terms

Italics are often used for a key term in a discussion or for a technical term, especially when it is accompanied by its definition. Italicize the term the first time it is used. Thereafter, put the term in roman type.

This flower has a ***zygomorphic*** (bilateral symmetry) structure.

### 28.88 For Foreign Words and Scientific Names

Use italics for foreign words that have not been adopted into the English language; italics are also used to denote scientific names.

Say ***arrivederci*** to your fears and try new activities. (foreign word)

The voyageurs discovered the shy ***Castor canadensis,*** or North American beaver. (scientific name)

## 28.89 Parentheses

### 28.90 To Enclose Explanatory or Supplementary Material

Use **parentheses** to enclose explanatory or supplementary material that interrupts the normal sentence structure.

Students use *The College Writer* (*TCW*) in this class.

### 28.91 To Set Off Numbers in a List

Use parentheses to set off numbers used with a series of words or phrases.

Dr. Beck told us **(1)** plan ahead, **(2)** stay flexible, and **(3)** follow through.

### 28.92 For Parenthetical Sentences

When using a full "sentence" within another sentence, do not capitalize it or use a period inside the parentheses.

Your friend doesn't have the assignment (**he was just thinking about calling you**), so you'll have to make a few more calls.

When the parenthetical sentence comes after the main sentence, capitalize and punctuate it the same way you would any other complete sentence.

But Mom doesn't say boo to Dad; she's always sweet to him. **(Actually she's sort of sweet to everybody.)**
—Norma Fox Mazer, *Up on Fong Mountain*

### 28.93 To Set Off References

Use parentheses to set off references to authors, titles, pages, and years.

The statistics are alarming **(see page 9)** and demand action.

**Note:** For unavoidable parentheses within parentheses ( . . . [ . . . ] . . . ), use brackets. Avoid overuse of parentheses by using commas instead.

## 28.94 Diagonal

### 28.95 To Form Fractions or Show Choices

Use a **diagonal** (also called a *slash*) to form a fraction. Also place a diagonal between two words to indicate that either is acceptable.

My **walking/running** shoe size is **5 1/2**; my dress shoes are **6 1/2**.

### 28.96 When Quoting Poetry

When quoting poetry, use a diagonal (with one space before and after) to show where each line ends in the actual poem.

A dryness is upon the house / My father loved and tended. / Beyond his firm and sculptured door / His light and lease have ended.
—Gwendolyn Brooks, "In Honor of David Anderson Brooks, My Father"

## 28.97 Brackets

### 28.98 With Words That Clarify

Use **brackets** before and after words that are added to clarify what another person has said or written.

"They'd [**the sweat bees**] get into your mouth, ears, eyes, nose. You'd feel them all over you."
—Marilyn Johnson and Sasha Nyary, "Roosevelts in the Amazon"

**Note:** The brackets indicate that the words *the sweat bees* are not part of the original quotation but were added for clarification.

### 28.99 Around Comments by Someone Other Than the Author

Place brackets around comments that have been added by someone other than the author or speaker.

"In conclusion, *docendo discimus*. Let the school year begin!" [**Huh?**]

### 28.100 Around Editorial Corrections

Place brackets around an editorial correction or addition.

"Brooklyn alone has 8 percent of lead poisoning [**victims**] nationwide," said Marjorie Moore.
—Donna Actie, student writer

### 28.101 Around the Word *Sic*

Brackets should be placed around the word *sic* (Latin for "so" or "thus") in quoted material; the word indicates that an error appearing in the quoted material was made by the original speaker or writer.

"There is a higher principal [**sic**] at stake here: Is the school administration aware of the situation?"

## 28.102 Exclamation Point

### 28.103 To Express Strong Feeling

Use an **exclamation point** to express strong feeling. It may be placed at the end of a sentence (or an elliptical expression that stands for a sentence). Use exclamation points sparingly.

"That's not the point," said Wangero. "These are all pieces of dresses Grandma used to wear. She did all this stitching by hand. **Imagine!**"
—Alice Walker, "Everyday Use"

Su-su-something's crawling up the back of my neck!
—Mark Twain, *Roughing It*

She was on tiptoe, stretching for an orange, when they heard, "**HEY YOU!**"
—Beverley Naidoo, *Journey to Jo'burg*

## 28.104 Apostrophe

### 28.105 In Contractions

Use an **apostrophe** to show that one or more letters have been left out of two words joined to form a contraction.

**don't** → **o** is left out     **she'd** → **woul** is left out     **it's** → **i** is left out

> **Note:** An apostrophe is also used to show that one or more numerals or letters have been left out of numbers or words.
>
> class of **'02** → **20** is left out     good **mornin'** → **g** is left out

### 28.106 To Form Plurals

Use an apostrophe and an *s* to form the plural of a letter, a number, a sign, or a word discussed as a word.

A → **A's**     t → **t's**     + → **+'s**

You use too many **and's** in your writing.

Use only an *s* to form the plural of a number or an abbreviation.

1950s     2s and 3s     $10s and $20s     BAs     MFAs     PhDs     TVs

> **Note:** If two apostrophes are called for in the same word, omit the second one.
>
> Follow closely the **do's** and **don'ts** (not **don't's**) on the checklist.

### 28.107 To Form Singular Possessives

The possessive form of singular nouns is usually made by adding an apostrophe and an *s*.

**Spock's** ears     my **computer's** memory

> **Note:** When a singular noun of more than one syllable ends with an *s* or a *z* sound, the possessive may be formed by adding just an apostrophe—or an apostrophe and an *s*.

When the singular noun is a one-syllable word, however, the possessive is usually formed by adding both an apostrophe and an *s*.

**Dallas'** sports teams *or* **Dallas's** sports teams (two-syllable word)
**Kiss's** last concert     my **boss's** generosity (one-syllable words)

### 28.108 To Form Plural Possessives

The possessive form of plural nouns ending in *s* is made by adding just an apostrophe.

the **Joneses'** great-grandfather     **bosses'** offices

> **Note:** For plural nouns not ending in *s*, add an apostrophe and *s*.
>
> **women's** health issues     **children's** program

### 28.109 To Determine Ownership

You will punctuate possessives correctly if you remember that the word that comes immediately before the apostrophe is the owner.

**girl's** guitar *(girl is the owner)*     **girls'** guitar *(girls are the owners)*

### 28.110 To Show Shared Possession

When possession is shared by more than one noun, use the possessive form for the last noun in the series.

Jason, Kamil, and **Elana's** sound system
(All three own the same system.)

**Jason's, Kamil's,** and **Elana's** sound systems
(Each owns a separate system.)

### 28.111 In Compound Nouns

The possessive of a compound noun is formed by placing the possessive ending after the last word.

his **mother-in-law's** name (singular)
the **secretary of state's** career (singular)
their **mothers-in-law's** names (plural)
the **secretaries of state's** careers (plural)

### 28.112 With Indefinite Pronouns

The possessive form of an indefinite pronoun is made by adding an apostrophe and an *s* to the pronoun. (See 25.20.)

**everybody's** grades  **no one's** mistake  **one's** choice

In expressions using *else*, add the apostrophe and *s* after the last word.

**anyone else's**  **somebody else's**

### 28.113 To Show Time or Amount

Use an apostrophe and an *s* with an adjective that is part of an expression indicating time or amount.

**yesterday's** news  a **day's** wage  a **month's** pay

### 28.114 Punctuation Marks

| | | | | | |
|---|---|---|---|---|---|
| ´ (é) | Accent, acute | : | Colon | ¶ | Paragraph |
| ` (è) | Accent, grave | , | Comma | ( ) | Parentheses |
| < > | Angle brackets | † | Dagger | . | Period |
| ' | Apostrophe | — | Dash | ? | Question mark |
| * | Asterisk | / | Diagonal/slash | " " | Quotation marks |
| { } | Braces | ¨ (ä) | Dieresis | § | Section |
| [ ] | Brackets | ... | Ellipsis | ; | Semicolon |
| ^ | Caret | ! | Exclamation point | ~ (ñ) | Tilde |
| ç | Cedilla | - | Hyphen | ___ | Underscore |
| ^ (â) | Circumflex | ..... | Leaders | | |

# Punctuation Exercises:

## Quotation Marks, Apostrophes, and Other Marks

### A. Quotation Marks and Italics (Underlining)

For each sentence, indicate the correct use of quotation marks or italics (underlining).

1. I read the article Five Cures for Writer's Block in the magazine Writer's Digest.
2. When I used the word interesting, I really meant the word bizarre.
3. The receptionist said, The doctor will be available shortly. While you wait, why don't you read the article New Vaccine in Time magazine?
4. Did the judge just say, Apolo Ohno is disqualified?
5. The music on the album Solar Plexus is what people call jazz fusion.
6. Where is Bill? asked Jacob. Didn't he say he'd be right back?
7. The short story Coffee appeared in the anthology Wake Up.
8. I played The Llama Song; my roommate objected.
9. My roommate said that he had heard that song enough.
10. Doesn't the law state, Any male 18 or over needs to sign up for the draft?

### B. Parentheses, Brackets, Diagonals, Exclamation Points

For each sentence, indicate the correct use of these marks.

1. The TA teaching assistant in my psychology class is great.
2. "I think that I shall never see A poem lovely as a tree." Joyce Kilmer
3. He signed the letter "Your fiend sic Fred."
4. This is not an either or proposition.
5. I want to 1 finish the paper, 2 revise the paper, and 3 be done with the paper.

### C. Apostrophes

For each item, write the word or words, inserting apostrophes correctly.

1. didnt
2. dos and donts
3. Pranjals scooter
4. Jane and Jills room
5. anyones folder
6. mother-in-laws hat
7. Lynnes job
8. wouldve
9. two *ands* and three *ors*
10. mens magazine

# Chapter 29

# Checking Mechanics

## 29.01 Capitalization

### 29.02 Proper Nouns and Adjectives

**Capitalize** all proper nouns and all proper adjectives (adjectives derived from proper nouns). The chart below provides a quick overview of capitalization rules. The pages following explain specific or special uses of capitalization.

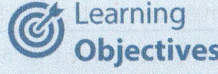

**Learning Objectives**

By working through this chapter, you will be able to

- apply conventions of capitalization.
- form plurals correctly.
- recognize when to express numbers as words or numerals.
- identify common abbreviations.
- identify common acronyms and initialisms.
- apply basic spelling rules.

### Capitalization at a Glance

| | |
|---|---|
| Days of the week | Sunday, Monday, Tuesday |
| Months | June, July, August |
| Holidays, holy days | Thanksgiving, Easter, Hanukkah |
| Periods, events in history | Middle Ages, World War I |
| Special events | Tate Memorial Dedication Ceremony |
| Political parties | Republican Party, Socialist Party |
| Official documents | the Declaration of Independence |
| Trade names | Oscar Mayer hot dogs, Mazda Miata |
| Formal epithets | Alexander the Great |
| Official titles | Mayor Jeannie Hefty, Senator Ben Sasse |
| Official state nicknames | the Badger State, the Aloha State |
| Geographical names | |
|    Planets, heavenly bodies | Earth, Jupiter, the Milky Way |
|    Continents | Australia, South America |
|    Countries | Ireland, Grenada, Sri Lanka |
|    States, provinces | Ohio, Utah, Nova Scotia |
|    Cities, towns, villages | El Paso, Burlington, Sioux Center |
|    Streets, roads, highways | Park Avenue, Route 66, Interstate 90 |
|    Sections of the United States and the world | the Southwest, the Far East |
|    Landforms | the Rocky Mountains, the Kalahari Desert |
|    Bodies of water | the Nile River, Lake Superior, Bee Creek |
|    Public areas | Central Park, Yellowstone National Park |

### 29.03 First Words

Capitalize the first word in every sentence and the first word in a full-sentence direct quotation. (Also see 28.80.)

**Attending** the orientation for new students is a good idea.

Max suggested, "**Let's** take the guided tour of the campus first."

### 29.04 Sentences in Parentheses

Capitalize the first word in a sentence that is enclosed in parentheses if that sentence is not contained within another complete sentence.

The bookstore has the software. (**Now** all I need is my computer.)

**Note:** Do *not* capitalize a sentence that is enclosed in parentheses and is located in the middle of another sentence. (Also see 28.92.)

Your college will probably offer everything (**this** includes general access to printers) that you'll need for a successful year.

### 29.05 Sentences Following Colons

Capitalize a complete sentence that follows a colon when that sentence is a formal statement, a quotation, or a sentence that you want to emphasize. (Also see 28.52.)

Sydney Harris had this to say about computers: "**The** real danger is not that computers will begin to think like people, but that people will begin to think like computers."

### 29.06 Salutation and Complimentary Closing

In a letter, capitalize the first and all major words of the salutation. Capitalize only the first word of the complimentary closing.

**Dear Personnel Director:**     **Sincerely** yours,

### 29.07 Sections of the Country

Words that indicate sections of the country are proper nouns and should be capitalized; words that simply indicate a direction are not proper nouns.

Many businesses move to the **South**. (section of the country)

They move **south** to cut fuel costs and other expenses. (direction)

### 29.08 Languages, Ethnic Groups, Nationalities, and Religions

Capitalize languages, ethnic groups, nationalities, and religions.

**African American   Latinx   Navajo   French   Islam**

Nouns that refer to the Supreme Being and holy books are capitalized.

**God   Allah   Jehovah   the Koran   Exodus   the Bible   Christ**

## 29.09 Titles

Capitalize the first word of a title, the last word, and every word in between except articles (*a, an, the*), short prepositions, *to* in an infinitive, and coordinating conjunctions. Follow this rule for titles of books, newspapers, magazines, poems, plays, songs, articles, films, works of art, and stories.

| | |
|---|---|
| *Going to Meet the Man* | *The Los Angeles Times* |
| "Nothing Gold Can Stay" | "Jobs in the Cyber Arena" |
| *A Midsummer Night's Dream* | *The War of the Roses* |

**Note:** When citing titles in a bibliography, check the style manual you've been asked to follow. For example, in APA style, only the first word of a title is capitalized.

## 29.10 Organizations

Capitalize the name of an organization or a team and its members.

| | |
|---|---|
| **American Indian Movement** | **Democratic Party** |
| **Tampa Bay Buccaneers** | **Tucson Drama Club** |

## 29.11 Abbreviations

Capitalize abbreviations of titles and organizations. (Some other abbreviations are also capitalized. See 29.32.)

MD    PhD    NAACP    CE    BCE    GPA    AD 2017    TV    CST

## 29.12 Letters

Capitalize letters used to indicate a form or shape.

**U**-turn    **I**-beam    **S**-curve    **V**-shaped    **T**-shirt

## 29.13 Words Used as Names

Capitalize words like *father, mother, uncle, senator,* and *professor* when they are parts of titles that include a personal name or when they are substituted for proper nouns (especially in direct address).

Hello, **Senator Tim Scott**. (*Senator* is part of the name.)
Our **senator** is an environmentalist.
Who was your chemistry **professor** last quarter?
I had **Professor** Williams for Chemistry 101.

**Note:** To test whether a word is being substituted for a proper noun, simply read the sentence with a proper noun in place of the word. If the proper noun fits in the sentence, the word being tested should be capitalized. Usually the word is not capitalized if it follows a possessive—*my, his, our, your,* and so on.

Did **Dad (Brad)** pack my bluetooth headphones? (*Brad* works in this sentence.)

Did your **dad (Brad)** pack the bluetooth headphones? (*Brad* does not work in this sentence; the word *dad* follows the possessive *your*.)

## 29.14 Titles of Courses

Words such as *technology, history,* and *science* are proper nouns when they are included in the titles of specific courses; they are common nouns when they name a field of study.

> Who teaches **Art History 202?** (title of a specific course)
>
> Professor Bunker loves teaching **history.** (a field of study)

**Note:** The words *freshman, sophomore, junior,* and *senior* are not capitalized unless they are part of an official title.

> The **seniors** who maintained high GPAs were honored at the **Mount Mary Senior Honors Banquet.**

## 29.15 Internet and World Wide Web

The words *Internet* and *World Wide Web* are always capitalized because they are considered proper nouns. When your writing includes a web address (URL), capitalize any letters that the site's owner does (on printed materials or on the site itself). Not only is it respectful to reprint a web address exactly as it appears elsewhere, but, in fact, some web addresses are case-sensitive and must be entered into a browser's address bar exactly as presented.

> When doing research on the **Internet,** be sure to record each site's **web** address (**URL**) and each contact's **email** address.

**Note:** Some people include capital letters in their email addresses to make certain features evident. Although email addresses are not case-sensitive, repeat each letter in print just as its owner uses it.

---

### Avoid Capitalization Errors

Do not capitalize any of the following:

- A prefix attached to a proper noun
- Seasons of the year
- Words used to indicate direction or position
- Common nouns and titles that appear near, but are not part of, a proper noun

| Capitalize | Do Not Capitalize |
|---|---|
| American | un-American |
| January, February | winter, spring |
| The South has great BBQ. | Turn south at the stop sign. |
| Duluth City College | a Duluth college |
| Prime Minister Justin Trudeau | the prime minister of Canada |
| President Ford | the president of the United States |
| Earth (the planet) | earthmover |
| Internet | email |

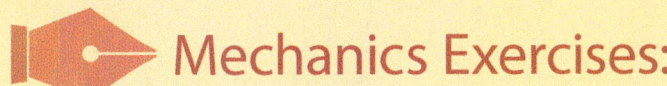
# Mechanics Exercises:

## Capitalization

### A. Capitalization Practice
For each sentence, write the correct form of any incorrectly capitalized or lowercased words.
1. The Vice President will speak in topeka, Kansas, on thursday.
2. What Jarrod meant to say is this: the dallas cowboys have enough talent to win the Super bowl.
3. The double rainbow in Yellowstone national park seemed like an act of god.
4. Does starbucks high-speed internet?
5. The vehicle in question was driving North along interstate 55 before making a u-turn.
6. are you taking introduction to mass communication 101 with professor Williams next semester?
7. I'm going to the south to visit my brother in the peach state.
8. A story in the *San Francisco chronicle* quoted the Secretary of Agriculture saying, "we are concerned with the development of our farmland."
9. Send me an email if you want to go with me to the civil war reenactment.
10. The french restaurant serves an amazing aged Cheese platter.

### B. Using Capitalization
For each line of the following email message, write the correct form of any incorrectly capitalized or lowercased words.

| | |
|---|---|
| dear Dr. Cruz, | 1 |
| Thank You for letting me shadow you for a day at St. Vincent Hospital. I very | 2 |
| much enjoyed observing the arthroscopic surgery and was impressed with the | 3 |
| expertise of the hospital's Staff! I hope we can meet up soon to discuss questions | 4 |
| about my Human functional anatomy 410 course. | 5 |
| Best Wishes, | 6 |
| Kimbra Jenson | 7 |

### C. Capitalization Errors
Write the correct form of any incorrectly capitalized or lowercased words.

| | | | |
|---|---|---|---|
| summer | prime minister | David Cameron | md |
| President | the bible | spanish | |

## 29.16 Plurals

### 29.17 Nouns Ending in a Consonant

Some nouns remain unchanged when used as plurals (*species, moose, halibut,* and so on), but the plurals of most nouns are formed by adding an *s* to the singular form.

    dorm—**dorms**   credit—**credits**   midterm—**midterms**

The plurals of nouns ending in *sh, ch, x, s,* and *z* are made by adding *es* to the singular form.

    lunch—**lunches**   wish—**wishes**   class—**classes**

### 29.18 Nouns Ending in *y*

The plurals of common nouns that end in *y* (preceded by a consonant) are formed by changing the *y* to *i* and adding *es*.

    dormitory—**dormitories**   sorority—**sororities**   duty—**duties**

The plurals of common nouns that end in *y* (preceded by a vowel) are formed by adding only an *s*.

    attorney—**attorneys**   monkey—**monkeys**   toy—**toys**

The plurals of all proper nouns ending in *y* (whether preceded by a consonant or a vowel) are formed by adding an *s*.

    the three **Kathys**   the five **Faheys**

### 29.19 Nouns Ending in *o*

The plurals of words ending in *o* (preceded by a vowel) are formed by adding an *s*.

    radio—**radios**   cameo—**cameos**   studio—**studios**

The plurals of most nouns ending in *o* (preceded by a consonant) are formed by adding *es*.

    echo—**echoes**   hero—**heroes**   tomato—**tomatoes**

Musical terms always form plurals by adding an *s*; check a dictionary for other words of this type.

    alto—**altos**   banjo—**banjos**   solo—**solos**   piano—**pianos**

### 29.20 Nouns Ending in *f* or *fe*

The plurals of nouns that end in *f* or *fe* are formed in one of two ways: If the final *f* sound is still heard in the plural form of the word, simply add *s*; if the final sound is a *v* sound, change the *f* to *ve* and add an *s*.

    **Plural ends with *f* sound:**   roof—**roofs**   chief—**chiefs**
    **Plural ends with *v* sound:**   wife—**wives**   loaf—**loaves**

> **Note:** The plurals of some nouns that end in *f* or *fe* can be formed by either adding *s* or changing the *f* to *ve* and adding an *s*.
>
>     **Plural ends with either sound:**   hoof—**hoofs, hooves**

## 29.21 Irregular Spelling

Many foreign words (as well as some of English origin) form a plural by taking on an irregular spelling; others are now acceptable with the commonly used *s* or *es* ending. Take time to check a dictionary.

    child—**children**    alumnus—**alumni**    syllabus—**syllabi, syllabuses**
    goose—**geese**    datum—**data**    radius—**radii, radiuses**

## 29.22 Words Discussed as Words

The plurals of symbols, letters, figures, and words discussed as words are formed by adding an apostrophe and an *s*.

    Many colleges have now added **A/B's** and **B/C's** as standard grades.

> **Note:** Omit the apostrophe when the omission does not cause confusion.
>     YMCAs    CDs    TVs    MDs    fours

## 29.23 Nouns Ending in *ful*

The plurals of nouns that end with *ful* are formed by adding an *s* at the end of the word.

    three **teaspoonfuls**    two **tankfuls**    four **bagfuls**

## 29.24 Compound Nouns

The plurals of compound nouns are usually formed by adding an *s* or an *es* to the important word in the compound. (Also see 28.56.)

    **brothers**-in-law    **maids** of honor    **secretaries** of state

## 29.25 Collective Nouns

Collective nouns do not change in form when they are used as plurals.

    **class** (a unit—singular form)
    **class** (individual members—plural form)

Because the spelling of the collective noun does not change, it is often the pronoun used in place of the collective noun that indicates whether the noun is singular or plural. Use a singular pronoun (**its**) to show that the collective noun is singular. Use a plural pronoun (**their**) to show that the collective noun is plural.

    The class needs to change **its** motto.
    (The writer is thinking of the group as a unit.)
    The class brainstormed with **their** professor.
    (The writer is thinking of the group as individuals.)

> **ESL Note:** To determine whether a plural requires the article *the*, you must first determine whether it is definite or indefinite. Definite plurals use *the*, whereas indefinite plurals do not require any article. (See 31.06.)

## 29.26 Numbers

### 29.27 Numerals or Words

**Numbers** from one to one hundred are usually written as words; numbers 101 and greater are usually written as numerals. (APA style uses numerals for numbers 10 and higher.) Hyphenate numbers written as two words if less than one hundred.

> **two**   **seven**   **ten**   **twenty-five**   **106**   **1,079**

The same rule applies to the use of ordinal numbers.

> **second**   **tenth**   **twenty-fifth**   **ninety-eighth**   **106th**   **333rd**

If numbers greater than 101 are used infrequently in a piece of writing, you may spell out those that can be written in one or two words.

> **two hundred**   **fifty thousand**   **six billion**

You may use a combination of numerals and words for very large numbers.

> **1.5 million**   **3 billion to 3.2 billion**   **6 trillion**

Numbers being compared or contrasted should be kept in the same style.

> **8** to **11** years old *or* **eight** to **eleven** years old

Particular decades may be spelled out or written as numerals.

> the **'80s** and **'90s** *or* the **eighties** and **nineties**

### 29.28 Numerals Only

Use numerals for the following forms: decimals, percentages, pages, chapters (and other parts of a book), addresses, dates, telephone numbers, identification numbers, and statistics.

> | | | | |
> |---|---|---|---|
> | 26.2 | 8 percent | chapter 7 | 8 May 2020 |
> | pages 287–289 | Highway 36 | (212) 555-1234 | Joshua 1: 9 |
> | 398-55-0000 | a vote of 23 to 4 | May 8, 2020 | 315 Burr Oak Road |

> **Note:** Abbreviations and symbols are often used in charts, graphs, footnotes, and so forth, but typically they are not used in texts.
> He is **five feet one inch** tall and **ten years old**.
> She walked **three and one-half miles** through **twelve inches** of snow.

However, abbreviations and symbols may be used in scientific, mathematical, statistical, and technical texts (APA style).

> Between **20%** and **23%** of the cultures yielded positive results.
> Your **245B** model requires **220V**.

Always use numerals with abbreviations and symbols.

> **5'4"**   **8%**   **10 in.**   **3 tbsp.**   **6 lb. 8 oz.**   **90°F**

Use numerals after the name of local branches of labor unions.

> The Office and Professional Employees International Union, Local **8**

## 29.29 Hyphenated Numbers

Hyphens are used to form compound modifiers indicating measurement. They are also used for inclusive numbers and written-out fractions.

 a **three-mile** trip     a **2,500-mile** road trip
 **one-sixth** of the pie    a **thirteen-foot** clearance
 **three-eighths** of the book

## 29.30 Time and Money

If time is expressed with an abbreviation, use numerals; if it is expressed in words, spell out the number.

 **4:00** a.m. *or* **four** o'clock (not 4 o'clock)
 the **5:15** p.m. train
 a **seven o'clock** wake-up call

If money is expressed with a symbol, use numerals; if the currency is expressed in words, spell out the number.

 **$20** or **twenty** dollars (not 20 dollars)

Abbreviations of time and of money may be used in text.

 The concert begins at **7:00** p.m., and tickets cost **$30**.

## 29.31 Words Only

Use words to express numbers that begin a sentence.

 **Fourteen** students "forgot" their assignments.
 **Three hundred** contest entries were received.

> **Note:** Change the sentence structure if this rule creates a clumsy construction.
>  **Six hundred thirty-nine** students are new to the campus this fall. (Clumsy)
>  This fall, **639** students are new to the campus. (Better)

Use words for numbers that precede a compound modifier that includes a numeral. (If the compound modifier uses a spelled-out number, use numerals in front of it.)

 She sold **twenty 35-millimeter** cameras in one day.
 The chef prepared **24 eight-ounce** filets.

Use words for the names of numbered streets of one hundred or fewer.

 **Ninth** Avenue
 123 **Forty-fourth** Street

Use words for the names of buildings if that name is also its address.

 **One Thousand** State Street    **Two Fifty** Park Avenue

Use words for references to particular centuries.

 the **twenty-first** century    the **fourth** century BCE

# Mechanics Exercises:

## Plurals and Numbers

### A. Plurals
For each of the following words, write the correct plural form.

1. team
2. party
3. ratio
4. shelf
5. child
6. sister-in-law
7. video
8. bucketful
9. choir
10. serf

### B. Numbers
For each sentence below, write the correct form of any incorrectly used numbers.

1. 4 tiny ducklings crossed a driveway near Six Hundred and Nine Lewis Street.
2. Out of all my friends, Alex woke up 1st around 6 o'clock.
3. The 6 cheeseburgers cost 12 dollars.
4. I read only fifty % of chapter three.
5. At half past 2 the temperature was still seventy degrees Fahrenheit.
6. The recipe calls for two tsp. salt and three oz. butter.

### C. Mechanics Practice
In the following paragraph, correct any number errors by writing the line number and the correct form. Also write the plural of each underlined word.

> Let me tell you how to grill some wonderful steak. First, consider buying    1
> your meat from a butcher rather than from local grocery. The ideal steak cut    2
> is between one and a half to 2 inches thick. Next, you will need to prepare the    3
> steaks for grilling. Start by trimming excess fat to about one-quarter of an    4
> inch thick and seasoning the meat with two tsp. of salt and cracked pepper.    5
> Then, when the grill has preheated, grill the steaks for 16 to twenty minutes.    6
> If you so choose, rotate the steaks forty-five degrees on both sides for nice    7
> diamond grill mark. When the steaks are done, turn off the grill and enjoy.    8
> And remember, steak goes great with potato and fresh mushroom.    9

## 29.32 Abbreviations

An **abbreviation** is the shortened form of a word or a phrase. These abbreviations are always acceptable in both formal and informal writing:

Mr.   Mrs.   Ms.   Dr.   Jr.   a.m. (A.M.)   p.m. (P.M.)   BS   MFA   PhD

**Note:** In formal writing, do not abbreviate the names of states, countries, months, days, units of measure, or courses of study. Do not abbreviate the words *Street, Road, Avenue, Company*, and similar words when they are part of a proper name. Also, do not use signs or symbols (%, &, #, @) in place of words. (The dollar sign, however, is appropriate when numerals are used to express an amount of money. See 29.30.)

**Also Note:** When abbreviations are called for (in charts, lists, bibliographies, notes, and indexes, for example), standard abbreviations are preferred. Reserve the postal abbreviations for ZIP code addresses.

### Correspondence Abbreviations

#### States/Territories

| | Standard | Postal |
|---|---|---|
| Alabama | Ala. | AL |
| Alaska | Alaska | AK |
| Arizona | Ariz. | AZ |
| Arkansas | Ark. | AR |
| California | Cal. | CA |
| Colorado | Colo. | CO |
| Connecticut | Conn. | CT |
| Delaware | Del. | DE |
| District of Columbia | D.C. | DC |
| Florida | Fla. | FL |
| Georgia | Ga. | GA |
| Guam | Guam | GU |
| Hawaii | Hawaii | HI |
| Idaho | Idaho | ID |
| Illinois | Ill. | IL |
| Indiana | Ind. | IN |
| Iowa | Ia. | IA |
| Kansas | Kans. | KS |
| Kentucky | Ky. | KY |
| Louisiana | La. | LA |
| Maine | Me. | ME |
| Maryland | Md. | MD |
| Massachusetts | Mass. | MA |
| Michigan | Mich. | MI |
| Minnesota | Minn. | MN |
| Mississippi | Miss. | MS |
| Missouri | Mo. | MO |
| Montana | Mont. | MT |
| Nebraska | Neb. | NE |
| Nevada | Nev. | NV |
| New Hampshire | N.H. | NH |
| New Jersey | N.J. | NJ |
| New Mexico | N. Mex. | NM |
| New York | N.Y. | NY |
| North Carolina | N.C. | NC |
| North Dakota | N. Dak. | ND |
| Ohio | Ohio | OH |
| Oklahoma | Okla. | OK |
| Oregon | Ore. | OR |
| Pennsylvania | Pa. | PA |
| Puerto Rico | P.R. | PR |
| Rhode Island | R.I. | RI |
| South Carolina | S.C. | SC |
| South Dakota | S. Dak. | SD |
| Tennessee | Tenn. | TN |
| Texas | Tex. | TX |
| Utah | Utah | UT |
| Vermont | Vt. | VT |
| Virginia | Va. | VA |
| Virgin Islands | V.I. | VI |
| Washington | Wash. | WA |
| West Virginia | W. Va. | WV |
| Wisconsin | Wis. | WI |
| Wyoming | Wyo. | WY |

#### Canadian Provinces

| | Standard | Postal |
|---|---|---|
| Alberta | Alta. | AB |
| British Columbia | B.C. | BC |
| Manitoba | Man. | MB |
| New Brunswick | N.B. | NB |
| Newfoundland and Labrador | N.F. Lab. | NL |
| Northwest Territories | N.W.T. | NT |
| Nova Scotia | N.S. | NS |
| Nunavut | | NU |
| Ontario | Ont. | ON |
| Prince Edward Island | P.E.I. | PE |
| Quebec | Que. | QC |
| Saskatchewan | Sask. | SK |
| Yukon Territory | Y.T. | YT |

#### Address Abbreviations

| | Standard | Postal |
|---|---|---|
| Apartment | Apt. | APT |
| Avenue | Ave. | AVE |
| Boulevard | Blvd. | BLVD |
| Circle | Cir. | CIR |
| Court | Ct. | CT |
| Drive | Dr. | DR |
| East | E. | E |
| Expressway | Expy. | EXPY |
| Freeway | Frwy. | FWY |
| Heights | Hts. | HTS |
| Highway | Hwy. | HWY |
| Hospital | Hosp. | HOSP |
| Junction | Junc. | JCT |
| Lake | L. | LK |
| Lakes | Ls. | LKS |
| Lane | Ln. | LN |
| Meadows | Mdws. | MDWS |
| North | N. | N |
| Palms | Palms | PLMS |
| Park | Pk. | PK |
| Parkway | Pky. | PKY |
| Place | Pl. | PL |
| Plaza | Plaza | PLZ |
| Post Office Box | P.O. Box | PO BOX |
| Ridge | Rdg. | RDG |
| River | R. | RV |
| Road | Rd. | RD |
| Room | Rm. | RM |
| Rural | R. | R |
| Rural Route | R.R. | RR |
| Shore | Sh. | SH |
| South | S. | S |
| Square | Sq. | SQ |
| Station | Sta. | STA |
| Street | St. | ST |
| Suite | Ste. | STE |
| Terrace | Ter. | TER |
| Turnpike | Tpke. | TPKE |
| Union | Un. | UN |
| View | View | VW |
| Village | Vil. | VLG |
| West | W. | W |

# Common Abbreviations

**abr.** abridged, abridgment
**AC, ac** alternating current, air-conditioning
**ack.** acknowledgment
**AM** amplitude modulation
**A.M., a.m.** before noon (Latin *ante meridiem*)
**AP** advanced placement
**ASAP** as soon as possible
**avg., av.** average
**BA** bachelor of arts degree
**BBB** Better Business Bureau
**BCE** before common era
**bibliog.** bibliography
**biog.** biographer, biographical, biography
**BS** bachelor of science degree
**C** 1. Celsius 2. centigrade 3. coulomb
**c.** 1. circa (about) 2. cup(s)
**cc** 1. cubic centimeter 2. carbon copy 3. community college
**CDT, C.D.T.** central daylight time
**CE** common era
**CEEB** College Entrance Examination Board
**chap.** chapter(s)
**cm** centimeter(s)
**c/o** care of
**COD, c.o.d.** 1. cash on delivery 2. collect on delivery
**co-op** cooperative
**CPA** Certified Public Accountant
**CST, C.S.T.** central standard time
**cu** 1. cubic 2. cumulative
**D.A.** district attorney
**d.b.a., d/b/a** doing business as
**DC, dc** direct current
**DDS** Doctor of Dental Surgery
**dec.** deceased
**dept.** department
**disc.** discount
**DST** daylight saving time
**dup.** duplicate
**ed.** edition, editor
**EDT** eastern daylight time
**EdD** Doctor of Education
**e.g.** for example (Latin *exempli gratia*)
**EST** eastern standard time
**etc.** and so forth (Latin *et cetera*)
**F** Fahrenheit, French, Friday
**FM** frequency modulation
**F.O.B., f.o.b.** free on board
**FYI** for your information
**g** 1. gravity 2. gram(s)
**gal.** gallon(s)
**gds.** goods
**gloss.** glossary

**GNP** gross national product
**GPA** grade point average
**hdqrs.** headquarters
**HIV** human immunodeficiency virus
**hp** horsepower
**Hz** hertz
**ibid.** in the same place (Latin *ibidem*)
**id.** the same (Latin *idem*)
**i.e.** that is (Latin *id est*)
**illus.** illustration
**inc.** incorporated
**IQ, I.Q.** intelligence quotient
**IRS** Internal Revenue Service
**ISBN** International Standard Book Number
**JD** Juris Doctor
**JP, J.P.** justice of the peace
**K** 1. kelvin (temperature unit) 2. Kelvin (temperature scale)
**kc** kilocycle(s)
**kg** kilogram(s)
**km** kilometer(s)
**kn** knot(s)
**kw** kilowatt(s)
**L** liter(s), lake
**lat.** latitude
**l.c.** lowercase
**lit.** literary; literature
**log** logarithm, logic
**long.** longitude
**Ltd., ltd.** limited
**m** meter(s)
**MA** master of arts degree
**man.** manual
**MBA** Master of Business Administration
**MC** master of ceremonies
**MD** doctor of medicine (Latin *medicinae doctor*)
**mdse.** merchandise
**MDT** mountain daylight time
**mfg.** manufacture, manufacturing
**mg** milligram(s)
**mi.** 1. mile(s) 2. mill(s) (monetary unit)
**misc.** miscellaneous
**mL** milliliter(s)
**mm** millimeter(s)
**mpg, m.p.g.** miles per gallon
**mph, m.p.h.** miles per hour
**MS** 1. manuscript 2. multiple sclerosis
**Ms.** title of courtesy for a woman
**MS** master of science degree
**MST** mountain standard time
**NE** northeast
**neg.** negative

**N.S.F., n.s.f.** not sufficient funds
**NW** northwest
**oz, oz.** ounce(s)
**PA** public-address system
**pct.** percent
**pd.** paid
**PDT** Pacific daylight time
**PFC, Pfc.** private first class
**pg., p.** page
**PhD** doctor of philosophy
**P.M., p.m.** after noon (Latin *post meridiem*)
**POW, P.O.W.** prisoner of war
**pp.** pages
**ppd.** 1. postpaid 2. prepaid
**PR, P.R.** public relations
**PSAT** Preliminary Scholastic Aptitude Test
**psi, p.s.i.** pounds per square inch
**PST,** Pacific standard time
**PTA, P.T.A.** Parent-Teacher Association
**R.A.** residence assistant
**RF** radio frequency
**R.P.M., rpm** revolutions per minute
**R.S.V.P., r.s.v.p.** please reply (French *répondez s'il vous plaît*)
**SAT** Scholastic Aptitude Test
**SE** southeast
**SOS** 1. international distress signal 2. any call for help
**Sr.** 1. senior (after surname) 2. sister (religious)
**SRO, S.R.O.** standing room only
**std.** standard
**SW** southwest
**syn.** synonymous, synonym
**tbs., tbsp.** tablespoon(s)
**TM** trademark
**UHF, uhf** ultrahigh frequency
**v** 1. physics: velocity 2. volume
**V** electricity: volt
**VA** Veterans Administration
**VHF, vhf** very high frequency
**VIP** informal: very important person
**vol.** 1. volume 2. volunteer
**vs.** versus, verse
**W** 1. electricity: watt(s) 2. physics: (also **w**) work 3. west
**whse., whs.** warehouse
**whsle.** wholesale
**wkly.** weekly
**w/o** without
**wt.** weight
**www** World Wide Web

Chapter 29 | Checking Mechanics     607

## 29.33 Acronyms and Initialisms

### 29.34 Acronyms

An **acronym** is an abbreviation that forms a pronounceable word. Even though acronyms are abbreviations, they require no periods.

| | |
|---|---|
| radar | radio detecting and ranging |
| CARE | Cooperative for Assistance and Relief Everywhere |
| NASA | National Aeronautics and Space Administration |
| VISTA | Volunteers in Service to America |
| FICA | Federal Insurance Contributions Act |

### 29.35 Initialisms

An **initialism** is similar to an acronym except that the initials used to form this abbreviation are pronounced individually.

| | |
|---|---|
| CIA | Central Intelligence Agency |
| FBI | Federal Bureau of Investigation |
| FHA | Federal Housing Administration |

#### Common Acronyms and Initialisms

| | | | | |
|---|---|---|---|---|
| AIDS | acquired immune deficiency syndrome | | OSHA | Occupational Safety and Health Administration |
| APR | annual percentage rate | | PAC | political action committee |
| CAD | computer-aided design | | PIN | personal identification number |
| CAM | computer-aided manufacturing | | POP | point of purchase |
| CETA | Comprehensive Employment and Training Act | | PSA | public service announcement |
| FAA | Federal Aviation Administration | | REA | Rural Electrification Administration |
| FCC | Federal Communications Commission | | RICO | Racketeer Influenced and Corrupt Organizations (Act) |
| FDA | Food and Drug Administration | | ROTC | Reserve Officers' Training Corps |
| FDIC | Federal Deposit Insurance Corporation | | SADD | Students Against Destructive Decisions |
| FEMA | Federal Emergency Management Agency | | SASE | self-addressed stamped envelope |
| | | | SPOT | satellite positioning and tracking |
| FHA | Federal Housing Administration | | SSA | Social Security Administration |
| FTC | Federal Trade Commission | | SUV | sport-utility vehicle |
| IRS | Internal Revenue Service | | SWAT | Special Weapons and Tactics |
| MADD | Mothers Against Drunk Driving | | TDD | telecommunications device for the deaf |
| NAFTA | North American Free Trade Agreement | | TMJ | temporomandibular joint |
| NATO | North Atlantic Treaty Organization | | TVA | Tennessee Valley Authority |
| OEO | Office of Economic Opportunity | | VA | Veterans Administration |
| ORV | off-road vehicle | | WHO | World Health Organization |

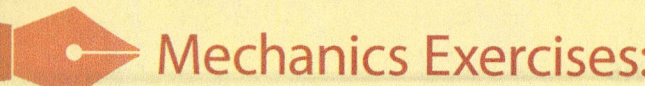 Mechanics Exercises:

# Abbreviations, Acronyms, and Initialisms

### A. Abbreviations

Indicate whether the following abbreviations would be acceptable in a formal piece of writing. Write "yes" for appropriate and "no" for inappropriate.

1. MN
2. Sask.
3. Dr.
4. R.A.
5. P.M.
6. Jr.
7. Ave.
8. Misc.
9. Mrs.
10. $5.25

### B. Acronyms and Initialisms

Indicate whether each term is an acronym or an initialism.

1. PSA
2. FDA
3. MADD
4. NATO
5. NASA
6. TMJ
7. VA
8. SWAT
9. IRS
10. FAA

### C. Mechanics Practice

For each sentence, write the correct abbreviation, acronym, or initialism of the underlined word or words.

1. <u>Mister</u> Anderson of the <u>Federal Deposit Insurance Corporation</u> called today regarding the bank's membership status.
2. We cruised south on Falcon <u>Drive</u> in our new <u>sport-utility vehicle</u>.
3. The student's low <u>grade point average</u> negated a high score on the <u>Scholastic Aptitude Test</u>.
4. Do you know the <u>latitude</u> and <u>longitude</u> of Key West, <u>Florida</u>?
5. You can add two <u>teaspoons</u> salt and one <u>tablespoon</u> basil for extra flavor.

## 29.36 Basic Spelling Rules

### 29.37 Write *i* Before *e*

Write *i* before *e* except after *c*, or when sounded like *a* as in *neighbor* and *weigh*.

believe   relief   receive   eight

**Note:** This sentence contains eight exceptions:
**Neither sheik dared leisurely seize either weird species of financiers.**

### 29.38 Words with Consonant Endings

When a one-syllable word (*bat*) ends in a consonant (*t*) preceded by one vowel (*a*), double the final consonant before adding a suffix that begins with a vowel (*batting*).

sum—**summary**   god—**goddess**

**Note:** When a multisyllable word (*control*) ends in a consonant (*l*) preceded by one vowel (*o*), the accent is on the last syllable (*con trol´*), and the suffix begins with a vowel (*ing*)—the same rule holds true: Double the final consonant (*controlling*).

prefer—**preferred**   begin—**beginning**
forget—**forgettable**   admit—**admittance**

### 29.39 Words with a Final Silent *e*

If a word ends with a silent *e*, drop the *e* before adding a suffix that begins with a vowel. Do *not* drop the *e* when the suffix begins with a consonant.

state—**stating**—**statement**   like—**liking**—**likeness**
use—**using**—**useful**   nine—**ninety**—**nineteen**

**Note:** Exceptions are **judgment, truly, argument, ninth.**

### 29.40 Words Ending in *y*

When *y* is the last letter in a word and the *y* is preceded by a consonant, change the *y* to *i* before adding any suffix except those beginning with *i*.

fry—**fries, frying**   hurry—**hurried, hurrying**
lady—**ladies**   ply—**pliable**
happy—**happiness**   beauty—**beautiful**

**Note:** When forming the plural of a word that ends with a *y* that is preceded by a vowel, add *s*.

toy—**toys**   play—**plays**   monkey—**monkeys**

*Tip:* Never trust your spelling to even the best spell checker. Carefully proofread and use a dictionary for words you know your spell checker does not cover.

## 29.41 Commonly Misspelled Words

The commonly misspelled words that follow are hyphenated to show where they would logically be broken at the end of a line.

### A

ab-bre-vi-ate
abrupt
ab-scess
ab-sence
ab-so-lute (-ly)
ab-sorb-ent
ab-surd
abun-dance
ac-a-dem-ic
ac-cede
ac-cel-er-ate
ac-cept (-ance)
ac-ces-si-ble
ac-ces-so-ry
ac-ci-den-tal-ly
ac-com-mo-date
ac-com-pa-ny
ac-com-plice
ac-com-plish
ac-cor-dance
ac-cord-ing
ac-count
ac-crued
ac-cu-mu-late
ac-cu-rate
ac-cus-tom (-ed)
ache
achieve (-ment)
ac-knowl-edge
ac-quaint-ance
ac-qui-esce
ac-quired
ac-tu-al
adapt
ad-di-tion (-al)
ad-dress
ad-e-quate
ad-journed
ad-just-ment
ad-mi-ra-ble
ad-mis-si-ble
ad-mit-tance
ad-van-ta-geous
ad-ver-tise-ment
ad-ver-tis-ing
ad-vice (n.)
ad-vis-able
ad-vise (v.)
ad-vis-er
ae-ri-al
af-fect
af-fi-da-vit
a-gainst
ag-gra-vate
ag-gres-sion
a-gree-able
a-gree-ment
aisle
al-co-hol
a-lign-ment
al-ley
al-lot-ted
al-low-ance
all right
al-most
al-ready
al-though
al-to-geth-er
a-lu-mi-num
al-um-nus
al-ways
am-a-teur
a-mend-ment
a-mong
a-mount
a-nal-y-sis
an-a-lyze
an-cient
an-ec-dote
an-es-thet-ic
an-gle
an-ni-hi-late
an-ni-ver-sa-ry
an-nounce
an-noy-ance
an-nu-al
a-noint
a-non-y-mous
an-swer
ant-arc-tic
an-tic-i-pate
anx-i-ety
anx-ious
a-part-ment
a-pol-o-gize
ap-pa-ra-tus
ap-par-ent (-ly)
ap-peal
ap-pear-ance
ap-pe-tite
ap-pli-ance
ap-pli-ca-ble
ap-pli-ca-tion
ap-point-ment
ap-prais-al
ap-pre-ci-ate
ap-proach
ap-pro-pri-ate
ap-prov-al
ap-prox-i-mate-ly
ap-ti-tude
ar-chi-tect
arc-tic
ar-gu-ment
a-rith-me-tic
a-rouse
ar-range-ment
ar-riv-al
ar-ti-cle
ar-ti-fi-cial
as-cend
as-cer-tain
as-i-nine
as-sas-sin
as-sess (-ment)
as-sign-ment
as-sist-ance
as-so-ci-ate
as-so-ci-a-tion
as-sume
as-sur-ance
as-ter-isk
ath-lete
ath-let-ic
at-tach
at-tack (-ed)
at-tempt
at-tend-ance
at-ten-tion
at-ti-tude
at-tor-ney
at-trac-tive
au-di-ble
au-di-ence
au-dit
au-thor-i-ty
au-to-mo-bile
au-tumn
aux-il-ia-ry
a-vail-a-ble
av-er-age
aw-ful
aw-ful-ly
awk-ward

### B

bac-ca-lau-re-ate
bach-e-lor
bag-gage
bal-ance
bal-loon
bal-lot
ba-nan-a
ban-dage
bank-rupt
bar-gain
bar-rel
base-ment
ba-sis
bat-tery
beau-ti-ful
beau-ty
be-com-ing
beg-gar
be-gin-ning
be-hav-ior
be-ing
be-lief
be-lieve
ben-e-fi-cial
ben-e-fit (-ed)
be-tween
bi-cy-cle
bis-cuit
bliz-zard
book-keep-er
bought
bouil-lon
bound-a-ry
break-fast
breath (n.)
breathe (v.)
brief
bril-liant
Brit-ain
bro-chure
brought
bruise
bud-get
bul-le-tin
buoy-ant
bu-reau
bur-glar
bury
busi-ness
busy

### C

caf-e-te-ria
caf-feine
cal-en-dar
cam-paign
can-celed
can-di-date
can-is-ter
ca-noe
ca-pac-i-ty
cap-i-tal
cap-i-tol
cap-tain
car-bu-ret-or
ca-reer
car-i-ca-ture
car-riage
cash-ier
cas-se-role
cas-u-al-ty
cat-a-log
ca-tas-tro-phe
caught
cav-al-ry
cel-e-bra-tion

cem-e-ter-y
cen-sus
cen-tu-ry
cer-tain
cer-tif-i-cate
ces-sa-tion
chal-lenge
chan-cel-lor
change-a-ble
char-ac-ter (-is-tic)
chauf-feur
chief
chim-ney
choc-o-late
choice
choose
Chris-tian
cir-cuit
cir-cu-lar
cir-cum-stance
civ-i-li-za-tion
cli-en-tele
cli-mate
climb
clothes
coach
co-coa
co-er-cion
col-lar
col-lat-er-al
col-lege
col-le-giate
col-lo-qui-al
colo-nel
col-or
co-los-sal
col-umn
com-e-dy
com-ing
com-mence
com-mer-cial
com-mis-sion
com-mit
com-mit-ment
com-mit-ted
com-mit-tee
com-mu-ni-cate
com-mu-ni-ty
com-par-a-tive
com-par-i-son
com-pel
com-pe-tent
com-pe-ti-tion

com-pet-i-tive-ly
com-plain
com-ple-ment
com-plete-ly
com-plex-ion
com-pli-ment
com-pro-mise
con-cede
con-ceive
con-cern-ing
con-cert
con-ces-sion
con-clude
con-crete
con-curred
con-cur-rence
con-demn
con-de-scend
con-di-tion
con-fer-ence
con-ferred
con-fi-dence
con-fi-den-tial
con-grat-u-late
con-science
con-sci-en-tious
con-scious
con-sen-sus
con-se-quence
con-ser-va-tive
con-sid-er-ably
con-sign-ment
con-sis-tent
con-sti-tu-tion
con-tempt-ible
con-tin-u-al-ly
con-tin-ue
con-tin-u-ous
con-trol
con-tro-ver-sy
con-ven-ience
con-vince
cool-ly
co-op-er-ate
cor-dial
cor-po-ra-tion
cor-re-late
cor-re-spond
cor-re-spond-
  ence
cor-rob-o-rate
cough
coun-cil

coun-sel
coun-ter-feit
coun-try
cour-age
cou-ra-geous
cour-te-ous
cour-te-sy
cous-in
cov-er-age
cred-i-tor
cri-sis
crit-i-cism
crit-i-cize
cru-el
cu-ri-os-i-ty
cu-ri-ous
cur-rent
cur-ric-u-lum
cus-tom
cus-tom-ary
cus-tom-er
cyl-in-der

D

dai-ly
dair-y
dealt
debt-or
de-ceased
de-ceit-ful
de-ceive
de-cid-ed
de-ci-sion
dec-la-ra-tion
dec-o-rate
de-duct-i-ble
de-fend-ant
de-fense
de-ferred
def-i-cit
def-i-nite (-ly)
def-i-ni-tion
del-e-gate
de-li-cious
de-pend-ent
de-pos-i-tor
de-pot
de-scend
de-scribe
de-scrip-tion
de-sert
de-serve

de-sign
de-sir-able
de-sir-ous
de-spair
des-per-ate
de-spise
des-sert
de-te-ri-o-rate
de-ter-mine
de-vel-op
de-vel-op-ment
de-vice
de-vise
di-a-mond
di-a-phragm
di-ar-rhe-a
dic-tio-nary
dif-fer-ence
dif-fer-ent
dif-fi-cul-ty
di-lap-i-dat-ed
di-lem-ma
din-ing
di-plo-ma
di-rec-tor
dis-agree-able
dis-ap-pear
dis-ap-point
dis-ap-prove
dis-as-trous
dis-ci-pline
dis-cov-er
dis-crep-an-cy
dis-cuss
dis-cus-sion
dis-ease
dis-sat-is-fied
dis-si-pate
dis-tin-guish
dis-trib-ute
di-vide
di-vis-i-ble
di-vi-sion
doc-tor
doesn't
dom-i-nant
dor-mi-to-ry
doubt
drudg-ery
du-pli-cate
dye-ing
dy-ing

E

ea-ger-ly
ear-nest
eco-nom-i-cal
econ-o-my
ec-sta-sy
e-di-tion
ef-fer-ves-cent
ef-fi-ca-cy
ef-fi-cien-cy
eighth
ei-ther
e-lab-o-rate
e-lec-tric-i-ty
el-e-phant
el-i-gi-ble
e-lim-i-nate
el-lipse
em-bar-rass
e-mer-gen-cy
em-i-nent
em-pha-size
em-ploy-ee
em-ploy-ment
e-mul-sion
en-close
en-cour-age
en-deav-or
en-dorse-ment
en-gi-neer
En-glish
e-nor-mous
e-nough
en-ter-prise
en-ter-tain
en-thu-si-as-tic
en-tire-ly
en-trance
en-vel-op (v.)
en-ve-lope (n.)
en-vi-ron-ment
equip-ment
equipped
e-quiv-a-lent
es-pe-cial-ly
es-sen-tial
es-tab-lish
es-teemed
et-i-quette
ev-i-dence
ex-ag-ger-ate
ex-ceed
ex-cel-lent

## Handbook

ex-cept
ex-cep-tion-al-ly
ex-ces-sive
ex-cite
ex-ec-u-tive
ex-er-cise
ex-haust (-ed)
ex-hi-bi-tion
ex-hil-a-ra-tion
ex-is-tence
ex-or-bi-tant
ex-pect
ex-pe-di-tion
ex-pend-i-ture
ex-pen-sive
ex-pe-ri-ence
ex-plain
ex-pla-na-tion
ex-pres-sion
ex-qui-site
ex-ten-sion
ex-tinct
ex-traor-di-nar-y
ex-treme-ly

### F

fa-cil-i-ties
fal-la-cy
fa-mil-iar
fa-mous
fas-ci-nate
fash-ion
fa-tigue (-d)
fau-cet
fa-vor-ite
fea-si-ble
fea-ture
Feb-ru-ar-y
fed-er-al
fem-i-nine
fer-tile
fic-ti-tious
field
fierce
fi-ery
fi-nal-ly
fi-nan-cial-ly
fo-li-age
for-ci-ble
for-eign
for-feit
for-go

for-mal-ly
for-mer-ly
for-tu-nate
for-ty
for-ward
foun-tain
fourth
frag-ile
fran-ti-cal-ly
freight
friend
ful-fill
fun-da-men-tal
fur-ther-more
fu-tile

### G

gad-get
gan-grene
ga-rage
gas-o-line
gauge
ge-ne-al-o-gy
gen-er-al-ly
gen-er-ous
ge-nius
gen-u-ine
ge-og-ra-phy
ghet-to
ghost
glo-ri-ous
gnaw
go-ril-la
gov-ern-ment
gov-er-nor
gra-cious
grad-u-a-tion
gram-mar
grate-ful
grat-i-tude
grease
grief
griev-ous
gro-cery
grudge
grue-some
guar-an-tee
guard
guard-i-an
guer-ril-la
guess
guid-ance

guide
guilty
gym-na-si-um
gyp-sy
gy-ro-scope

### H

hab-i-tat
ham-mer
hand-ker-chief
han-dle (-d)
hand-some
hap-haz-ard
hap-pen
hap-pi-ness
ha-rass
har-bor
hast-i-ly
hav-ing
haz-ard-ous
height
hem-or-rhage
hes-i-tate
hin-drance
his-to-ry
hoarse
hol-i-day
hon-or
hop-ing
hop-ping
horde
hor-ri-ble
hos-pi-tal
hu-mor-ous
hur-ried-ly
hy-drau-lic
hy-giene

### I

i-am-bic
i-ci-cle
i-den-ti-cal
id-io-syn-cra-sy
il-leg-i-ble
il-lit-er-ate
il-lus-trate
im-ag-i-nary
im-ag-i-na-tive
im-ag-ine
im-i-ta-tion
im-me-di-ate-ly

im-mense
im-mi-grant
im-mor-tal
im-pa-tient
im-per-a-tive
im-por-tance
im-pos-si-ble
im-promp-tu
im-prove-ment
in-al-ien-able
in-ci-den-tal-ly
in-con-ve-nience
in-cred-i-ble
in-curred
in-def-i-nite-ly
in-del-ible
in-de-pend-ence
in-de-pend-ent
in-dict-ment
in-dis-pens-able
in-di-vid-u-al
in-duce-ment
in-dus-tri-al
in-dus-tri-ous
in-ev-i-ta-ble
in-fe-ri-or
in-ferred
in-fi-nite
in-flam-ma-ble
in-flu-en-tial
in-ge-nious
in-gen-u-ous
in-im-i-ta-ble
in-i-tial
ini-ti-a-tion
in-no-cence
in-no-cent
in-oc-u-la-tion
in-quir-y
in-stal-la-tion
in-stance
in-stead
in-sti-tute
in-struc-tor
in-sur-ance
in-tel-lec-tu-al
in-tel-li-gence
in-ten-tion
in-ter-cede
in-ter-est-ing
in-ter-fere
in-ter-mit-tent
in-ter-pret (-ed)

in-ter-rupt
in-ter-view
in-ti-mate
in-va-lid
in-ves-ti-gate
in-ves-tor
in-vi-ta-tion
ir-i-des-cent
ir-rel-e-vant
ir-re-sis-ti-ble
ir-rev-er-ent
ir-ri-gate
is-land
is-sue
i-tem-ized
i-tin-er-ar-y

### J

jan-i-tor
jeal-ous (-y)
jeop-ar-dize
jew-el-ry
jour-nal
jour-ney
judg-ment
jus-tice
jus-ti-fi-able

### K

kitch-en
knowl-edge
knuck-le

### L

la-bel
lab-o-ra-to-ry
lac-quer
lan-guage
laugh
laun-dry
law-yer
league
lec-ture
le-gal
leg-i-ble
leg-is-la-ture
le-git-i-mate
lei-sure
length

let-ter-head
li-a-bil-i-ty
li-a-ble
li-ai-son
lib-er-al
li-brar-y
li-cense
lieu-ten-ant
light-ning
lik-able
like-ly
lin-eage
liq-ue-fy
liq-uid
lis-ten
lit-er-ary
lit-er-a-ture
live-li-hood
log-a-rithm
lone-li-ness
loose
lose
los-ing
lov-able
love-ly
lun-cheon
lux-u-ry

## M

ma-chine
mag-a-zine
mag-nif-i-cent
main-tain
main-te-nance
ma-jor-i-ty
mak-ing
man-age-ment
ma-neu-ver
man-u-al
man-u-fac-ture
man-u-script
mar-riage
mar-shal
ma-te-ri-al
math-e-mat-ics
max-i-mum
may-or
mean-ness
meant
mea-sure
med-i-cine
me-di-eval

me-di-o-cre
me-di-um
mem-o-ran-dum
men-us
mer-chan-dise
mer-it
mes-sage
mile-age
mil-lion-aire
min-i-a-ture
min-i-mum
min-ute
mir-ror
mis-cel-la-neous
mis-chief
mis-chie-vous
mis-er-a-ble
mis-ery
mis-sile
mis-sion-ary
mis-spell
mois-ture
mol-e-cule
mo-men-tous
mo-not-o-nous
mon-u-ment
mort-gage
mu-nic-i-pal
mus-cle
mu-si-cian
mus-tache
mys-te-ri-ous

## N

na-ive
nat-u-ral-ly
nec-es-sary
ne-ces-si-ty
neg-li-gi-ble
ne-go-ti-ate
neigh-bor-hood
nev-er-the-less
nick-el
niece
nine-teenth
nine-ty
no-tice-able
no-to-ri-ety
nu-cle-ar
nui-sance

## O

o-be-di-ence
o-bey
o-blige
ob-sta-cle
oc-ca-sion
oc-ca-sion-al-ly
oc-cu-pant
oc-cur
oc-curred
oc-cur-rence
of-fense
of-fi-cial
of-ten
o-mis-sion
o-mit-ted
op-er-ate
o-pin-ion
op-po-nent
op-por-tu-ni-ty
op-po-site
op-ti-mism
or-di-nance
or-di-nar-i-ly
orig-i-nal
out-ra-geous

## P

pag-eant
pam-phlet
par-a-dise
para-graph
par-al-lel
par-a-lyze
pa-ren-the-ses
pa-ren-the-sis
par-lia-ment
par-tial
par-tic-i-pant
par-tic-i-pate
par-tic-u-lar-ly
pas-time
pa-tience
pa-tron-age
pe-cu-liar
per-ceive
per-haps
per-il
per-ma-nent
per-mis-si-ble
per-pen-dic-u-lar

per-se-ver-ance
per-sis-tent
per-son-al (-ly)
per-son-nel
per-spi-ra-tion
per-suade
phase
phe-nom-e-non
phi-los-o-phy
phy-si-cian
piece
planned
pla-teau
plau-si-ble
play-wright
pleas-ant
plea-sure
pneu-mo-nia
pol-i-ti-cian
pos-sess
pos-ses-sion
pos-si-ble
prac-ti-cal-ly
prai-rie
pre-cede
pre-ce-dence
pre-ced-ing
pre-cious
pre-cise-ly
pre-ci-sion
pre-de-ces-sor
pref-er-a-ble
pref-er-ence
pre-ferred
prej-u-dice
pre-lim-i-nar-y
pre-mi-um
prep-a-ra-tion
pres-ence
prev-a-lent
pre-vi-ous
prim-i-tive
prin-ci-pal
prin-ci-ple
pri-or-i-ty
pris-on-er
priv-i-lege
prob-a-bly
pro-ce-dure
pro-ceed
pro-fes-sor
prom-i-nent
pro-nounce

pro-nun-ci-a-tion
pro-pa-gan-da
pros-e-cute
pro-tein
psy-chol-o-gy
pub-lic-ly
pump-kin
pur-chase
pur-sue
pur-su-ing
pur-suit

## Q

qual-i-fied
qual-i-ty
quan-ti-ty
quar-ter
ques-tion-naire
quite
quo-tient

## R

raise
rap-port
re-al-ize
re-al-ly
re-cede
re-ceipt
re-ceive
re-ceived
rec-i-pe
re-cip-i-ent
rec-og-ni-tion
rec-og-nize
rec-om-mend
re-cur-rence
ref-er-ence
re-ferred
reg-is-tra-tion
re-hearse
reign
re-im-burse
rel-e-vant
re-lieve
re-li-gious
re-mem-ber
re-mem-brance
rem-i-nisce
ren-dez-vous
re-new-al
rep-e-ti-tion

rep-re-sen-ta-tive
req-ui-si-tion
res-er-voir
re-sis-tance
re-spect-a-bly
re-spect-ful-ly
re-spec-tive-ly
re-spon-si-bil-i-ty
res-tau-rant
rheu-ma-tism
rhyme
rhythm
ri-dic-u-lous
route

## S

sac-ri-le-gious
safe-ty
sal-a-ry
sand-wich
sat-is-fac-to-ry
Sat-ur-day
scarce-ly
scene
scen-er-y
sched-ule
schol-ar-ship
sci-ence
scis-sors
sec-re-tary
seize
sen-si-ble
sen-tence
sen-ti-nel
sep-a-rate
ser-geant
sev-er-al
se-vere-ly
shep-herd
sher-iff
shin-ing
siege
sig-nif-i-cance
sim-i-lar
si-mul-ta-ne-ous
since
sin-cere-ly
ski-ing
sol-dier
sol-emn
so-phis-ti-cat-ed
soph-o-more

so-ror-i-ty
source
sou-ve-nir
spa-ghet-ti
spe-cif-ic
spec-i-men
speech
sphere
spon-sor
spon-ta-ne-ous
sta-tion-ary
sta-tion-ery
sta-tis-tic
stat-ue
stat-ure
stat-ute
stom-ach
stopped
straight
strat-e-gy
strength
stretched
study-ing
sub-si-dize
sub-stan-tial
sub-sti-tute
sub-tle
suc-ceed
suc-cess
suf-fi-cient
sum-ma-rize
su-per-fi-cial
su-per-in-tend-ent
su-pe-ri-or-i-ty
su-per-sede
sup-ple-ment
sup-pose
sure-ly
sur-prise
sur-veil-lance
sur-vey
sus-cep-ti-ble
sus-pi-cious
sus-te-nance
syl-la-ble
sym-met-ri-cal
sym-pa-thy
sym-pho-ny
symp-tom
syn-chro-nous

## T

tar-iff
tech-nique
tele-gram
tem-per-a-ment
tem-per-a-ture
tem-po-rary
ten-den-cy
ten-ta-tive
ter-res-tri-al
ter-ri-ble
ter-ri-to-ry
the-ater
their
there-fore
thief
thor-ough (-ly)
though
through-out
tired
to-bac-co
to-geth-er
to-mor-row
tongue
to-night
touch
tour-na-ment
tour-ni-quet
to-ward
trag-e-dy
trai-tor
tran-quil-iz-er
trans-ferred
trea-sur-er
tru-ly
Tues-day
tu-i-tion
typ-i-cal
typ-ing

## U

unan-i-mous
un-con-scious
un-doubt-ed-ly
un-for-tu-nate-ly
unique
u-ni-son
uni-ver-si-ty
un-nec-es-sary
un-prec-e-

dent-ed
un-til
up-per
ur-gent
us-able
use-ful
using
usu-al-ly
u-ten-sil
u-til-ize

## V

va-can-cies
va-ca-tion
vac-u-um
vague
valu-able
va-ri-ety
var-i-ous
veg-e-ta-ble
ve-hi-cle
veil
ve-loc-i-ty
ven-geance
vi-cin-i-ty
view
vig-i-lance
vil-lain
vi-o-lence
vis-i-bil-i-ty
vis-i-ble
vis-i-tor
voice
vol-ume
vol-un-tary
vol-un-teer

## W

wan-der
war-rant
weath-er
Wednes-day
weird
wel-come
wel-fare
where
wheth-er
which
whole
whol-ly
whose
width
wom-en

worth-while
wor-thy
wreck-age
wres-tler
writ-ing
writ-ten
wrought

## Y

yel-low
yes-ter-day
yield

## 29.42 Steps to Becoming a Better Speller

1. **Be patient.**
   Becoming a good speller takes time.

2. **Check the correct pronunciation of each word you are attempting to spell.**
   Knowing the correct pronunciation of each word can help you to remember its spelling.

3. **Note the meaning and history of each word as you are checking the dictionary for the pronunciation.**
   Knowing the meaning and history of a word provides you with a better notion of how the word is properly used, and it can help you remember the word's spelling.

4. **Before you close the dictionary, practice spelling the word.**
   You can do so by looking away from the page and trying to "see" the word in your "mind's eye." Write the word on a piece of paper. Check the spelling in the dictionary and repeat the process until you are able to spell the word correctly.

5. **Learn some spelling rules.**
   The four rules in this handbook (page 621) are four of the most useful—although there are others.

6. **Make a list of the words that you misspell.**
   Select the first ten words and practice spelling them.
   **First:** Read each word carefully; then write it on a piece of paper. Look at the written word to see that it's spelled correctly. Repeat the process for those words that you misspelled.
   **Then:** Ask someone to read the words to you so you can write them again. Then check for misspellings. Repeat both steps with your next ten words.

7. **Write often.**
   As noted educator Frank Smith said,

   *"There is little point in learning to spell if you have little intention of writing."*

## Mechanics Exercises:

# Spelling

Correct any spelling errors in the following letter by writing the line number and the correct spelling of the word(s).

Dear Dr. Hanson:

I wanted to pass along an updat regarding my project for the Undergraduate Recearch Conference. I'm makin great progress, but I have a few questions. I'll start with my progress:

- As of Febuary 21, my primary and secondary research is in excelent order.
- I've completed writng, revising, and editing my literature review.
- I beleive I will finish a first draft by the end of the week.

Here are my questions for you:

- Should I make a PowerPoint version for my presentation?
- Who is in charge of advertiseing for the event?
- How soon from now will room asignments be announced?

I've really enjoyed researching the relationship between stress and eating habits among college students. You'll find the introduction to my presentation in the enclosed pamflet.

Thanks for takin the time to read over these materials.

Sincerely,
Jim White

# Chapter 30

# Using the Right Word

The following glossary contains words that are commonly confused.

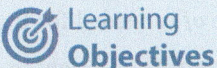

## Learning Objectives

By working through this chapter, you will be able to

- distinguish the meaning of commonly confused words.
- identify the right word for your writing.

**a, an** Use *a* as the article before words that begin with consonant sounds and before words that begin with the long vowel sound *u* (yü). Use *an* before words that begin with other vowel sounds.

> **An** administrator showed Kris **an** easy way to get to class.
> **A** uniform is required attire for **a** cafeteria worker.

**a lot, alot, allot** *Alot* is not a word; *a lot* (two words) is a vague descriptive phrase that should be used sparingly, especially in formal writing. *Allot* means to give someone a share.

> Prof Dubi **allots** each of us five spelling errors per semester, and he thinks that's **a lot**.

**accept, except** The verb *accept* means "to receive or believe"; the preposition *except* means "other than."

> The instructor **accepted** Mike's story about being late, but she wondered why no one **except** Mike had forgotten about the change to daylight saving time.

**adapt, adopt, adept** *Adapt* means "to adjust or change to fit"; *adopt* means "to choose and treat as your own" (a child, an idea). *Adept* is an adjective meaning "proficient or well trained."

> After much thought and deliberation, we agreed to **adopt** the black beagle from the shelter. Now we have to agree on how to **adapt** our lifestyle to fit our new roommate, who is quite **adept** at getting food off the kitchen counter.

**adverse, averse** *Adverse* means "hostile, unfavorable, or harmful." *Averse* means "to have a definite feeling of distaste—disinclined."

> Groans and other **adverse** reactions were noted as the new students, **averse** to strenuous exercise, were ushered past the X-5000 pump-and-crunch machine.

**advice, advise** *Advice* is a noun meaning "information or recommendation"; *advise* is a verb meaning "to recommend."

> Successful people will often give you sound **advice**, so I **advise** you to listen.

**affect, effect** *Affect* means "to influence"; the noun *effect* means "the result."

> The employment growth in a field will **affect** your chances of getting a job. The **effect** may be a new career choice.

**aid, aide** As a verb, *aid* means "to help"; as a noun, *aid* means "the help given." An *aide* is a person who acts as an assistant.

**all, of** *Of* is seldom needed after *all*.
>**All** the reports had an error in them.
>**All** the speakers spoke French.
>**All of** us voted to reschedule the meeting.
>(Here *of* is needed for the sentence to make sense.)

**all right, alright** *Alright* is the incorrect form of *all right*. (**Note:** The following are spelled correctly: *always, altogether, already, almost*.)

**allude, elude** *Allude* means "to indirectly refer to or hint at something"; *elude* means "to escape attention or understanding altogether."
>Ravi often **alluded** to wanting a supper invitation by mentioning the "awfully good" smells from the kitchen. These hints never **eluded** Ma's good heart.

**allusion, illusion** *Allusion* is an indirect reference to something or someone, especially in literature; *illusion* is a false picture or idea.
>Did you recognize the **allusion** to David in the reading assignment? Until I read that part, I was under the **illusion** that the young boy would run away from the bully.

**already, all ready** *Already* is an adverb meaning "before this time" or "by this time." *All ready* is an adjective form meaning "fully prepared." (**Note:** Use *all ready* if you can substitute *ready* alone in the sentence.)
>By the time I was a junior in high school, I had **already** taken my SATs. That way, I was **all ready** to apply early to college.

**altogether, all together** *Altogether* means "entirely." *All together* means "in a group" or "all at once." (**Note:** Use *all together* if you can substitute *together* alone in the sentence.)
>**All together** there are 35,000 job titles to choose from. That's **altogether** too many to even think about.

**among, between** *Among* is used when emphasizing distribution throughout a body or a group of three or more; *between* is used when emphasizing distribution to two individuals.
>There was discontent **among** the relatives after learning that their aunt had divided her entire fortune **between** a canary and a favorite waitress at the local cafe.

**amoral, immoral** *Amoral* means "neither moral (right) nor immoral (wrong)"; *immoral* means "wrong, or in conflict with traditional values."
>Carnivores are **amoral** in their hunt; poachers are **immoral** in theirs.

**amount, number** *Amount* is used for bulk measurement. *Number* is used to count separate units. (See also **fewer**.)
>The **number** of new instructors hired next year will depend on the **amount** of revenue raised by the new sales tax.

**and etc.** Don't use *and* before *etc.* since *et cetera* means "and the rest."
  Did you remember your textbook, notebook, handout, **etc.**?

**annual, biannual, semiannual, biennial, perennial** An *annual* event happens once every year. A *biannual* event happens twice a year (*semiannual* is the same as *biannual*). A *biennial* event happens every two years. A *perennial* event happens throughout the year, every year.

**anxious, eager** Both words mean "looking forward to," but *anxious* also connotes fear or concern.
  The professor is **eager** to move into the new building, but she's a little **anxious** that students won't be able to find her new office.

**anymore, any more** *Anymore* (an adverb) means "any longer"; *any more* means "any additional."
  We won't use that textbook **anymore**; call if you have **any more** questions.

**any one (of), anyone** *Any one* means "any one of a number of people, places, or things"; *anyone* is a pronoun meaning "any person."
  Choose **any one** of the proposed weekend schedules. **Anyone** wishing to work on Saturday instead of Sunday may do so.

**appraise, apprise** *Appraise* means "to determine value." *Apprise* means "to inform."
  Because of the tax assessor's recent **appraisal** of our home, we were **apprised** of an increase in our property tax.

**as** Don't use *as* in place of *whether* or *if*.
  I don't know **as** I'll accept the offer. (Incorrect)
  I don't know **whether** I'll accept the offer. (Correct)

Don't use *as* when it is unclear whether it means *because* or *when*.
  We rowed toward shore **as** it started raining. (Unclear)
  We rowed toward shore **because** it started raining. (Correct)

**assure, ensure, insure** (See insure.)

**bad, badly** *Bad* is an adjective, used both before nouns and as a predicate adjective after linking verbs. *Badly* is an adverb.
  Christina felt **bad** about serving us **bad** food.
  Larisa played **badly** today.

**beside, besides** *Beside* means "by the side of." *Besides* means "in addition to."
  **Besides** the two suitcases you've already loaded into the trunk, remember the smaller one **beside** the van.

**between, among** (See among.)

**bring, take** *Bring* suggests the action is directed toward the speaker; *take* suggests the action is directed away from the speaker.
  If you're not going to **bring** the video to class, **take** it back to the resource center.

# Using the Right Word Exercises:

## Using the Right Word: I

### A. Selecting the Right Word
Choose the correct word from those in parentheses for each sentence.
1. Hunter was (*accepted, excepted*) into a summer internship program at an accounting firm.
2. The celebrity was unable to (*allude, elude*) the paparazzi outside of the night club.
3. Juan is quite (*adapt, adopt, adept*) at playing the electric guitar.
4. Does (*anyone, any one*) know of a scenic location for a Sunday picnic?
5. I feel (*anxious, eager*) around people who are loud and outgoing.
6. Today was a good day because it did not go as (*bad, badly*) as yesterday.
7. (*Altogether, All together*) thirty-five people waited outside of the movie theater for the premiere of the new movie.
8. Are you under the (*allusion, illusion*) that the young businessperson will abandon her friends?
9. The new round of layoffs may (*affect, effect*) my position with the company.
10. What (*amount, number*) of money will it take to purchase a plane ticket to Japan?

### B. Replacing Incorrect Words
For each sentence below, identify the misused words and correct them.
1. Phil appraised his buddy about the affects of driving a car more than 3,000 miles without a oil change.
2. Do you mean to elude to my need for some fashion advise?
3. A strong friendship among Cary and Nyssa helped get them through an averse situation.

**can, may** In formal contexts, *can* is used to mean "being able to do"; *may* is used to mean "having permission to do."

    **May** I borrow your bicycle to get to the library? Then I **can** start working on our group project.

**capital, capitol** The noun *capital* refers to a city or to money. The adjective *capital* means "major or important" or "seat of government." *Capitol* refers to a building.

    The **capitol** is in the **capital** city for a **capital** reason. The city government contributed **capital** for the building expense.

**cent, sent, scent** *Cent* is a coin; *sent* is the past tense of the verb "send"; *scent* is an odor or a smell.

    For forty-nine **cents**, I **sent** my friend a love poem in a perfumed envelope. She adored the **scent** but hated the poem.

**chord, cord** *Chord* may mean "an emotion or a feeling," but it also may mean "the combination of three or more tones sounded at the same time," as with a guitar *chord*. A *cord* is a string or a rope.

    The guitar player strummed the opening **chord**, which struck a responsive **chord** with the audience.

**chose, choose** *Chose* (choz) is the past tense of the verb *choose* (chüz).

    For generations, people **chose** their careers based on their parents' careers; now people **choose** their careers based on the job market.

**climactic, climatic** *Climactic* refers to the climax, or high point, of an event; *climatic* refers to the climate, or weather conditions.

    Because we are using the open-air amphitheater, **climatic** conditions will just about guarantee the wind gusts we need for the **climactic** third act.

**coarse, course** *Coarse* means "of inferior quality, rough, or crude"; *course* means "a direction or a path taken." *Course* also means "a class or a series of studies."

    A basic writing **course** is required of all students.

    Due to years of woodworking, the instructor's hands are rather **coarse**.

**compare with, compare to** Things in the same category are *compared with* each other; things in different categories are *compared to* each other.

    **Compare** Christopher Marlowe's plays **with** William Shakespeare's plays.

    My brother **compared** reading *The Tempest* **to** visiting another country.

**complement, compliment** *Complement* means "to complete or go well with." *Compliment* means "to offer an expression of admiration or praise."

    We wanted to **compliment** Zach on his decorating efforts; the bright yellow walls **complement** the purple carpet.

**comprehensible, comprehensive** *Comprehensible* means "capable of being understood"; *comprehensive* means "covering a broad range, or inclusive."

    The theory is **comprehensible** only to those who have a **comprehensive** knowledge of physics.

**comprise, compose** *Comprise* means "to contain or consist of"; *compose* means "to create or form by bringing parts together."

>Fruitcake **comprises** a variety of nuts, candied fruit, and spice.

>Fruitcake is **composed of** (not *comprised of*) a variety of ingredients.

**conscience, conscious** A *conscience* gives one the capacity to know right from wrong. *Conscious* means "awake or alert, not sleeping or comatose."

>Your **conscience** will guide you, but you have to be **conscious** to hear what it's "saying."

**continual, continuous** *Continual* often implies that something is happening often, recurring; *continuous* usually implies that something keeps happening, uninterrupted.

>The **continuous** loud music during the night gave the building manager not only a headache but also **continual** phone calls.

**counsel, council, consul** When used as a noun, *counsel* means "advice"; when used as a verb, *counsel* means "to advise." *Council* refers to a group that advises. A *consul* is a government official appointed to reside in a foreign country.

>The city **council** was asked to **counsel** our student **council** on running an efficient meeting. Their **counsel** was very helpful.

**decent, descent, dissent** *Decent* means "good." *Descent* is the process of going or stepping downward. *Dissent* means "disagreement."

>The food was **decent**.

>The elevator's fast **descent** clogged my ears.

>Their **dissent** over the decisions was obvious in their sullen expressions.

**desert, dessert** *Desert* is barren wilderness. *Dessert* is food served at the end of a meal. The verb *desert* means "to abandon."

**different from, different than** Use *different from* in formal writing; use either form in informal or colloquial settings.

>Rafael's interpretation was **different from** Andrea's.

**discreet, discrete** *Discreet* means "showing good judgment, unobtrusive, modest"; *discrete* means "distinct, separate."

>The essay question had three **discrete** parts.

>Her roommate had apparently never heard of quiet, **discreet** conversation.

**disinterested, uninterested** Both words mean "not interested." However, *disinterested* is also used to mean "unbiased or impartial."

>A person chosen as an arbitrator must be a **disinterested** party.

>Professor Eldridge was **uninterested** in our complaints about the assignment.

**effect, affect** (See affect.)

**elicit, illicit** *Elicit* is a verb meaning "to bring out." *Illicit* is an adjective meaning "unlawful."

>It took a hand signal to **elicit** the **illicit** exchange of cash for drugs.

**eminent, imminent** *Eminent* means "prominent, conspicuous, or famous"; *imminent* means "ready or threatening to happen."

> With the island's government about to collapse, assassination attempts on several **eminent** officials seemed **imminent**.

**ensure, insure, assure** (See *insure*.)

**except, accept** (See *accept*.)

**explicit, implicit** *Explicit* means "expressed directly or clearly defined"; *implicit* means "implied or unstated."

> The professor **explicitly** asked that the experiment be wrapped up on Monday, **implicitly** demanding that her lab assistants work on the weekend.

**farther, further** *Farther* refers to a physical distance; *further* refers to additional time, quantity, or degree.

> **Further** research showed that walking **farther** rather than faster would improve his health.

**fewer, less** *Fewer* refers to the number of separate units; *less* refers to bulk quantity.

> Because of spell checkers, students can produce papers containing **fewer** errors in **less** time.

**figuratively, literally** *Figuratively* means "in a metaphorical or analogous way—describing something by comparing it to something else"; *literally* means "actually."

> The lab was **literally** filled with sulfurous gases—**figuratively** speaking, dragon's breath.

**first, firstly** Both words are adverbs meaning "before another in time" or "in the first place." However, do not use *firstly*, which is stiff and unnatural sounding.

> **Firstly** I want to see the manager. (Incorrect)
>
> **First** I want to see the manager. (Correct)

*Note:* When enumerating, use the forms *first, second, third, next, last*—without the *ly*.

**fiscal, physical** *Fiscal* means "related to financial matters"; *physical* means "related to material things."

> The school's **fiscal** work is handled by its accounting staff.
>
> The **physical** work is handled by its maintenance staff.

**for, fore, four** *For* is a conjunction meaning "because" or is a preposition used to indicate the object or recipient of something; *fore* means "earlier" or "the front"; *four* is the word for the number 4.

> The crew brought treats **for** the barge's **four** dogs, who always enjoy the breeze at the **fore** of the vessel.

**former, latter** When two things are being discussed, *former* refers to the first thing, and *latter* to the second.

> Our choices are going to a movie or eating at the Pizza Palace: The **former** is too expensive, and the **latter** too far away.

# Using the Right Word Exercises:

## Using the Right Word: II

### A. Selecting the Right Word
Choose the correct word from those in parentheses for each sentence.

1. The (*capital, capitol*) building looked radiant with the fall sunshine beaming on its white dome.
2. That jacket would (*complement, compliment*) the colors of your dress.
3. The museum had three (*discreet, discrete*) levels, each with a different theme.
4. Darren took (*counsel, council, consul*) from his internship coordinator regarding his career path.
5. Would you (*comprise, compose*) an updated report on our position in the New York power and electric industry?
6. Our destination along Interstate 43 was (*farther, further*) than we expected.
7. The (*climactic, climatic*) point of the baseball game occurred when Vicki caught a foul ball.
8. Our (*decent, descent, dissent*) of Pike's Peak Mountain was a scary experience.
9. I was so sleepy that I felt barely (*conscience, conscious*).
10. The (*cent, sent, scent*) coming from the garbage left us all gagging for fresh air.

### B. Replacing Incorrect Words
For each sentence below, identify the misused words and correct them.

1. Our second coarse was descent, but the desert was the real winner.
2. The farther we delay restructuring our finances, the worse our physical situation will be.
3. My aunt is firstly a good judge of character and second an imminent authority on all things West Virginia.

**good, well** *Good* is an adjective; *well* is nearly always an adverb. (When used to indicate state of health, *well* is an adjective.)

    A **good** job offers opportunities for advancement, especially for those who do their jobs **well**.

**heal, heel** *Heal* (a verb) means "to mend or restore to health"; a *heel* (noun) is the back part of a human foot.

**healthful, healthy** *Healthful* means "causing or improving health"; *healthy* means "possessing health."

    **Healthful** foods and regular exercise build **healthy** bodies.

**I, me** *I* is a subject pronoun; *me* is used as an object of a preposition, a direct object, or an indirect object. (See 25.26.) (A good way to know if *I* or *me* should be used in a compound subject is to eliminate the other subject; the sentence should make sense with the pronoun—*I* or *me*—alone.)

    My roommate and **me** went to the library last night. (Incorrect)

    My roommate and **I** went to the library last night. (Correct: Eliminate "my roommate and"; the sentence still makes sense.)

    Rasheed gave the concert tickets to Erick and **I**. (Incorrect)

    Rasheed gave the concert tickets to Erick and **me**. (Correct: Eliminate "Erick and"; the sentence still makes sense.)

**illusion, allusion** (See *allusion*.)

**immigrate (to), emigrate (from)** *Immigrate* means "to come into a new country or environment." *Emigrate* means "to go out of one country to live in another."

    **Immigrating** to a new country is a challenging experience.

    People **emigrating** from their homelands face unknown challenges.

**imminent, eminent** (See *eminent*.)

**imply, infer** *Imply* means "to suggest without saying outright"; *infer* means "to draw a conclusion from facts." (A writer or a speaker *implies*; a reader or a listener *infers*.)

    Dr. Rufus **implied** I should study more; I **inferred** he meant my grades had to improve, or I'd be repeating the class.

**ingenious, ingenuous** *Ingenious* means "intelligent, discerning, clever"; *ingenuous* means "unassuming, natural, showing childlike innocence and candidness."

    Gretchen devised an **ingenious** plan to work and receive college credit for it.

    Ramón displays an **ingenuous** quality that attracts others.

**insure, ensure, assure** *Insure* means "to secure from financial harm or loss," *ensure* means "to make certain of something," and *assure* means "to put someone's mind at rest."

    Plenty of studying generally **ensures** academic success.

    Nicole **assured** her father that she had **insured** her new car.

**interstate, intrastate** *Interstate* means "existing between two or more states"; *intrastate* means "existing within a state."

**irregardless, regardless** *Irregardless* is a nonstandard synonym for *regardless*.
> **Irregardless** of his circumstance, José is cheerful. (Incorrect)
> **Regardless** of his circumstance, José is cheerful. (Correct)

**it's, its** *It's* is the contraction of "it is." *Its* is the possessive form of "it."
> **It's** not hard to see why my husband feeds that alley cat; **its** pitiful limp and mournful mewing would melt any heart.

**later, latter** *Later* means "after a period of time." *Latter* refers to the second of two things mentioned.
> The **latter** of the two restaurants you mentioned sounds good.
> Let's meet there **later**.

**lay, lie** *Lay* means "to place." *Lay* is a transitive verb. (See 25.31.) Its principal parts are *lay, laid, laid*. (See 25.52.)
> If you **lay** another book on my table, I won't have room for anything else.
> Yesterday, you **laid** two books on the table.
> Over the last few days, you must have **laid** at least twenty books there.

*Lie* means "to recline." *Lie* is an intransitive verb. (See 25.31.) Its principal parts are *lie, lay, lain*.
> The cat **lies** down anywhere it pleases.
> It **lay** down yesterday on my tax forms.
> It has **lain** down many times on the kitchen table.

**learn, teach** *Learn* means "to acquire information"; *teach* means "to give information."
> Sometimes it's easier to **teach** someone else a lesson than it is to **learn** one yourself.

**leave, let** *Leave* means "to allow something to remain behind." *Let* means "to permit."
> Please **let** me help you carry that chair; otherwise, **leave** it for the movers to pick up.

**lend, borrow** *Lend* means "to give for temporary use"; *borrow* means "to receive for temporary use."
> I asked Haddad to **lend** me $15 for gas, but he said I'd have to find someone else to **borrow** the money from.

**less, fewer** (See **fewer**.)

**liable, libel** *Liable* is an adjective meaning "responsible according to the law" or "exposed to an adverse action"; the noun *libel* is a written defamatory statement about someone, and the verb *libel* means "to publish or make such a statement."
> Supermarket tabloids, **liable** for ruining many a reputation, make a practice of **libeling** the rich and the famous.

**liable, likely** *Liable* means "responsible according to the law" or "exposed to an adverse action"; *likely* means "in all probability."
> Rain seems **likely** today, but if we cancel the game, we are still **liable** for paying the referees.

**like, as** *Like* should not be used in place of *as*. *Like* is a preposition, which is followed by its object (a noun, a pronoun, or a noun phrase). *As* is a subordinating conjunction, which introduces a clause. Do not use *like* as a subordinating conjunction. Use *as* instead.

> You don't know her **like** I do. (Incorrect)
> You don't know her **as** I do. (Correct)
> **Like** the others in my study group, I do my work **as** any serious student would—carefully and thoroughly. (Correct)

**literally, figuratively** (See **figuratively**.)

**loose, lose, loss** The adjective *loose* (lüs) means "free, untied, unrestricted"; the verb *lose* (lüz) means "to misplace or fail to find or control"; the noun *loss* (los) means "something that is misplaced and cannot be found."

> Her sadness at the **loss** of her longtime companion caused her to **lose** weight, and her clothes felt uncomfortably **loose**.

**may, can** (See **can**.)

**maybe, may be** Use *maybe* as an adverb meaning "perhaps;" use *may be* as a verb phrase.

> She **may be** the fix-it person we've been looking for. **Maybe** she will solve our plumbing problems.

**miner, minor** A *miner* digs in the ground for ore. A *minor* is a person who is not legally an adult. The adjective *minor* means "of no great importance."

> The use of **minors** as coal **miners** is no **minor** problem.

**number, amount** (See **amount**.)

**OK, okay** This expression, spelled either way, is appropriate in informal writing; however, avoid using it in papers, reports, or formal correspondence of any kind.

> Your proposal is satisfactory [not okay] on most levels.

**oral, verbal** *Oral* means "uttered with the mouth"; *verbal* means "relating to or consisting of words and the comprehension of words."

> The actor's **oral** abilities were outstanding, her pronunciation and intonation impeccable, but I doubted the playwright's **verbal** skills after trying to decipher the play's meaning.

**passed, past** *Passed* is a verb. *Past* can be used as a noun, an adjective, or a preposition.

> That little pickup truck **passed** my 'Vette! (verb)
> My stepchildren hold on dearly to the **past**. (noun)
> I'm sorry, but my **past** life is not your business. (adjective)
> The officer drove **past** us, not noticing our flat tire. (preposition)

**peace, piece** *Peace* means "tranquility or freedom from war." A *piece* is a part or fragment.

> Someone once observed that **peace** is not a condition, but a process—a process of building goodwill one **piece** at a time.

# Using the Right Word Exercises:

## Using the Right Word: III

### A. Selecting the Right Word
Choose the correct word from those in parentheses for each sentence.

1. Raphael injured his (*heal, heel*) when he took out the trash shoeless.
2. (*Irregardless, Regardless*) of how you feel about the assignment, you have to get it done by Friday.
3. Could you (*borrow, lend*) me three quarters for laundry?
4. My car suffered (*miner, minor*) damage from last night's hailstorm.
5. You (*maybe, may be*) upset with me, but I hope you will soon forgive me.
6. Before you look to the future, you should recognize lessons from the (*passed, past*).
7. Can you (*insure, ensure, assure*) me that I will receive an annual review?
8. Andrew (*immigrated, emigrated*) from Australia.
9. The offender was found (*liable, libel*) for all medical expenses.
10. The Taj Mahal was incredible; I was most impressed by (*it's, its*) majesty.

### B. Replacing Incorrect Words
For each sentence below, identify the misused words and correct them.

1. Despite feeling under the weather, Andre was good enough to give a verbal presentation at a company meeting.
2. Teresa inferred I should look for a new job, while I implied she meant I had no chance for a promotion.
3. Before you lie down another box, make sure the shelf is sturdy enough; otherwise it is liable to collapse.

**people, person** Use *people* to refer to human populations, races, or groups; use *person* to refer to an individual or the physical body.

> What the American **people** need is a good insect repellent.
>
> The forest ranger recommends that we check our **persons** for wood ticks when we leave the woods.

**percent, percentage** *Percent* means "per hundred"; for example, 60 percent of 100 jelly beans would be 60 jelly beans. *Percentage* refers to a portion of the whole. Generally, use the word *percent* when it is preceded by a number. Use *percentage* when no number is used.

> Each person's **percentage** of the reward amounted to $125—25 **percent** of the $500 offered by Crime Stoppers.

**personal, personnel** *Personal* (an adjective) means "private." *Personnel* (a noun) are people working at a particular job.

> Although choosing a major is a **personal** decision, it can be helpful to consult with guidance **personnel**.

**perspective, prospective** *Perspective* (a noun) is a point of view or the capacity to view things realistically; *prospective* is an adjective meaning "expected in or related to the future."

> From my immigrant neighbor's **perspective**, any job is a good job.
>
> **Prospective** students wandered the campus on visitors' day.

**pore, pour, poor** The noun *pore* is an opening in the skin; the verb *pore* means "to gaze intently." *Pour* means "to move with a continuous flow." *Poor* means "needy or pitiable."

> **Pour** hot water into a bowl, put your face over it, and let the steam open your **pores**. Your **poor** skin will thank you.

**precede, proceed** To *precede* means "to go or come before"; *proceed* means "to move on after having stopped" or "go ahead."

> Our biology instructor often **preceded** his lecture with these words:
>
> "OK, sponges, **proceed** to soak up more fascinating facts!"

**principal, principle** As an adjective, *principal* means "primary." As a noun, it can mean "a school administrator" or "a sum of money." A *principle* (noun) is an idea or a doctrine.

> His **principal** gripe is lack of freedom. (adjective)
>
> My son's **principal** expressed his concerns to the teachers. (noun)
>
> After 20 years, the amount of interest was higher than the **principal**. (noun)
>
> The **principle** of *caveat emptor* guides most consumer groups. (noun)

**quiet, quit, quite** *Quiet* is the opposite of noisy. *Quit* means "to stop or give up." *Quite* (an adverb) means "completely" or "to a considerable extent."

> The meeting remained **quite quiet** when the boss told us he'd **quit**.

**quote, quotation** *Quote* is a verb; *quotation* is a noun.

> The **quotation** I used was from Ida B. Wells. You may **quote** me on that.

**real, very, really** Do not use the adjective *real* in place of the adverbs *very* or *really*.

> My friend's cake is usually **very** [not *real*] fresh, but this cake is **really** stale.

**right, write, wright, rite**  *Right* means "correct or proper"; it also refers to that which a person has a legal claim to, as in *copyright*. *Write* means "to inscribe or record." A *wright* is a person who makes or builds something. *Rite* is a ritual or ceremonial act.

Did you **write** that it is the **right** of the **shipwright** to perform the **rite** of christening—breaking a bottle of champagne on the bow of the ship?

**scene, seen**  *Scene* refers to the setting or location where something happens; it also may mean "sight or spectacle." *Seen* is the past participle of the verb "see."

An exhibitionist likes to be **seen** making a **scene**.

**set, sit**  *Set* means "to place." *Sit* means "to put the body in a seated position." *Set* is a transitive verb; *sit* is an intransitive verb (see 25.31).

How can you just **sit** there and watch as I **set** the table?

**sight, cite, site**  *Sight* means "the act of seeing" (a verb) or "something that is seen" (a noun). *Cite* (a verb) means "to quote" or "to summon to court." *Site* means "a place or location" (noun) or "to place on a site" (verb).

After **sighting** the faulty wiring, the inspector **cited** the building contractor for breaking two city codes at a downtown work **site**.

**some, sum**  *Some* refers to an unknown thing, an unspecified number, or a part of something. *Sum* is a certain amount of money or the result of adding numbers together.

**Some** of the students answered too quickly and came up with the wrong **sum**.

**stationary, stationery**  *Stationary* means "not movable"; *stationery* refers to the paper and envelopes used to write letters.

Odina uses **stationery** for craft projects; she drops her mail into a **stationary** mail receptacle on campus.

**take, bring**  (See bring.)

**teach, learn**  (See learn.)

**than, then**  *Than* is used in a comparison; *then* is an adverb that tells when.

Study more **than** you think you need to. **Then** you will probably be satisfied with your grades.

**their, there, they're**  *Their* is a possessive personal pronoun. *There* is an adverb used as a filler word or to point out location. *They're* is the contraction for "they are."

Look over **there**. **There** is a comfortable place for students to study for **their** exams, so **they're** more likely to do a good job.

**threw, through**  *Threw* is the past tense of "throw." *Through* (a preposition) means "from one side of something to the other."

In a fit of frustration, Sachiko **threw** his cell phone right **through** the window.

**to, too, two**  *To* is a preposition that can mean "in the direction of." *To* is also used to form an infinitive. *Too* (an adverb) means "also" or "very." *Two* is the number 2.

**Two** causes of eye problems among students are lights that fail **to** illuminate properly and computer screens with **too** much glare.

**vain, vane, vein** *Vain* means "valueless or fruitless"; it may also mean "holding a high regard for oneself." *Vane* is a flat piece of material set up to show which way the wind blows. *Vein* refers to a blood vessel or a mineral deposit.

> The weather **vane** indicates the direction of the wind; the blood **vein** determines the direction of flowing blood; and the **vain** mind moves in no particular direction, content to think only about itself.

**vary, very** The verb *vary* means "to change"; the adverb *very* means "to a high degree."

> To ensure the **very** best employee relations, the workloads should not **vary** greatly from worker to worker.

**verbal, oral** (See *oral*.)

**waist, waste** The noun *waist* refers to the part of the body just above the hips. The verb *waste* means "to squander" or "to wear away, decay"; the noun *waste* refers to material that is unused or useless.

> His **waist** is small because he **wastes** no opportunity to exercise.

**wait, weight** *Wait* means "to stay somewhere expecting something." *Weight* refers to a degree or unit of heaviness.

> The **weight** of sadness eventually lessens; one must simply **wait** for the pain to dissipate.

**ware, wear, where** The noun *ware* refers to a product that is sold; the verb *wear* means "to have on or to carry on one's body"; the adverb *where* asks the question "In what place?" or "In what situation?"

> The designer boasted, "**Where** can one **wear** my **wares**? Anywhere."

**weather, whether** *Weather* refers to the condition of the atmosphere. *Whether* refers to a possibility.

> **Weather** conditions affect all of us, **whether** we are farmers or plumbers.

**well, good** (See *good*.)

**which, that** (See 28.27.)

**who, which, that** *Who* refers to people. *Which* refers to nonliving objects or to animals. (*Which* should never refer to people.) *That* may refer to animals, people, or nonliving objects. (See also 28.27.)

**who, whom** *Who* is used as the subject of a verb; *whom* is used as the object of a preposition or as a direct object.

> Captain Mather, to **whom** the survivors owe their lives, is the man **who** is being honored today.

**who's, whose** *Who's* is the contraction for "who is." *Whose* is a possessive pronoun.

> **Whose** car are we using, and **who's** going to pay for the gas?

**your, you're** *Your* is a possessive pronoun. *You're* is the contraction for "you are."

> If **you're** like most Americans, you will have held eight jobs by **your** fortieth birthday.

# Using the Right Word Exercises:

## Using the Right Word: IV

### A. Selecting the Right Word

Choose the correct word from those in parentheses for each sentence.

1. The (*principal, principle*) of relativity applies to any scientific investigation.
2. Vince gave an interesting (*perspective, prospective*) on the importance of workplace writing proficiency.
3. The large piece of rock that fell from the cliff face remained (*stationary, stationery*) near the entrance to the hiking trail.
4. Have you decided (*weather, whether*) to take your boyfriend to your Thanksgiving dinner?
5. If (*your, you're*) planning to begin work on Monday, we'll have the training materials ready for you.
6. Latoya tried in (*vain, vane, vein*) to find her missing car keys.
7. I think Christopher Nolan's *Inception* is even better (*than, then*) *The Dark Knight*.
8. The professor reminded her students to (*sight, cite, site*) any sources they use in their papers.
9. Mack and Gordon discussed (*who's, whose*) car they should take to the mall.
10. Although not recommended, pulling an all-night study session is considered a (*right, write, wright, rite*) of passage among college students.

### B. Replacing Incorrect Words

For each sentence below, identify the misused words and correct them.

1. The company began making personal changes by interviewing perspective suitors.
2. Students whom wish to proceed with the medical mission trip will need to bring there applications to the volunteer office.
3. Hopefully the some of my two checks will not go to waist at the casino.

# Chapter 31

# Multilingual and ESL Guidelines

English may be your second, third, or fifth language. As a multilingual learner, you bring to your writing the culture and knowledge of the languages you use. This broader perspective enables you to draw on many experiences and greater knowledge as you write and speak. Whether you are an international student or someone who has lived in North America a long time and is now learning more about English, this chapter provides you with important information about writing in English.

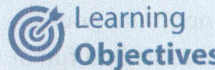

**Learning Objectives**

By working through this chapter, you will be able to

- use nouns, articles, and other noun markers correctly.
- use verb tenses as well as objects and complements of verbs correctly.
- place adjectives and adverbs in the correct sentence position.
- distinguish common prepositions.
- recognize basic sentence patterns.
- avoid common sentence problems.
- identify common idioms.

## 31.01 Five Parts of Speech

## 31.02 Noun

### 31.03 Count Nouns

**Count nouns** refer to things that can be counted. They can have *a*, *an*, *the*, or *one* in front of them. One or more adjectives can come between the articles *a*, *an*, *the*, or *one* and a singular count noun.

> **an** apple, **one** orange, **a** plum, **a** purple plum

Count nouns can be singular, as in the examples above, or plural, as in the examples below.

> plums, apples, oranges

**Note:** When count nouns are plural, they can have the article *the*, a number, or one or more demonstrative adjectives in front of them. (See 31.09 and 31.11)

> I used **the** plums to make a pie.
>
> He placed **five red** apples on my desk.
>
> **These** oranges are so juicy!

The *number* of a noun refers to whether it names a single thing (*book*), in which case its number is *singular*, or whether it names more than one thing (*books*), in which case the number of the noun is *plural*.

**Note:** There are different ways in which the plural form of nouns is created. For more information, see 29.16–29.25.

### 31.04 Noncount Nouns

**Noncount nouns** refer to things that cannot be counted. Do not use *a*, *an*, or *one* in front of them. They have no plural form, so they always take a singular verb. Some nouns that end in *s* are not plural; they are noncount nouns.

> fruit, furniture, rain, thunder, advice, mathematics, news

**Abstract nouns** name ideas or conditions rather than people, places, or objects. Many abstract nouns are noncount nouns.

> The students had **fun** at the party. Good **health** is a wonderful gift.

**Collective nouns** name a whole category or group and are often noncount nouns.

> homework, furniture, money

**Note:** The parts or components of a group or category named by a noncount noun are often count nouns. For example, *report* and *assignment* are count nouns that are parts of the collective, noncount noun *homework*.

### 31.05 Two-Way Nouns

Some nouns can be used as either count or noncount nouns, depending on what they refer to.

> I would like a **glass** of water. (count noun)
>
> **Glass** is used to make windows. (noncount noun)

## 31.06 Articles and Other Noun Markers

### 31.07 Specific Articles

Use articles and other noun markers or modifiers to give more information about nouns. The **specific** (or **definite**) **article** *the* is used to refer to a specific noun.

> I found **the** book I misplaced yesterday.

### 31.08 Indefinite Articles and Indefinite Adjectives

Use the **indefinite article** *a* or *an* to refer to a nonspecific noun. Use *an* before singular nouns beginning with the vowels *a, e, i, o,* and *u*. Use *a* before nouns beginning with all other letters of the alphabet, the consonants. Exceptions do occur: *a* unit; *a* university.

> I always take **an** apple to work.
>
> It is good to have **a** book with you when you travel.

**Indefinite adjectives** can also mark nonspecific nouns—*all, any, each, either, every, few, many, more, most, neither, several, some* (for singular and plural count nouns); *all, any, more, most, much, some* (for noncount nouns).

> **Every** student is encouraged to register early.
>
> **Most** classes fill quickly.

> **31.09 Determining Whether to Use Articles**
>
> Listed below are a number of guidelines to help you determine whether to use an article and which one to use.
>
> Use *a* or *an* with singular count nouns that do not refer to one specific item.
>
> > **A zebra** has black and white stripes. **An apple** is good for you.
>
> Do not use *a* or *an* with plural count nouns.
>
> > **Zebras** have black and white stripes. **Apples** are good for you.
>
> Do not use *a* or *an* with noncount nouns.
>
> > **Homework** needs to be done promptly.
>
> Use *the* with singular count nouns that refer to one specific item.
>
> > **The apple** you gave me was delicious.
>
> Use *the* with plural count nouns.
>
> > **The zebras** at Brookfield Zoo were healthy.
>
> Use *the* with noncount nouns.
>
> > **The money** from my uncle is a gift.
>
> Do not use *the* with most singular proper nouns.
>
> > **Mother Theresa** loved the poor and downcast.
>
> **Note:** There are many exceptions: *the* Sahara Desert, *the* University of Minnesota, *the* Fourth of July, *The New York Times*
>
> Use *the* with plural nouns.
>
> > **the Joneses** (both Mr. and Mrs. Jones), **the Rocky Mountains, the United States**

## 31.10 Possessive Adjectives

The possessive case of nouns and pronouns can be used as adjectives to mark nouns.

**possessive nouns:** *Tanya's, father's, store's*

> The car is **Tanya's**, not her **father's.**

**possessive pronouns:** *my, your, his, her, its, our*

> **My** hat is purple.

## 31.11 Demonstrative Adjectives

Demonstrative pronouns can be used as adjectives to mark nouns.

**Demonstrative adjectives:** *this, that, these, those* (for singular and plural count nouns); *this, that* (for noncount nouns)

> **Those** chairs are lovely. Where did you buy **that** furniture?

# Grammar Exercises:

## Nouns, Articles, and Other Noun Markers

### A. Count and Noncount Nouns

Make a list of count nouns from the following paragraph. Next make a list of noncount nouns.

1 We live in a time of confusing economics. On the one hand, it is
2 necessary to spend money to keep the economy stimulated. Manufacturers
3 use every psychological trick they can identify to coax consumers to buy
4 more products. As a matter of fact, advertisers work to make the public want
5 things it doesn't actually need. On the other hand, citizens are expected to
6 invest and save for emergencies and for their retirement. Shame is used as a
7 motivator to accomplish this. Unfortunately, in a world where citizens have
8 been relabeled as consumers, the psychology of sales too often outweighs the
9 shadow of shame.

### B. Articles and Other Noun Markers

For each numbered blank, write an appropriate article or noun marker as needed. (If none is needed, write "none needed.") Then identify each added article or adjective by type (specific article, indefinite article, indefinite adjective, possessive adjective, demonstrative adjective, or quantifier).

Does (1)_____ family own a dog? If so, what made you choose (2)_____ breed instead of a different one? In (3)_____ house, we have (4)_____ dogs. (5)_____ dog is a Chihuahua and (6)_____ other is (7)_____ Bichon Frise. The Chihuahua barks at (8)_____ people but not at others. Well, to be truthful, he always barks at (9)_____ strangers, but seldom at a family member or (10)_____ friend. (11)_____ Bichon Frise is too friendly and excited to bark. He jumps on each and (12)_____ person who visits us. Scientists say that (13)_____ dogs originally descended from (14)_____ wolf. From my observation of (15)_____ Chihuaha and Bichon Frise, it is obvious that different dogs descended differently.

## 31.12 Quantifiers

**Expressions of quantity and measure** are often used with nouns. Below are some of these expressions and guidelines for using them.

The following expressions of quantity can be used with count nouns: *each, every, both, a couple of, a few, several, many, a number of.*

>We enjoyed **both** concerts we attended. **A couple of** songs performed were familiar to us.

Use a number to indicate a specific quantity of a continuum.

>I saw **fifteen** cardinals in the park.

To indicate a specific quantity of a noncount noun, use *a* + quantity (such as *bag, bottle, bowl, carton, glass,* or *piece*) + *of* + noun.

>I bought **a carton of milk, a head of lettuce, a piece of cheese,** and **a bag of flour** at the grocery store.

The following expressions can be used with noncount nouns: *a little, much, a great deal of.*

>We had **much** wind and **a little** rain as the storm passed through yesterday.

The following expressions of quantity can be used with both count and noncount nouns: *no/not any, some, a lot of, lots of, plenty of, most, all, this, that.*

>I would like **some** apples *(count noun)* and **some** rice *(noncount noun),* please.

## 31.13 Verb

As the main part of the predicate, a verb conveys much of a sentence's meaning. Using verb tenses and forms correctly ensures that your readers will understand your sentences as you intend them to. For a more thorough review of verbs, see 25.29–25.52.

## 31.14 Progressive (Continuous) Tenses

Progressive or continuous tense verbs express action in progress (see 25.40–25.43).

To form the **present progressive** tense, use the helping verb *am, is,* or *are* with the *ing* form of the main verb.

>He **is washing** the car right now.
>Kent and Chen **are studying** for a test.

To form the **past progressive** tense, use the helping verb *was* or *were* with the *ing* form of the main verb.

>Yesterday he **was working** in the garden all day.
>Julia and Juan **were watching** a movie.

To form the future progressive tense, use *will* or a phrase that indicates the future, the helping verb *be,* and the *ing* form of the main verb.

>Next week he **will be painting** the house.
>He **plans to be painting** the house soon.

Note that some verbs are generally not used in the progressive tenses, such as the following groups of frequently used verbs:
- Verbs that express thoughts, attitudes, and desires: *know, understand, want, prefer*
- Verbs that describe appearances: *seem, resemble*
- Verbs that indicate possession: *belong, have, own, possess*
- Verbs that signify inclusion: *contain, hold*

Kala **knows** how to ride a motorcycle.
NOT THIS: Kala is **knowing** how to ride a motorcycle.

## 31.15 Objects and Complements of Verbs

Active transitive verbs take objects. These can be direct objects, indirect objects, or object complements. Linking verbs take subject complements—predicate nominatives or predicate adjectives—that rename or describe the subject.

### 31.16 Infinitives as Objects

**Infinitives** can follow many verbs, including these: *agree, appear, attempt, consent, decide, demand, deserve, endeavor, fail, hesitate, hope, intend, need, offer, plan, prepare, promise, refuse, seem, tend, volunteer, wish.* (See 25.49 for more on infinitives.)

He **promised to bring** some samples.

The following verbs are among those that can be followed by a noun or pronoun plus the infinitive: *ask, beg, choose, expect, intend, need, prepare, promise, want.*

I **expect you to be** there on time.

**Note:** Except in the passive voice, the following verbs must have a noun or pronoun before the infinitive: *advise, allow, appoint, authorize, cause, challenge, command, convince, encourage, forbid, force, hire, instruct, invite, order, permit, remind, require, select, teach, tell, tempt, trust.*

I will **authorize Emily to use** my credit card.

**Unmarked infinitives** (no *to*) can follow these verbs: *have, help, let, make.*

These glasses **help me see** the board.

### 31.17 Gerunds as Objects

**Gerunds** can follow these verbs: *admit, avoid, consider, deny, discuss, dislike, enjoy, finish, imagine, miss, postpone, quit, recall, recommend, regret.* (Also see 25.48.)

I **recommended hiring** Ian for the job.

Here *hiring* is the direct object of the active verb *recommended*, and *Ian* is the object of the gerund.

## 31.18 Infinitives or Gerunds as Objects

Either **gerunds** or **infinitives** can follow these verbs: *begin, continue, hate, like, love, prefer, remember, start, stop, try.*

> I **hate having** cold feet. I **hate to have** cold feet. (In either form, the verbal phrase is the direct object of the verb hate.)

**Note:** Sometimes the meaning of a sentence will change depending on whether you use a gerund or an infinitive.

> I stopped to smoke. (I *stopped* weeding the garden *to smoke* a cigarette.)
> I stopped smoking. (I no longer smoke.)

## 31.19 Common Modal Auxiliary Verbs

**Modal auxiliary verbs** are a kind of auxiliary verb. (See 25.32.) They help the main verb express meaning. Modals are sometimes grouped with other helping or auxiliary verbs.

Modal verbs must be followed by the base form of a verb without *to* (not by a gerund or an infinitive). Also, modal verbs do not change form; they are always used as they appear in the following chart.

| Modal | Expresses | Sample Sentence |
|---|---|---|
| can | ability | I *can* make tamales. |
| could | ability | I *could* babysit Tuesday. |
|  | possibility | He *could* be sick. |
| might | possibility | I *might* be early. |
| may, might | possibility | I *may* sleep late Saturday. |
|  | request | *May* I be excused? |
| must | strong need | I *must* study more. |
| have to | strong need | I *have to* (have got to) exercise. |
| ought to | feeling of duty | I *ought to* (should) help Dad. |
| should | advisability | She *should* retire. |
|  | expectation | I *should* have caught that train. |
| shall | intent | *Shall* I stay longer? |
| will | intent | I *will* visit my grandma soon. |
| would | intent | I *would* live to regret my offer. |
|  | repeated action | He *would* walk in the meadow. |
| would + you | polite request | *Would you* help me? |
| could + you | polite request | *Could you* type this letter? |
| will + you | polite request | *Will you* give me a ride? |
| can + you | polite request | *Can you* make supper tonight? |

### 31.20 Common Two-Word Verbs

This chart lists some common verbs in which two words—a verb and a preposition—work together to express a specific action. A noun or pronoun is often inserted between the parts of the two-word verb when it is used in a sentence: *break it down, call it off.*

| | |
|---|---|
| **break down** | to take apart or fall apart |
| **call off** | cancel |
| **call up** | make a phone call |
| **clear out** | leave a place quickly |
| **cross out** | draw a line through |
| **do over** | repeat |
| **figure out** | find a solution |
| **fill in/out** | complete a form or an application |
| **fill up** | fill a container or tank |
| *  **find out** | discover |
| *  **get in** | enter a vehicle or building |
| *  **get out of** | leave a car, a house, or a situation |
| *  **get over** | recover from a sickness or a problem |
| **give back** | return something |
| **give in/up** | surrender or quit |
| **hand in** | give homework to a teacher |
| **hand out** | give someone something |
| **hang up** | put down a phone receiver |
| **leave out** | omit or don't use |
| **let in/out** | allow someone or something to enter or go out |
| **look up** | find information |
| **mix up** | confuse |
| **pay back** | return money or a favor |
| **pick out** | choose |
| **point out** | call attention to |
| **put away** | return something to its proper place |
| **put down** | place something on a table, the floor, and so on. |
| **put off** | delay doing something |
| **shut off** | turn off a machine or light |
| *  **take part** | participate |
| **talk over** | discuss |
| **think over** | consider carefully |
| **try on** | put on clothing to see if it fits |
| **turn down** | lower the volume |
| **turn up** | raise the volume |
| **write down** | write on a piece of paper |

*  These two-word verbs should not have a noun or pronoun inserted between their parts.

## 31.21 Spelling Guidelines for Verb Forms

The same spelling rules that apply when adding a suffix to other words apply to verbs as well. Most verbs need a suffix to indicate tense or form. The third-person singular form of a verb, for example, usually ends in *s*, but it can also end in *es*. Formation of *ing* and *ed* forms of verbs and verbals needs careful attention, too. Consult the rules below to determine which spelling is correct for each verb. (For general spelling guidelines, see 29.36.)

 There may be exceptions to these rules when forming the past tense of irregular verbs because the verbs are formed by changing the word itself, not merely by adding *d* or *ed*. (See 25.52 for a chart of irregular verbs.)

## 31.22 Past Tense: Adding *ed*

**Add *ed* . . .**

- When a verb ends with two consonants:
  touch—**touched**   ask—**asked**   pass—**passed**
- When a verb ends with a consonant preceded by two vowels:
  heal—**healed**   gain—**gained**
- When a verb ends in *y* preceded by a vowel:
  annoy—**annoyed**   flay—**flayed**
- When a multisyllable verb's last syllable is not stressed (even when the last syllable ends with a consonant preceded by a vowel):
  budget—**budgeted**   enter—**entered**   interpret—**interpreted**

**Change *y* to *i* and add *ed*** when a verb ends in a consonant followed by *y*:
  liquefy—**liquefied**   worry—**worried**

**Double the final consonant and add *ed* . . .**

- When a verb has one syllable and ends with a consonant preceded by a vowel:
  wrap—**wrapped**   drop—**dropped**
- When a multisyllable verb's last syllable (ending in a consonant preceded by a vowel) is stressed:
  admit—**admitted**   confer—**conferred**   abut—**abutted**

## 31.23 Past Tense: Adding *d*

**Add *d* . . .**

- When a verb ends with *e*:
  chime—**chimed**   tape—**taped**
- When a verb ends with *ie*:
  tie—**tied**   die—**died**   lie—**lied**

## 31.24 Present Tense: Adding *s* or *es*

**Add *es* . . .**

- When a verb ends in *ch, sh, s, x,* or *z*:
  watch—**watches**   fix—**fixes**

- To *do* and *go*:
  do—**does**   go—**goes**

**Change *y* to *i* and add *es*** when the verb ends in a consonant followed by *y*:
  liquefy—**liquefies**   quantify—**quantifies**

**Add *s*** to most other verbs, including those already ending in *e* and those that end in a vowel followed by *y*:
  write—**writes**   buy—**buys**

## 31.25 Present Tense: Adding *ing*

**Drop the *e* and add *ing*** when the verb ends in *e*:
  drive—**driving**   rise—**rising**

**Double the final consonant and add *ing* . . .**

- When a verb has one syllable and ends with a consonant preceded by a single vowel:
  wrap—**wrapping**   sit—**sitting**

- When a multisyllable verb's last syllable (ending in a consonant preceded by a single vowel) is stressed:
  forget—**forgetting**   begin—**beginning**   abut—**abutting**

**Change *ie* to *y* and add *ing*** when a verb ends with *ie*:
  tie—**tying**   die—**dying**   lie—**lying**

**Add *ing* . . .**

- When a verb ends with two consonants:
  touch—**touching**   ask—**asking**   pass—**passing**

- When a verb ends with a consonant preceded by two vowels:
  heal—**healing**   gain—**gaining**

- When a verb ends in *y*:
  buy—**buying**   study—**studying**   cry—**crying**

- When a multisyllable verb's last syllable is not stressed (even when the last syllable ends with a consonant preceded by a vowel):
  budget—**budgeting**   enter—**entering**   interpret—**interpreting**

**Note:** Never trust your spelling to even the best computer spell checker. Carefully proofread. Use a dictionary for questionable words your spell checker may miss.

Chapter 31 | Multilingual and ESL Guidelines 643

# Grammar Exercises:

## Verbs, Objects, and Complements

### A. Errors in Context

Correct any verb, object, and complement errors in the sentences below. Write down the error, crossed out, with the correction beside it.

(1) Evolutionary psychologist Robert Dunbar suggest that brain size directly affects behavior in terms of how many individuals a mammal can to care about. (2) A chimpanzee is possessing an emotional connection with about 50 other chimpanzees. (3) If a tribe's size grow beyond that, the group tends fighting. (4) Studies of human brain size predict that humans are having the ability to care for roughly 150 other people, and Dunbar says research bears that out. (5) Fortunately, humans decide building hierarchies to support larger societies. (6) Also, people can conceiving of a universal family of humanity. (7) Can you to think that way?

### B. Forming Tenses

Write the correct past tense for each of the verbs listed below. (Note that some of these verbs have irregular past-tense forms.)

1. say _____
2. go _____
3. derive _____
4. maintain _____

Write the correct present tense form (adding *s* or *es*) for each of these verbs.

1. will _____
2. come _____
3. wonder _____
4. verify _____

Write the correct present tense form (adding *ing*) for each of these verbs.

1. activate _____
2. portray _____
3. begin _____
4. start _____

## 31.26 Adjective

### 31.27 Placing Adjectives

You probably know that an adjective often comes before the noun it modifies. When several adjectives are used in a row to modify a single noun, it is important to arrange the adjectives in the well-established sequence used in English writing and speaking. The following list shows the usual order of adjectives. (Also see 28.18.)

> **First, place . . .**
> 1. articles . . . . . . . . . . . . . . . . . . . . . . . . . . . . . . . . . . . . . . . . . . . . . . . . . . . . . . . . . . a, an, the
>    demonstrative adjectives . . . . . . . . . . . . . . . . . . . . . . . . . . . . . . . . . . . . . . . that, those
>    possessives . . . . . . . . . . . . . . . . . . . . . . . . . . . . . . . . . . . . . . . . . . . . . . . my, her, Misha's
>
> **Then place words that . . .**
> 2. indicate time . . . . . . . . . . . . . . . . . . . . . . . . . . . . . . . . . . . . . . . . . . . . first, next, final
> 3. tell how many . . . . . . . . . . . . . . . . . . . . . . . . . . . . . . . . . . . . . . . . . . . . one, few, some
> 4. evaluate . . . . . . . . . . . . . . . . . . . . . . . . . . . . . . . . . . . . . . . beautiful, dignified, graceful
> 5. tell what size . . . . . . . . . . . . . . . . . . . . . . . . . . . . . . . . . . . . . . . big, small, short, tall
> 6. tell what shape . . . . . . . . . . . . . . . . . . . . . . . . . . . . . . . . . . . . . . . . . . . . round, square
> 7. describe a condition . . . . . . . . . . . . . . . . . . . . . . . . . . . . . . . . . . . . . messy, clean, dark
> 8. tell what age . . . . . . . . . . . . . . . . . . . . . . . . . . . . . . . . . . . . . old, young, new, antique
> 9. tell what color . . . . . . . . . . . . . . . . . . . . . . . . . . . . . . . . . . . . . . . . . blue, red, yellow
> 10. tell what nationality . . . . . . . . . . . . . . . . . . . . . . . . . . . . . . . English, Chinese, Mexican
> 11. tell what religion . . . . . . . . . . . . . . . . . . . . . . . . . . . . . . . . . Buddhist, Jewish, Protestant
> 12. tell what material . . . . . . . . . . . . . . . . . . . . . . . . . . . . . . . . . . . satin, velvet, wooden
>
> **Finally, place nouns . . .**
> 13. used as adjectives . . . . . . . . . . . . . . . . . . . . . . . . . . computer [monitor], spice [rack]
>    **my second try** (1 + 2 + noun)
>    **gorgeous young white swans** (4 + 8 + 9 + noun)

### 31.28 Present and Past Participles as Adjectives

Both the **present participle** and the **past participle** can be used as adjectives. (Also see 25.50.) Exercise care in choosing whether to use the present participle or the past participle. A participle can come either before a noun or after a linking verb.

A **present participle** used as an adjective should describe a person or thing that is causing a feeling or situation.

> His **annoying** comments made me angry.

A **past participle** should describe a person or thing that experiences a feeling or situation.

> He was **annoyed** because he had to wait so long.

> **Note:** Within each of the following pairs, the present (*ing* form) and past (*ed* form) participles have different meanings.
>
> annoying/annoyed     depressing/depressed     fascinating/fascinated
> boring/bored     exciting/excited     surprising/surprised
> confusing/confused     exhausting/exhausted

## 31.29 Nouns as Adjectives

Nouns sometimes function as adjectives by modifying another noun. When a noun is used as an adjective, it is always singular.

Many European cities have **rose** gardens.

Marta recently joined a **book** club.

**Note:** Try to avoid using more than two nouns as adjectives for another noun. These "noun compounds" can get confusing. Prepositional phrases may get the meaning across better than long noun strings.

**Correct:** Omar is a **crew** member in the **restaurant** kitchen during **second** shift.

**Not correct:** Omar is a **second-shift restaurant kitchen crew** member.

## 31.30 Adverb

### 31.31 Placing Adverbs

Consider the following guidelines for placing adverbs correctly. See 25.58 for more information about adverbs.

**Place adverbs that tell how often** (*frequently, seldom, never, always, sometimes*) after a helping (auxiliary) verb and before the main verb. In a sentence without a helping verb, adverbs that tell *how often* are placed before an action verb but after a linking verb.

The salesclerk will **usually** help me.

**Place adverbs that tell when** (*yesterday, now, at five o'clock*) at the end of a sentence.

Auntie El came home **yesterday.**

**Adverbs that tell where** (*upside-down, around, downstairs*) usually follow the verb they modify. Many prepositional phrases (*at the beach, under the stairs, below the water*) function as adverbs that tell where.

We waited **on the porch.**

**Adverbs that tell how** (*quickly, slowly, loudly*) can be placed either at the beginning, in the middle, or at the end of a sentence—but not between a verb and its direct object.

**Softly** he called my name. He **softly** called my name. He called my name **softly.**

**Place adverbs that modify adjectives** directly before the adjective.

That is a **most** unusual dress.

**Adverbs that modify clauses** are most often placed in front of the clause, but they can also go inside or at the end of the clause.

**Fortunately,** we were not involved in the accident.
We were not involved, **fortunately,** in the accident.
We were not involved in the accident, **fortunately.**

**Note:** Adverbs that are used with verbs that have direct objects must *not* be placed between the verb and its object.

**Correct:** Luis **usually** catches the most fish.   **Usually,** Luis catches the most fish.

**Not correct:** Luis catches **usually** the most fish.

## 31.32 Preposition

A **preposition** combines with a noun to form a prepositional phrase, which acts as a modifier—an adverb or an adjective. See 25.63–25.64 for a list of common prepositions and for more information about prepositions.

### 31.33 Using *in, on, at,* and *by*

*In, on, at,* and *by* are four common prepositions that refer to time and place. Here are some examples of how these prepositions are used in each case.

> **To show time**
> 
> **on** a specific day or date: ***on*** June 7, ***on*** Wednesday
> **in** part of a day: ***in*** the afternoon
> **in** a year or month: ***in*** 2016, ***in*** April
> **in** a period of time: completed ***in*** an hour
> **by** a specific time or date: ***by*** noon, ***by*** the fifth of May
> **at** a specific time of day or night: ***at*** 3:30 this afternoon
> 
> **To show place**
> 
> **at** a meeting place or location: ***at*** school, ***at*** the park
> **at** the edge of something: standing ***at*** the bar
> **at** the corner of something: turning ***at*** the intersection
> **at** a target: throwing a dart ***at*** the target
> **on** a surface: left ***on*** the floor
> **on** an electronic medium: ***on*** the Internet, ***on*** television
> **in** an enclosed space: ***in*** the box, ***in*** the room
> **in** a geographic location: ***in*** New York City, ***in*** Germany
> **in** a print medium: ***in*** a journal
> **by** a landmark: ***by*** the fountain

**Note:** Do not insert a preposition between a transitive verb and its direct object. Intransitive verbs, however, are often followed by a prepositional phrase (a phrase that begins with a preposition).

I **cooked** hot dogs on the grill. (transitive verb)

I **ate** in the park. (intransitive verb)

### 31.34 Phrasal Prepositions

Some prepositional phrases begin with more than one preposition. These **phrasal prepositions** are commonly used in both written and spoken communication. A list of common phrasal prepositions follows:

| | | | |
|---|---|---|---|
| according to | because of | in case of | on the side of |
| across from | by way of | in spite of | up to |
| along with | except for | instead of | with respect to |

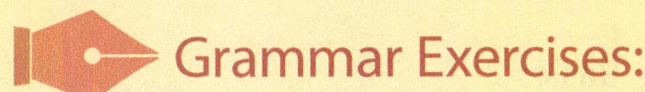

# Grammar Exercises:

## Adjectives, Adverbs, Prepositions

### A. Adjective Order
Rewrite the following phrases to place the adjectives in the proper order.
1. sandstone first square several red gigantic the blocks
2. a sticky brown few last delicious figs
3. rough-barked old some round huge trees

### B. Present and Past Participles
Choose the correct adjective form (present or past participle) in each case below.
1. Deborah was <u>annoying/annoyed</u> that her wedding dress was not finished.
2. The <u>exciting/excited</u> day was quickly approaching, but the preparation was making her <u>exhausting/exhausted</u>.
3. Then <u>surprising/surprised</u> news arrived: An old high school friend was coming to help!
4. Her fiancé Trevor was <u>confusing/confused</u> at first that her old friend, Michael, was willing to be a "bridesmaid."
5. Trevor figured that Michael must be a <u>fascinating/fascinated</u> fellow.

### C. *At, By, In,* or *On*
Write the best preposition—*at, by, in,* or *on*—for each blank in the sentences below.
1. _____ what time do you get up most mornings?
2. Do you come to school _____ car, _____ bike, _____ bus, or do you walk?
3. After school, I have to work _____ a pizza parlor most evenings.
4. The pizza restaurant is _____ the downtown area, _____ the public library.
5. I like pizza with mushrooms _____ it.
6. The place I work posts free coupons _____ its Web site.
7. The current coupon expires _____ June 8.
8. We have tables, so you can eat _____ the store if you like.
9. Our pizzas are cooked _____ a wood-burning oven.
10. Once, I cooked a pizza _____ my grill at home, over charcoal.

## 31.35 Understanding Sentence Basics

Simple sentences in the English language follow the five basic patterns shown below. (See chapter 26 for more information.)

### Subject + Verb

⌜—S—⌝ ⌜—V—⌝
**Naomie winked.**

Some verbs like *winked* are intransitive. Intransitive verbs do not need a direct object to express a complete thought. (See 25.31.)

### Subject + Verb + Direct Object

⌜—S—⌝ ⌜—V—⌝ ⌜—DO—⌝
**Harris grinds his teeth.**

Some verbs like *grinds* are transitive. Transitive verbs *do* need a direct object to express a complete thought. (See 25.31.)

### Subject + Verb + Indirect Object + Direct Object

⌜—S—⌝ ⌜—V—⌝ ⌜—IO—⌝ ⌜—DO—⌝
**Elena offered her friend an anchovy.**

The direct object names who or what receives the action; the indirect object names to whom or for whom the action was done.

### Subject + Verb + Direct Object + Object Complement

⌜———S———⌝ ⌜—V—⌝ ⌜—DO—⌝ ⌜————OC————⌝
**The chancellor named Ravi the outstanding student of 2019.**

The object complement renames or describes the direct object.

### Subject + Linking Verb + Predicate Nominative (or Predicate Adjective)

⌜—S—⌝ LV ⌜————PN————⌝      ⌜—S—⌝ LV ⌜———PA———⌝
**Paula is a computer programmer.**    **Paula is very intelligent.**

A linking verb connects the subject to the predicate noun or predicate adjective. The predicate noun renames the subject; the predicate adjective describes the subject.

## 31.36 Inverted Order

In the sentence patterns above, the subject comes before the verb. In a few types of sentences, such as those below, the subject comes *after* the verb.

LV ⌜—S—⌝ ⌜—PN—⌝          LV ⌜———S———⌝
**Is Larisa a poet?**         **There was a meeting.**
(A question)                  (A sentence beginning with "there")

## 31.37 Sentence Problems

This section looks at potential trouble spots and sentence problems. For more information about English sentences, their parts, and how to construct them, see chapter 26. Chapter 27 covers the types of problems and errors found in English writing. The guide to avoiding sentence problems found at 27.42 is an excellent editing tool.

### 31.38 Double Negatives

When making a sentence negative, use *not* or another negative adverb (*never, rarely, hardly, seldom,* and so on), but not both. Using both results in a double negative (see 27.40).

### 31.39 Subject–Verb Agreement

Be sure the subject and verb in every clause agree in person and number. (See 27.01–27.15.)

The **student was** rewarded for her hard work.
The **students were** rewarded for their hard work.
The **instructor,** as well as the students, **is** expected to attend the orientation.
The **students,** as well as the instructor, **are** expected to attend the orientation.

### 31.40 Omitted Words

Do not omit subjects or the expletives *there* or *here*. In all English clauses and sentences (except imperatives in which the subject *you* is understood), there must be a subject.

**Correct:** Your mother was very quiet; **she** seemed to be upset.
*Not correct:* Your mother was very quiet; seemed to be upset.

**Correct:** **There** is not much time left.
*Not correct:* Not much time left.

### 31.41 Repeated Words

Do not repeat the subject of a clause or sentence.

**Correct:** The doctor prescribed an antibiotic.
*Not correct:* The doctor, **she** prescribed an antibiotic.

Do not repeat an object in an adjective dependent clause.

**Correct:** I forgot the flowers that I intended to give to my hosts.
*Not correct:* I forgot the flowers that I intended to give **them** to my hosts.

**Note:** Sometimes the relative pronoun that begins the adjective dependent clause is omitted but understood.

I forgot the flowers I intended to give to my hosts.
(The relative pronoun *that* is omitted.)

### 31.42 Conditional Sentences

**Conditional sentences** express a situation requiring that a condition be met in order to be true. Selecting the correct verb tense for use in the two clauses of a conditional sentence can be problematic. Below you will find an explanation of the three types of conditional sentences and the verb tenses that are needed to form them.

1. **Factual conditionals:** The conditional clause begins with *if, when, whenever,* or a similar expression. Furthermore, the verbs in the conditional clause and the main clause should be in the same tense.

    **Whenever** we **had** time, we **took** a break and **went** for a swim.

2. **Predictive conditionals** express future conditions and possible results. The conditional clause begins with *if* or *unless* and has a present tense verb. The main clause uses a modal (*will, can, should, may, might*) plus the base form of the verb.

    **Unless** we **find** a better deal, we **will buy** this sound system.

3. **Hypothetical past conditionals** describe a situation that is unlikely to happen or that is contrary to fact. To describe situations in the past, the verb in the conditional clause is in the past perfect tense, and the verb in the main clause is formed from *would have, could have,* or *might have* plus the past participle.

    If we **had started out** earlier, we **would have arrived** on time.

**Note:** If the hypothetical situation is a present or future one, the verb in the conditional clause is in the past tense, and the verb in the main clause is formed from *would, could,* or *might* plus the base form of the verb.

If we **bought** groceries once a week, we **would** not **go** to the store so often.

### 31.43 Quoted and Reported Speech

**Quoted speech** is the use of exact words from another source in your own writing; you must enclose these words in quotation marks. It is also possible to report nearly exact words without quotation marks. This is called **reported speech,** or indirect quotation. (See 28.73–28.83 for a review of the use of quotation marks.)

*Direct quotation:* Felicia said, "Don't worry about tomorrow."

*Indirect quotation:* Felicia said that you don't have to worry about tomorrow.

In the case of a question, when a direct quotation is changed to an indirect quotation, the question mark is not needed.

*Direct quotation:* Ahmad asked, "Who of you will give me a hand?"

*Indirect quotation:* Ahmad asked who of us would give him a hand.

Notice how pronouns are often changed in indirect quotations.

*Direct quotation:* My friends said, "**You**'re crazy."

*Indirect quotation:* My friends said that **I** was crazy.

**Note:** In academic writing, the use of another source's spoken or written words in one's own writing without proper acknowledgment is called *plagiarism*. Plagiarism is severely penalized in academic situations. (See chapter 21.)

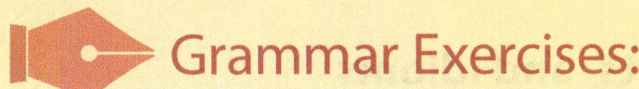

# Grammar Exercises:

## Sentence Problems

### A. Errors in Context

Correct the error(s) in each sentence below. Write down the error, crossed out, with the correction beside it.

(1) Flying by commercial jet can be a great way to travel if you have a long way to go and needs to get there quickly. (2) You can't never ignore, however, that the convenience comes with a price. (3) Security checks is becoming more intrusive every year. (4) Also, airlines they are reducing flights, crowding planes, and charging for services like meals. (5) If you wanted a leisurely vacation, you do better to choose different transportation. (6) An ocean voyage it takes longer but doesn't cause no jet lag. (7) People makes the same mistake with their road trips. (8) They gets in a car and rushes down the highway to a destination. (9) If they took a train instead, they relax and watch the countryside. (10) A jeep or a motorcycle are another great way to make a road trip. (11) Because these vehicles are open to the air, can feel in touch with the terrain. (12) If you were to travel back roads, you enjoy the journey as much as the arrival.

### B. Quoted and Reported Speech

Rewrite direct quotations as indirect quotations and vice versa.
1. Kimi told Hal, "I pay my bills with income from my online writing."
2. "How did you get started?" he asked.
3. She answered that their friend Toi had introduced her to a site for essayists.
4. She told him, "I had to fill out an application and submit a sample of work."
5. She said they made her revise her biography several times before accepting it.

### C. Defining Problems

In your own words, define each of the following sentence problems or types.
1. Double negatives
2. Omitted words
3. Repeated words
4. Conditional sentences
5. Quoted speech
6. Reported speech

## 31.44 Numbers, Word Parts, and Idioms

### 31.45 Numbers

As a multilingual/ESL learner, you may be accustomed to a way of writing numbers that is different from the way it is done in North America. Become familiar with the North American conventions for writing numbers. See 29.26–29.31 for more on how numbers are written and punctuated in both word and numeral forms.

#### 31.46 Using Punctuation with Numerals

Note that the **period** is used to express percentages (5.5%, 75.9%) and the **comma** is used to organize large numbers into units (7,000; 23,100; 231,990,000). Commas are not used, however, in writing the year (2020).

#### 31.47 Cardinal Numbers

**Cardinal numbers** (such as *one, two, three*) are used when counting a number of parts or objects. Cardinal numbers can be used as nouns (she counted to **ten**), pronouns (I invited many guests, but only **three** came), or adjectives (there are **ten** boys here).

Write out in words the numbers one through one hundred. Numbers 101 and greater are often written as numerals. (See 29.27.)

#### 31.48 Ordinal Numbers

**Ordinal numbers** show place or succession in a series: the fourth row, the twenty-first century, the tenth time, and so on. Ordinal numbers are used to talk about the parts into which a whole can be divided, such as a fourth or a tenth, and as the denominator in fractions, such as one-fourth or three-fifths. Written fractions can also be used as nouns (I gave him **four-fifths**) or as adjectives (a **four-fifths** majority).

> **Note:** See the list that follows for names and symbols of the first twenty-five ordinal numbers. Consult a college dictionary for a complete list of cardinal and ordinal numbers.

| | | | | | |
|---|---|---|---|---|---|
| First | 1st | Tenth | 10th | Nineteenth | 19th |
| Second | 2nd | Eleventh | 11th | Twentieth | 20th |
| Third | 3rd | Twelfth | 12th | Twenty-first | 21st |
| Fourth | 4th | Thirteenth | 13th | Twenty-second | 22nd |
| Fifth | 5th | Fourteenth | 14th | Twenty-third | 23rd |
| Sixth | 6th | Fifteenth | 15th | Twenty-fourth | 24th |
| Seventh | 7th | Sixteenth | 16th | Twenty-fifth | 25th |
| Eighth | 8th | Seventeenth | 17th | | |
| Ninth | 9th | Eighteenth | 18th | | |

## 31.49 Prefixes, Suffixes, and Roots

Following is a list of many common word parts and their meanings. Learning them can help you determine the meaning of unfamiliar words as you come across them in your reading. For instance, if you know that *hemi* means "half," you can conclude that *hemisphere* means "half of a sphere."

| Prefixes | Meaning | Suffixes | Meaning |
|---|---|---|---|
| a, an | not, without | able, ible | able, can do |
| anti, ant | against | age | act of, state of |
| co, con, com | together, with | al | relating to |
| di | two, twice | ate | cause, make |
| dis, dif | apart, away | en | made of |
| ex, e, ec, ef | out | ence, ency | action, quality |
| hemi, semi | half | esis, osis | action, process |
| il, ir, in, im | not | ice | condition, quality |
| inter | between | ile | relating to |
| intra | within | ish | resembling |
| multi | many | ment | act of, state of |
| non | not | ology | study, theory |
| ob, of, op, oc | toward, against | ous | full of, having |
| per | throughout | sion, tion | act of, state of |
| post | after | some | like, tending to |
| super, supr | above, more | tude | state of |
| trans, tra | across, beyond | ward | in the direction of |
| tri | three | | |
| uni | one | | |

| Roots | Meaning | Roots | Meaning |
|---|---|---|---|
| acu | sharp | ject | throw |
| am, amor | love, liking | log, ology | word, study, speech |
| anthrop | man | man | hand |
| aster, astr | star | micro | small |
| auto | self | mit, miss | send |
| biblio | book | nom | law, order |
| bio | life | onym | name |
| capit, capt | head | path, pathy | feeling, suffering |
| chron | time | rupt | break |
| cit | to call, start | scrib, script | write |
| cred | believe | spec, spect, spic | look |
| dem | people | tele | far |
| dict | say, speak | tempo | time |
| erg | work | tox | poison |
| fid, feder | faith, trust | vac | empty |
| fract, frag | break | ver, veri | true |
| graph, gram | write, written | zo | animal |

# Handbook

## Grammar Exercises:

# Numbers and Word Parts

### A. Punctuating Numerals

For the following numbers, add or correct punctuation as necessary to suit North American style. (Some of the numbers are already correct, and two items need to be punctuated correctly as percentages.)

- **A.** 3000
- **B.** 44
- **C.** 9.400.207,33
- **D.** 200,000,01
- **E.** 600000009
- **F.** 23,7%
- **G.** Dec. 21 2012
- **H.** 100
- **I.** 1.877,14
- **J.** 17,7%

### B. Numbers in Text

Write each number below as it should appear in text.

- **A.** 900
- **B.** 4/5
- **C.** 99
- **D.** 24
- **E.** 101
- **F.** 42
- **G.** 17
- **H.** 1/3
- **I.** 70
- **J.** 1,001

### C. Prefixes, Suffixes, and Roots

Break each of the following terms into its component parts (prefix, root, and/or suffix) and define it in your own words.

1. semiserious
2. pseudonym
3. toxicology
4. bibliography
5. verified
6. coauthor
7. westward
8. microfinance
9. antipathy
10. international
11. infantile
12. postponement
13. astrophysics
14. ticklish
15. multihued
16. incredulous

## 31.50 Idioms

Idioms are phrases that are used in a special way. An idiom can't be understood just by knowing the meaning of each word in the phrase. It must be learned as a whole. For example, the idiom to *bury the hatchet* means to "settle an argument," even though the individual words in the phrase mean something much different. These pages list some of the common idioms in American English.

|  |  |
|---|---|
| **a bad apple** | One troublemaker on a team may be called **a bad apple.** *(a bad influence)* |
| **an axe to grind** | Mom has **an axe to grind** with the owners of the dog that dug up her flower garden. *(a problem to settle)* |
| **as the crow flies** | She lives only two miles from here **as the crow flies.** *(in a straight line)* |
| **beat around the bush** | Dad said, "Where were you? Don't **beat around the bush.**" *(avoid getting to the point)* |
| **benefit of the doubt** | Ms. Hy gave Henri the **benefit of the doubt** when he explained why he fell asleep in class. *(another chance)* |
| **beyond the shadow of a doubt** | Salvatore won the 50-yard dash **beyond the shadow of a doubt.** *(for certain)* |
| **blew my top** | When my money was stolen, I **blew my top.** *(showed great anger)* |
| **bone to pick** | Nick had a **bone to pick** with Adrian when Nick learned they both liked the same girl. *(problem to settle)* |
| **break the ice** | Shanta was the first to **break the ice** in the room full of new students. *(start a conversation)* |
| **burn the midnight oil** | Carmen had to **burn the midnight oil** the day before the big test. *(work late into the night)* |
| **chomping at the bit** | Dwayne was **chomping at the bit** when it was his turn to bat. *(eager, excited)* |
| **cold shoulder** | Alicia always gives me the **cold shoulder** after our disagreements. *(ignores me)* |
| **cry wolf** | If you **cry wolf** too often, no one will come when you really need help. *(say you are in trouble when you aren't)* |
| **drop in the bucket** | My donation was a **drop in the bucket.** *(a small amount compared with what's needed)* |
| **face the music** | José had to **face the music** when he got caught cheating on the test. *(deal with the punishment)* |
| **flew off the handle** | Tramayne **flew off the handle** when he saw his little brother playing with matches. *(became very angry)* |
| **floating on air** | Teresa was **floating on air** when she read the letter. *(feeling very happy)* |

|  |  |
|---|---|
| food for thought | The coach gave us some **food for thought** when she said that winning isn't everything. *(something to think about)* |
| get down to business | In five minutes you need to **get down to business** on this assignment. *(start working)* |
| get the upper hand | The other team will **get the upper hand** if we don't play better in the second half. *(probably win)* |
| go overboard | The teacher told us not **to go overboard** with fancy lettering on our posters. *(do too much)* |
| hit the ceiling | Rosa **hit the ceiling** when she saw her sister painting the television. *(was very angry)* |
| hit the hay | Patrice **hit the hay** early because she was tired. *(went to bed)* |
| in a nutshell | **In a nutshell,** Coach Roby told us to play our best. *(to summarize)* |
| in the nick of time | Zong grabbed his little brother's hand **in the nick of time** before he touched the hot pan. *(just in time)* |
| in the same boat | My friend and I are **in the same boat** when it comes to doing Saturday chores. *(have the same problem)* |
| iron out | Jamil and his brother were told to **iron out** their differences about cleaning their room. *(solve, work out)* |
| it stands to reason | **It stands to reason** that if you keep lifting weights, you will get stronger. *(it makes sense)* |
| knuckle down | Grandpa told me to **knuckle down** at school if I want to be a doctor. *(work hard)* |
| learn the ropes | Being new in school, I knew it would take some time to **learn the ropes**. *(get to know how things are done)* |
| let's face it | "**Let's face it!**" said Mr. Sills. "You're a better long distance runner than you are a sprinter." *(let's admit it)* |
| let the cat out of the bag | Tia **let the cat out of the bag** and got her sister in trouble. *(told a secret)* |
| lose face | If I strike out again, I will **lose face**. *(be embarrassed)* |
| nose to the grindstone | If I keep my **nose to the grindstone,** I will finish my homework in one hour. *(working hard)* |
| on cloud nine | Walking home from the party, I was **on cloud nine**. *(feeling very happy)* |
| on pins and needles | I was **on pins and needles** as I waited to see the doctor. *(feeling nervous)* |
| over and above | **Over and above** the assigned reading, I read two library books. *(in addition to)* |

| | |
|---|---|
| put his foot in his mouth | Chivas **put his foot in his mouth** when he called his teacher by the wrong name. *(said something embarrassing)* |
| put your best foot forward | Grandpa said that whenever you do something, you should **put your best foot forward.** *(do the best that you can do)* |
| rock the boat | The coach said, "Don't **rock the boat** if you want to stay on the team." *(cause trouble)* |
| rude awakening | I had a **rude awakening** when I saw the letter *F* at the top of my Spanish quiz. *(sudden, unpleasant surprise)* |
| save face | Grant tried to **save face** when he said he was sorry for making fun of me in class. *(fix an embarrassing situation)* |
| see eye to eye | My sister and I finally **see eye to eye** about who gets to use the phone first after school. *(are in agreement)* |
| sight unseen | Grandma bought the television **sight unseen.** *(without seeing it first)* |
| take a dim view | My brother will **take a dim view** if I don't help him at the store. *(disapprove)* |
| take it with a grain of salt | If my sister tells you she has no homework, **take it with a grain of salt.** *(don't believe everything you're told)* |
| take the bull by the horns | This team needs to **take the bull by the horns** to win the game. *(take control)* |
| through thick and thin | Max and I will be friends **through thick and thin.** *(in good times and in bad times)* |
| time flies | When you're having fun, **time flies.** *(time passes quickly)* |
| time to kill | We had **time to kill** before the ballpark gates would open. *(extra time)* |
| under the weather | I was feeling **under the weather,** so I didn't go to school. *(sick)* |
| word of mouth | We found out who the new teacher was by **word of mouth.** *(talking to other people)* |

**Note:** Like idioms, collocations are groups of words that often appear together. They may help you identify different senses of a word; for example, *old* means slightly different things in these collocations: *old man, old friends.* You will find sentence construction easier if you check for collocations.

# Handbook

# Grammar Exercises:

## Idioms

### A. Using Idioms
Replace the underlined words with appropriate idioms.

Here's (1) something to think about. In order for a democracy to succeed, its citizens must participate. That just (2) makes sense. But (3) let's admit it, far too many U.S. citizens just don't vote. What excuse do they give? Many say, "My vote doesn't matter; it's just (4) a small amount compared to what's needed." I (5) disapprove of this excuse. It's time for these people to (6) deal with the negative effects concerning this abdication of responsibility. Notice that word "abdication." In a democracy, every person is a king. We are all (7) facing the same problem. I'm not saying we need (8) to do too much with our political involvement. However, we should at least vote, and that means researching the issues to avoid (9) being embarrassed because of our choices.

### B. Defining Idioms
Using your own words, define the following idioms.

1. benefit of the doubt
2. burn the midnight oil
3. floating on air
4. get down to business
5. let's face it
6. over and above
7. see eye to eye
8. a bad apple
9. flew off the handle
10. break the ice
11. food for thought
12. iron out
13. lose face
14. hit the ceiling
15. on cloud nine
16. learn the ropes
17. bone to pick
18. cold shoulder
19. as the crow flies
20. in a nutshell

# Grammar Exercises:

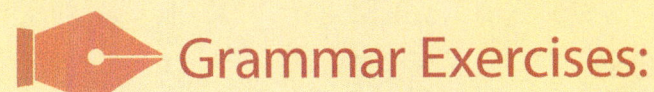

### A. Period, Comma, Quotation Marks, Question Mark, Apostrophe

Rewrite each of the following sentences, inserting punctuation where needed.

1. I asked Could I have an extension on my paper Professor Rubel
2. He responded Well Rob all the other papers have been turned in
3. Yes thats true I replied but no one elses paper will be as good as mine
4. Youd better be right said Professor Rubel How many days better will it be
5. I cringed and asked How about five days better
6. Professor Rubels eyebrows shot up Five days better will have to be phenomenal
7. Three days I asked sheepishly
8. Thats still very much better than everyone else Professor Rubel pointed out.
9. Okay what about one day better I responded
10. I think thats the level of better that you can do Rob One day it is

### B. Title Capitalization, Quotation Marks, Italics

For each sentence, rewrite titles, correctly capitalizing them and using quotation marks or italics (underlining) as needed.

1. In the New york times, I read the article, Four representatives Charged In ethics Probe.
2. The music album Sea of cowards by the band The Dead Weather includes the song I'm mad.
3. I read the chapter An empire Crumbles in the novel The shadow of Reichenbach falls, which was reviewed well in the library journal.
4. Have you read the poem the Fiddler Of Dooney in the collection W.b. Yeats: selected Poems?
5. In John Steinbeck's book The acts of King Arthur And his noble Knights, I most enjoyed the chapter the Noble tale of Sir Lancelot Of The Lake.
6. A chapter entitled Management writing has been added to the second edition of the handbook Write For Business.
7. We went to the Riverside Theater to see Adam Lambert sing his song For your entertainment.
8. The radio show Performance today stars Fred Child.
9. The song Joyful, Joyful comes from Beethoven's symphony Ode to joy.
10. We'll sail to Mexico aboard a boat called The lark Of The sea.

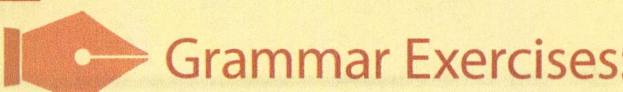
## Grammar Exercises:

### A. Capitalization, Plurals

Correct the capitalization and plural errors in each sentence by writing the correct word or words.

1. Some Holidays fall on different daies of the week.
2. A holiday like the fourth of july or halloween can fall on only one Date but on any day.
3. Holidaies such as Memorial day or Labor day always fall on a Monday.
4. In the badger state, christmas is often white, but in the aloha state, it never is.
5. Festivals such as taste of chicago or milwaukee's summerfest stretch out over weekes.
6. In that way, these celebrationes are similar to chinese new year, which lasts for many daies.
7. On new year's eve in the west, husbands dance with their wifes and leave their childs with babysitters.
8. Reveleres often have a few glassesful of wine or champagne to celebrate New year's eve.
9. It's funny how most Americanes don't know when columbus day is, which celebrates Columbus's discovery of the new world.
10. It's also strange how many earthlings don't know if earth day is in march, april, or may.

### B. Numbers and Spelling

Correct the number and spelling errors in each sentence by writing the correct form or words.

1. Do monkies and other great aps like to eat French frys?
2. 300 million Americans seem to like frys, as do many of the 6,000,000,000 others in the world.
3. Fries and a 4- or eight-ounce burger is a common meal for Americans.
4. If you drive through before eleven a.m., you'll get hashes brown instead of frys at most fast-food places.
5. One eight-ounce burger can pack a whopping four hundred fifty calories.
6. The local fast-food restaurant employs 43 people, with 2 Steve's and 3 Jacob's.
7. They cut about three hundred tomatos every day.
8. In addition to 11 fry cooks, they employ 3 cheves.
9. They advertise over 1,000,000,000 served.
10. On each burger, they squirt one teaspoon of ketchup and one half teaspoon of mustard.

# Grammar Exercises:

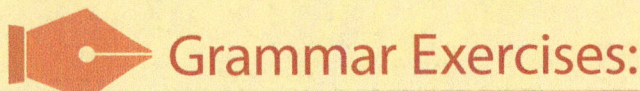

## Spelling

Write the correct spelling of each word below.

1. abundence
2. acommodate
3. aquiesce
4. advize
5. althrough
6. annoint
7. biscut
8. celibration
9. comission
10. concieve
11. confidencial
12. consientous
13. deseased
14. dependant
15. disipline
16. eficiency
17. essencial
18. exhorbitant
19. extreem
20. Feberary
21. freind
22. harrass
23. interupt
24. irigate
25. judgement
26. laundary
27. licence
28. ofen
29. opperate
30. parlament
31. personell
32. preferrance
33. previlant
34. procede
35. pumkin
36. questionaire
37. reccurrence
38. rehersal
39. restaraunt
40. reumatism
41. sceen
42. seperate
43. simmilar
44. speciman
45. stomache
46. sumerize
47. surveylance
48. unneccessary
49. useable
50. vegtable
51. villian
52. volunter
53. wether
54. wholely
55. writen
56. yeild

# Grammar Exercises:

## Usage

Correct the usage in the following document by writing down the line number and the usage errors, crossed out, with the correct words beside them.

When I sat down to eat at Leon's Texas Grill, I remembered a friend's advise: 1
"Alright, get ready for allot of food." His prediction was all together accurate. 2
When I smelled the delicious aroma of beef brisket on the barbecue, I was anxious 3
to get some of my own. I wanted it bad. But the brisket was complimented by 4
beans, potato salad, and other sides. Leon's also offered spicy sausage, steaks, 5
and more meats than I could chose from. I decided that the first coarse would 6
be brisket with beans. I had a guilty conscious as I ate fore hunks of brisket and 7
went back for more. Everything tasted so well. I was under no allusion that I 8
would be loosing wait tonight. 9

Brisket would normally be vary tough, but slow grilling assures its tenderness. 10
Brisket often cooks for hours and is only latter served to customers. What an 11
ingenuous way to make tough meat flavorful and delicious! I was liable to 12
literally eat everything in the restaurant, and then loose conscienceness. 13

I was in the midst of my third helping when one of the restaurant's personal past 14
me with a cart that had peaces of cake and pie and other types of desert. My pour 15
stomach was already quiet full, and I felt real sleepy, but from my prospective, 16
I wasn't going to be getting back here anytime soon. Those were sum of the 17
most delicious sweets I'd ever scene. I looked threw all the options their and 18
picked too cupcakes. I was being vary gluttonous, and my waste would reveal 19
my indiscretions. 20

After my meal, I wished I could meet the man whom established this restaurant. 21
I would have told him, "Leon, your my hero." Then, a second latter, I would've 22
past out. 23

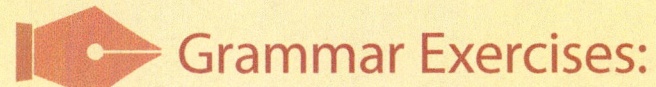
# Grammar Exercises:

### A. Noun, Pronoun, Verb, Adjective, Adverb
Identify each underlined word as a noun (n), a pronoun (pron), a verb (v), an adjective (adj), or an adverb (adv).

(1) <u>You</u> may not (2) <u>think</u> much about that (3) <u>green</u> stuff under your feet—yes, (4) <u>grass</u>—but it has conquered the world. Grass didn't exist at all until the (5) <u>late</u> Cretaceous period, but once it (6) <u>arrived</u> on the scene, (7) <u>it</u> took over. Whole animal (8) <u>species</u> grew up to graze upon this (9) <u>hardy</u> plant, eating both the leaves and the (10) <u>heads</u> of grain. Some types of grass, such as barley, (11) <u>produce</u> grains that humans (12) <u>also</u> eat. Farm kids (13) <u>often</u> pluck a long stalk of grass and chew on (14) <u>it</u>, but you wouldn't be able to chew on the (15) <u>largest</u> stalks from the grass family—the giant bamboo. Unlike its (16) <u>tiny</u> cousins, bamboo plants grow (17) <u>so</u> rapidly that they have been purported to be used to torture people. (18) <u>Maybe</u> they are just getting back at (19) <u>us</u> for (20) <u>always</u> walking on top of them.

### B. Coordinating, Correlative, and Subordinating Conjunctions
Create a three-column table, labeling the columns "Coordinating," "Correlative," and "Subordinating." Then sort the following conjunctions, writing them in their correct columns.

| | | |
|---|---|---|
| as long as | so that | whenever |
| after | so | as |
| yet | or | whereas |
| both/and | even though | until |
| when | for | nor |
| because | where | not only/but also |
| either/or | as if | and |
| though | in order that | provided that |
| before | whether/or | |
| neither/nor | but | |
| while | since | |
| although | unless | |

## 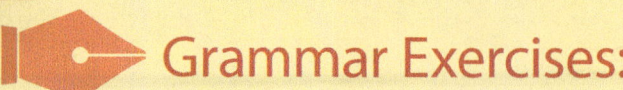 Grammar Exercises:

### A. Fragments

Turn each fragment into a sentence by adding what is missing (a subject, a verb, a subject and a verb, or a complete thought).
1. During the big game.
2. When we scored the winning goal.
3. Shouted our fight song.
4. Just before the whistle blew.
5. Smiling from ear to ear.
6. The scoreboard overhead.
7. With looks of amazement.
8. In order to commemorate the win.
9. The college newspaper.
10. Whenever we win a big game.

### B. Other Sentence Errors

Rewrite each sentence, fixing the comma splice, run-on, agreement error, or nonstandard language.
1. The team fought like never before they won in overtime.
2. Each team member gave their all.
3. Three touchdowns, three extra points, and a field goal sets the score at 24-21.
4. Tim, Jake, and Kurt, they played their best games ever.
5. Tim broke his passing record, Jake beat his rushing yards.
6. Kurt been kicking the ball through the goalposts every time.
7. You should of been there.
8. I'm gonna watch every game this year.
9. Coach Carlson say he's never had such a good team.
10. I is planning to try out next year.

### C. Dangling/Misplaced Modifiers

Rewrite each sentence to correct the dangling or misplaced modifiers.
1. After watching from the stands for the whole game, the team scored the winning field goal.
2. I congratulated the linebacker for tackling the quarterback on his way to the locker room.
3. A kicker once punted the ball from our second string.
4. A cheerleader climbed to the top of the pyramid with red hair.
5. After kicking the winning field goal, the other team left looking dejected.

# Index

## A

*A/an,* 617
*A lot/alot/allot,* 617
**Abbreviations,** *ch.* 29.32
  Acronyms and initialisms, *ch.* 29.34
  Capitalization, *ch.* 29.11
  Common, 606
  Correspondence, *ch.* 29.32
  Punctuation of, *ch.* 28.03
**Absolute** phrase, *ch.* 26.22
**Abstract** noun, *ch.* 25.07
**Abstracts,**
  APA, 509, 511
  Citation of, 502
  Writing, 445, 511
**Academic** style, 91–93
  Active or passive voice, 91, *ch.* 25.44, 25.45
*Accept/except,* 617
**Acronyms,** *ch.* 29.34
**Action** verb, *ch.* 25.31
**Active** voice, 91, *ch.* 25.44, 25.45
*Adapt/adopt/adept,* 617
**Address,**
  Abbreviations, *ch.* 29.32
  Direct, *ch.* 28.31
  Punctuation of, *ch.* 28.28
**Adjective,** *ch.* 25.54
  Clause, *ch.* 26.27
  Comparative, *ch.* 25.57
  Compound, *ch.* 28.66
  Forms of, *ch.* 25.57
  Infinitive phrase, acting as, *ch.* 25.49
  Nouns as, *ch.* 31.29
  Participial phrase, acting as, *ch.* 25.50
  Placing, *ch.* 31.27
  Positive, *ch.* 25.57
  Possessive, *ch.* 31.10
  Predicate, *ch.* 25.56
  Prepositional phrase, acting as, *ch.* 25.64
  Proper, *ch.* 25.55
  Separating with commas, *ch.* 28.18
  Superlative, *ch.* 25.57
**Adverb,** *ch.* 25.58, 31.30
  Clause, *ch.* 26.26
  Comparative, *ch.* 25.60
  Conjunctive, *ch.* 26.38, 28.42
  Forms of, *ch.* 25.60
  Placing, *ch.* 31.31
  Positive, *ch.* 25.60
  Superlative, *ch.* 25.60
*Adverse/averse,* 617
*Advice/advise,* 617
*Affect/effect,* 617
**Agreement,**
  Pronoun-antecedent, *ch.* 27.16
  Subject-verb, *ch.* 27.01
*Aid/aide,* 618
**Aiming** for writing excellence, 6–7
*All, of,* 618
*All right/alright,* 618
**Alliteration,** 291
*Allude/elude,* 618
**Allusion,** 288
*Allusion/illusion,* 618
*Already/all ready,* 618
*Altogether/all together,* 618
**Ambiguous** wording, *ch.* 27.32
*Among/between,* 618
*Amoral/immoral,* 618
*Amount/number,* 618
**Analogies,** 288
  Paragraph, 67
**Analysis,**
  Of documents and artifacts, 394–395
  Literary, 271–294
  Rhetorical situation, 8
**Analytical** writing, 163–294
  Cause-effect, 247–270
  Classification, 185–204
  Comparison-contrast, 227–246
  Definition, 163–184
  Literary analysis, 271–294
  Process, 205–226
**Analyze,** key word, 9
**Anapestic** foot, 291
*And,*
  Comma before, *ch.* 28.16, 28.17
*And etc.,* 619
**Anecdote,** 143, 288
**Annotated** bibliography, 376–377
**Annotating,** 28, 380
*Annual/biannual/semiannual/biennial/perennial,* 619
**Antagonist,** 288
**Antecedent,**
  Agreement with pronoun, *ch.* 27.16
**Antithesis,** 289
*Anxious/eager,* 619
*Any one (of)/any one,* 619
*Anymore/any more,* 619
**APA** documentation format, 491–520
  Abstract, 511
  Format guidelines, 509
  Parenthetical references, 494–497
  Reference entries, 498–508
  Sample research paper, 510–519
**Apostrophe,** *ch.* 28.104
**Appeals,** 306–307
**Appositive,**
  Phrase, *ch.* 26.21, 94
*Appraise/apprise,* 619
**Argumentation,**
  Engaging the opposition, 306
  Essays of, 330–352
  Identifying fallacies, 313–317
  Making and qualifying claims, 308–309
  Preparing your argument, 301–304
  Rogerian, 302–303
  Supporting claims, 310
  Toulmin, 301–302
  Using appeals, 306–307
**Articles,**
  *A/an,* 617
  Indefinite, *ch.* 31.08
  When to use, *ch.* 31.06
**Arts,** writing about, 271–294
*As,* 619
*As/like,* 627
**Assignment,** understanding the, 8, 110
**Assonance,** 291
*Assure/ensure/insure,* 625
**Attributive** phrase, 437, 438
**Audience,** 8, 110, 272
**Auxiliary** verbs, *ch.* 25.32
*Averse/adverse,* 617
**Avoiding** plagiarism, 422–427
  Other source abuses, 426–427
  Recognizing plagiarism, 422–423
  Understanding the problem, 424
  Using sources credibly, 420–421

## B

*Bad/badly,* 619
**Bandwagon,** 314
**"Be"** verbs,
  Avoid overusing, 102
*Beside/besides,* 619
*Between/among,* 618
*Biannual/semiannual/biennial/annual/perennial,* 619
**Biased** language, avoiding, 105–107
**Bibliography,**
  Annotated, 376–377
  APA references, 498–508
  MLA citations, 464–474
  Working, 372
**Blank** verse, 291
**Blogs,** 385, 472
**Body,**
  Essay, 60, 66–69
**Books,**
  APA reference entries, 499–501
  MLA works-cited entries, 468–469
  As research tools, 402
**Boolean** operators, 371
*Borrow/lend,* 626
**Brackets,** 384, 439, 496, *ch.* 28.97
**Brainstorming,** 11, 364
*Bring/take,* 619
**Broad** generalization, 315

## C

**Call** number, 400, 401
*Can/may,* 621
*Capital/capitol,* 621
**Capitalization,** *ch.* 29.01
**Case,**
  Nouns, *ch.* 25.11
  Pronouns, *ch.* 25.26
**Case** study in literary analysis, 271–294
  Approaches to criticism, 199–201
  Models and readings, 277–287
  Strategies, 272–277
  Writing guidelines, 292–293
**Cause-effect,**
  Essays of, 254–267

# Index

Graphic organizer, 253
Guidelines, 268–269
Paragraph, 252
Patterns, 252–253
Reading, 254–267
Strategies, 250–253
Thesis, 252–253
*Cent/sent/scent,* 621
**Checking** mechanics, 595–616
**Checklists,**
  Proofreading, 90
  Traits, 124
*Chord/cord,* 621
*Chose/choose,* 621
*Cite/site/sight,* 630
**Citing** sources, 436–438
  APA style, 492–508
  MLA style, 454–474
**Claims,**
  Engaging the opposition, 305
  Making and qualifying, 308–309
  Supporting, 310–312
**Clarity,**
  Using brackets for, *ch.* 28.98
  Using comma for, *ch.* 28.38
  Word choice, 102
**Classification,**
  Essays of, 191–201
  Graphic organizer, 190
  Guidelines, 202–203
  Paragraph, 189
  Patterns, 190
  Reading, 191–201
  Strategies, 188–190
  Thesis, 189–190
**Clause,** *ch.* 26.23
  Adjective, *ch.* 26.27
  Adverb, *ch.* 26.26
  Conjunctions with, *ch.* 25.69
  Dependent, *ch.* 26.24, 26.39, 26.40
  Independent, *ch.* 26.24, 26.37, 26.39
  Noun, *ch.* 26.28
  Restrictive and nonrestrictive, *ch.* 28.24
**Cliché,** 103
*Climactic/climatic,* 621
**Climax,** 288
**Closings,** 60, 70–71
**Clustering,** 12, 111
*Coarse/course,* 621
**Coherence,**
  In paragraph, 83–84
**Collaborative** revising, 86–87
**Collective** noun, *ch.* 29.25
**Colloquial** language, *ch.* 27.37
**Colon,** *ch.* 28.47
  Capitalizing after, *ch.* 29.05
**Combining** sentences, 94–97
**Comma,** *ch.* 28.15–28.38
  Splice, *ch.* 27.27
  With quotation marks, *ch.* 28.76
**Command,** punctuation of, *ch.* 28.02
**Common** noun, *ch.* 25.04
**Comparative** form,

Adjectives, 233, *ch.* 25.57
Adverbs, *ch.* 25.60
*Compare with/compare to,* 621
**Comparison-contrast,**
  Essays of, 234–243
  Graphic organizer, Venn diagram, 230–231
  Guidelines, 244–245
  Paragraph, 231
  Patterns, 233
  Reading, 234–243
  Strategies, 230–233
  Thesis, 232–233
  Transitions, 84
*Complement/compliment,* 621
**Complete**
  Predicate, *ch.* 26.11
  Subject, *ch.* 26.04
**Complex** sentence, *ch.* 26.39
**Compound,**
  Adjective, *ch.* 28.66
  Noun, *ch.* 28.111
  Number, *ch.* 28.58
  Predicate, *ch.* 26.12
  Sentence, *ch.* 26.38
  Subject, *ch.* 26.05
  Word, *ch.* 28.56
**Compound-complex** sentence, *ch.* 26.40
*Comprehensible/comprehensive,* 621
*Comprise/compose,* 622
**Concessions,** making, 305
**Concluding** paragraph, 70
  Transitions, 84
**Concrete** noun, *ch.* 25.06
**Conditional** sentence, *ch.* 26.35
**Conflict,** 288
**Conjunction,**
  Coordinating, *ch.* 25.67
  Correlative, 94, 99, *ch.* 25.68
  Subordinating, *ch.* 25.69
**Conjunctive** adverb, *ch.* 26.38, 28.42
*Conscience/conscious,* 622
**Consonance,** 291
**Construction,** sentence, shifts in, *ch.* 27.20
*Consul/counsel/council,* 622
*Continual/continuous,* 622
**Contractions,** 93, *ch.* 28.105
**Contrasted** elements, *ch.* 28.36
**Coordinating** conjunction, *ch.* 25.67
  Between independent clauses, *ch.* 28.16
*Cord/chord,* 621
**Correction** and proofreading symbols, inside back cover
**Correlative** conjunctions, 94, 99, *ch.* 25.68
**Couplet,** 291
*Course/coarse,* 621
**Critical** reading, 19–35
  Engaging with social media, 32–33
  Notes, 28–29
  Responding to a text, 30

SQ3R strategy, 22–23
Summarizing a text, 31
**Critical** thinking, 20–21, 24–27
**Critical** viewing, 35–46
  Detecting misinformation, 44–45
  Images, 36–39
  Video, 42–43
  Evaluation, 40–41

## D

**Dactylic** foot, 291
**Dangling** modifiers, *ch.* 27.31
**Dash,** *ch.* 28.67
**Databases,** 370–371, 404
  Citing, 468, 470, 505
**Dates,** punctuation of, *ch.* 28.28
*Decent/descent/dissent,* 622
**Declarative** sentence, *ch.* 26.31
**Deductive** reasoning, 51, 312
**Definition,**
  Essays of, 170–181
  Graphic organizer, 169
  Guidelines, 182–183
  Moves, 169
  Paragraph, 167
  Reading, 164–167, 170–181
  Thesis, 168
**Delayed** subject, *ch.* 27.04
**Demonstrative** pronoun, *ch.* 25.22
**Denouement,** 288
**Dependent** clause, *ch.* 26.24, 26.39, 26.40
**Description,**
  Principles, 144–145
*Desert/dessert,* 622
**Details,**
  Connecting, 83–84
  Five W's, 14
  Organizing, 50–51
  Specific, 85
  Supporting, 67–69, 85
  Types of, 85
**Development,**
  Of an essay, 109–122
  Of ideas, 50–51
  Middle, 66–69
  Subject, 50–51
**Dewey** decimal system, 401
**Dialogue,** 143
  Punctuation of, *ch.* 28.30, 28.71
**Diction,** 288
*Different from/different than,* 622
**Dimeter,** 291
**Direct** address, *ch.* 28.31
**Direct** object, *ch.* 25.12, 26.13
**Direct** quotation, 384, *ch.* 28.80, 31.43
**Disabilities,** acceptable terms, 106
*Discreet/discrete,* 622
*Disinterested/uninterested,* 622
*Dissent/decent/descent,* 622
**Dividing** words, *ch.* 28.65
**Documentation** in research paper, 436–429, 454, 492
  APA references, 492, 498–508
  MLA works cited, 454, 464–474

**Double-entry** notebook, 29, 381
**Double** negative, *ch.* 27.40, 31.38
**Double** preposition, *ch.* 27.38
**Double** subject, *ch.* 31.41
**Drafting,** 59–72
  Coherent structure, 60, 83
  Ending, 70–71
  First, 59–71, 114
  Middle, 66–69
  Moves, 67–69
  Openings, 64–65
  Research paper, 429–452

### E

*Eager/anxious,* 619
**Editing,** 89–108
  Biased words, 105–107
  Expletives, 100
  Jargon/clichés, 103
  Negative constructions, 100
  Nominal constructions, 100
  Parallel structure, 91
  Proofreading, 108 *See also* Handbook
  Sentence problems, 91
  Sentence style, 92–101
  Word choice, 102–107
  Wordiness, 101
*Effect/affect,* 617
**Electronic** sources,
  APA reference entries, 504–507
  MLA works-cited entries, 472
*Elicit/illicit,* 623
**Ellipsis,** *ch.* 28.05
**Email,** citing, 471
*Emigrate/immigrate,* 625
*Eminent/imminent,* 623
**Emphasis,** *ch.* 28.38, 28.50, 28.72
**Encyclopedia,** 385, 403
**Endings,** 60, 70–71
*Ensure/insure/assure,* 625
**ESL guidelines,** 633–664
  Adjectives, *ch.* 31.26
  Adverbs, *ch.* 31.30
  Articles, *ch.* 31.06
  Gerund, *ch.* 31.18
  Idioms, *ch.* 31.50
  Infinitives, *ch.* 31.18
  Modal verbs, *ch.* 31.19
  Nouns, count/noncount, *ch.* 31.02, 31.03, 31.04
  Numbers, *ch.* 31.45
  Prefixes, suffixes, roots, *ch.* 31.49
  Preposition, *ch.* 31.32
  Sentence problems, *ch.* 31.37
  Verbs, *ch.* 31.13, 31.20
**Essay,**
  Argumentation, 321–356
  Cause-effect, 247–270
  Classification, 185–204
  Comparison-contrast, 227–246
  Definition, 163–184
  Drafting, 59–72
  Editing, 89–108
  Ending, 70–71
  Expository. *See* Expository writing
  Middle, 66–69
  One writer's process, 109–136
  Opening, 64–65
  Persuasive, 321–356
  Planning, 47–58
  Process, 205–226
  Proofreading, 108
  Research, 429–452, 453–490, 491–520
  Revising, 73–88
  Structure, 60–71
  Thesis statement, 48–49, 76, 146–147, 168–169, 189–190, 210–211, 232–233, 252–253, 328–329
**Ethnic** groups,
  Acceptable terms, 105
**Evaluation,**
  Images, 40–41
  Sources, 27, 385–389
**Evidence,** using, 76, 310–311, 435
*Except/accept,* 617
**Exclamation** point, *ch.* 28.77, 28.102
**Exclamatory** sentence, *ch.* 26.34
**Expanding** sentences, 95
**Experiment,** lab, and field reports, 445–451
**Explanatory** words, *ch.* 28.35
*Explicit/implicit,* 623
**Exposition,** 289
**Expository** writing,
  Analysis of a process, 205–226
  Cause-effect, 247–270
  Classification, 185–204
  Comparison-contrast, 227–246
  Definition, 163–184

### F

**Fallacies** of logic, 313–317
**Falling** action, 289
*Farther/further,* 623
*Fewer/less,* 623
**Figurative** language, 273, 291
*Figuratively/literally,* 623
**Figure** of speech, 289
**Film** review, 284–287
**First** draft, 59–71, 114
*First/firstly,* 623
*Fiscal/physical,* 623
**Five** W's, 14
**Focus,** 48, 65, 82, 364–365
**Foot,** 291
*For/fore/four,* 623
**Formatting,**
  APA style, 509
  MLA style, 475–479
*Former/latter,* 623
**Forms** of writing,
  Analysis, literary, 271–294
  Analytical, 163–270
  Essay. *See* Essay
  Expository. *See* Expository writing
  Narrative, 137–162
  Persuasive, 295–356

Report. *See* Report writing
Review. *See* Review
**Fragment,** sentence, *ch.* 27.26
**Freewriting,** 12–13
*Further/farther,* 623
**Future** perfect tense, *ch.* 25.43
**Future** tense, *ch.* 25.43

### G

**Gender,**
  Noun, *ch.* 25.10
  Pronoun, *ch.* 25.27
**Gender** references, 107
**Generalization,** 315
**Genre,** 289
**Gerund,** *ch.* 25.48, 31.17, 31.18
**Gerund** phrase, *ch.* 26.18
*Good/well,* 625
**Grammar,** 523–543
**Graphic** organizers,
  Cause/effect, 253
  Classification, 190
  Cluster, 12, 111
  Comparison, 233
  Definition, 169
  Problem/solution web, 329
  Process analysis, 211
  Venn diagram, 231, 304
**Guidelines** for reading, 19–34
**Guidelines** for writing,
  About literature and the arts, 292–293
  Argumentative essay, 353–355
  Cause-effect essay, 268–269
  Classification essay, 202–203
  Comparison-contrast essay, 244–245
  Definition essay, 182–183
  Literary analysis, 292–293
  Narration, reflection, and description essay, 160–161
  Personal essay, 160–161
  Persuasive essay, 353–355
  Position paper, 353–355
  Problem/solution essay, 353–355
  Process writing, 224–225
  Research papers,
    APA, 491–520
    MLA, 453–490

### H

**Half-truths,** 315
**Handbook,** 523–664
**Hasty** generalization, 315
*Heal/heel,* 625
*Healthful/healthy,* 625
**Helping** (auxiliary) verb, *ch.* 25.32
**Heptameter,** 291
**Hexameter,** 291
**Humanities,** 129
**Hyperbole,** 289
**Hyphen,** *ch.* 28.55

### I

*I/me,* 625
**Iambic,** 291

# Index

**Ideas,** 4, 6
  Generating, 10–17, 48–55
  Revising, 75–76
**Idioms,** *ch.* 31.50
*Illicit/elicit,* 623
*Illusion/allusion,* 618
**Illustration.** *See* Anecdote
  Paragraph, 67
**Imagery,** 289
*Immigrate/emigrate,* 625
*Imminent/eminent,* 623
*Immoral/amoral,* 618
**Imperative** mood, *ch.* 25.46
**Imperative** sentence, *ch.* 26.33
*Implicit/explicit,* 623
*Imply/infer,* 625
**Incomplete** comparison, *ch.* 27.34
**Indefinite** pronoun, *ch.* 25.20, 27.14, 27.15
  Agreement with antecedent, *ch.* 27.13, 27.14, 27.15
  Agreement with verb, *ch.* 27.13, 27.14, 27.15
  Possessive, *ch.* 28.112
  Unclear reference, *ch.* 27.33
**Independent** clause, *ch.* 26.24
  Punctuation of, *ch.* 26.37, 26.39
**Indicative** mood, *ch.* 25.46
**Indirect** object, *ch.* 25.12, 26.14
**Indirect** question, *ch.* 28.02, 28.11
**Indirect** quotation, *ch.* 31.43
**Inductive** reasoning, 51, 312
**Infinitive,** *ch.* 25.49, 26.02, 31.16
  Phrase, *ch.* 26.18
**Information,**
  Avoiding other source abuses, 426–428
  Avoiding plagiarism, 424–425
  Evaluation of, 27, 385–389
  Searching for, 375–409
  Sites, 369
  Sources, primary, secondary, and tertiary, 366–367
*Ingenious/ingenuous,* 625
**Initialisms,** *ch.* 29.35
**Initials,** *ch.* 28.03, 29.35
*Insure/ensure/assure,* 625
**Intensive** pronoun, *ch.* 25.15, 25.18
**Interjection,** *ch.* 25.71, 28.33
**Internet,**
  Source documentation, 472–473, 504–507
  Using for research, 405–409
**Interpret** images, 38–39
**Interrogative,**
  Pronoun, *ch.* 25.21
  Sentence, 96, *ch.* 26.32
**Interrupted** speech, *ch.* 28.71
**Interruption,** punctuation of, *ch.* 28.34
*Interstate/intrastate,* 625
**Interview,**
  Conducting an, 396–397
**Intransitive** verb, *ch.* 25.31
**Introduction,**
  Drafting, 61, 64–65

**Introductory** phrase, 94, *ch.* 28.22
  Comma rule, *ch.* 28.22
**Introductory** series, *ch.* 28.69
**Inverted** sentence, *ch.* 27.04
**Irony,** 289
*Irregardless/regardless,* 626
**Irregular,**
  Adverbs, *ch.* 25.62
  Verbs, *ch.* 25.52
**Italics,** *ch.* 28.84
*It's/its,* 626

## J
**Jargon,** 92, 103
**Journal** writing, 11

## K
**Keyword** searching, 370–371, 404

## L
**Lab** reports. *See* Experiment, lab, and field reports
  Model, 445–451
**Language,**
  Addressing
    Age, 105
    Disability, 106
    Ethnicity, 105
    Gender, 107
    Occupation, 107
  Capitalizing, 595–508
  Clichés, 103
  Constructing sentences, 545–554
  Jargon, 92, 103
  Level of, 93
  Nonstandard, *ch.* 27.36
  Parts of speech, 523–543, 633–646
  Usage, 617–632
  Using fair language, 105–107
*Later/latter,* 626
*Latter/former,* 623
*Lay/lie,* 626
*Learn/teach,* 626
*Leave/let,* 626
*Lend/borrow,* 626
*Less/fewer,* 623
*Liable/libel,* 626
*Liable/likely,* 626
**Library,** 399–404
  Electronic databases, 404
  Reference works, 403
*Like/as,* 627
**Linking** verb, *ch.* 25.34, 27.10
**List,** colon before, *ch.* 28.53
**Listing,** 11, 52
  Brainstorming, 11
*Literally/figuratively,* 623
**Literary** analyses,
  Approaches, 199–201, 272–276
  Guidelines, 292–293
  Samples, 277–287
  Strategies, 272–276
**Literary** terms, 288–290
**Literature,** writing about, 271–294
**Logic,**
  Appeals to, 307

Fallacies of, 313–316
Inductive/deductive patterns, 51, 312
*Loose/lose/loss,* 627

## M
**Mapping,** 26, 52–55
*May/can,* 621
*Maybe/may be,* 627
*Me/I,* 625
**Mechanics** of writing, 595–616
**Metaphor,** 144, 289
**Metasearch** tools, Internet, 405
**Methods** of organization. *See* Development
**Metonymy,** 291
*Miner/minor,* 627
**Misplaced** modifier, *ch.* 27.30
**MLA** documentation style, 453–490
  Guidelines, 454–455, 475–479
  In-text citations, 456–463
  Sample research paper, 480–489
  Works-cited references, 464–474
**Modals,** *ch.* 31.19
**Modifiers,**
  Dangling, *ch.* 27.31
  Equal, *ch.* 28.19
  Misplaced, *ch.* 27.30
**Monometer,** 291
**Mood,**
  Grammar, *ch.* 25.46
  Literary term, 290
**Moves,** writing, 67–69
  Applying, 68
  Analogy, 67
  Cause-effect, 253
  Classification, 190–191
  Comparison, 67, 233–234
  Definition, 169–170
  Example, 67
  Illustration, 67
  Personal essays, 147–148
  Persuasive essays, 329
  Process, 211–212
  Stretching an idea, 69
  Tension, 69
**Movie** review, 284–287
**Multimodal** projects, 134–135

## N
**Names,** words used as, *ch.* 29.13
**Narrative,**
  Anecdotes, 143
  Essays of, 149–159
  Guidelines, 160–161
  Paragraph, 143
  Principles, 142–143
**Narrative** writing, 137–162
**Negative,** double, *ch.* 27.40, 31.38
**Nominative** case,
  Noun, *ch.* 25.11
  Pronoun, *ch.* 25.26
**Nonprint** sources,
  APA reference entries, 504–508
  MLA works cited entries, 470–473

Nonrestrictive phrase and clause, *ch.* 28.24
**Nonstandard** language, *ch.* 27.36
**Note cards,** 379
**Note taking,** 17, 28–31
　Bibliography, 379–381
　Copy-and-annotate system, 28, 380
　Double-entry notebook, 29, 381
　Electronic, 380
　Paraphrasing, 382–384, 436–437
　Quoting directly, 17, 382–384
　Summarizing, 31, 382–383
**Noun,** *ch.* 25.01, 31.02
　Abstract, *ch.* 25.07
　Capitalization, *ch.* 29.02
　Cases of, *ch.* 25.11
　Classes of, *ch.* 25.02
　Clause, *ch.* 26.28
　Collective, *ch.* 25.05
　Common, *ch.* 25.04
　Compound, *ch.* 28.111
　Concrete, *ch.* 25.06
　Count/noncount, *ch.* 31.03, 31.04
　Gender of, *ch.* 25.10
　Infinitive phrase, acting as, *ch.* 26.18
　Number of, *ch.* 25.09
　Plural, *ch.* 27.09
　Possessives, *ch.* 28.106, 28.107, 28.108
　Proper, *ch.* 25.03
　Specific, 102
**Noun** clause, *ch.* 26.28
**Nouns** as adjectives, *ch.* 31.29
**Number,**
　Agreement in, *ch.* 27.02
　Noun, *ch.* 25.09
　Pronoun, *ch.* 25.24, 25.28
　Verb, *ch.* 25.38
*Number/amount,* 618
**Numbers,** *ch.* 29.26
　Commas in, *ch.* 28.29
　Compound, *ch.* 28.58
　Joining, *ch.* 28.63
　In a list, *ch.* 28.91
　Numerals or words, *ch.* 29.27, 29.28, 29.31

## O

**OAQS,** 87
**Object,**
　Direct, *ch.* 25.12, 26.13
　Indirect, *ch.* 25.12, 26.14
　Of preposition, *ch.* 25.63, 31.32
　Of verb, *ch.* 26.13, 26.14
　Verbals as, *ch.* 25.47
**Objective** case,
　Noun, *ch.* 25.11
　Pronoun, *ch.* 25.26
**Observations** as primary research, 398
**Octave,** 291
**Octometer,** 291
*OK/okay,* 627
**Omitted** words, 439, *ch.* 28.06

**One** writer's process, 109–124
**Onomatopoeia,** 291
**Openings,** 60, 64–65, 77
**Opposition,** engaging the, 305
*Oral/verbal,* 627
**Organization,**
　Methods of development, 50–51, 77–78
　Major moves, 60
　Outlines, 52–54
　Paragraphs, 61–63
　Of research, 373–374
　Writing organizers, 55, 148, 169, 190, 211, 233, 253, 329
**Organizers,** graphic. *See* Graphic organizers
**Outlines,** 26, 52–54
　Developing, 52–54
　Sentence, 54
　Topic, 53

## P

**Paradox,** 290
**Paragraph,**
　Analogy, 67
　Argumentative, 328
　Body, 61, 62
　Cause/effect, 252
　Classification, 189
　Closing, 70
　Coherence, 83–84
　Compare-contrast, 67, 231
　Completeness, 85
　Concluding, 61
　Connecting details, 83–84
　Definition, 167
　Drafting, 61–63
　Ending, 70
　Illustration, 67
　Introductory, 61, 64–65
　Middle, 61, 62
　Moves, 67–69
　Narrative, 143
　Opening, 64–65
　Process, 210
　Revising, 80–85
　Sentence variety, 96–97
　Structure, 62
　Topic sentence, 62, 81
　Transition, 61, 84
　Unity, 81–82
**Parallel** structure, 91
**Paraphrasing,** 382–384, 436–437
　Avoiding plagiarism, 436–437
**Parentheses,** *ch.* 28.89
　Capitalization in, *ch.* 29.04
　Periods in, *ch.* 28.02
　Questions in, *ch.* 28.14
**Parenthetical** expressions,
　Appositive, 94, *ch.* 26.21
　Explanatory phrase, *ch.* 28.35
**Parenthetical** references,
　APA, 494–497
　MLA, 456–463
**Participial** phrase, ch. 26.18

**Participle,** *ch.* 25.50
　As adjectives, *ch.* 31.28
**Parts** of speech, 523–543, 633–646
**Passive** voice, 91, 98, *ch.* 25.44–45
　Weaknesses/strengths, 98
*Past/passed,* 627
**Past** perfect tense, *ch.* 25.42
**Past** tense, *ch.* 25.42, 25.53
**Pause,** *ch.* 28.08
*Peace/piece,* 627
**Peer** reviewing, 86–87
**Pentameter,** 291
*People/person,* 629
*Percent/percentage,* 629
*Perennial/annual/biannual/ semiannual/biennial,* 619
**Period,** *ch.* 28.01
**Periodicals,**
　APA reference entries, 502–503
　MLA works-cited entries, 470–471
**Person,**
　Shift in, *ch.* 27.21
*Person/people,* 629
**Personal,**
　Anecdotes, 143
　Description, 144–145
　Essays, 149–159
　Guidelines, 160–161
　Moves, 147
　Narrative, 142–143
　Reflection, 145
　Strategies for, 142–148
　Thesis, 146
　Writing, 137–162
*Personal/personnel,* 629
**Personal** pronouns, *ch.* 25.17, 25.28
**Personification,** 144, 289
*Perspective/prospective,* 629
**Persuasive** writing, 321–356
　Essays of, 330–352
　Graphic organizer, 329
　Guidelines, 353–355
　Principles, 324–329
　Reading, 330–352
　Thesis, 328
**Phrasal** preposition, *ch.* 31.34
**Phrase,** *ch.* 26.15
　Absolute, *ch.* 26.22
　Appositive, 94, *ch.* 26.21
　Explanatory, *ch.* 28.35
　Introductory, 94, *ch.* 28.22
　Prepositional, *ch.* 25.64
　Restrictive, nonrestrictive, *ch.* 28.24
　Transitional, *ch.* 28.44
　Verb, *ch.* 26.17
　Verbal, *ch.* 25.47, 25.51
*Physical/fiscal,* 623
**Plagiarism,** avoiding, 424–425
　Avoiding other source abuses, 426–428
　Recognizing, 422–423
　Using sources in writing, 436–439
　Developing a research plan, 373

# Index

**Planning,** 47–58, 359–374
**Plot,** 276, 290
**Plurals,**
    Nouns, *ch.* 25.09, 27.09
    Number, *ch.* 28.106
    Possessives, *ch.* 28.106, 28.108
    Pronouns, *ch.* 25.18, 25.24, 25.25, 27.15
    Spelling, *ch.* 29.16
    Verbs, *ch.* 25.38, 25.39, 27.02
**Poetry,**
    Analysis, 292–294
    Punctuation of, *ch.* 28.96
    Terms, 291
    Writing about, 277–280
**Point** of view, 290, 430
*Pore/pour/poor,* 629
**Position** paper,
    Essays of, 330–352
    Guidelines, 353–355
    Strategies, 324
**Positive** form,
    Adjectives, *ch.* 25.57
    Adverbs, *ch.* 25.60
**Possessive** case,
    Noun, *ch.* 25.11
    Pronoun, *ch.* 25.26
**Possessives,** forming, *ch.* 28.107, 28.108
*Precede/proceed,* 629
**Predicate.** *See also* Verb
    Complete, *ch.* 26.11
    Compound, *ch.* 26.12
    Simple, *ch.* 26.10
**Predicate** adjective, *ch.* 25.56, 31.35
**Predicate** nominative, *ch.* 25.11
**Predicate** noun, *ch.* 25.11
**Prefixes,** *ch.* 31.49
**Preposition,** *ch.* 25.63, 31.32
    Double, avoiding, *ch.* 27.38
    Phrasal, *ch.* 25.64
    Using *in, on, at, by, ch.* 31.33
**Prepositional** phrase, *ch.* 25.64, 26.20
**Present** perfect tense, *ch.* 25.41
**Present** tense, *ch.* 25.41
**Prewriting,** 3–18, 47–58
**Primary** sources, 366, 390–398
*Principal/principle,* 629
**Problem/solution** essay,
    Essays of, 330–352
    Graphic organizer, 329
    Guidelines, 353–355
    Principles, 326–327
    Reading, 330–352
    Thesis, 328
**Process** analysis, 205–226
    Essays of, 212–223
    Graphic organizer, 211
    Guidelines, 224–225
    Reading, 212–223
    Strategies, 209–211
    Thesis, 210–211
**Process** of writing,
    Drafting, 59–72
    Editing and proofreading, 89–108

    Getting started, 3–18
    One writer's process, 109–124
    Planning, 47–58
    Revising, 73–88
**Pronoun,** *ch.* 25.13
    Agreement with verb, *ch.* 27.16
    Antecedent, *ch.* 25.14, 27.16, 27.19
    Cases of, *ch.* 25.26
    Classes, *ch.* 25.15, 25.16
    Demonstrative, *ch.* 25.22
    Gender of, *ch.* 25.27
    Indefinite, *ch.* 25.20, 27.13, 27.14, 27.15
    Intensive, *ch.* 25.15, 25.18
    Interrogative, *ch.* 25.15, 25.21
    Nominative, *ch.* 25.18, 25.26
    Number of, *ch.* 25.24, 25.28
    Objective, *ch.* 25.26, 25.28
    Person of, *ch.* 25.25, 25.28
    Personal, *ch.* 25.17, 25.28
    Plural, *ch.* 25.18
    Possessive, *ch.* 25.26
    Reciprocal, *ch.* 25.15
    Reflexive, *ch.* 25.18
    Relative, *ch.* 25.19, 27.12
    Singular they, 107, *ch.* 27.17
**Proofreader's** guide, 523–664
**Proofreading,** 4, 90
    Symbols, inside back cover
**Proper** adjective, *ch.* 25.55
**Proper** noun, *ch.* 25.03
**Proposal,** research, 360–361
*Prospective/perspective,* 629
**Protagonist,** 290
**Punctuation,** 571–594
**Purpose,** 40, 74, 80, 142, 166, 188, 209, 230, 250, 272, 324, 430

## Q

**Qualifiers,** 301, 309
**Quatrain,** 291
**Question** mark, *ch.* 28.09
**Questions,**
    Interview, 396
    For surveys, 392
*Quiet/quit/quite,* 629
**Quintet,** 291
**Quotation** marks, *ch.* 28.73
**Quotations,** *ch.* 28.73
    Dialogue, 143, *ch.* 28.30
    Indirect, *ch.* 28.79, 31.43
    Introductions to, *ch.* 28.52
    In research writing, 17, 382–384
    Of poetry, 462, *ch.* 28.96
    Quotation within a quotation, 471, *ch.* 28.83
    Quoted questions, *ch.* 28.12
*Quote/quotation,* 629

## R

**Reading,**
    Critical, 19–34
    Literature, 271–294
    *See* Modes chapters
*Real/very/really,* 629
**Reasoning,**

    Develop a line of, 301–311
    Inductive and deductive, 51, 312
**Reciprocal** pronoun, *ch.* 25.15
**Redundancy,** 101
**Reference** entries,
    APA, 498–508
**References,** parenthetical,
    APA in-text citations, 492–497
    MLA in-text citations, 454–463
**Reflective** writing,
    Anecdotes, 143
    Essays, 149–159
    Guidelines, 146–148, 160–161
    Writing principles, 145
**Reflexive** pronoun, *ch.* 25.18
**Refrain,** 291
*Regardless/irregardless,* 626
**Relative** pronoun, *ch.* 25.19
**Report** writing,
    Science IMRAD, 445–451
**Research,** 375–410
    Conducting primary, 390–396
    Conducting secondary, 399–409
    Ethics, 411–428
**Research** paper,
    Abstract, 445
    Bibliography,
        Annotated, 376–377
        Working, 17, 372
    Conducting,
        Interviews, 396–397
        Surveys, 392–393
    Developing a plan, 373
    Documenting sources. *See* Sources
        APA, 491–509
        MLA, 453–479
    Drafting, 429–439
    Flowchart, 362
    Frame of mind, 363
    Guidelines,
        APA, 491–520
        MLA, 453–490
    Information resources/sites, 368–369
    Keyword searches, 405–407
    Note-taking, 379–381
    Paraphrasing sources, 382–383
    Plagiarism, avoiding, 424–425
    Plagiarism, unintentional, 426–427
    Planning and doing research, 375–410
    Practicing research ethics, 411–428
    Sample papers,
        APA, 510–519
        MLA, 480–489
    Sources, evaluating, 27, 33, 385–389
    Strategies,
        Books, 402
        Free-Web, 405–409
        Periodicals, 404
    Summarizing sources, 31, 382–383
    Thesis, 365, 431
    Topic, 364
    Using the library, 399–404
    Using sources, 378–388, 436–439

# Index

**Resolution,** 290
**Restrictive** appositives, *ch. 28.20*
**Restrictive** phrases/clauses, *ch. 28.24*
**Review,**
   Film, 284–287
   Poem, 277–280
   Short story, 281–283
**Revising,** 73–88
   Collaborative, 86–87
   Essay, 73–87
   Ideas/organization, 75–78
   OAQS method, 87
   Paragraphs, 80–85
   Voice/style, 79
**Rhetorical** situation, 8, 22, 32, 55, 142, 166, 188, 209, 230, 250, 272, 324
   Prewriting, 8, 55
   Reading, 22, 32
   Viewing, 38
**Rhetorical** modes, 132–133
**Rhythm,** 291
*Right/write/wright/rite,* 630
**Rising** action, 290
**Roots,** list of, *ch. 31.49*
**Run-on** sentence, *ch. 27.28*

## S

**Satire,** 290
*Scene/seen,* 630
*Scent/sent/cent,* 621
**Sciences,** writing in, natural and applied, 131
   Social, 130
**Search** engines, 406–407
**Searching** for information, 14–17, 362–374
   Keyword, 405–407
**Secondary** sources, 366, 399–404, 405–409
*Semiannual/biannual/perennial/annual/biennial,* 619
**Semicolon,** *ch. 28.40*
**Sentence,**
   Capitalization, *ch. 29.03*
   Combining, 94–97
   Constructing, 94–97, 545–554
   Cumulative, 95, 97
   Errors. *See* Sentence problems
   Expanding, 95
   Kinds of, 62, 97, *ch. 26.30*
   Structure, 96–97, 545–554
      Parallel, 91
   Style, 92–95
   Subject–verb agreement, *ch. 27.01*
   Topic, 62, 80–81
   Types of, 62, *ch. 26.30*
   Types of errors, 555–567
   Variety, 96, *ch. 25.29*
**Sentence** outline, 54
**Sentence** problems,
   Ambiguous wording, *ch. 27.32, 27.35*
   Avoiding, 555–567
   Comma splices, *ch. 27.27*
   Double negative, *ch. 27.40, 31.38*

**Fragments,** *ch. 27.26*
**Modifiers,** misplaced and dangling, *ch. 27.29*
**Nonstandard** language, *ch. 27.36, 27.41*
**Omitted** words, *ch. 31.40*
**Pronoun–antecedent** agreement, *ch. 27.16*
**Repeated** words, *ch. 31.41*
**Run-ons,** *ch. 27.28*
**Shifts** in construction, *ch. 27.20*
**Subject–verb** agreement, *ch. 27.01*
**Series,**
   Comma with, *ch. 28.17*
   Dash with, *ch. 28.69*
   Hyphen with, *ch. 28.60*
   Semicolon in, *ch. 28.46*
*Set/sit,* 630
**Setting,** 143, 290
**Sexism,** avoiding, 107, *ch. 27.17*
**Shared** possession, *ch. 28.110*
**Shift** in
   Construction, *ch. 27.20*
   Person, *ch. 27.21*
   Tense, *ch. 27.22*
   Voice, *ch. 27.23*
**Short** story, review, 281–283
*Sic, ch. 28.101*
*Sight/cite/site,* 630
**Simile,** 144, 289
**Simple,**
   Predicate, *ch. 26.10*
   Sentence, 94–95, *ch. 26.37*
   Subject, *ch. 26.03*
**Singular.** *See* Number *and* Plurals
   Nouns, *ch. 25.09*
   Number, *ch. 27.02*
   Possessives, *ch. 28.107*
   Pronouns, *ch. 25.24, 27.17*
   Subjects, *ch. 27.06, 27.07*
   *They,* 107, *ch. 27.17*
   Verbs, *ch. 25.38*
**Slang,** 92, *ch. 27.41*
**Slash,** 436, *ch. 28,94*
**Social** media, evaluating, 32–33
**Social** science, 130
*Some/sum,* 630
**Sources,**
   Annotating, 28, 380
   Avoiding source abuses, 426–428
   Documenting, 378–389, 430–436
      *See also* APA documentation style and MLA documentation style
   Evaluating, 27, 385–389
   Integrating, 436–439
   Locating,
      *See also* Using the library and Internet
   Online, 387, 405–407
   Primary, 366, 390–398
   Secondary, 366, 399–404, 405–409
   Tertiary, 367, 408–409
**Specific** details, 85

**Speech,** parts of, 522–543, 633–655
**Speech,** quoted, *ch. 31.43*
**Spelling,**
   Commonly misspelled words, *ch. 29.41*
   Plurals of words, *ch. 29.16*
   Rules, *ch. 29.36*
**Splice,** comma, *ch. 27.27*
**Spondaic** foot, 291
**SQ3R** reading strategy, 22–23
**Stanza,** 291
*Stationary/stationery,* 630
**Strategies,**
   Argumentation and persuasion, 295–320
   Drafting, 59–71
   Editing, 89–108
   Prewriting, 3–17, 47–57
   Proofreading, 90, *See also* Handbook
   Reading, 19–34
   Revising, 73–87
   Viewing, 35–45
**Structure,**
   Essay, 60–71
   Paragraph, 61–62
   Parallel, 91
   Sentence, 96–97
**Style,**
   Academic style, 92–93
   Active/passive voice, 91, 98
   Level of formality, 93
   Personal pronouns, 92
   Primer, 94–95
   Revising for voice/style, 79, 91–102
   Sentence style, 92–102
   Technical terms/jargon, 92–93
   Unnecessary modifiers, 101
**Subject,** rhetorical situation, 8, 22, 32, 43, 55
**Subject,** selecting, 10–13
**Subject** of a sentence, *ch. 26.02*
   Agreement with verb, *ch. 27.01*
   Compound, *ch. 26.05*
**Subjunctive** mood, *ch. 25.46*
**Submitting** an essay, 4
**Subordinating** conjunction, *ch. 25.69*
**Suffixes,** *ch. 31.49*
*Sum/some,* 630
**Summarize,** key word, 9
**Summarizing,** 31, 382–383
**Superlative** form,
   Adjectives, *ch. 25.57*
   Adverbs, *ch. 25.60*
**Supporting** details, 85
   In arguments, 310–312
**Surveys,** 392–393
**Symbols,** *ch. 29.28*
   Proofreading and correction, inside back cover

## T

*Take/bring,* 619
*Teach/learn,* 626
**Tense** of verbs, *ch. 25.40*

# Index

**Tense,** shift in, *ch.* 27.22
**Term** papers, *See* Research writing
**Tetrameter,** 291
*Than/then,* 630
*That/who/which,* 631
*Their/there/they're,* 630
**Theme,** 290
**Thesis** statement, 48–49, 76, 146–147, 168–169, 189–190, 210–211, 232–233, 252–253, 328–329
**Thinking,**
    Building arguments, 295–320
    Critical reading, 19–34
    Critical viewing, 35–46
    Fallacies of, 313–317
*Threw/through,* 630
**Time,**
    Nouns, *ch.* 27.11,
    Numerals, *ch.* 29.27, 29.28
    Punctuation of, *ch.* 28.49, 28.113
**Titles,**
    Capitalization, *ch.* 29.09, 29.14
    For men and women, 107
    Punctuation, *ch.* 28.37, 28.74, 28.86
    As subjects, *ch.* 27.05
    Used as names, *ch.* 29.13
*To/too/two,* 630
**Tone,** 93, 290
**Topic** outline, 53
**Topic** sentence, 62, 80–81
**Topics,**
    Explore possible, 10–13
    Focus, 48–49
    Selecting, 10–13
**Toulmin** argumentation, 301–303
**Traits** of college writing, 6–7, 124
**Transitions,** 83–84
    Paragraph, 83–84
    Phrase, *ch.* 28.23, 28.43
    Useful linking, 84
**Transitive** verb, *ch.* 25.31
**Trimeter,** 291
**Triplet,** 291
**Trochaic** foot, 291
**Types** of sentences, 62, *ch.* 26.30
**Typography,** 57

## U

**Unclear** wording, 316, *ch.* 27.32
**Underlining,** as italics, *ch.* 28.84
**Understatement,** 289
**Understood** subject, *ch.* 26.06, 26.33
*Uninterested/disinterested,* 622
**Unity.** *See* Coherence
**Unparallel** construction, 99, *ch.* 27.24
**Using** the right word, 617–632

## V

*Vain/vane/vein,* 631
**Varied** sentence structure, 96, *ch.* 25.29
*Vary/very,* 631
**Venn** diagram, 230–231, 304
**Verb,** 102, *ch.* 25.29, 31.13
    Action, *ch.* 25.31
    Agreement with subject, *ch.* 27.01

Auxiliary, *ch.* 25.32
Classes of, *ch.* 25.30
Complements, *ch.* 31.15
Complete, *ch.* 26.11
Compound, *ch.* 26.12
Forms of, *ch.* 25.37
Future tense, *ch.* 25.43
Helping, *ch.* 25.32
Intransitive, *ch.* 25.31
Irregular, *ch.* 25.52
Linking, *ch.* 25.34
Modal, *ch.* 31.19
Mood of, *ch.* 25.46
Number of, *ch.* 25.38
Past tense, *ch.* 25.42
Person of, *ch.* 25.39
Phrase, *ch.* 26.17
Present tense, *ch.* 25.41
Simple, *ch.* 26.10
Tense of, *ch.* 25.40
Transitive, *ch.* 25.31
Two-word, *ch.* 31.20
Vivid, 102
Voice of, 91, 98, *ch.* 25.44–45
*Verbal/oral,* 631
**Verbals,** *ch.* 25.47, 25.51
**Verse,** 291
*Very/real/really,* 631
**Viewing,** critically, 35–46
    Critiquing a video, 42–43
    Detecting misinformation, 44–45
    Evaluating images, 40–41
    Interpreting images, 38–39
**Vivid** verbs, 102
**Voice,**
    Active, 91, 98, *ch.* 25.44–45
    Energy, 96–97
    Passive, 91, 98, *ch.* 25.44–45
    Shift in, *ch.* 27.23

## W

*Waist/waste,* 631
*Wait/weight,* 631
*Ware/wear/where,* 631
*Weather/whether,* 631
*Well/good,* 631
*Who/which/that,* 631
*Who/whom,* 631
*Who's/whose,* 631
**Wikipedia,** strengths and weaknesses, 408–409
**Word** choice, 6, 102–107, 124
**Word** clustering, 12, 26, 111
**Word** division, *ch.* 28.65
**Wording,** ambiguous, 316, *ch.* 27.32
**Words,**
    Biased, 105–107
    Compound, *ch.* 28.56, 28.111
    Dividing, *ch.* 28.65
    Jargon/clichés, 103
    Special, *ch.* 28.75
    Specific, 102
    Unclear, 316, *ch.* 27.32
**Working** bibliography, 372
**Working** thesis, 365, 431

**Works-cited** entries,
    MLA, 454, 464–474
*Write/wright/right/rite,* 631
**Writing,**
    Abstracts, 445, 511
    To analyze, 163–294
    Annotated bibliography, 376–377
    A definition, 163–184
    Descriptions, 144–145
    Essays, 163–294, 321–356
    About literature, 271–294
    Literature reviews, 412–417
    Paragraphs, 61–64, 80–85
    Paraphrases, 382, 384
    Personal, 137–162
    To persuade, 295–320, 321–356
    Reflections, 145
    Research papers, 429–452, 453–490, 491–520
        Sample APA paper, 510–519
        Sample humanities essay, 440–444
        Sample IMRAD report, 445–451
        Sample MLA paper, 479–489
    Summaries, 31, 382–383
    Thesis statements, 48–49, 76, 146–147, 168–169, 189–190, 210–211, 232–233, 252–253, 328–329, 365
    Traits, 6–7, 124
**Writing** across the curriculum, 128–131
    Modes of college writing, 132–133
**Writing** assignments. *See* Activities
**Writing** excellence,
    Traits of, 6–7, 124
**Writing** moves, 60, 61–70, 142–159, 166–181, 188–201, 209–223, 229–233, 249–267, 324–352
**Writing** process, 3–124
    Drafting, 59–72
    Editing and proofreading, 89–108
    Getting started, 3–18
    Group revising, 86–87
    Planning, 47–58
    Revising, 73–88
**Writing,** research, 357–520

## Y

**You** understood, in imperative sentences, 96, *ch.* 25.46, 26.06, 26.33
*Your/you're,* 631